Slovenia

a Lonely Planet travel survival kit

Steve Fallon

Slovenia

1st edition

Published by
   Lonely Planet Publications
   Head Office: PO Box 617, Hawthorn, Vic 3122, Australia
   Branches: 155 Filbert St, Suite 251, Oakland, CA 94607, USA
      10 Barley Mow Passage, Chiswick, London W4 4PH, UK
      71 bis rue du Cardinal Lemoine, 75005 Paris, France

Printed by
   SNP Printing Pte Ltd., Singapore

Photographs by
   Steve Fallon (SF)
   Promotion Centre Ljubljana (PCL)
   Joco Žnidaršič/Ministry of Economic Affairs (JŽ)

   Front cover: Urbanc House (Centromerkur department store), Ljubljana (SF)
   Spine: Medieval fresco in the Church of St John the Baptist, Bohinj, Gorenjska (SF)
   Title page: Kokra Saddle (Kokrsko Sedlo) in the Kamnik Alps, Gorenjska (JŽ)

Published
   October 1995

**Although the authors and publisher have tried to make the information as
accurate as possible, they accept no responsibility for any loss, injury or
inconvenience sustained by any person using this book.**

National Library of Australia Cataloguing in Publication Data

Fallon, Steve
   Slovenia

   1st ed.
   Includes index.
   ISBN 0 86442 309 8.

   1. Slovenia – Guidebooks.
   I. Fallon, Steve II. Title. (Series: Lonely Planet travel survival kit)

914.97304

text & maps © Lonely Planet 1995
photos © photographers as indicated 1995
climate charts compiled from information supplied by Patrick J Tyson, © Patrick J Tyson, 1995

Steve Fallon

Born in Boston, Massachusetts, Steve Fallon says he can't remember a time when he was not obsessed with travel, other cultures and languages. As a teenager he worked an assortment of jobs to finance trips to Europe and South America, and he graduated from Georgetown University in 1975 with a Bachelor of Science in modern languages. The following year he taught English at the University of Silesia near Katowice, Poland. After he had worked for several years for a Gannett newspaper and obtained a master's degree in journalism, his fascination with the 'new' Asia took him to Hong Kong, where he lived and worked for 13 years for a variety of publications and was editor of *Business Traveller* magazine. In 1987, he put journalism on hold when he opened Wanderlust Books, Asia's only travel bookshop. Steve lived in Budapest for two years where he wrote *Hungary – a travel survival kit* before moving to London in 1994.

From the Author

This one, too, is for Michael Rothschild, whose patience, support, love and enthusiasm is always a source of inspiration, and also for my father, Thomas Fallon (1916-74), who still travels with me after all these long years.

A number of people assisted in the research and preparation of *Slovenia – a travel survival kit*, in particular: Gregor Avguštin of the tourist office in Škofja Loka; Jure Golob of Knjigarna Konzorcij, Ljubljana; Jože Halas of the Dolenjska Museum, Novo Mesto; Suzana Lutar of the Vas travel agency, Ljubljana; Aleksander 'Sašo' Riznič of Video Art, Črnomelj; Jernej Skubic at the Stična Abbey; Sandy Svetličič of the Areh hotel, Maribor Pohorje; Darko Viler of the Municipal Museum, Idrija; Jure Žerovec of the Government Public Relations and Media Office, Ljubljana and a prolific correspondent named Drago in Celje (Drago, phone home). Their enthusiasm for Slovenia and things Slovenian is both fetching and catching and made my visits to their country memorable, more comfortable and interesting. *Najlepša hvala, gospe in gospodje!*

I am also grateful to the following people for their help along the way: Alenka Brežnik of Kompas Holidays, Ljubljana; Alenka Dermastia of the Enciklopedija Slovenije, Ljubljana; Lea Dolinšek of the CTEP, Ljubljana; the staff at the Erazem travel agency, Ljubljana; Andrej Klemenčič of the Ministry of Finance, Ljubljana; Matjaž Kos of Geodetski Zavod Slovenije, Ljubljana; Marko Langmaid of the Ptuj Regional Museum; Tanja Makovec at the tourist office in Kamnik; Miha Rott of the Government Public Relations and Media Office, Ljubljana; Robert Saksida of the Ljubljana Promotion Centre; Janko Štebej of Kompas Holidays, Ljubljana; Zdenka Strašnik at the US Embassy, Ljubljana; Liljana Vavpotič of Kompas Turizem, Ljubljana; Eržen Vroš of the Anthony Mine Shaft Museum, Idrija; Violeta Zgonik of the Ljubljana Promotion Center; Barbara Zupanc at the Ministry of

Economic Affairs, Ljubljana, and Silva Zupančvič of Kompas in Budapest.

Finally, special thanks again to the girls who are *almost* always there, Whitey Tengerkutya and Sophie Foxx-Benjamin, now awaiting release from incarceration somewhere in Essex for a 'crime' they did not commit.

From the Publisher

This book was edited at Lonely Planet in Melbourne, Australia, by Chris Wyness with the help of Jane Fitzpatrick, Anne Mulvaney, Mary Neighbour and Janet Austin, who also helped with the proofreading. Additional proofreading was done by Steve Womersley and Stephen Townshend. Sharon Wertheim produced the index. The maps, layout, illustrations and design were done by Michelle Stamp. Additional illustrations were done by Tamsin Wilson and Jane Hart. The cover was designed by Simon Bracken and Andrew Tudor. Special thanks to Dan 'the Magician' Levin for his computer wizardry in creating Slovenian accents.

Warning & Request

Things change – prices go up, schedules change, good places go bad and bad places go bankrupt – nothing stays the same. So if you find things better or worse, recently opened or long since closed, please write and tell us and help make the next edition better.

Your letters will be used to help update future editions and, where possible, important changes will also be included in a Stop Press section in reprints.

We greatly appreciate all information that is sent to us by travellers. Back at Lonely Planet we employ a hard-working readers' letters team to sort through the many letters we receive. The best ones will be rewarded with a free copy of the next edition or another Lonely Planet guide if you prefer. We give away lots of books, but, unfortunately, not every letter/postcard receives one.

Contents

Map Legend

BOUNDARIES

.... International Boundary

.... Provincial Boundary

ROUTES

.... Freeway

.... Highway

.... Major Road

.... Unsealed Road or Track

.... City Road

.... City Street

.... Railway

.... Underground Railway

.... Tram

.... Walking Track

.... Walking Tour

.... Ferry Route

.... Cable Car or Chair Lift

AREA FEATURES

.... Park, Gardens

.... Built-Up Area

.... Pedestrian Mall

.... Market

.... Cemetery

.... Reef

.... Beach or Desert

.... Rocks

HYDROGRAPHIC FEATURES

.... Coastline

.... River, Creek

.... Intermittent River or Creek

.... Lake, Intermittent Lake

.... Salt Lake

.... Canal

.... Swamp

SYMBOLS

✪ CAPITAL		.... National Capital
◉ Capital		.... Regional Capital
🕸 CITY		.... Major City
● City		.... City
● TOWN		.... Town
● Village		.... Village
■		.... Place to Stay
▼		.... Place to Eat
♟		.... Pub, Bar, Disco
✉	☎	.... Post Office, Telephone
❶	⑤	.... Tourist Information, Bank
⊖	℗	.... Transport, Parking
🏛	🏠	.... Museum, Youth Hostel
⌸	🏕	Caravan Park, Camping Ground
🕆	✚	.... Church, Cathedral
☪	✡	.... Mosque, Synagogue
卍	🕉	Buddhist Temple, Hindu Temple

✚	★	.... Hospital, Police Station
✈	✝	.... Airport, Airfield
▭	🐘	.....Swimming Pool or Baths, Zoo
❖	✿	.........Shopping Centre, Gardens
⚐	⚘	..... Ski Field, Winery or Vineyard
←	A25	One Way Street, Route Number
	∴	...... Archaeological Site or Ruins
🏛	▣	... Palace or Stately Home, Tomb
🏰	⚱	.... Castle, Monument or Tower
⌢	⌂	.... Cave, Hut or Chalet
▲	❋	.... Mountain or Hill, Lookout
🕆	⚑	.... Lighthouse, Beach
)(	◎	.... Pass, Spring
		.... Ancient or City Wall
		.... Rapids, Waterfalls
		.... Cliff or Escarpment, Tunnel
		.... Railway Station

Note: not all symbols displayed above appear in this book

Introduction

It's a tiny place – there's no disputing that – with a surface area of just over 20,000 sq km and fewer than 2 million people. But 'good things come in small packages', and never was that old chestnut more appropriate than in describing Slovenia (Slovenija), an independent republic bordering Italy, Austria, Hungary and Croatia.

The national tourist office makes ample use of clichés, too, calling Slovenia 'Europe in miniature', 'the sunny side of the Alps' and 'a green treasure of Europe'. And it's all true. Slovenia has everything – from beaches, snow-capped mountains and wide plains blanketed in sunflowers and grape vines to Gothic churches, Baroque palaces and Art-Nouveau bank buildings. And with just under half of its total area covered in forest, Slovenia is one of the world's 'greenest' countries.

There are several important things to remember about Slovenia, points that are often misunderstood or overlooked. First, this is Slovenia not Slovakia. The latter

declared itself independent from its erstwhile sibling, the Czech Republic, in January 1993. Even the *New York Times* has been known to mix that one up.

Second, Slovenia is not part of the Balkans – geographically (the Kolpa River is the border), historically or psychologically – and no more resembles the nations of that volatile region than do Austria, Hungary or Italy. Throughout their history, the Slovenian people have had very close cultural and economic ties with Europe and have been influenced much more from the west than from the east or south. This may seem odd when you take a very close look at a map of the country. If you imagine the city of Murska Sobota to be an 'eye', the Julian Alps and the north-west to be a clump of 'tail feathers' and Bela Krajina and southern Primorska to be 'feet', you'll see a chicken scurrying toward Hungary. In fact, Slovenia is heading in the opposite direction in these last few years of the 20th century.

Third, and most important, Slovenia is a

very safe country. Except for a brief period in June and July 1991 when rump Yugoslavia attempted to stop its smallest child from leaving its decayed and collapsing 'home', there has been no fighting, no war and no terrorism. While Croatia and Bosnia-Hercegovina became embroiled in the bitterest conflict in Europe since WW II, Slovenes got on with what they have always done best: working hard, making money and keeping out of the limelight.

In a very short time, Slovenia has gone from being a *narod* (a nation of people) to a *nacija* (a nation-state), and that's just what the vast majority (90%) of its people wanted when they voted for independence in December 1990. But the 'evening dreams' that President Milan Kurčan spoke about on that first Independence Day in June 1991 are long over and the 'new day', with all its shams and demands, has arrived. Sometimes you get the impression that people here are a little scared about no longer 'renting' but 'owning'; that they are searching for old heroes and are on the lookout for new ones.

Slovenes are proud of their new-found freedom and, despite the difficulties that lie ahead as the country shapes itself into a nation, they are determined to find their own way without anyone's help. They might need new heroes to show them the way, but they'll find them themselves.

God's blessing on all nations,
Who long and work for that bright day
When o'er earth's habitations
No war, no strife shall hold its sway;
Who long to see
That all men free
No more shall foes, but neighbours be.
A Toast to Freedom, **France Prešeren (1800-49)**

Facts about the Country

HISTORY
Early Inhabitants

The area of present-day Slovenia and its surrounding borders has been settled since the Palaeolithic Age. Tools made of bone and dating back to between 100,000 and 60,000 BC have been found in a cave at Mt Olševa, north of the Upper Savinja Valley, and remains of Palaeolithic man have been unearthed at Krapina, south-east of Rogaška Slatina in Croatia.

During the Copper Age (around 2000 to 900 BC), marsh dwellers farmed and raised cattle in the area south of present-day Ljubljana called Ljubljansko Barje at Lake Cerknica. They lived in round huts set on stilts and traded with other peoples along the so-called Amber Road linking the Balkans with Italy and northern Europe. Finds dating from this period are extensive and include daggers, hatchets, pots and hoes.

The Ljubljana Marsh people were overwhelmed around the year 700 BC by Illyrian tribes from the south who brought with them iron tools and weapons. They settled largely in today's Dolenjska province, built hilltop forts and reached their economic and cultural peak between 650 and 550 BC during what is now called the Hallstatt period. Priceless objects such as iron helmets, gold jewellery and embossed pails called situlae have been found in tombs near Stična and at Vače near Litija.

In about 400 BC, Celtic tribes from France, Germany and the Czech lands began pushing south toward the Balkans. They mixed with the local population and established the first 'state' on Slovenian soil, the Noric kingdom.

The Romans

In 181 BC, the Romans established the colony of Aquileia (Oglej in Slovene) on the Gulf of Trieste in order to protect the empire from tribal incursions. Among its visitors was Julius Caesar, for whom the Julian Alps are named. In the second decade AD, the Romans annexed the Noric kingdom and

---

Patriarchate of Aquileia

You'd never guess from its present size and population (a mere 3500 people) but the Friulian town of Aquileia (Oglej in Slovene), north of Grado on the Gulf of Trieste, played a pivotal role in Slovenian history and for many centuries its bishops (or 'patriarchs') ruled much of Carniola (Kranjska).

Founded as a powerful Roman colony in the 2nd century AD, Aquileia fell to a succession of tribes during the Great Migrations and had lost its political and economic importance by the end of the 6th century. But Aquileia had been made the metropolitan see for Venetia, Istria and Carniola and when the Church declared some of Aquileia's teachings heretical it broke from Rome. The schism lasted only a century and when it was resolved, Aquileia was recognised as a separate patriarchate.

Aquileia's ecclesiastical importance grew during the mission of Paolino II to the Avars and Slovenes in the late 8th century, and it acquired feudal estates and extensive political privileges (including the right to coin money) from the Frankish, and later the German, kings. It remained a feudal principality until 1420 when the Venetian Republic conquered Friuli and Venetians were appointed patriarchs for the first time. Aquileia retained some of its holdings in Slovenia and elsewhere for the next 300 years. But the final blow came in 1751 when Pope Benedicts XIV created the archbishoprics of Udine and Gorizia. The once-powerful Patriarchate of Aquileia had outlasted its usefulness and was dissolved forever. ■

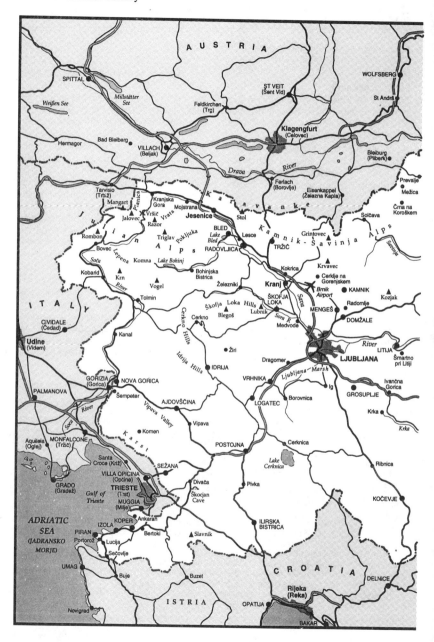

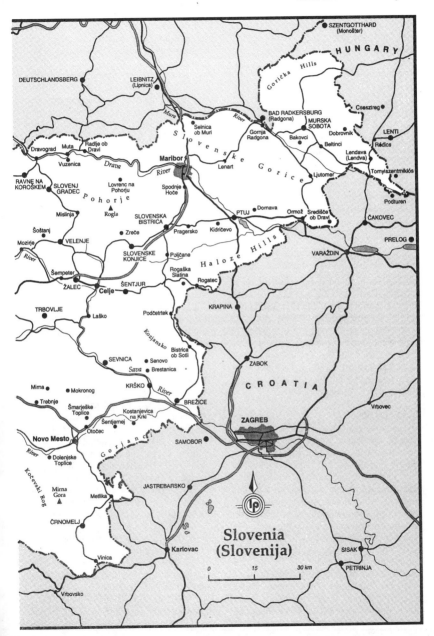

Slovenia
(Slovenija)

0   15   30 km

moved into the rest of Slovenia and Istria, completing the takeover by the 2nd century AD.

The Romans divided the area into the provinces of Noricum (southern Austria, Koroška, western Štajerska), Upper and Lower Pannonia (eastern Štajerska, Dolenjska, much of Gorenjska) and Histria, and built roads connecting their new military settlements. From these bases developed the important towns of Emona (Ljubljana), Celeia (Celje), Poetovio (Ptuj) and Virunum (near Klagenfurt, Austria), which had sophisticated fortifications, housing, baths, temples and later chapels. Many reminders of the Roman presence have been preserved in Ljubljana, Ptuj, Celje and Šempeter, west of Celje.

The Great Migrations

In the middle of the 5th century, the Huns, led by Attila, invaded Italy via Slovenia, attacking Poetovio, Celeia and Emona along the way. Aquileia fell to the Huns in 452, but Attila's empire was short-lived and soon eclipsed by the Germanic Ostrogoths. In their wake came the Langobards, another Germanic tribe that had also occupied much Slovenian territory. In 568 they struck out for Italy, taking Aquileia and eventually conquering the Venetian mainland.

The Early Slavs

The ancestors of today's Slovenes arrived from the Carpathian Basin in the 6th century and settled in the Sava, Drava and Mura river valleys and the eastern Alps. At the same time, under pressure from the Avars, a powerful Mongol people with whom they had formed a tribal alliance, the early Slavs continued to migrate west to the Friulian Plain and the Adriatic Sea, north to the sources of the rivers Drava and Mura and east as far as Lake Balaton in Hungary. In the end the community of about 200,000 occupied a total land area of about 70,000 sq km.

At that time these people were called Sclavi or Sclaveni, as were most Slavs. Later these 'proto-Slovenes' would be identified by their region: Carniolan, Styrian, Carin-

thian. It wasn't until the late 18th century during a period of national consciousness that the name Slovenci or Sloveni came into common use.

In their original homelands – bordered by the Baltic Sea to the north, the Carpathians to the south, the Oder River to the west and the Dnieper to the east – the Slavs were a peaceful people, living in forests or along rivers and lakes, breeding cattle and farming by slash-and-burn methods. They were a superstitious people who saw vile ('fairies' both good and bad) everywhere and paid homage to a pantheon of gods and goddesses: Svarog, the creator of light; Perun, god of storms, lightning and thunder; Vales, the protector of cattle. As a social group they made no class distinctions (which is why some historians say they never succeeded in establishing a kingdom or a state). But a leader – a župan (now the word for 'mayor') or vojvoda (duke) – was selected in times of great danger.

The docile nature of these people changed, however, during the migratory periods and they became more warlike and aggressive.

The Duchy of Carantania

When the Avars failed in their bid to take Byzantium in 626, the Alpine Slavs united under their leader Veluk and joined forces with the Frankish chief Samo to fight the Avars. The Slavic tribal union became the Duchy of Carantania (Karantanija) with its seat at Krn Castle in Karnburg (now Austria). Carantania was the first Slavic state and its borders extended from the valley of the Sava River as far as Leipzig including Moravia, Bohemia and Lower Austria.

By the early 8th century, a new class of ennobled commoners (kosezi) had emerged, and it was they who, using the Slovene language, publicly elected and crowned the new knez (grand duke) on the 'duke's rock' in the courtyard of Krn Castle. Such a democratic process was unique in feudal Europe, and it influenced Thomas Jefferson in the formation of his contractual theory and the writing of the American Declaration of Independence.

Expansion of the Franks

In 748 the Frankish empire of the Carolingians incorporated Carantania as a vassal state called Carinthia and attempted to convert the population to Christianity. Because of this foreign domination, the new religion was resisted at first. However, Irish monks under the auspices of the Diocese of Salzburg in the late 8th century made use of the vernacular and were more successful in claiming converts.

By the early 9th century, religious authority on Slovenian territory was shared between Salzburg and the Patriarchate of Aquileia (the Drava River remained the border until the 18th century) so that no local ecclesiastical centre could develop on its own. At the same time, the weakening Frankish authorities replaced the Slovenian nobles with German counts to help retain what little power they had left. The nobles were absorbed into the new system and Germanicised while the local peasantry was reduced to serfdom. This would later become one of the key obstacles to Slovenian national and cultural development.

Prince Kocelj & the Carinthian Kingdom

With the total collapse of the Frankish state in the second half of the 9th century, a Carinthian prince named Kocelj established an independent Slovenian 'kingdom' (869-74) in Lower Pannonia, the area stretching south-east from Styria (Štajerska) to the Mura, Drava and Danube rivers. It was to Lower Pannonia that the Macedonian brothers Cyril and Methodius, the 'apostles of the Slavs', had first brought the translations of the Scriptures to the Slovenes (in 863). And it was here that calls for a Slavic archdiocese were first heard.

Magyar Invasion & German Ascendancy

Slovenian independence was not to last long. In about the year 900, the fearsome Magyars, expert horsemen and archers, invaded and subjugated the Slovenian regions of Lower Pannonia and along the Sava, cutting them off from Carinthia. They intended to go farther but were defeated by German and Slovenian soldiers under King Otto I at Augsburg in 955.

The Germans decided to revive Carinthia, dividing the area into six border counties or marches. By the early 11th century, these would develop into the Slovenian provinces that would remain basically unchanged until 1918: Carniola (Kranjska), Carinthia (Koroška), Styria (Štajerska), Gorica (Goriška) and the White March (Bela Krajina).

A drive for complete Germanisation of the Slovenian lands began in the 10th century. Land was divided between the nobility and the church, and German gentry was settled on it. But except for the foreign nobles and administrators, the territory remained essentially Slovenian. That these people were able to preserve their identity through German and later Austrian rule was due largely to intensive educational work conducted by the clergy.

Most of Slovenia's important castles and towns were built between the 10th and 13th centuries, as were many Christian monasteries (Stična, Kostanjevica).

Early Habsburg Rule

The Austro-German monarchy (the Austrian Habsburg Empire from 1804) held control over Slovenian territory from the early 14th century until the end of WW I. It dominated the local population in every sense, stifled national aspirations and stunted political and cultural development.

In the early Middle Ages, the Habsburgs were just one of many German aristocratic families struggling for hegemony on Slovenian soil. Others, such as the Andechs, Spanheims and Žoneks (later the Celje counts), were equally powerful at various times. But as dynasties intermarried or died out, the Habsburgs consolidated their power. Between the late 13th and the early 16th centuries, almost all the lands inhabited by the Slovenes passed under the Habsburgs with the exception of Istria and the Littoral (controlled by Venice until 1797), and Prekmurje, which belonged to the Hungarian crown. Most of Kranjska, Koroška and western Štajerska were united under the Habsburgs by the middle of the 14th century, and the area around Celje, Gorica and parts of Prekmurje followed in the 15th and 16th centuries. Until the 17th century, rule was not directly imposed but administered by diets (parliaments) of 'resident princes', prelates, feudal lords and representatives from the towns, who dealt with matters like taxation.

By this time Slovenian territory totalled about 24,000 sq km, not far from its present size. Not only did more towns and boroughs receive charters and rights, but the country began to develop economically with the opening of ironworks at Kropa and mines at Idrija. And as economic progress reduced the cultural differences among the repressed rural population, they became united against their feudal lords.

Peasant Uprisings & the Reformation

More than 100 peasant uprisings and revolts occurred between 1358 (at Stična) and 1848 (at Ig), but they reached their peak between 1478 and 1573. Together with the Protestant Reformation in the 16th century, they are considered a cornerstone of Slovenian national awakening.

Attacks by the Ottoman Turks on southeastern Europe began in 1408 and continued for more than two and a half centuries, almost reaching Vienna on several occasions. By the start of the 16th century, thousands of Slovenes had been killed or were taken prisoner. The assaults helped to radicalise the peasants and landless labourers who were required to raise their own defences as well as continue to pay tribute and work for the feudal lords. At the same time, the population was growing and small farms were being divided up even further.

In most of the uprisings, peasant 'unions' demanded a reduction in payments, the democratic election of parish priests and, in at least one case, the formation of a peasant state under direct control of the emperor. The three most violent uprisings were in 1478 in Koroška, one in 1515 which encompassed almost the entire Slovenian territory, and the 1573 revolt by some 12,000 Slovenian and Croatian peasants led by Ambrož 'Matija' Gubec. Castles were occupied and pulled down and lords executed. But none of the revolts succeeded.

The Reformation in Slovenia, from 1540 onward, was closely associated with the nobility and the emerging middle class, and was generally ignored by the rural population except for those who lived or worked on lands owned by the Church. But the effects of this great reform movement cannot be underestimated. Though only 1% of the current population is Protestant, the Reformation gave Slovenia its first books in the vernacular – some 50 in all. Not only did this raise the educational level of Slovenes but it also lifted the status of the language itself, the first real affirmation of Slovenian culture.

Counter-Reformation & Progress

The wealthy 'middle class' had lost interest in the Reformation by the time it had peaked in the 1580s because of the widening economic gap between that class and the nobility. They turned to the Catholic resident princes who quashed it through religious commissions and trials, and banished noble families or individuals who persisted in the new belief.

With economic improvements in the early 18th century, after almost a century of decline brought on by the losses of the Counter-Reformation and the Thirty Years' War (1618-48) to gain control of Germany, Empress Maria Theresa (ruled 1740-80) introduced a series of reforms. These included the establishment of a new state administration with a type of provincial government, the abolition of customs duties between provinces of the Empire, the building of new roads, and the introduction of state-controlled secondary schools and obligatory elementary schools in German.

Her son, Joseph II (1780-90), went several steps further. He abolished serfdom in 1782, paving the way for the formation of a Slovenian bourgeoisie, and allowed complete religious freedom to Calvinists, Lutherans and Jews. He also dissolved the all-powerful (and corrupt) religious orders.

Though Joseph II rescinded many of the reforms (including the emancipation of the peasantry) on his deathbed, they had a major effect on the economy. Agricultural production improved, manufacturing intensified and shipping from Austria's main port at Trieste increased substantially. The reforms also produced a flowering of arts and letters in Slovenia, with the playwright and historian Anton Tomaž Linhart and the poet and journalist Valentin Vodnik producing their finest and most influential works at this time. The first Slovene-language newspaper, *Lublanske Novize*, was launched in 1797.

Napoleon & the Illyrian Provinces

The French Revolution of 1789 had convinced the Austrian rulers to halt the reform movement, and a period of reaction began that would continue until the Revolution of 1848. In the meantime there was a brief interlude – almost a footnote in history – that would have a profound effect on Slovenia and the future of the Slovenian nation.

After the defeat of the Austrians by the French at Wagram in 1809, Napoleon cut the Habsburg Empire off from the Adriatic. He created six 'Illyrian Provinces' from Slovenian and Croatian regions, including Koroška, Kranjska, Gorica, Istria and Trieste, and made Ljubljana the capital.

Though the Illyrian Provinces only lasted four years (1809-13), France instituted a number of reforms – equality before the law, use of Slovene in primary and lower secondary schools and public offices – and gained the support of certain Slovenian intellectuals including Vodnik. Most important, the Illyrian Provinces and the progressive influence of the French Revolution brought the issue of national awakening to the political arena for Slovenes for the first time.

Romantic Nationalism & the 1848 Revolution

Austrian rule, restored in 1814, was now guided by the iron-fisted Prince Clemens von Metternich. He immediately re-established the Austrian feudal system and attempted to suppress every national movement in the Empire. But the process of change in the wake of industrial revolution had started in Europe and had spread among the Slovenes too. It could no longer be stopped.

The period of Romantic Nationalism (1814-48) in Slovenia was one of intensive literary and cultural activity and set the stage for the promulgation of the first Slovenian political programme. Though many influential writers published at this time (Matija Čop, Bishop Anton Martin Slomšek, Andrej Smole), no one so dominated the period as the poet France Prešeren. His bitter-sweet verse, progressive ideas, demands for political freedom and longings for the unity of all Slovenes (Slovenšna Cela) caught the imagination of the nation and have never let it go.

Despite this, the revolution that swept Europe in early 1848 found Slovenia politically weak and relatively unprepared. But it did bring two positive results. First, it did away with absolutism and freed the peasantry from its remaining feudal obligations (though at a price – literally). Second, it provided intellectuals with the opportunity to launch their first national political programme, one that came under the banner Zedinjena Slovenija ('United Slovenia').

The United Slovenia programme, first drawn up by the Slovenija Society in Vienna, called for the unification of all historic Slovenian regions within an autonomous unit of the Austrian monarchy. It also called for the use of Slovene in all schools and offices and the establishment of a local university.

The demands were rejected as they would have required the reorganisation of the Austrian Empire on an ethnic basis. It must be remembered that the Slovenes of the time were not contemplating total independence.

Indeed, most looked upon the Habsburg Empire as a protective mantle for small nations against larger ones they considered predators, such as Italy, Germany and Serbia.

Constitutional Period

The only tangible result for the Slovenes in the 1848 Austrian Constitution was that laws would henceforth be published in Slovene and that the first Slovenian flag should be three horizontal stripes of white, blue and red. The United Slovenia programme would remain the basis of all Slovenian political demands up to 1918, and political-cultural clubs and circles began to appear all over the territory.

The rest of the 19th century and the decade before WW I was marked by economic development for the ruling classes; for example a railway from Vienna to Ljubljana was built in 1849, industrial companies were formed at Kranj and Trbovlje, and a mill built at Ajdovščina. However, conditions declined for the peasantry whose traditional sources of income were being eroded. Between 1850 and 1910, more than 300,000 Slovenes emigrated – 56% of the population.

Some advances were made on the political front. Out of the *čitalnice* (reading clubs) and the *tabori* (camps in which Slovenes of many different beliefs rallied) grew political movements. Parties first appeared toward the end of the 19th century, with the Clerical Party of newspaper editor Janez Bleiweis representing the conservative side, the Liberal Party representing the left, and the Social Democratic Party advocating a new idea: union with the other southern Slavs ('Yugoslavs'). This idea was propounded from the 1860s onward by the distinguished Croatian Bishop Josip Strossmayer, whose name adorns the streets of many Slovenian towns and cities. The writer and socialist Ivan Cankar called for an independent Yugoslav state in the form of a federal republic.

WW I & the Kingdom of Serbs, Croats & Slovenes

At the outbreak of WW I in 1914 Slovenian political parties generally remained faithful to Austria-Hungary (as the Empire was known from 1867). With the heavy loss of life and destruction of property, however, support grew for an autonomous democratic state within the Habsburg monarchy, as was put forward in the May 1917 Declaration of the Yugoslav Club. With the defeat of Austria-Hungary and the dissolution of the Habsburg dynasty in 1918, Slovenes, Croats and Serbs banded together and declared themselves to be an independent state with the capital at Zagreb. Due to a perceived threat from Italy, however, the state joined up with Serbia and Montenegro in December 1918 under the name of the Kingdom of Serbs, Croats and Slovenes. The Serbian statesman Stojan Protić became prime minister while the Slovene leader of the Clerical Party, Anton Korošec, was named vice-premier.

The peace treaties signed at Paris and Rapallo had given large amounts of Slovenian and Croatian territory to Italy (Primorska, Istria), Austria (Koroška) and Hungary (part of Prekmurje), and almost half a million Slovenes now lived in those countries (some, like the ethnic Slovenes in Koroška, had voted to do so). The loss of more than a quarter of its population and a third of its land would remain the single most important issue facing Slovenia between the wars.

The Kingdom of Serbs, Croats and Slovenes, which lasted in one form or another until 1940, was dominated by the notion of 'Yugoslav unity', Serbian control, imperialistic pressure from Italy and political intrigue. Slovenia was reduced to little more than a province in this centralist kingdom – a position supported by both the liberal bourgeoisie and the socialist parties for entirely different reasons. The Slovenes did enjoy cultural and linguistic autonomy, however, and economic progress was rapid.

Following the assassination of the leaders of the most powerful Serbian and Croatian parties, King Alexander seized absolute power in 1929, abolished the constitution and proclaimed the Kingdom of Yugoslavia. Alexander was murdered by a Macedonian terrorist in 1934 and his cousin, Prince Paul, was named regent until Alexander's son Peter came of age.

The political climate changed in Slovenia when the Clerical Party joined the new centralist government of Milan Stojadinović in 1935, proving how hollow the party's calls for Slovenian autonomy had been. As a result, splinter groups from both the Clerical and Liberal parties began to seek closer contacts with the workers' movements. In 1937 the Communist Party of Slovenia (KPS) was formed under the tutelage of the Croat Josip Broz Tito (1892-1980) and the Communist Party of Yugoslavia (KPJ).

WW II & the Partisan Struggle
Yugoslavia avoided getting involved in the war until March 1941 when Prince Paul, under pressure from Berlin and Rome, signed a treaty with the Axis powers. He was overthrown in a coup backed by the British, who installed King Paul II. Paul at first attempted neutrality, but German armies invaded Yugoslavia in April and the Yugoslav army capitulated in less than two weeks.

Slovenia was split up among Germany (Štajerska, Gorenjska and Koroška), Italy (Ljubljana, Primorska, Notranjska, Dolenjska and Bela Krajina) and Hungary (Prekmurje). Repression and deportations – with the help of Slovenian collaborators called Domobranci (Home Guards) – were the order of the day, especially in Štajerska, where ethnic Germans were settled from various parts of Europe.

To counter this the Slovenian Communists and other left-wing groups formed a 'Liberation Front' (Osvobodilne Fronte), and Slovenes took up arms to resist occupiers for the first time since the peasant uprisings. The OF, dedicated to the principles of a united Slovenia in a Yugoslav republic, joined the all-Yugoslav Partisan army of the KPJ and its secretary-general, Josip Tito. Under the Dolomites Proclamation (1943), the KPS was given the leading role in the front. The Partisans received assistance from the Allies and, given the terrain and long tradition of guerrilla warfare in the Balkans, were the most organised and successful of any resistance movement during the war.

Italy surrendered in 1943, and the following year, despite the support of the fascist Ustaša nationalists in Croatia and later the Četniks in Serbia, the Germans were forced to evacuate Belgrade. Slovenia wasn't fully liberated until May 1945.

Of immediate concern to Slovenia after the war was the status of the liberated areas along the Adriatic. A treaty signed in Paris in 1946 put Trieste and its surrounds under Anglo-American administration (Zone A), and the Koper and Buje (Istria) areas under Yugoslav control (Zone B). In 1954, Zone A (with both its Italian and ethnic Slovenian populations) became the Italian province of Trieste. Koper and a 47-km stretch of coast went to Slovenia, and Istria to Croatia. The Belvedere Treaty (1955) guaranteed Austria its 1938 borders, including most of Koroška.

Tito & Socialist Yugoslavia
Tito had been elected head of the Anti-Fascist Assembly for the National Liberation of Yugoslavia (AVNOJ) in November 1943, which provided for a federal republic. Immediately after the war he moved quickly to consolidate his power under the Communist banner.

It soon became clear that, despite the efforts of Slovenian Communist leader Edvard Kardelj to have them enshrined in the new constitution, Slovenia's rights to self-determination and autonomy within the framework of a federal Yugoslavia would be very limited beyond education and culture. Serbian domination from Belgrade would continue and in some respects be even more centralist than under the Kingdom of Yugoslavia.

Although Tito distanced himself from Stalin and domination by the Soviet Union as early as 1948, risking invasion, his efforts to create a Communist state, with all the usual arrests, show trials, purges and concentration camps (on the island of Goli in the Adriatic), continued into the mid-1950s. Industry was nationalised, private ownership

Tito

of agricultural land limited to 20 hectares, and a central economy installed.

But isolation from the markets of the Soviet bloc soon forced Tito to look to the West. Yugoslavia introduced features of a market economy (including workers' self-management), though what was now called the League of Communists would retain its decisive political role. Greater economic reforms in the mid-1960s (especially under Stane Kavčič in Slovenia), as well as relaxed police control and border controls for both foreign tourists and Yugoslavs, brought greater prosperity and freedom, but the Communist Party saw such democratisation as a threat to its power. A purge against the reformists in government was carried out in 1971-72, and many politicians and directors were pensioned off for their 'liberalism' and 'entrepreneurial thinking'. A new constitution in 1974 gave the republics more independence (and autonomy to the ethnic Albanian province of Kosovo in Serbia), but what were to become known as the 'leaden years' in Yugoslavia lasted throughout the 1970s until Tito's death in 1980. Economically, though, Slovenia was the most advanced republic in Yugoslavia by the end of the decade.

Crisis, Renewal & Change

The economic decline in Yugoslavia in the early 1980s led to inter-ethnic conflict, especially between Serbs and Albanians in Kosovo. Serbia proposed scrapping elements of the 1974 constitution in favour of more uniformity of the state in the economic and cultural areas. This, of course, was anathema to Slovenes who saw themselves threatened.

In 1987, the liberal magazine *Nova Revija* in Ljubljana published an article outlining a new Slovenian national programme: political pluralism, democracy, a market economy and independence for Slovenia, possibly within a Yugoslav confederation. The new liberal leader of the Slovenian Communists, Milan Kurčan, did not oppose this new national programme and new political parties began emerging. The de facto head of the central government in Belgrade, the Serbian Communist leader Slobodan Milošević, decided to put pressure on Slovenia.

In June 1988, three Slovenian journalists with the weekly *Mladina* (Youth) and a junior army officer named Janez Janša, who had given them 'military secrets', were put on trial by a military court and sentenced to prison. (Janša would serve as minister of defence for the first 15 months after independence.) Mass demonstrations were held throughout the country in support of the four.

In the autumn, Serbia unilaterally scrapped the autonomy of Kosovo (where 80% of the population was ethnically Albanian). Slovenes were shocked by the move, fearing the same could happen to them. A rally in Ljubljana the following February, organised jointly by the Slovenian government and the opposition, condemned the move.

In the spring of 1989 the new opposition parties published the May Declaration demanding a sovereign state for Slovenes based on democracy and respect for human rights. Of course, it wasn't all about political altruism. In September, the Slovenian Parliament amended the constitution to legalise management of its own resources (much more money was still going out of Slovenia than coming in) and peace-time command of the armed forces. Serbia announced plans to hold a 'meeting of truth' in Ljubljana on its intentions. When Slovenia banned it, Serbia and the other republics except Croatia announced an economic boycott of Slovenia, cutting off 25% of its exports. In January 1990 Slovenian delegates walked out on an extraordinary congress of the League of Communists, thereby sounding the death knell of the party.

Independence

In April 1990, Slovenia became the first Yugoslav republic to hold free elections and slough off 45 years of Communist rule. DEMOS, a coalition of seven opposition parties, won 55% of the vote, and Kurčan, head of what was now called the Party of Democratic Renewal, was elected 'president of the presidency'. The leader of the Christian Democrats, Lojze Peterle, became prime minister.

In the summer, after Serbia had rejected Slovenian and Croatian proposals for a confederation and threatened to declare a state of emergency, the Slovenian Parliament adopted a 'declaration on the sovereignty of the state of Slovenia'. Henceforth Slovenia's own constitution would direct its political, economic and judicial systems; federal laws would apply only if they were not in contradiction to it. A referendum on the question of independence was scheduled for later in the year.

On 23 December 1990, 89% of the electorate voted overwhelmingly (by 90%) for an independent republic to be effective within six months. The presidency of the Yugoslav Federation in Belgrade called the move secessionist and an anti-constitutional

---

New Age in Slovenia

Slovenia had to come up with a national flag and coat of arms at rather short notice and not everyone is happy with the result. Some say the flag resembles a football banner; others complain it looks too much like the flags and seals in neighbouring countries (like Croatia).

Though the flag's colours (white, blue and red) were decided in 1848, the national seal is a new design. In order to clear up any confusion, the government's information office has offered Slovenes and the world an explanation of 'what it all means' on both a national and a universal level, as follows:

'On a national level, the outline of Triglav above a wavy line represents a recognisable sign of the Slovenian regional space, which has been created between the mountain world to the north and west, the Adriatic Sea to the south and the plains of the former Pannonian Sea to the east. The three six-pointed stars of the Counts of Celje symbolise the cultural-statesmanship tradition of the Slovenian lands in relation to their inclusion in the currents of European history.'

And then there's the 'universal' explanation – one that would do any Californian new-ager proud. 'The symbol of a mountain with a water surface along the foothills is a universal archetype symbolising the basic equilibrium of the world. On a human level it also demonstrates the balance between man and woman and, on a planetary level, the balance between civilisation and nature. Such a symbol is understandable to people, irrespective of the cultural background from which they come since it touches a primal exemplar which is rooted deep in the subconscious. In addition it is a sign of the future as a postmodern time which once again respects equilibrium on every level. The three gold stars above symbolise spiritual-ethical principles in relation to which the equilibrium is restored. Their triangular disposition is a symbol of pluralist dynamics.' So now you know. ■

act. Serbia then proceeded to raid the Yugoslav monetary system and misappropriated almost the entire monetary issue planned for Yugoslavia in 1991: US$2 billion. Seeing the writing on the wall, the Slovenian government began stockpiling weapons and on 25 June 1991 Slovenia pulled out of the Yugoslav Federation for good. 'This evening dreams are allowed,' President Kurčan told the jubilant crowd in Kongresni trg (Congress Square) the following night. 'Tomorrow is a new day.'

Indeed, it was. On 27 June the Yugoslav army began marching on Slovenia but met great resistance from the Territorial Defence Forces, the police and the general population. Within several days, units of the federal army began disintegrating; Belgrade threatened aerial bombardment and total war, as would soon follow in the Croatian cities of Vukovar and Dubrovnik.

The military action had not come totally unprovoked. To dramatise their bid for independence and to generate support from a less-than-sympathetic West, which hoped to see Yugoslavia continue to exist in some form or another, Slovenian leaders had baited Belgrade by attempting to take control of the border crossings first. It is now believed that Belgrade did not expect Slovenia to resist to the degree that it did and that a show of force would be sufficient for it to back down.

As no territorial claims or minority issues were involved, the Yugoslav government agreed on 7 July to a truce brokered by leaders of the European Community (EC). Under the so-called Brioni Declaration, Slovenia would put further moves to assert its independence on hold for three months, provided it was granted recognition by the EC after that time. The war had lasted just 10 days and had taken the lives of 66 people.

To everyone's surprise, Belgrade announced that it would withdraw the federal army from Slovenian soil within three months, and this actually took place on 25 October. In late December, Slovenia got a new constitution and the EC formally recognised the country on 15 January 1992.

Slovenia was admitted to the United Nations on 22 May as the 176th state.

GEOGRAPHY

Slovenia is a Central European country with a surface area of only 20,256 km – about 0.2% of Europe's total land mass. Compare it with Wales, Israel or half of Switzerland and you'll get the picture. It borders Austria for 324 km to the north and Croatia for 546 km to the south and south-east. Much shorter frontiers are shared with Italy (235 km) to the west and Hungary (102 km) to the north-east.

Geographers divide Slovenia into as many as 13 different areas, but there are basically six topographies: the Alps, including the Julian Alps, the Kamnik-Savinja Alps, the Karavanke chain and the Pohorje Massif to the north and north-east; the pre-Alpine hills of Idrija, Cerkno, Škofja Loka and Posavje spreading across the entire southern side of the Alps; the Dinaric karst (a limestone region of underground rivers, gorges and caves) below the hills and encompassing the 'true' or 'original' Karst plateau (from which all other karst regions around the world take their name) between Ljubljana and the Italian border; the Slovenian Littoral, 47 km of coastline along the Adriatic Sea; the 'lowlands', comprising about one-fifth of the territory in various parts of the country; and the essentially flat Pannonian plain to the east and north-east.

Much of the interior of Slovenia is drained by the rivers Sava, which rises near Bohinj and Kranjska Gora, and Drava from Austria; they both empty into the Danube. Other important rivers are the western Soča, which flows into the Adriatic, the Mura in the north-east, the Krka to the south-east and the Kolpa, which forms part of the south-eastern border with Croatia. There are several 'intermittent' rivers (Unica, Pivka, Reka), which disappear into karst caves, only to resurface again later under different names. Slovenia's largest lakes are Cerknica, which is dry for part of the year, and Bohinj.

Main Regions

The topographical divisions do not accurately reflect Slovenia's cultural and historical differences nor do the 58 administrative občine (communes) help the traveller much. Instead, Slovenia is best viewed as a country with a capital city (Ljubljana) and eight traditional provinces or regions (*regije*): Gorenjska, Primorska, Notranjska, Dolenjska, Bela Krajina, Štajerska, Prekmurje and Koroška.

Greater Ljubljana, by far the nation's largest city with nearly 330,000 people, is pinched between two groups of hills to the west and east and a non-arable 'marshland' (Ljubljansko Barje) to the south. It is not exactly in the centre of the country but close to it. Gorenjska, the country's most mountainous province to the north and north-west, contains Slovenia's highest peaks, including Mt Triglav (2864 metres). The provincial centre is Kranj. Primorska, a very diverse region of hills, valleys, karst and a short coastline on the north-western side of the Istrian peninsula, forms the country's western border. It has two 'capitals', Nova Gorica and Koper, and the Italian minority is based here. Notranjska, to the south and south-west of Ljubljana, is an underdeveloped area of forests and karst – Slovenia's 'last frontier'. Its main towns are Postojna and Cerknica.

Dolenjska lies south of the Sava River and counts several distinct areas, including the Krka Valley, the hilly Kočevje and Posavje regions. Novo Mesto is the main city here. Bela Krajina, a land of rolling hills, birch groves and folk culture, is below Dolenjska and has centres at Metlika and Črnomelj.

Štajerska, Slovenia's largest regija, stretches eastward and is a land of mountains, rivers, valleys, vineyards and ancient towns. Maribor and Celje are the centres and Slovenia's second- and third-largest cities. Prekmurje, 'beyond the Mura River' in Slovenia's extreme north-east, is basically a flat plain though there are hills to the north. A large Hungarian minority lives within its

Provinces of Slovenia

borders, and the centre is Murska Sobota. Sitting north of Štajerska, little Koroška, with centres at Slovenj Gradec and Dravograd, is all that is left of the once great historical province of Carinthia.

Habitation

Slovenia is predominantly hilly or mountainous; about 90% of the surface is over 300 metres above sea level. Forest, some of it virgin, covers just under half of the country, making Slovenia one of the greenest countries in the world. Agricultural land (fields, orchards, vineyards, pastures, etc) account for 43% of the total. The population density is 99 people per sq km, with the urban-rural ratio split almost exactly in half. The five largest settlements in Slovenia are Ljubljana (330,000), Maribor (108,000), Celje (42,000), Kranj (37,300) and Koper (25,300).

Cities and towns such as Ljubljana, Celje, Ptuj and Koper were built on the foundations of Roman or even pre-Roman settlements, while others are essentially new (Nova Gorica) or still developing (Kranj). Many cities in Slovenia are ringed by housing estates. Traditional farmhouses are quite different in the Alps, the Karst region, Pannonia and central Slovenia, though modern 'European' housing appears everywhere. The hayrack *(kazolec)*, the most distinctly Slovenian of all folk architecture, can be seen everywhere except in Prekmurje and in some parts of Primorska.

Pollution

Though Slovenia is a very 'green' country in both senses of the word (virtually all printed matter issued by the government is on recycled paper), pollution is a problem, particularly in the rivers Sava and Mura and the lower Savinja. Rain has washed all sorts of filth dumped in the Karst region underground, and waste carried by the 'disappearing' Unica and Ljubljanica rivers threaten the Ljubljana Marsh.

Air pollution is also a big worry. Nitrogen oxide emitted by cars on the highway connecting Gorenjska with the coast is dam-

aging the pine forests of Notranjska, and it's also damaging buildings, outdoor sculptures and other artwork in many historical cities. Sulphur dioxide levels are high in cities and towns such as Šoštanj, Trbovlje and Ljubljana where coal is burned in thermo-electric power stations. The nation's sole nuclear power plant (at Krško in Dolenjska) currently provides 37% of electric power but half is owned by Croatia.

Steps are being taken to clean up the mess with the construction of water-purifying plants, the monitoring of some 1300 companies discharging waste and the introduction of gas heating. Pollution levels rarely exceed those permitted in the rest of Central and Western Europe, and warnings are issued periodically.

CLIMATE

In general, Slovenia is temperate with four seasons, but the topography creates three individual climates. The north-west has an Alpine climate with strong influences from the Atlantic and abundant precipitation. Temperatures in the Alpine valleys are moderate in summer but cold in winter. The coast and a large part of Primorska as far as the Soča Valley has a Mediterranean climate with warm, sunny weather much of the year and mild winters (though the bora, a cold and dry north-easterly wind from the Adriatic, can be fierce at times). Most of eastern Slovenia has a Continental climate with hot (in recent years very hot) summers and cold winters.

Slovenia gets most of its rain in the spring (May and June) and autumn (October and November); precipitation amounts vary but average about 1600 millimetres a year. January is the coldest month with an average annual temperature of -2˚ C and July is the warmest (21˚ C). The mean average temperature in Ljubljana is 10˚ C. The annual number of hours of sunshine ranges between 1850 and 2350, with Ljubljana getting about 1900. The climate charts on these pages show you what to expect and when to expect it in various parts of the country.

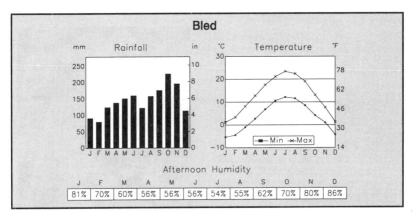

Bled

J	F	M	A	M	J	J	A	S	O	N	D
81%	70%	60%	56%	56%	56%	54%	55%	62%	70%	80%	86%

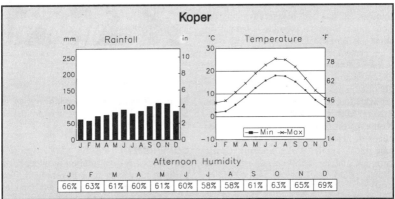

Koper

J	F	M	A	M	J	J	A	S	O	N	D
66%	63%	61%	60%	61%	60%	58%	58%	61%	63%	65%	69%

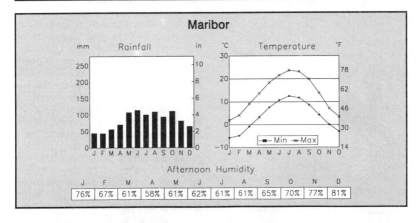

Maribor

J	F	M	A	M	J	J	A	S	O	N	D
76%	67%	61%	58%	61%	62%	61%	61%	65%	70%	77%	81%

FLORA & FAUNA

Slovenia is home to 2900 plant species, and about 70 of them – many in the Alps – are unique to the country or were first classified here. Triglav National Park is especially rich in endemic flowering plants, including the Triglav 'rose' (actually a pink cinquefoil), the blue Froelich's gentian, yellow hawk's beard, Julian poppy and the purple Zois bell flower.

Common European animals live here in abundance, such as deer, boar, chamois, bear and lynx (all of which are hunted), as well as some rare species such as the moor tortoise, cave hedgehog, scarab beetle and various types of dormice. Two species unique to Slovenia are *Proteus anguinus*, the unique 'human fish' that lives in karst caves, and the Soča trout. Slovenia provides a habitat for some 344 bird species.

At present, there is only one national park – the 84,800-hectare Triglav National Park encompassing almost all of the Julian Alps – although a proposal is before Parliament to set aside four more in the Kamnik Alps, the Pohorje Massif, the Karst and the Kočevje-Kolpa region. There are another two-dozen zones designated as regional parks. These can be as small as the Snežnik Castle complex and the Sečovlje salt pans or as

Zois bell flower

large as Robanov Kot, a pristine valley in Štajerska, or Rakov Škocjan in Notranjska.

GOVERNMENT

Slovenia's 1991 constitution provides for a parliamentary system of government. The National Assembly consists of 90 deputies elected to the State Chamber for four years by proportional representation and a 40-member National Council, which performs an advisory role. Council members are elected for five-year terms by regions and interest groups. The head of state, the president, is also the supreme commander of the armed forces and is chosen by the National Assembly for five years. Executive power is vested in the prime minister and a 15-member cabinet. Judges exercise judicial authority and their appointment is for life.

Slovenia has seven leading political parties: the Liberal Democrats (LDS; now including members of the former Greens Party), the Christian Democrats (SKD), the Associated List of Social Democrats (ZLSD), the Slovenian National Party

Deer

(SNS), the Social Democrats (SDSS), the Slovenian People's Party (SLS) and the Democratic Party (DS). Their political leanings run the spectrum from the far right (SLS) and right (SDSS) to the centre (LDS) and the centre-left (ZLSD).

In the first elections held in independent Slovenia (December 1992), which resulted in the present government, a coalition of four parties (Liberal Democrats, Christian Democrats, Associated List and Social Democrats) won more than 60% of the vote with 63 deputies taking seats. The leader of the Liberal Democrats, Janez Drnovšek, was named prime minister. Milan Kurčan was elected president of the republic with 64% of the vote. The next parliamentary elections are scheduled for autumn 1996. Municipal (občina) elections in December 1994 saw independents and the Christian Democrats win a third of the contests for mayor, with heavy losses for the left.

The Hungarian and Italian ethnic communities are guaranteed certain rights under the constitution including education in their own language and the right to publish in it. They are also guaranteed representation in the National Assembly by one deputy each. The law on foreigners applies to those individuals of other nationalities in Slovenia who did not obtain citizenship by December 1991.

Slovenia is a member of the Alps-Adriatic Association, a regional group bringing together Hungary, Croatia, Bavaria and adjacent regions of Austria and Italy for multilateral cooperation in many fields. Its relations with Austria are good, despite neo-Nazi attacks on a Slovenian-language school and publishing house in Klagenfurt in 1993 and 1994. Relations between Slovenia and Hungary are warm for the region, even with the 8500 ethnic Magyars living in Prekmurje and the estimated 5000 Slovenes in southwest Hungary. There are, however, a lot of problems with Italy and with Croatia.

Difficulties with its neighbour to the west stem from the land claims of Italian citizens expelled from Slovenia (then Yugoslavia) after WW II. Italy has even gone so far as to grant citizenship to everyone born in Italian-occupied land up to 1943, which would include such 'un-Italian' places as Idrija and Postojna. In late 1994 the deadline for such applications was extended for another year.

Slovenia has a long list of disputes with Croatia, including debates over customs tariffs, fishing rights, the status of Croatian 'guest workers' in Slovenia and Croatia's foreign-exchange balance with Ljubljanska Banka. One of the biggest disagreements is over the exact position of the border in Piran Bay off Sečovlje. Slovenia claims the entire bay.

Slovenia was admitted into the Council of Europe in May 1993. Negotiations over membership in the European Union (EU) was blocked by Italy until March 1995 when Rome dropped its veto. Slovenia will probably be the first 'reformed' country of Central or Eastern Europe to be admitted.

ECONOMY

After a few tough years, Slovenia has emerged as one of the strongest economies of the former socialist countries of Eastern and Central Europe. Inflation has dropped, employment is on the rise and income per capita is likely to surpass those of Greece, Portugal and Ireland in the near future.

But for many Slovenes, the economic picture remains unclear. While real wages rose by 6% in 1994, inflation remains stubbornly high. It zoomed up to 200% in 1992 after independence and has steadily decreased since, but it is expected to remain at 15% through 1995. Unemployment continues to hover around 15%.

Slovenia has never been a poor country. Prior to independence it was by far the wealthiest republic of Yugoslavia. Although it represented only 8% of the total population, the industrious Slovenes produced up to 20% of the gross domestic product and exported more than a quarter of its goods. A favourite saying was that 'Laws are written in Belgrade, read in Zagreb and carried out in Slovenia'.

The negative effects of the loss of its

markets in the former Yugoslavia (30% of its exports) and the pain caused by reforms needed to modernise the economy are fading away. The country has been able to bounce back largely because its highly educated populace quickly reoriented itself towards Western Europe. Shipments from the former Yugoslavia have halved in the past two years. Germany, Italy, France and Austria now constitute Slovenia's main trading partners.

With hindsight, Slovenia was fortunate not to be the site of many large industrial conglomerates that in today's economic climate would prove unviable to maintain. Although Slovenia still has its share of Communist-style dinosaur industrial plants, the country's furniture, textile and paper sectors produce high-quality goods that can be sold throughout Europe. Skis, for example, are one of the country's niche products.

Anyone searching for smokestacks and mines can find steel mills at Jesenice or coal mines east of Ljubljana at Trbovlje and Hrastnik. But more typically, the landscape is now dotted with upgraded factories as manufacturers benefit from foreign investment. Renault assembles Clio cars at Novo Mesto, and the Gorenje appliance manufacturer is partly owned by a German company that is modernising its production and marketing.

Foreign investment is not as high as originally expected; Slovenia got a slow start in reforming laws that would entice large companies into the country. For instance, it is not legal for foreigners to buy land, though they can lease it for 100 years. Also, foreign investors are forbidden to take part directly in privatisations. They may buy shares only from the Slovenian Development Fund, a government agency that receives 20% of all shares in enterprises that are being sold by the state. However, foreign enterprises have no restrictions on participating in joint ventures and can own 100% of a company.

Mass privatisation in Slovenia came about much later than in Hungary, Poland and the Czech Republic. Although a privatisation law was passed in 1992, the mechanics of transforming ownership did not start to get under way until late 1994. Private enterprises might be in the majority in numerical terms, but as of early 1995 an astonishing 79% of employed workers still worked for the state.

In Slovenia 'transformation of ownership' is used in place of the term 'privatisation'. This is partly because there was not enough private capital available in the country for companies to be sold outright. More importantly, it is because when it was a part of the former Yugoslavia, Slovenia maintained a system of workers' councils that owned shares in enterprises, as well as a system of worker self-management. There was no central-based government ministry or conglomerate that could claim direct ownership of any enterprise.

Under the Slovenian 'transformation of ownership' scheme, all citizens receive certificates that entitle them to buy shares in companies. Employees get 20% of all shares in enterprises that are being sold. Of the balance, 40% are sold to domestic investors, 20% to the Slovenian Development Fund, 10% to the national pension fund and 10% to a fund compensating former owners or their heirs. The whole process was expected to run throughout 1995.

One of Slovenia's fastest growing economic sectors is tourism, though the levels of tourists have yet to rise to pre-1991 levels. In 1994, Slovenia was expected to earn US$600 million from tourism. The majority of visitors come from Italy, Germany and Austria.

Agriculture plays a remarkably minor role in the economy, considering how rural Slovenia appears at first. It comprises only 6% of gross domestic product, as opposed to industry at 39% (manufacturing is 30% of that figure) and services at 55%.

Fewer than one in 10 Slovenes now lives off farming alone – in 1960 nearly half the population were engaged full-time in agriculture. But as Slovenes love the countryside, it is estimated that a quarter of the population farms to some degree, growing grapes or raising bees for honey. The most important farm products are wheat, corn, potatoes, pears, apples and grapes.

There is also a disproportionately large number of chickens per head of population: an astounding 13 million of them. The country is virtually self-sufficient in food production.

POPULATION & PEOPLE

The last census in Slovenia (1991) counted just under 1,966,000 people. The vast majority (88%) are Slovenes, descendants of the Southern Slavs who settled in what is now Slovenia and parts of Italy, Austria and Hungary from the 6th century AD. Other groups identify themselves as Croats (2.7%), Serbs (2.5%) and simply 'Muslims' (1.3%). There are also 8500 ethnic Hungarians and 2300 Gypsies, largely in Prekmurje, as well as 3000 Italians in Primorska.

The Italians and Hungarians are considered indigenous minorities with rights protected under the constitution, and they have special deputies looking after their interests in Parliament. Though some members of the other groups have lived and worked in Slovenian towns and cities for many years, most are recent arrivals – refugees and economic immigrants from the fighting in former Yugoslav republics like Bosnia and Croatia. Their status as non-citizens in Slovenia remains hazy and many Slovenes have very racist feelings about them. Up to 30,000 migrants cross over the border from Croatia each day to work in Slovenia.

Ethnic Slovenes living outside the national borders number about 400,000, with the vast majority (almost 75%) in the USA and Canada. (Cleveland, Ohio, is the largest 'Slovenian' city outside Slovenia.)

Life expectancy is increasing in Slovenia but still relatively low by Western European standards: 69 years for men and 77 years for women. The birth rate in Slovenia is also low – 10 per 1000 population against 14 in the UK and 15 in Australia. The age structure is therefore old with an average of 34 years for men and 38 years for women. Almost 30% of the parents of the 20,000 children born in 1992 were unmarried.

EDUCATION

Slovenia is a highly educated society with a literacy rate of more than 99%.

Primary school *(osnovna šola)* is compulsory and free for eight years until the age of 15. Secondary school *(srednja šola)* can be a two-year apprenticeship, a three-year vocational course or *gimnazija* (high school), which lasts four years and prepares pupils for university. Ethnic Italians and Hungarians can choose to be taught in their mother tongues at some 18 elementary schools and 46 secondary-school departments largely in Prekmurje and Primorska.

Slovenia has only two universities – the University of Ljubljana and a smaller one at Maribor – with a total enrollment of about 33,500 students. Competition for places is stiff, and secondary-school pupils must take exams to be accepted into most faculties. The largest number of students are enrolled at the Technical Faculty at the University of Maribor and the Faculty of Economics in Ljubljana. About 9% of the population has some sort of university degree.

Slovenia has a strong tradition in the sciences and has produced many great scientists – from the 17th century polymath Janez Vajkard Valvasor and Gabriel Gruber, who regulated the Ljubljanica River in the late 18th century, to the patron Žiga Zois and Friderik Pregl, who won the Nobel Prize in 1923 for organic chemistry. The Slovenian Academy of Arts & Sciences has a research centre with 14 institutes supporting the study of all aspects of science as well as history and culture.

ARTS & CULTURE
Painting, Sculpture & Architecture

The apogee of folk painting in Slovenia is the traditional beehive panel *(panjska končnica)* illustrated with folk motifs that was so popular in the 18th and 19th centuries and has enjoyed something of a comeback in recent years. For more information, see the Radovljica section of the Gorenjska chapter.

Romanesque architecture can be found in many parts of Slovenia, including the churches at Stična Abbey, Muta and

Dravograd in Koroška and Podsreda Castle, but fine art is rare, surviving only as illuminated manuscripts. Gothic painting and sculpture is another matter with excellent works – some commissioned by burghers and wealthy landowners – at Ptujska Gora (the carved altar in the Church of the Virgin Mary), Bohinj (frescoes in St John the Baptist's Church) and Hrastovlje (*Dance of Death* wall painting at the Church of the Holy Trinity). Famous painters of this time were Johannes de Laibaco, who decorated the Church of the Assumption in Muljava, Jernej of Loka, who worked mostly around Škofja Loka, and Johannes Aquila of Radgona, who did the frescoes in the magnificent church at Martjanci. Much Gothic architecture in Slovenia is of the late period, as the earthquake of 1511 destroyed many buildings (though Koper's Venetian Gothic Loggia and Praetorian Palace date back a century earlier). Renaissance architecture is mostly limited to secular buildings (the town houses in Škofja Loka and Kranj, Brdo Castle).

Italian-influenced Baroque abounds in Slovenia, and you'll find great architectural examples everywhere, particularly in Ljubljana (Ursuline Church of the Holy Trinity and the cathedral). For sculpture, look at Jožef Straub's plague pillar in Maribor, the golden altar in the Church of the Annunciation at Crngrob, or the work of Francesco Robba in Ljubljana (Fountain of the Carniolan Rivers in Mestni trg). Fortunat Bergant, who painted the Stations of the Cross at the Stična Abbey church, was a master of Baroque painting.

Classicism prevailed in Slovenian architecture (Kazina building in Kongresni trg in Ljubljana, the Tempel pavilion in Rogaška Slatina) in the first half of the 18th century, and also in the works of the painter Franc Kavčič and the Romantic portraits and landscapes of Josip Tominc and Matevž Langus. Realism came later in the works of the artists Ivana Kobilca, Jurij Šubic and Anton Ažbe in the second half of the 18th century, but the most important painters were the Impressionists Rihard Jakopič, Matija Jama,

Ivan Grohar and Matej Sternen, who exhibited together in Ljubljana in 1900.

The turn of the century was also the time when the Secessionist (or Art-Nouveau) architects Maks Fabiani and Ivan Vurnik began changing the face of Ljubljana after the devastating 1895 earthquake (Miklošičev Park, Prešeren Monument, the Cooperative Bank on Miklošičeva cesta). But no architect has had a greater impact on his city or nation than Jože Plečnik, a man who defies easy definition (see the Ljubljana chapter).

In the 20th century, the expressionist school of Božidar Jakac and the brothers France and Tone Kralj gave way to the 'Club of Independents' (the painters Zoran Mušič, Maks Sedej and France Mihelič) and later the sculptors Alojzij Gangl, Franc Berneker, Jakob Savinšek and Lojze Dolinar. The last two would later create 'masterpieces' of Socialist Realism under the Tito regime without losing their credibility or (sometimes) their artistic sensibilities. Favourite artists of recent years include Janez Bernik, Rudi Španzel (who designed the new *tolar* notes) and Jože Tisnikar, a naive painter from Slovenj Gradec with a unique style.

Postmodernist painting and sculpture has been dominated since the 1980s by the multimedia group Neue Slowenische Kunst (NSK) and the five-member artists' cooperative IRWIN. The latter, founded in 1983, spurns the sacred myth of the individual artist by exhibiting only as an anonymous group with jarring ideological or historical symbols juxtaposed in such a way as to bring out new meanings.

Ljubljana has hosted the International Biennial of Graphic Art since 1955. The Biennial of Slovenian Graphic Art takes place in Novo Mesto during even-numbered years.

Folk Music

Slovenian music is rooted in folk songs sung as part of rituals or ceremonies that were brought to present-day Slovenia by the early Slavs in the 6th century. Folk music *(ljudska glasba)* has developed independently from other forms of music over the centuries. The collection and classification of children's songs, wedding marches and fables set to music began in the nationalistic Romantic period of the 19th century, and today the Institute of Music & National Manuscripts is charged with this task.

Mira and Matija Terlep of the trio Trutamora Slovenica have examined literature and conducted field surveys in an attempt to rediscover the roots of Slovenian folk music. Their compact disc *Sound Image of Slovene Regions No 4* features reconstructions of old Slovenian folk songs played on original folk instruments such as the *cymbalom* (a curious stringed instrument played with sticks), zither, *zvegla* (wooden cross flute), ocarina (a clay flute), *šurle* (Istrian double flute), panpipes, Jew's harp, *gudalo* (earthenware bass) and even a rattle made from a dried pumpkin.

Classical & Popular Music

The conversion of the Slavs to Christianity from the 8th century onward brought the development of choral singing – the oldest sacred song dates from 1440 – in churches and monasteries. By the end of the Middle Ages, secular music had developed to the same degree as music elsewhere in Europe. The most important composer in the late 16th century was Jakob Gallus, who wrote madrigals and choral songs as well as 16 Masses. An outstanding composer of Renaissance music was Izak Poš.

Baroque music had gone out of fashion by the time the Filharmonija was founded in Ljubljana in 1701, and classicist forms were all the rage. The first Slovenian opera *(Belin)* was written by Jakob Francisek Zupan in 1780, and Janez Novak composed classicist music for a comedy written by Slovenia's first playwright, Anton Tomaž Linhart. The 19th century Romantics such as Benjamin Ipavec, Fran Gerbič and Anton Foerster incorporated traditional Slovenian elements into their music as a way of expressing their nationalism, as did the composer Hugo Wolf who was born in Slovenj Gradec in 1860.

Slovenian music between the wars was best represented by the expressionist Marij Kogoj and the modernist Slavko Osterc. Contemporary composers whose reputations go well beyond the borders of Slovenia include Primož Ramovš, Lojze Lebič and the ultramodernist Vinko Globokar who lives in Paris. Opera buffs won't want to miss the chance to hear Marjana Lipovšek, the country's foremost mezzo-soprano.

Popular music runs the gamut from Slovenian *chanson* (best exemplified by Vita Mavrič) and jazz to Latin and house disco, but it was punk music in the late 1970s and early 1980s that put Slovenia on the world stage. The most celebrated groups were Pankrti, Kuzle, Borghesia and Laibach (part of the NSK movement). These groups were imitated throughout Eastern Europe. (Laibach's leader, Tomaž Hostnik, died tragically in 1983 when he hanged himself from a kazolec, the traditional Slovenian hayrack.) Other groups to watch for are Miladojka Youneed, 2227 and the reunited Niet.

Dance

Slovenian dance also finds its origins in folk culture. Folk dance *(ljudski ples)* has a long tradition in Slovenia: polkas, circle dances, Hungarian-style czardas. The first ballet group was established in 1918 as part of the Ljubljana Opera, and a ballet school was established within the National Theatre. The Ljubljana Ballet Company still performs at the Opera House and there's another company in Maribor.

Avante-garde dance is best exemplified by Betontanc, a dance company directed by Matjaž Pograjc that mixes live music and theatrical elements with sharp political comment. In the rock ballet *Thieves of Wet Handkerchiefs*, members of the troupe murder one another and then are resurrected.

Literature

Irish monks probably introduced the Latin alphabet to the Slavs living in Slovenia in the 8th century, and Sts Cyril and Methodius gave them their first translations of the Scriptures a century later.

The oldest example of written Slovene (or any Slavic language for that matter) is contained in the *Freising Texts (Brižinski Spomeniki)* dating from around 970. They contain a sermon on sin and penance and instructions for general confession. Oral poetry, such as the seminal tale of *Fair Vida (Lepa Vida)*, flourished throughout the Middle Ages, but it was the Reformation that saw the first book in Slovene, a catechism published by Primož Trubar in 1550. A complete translation of the Bible by Jurij Dalmatin followed in 1584, and Adam Bohorič published a grammar of Slovene in Latin (with the lovely title *Spare Winter Hours*) about the same time. Almost everything else published until the late 18th century was in Latin or German, including Janez Vajkard Valvasor's laudatory account of Slovenia, *The Glory of the Duchy of Carniola* (1689).

The Enlightenment and the reforms of Habsburg rulers Maria Theresa and her son, Joseph II, raised the educational and general cultural level of the Slovenian nation. In large part due to the support and philanthropy of Baron Žiga Zois (1747-1819), Slovenia gained its first dramatist (Anton Tomaž Linhart), poet (the Franciscan priest Valentin Vodnik) and modern grammarian

France Prešeren: A National Poet

Slovenia's most beloved poet was born in Vrba near Bled in 1800 and educated in Ljubljana and Vienna, where he received a law degree in 1828. Most of his working life was spent as an articled clerk in the office of a Ljubljana lawyer. By the time he opened his own practice in Kranj in 1846 he was already a sick and dispirited man. He died in 1849.

Although Prešeren published only one volume of poetry in his lifetime *(Poezije,* 1848), he left behind a legacy of work printed in the literary magazines *Kranjska Čbelica (Carniolan Bee)* and the German-language *Illyrisches Blatt.* His verse set new standards for Slovenian literature at a time when German was the literary language and his lyric poems, such as the masterpiece *Sonetni Venec (Garland of Sonnets,* 1834), are among the most sensitive, original and eloquent works in Slovene. In later poems he expressed a national consciousness that he tried to instil in his compatriots. *Krst pri Savici (Baptism at the Savica Waterfall,* 1836) is such a work.

Prešeren's life was one of sorrow and disappointment which he met with stoicism and resignation. The sudden death of his close friend and mentor, the literary historian Matija Čop, in 1835 and an unrequited love affair with an heiress called Julija Primic brought him close to suicide. (Julija later married a German, and Slovenes like to point out, with a certain amount of *Schadenfreude,* that she was unhappy with her husband.) It was during this time that he produced his best poems.

In reality, Prešeren was a drunkard, a philanderer, a social outcast and perhaps even vain. He refused to have his portrait painted and any likenesses you see of him – including the rather dashing one on the 1000 SIT note – were done from memory after his death.

But Prešeren was the first to demonstrate the full literary potential of Slovene, and his body of verse – lyric poems, epics, satire, and narrative verse – has inspired Slovenes at home and abroad for generations. ∎

(Jernej Kopitar). But it was during the Romantic period that Slovenian literature truly came of age. This period produced the nation's greatest poet and hero, France Prešeren. The *Carniolan Bee (Kranjska Čbelica)*, an 'almanac' to which Prešeren contributed, was an important literary and nationalist forum in the 1830s and 1840s.

In the latter half of the 19th century, Fran Levstik (1831-87) brought the writing and interpretation of oral folk tales to new heights with his *Martin Krpan* (see the Notranjska chapter), but it was Josip Jurčič (1844-81) who published the first full-length novel in Slovene. *The Tenth Brother (Deseti Brat*; 1866) is the tragic and very realistic tale of an illegitimate son's desire for revenge. The lyrical poets Simon Jenko (1835-69) and priest Simon Gregorčič (1844-1906) wrote original and powerful verse.

The period from the turn of the 20th century up to WW II was dominated by two men who single-handedly introduced modernism into Slovenian literature: the poet Oton Župančič (1878-1949) and the novelist and playwright Ivan Cankar (1876-1918). The latter has been called 'the outstanding master of Slovenian prose' and his works, notably *The Ward of Our Lady of Mercy (Hiša Marije Pomočnice)* and *The Bailiff Yerney and His Rights (Hlapec Jernej in Njegova Pravica)*, influenced a generation of younger writers.

Slovenian literature immediately before and after WW II was influenced by Socialist Realism and the Partisan struggle (the novels of Voranc Prežihov, and poems by Matej Bor), but since then Slovenia has tended to follow Western European literary trends: late expressionism, symbolism (the poetry of Edvard Kocbek) and existentialism (the novels of Vitomil Zupan). Writers and poets using avante-garde techniques include Rudi Šeligo (1935-), Tomaž Šalamun (1941-) and Drago Jančar (1948-).

RELIGION

Although Protestantism had a very strong foothold in Slovenia in the 16th century, most Slovenes today – about 80% – are Roman Catholic (at least in name). An archbishop (currently Alojzij Šuštar) sits in Ljubljana and there are bishoprics at Maribor and Koper.

Other religious communities in Slovenia include Eastern Orthodox Christians (2.4%), Muslims (1%) and Protestants (1%). Most Protestants in Slovenia belong to the Evangelical (Lutheran) church based in Murska Sobota in Prekmurje.

Jews have played a very minor role in Slovenia since they were first banished from the territory in the 15th century. Although the remains of a synagogue still stand in Maribor and there was one in Ljubljana until WW II, no temple functions in Slovenia today. The rabbi from Zagreb occasionally holds services for the tiny community in Ljubljana when numbers suffice.

As in most of Central and Western Europe today, religion doesn't appear to be much of an issue for most people in Slovenia, particularly among the young, and churches are seldom more than half-full outside the most important holy days of Easter, Christmas and the Assumption of Mary.

LANGUAGE

The French novelist Charles Nodier (1780-1844), who lived and worked in Ljubljana for a couple of years in the early 19th century, once wrote that Slovenia was like 'an Academy of Arts and Sciences' because of the people's flair for speaking foreign languages. Monsieur Nodier would be happy to know that they still have that talent almost two centuries down the track.

Virtually everyone in Slovenia speaks at least one other language. In the 1991 census, 88% said they knew Croatian and Serbian, 45% German, 37% were conversant in English and 17% spoke Italian. But those figures require further explanation.

Italian is really only useful in Primorska and small parts of Notranjska. German, once the language of education and the elite, is spoken mostly by older people, especially in Koroška, Štajerska and northern Gorenjska. There may be fewer speakers of English than

German overall, but it is definitely the preferred language of the young, with 84% of all students claiming knowledge of it. Most speak English very well indeed, even if they pepper their speech with 'Slovenglish' slang like 'full cool', meaning 'very hip' or 'fashionable'.

The fact that you will rarely have difficulty in making yourself understood and that you will never 'need' Slovene shouldn't stop you from learning a few words and phrases of this rich language. More than anything else, Slovene has kept the Slovenian nation (narod) alive and united as a culture over centuries of domination and brutality. And despite all attempts to destroy it, it is very much alive, dynamic and organic. Any effort on your part to speak it will be rewarded one-hundredfold.

Slovene (Slovenščina) is a South Slavic language written in the Roman alphabet. It is closely related to Croatian and Serbian, but the languages are not mutually intelligible. Linguists have counted no fewer than 50 dialects and subdialects in little Slovenia, though the 'purest' form of the language is said to be spoken in north-western Dolenjska.

Slovene is grammatically complex with six cases for nouns, adjectives and pronouns, three genders and four verb tenses. In addition to singular and plural, Slovene has something very rare in linguistics: the dual number. It's one *miza* (table) and three or more *mize* (tables) but two *mizi*. It may not sound too complicated at first, but remember that there are special case endings for masculine, feminine and neuter nouns in the singular, the plural *and* the dual.

More bad news is that there are a lot of irregularities in verbal conjugations and noun declensions. And the good news? Adjectives precede the noun as in English and there are no articles: 'a table' or 'the table' is just 'table'.

Pronunciation

The Slovenian alphabet has 25 letters. It drops the letters q, w, x and y but adds the following in both upper and lower case: č, š

and ž. (That little mark on top is called a carrot in English and a *strešica*, or 'little roof', in Slovene.)

Like English, Slovene is not a 'one-for-one' language: the pronunciation of a vowel and some consonants can change from word to word even though the same letter is used in the spelling. Stress – where the emphasis falls on a word – is also irregular and, as in English, has to be learned word by word.

It's a simplification, but you could say that consonants in Slovene are pronounced more or less as they are in English with the following exceptions:

c	'ts' as in 'hats' even at the beginning of a word
č	'ch' as in 'church'
d	like the 'j' in 'joke'
j	'y' as in 'yes' or 'y' in 'aye' if preceded by a vowel *(maj* for 'May', čaj for 'tea', etc)
l	'l' as in 'leap' except at the end of a syllable or before a vowel when it's like the 'w' in 'know' *(pol* for 'half', *kal* for 'bud', etc)
lj	like 'li' in 'million' or the French word *lieu*
nj	'ni' in 'onion' or the 'gn' in 'cognac'
r	a slightly trilled Spanish or Scottish 'r' pronounced with the tip of your tongue
š	'sh' as in 'ship'
šč	like the 'sh' and 'ch' of 'fresh chips' said quickly
v	like 'v' in 'vat' except at the end of a syllable or before a vowel when it's like the 'w' in 'know' (Triglav, *nov* for 'new', etc)
ž	like the 's' in 'measure' or 'pleasure' even at the beginning of a word

Don't be daunted by vowel-less words like *trg* (square), which is pronounced more like 'terg' or by consonant clusters as in the word for key, *ključ*. It's 'klyooch'.

Vowels in Slovene (a, e, i, o, u) are much more difficult than consonants for a foreigner to pronounce. Each one has several different pronunciations, depending on whether it's stressed, unstressed, long or short. The letter e, for example, can sound like the 'a' in 'gate', the 'e' in 'there' or the 'e' in 'bet'. In Slovenian dictionaries these differences are shown with accent marks (é, ê, è) to help foreigners and youngsters learn proper pronunciation but the accents *never* appear elsewhere in the written language. Don't worry about it; no one is going to lose any sleep if you pronounce Bohinj as 'BOW-heen' instead of the correct 'BAW-heen'.

The following is thus a very rough guide to pronouncing Slovenian vowels.

a	'a' in 'father' or 'u' in 'cut'
e	'e' in 'bet'
i	'ee' in 'feet' but also very commonly like the 'i' in 'hit'
o	'o' in 'hot' but also like 'o' in 'open'
u	'oo' in 'soon' but shorter

For more words and phrases in Slovene, see the Food and Drinks sections in the Facts for the Visitor chapter or the Glossary in the back of the book.

Greetings & Civilities

Hello.	*Dober dan.* (formal)
	Zdravo. (familiar)
Goodbye.	*Nasvidenje.*
Good morning.	*Dobro jutro.*
Good day/afternoon.	*Dober dan.*
Good evening.	*Dober večer.*
Please.	*Prosim.*
Thank you	*Hvala*
(very much).	*(lepa).*
You're welcome.	*Prosim/Ni za kaj.*
Yes.	*Da.*
	Ja. (more common)
No.	*Ne.*
Maybe.	*Mogoče.*
Excuse me/I am sorry.	*Oprostite.*
How are you?	*Kako ste?* (formal)
	Kako si? (familiar)
I'm fine, thanks.	*(Jaz) Sem dobro, hvala.*

Essentials

Please write it down.	*Prosim, zapišite si.*

Please show me (on the map).	*Prosim pokažite mi (na mapi).*
I understand.	*Razumem.*
I don't understand.	*Ne razumem.*
I don't speak...	*Ne govorim...*
Do you speak English?	*Ali govorite angleško?*
Does anyone speak English?	*Ali kdo govori angleško?*
Where/What country are you from?	*Od kod ste?/Iz katere dežele ste?*
I am from...	*Sem iz...*
Age?/How old are you?	*Starost?/Koliko ste stari?*
I am...years old.	*Imam...let.*
I have a visa/permit.	*Imam vizum/dovoljenje.*

Surname	*Priimek*
Given name	*Krstno ime*
Date of birth/place of birth	*Datum/kraj rojstva*
Nationality	*Državljanstvo*
Male/Female	*Moški/Ženska*
Passport	*Potni list*

Help!	*Na pomoč!*
Go away!	*Pojdite stran!*
Call...	*Pokličite...*
a doctor	*zdravnika*
the police.	*policijo.*

Small Talk

What is your name?	*Kako vam je ime?* (formal)
	Kako ti je ime? (familiar)
My name is...	*Moje ime je....*
I'm a tourist/student.	*Sem turist/študent.*
Are you married?	*Ali ste poročeni?*
Do you like...?	*Ali imate radi...?*
I like it very much.	*Imam zelo rad.*
I don't like...	*Ne maram...*
Just a minute.	*Samo trenutek.*
May I?	*Ali lahko?*
It's all right.	*Je v redu.*
No problem.	*Brez problema.*
How do you say... (in Slovene)?	*Kako se reče... (poslovensko)?*

Getting Around

I want to go to...	*Rad bi šel v...*
I want to book a seat for...	*Rad bi rezerviral sedež za...*

What time does... leave/arrive?	*Ob kateri uri je... odhod/prihod?*
Where does the ...leave from?	*Od kje je ...odhod/prihod?*
bus/tram	*avtobusa*
train	*vlaka*
boat	*ladja*
ferry	*trajekt*
hydrofoil	*gliser*
airplane	*letalo*

How long does the trip take?	*Koliko dolgo traja potovanje?*
The train is delayed/is early.	*Vlak ima zamudo/je zgodnji.*
The train is on time.	*Vlak prihaja pravočasno.*
The train is cancelled.	*Vožnja je stornirana.*
Do I need to change?	*Ali moram presesti?*
You must change trains/platform.	*Presesti morate vlak/peron.*

left-luggage office/locker	*garderoba*
one-way ticket	*enosmerna vozovnica*
platform	*peron*
return ticket	*povratna vozovnica*
(bus/train) station	*(avtobusna/železniška) postaja*
ticket	*vozovnica*
ticket office	*(avtobusna/železniška) blagajna*
timetable	*vozni red*

I'd like to hire a...	*Rad bi najel...*
bicycle	*kolo*
motorcyle	*motorno kolo*
car	*avto*
guide	*vodiča*
horse	*konja*

Directions

How do I get to...?	*Kako pridem do...?*
Where is...?	*Kje je...?*
Is it near/far?	*Ali je blizu/daleč?*
What street/road/street number is this?	*Katera ulica/cesta/ulična številka je to?*
What town/suburb is this?	*Katero mesto/predmestje je to?*

(Go) straight ahead.	*(Pojdite) naravnost naprej.*
(Turn)	*(Obrnite)*
left/right...	*levo/desno...*
at the traffic lights	*pri semaforju*
at the next/ second/third corner	*pri naslednem/ drugem/tretjem ovinku*

up/down	*zgoraj/spodaj*
behind/opposite	*za/nasproti*
east/west	*vzhod/zahod*
north/south	*sever/jug*
here/there/ everywhere	*tu/tam/povsod*

Useful Signs

Entrance	*Vhod*
Entry Fee (Admission)	*Vstopnina*
Exit	*Izhod*
Full	*Polno/Zasedeno*
Gents	*Moški*
Information	*Informacija*
Ladies	*Ženske*
Open/Closed	*Odprto/Zaprto*
Police	*Policija*
Prohibited	*Prepovedano*
Pull	*Vleci*
Push	*Rini*
Rooms Available	*Sobe Proste*
Toilets	*Stranišče/WC*

Around Town

Where is the/a...?	*Kje je...?*
bank/exchange office	*banka/menjalnica*
city centre	*središče mesta/center*

embassy	*ambasada*
post office	*pošta*
public toilet	*javno stranišče*
telephone centre	*telefonska centrala*
tourist office	*turistični urad*

I want to make a telephone call.	*Rad bi telefoniral.*
I'd like to change some money.	*Rad bi zamenjal nekaj denarja.*
I'd like to change some travellers' cheques.	*Rad bi zamenjal nekaj potovalne čeke.*

abbey	*opatija*
beach	*plaža*
bridge	*most*
castle	*grad*
cathedral	*stolnica*
church	*cerkev*
hospital	*bolnišnica*
island	*otok*
lake	*jezero*
main square	*glavni trg*
market	*tržnica*
mosque	*mošeja/džamija*
old city (town)	*staro mesto*
palace	*palača*
ruins	*ruševine*
sea	*morje*
square	*trg*
tower	*stolp*

Accommodation

I'm looking for...	*Iščem...*
the youth hostel	*počitniški dom*
the camping ground	*kamping*
a hotel	*hotel*
a guesthouse	*gostišče/penzion*
the manager/ owner	*direktorja/lastnik*

What is the address?	*Na katerem naslovu je?*

Do you have a ...available?	*Ali imate...prosto?*
bed	*posteljo*
cheap room	*poceni sobo*
single/double room	*enoposteljno/ dvoposteljno sobo*

for one night/two nights	*za eno noč/za dve noči*
How much is it per night/per person?	*Koliko stane na noč/na osebo?*
Is breakfast included?	*Ali je zajtrk vključen?*
Is service included?	*Ali je postrežba vključena?*
Can I see the room?	*Lahko vidim sobo?*
Where is the toilet?	*Kje je stranišče/WC?*
It is very dirty/ noisy/expensive.	*Je zelo umazana/ glasna/draga.*
I am/We are leaving now.	*Danes odhajam/ odhajamo.*

Do you have...?	*Ali imate...?*
a clean sheet	*cisto rjuho*
hot water	*toplo vodo*
a key	*ključ*
a shower	*tuš*

Food

I am hungry/thirsty.	*Lačen/žejen sem.*
breakfast	*zajtrk*
lunch	*kosilo*
dinner	*večerja*
set menu	*menu*
food stall	*kiosk*
grocery store	*samopostrežba*
delicatessen	*delikatesa*
market	*tržica*
restaurant	*restavracija*
waiter/waitress	*natakar/natakarica*

I would like the set lunch, please.	*Lahko dobim menu, prosim.*
Is service included in the bill?	*Ali je napitnina vključena?*
I am a vegetarian.	*Vegetarijanec sem.*
I would like some...	*Rad bi nekaj...*
Another, please.	*Še enkrat, prosim.*

The bill (check), please.	*Račun, prosim.*
I don't eat...	*Ne jem...*

beer	*pivo*
bread	*kruh*
butter	*maslo*
cheese	*sir*
chicken	*piščanec*
coffee	*kava*
eggs	*jajca*
fish	*riba*
food	*hrana*
fruit	*sadje*
fruit juice	*sadni sok*
meat	*meso*
milk	*mleko*
mineral water	*mineralna voda*
pepper	*poper*
pork	*svinjina*
salt	*sol*
soup	*juha*
sugar	*sladkor*
tea	*čaj*
vegetables	*zelenjava*
wine	*vino*

hot/cold	*topel/hladen*
with/without	*z/brez*

Shopping

How much does it cost?	*Koliko stane?*
I would like to buy it.	*Rad bi kupil.*
It's too expensive for me.	*Predrago je zame.*
Can I look at it?	*Ali lahko pogledam?*
I'm just looking.	*Samo gledam.*
I'm looking for...	*Iščem...*
the chemist	*lekarno*
clothing	*oblačila*
souvenirs	*spominke*
Do you take travellers' cheques?	*Ali vzamete potovalne čeke?*
Do you have another colour/size?	*Ali imate drugo barvo/velikost?*

big/bigger	*velik/večji*
small/smaller	*majhen/manjši*
more/less	*več/manj*
cheap/cheaper	*poceni/cenejši*

Time & Dates

When?	*Kdaj?*
today	*danes*
tonight	*danes zvečer*
tomorrow	*jutri*
the day after tomorrow	*pojutrišnjem*
yesterday	*včeraj*
all day/every day	*ves dan/vsak dan*

Monday	*ponedeljek*
Tuesday	*torek*
Wednesday	*sreda*
Thursday	*četrtek*
Friday	*petek*
Saturday	*sobota*
Sunday	*nedelja*

January	*januar*
February	*februar*
March	*marec*
April	*april*
May	*maj*
June	*junij*
July	*julij*
August	*avgust*
September	*september*
October	*oktober*
November	*november*
December	*december*

What time is it?	*Koliko je ura?*
It's...o'clock	*Ura je...*
in the morning	*zjutraj*
in the evening	*zvečer*
1.15	*četrt na dve* ('one quarter of two')
1.30	*pol dveh* ('half of two')
1.45	*tri cetrt na dve* ('three quarters of two')

Numbers

0	*nič*	80	*osemdeset*
1	*ena*	90	*devetdeset*
2	*dve*	100	*sto*
3	*tri*	101	*sto ena*
4	*štiri*	110	*sto deset*
5	*pet*	1000	*tisoč*
6	*šest*	one million	*milijon*
7	*sedem*		
8	*osem*		
9	*devet*		
10	*deset*		
11	*enajst*		
12	*dvanajst*		
13	*trinajst*		
14	*štirinajst*		
15	*petnajst*		
16	*šestnajst*		
17	*sedemnajst*		
18	*osemnajst*		
19	*devetnajst*		
20	*dvajset*		
21	*enaindvajset*		
22	*dvaindvajset*		
30	*trideset*		
40	*štirideset*		
50	*petdeset*		
60	*šestdeset*		
70	*sedemdeset*		

Health

I'm diabetic/ epileptic/ asthmatic.	*Sem diabetik/ epileptik/ astmatik.*
I'm allergic to antibiotics/ penicillin.	*Alergičen sem na antibiotike/ penicilin.*
antiseptic	*antiseptičen/ razkužilo*
aspirin	*aspirin*
condoms	*kondomi*
contraceptive	*kontracептično sredstvo*
diarrhoea	*driska*
medicine	*zdravilo*
nausea	*slabost*
sunblock cream	*zaščita proti soncu*
tampons	*tamponi*

Facts for the Visitor

VISAS & EMBASSIES

Slovenia has relaxed its entry requirements considerably since the early days of independence and, in most cases, a valid passport is sufficient for a stay of up to three months. Citizens of Australia, Canada, the EU, Israel, Japan, New Zealand and the USA do not require visas. At the same time, those from any EU country as well as Switzerland can enter Slovenia on just a valid personal identity document, but in this case their visit may not exceed 30 days. Contact any Slovenian embassy, consulate or tourist bureau abroad for recent changes in the regulations. The staff at a branch of Adria Airways, the Slovenian national carrier, should also be able to help. For addresses, see Air in the Getting There & Away chapter.

Those who do require visas (including South African citizens at the time of writing) can get them at any of the Slovenian embassies or consulates listed here for up to 90 days. They cost DM50/£21/US$35, and you may have to show a return or onward ticket. Photographs are not required.

Visas are also available at border crossings (see Car & Motorbike in the Getting There & Away chapter), at Brnik Airport near Ljubljana and upon arrival at Portorož on the *Prince of Venice* catamaran from Italy. There they cost 1500 SIT and photos are not necessary. Theoretically, visas can also be acquired on trains, but you may have to get off and queue, in which case you could miss your onward connection. If you do plan to enter Slovenia by rail, it is strongly advised that you get your visa in advance at a Slovenian embassy or consulate.

Your hotel, hostel, camp site or private room arranged through an agency will register your name and address with the municipal government office (občina) as required by law; that's why they have to take your passport away – at least for the first night. If you are staying elsewhere (eg with relatives or friends), your host will have to take care of this for you and it must be done within three days.

If you want to stay in Slovenia longer than three months, the easiest thing to do is simply cross the border into Italy or Austria and return. Otherwise you will have to apply for a temporary residence permit at the Foreigners Office (Urad za Tujce; ☎ 061-131 0166) in the Kresija building near the market at Adamič-Lundrovo nabrežje 2 in Ljubljana.

Slovenian Embassies & Consulates

In addition to the embassies listed here, Slovenia has honorary consuls in Sydney (☎ 02-314 5116, however, from July 1996 the number will be 02-9314 5116), Australia, and in Cleveland, Ohio (☎ 216-589 9220), in the USA.

Australia
    Advance Bank Centre, Level 6, 60 Marcus Clark St, Canberra, ACT 2601 (☎ 06-243 4830)
Austria
    Nibelungengasse 13, A-1010 Vienna (☎ 0222-586 1304)
    Bahnhofstrasse 22/2, 9020 Klagenfurt (☎ 0463-54 150)
Belgium
    Ave Louise 179, 1050 Brussels (☎ 02-649 9099)
Canada
    150 Metcalfe St, Suite 2101, Ottawa, Ont K2P 1P1 (☎ 613-565 5781)
Croatia
    Savska cesta 41/IX, 41000 Zagreb (☎ 041-517 401)
Czech Republic
    Pod hradbami 15, 16000 Prague 6 (☎ 02-320 872)
France
    21 rue Bouquet de Longchamp, 75016 Paris (☎ 1-47 55 65 90)
    40 allée de la Robertsau, 67000 Strasbourg (☎ 88 36 60 25)
Germany
    Siegfriedstrasse 28, 5300 Bonn 2 (☎ 0228-858 031)
    Lindwurm Strasse 10, 8045 Munich (☎ 089-543 9819)
Hungary
    Lendvay utca 23, 1062 Budapest (☎ 1-153 2374)

Italy

Via Ludovico Pisano 10, 00197 Rome (☎ 06-808 1075)

Via Carducci 29, 34100 Trieste (☎ 040-636 161)

Japan

5-15 Akasaka, 7-chome, Minato-ku, Tokyo 107 (☎ 3-55 70 62 75)

Macedonia

Bulevar Partizanski Odredi 3, 91000 Skopje (☎ 091-116 213)

Russia

Gruzinsky pereulok 3, Suite 41, 123056 Moscow (☎ 095-254 3531)

Spain

Calle Salustiano Olózoga 5, IV-iz, 28001 Madrid (☎ 91-575 6556)

Sweden

Klarabergsgatan 33, 3tr, 11121 Stockholm (☎ 08-217 980)

Switzerland

Schwanengasse 9/II, CH-3011 Bern (☎ 031-312 4418)

UK

Suite 1, Cavendish Court, 11-15 Wigmore St, London W1H 9LA (☎ 0171-495 7775)

USA

1525 New Hampshire Ave NW, Washington, DC 20036 (☎ 202-667 5363)

600 Third Ave, 24th floor, New York, NY 10016 (☎ 212-370 3006)

Foreign Embassies in Slovenia

Selected countries with representation in Ljubljana – either full embassies or consulate holdovers from pre-independence days – appear below. If telephoning from outside the capital within Slovenia, remember to dial 061 first. Citizens of countries not listed here (such as Australia, Canada and South Africa) should contact their embassies in Vienna or Budapest.

Austria

Štrekljeva ulica 5 (☎ 213 436)

Belgium

Snežniška ulica 10 (☎ 219 210)

Bosnia-Hercegovina

Celovška cesta 199 (☎ 159 1249)

Croatia

Gruberjevo nabrežje 6 (☎ 125 7287)

Czech Republic

Kolarjeva ulica 30 (☎ 132 8035)

France

Železna cesta 18/VI (☎ 173 4441)

Germany

Prešernova cesta 27 (☎ 216 166)

Hungary

Dunajska cesta 22/IV (☎ 131 5168)

Italy

Snežniška ulica 8 (☎ 126 2194)

Macedonia

Dunajska cesta 104 (☎ 168 4454)

Netherlands

Dunajska cesta 22/I (☎ 328 978)

Romania

Nanoška ulica 8 (☎ 268 702)

Russia

Rožna Dolina, Cesta II, No 7 (☎ 123 1236)

Switzerland

Šmartinska cesta 130 (☎ 140 5231)

Turkey

Livarska ulica 4 (☎ 132 2012)

UK

Trg Republike 3/IV (☎ 125 7191)

USA

Pražakova ulica 4 (☎ 301 427)

DOCUMENTS

Foreigners travelling in Slovenia do not require any special documentation beyond a valid passport (with visa if necessary) or identity card. While it is always prudent to carry your passport or ID card with you while travelling, hotels, hostels, camping grounds and other types of accommodation in Slovenia almost always hold your papers until you check out – which can make it difficult cashing travellers' cheques.

CUSTOMS

Travellers can bring in the usual personal effects, a couple of cameras and electronic goods for their own use, 200 cigarettes, a generous four litres of spirits but only a litre of wine (remember: viniculture is a big business here). The import or export of more than DM1000 in Slovenian tolars without permission from the Bank of Slovenia is forbidden.

Customs inspections at most border crossings and Brnik Airport are cursory or nonexistent and visitors need only make an oral declaration. However, officers are rather strict about enforcing laws regarding pets, and you may have to turn around – as I almost had to – if Fido's (or Pussy's) papers aren't in order. Basically, a rabies vaccination certificate (in English, German or Italian if you can't manage Slovene) must be at least 30 days old but no older than six months. A veterinarian's certificate of health must be no more than 10 days old.

MONEY

Slovenia's currency, the tolar, is abbreviated as SIT in accordance with the international currency-coding system. Prices in shops, at restaurants and train and bus fares are always in tolars, but hotels, guesthouses and even camping grounds use Deutschmarks as the tolar is linked to it. For that reason, most forms of accommodation listed in this guide are quoted in DM. You are never required to pay in the German currency though.

It is very simple to change cash and travellers' cheques at banks, post offices, travel agencies and *menjalnice*, the private exchange offices that have sprung up like mushrooms after rain in recent years. Look for any of the following words to guide you: Menjalnica, Prevzem Menjalnic or Devizna Blagajna.

There's no black market in Slovenia, but exchange rates can vary tremendously, so it pays to keep your eyes open. For example, on the very same day I got 119 SIT for US$1 at Ljubljanska Banka's main branch on Trg Republike in Ljubljana and 112 SIT at Gorenjska Banka on Prešernova ulica in Kranj – a difference of almost 6%. Banks take a commission *(provizija)* of 1% or none at all, but tourist offices, travel agencies, exchange bureaus and hotels have high fees – sometimes up to 5%.

Banks usually pay a higher rate for travellers' cheques than for cash but some private exchange offices (not travel agencies) do the opposite. Post offices are not the best places to change money as some may only want to accept cash, and when they do take travellers' cheques it will be at a poor rate.

You can usually exchange excess tolars back into US dollars or Deutschmarks (the 24-hour exchange office at Ljubljana's train station is a good place), but exchange receipts may be required. Some offices will refuse to change them back, and tolars are nearly impossible to get rid of outside Slovenia so only change what you need.

Spend what's left over on long-distance telephone calls or put something in the poor box at a church.

Slovenia, which had relatively liberal currency-exchange laws even when it was a part of Yugoslavia, is also a good place to trade one hard currency for another – US dollars for Deutschmarks, say – without having to have it converted into tolars first. You can also get cash dollars or Deutschmarks for your travellers' cheques at most banks for a flat 3% commission.

Ljubljanska Banka branches will cash Eurocheques for up to 25,000 SIT (or the equivalent).

Currency

The Slovenian tolar, a new currency with a distinguished pedigree, is theoretically divided into 100 *stotinov* but nowadays you'll encounter only the 50 *stotin* version of these worthless aluminium coins. More substantial brassy coins of one tolar, two *tolarja* and five *tolarji* have been in circulation since 1992.

Slovenia's truly colourful paper money designed by the postmodernist artist Rudi Španzel comes in eight denominations: 10, 20, 50, 100, 200, 500, 1000 and 5000 SIT. They bear the likenesses of Slovenian writers, historians, artists, scientists, architects and musicians; thankfully, there's not a general among them.

The 10 SIT note bears the portrait of Primož Trubar (1508-86), the Protestant reformer and translator, while the 20 SIT note portrays the historian and geographer Janez Vajkard Valvasor (1641-93). The 50 SIT note has the mathematician Jurij Vega (1754-1802).

The 100 SIT bill takes us into the 20th century with the stern-faced Impressionist painter Rihard Jakopič (1869-1943). Jakob Gallus (1550-91), a composer who worked mostly in Prague, is on the 200 SIT note, while the architect Jože Plečnik (1872-1955) is portrayed on the 500 SIT note. The Romantic poet and patriot France Prešeren (1800-49) is on the 1000 SIT note and, in a bow to political correctness, a woman – the

Realist painter Ivana Kobilca (1861-1926) – takes pride of place on the 5000 SIT note. There are plans to issue a 10,000 SIT note, which will probably feature Ivan Cankar (1876-1918), the writer who has been called the 'outstanding master of Slovenian prose'.

Exchange Rates

As the tolar remains tied to the Deutschmark, it will continue to reflect fluctuations in the German currency's value for the foreseeable future. As a result, the following exchange rates for cash/travellers' cheques should be viewed as a guide only.

Australia	A$1	=	82/85 SIT
Austria	ASch 1	=	11/12 SIT
Canada	C$1	=	79/81 SIT
Germany	DM1	=	181/182 SIT
European Union	ECU 1	=	150 SIT**
Italy	ItL 100	=	6.5/6.6 SIT
Czech Republic	Kčs 1	=	4.5 SIT*
New Zealand	NZ$1	=	76 SIT*
South Africa	SAfr R1	=	33 SIT*
Switzerland	Sfr 1	=	97/99 SIT
UK	UK£1	=	177/184 SIT
USA	US$1	=	112/116 SIT
Japan	¥100	=	124/129 SIT

*cash only
**cheques only

Exchange rates for other currencies in the region, like the Croatian kuna and the Hungarian forint, change so rapidly that any quotation can be obsolete almost immediately. Embassies can help you with the official rate, but if you want to know what the *real* (ie black-market) rate is in some of these countries, ask the hawkers at any flea market near the border.

Credit Cards

Visa, MasterCard and American Express cards are widely accepted at up-market restaurants, shops, hotels, car-rental firms and some travel agencies. Otherwise, you'll have to rely on cash.

There are no automatic teller machines (ATMs) open to foreign-account holders at present in Slovenia, but clients of Visa can get cash advances in tolars from any A Banka branch. If you have problems with your Visa card, contact the Visa Centre (☎ 061-302 055) in the office complex at Slovenska cesta 56 in Ljubljana. They can't replace a lost or stolen card, but they can put a stop-payment order on it. The centre can also replace lost or stolen Visa, Thomas Cook, Bank of America and Barclay's Bank travellers' cheques.

American Express customers who have problems with their card or need money

---

The Almighty Tolar

The Slovenian tolar, the currency that sounds suspiciously like 'dollar', actually shares the same origin and etymology as its more worldly cousin.

Both 'tolar' and 'dollar' are modified forms of the German word *thaler*, the name of a silver coin first struck in 1518 under Emperor Charles V of Germany, also King of Spain and the Spanish colonies in the New World. The silver was mined at a place called St Joachimsthal (Joachim's Dale) in Bohemia, and the coin circulated in Germany from the 16th century onward under various names: thaler, daler, dalar and tallero. The thaler was replaced by the mark as the German monetary unit in 1873.

The Spanish peso – the celebrated 'piece of eight' of sea ditties – circulated in the Spanish and English colonies in 17th century America and was known as a 'dollar' to English speakers. In 1792, the fledgling US government bowed to this familiarity and adopted it as its official currency. Canada followed in 1858, as did Australia in 1966 and New Zealand a year later.

In October 1991, as the last of the Yugoslav army left Slovenia, the central bank issued its own tolar coupons to replace the Yugoslav dinars in circulation. A year later Slovenia had its own currency. ∎

should contact Atlas (☎ 061-222 711) at Mestni trg 8 in Ljubljana. They can replace cards (though you must know the account number) and make refunds for lost or stolen American Express travellers' cheques. Green Card holders can get up to US$200 in cash tolars and US$1000 in US dollar travellers' cheques; anyone with a Gold Card can get the tolar cash equivalent of US$500 and US$1500 in dollar cheques. The advance must be approved by the head office in Zagreb, but that usually only takes a few minutes. Payment is actually made by Ljubljanska Banka at Trg Republike 2.

Eurocard and MasterCard clients should go to Ljubljanska Banka (☎ 061-125 0155) on Trg Republike.

Costs

Though prices are increasing, with imported items costing as much as they do in Western Europe, Slovenia remains much cheaper than nearby Italy and Austria. But don't expect it to be a bargain basement like Hungary; everything costs at least 50% more here.

If you stay at private rooms or guesthouses, eat at medium-priced restaurants and travel 2nd class, you should get by on under US$40 a day. Those putting up at hostels or college dormitories, eating *burek* (meat- or cheese-filled pastries) for lunch and at self-service restaurants at night will cut costs considerably. Travelling in a little more style and comfort – occasional restaurant splurges with bottles of wine, an active nightlife, small hotels/guesthouses with 'character' – will cost about US$65 a day.

Tipping & Bargaining

Tipping is not really necessary at Slovenian restaurants (many take a 10% service charge anyway), bars or hotels, but no one is going to complain if you hand them a gratuity. Taxi drivers are almost never tipped, but you can round up if you have been happy with the ride or for the sake of convenience to a maximum 10%.

As in Eastern Europe, bargaining was not the done thing under Communism; everyone paid the same amount by weight and volume. Nowadays vendors at flea markets and individuals selling folk crafts may be open to haggling, but even this is not very common. At hotels enjoying less-than-full occupancy during the off-season, you may be able to get a *popust* (discount) of up to 25%.

Consumer Taxes

A 'circulation tax' called Prometni Davek (PD), and not unlike Value-Added Tax (VAT), covers the purchase of most goods and services, from imported electronic equipment and top-class hotels (20%) to books (10%) and car rentals (5%). It is usually included in the quoted price of goods but not some services, so beware.

Visitors can claim refunds on total purchases of 11,000 SIT or more (not including tobacco products or spirits) through Kompas MTS, which has offices at Brnik Airport and about 30 border crossings; they are marked with an asterisk (*) in the Car & Motorbike section of the Getting There & Away chapter. But in order to make the claim, you must have a European Tax-free Shopping (ETS) cheque correctly filled out by the salesperson at the time of purchase and have it stamped by a Slovenian customs officer at the border. You can then collect your refund – minus commission – from the nearby Kompas MTS payment office in cash.

Most towns and cities levy a 'tourist tax' on visitors staying the night.

WHEN TO GO

April to September are the best months to be in Slovenia as the days are long and the weather is warm. Snow can linger in the mountains as late as June, but spring (April and May) is a good time to be in the lowlands and valleys when everything is fresh and in blossom (though April can be a bit wet). In July and August, hotel rates are increased and there are lots of tourists, especially on the coast. September is an excellent month to visit Slovenia as the summer crowds have vanished, and it's the best time for hiking and climbing. October and November can be rainy but winter (December to March) is for skiers. Remember though that Slovenian school kids get their Christmas holidays in December/January and a week off in early February specifically to learn how to ski. The slopes will be packed at those times.

WHAT TO BRING

You don't have to remember any particular items of clothing – a warm sweater (even in summer) for the mountains at night, perhaps, and an umbrella in the spring or autumn – unless you plan to do some serious hiking or other sport. In general, Slovenian society dresses casually (though a bit smarter in Ljubljana) when it goes out on the town.

A swimsuit for the beach, pool or mixed-sex thermal spas and a towel and thongs (flip-flops) for mouldy showers in hostels and guesthouses are mandatory. Soap, tooth-paste and toilet paper are readily obtainable almost anywhere, as are tampons and condoms, both locally made and imported.

A sleeping sheet with pillow cover (case) is a good idea if you plan to stay in hostels or college dormitories. A padlock is useful to secure your hostel locker. A pocket knife is helpful for all sorts of things. Make sure it includes such essentials as a bottle opener and a strong corkscrew.

Slovenes drink lots of herbal teas and tisanes but if you like your cuppa strong and black, you're out of luck. Bring along a cup, coil water heater and tea bags to make your own.

Other optional items include a compass (to help orient yourself in the mountains and while driving), a torch (flashlight), an adapter plug for electrical appliances, a universal sink plug, sunglasses, a few clothes pegs and a length of cord to use as a washing line, and pre-moistened towelettes or a large cotton handkerchief that you can soak in fountains and use to cool off while touring towns and cities in the hot summer months. And don't forget sunscreen lotion – even in the cooler months. Those rays in the mountains can be fierce.

TOURIST OFFICES
Local Tourist Offices

For a country so keen on getting visitors through its doors, tourism is not very well organised on either the national or local level. Outside large cities like Ljubljana and Maribor or very popular destinations in the Alps or on the coast, it can be very difficult to obtain information in any language. Even some of the foreign offices, such as the one in London, can be less than helpful.

The best tourist office in Slovenia – bar none – is the Tourist Information Centre (TIC; ☎ 061-224 222; fax 222 115) in Ljubljana. They know everything about Slovenia. Bled, Bohinj (at Ribčev Laz), Izola, Kamnik, Kranj, Kranjska Gora and Škofja Loka also have excellent tourist offices. If there is no office in a town or city you're visiting, seek assistance at a branch of one of the national travel agencies or from hotel or museum staff.

Travel Agencies

The head offices (all in Ljubljana; telephone code 061) of Slovenia's five most important travel agencies appear below. For the addresses and telephone numbers of branch offices in Ljubljana and the provinces, see the Information sections for each town.

Emona Globtour
    Šmartinska cesta 130 (☎ 140 1044; fax 441 325)
Kompas Holidays
    Slovenska cesta 36 (☎ 132 1053; fax 219 111)
Kompas Turizem
    Pražakova ulica 4 (☎ 133 4180; fax 317 180)
Slovenijaturist
    Slovenska cesta 58 (☎ 131 5288; fax 328 884)
Vas (rural tourism)
    Miklošičeva cesta 4 (☎ 132 8093; fax 219 388)

Tourist Offices & Agencies Abroad

Slovenia – sometimes in conjunction with Kompas – maintains tourist offices in the following eight countries:

Austria
    Hilton Center, Landstrasser Hauptstrasse 2,
    A-1030 Vienna (☎ 0222-715 4010)
Czech Republic
    Thámova 34, 18000 Prague VIII (☎ 02-203 544)

Germany
Lessing Strasse 7-9, 61440 Oberursel (☎ 06171-64 1660)
Hungary
Hotel Buda Penta, Krisztina körút 41-43, 1013 Budapest (☎ 1-156 6333 ext 111)
Netherlands
Goudent 8, NL-4330 GC Middelburg (☎ 01180-35 790)
Switzerland
St Leodegarstrasse 2, CH-6006 Lucerne (☎ 041-528 515)
UK
2 Canfield Place, London NW6 3BT (☎ 0171-372 3767)
USA
122 East 42nd St, Suite 3006, New York, NY 10168-0072 (☎ 212-421 0551)

In addition, Kompas has representative offices in 13 cities worldwide, including:

Australia
3/257 Boundary St, Spring Hill, Queensland 4000 (☎ 07-3831 4400)
Austria
Zimmermann Gasse 13, A-1010 Vienna (☎ 0222-402 2042)
Canada
4060 Ste-Catherine St West, Suite 535, Montreal, Que H3Z 2Z3 (☎ 514-938 4041)
Czech Republic
Thakurova 6/II, 16000 Prague VI (☎ 02-311 0363)
France
23, rue Singer, 75016 Paris (☎ 1-45 20 65 84)
Germany
Toleranzstrasse 3a, 1080 Berlin (☎ 030-609 3079)
Mailuststrasse 6/VI, 6000 Frankfurt (☎ 069-233 025)
Strogenweg 8, 8000 Munich (☎ 089-904 6355)
Italy
Calle Castello 2139, 30122 Venice (☎ 041-520 6184)
Russia
Obolenskij pereulok 5, Suite 118, 119021 Moscow (☎ 095-249 2280)
Spain
Plaza Tetuan 14, Entresuelo B, 08010 Barcelona (☎ 93-265 1455)
USA
2826 East Commercial Blvd, Fort Lauderdale, FL 33308 (☎ 305-771 9200)
10662 El Adelante Ave, Fountain Valley, CA 92708 (☎ 714-378 0510)

Tourist Literature

The tourist offices and other agencies produce many brochures, pamphlets and booklets in English, some of them overly colourful and 'sing-song', others quite useful and well written. If a map or pamphlet is up to date, it will have 'Slovenija/Slovenia' printed prominently and alone on the front – not just a label pasted over 'Slovenia, Yugoslavia'.

The titles below are general ones; more specialised publications and local ones appear under other headings in this chapter or in the Information sections for each town.

Calendar of Events in Slovenia
An annual list of everything happening in Slovenia – from concerts and marathons to trade fairs and conferences
Kako Se Reče?/What Is It Called?
A slim, vest-pocket dictionary with key words and phrases in Slovene, English, French, Italian, German and Spanish
Fishing in Slovenia/Ribolov v Sloveniji
Details, seasons and prices for angling in a dozen different rivers and lakes
Holiday on a Farm
A complete list of almost 120 farms accepting paying guests in Slovenia's eight provinces
Holidays in a Saddle
A full list of the horse-riding centres in Slovenia
Hotel Rates in Slovenia
Virtually every type of accommodation (not just hotels) appears in this annual publication
Meet with an Unforgettable Experience: Camp Sites in Slovenia
Descriptions and photographs of the more than 40 registered camping grounds in the country
A Merry Wintertime on the Sunny Side of the Alps
This slim brochure describes the facilities and nearby accommodation at some 47 ski resorts and grounds in Slovenia – from Kranjska Gora to tiny Janina Hill in Rogaška Slatina
Slovenian Health Resorts
This pamphlet covers all aspects of spa tourism in Slovenia, with a listing of 16 resorts and their facilities
Slovenia in Figures
Every statistic you may (or may not) need to know about Slovenia – from unemployment rates to how much the average family spends on bread

USEFUL ORGANISATIONS

In addition to the organisations listed elsewhere in this chapter, the following may be helpful for visitors to Slovenia with special interests.

Archives of the Republic of Slovenia (Arhiv Republike Slovenije), Gruber Palace, Zvezdarska ulica 2, 61000 Ljubljana (☎ 061-125 1266). If you are searching for your Slovenian roots, check first with the municipal government *(mestna občina)* or county office (občina); they have birth and death certificates going back a century. Vital records beyond the 100-year limit are kept at the national archives.

Centre for Tourist & Economic Promotion (CTEP; ☎ 061-125 6172), Igriška ulica 5, 61000 Ljubljana. This is the umbrella organisation for tourist offices in Slovenia and produces brochures and pamphlets.

Slovenian Emigrants' Centre (Slovenska Izseljenska Matica), Cankarjeva ulica 1/II, 61000 Ljubljana (☎ 061-210 733). This office deals with ethnic Slovenes living abroad and publishes the quarterly magazine *Slovenija* in English.

BUSINESS HOURS

With very few exceptions, the opening times *(delovni čas)* of a business, museum or government office are posted on the front door.

Shops, groceries and department stores are open from about 8 am to 7 or 8 pm on weekdays and to 1 or 2 pm on Saturday. In winter they may close an hour earlier. Bank hours vary but generally they're from 8 am to 5 or 6 pm weekdays (often with a lunchtime break) and till noon on Saturday. The main post office in any city or town (usually the ones listed in the Information sections) is open from 7 am to 8 pm weekdays, till 1 pm or later on Saturday and from 9 to 11 am on Sunday. Branch offices close earlier on weekdays and at noon on Saturday. They are closed on Sunday.

Museums are usually open from 10 am to 6 pm Tuesday to Sunday but many, strapped for cash, have had to curtail their hours in recent years. Most government offices close at 3 pm.

HOLIDAYS

Slovenia has a total of 13 public holidays *(prazniki)*. If any of the following fall on a Sunday, then the Monday becomes the holiday.

1 & 2 January
    New Year's holidays
8 February
    Prešeren/Culture Day
March/April
    Easter Monday
27 April
    Insurrection Day
1 & 2 May
    Labour Day holidays
25 June
    National Day
15 August
    Assumption Day
31 October
    Reformation Day
1 November
    All Saints' Day
25 December
    Christmas Day
26 December
    Independence Day

Though not a public holiday, St Martin's Day (11 November) is important for on this day, must (pressed grape juice) officially becomes wine and can be sold as such. That evening families traditionally dine on goose, and some restaurants offer a *Martinovanje* dinner of goose and young wine accompanied by folk music.

On Palm Sunday (the Sunday before Easter), people carry a complex arrangement of greenery and ribbons called a *butara* to church to be blessed. The butare end up as home decorations or are placed on the graves of relatives. On the eve of St Gregory's Day (3 September), children in certain Gorenjska towns and villages (Tržič, Kropa) set afloat hundreds of tiny boats bearing candles – perhaps in memory of the saint's conversion of Britain in the 6th century AD.

Many towns celebrate Midsummer's Night (*Kresna Noč*; 23 June) by lighting a large bonfire, and St John's Eve (30 April) is the night for setting up the maypoles. A *žegnanje* is a fair or some sort of celebration held on the feast day of the patron saint of a church. Many of them take place throughout Slovenia on 15 August, the Assumption of the Virgin Mary, especially at Ptujska Gora near Ptuj and Sveta Gora north of Nova Gorica.

CULTURAL & SPORTING EVENTS

Major cultural and sporting events in Slovenia appear in the Festivals section for each town and city. The following abbreviated list gives you a taste of what to expect.

January
> Women's World Cup Slalom and Giant Slalom Competition (Golden Fox), Pohorje – One of the major international ski events for women held on the slopes south-west of Maribor in late January/early February

February
> Kurentovanje, Ptuj – A 'rite of spring' celebrated for 10 days up to Shrove Tuesday and the most popular Mardi Gras celebration in Slovenia (though others take place in Cerknica and Cerkno)

March
> Ski Jumping World Championships, Planica – Three days of high flying on skis near Kranjska Gora

April
> International Motocross Grand Prix of Slovenia, Orehova Vas (Štajerska)

May
> Tour de Slovénie, Otočec – International bicycle race around Slovenia starting in Dolenjska

June
> Festival Lent, Maribor – A two-week extravaganza of folklore and culture held in late June/early July with stages set up throughout the old part of town

July
> International Summer Festival, Ljubljana – The nation's premier cultural event (music, theatre and dance) from mid-July through August

August
> Piran Musical Evenings, Piran and Portorož – Concerts held in various locations

September
> Kravji Bal (Cows' Ball), Bohinj – A zany weekend in September of folk dance, music, eating and drinking to mark the return of the cows from their high pastures to the valleys

October
> Dormouse Night (Polharska Noč), Cerknica – Celebration and feast during the very short dormouse-hunting season

December
> Christmas concerts, Ljubljana and Postojna Cave

POST & TELECOMMUNICATIONS
Post

PTT Slovenija, recognised by its bright-yellow sign, offers a wide variety of services – from selling stamps and telephone cards

and tokens to sending faxes and changing money. The queues are never very long, but you can avoid a trip to the post office if you just want to mail a few postcards by buying stamps *(znamke)* at Delo or Tobak newsstands and dropping your mail into any of the yellow letterboxes on the street.

Look for the signs *Sprejem Pisemskih Pošiljk* if you're posting a letter and *Sprejem Paketov* if you've got a parcel. Domestic mail costs 12 SIT for up to 20 grammes and 22 SIT for up to 100. Postcards are 12 SIT. For international mail, the base rate is 70 SIT for 20 grammes or less, 120 SIT for up to 100 grammes and 44 SIT for a postcard. Then you have to add on the air-mail charge for every 10 grammes: 10 SIT for Europe, 15 SIT for North America, 16 SIT for most of Asia and 22 SIT for Australasia. Thus, standard-size postcards sent via air mail to friends in London, New York, Hong Kong or

Sydney will cost 54, 59, 60 or 66 SIT respectively.

Something mailed within Slovenia takes only a day or two, but international mail can be slow. Post to neighbouring countries and ones close by like Germany should take about five days. For Britain, count on a week and the USA about 10 days. Mail to Asia and Australia takes between 10 days and two weeks.

Poste restante is sent to the main post office in a city or town (in the capital, it goes to the one at Slovenska cesta 32, 61101 Ljubljana) where it is held for 30 days. American Express card-holders can have their mail addressed c/o the Atlas travel agency, Mestni trg 8, 61000 Ljubljana.

You can exchange cash and travellers' cheques at most post offices in Slovenia, but not Eurocheques.

Telephone

Slovenia's telephone system works, but it is rather antiquated. The easiest place to make long-distance calls as well as send telegrams and faxes is from a post office or telephone centre; the one at Pražakova ulica 3 in Ljubljana is open 24 hours a day. Simply go into one of the booths (sometimes you have to take a number first), make your call and then pay the cashier. Some booths have electronic metres telling you exactly how much you're spending as you chat away.

You can also use public telephones on the street, but these require a token *(žeton)* or a phone card *(telefonska kartica)*; they never take coins. Phone boxes that accept tokens are marked with a 'Ž'; those taking cards (rare outside Ljubljana) have a 'K'.

Tokens, available at post offices and some newsstands, come in three types. Token A (24 SIT) has five impulses and is used for brief local calls. Token B, with 25 impulses for 64 SIT, can be used for longer or domestic calls. Token C costs 104 SIT and has 50 impulses. You can only use the tokens once; they are not returned for later use.

The most common telephone card, and valid throughout most of the country, is the one issued by PTT Slovenija. It costs 266

SIT for 100 impulses and 446 SIT for 200; you'd need one of the latter for three minutes to the UK and at least two for the same conversation to the USA or Australia. A much more expensive card, issued and used in Primorska only, is called Telefonska Kartica Čip Impulz with 100 impulses for 900 SIT and 300 for 2200 SIT. With a 300 SIT Čip Impulz card you get only two minutes and 10 seconds to the UK and a mere one minute and 15 seconds to the USA or Australia.

Slovenian call boxes do not display their telephone numbers so it's impossible for the other party to phone you back. There are no 'country direct' services yet available, and most telephone credit cards like Sprint and AT&T still can't be used from Slovenia.

To call Slovenia from abroad, dial the international access code, 386 (the country code for Slovenia), the area code (minus the initial zero) and the number. There are 12 area codes in Slovenia and these are listed in the Information section of each city and town. Most have three digits (eg 061 in Ljubljana, 062 in Maribor), but a few areas of Koroška and Dolenjska have four digits (0602 is the code for Slovenj Gradec). Slovenian telephone numbers themselves can have between five and seven digits.

When making a domestic call from one area to another, you must use the code. To call abroad, dial 00 followed by the country and area codes and then the number.

Telephone numbers you may find useful include:

☎ 981 & 985 – general information
☎ 988 – directory assistance for Slovenia
☎ 989 – directory assistance for other countries
☎ 901 – international operator/collect calls
☎ 95 – time (in Slovene)

TIME

Slovenia lies in the Central European time zone. In winter the time is GMT plus one hour, while in summer it's GMT plus two hours. Clocks are advanced by one hour at 2 am on the last Sunday in March and turned back on the last Sunday in September.

Without taking daylight-saving time into account, when it's noon in Ljubljana (and the lunchtime siren blows), it's...

3 am in San Francisco and Vancouver
6 am in New York and Toronto
11 am in London and Dublin
noon in Belgrade, Berlin, Paris, Vienna and Warsaw
1 pm in Bucharest and Athens
2 pm in Moscow
7 pm in Hong Kong
8 pm in Tokyo
9 pm in Sydney
11 pm in Auckland

Like a lot of other European languages, Slovene tells the time by making reference to the next hour – not the last one. Thus 1.15 is 'one quarter of two', 1.30 is 'half of two' and 1.45 is 'three quarters of two'.

ELECTRICITY

The electric current in Slovenia is 220 volts, 50 Hz AC. Plugs are the standard European type with two pins. Do not attempt to plug an American appliance into a Slovenian outlet without a transformer.

LAUNDRY

With over 95% of all Slovenian households owning washing machines...well, good luck finding a self-serve laundrette! The best place to look for do-it-yourself washers and dryers is at hostels, college dormitories and camp sites (about a dozen have them), and there are a couple of places in Ljubljana that will do your laundry reasonably quickly (see Laundry in the Information section of that chapter). Hotels will take care of it, too – at a price. I had a load done at a hotel in Ptuj that cost me an extortionate 4000 SIT!

WEIGHTS & MEASURES

Slovenia uses the metric system exclusively. In supermarkets and outdoor markets, fresh food is sold by weight or by piece *(kos)*. When ordering by weight, you specify by kilo or decagramme *(dekagram)*. Fresh fish is almost always sold in restaurants by decagramme, usually abbreviated as *dag*. Fifty decagrammes is equal to half a kilo or roughly one pound. For those who need help with the metric system, there's a conversion table at the back of this book.

Beer is served in a *pivnica* (pub) in either a half-litre glass *(veliko pivo)* or a glass measuring one-third of a litre *(malo pivo)*. Wine comes in litre bottles or is ordered by the *deci* (decilitre, 0.1 litre). A 'normal' glass of wine is about two decilitres *(dva deci)* but no one is going to blink an eye if you order three or more.

BOOKS & MAPS

There's no shortage of books on Slovenia but the big problem is price: printed material of any kind is terribly expensive in this country. The useful *Atlas of Slovenia*, for example, will set you back 13,450 SIT, while an attractive, but by no means lavish, picture book on the history of urban development called *Naselbinska Kultura na Slovenskem* costs a whopping 17,850 SIT. *Discover Slovenia*, a 127-page paperback, is priced at 2205 SIT and even maps or simple town plans cost 500 to 600 SIT each. Remember that Slovenes, who earn a lot less than most of us, have to pay those prices too. Slovenia is the third-smallest literature market in Europe and a fiction 'best seller' in this country means 500 to 1000 copies.

Most of the following books can be purchased at any branch of Mladinska Knjiga. See the Information section of individual towns for addresses. Unless noted otherwise, the publishers are all based in Ljubljana.

History & Politics

The Slovenians from Earliest Times (Co-ordinating Committee of Slovenian Organisations in Victoria, Eltham, Australia) by Draga Gelt is an oversized, illustrated history published before independence, but it's very poorly written. A better bet is the new *Brief History of Slovenia* (Mihelač) by Janko Prunk.

Slovenija for Everyone (Vitrum) is an 'idiot's guide' to the nation's political, economic and judicial systems with all cultural, scientific and media associations listed. It is updated annually.

Culture
Discover Slovenia (Cankarjeva Založba) is not exclusively devoted to things cultural but contains a very enlightening section. It also introduces the nation's history, geography and key cities and towns. *Traditional Arts & Crafts in Slovenia* by Berk is a lavishly illustrated guide to local folk craft and lore.

Picture Books
There are plenty of these. The 80-page *Greetings from Slovenia*, available in English, German and Slovene, introduces the country's natural and cultural heritage with shots of daily life. The 244-page *Slovenia from the Air* in English, German and Slovene by Matjaž Kmecl et al has the standard 'Gosh!' photographs of Slovenia's mountains, lakes, coast and towns taken from on high.

A superb book, with excellent photos and text that delves into Slovenian culture, history and folklore, is *Mountains of Slovenia* (*Cankarjeva Založba*) by Matjaž Kmecl et al.

Travel Guides
You are holding the first complete guidebook to Slovenia in the English language, though Lonely Planet's *Mediterranean Europe on a Shoestring* and *Eastern Europe on a Shoestring* include a brief chapter on the country. The only other guide devoted exclusively to the country is the Italian-language *Slovenia* (ClupGuide, Milan) by Aldo Pavan, but it's not very practical.

Good local guides to the whole country are thin on the ground, but the *Slovenia Art Guide* (Marketing 013 ZTP) by Nace Šumi is an excellent illustrated primer to the country's architecture. For Ljubljana, choose *Walks in Old Ljubljana* (Marketing 013 ZTP) by Ivan Stopar or *Outdoor Sculpture in Ljubljana* (DZS) by Špelca Čopič et al.

A book entitled *500 Dobrih Zasebnih Gostišča v Sloveniji* (OZS) has 500 good private inns and restaurants throughout Slovenia. But it's just a listing of names, addresses, telephone numbers and opening hours; there are no reviews or recommendations.

Language
The best dictionary is the English-Slovene/Slovene-English *Moderni Slovar/Modern Dictionary* (Cankarjeva Založba) by Daša Komac. *Slovene for Travelers* (Požgaj, Kranj) by Miran Hladnik not only has conversational phrases by topic also but includes excellent cultural information and travel tips. If you think you really want to learn Slovene well on your own, you might try the bizarrely named *Slovene by Synthetic Method* (Philosophy Faculty, University of Ljubljana) by Jože Toporišič. It has four accompanying cassettes, but the course is dated and, frankly, a bit silly.

Maps & Atlases
If you can afford it, the 368-page *Atlas of Slovenia* (Mladinska Knjiga), weighing in at several kg, is the most complete, with 109 1:50 000-scale maps of the country and a dozen town plans. Much more useful is the *Atlas for Travellers in Slovenia* (AMZS) with 22 1:250 000 motoring maps, town plans and practical tips.

Slovenia's main cartographic institute is Geodetski Zavod Slovenije. They produce all sorts of general and specialised maps and atlases as well as plans to about 100 cities, towns and regions.

MEDIA
Newspapers & Magazines
Slovenia counts six daily newspapers, the most widely read being *Delo (Work)* and *Večer (Evening)*. Some three-dozen weeklies, biweeklies and monthlies cover topics as diverse as agriculture, finance and women's fashion. *Mladina (Youth)* is a liberal monthly covering political and social issues.

There are no English-language newspapers, though Vitrum publishes a good political and business newsletter called *Slovenia Weekly* and a magazine devoted to tourism, leisure and the arts called *Flaneur*. You can subscribe to them by contacting

Vitrum Publishing (☎ 061-133 4292; fax 133 2301) at Šaranovičeva ulica 12 in Ljubljana. An annual subscription to *Flaneur*, which appears three or four times a year, costs DM45. *Slovenia Weekly* is DM126. The Slovenian Emigrants' Centre (see the Useful Organisations section) publishes a glossy quarterly magazine in English called *Slovenija*. Subscription is US$25 a year.

M'zine, a bimonthly magazine that started with the Metelkova movement in Ljubljana three years ago but is now independent, will give you a good idea of counter-culture art and music trends, fashion and design in Slovenia. All the articles are summarised in English at the end.

TV & Radio

State-owned RTV Slovenija broadcasts on two channels: Slovenija 1 and Slovenija 2. A subsidiary called RTV Koper-Capodistria broadcasts in Italian on the coast. There are private channels and cable stations as well including Kanal A in Maribor, TV Primorska in Nova Gorica and Vaš Kanal in Novo Mesto. TV is not very good in Slovenia – you may have noticed all the satellite dishes on the roof tops – with 'talking heads' droning on for hours about the state of tourism and the like.

Radio Slovenija has three channels and special ones in Murska Sobota (Radio Murski Val) and Koper (Radio Koper-Capodistria) for the Hungarian and Italian minorities.

Between May and mid-September, Channel 1 broadcasts a weather report and sea conditions at 6.35 am in English and German followed by news and traffic information at 9.35 am. There's nightly news at 10 pm throughout the year. You can listen on MHz/FM frequencies 88.5, 90.0, 90.9, 91.8, 92.0, 92.9, 94.1 and 96.4.

Radio Student in Ljubljana can be heard on MHz frequencies 89.3 and 104.3.

FILM & PHOTOGRAPHY

Film and basic camera equipment (batteries, lens cleaner, etc) are available throughout Slovenia, though the largest selection is in Ljubljana. Film prices vary but 24 exposures of 100 ASA Kodacolor II, Agfa or Fujifilm will cost from 540 to 638 SIT; 36 exposures between 600 and 772 SIT. Ektachrome 100 is 1134 SIT.

Photo developers can be found in towns and cities nationwide and you can have your film processed in a matter of hours. One large outfit with fast processing is Mikrokop Kodak Express at Gregorčičeva ulica 9 in Ljubljana, open from 7 am to 7 pm weekdays. Some smaller agencies offer professional service at competitive rates. One good example in the capital is Foto Grad at Miklošičeva cesta 36. They are affiliated with Kodak and are open from 8 am to 6 pm on weekdays and till noon on Saturday.

Developing print film costs about 2000 SIT for 36 prints (10 x 15 cm). For 36 framed transparencies, expect to pay around 985 SIT.

HEALTH

No special inoculations are needed before visiting Slovenia, and tap water is 100% safe everywhere (though over-chlorinated on the coast). There are no troublesome snakes or creepy-crawlies to worry about, but mosquitoes can be a real pain around lakes and ponds. Make sure you're armed with insect repellent.

The standard of medical care in Slovenia is high and a constituent part of the nation's welfare system. And it is generous: women get a full year off work after having a child and the child's father can opt to take the leave instead if that's what the couple wants.

All foreigners are entitled to emergency medical aid at the very least; for subsequent treatment entitlement varies. Some EU countries (including the UK) have contractual agreements with Slovenia which allow their citizens free care while travelling in the country. This may require carrying a special form so check with your Ministry of Health or equivalent before setting out.

Others have to pay, and medical care and medicine can be very expensive in Slovenia for foreigners. The best idea if you're not covered is to buy temporary health insurance from ZZZS (☎ 061-132 2221) at Miklošičeva cesta 28 in Ljubljana. It costs less than 2000 SIT a month.

Pharmacies are usually open from 7 am to 8 pm and at least one in a town or city is open round the clock. A sign on the door of any pharmacy *(lekarna)* will help you locate the closest 24-hour service.

Remember that travel health depends on your predeparture preparations, your day-to-day health care while travelling and how you handle any medical problem or emergency that does develop.

A travel insurance policy to cover theft, loss and medical problems is a must, so consider this before you leave home. Remember, however, that some policies specifically exclude 'dangerous activities' such as scuba diving, skiing, mountaineering or even trekking.

STUDENT TRAVELLERS

The Student Organisation of the University of Ljubljana (ŠOU; ☎ 061-131 3282) at Kersnikova ulica 4 in the capital is a good place to mix with like-minded people. There's a small club/café there for socialising, and the organisation produces a useful brochure called *Slovenia for Foreign Students* in which, among lots of other things, the dates and locations of weekly student parties are listed. A branch of ŠOU called ŠKUC organises cultural activities such as theatre productions.

Two agencies in Ljubljana – Erazem and Mladi Turist – deal specifically with students and young travellers. See Travel Agencies in the Information section of that chapter for details.

TRAVEL WITH CHILDREN

They might not have a lot of kids – the average family numbers just over three people – but Slovenes love them and this is a very children-friendly country. The family goes everywhere together and you'll see youngsters dining with their parents in even the poshest restaurants.

A great place to visit with the kids (or even deposit them) is the Ranč Kaja & Grom (☎ 0609-616 553) in the village of Zaplana near Rovte, 30 km south-west of Ljubljana. The 'ranch' offers week-long riding and sports programmes (about US$415) for children on their own from nine years and up.

DISABLED TRAVELLERS

Facilities found throughout Slovenia include public telephones with amplifiers for the deaf, special traffic lights at pedestrian crossings that make a beeping noise for the blind, sloped pavements and ramps in government buildings for wheelchairs and reserved spaces in many car parks.

A group that looks after the interests and special needs of paraplegics – Zveza Paraplegikov Republike Slovenije (☎ 061-123 7138) at Štihova ulica 19 in Ljubljana – produces a special guide for its members but unfortunately it is in Slovene only. The TIC in Ljubljana can organise a guide for disabled people with advance notice.

GAY & LESBIAN TRAVELLERS

The gay branch of ŠOU called the Roza Klub (☎ 061-132 4089) publishes a monthly newspaper called *Kekec*, a magazine called *Revolver*, organises a disco every Sunday night at the Klub K4 in Ljubljana and runs a small coffee house/bar (Club Magnus) in the Metelkova squat. But there have been some conflicts recently about funding with the Ljubljana city government, so the future may not be very *roza*.

Lesbians should also contact ŠOV for information about the gay womens' group LL. There's a women-only club called Lilit in the same building as the Club Magnus.

The general age of consent in Slovenia is 14 years.

DANGERS & ANNOYANCES

Slovenia is not a violent or dangerous society. Firearms are strictly controlled, drunks are sloppy but docile and you'll see little of the vandalism and graffiti that plague cities like New York or London. About as bad as the 'handwriting on the wall' gets here is stuff like 'Ljubim Te Slovenija' ('I Love You Slovenia'). At the special traffic lights for the blind, which bear the sign 'Samo za Slepe' ('Only for the Blind'), wags frequently erase the second 'S', making it 'Samo za Lepe' ('Only for the Beautiful'). Gratefully, the organised crime tormenting the countries of Eastern Europe hasn't arrived in Slovenia.

Police say that 90% of all crimes reported involve thefts so take the usual precautions. Be careful of your purse or wallet in bus and train stations and where you may consider leaving it unattended (on the beach, in a hut while hiking). Lock your car at all times, park in well-lit areas and do not leave valuables visible.

In cities such as Ljubljana, Maribor or Koper, you might be approached occasionally by panhandlers who ask for and then demand money. But it's usually nothing serious. One problem can be drunks on the road – literally or behind the wheel – especially on St Martin's Day (11 November) when grape juice legally becomes new wine and everybody has got to have a sip or three.

In the event of an emergency, the following are the most important numbers which can be dialled nationwide:

☎ 92 – Police (Policija)
☎ 93 – Fire (Gasilci)
☎ 94 – First Aid/Ambulance (Prva Pomoč)
☎ 987 – Automobile assistance (AMZS)

WORK

Employment of foreigners in Slovenia is among the most restricted in Europe, and there are already some 34,000 labourers here from the former Yugoslav republics.

Travellers on tourist visas in Slovenia are not supposed to accept employment, but many end up teaching English (going rate: DM25 per hour) or even doing a little work for foreign firms without work permits. An organisation called Most (Bridge), part of the Service Civil International (SCI), organises summer work camps in Slovenia on projects ranging from ecology research in Novo Mesto to working with Gypsies near Murska Sobota. Contact a local branch of the SCI or the ŠOU student organisation in Ljubljana.

ACTIVITIES

Slovenes have a strong attachment to nature and they lead active, outdoor lives from an early age. From skiing and cycling to caving and bird-watching, Slovenia has it all and such activities are always affordable. Oddly, Slovenia is one of the few countries in Europe where football is not a national passion. The most popular spectator sport here is basketball.

Skiing

Skiing is by far the most popular recreational pursuit in Slovenia, and some people believe the sport was actually invented in the 17th century on the Bloke Plateau in Notranjska province. Everybody seems to take to the slopes or trails in season (mainly between December and March) and you can too – at almost four-dozen ski resorts and grounds.

Most of the biggest resorts are in the Julian Alps – Kranjska Gora (skiing up to 1810 metres), Vogel (1800 metres) above Bohinj, Krvavec (1450 metres) east of Kranj – but

other large resorts are in the Pohorje Massif, including those at the Maribor Pohorje (1347 metres) and Rogla (1517 metres). The highest altitude skiing is at Kanin (2200 metres) near Bovec, where the season often extends into May. These and other resorts have multiple chair lifts, tows and cable cars, ski schools, equipment rental and large resort hotels.

In recent years 'the sunny side of the Alps' has become more than just a cute slogan, and snowfall at the lower-lying resorts has been minimal or nonexistent. A large number of Slovenian aficionados have been heading for 'shady' Austria, where the skiing has been better. The ski resorts in Slovenia are most crowded over the Christmas holidays and in early February, when children get a week off from school to learn the sport.

Hiking & Climbing

Almost as many Slovenes hike as they do ski and one of the nicest things about this activity is that it gives you a chance to meet local people in an informal environment. Though many Slovenes are expert climbers, you don't have to be a mountaineer to 'conquer' Mt Triglav (2864 metres), the nation's highest peak.

Slovenia has an excellent system of trails – some 9000 km of them – and they are most commonly marked by a red circle with a white centre. At crossings, there are signs indicating distances and walking times. The Julian Alps, the Kamnik-Savinja Alps and the Pohorje Massif are the most popular places for hiking, but there are some wonderful trails in the lower hills and valleys as well.

The E6 European Hiking Trail running from the Baltic to the Adriatic enters Slovenia at Radlje in Koroška and continues for some 280 km to a point south of Mt Snežnik in Notranjska. The E7 European Hiking Trail, which connects the Atlantic with the Black Sea, crosses into Slovenia at Robič in Primorska, runs along the Soča Valley and then crosses through the southern part of Slovenia eastward to Bistrica ob Sotli in Štajerska before exiting into Croatia. The E6 and E7 trails are marked by a red circle with a yellow centre.

The Slovenian Alpine Trail, which opened in 1953, runs from Maribor to Ankaran on the coast via the Pohorje Massif, the Kamnik-Savinja Alps, the Julian Alps and the Cerkno and Idrija hills. You can also follow the Slovenian Geological Trail (Slovenska Geološka Pot) system in various parts of the country.

The Alpine Association of Slovenia (Planinska Zveza Slovenije; PZS) in Ljubljana, the umbrella organisation of 185 clubs with 90,000 paid members, is the font of all information and can organise guides. They also produce hiking maps and a very useful list of 165 mountain huts, refuges and bivouacs throughout Slovenia. They can tell you which huts are open and when, and whether you can book in advance via mobile phone. They also provide information about weather conditions and specific trails in Triglav National Park and elsewhere. More information about the PZS and the park appears in the Ljubljana and Gorenjska chapters.

A bivouac *(bivak)* is the most basic retreat, providing shelter only, while a refuge *(zavetišče)* has refreshments, sometimes accommodation but usually no water. A hut *(koča)* or house *(dom)* can be a simple cottage or a fairly grand establishment like some of the ones near Mt Triglav. A bed for the night, a simple meal and a hot drink shouldn't cost you more than about 1300 SIT. And if you were wondering how all the food in front of you got there, it was carried in by helicopter or on horseback. Some huts at lower altitudes are supplied by cable cars.

The centre for rock climbing is the Bohinj area.

Swimming

In summer, swimming is extremely popular on the coast, in the Bled and Bohinj lakes and the Krka and Kolpa rivers. Virtually every town of any size has a swimming pool open to the public and some, like the one at Portorož, uses heated sea water. Pools sometimes require you to wear a bathing cap;

disposable plastic ones are available from the pool attendant.

Boating & Windsurfing

Sailing is big on the Adriatic, and you can rent sailing boats at several locations along the coast, including the Portorož Marina. You can windsurf here, too, as well as on the lakes.

Kayaking, Canoeing & Rafting

These sports are practised anywhere there's running water but especially on the Sava River in Gorenjska (Šobec camp site near Bled), the Savinja River in Štajerska (Logar Valley, near Radmirje), the Krka River in Dolenjska (Žužemberk, Novo Mesto) and the Kolpa River in Bela Krajina (Vinica).

The best white-water rafting is on the Soča River, one of only a half-dozen rivers in the European Alps whose upper waters are still unspoiled. The centre is at Bovec. See that section in the Primorska chapter for details.

Fishing

Slovenia's rivers and Alpine lakes and streams are teeming with trout, grayling, pike and other fish. The best rivers for angling are the Soča, the Krka, the Kolpa, the Sava Bohinjka near Bohinj and the Unica in Notranjska. Lake fishing is excellent at Bled, Bohinj and Cerknica. But it's not a cheap sport; a daily fishing permit at the popular spots will cost you at least DM50 a day.

For information, licenses and seasons, contact the Fisheries Administration (Zavod za Ribištvo; ☎ 061-126 2019) at Župančičeva ulica 9 in Ljubljana weekdays between 7 am and 3 pm.

Hunting

Hunting is big business in Slovenia and many Europeans (especially Italians) will pay a lot of money to bag a deer, a brace of grouse, a boar or even a bear. (The latter have been making their way north from Croatia in search of more peaceful surroundings, they say.) Among the best areas are the virgin forests of Kočevski Rog and the Gorjanci Hills in Gorenjska.

The Slovenian Hunting Association (Lovska Zveza Slovenije; ☎ 061-214 947), at the same address as the Fisheries Administration in Ljubljana, can organise a guide or include you in a hunting party. In addition to a daily fee, you will be charged for each animal or bird killed. And how much is that? Well, for a prize bear of the highest category a foreign visitor will have to shell out DM12,500.

Horse Riding

Slovenia is a nation of horse riders, and one of the world's most famous horses, the Lipizzaner of the Spanish Riding School in Vienna, was bred here first at Lipica in Primorska. Some 17 centres registered with the Equestrian Association of Slovenia offer riding and lessons, but there are just as many smaller stables renting privately. One of the biggest, and most professional, outfits is the Kaval Equestrian Centre (☎ 067-54 506) at Prestranek Castle, about 6.5 km south of Postojna. You can contact them directly or get information from the Vas travel agency in Ljubljana.

Cycling

Slovenia is a wonderful country for bicycling and mountain biking; the *Slovenia Tourist Map* available for free everywhere lists cycling itineraries. Many towns and cities, including Ljubljana, Maribor, Ptuj, Novo Mesto, Kranj and Škofja Loka, have bicycle lanes and some even have special traffic lights.

Mountain bikes are for rent at Bled and Bohinj and the uncrowded roads around these resorts are a joy to cycle. Other excellent areas for cycling are the Upper Savinja Valley in Štajerska, the Soča Valley, the Krka Valley and, in Koroška, the Drava Valley. Remember that bikes are banned from the trails of Triglav National Park and all motorways.

It is not always easy to rent bicycles and mountain bikes in Slovenia. Places to rent them are listed in the Getting Around sections of each town. Your best bet is at camp sites or the tourist office. Buying one is not really an option; the cheapest mountain bike available at the Maximarket department store on Trg Republike in Ljubljana is about 35,000 SIT.

Prava Pot (☎ 061-131 7114) at Slovenska cesta 55b in Ljubljana organises cycling tours of Slovenia between June and September, including an eight-day trip of Dolenjska following the Krka River for under US$400 including meals and accommodation.

Caving
Of Slovenia's estimated 15,000 caves, two dozen are open to tourists. The vast majority of the richest ones – Škocjan, Postojna, Križna, Planina, Pivka, Predjama – are in the karst areas of Primorska and Notranjska but there are many ice caves as well, including one open to the public above the Upper Savinja Valley in Štajerska. Not all 24 of the karst caves are lit by electricity or open regular hours, though. You can learn to pothole – descending with a guide through tunnels into the bowels of the earth – in the Kanin Mountains near Bovec.

Cave diving is a popular sport in Slovenia, and its greatest proponent is Olivier Isler, who holds several world records and has invented a unique breathing apparatus that enriches exhaled air for extreme conditions and long dives. Cave diving has been done at Postojna, Škocjan and in the tunnel at Wild Lake (Divje Jezero) near Idrija.

Thermal Baths
Slovenia counts 16 thermal spa resorts, most of them in Štajerska, Dolenjska and Prekmurje and they are covered in this guide. They are excellent places not just for 'taking the cure' but for relaxing and meeting people.

Only two – Dolenjske Toplice and Radenci – are really spa towns, with that distinctive *fin-de-siècle* feel about them. Others, like Atomske Toplice and Terme Čatez, are loud, brashy places dedicated to all the hedonistic pursuits you care to imagine. The Banovci spa near Veržej, about 13 km south of Murska Sobota in Prekmurje, is reserved for naturists.

Many resorts use the trendier Italian *terme* for 'spa' instead of the proper Slovene word *toplice* or *zdravilišče* (health resort).

Golfing
There are 18-hole golf courses at Bled and at Mokrice Castle in Dolenjska and a nine-hole course in Lipica. Another golf course is due to open soon at Rogaška Slatina.

Bird-Watching
Although many Slovenes don't know it, Slovenia has some of the best bird-watching in Central Europe with well over 300 species spotted here. The Ljubljana Marsh (Ljubljansko Barje) and Lake Cerknica are especially good for seeing aquatic and other birds like the black heron and kestrel, and the arrival of the white storks in Prekmurje in April is a wonderful sight. There's no guidebook devoted specifically to Slovenian birds, but the *Collins Field Guide to the Birds of Britain and Europe* by Roger T. Peterson (UK£14.95) is very useful.

Language Courses
The most famous school for learning Slovene is the Centre for Slovene as a Second Language (☎ 061-125 0001) at the University of Ljubljana's Faculty of Arts, Aškerčeva cesta 2. They have two- and four-week summer courses for US$290 and US$550 as well as an intensive course running from October to May for US$1200. Prices do not include room and board.

Two other schools offering Slovene that get good reviews (and presumably results) are the Miklošič Educational Centre (☎ 061-133 4016) at Miklošičeva cesta 26 and the Štupar Center (☎ 061-132 7223) at Vojkova cesta 71.

HIGHLIGHTS
Historic Towns
The most attractive cities and towns in Slovenia – and the ones where you'll get a real feel for the past – are Ljubljana, Ptuj, Škofja Loka, Radovljica, Piran and Kranj.

Museums

The following museums stand out not just for what they contain but for how they display it: the Dolenjska Museum in Novo Mesto; the Posavje Museum in Brežice; the Blacksmith Museum in Kropa; the Municipal Museum in Idrija; the Saltworks Museum in Sečovlje; the Beekeeping Museum in Radovljica, and the Kobarid Museum.

Castles

Slovenia was once known as the 'country of castles' and counted over 1000 but wars and development have taken care of most of them. Of the remaining ones, the most dramatic castles (open to the public and in varying states of repair) are Bled Castle, Predjama Castle near Postojna, Snežnik Castle in Notranjska, Bogenšperk Castle in Dolenjska, Podsreda Castle in the Kozjansko region of Štajerska and Celje Castle.

Churches

The following are a half-dozen of Slovenia's most beautiful houses of worship: the Church of St John the Baptist at Bohinj; the Church of the Holy Trinity at Hrastovlje (Primorska); the Church of the Virgin Mary at Ptujska Gora near Ptuj; the Chapter Church of St Nicholas in Novo Mesto; the Church of the Assumption at Nova Štifta near Ribnica; and the Church of the Annunciation at Crngrob near Škofja Loka.

Natural Wonders

You won't soon forget the Vršič Pass and the Julian Alps in Triglav National Park, the Škocjan Caves, the Vintgar Gorge near Bled, the Upper Savinja Valley in Štajerska, the Soča River and the (True) Karst region.

ACCOMMODATION

Accommodation in Slovenia runs the gamut from riverside camp sites, cosy *gostišča* (inns) and farm houses to elegant castle hotels in Dolenjska and Štajerska. Slovenia counts some 90,000 beds in total – about one-third of them in hotels – so you'll seldom have trouble finding accommodation except at the height of the season (July and August) on the coast, at Bled or Bohinj or in Ljubljana.

Accommodation is never really cheap in Slovenia, and there are a lot of 'hidden' costs. First of all, virtually every municipality levies a tourist tax that can add 100 to 150 SIT to your bill (per person per night) and some places charge fees for registration, stays of less than three nights and even insurance. Hotels and camp sites invariably insist on holding your passport or identity document during your stay. This can be a real pain when trying to change money and even disastrous when the staff is not as efficient as they should be. I almost left town twice without mine.

Camping

In summer, camping is the cheapest way to go and there are conveniently located camping grounds *(kampi)* – about 40 'official ones and lots more independent ones – in all areas of the country. You don't always need a tent as some camp sites have inexpensive bungalows, too. The three best camping grounds for those who want to experience the mountains or the sea are Zlatorog on Lake Bohinj, Špik at Gozd Martuljek near Kranjska Gora and Jezero Fiesa near Piran, though they can be jammed in summer. Prices vary according to the site and the season, but expect to pay between DM6 and DM15 per person a night. Some camping grounds – like Šobec in Lesce near Bled – give a 10% discount if you stay more than five nights.

It is forbidden to camp 'rough' in Slovenia though many Slovenes do – without ever lighting a fire.

Private Rooms

The system of letting private rooms to travellers is not as developed or as widespread as it is in, say, Hungary, but you'll find them available through tourist offices and travel agencies at Bled, Bohinj, Bovec, Celje, Izola, Koper, Kranjska Gora, Ljubljana, Piran, Podčetrtek (Atomske Toplice), Portorož, Postojna, Radenci and Rogaška

Slatina. Make sure you understand exactly where you'll be staying; in cities some private rooms are far from the centre.

You don't have to go through agencies or tourist offices; any house with a sign reading *Sobe* means that rooms are available. Of course, you have no recourse if things don't work out, but if you've seen the room and understand the price, what could go wrong?

In Slovenia, private rooms are ranked according to category. Category I rooms have their own shower or bath, Category II rooms have running water in the room and a shower or bath in the corridor and Category III rooms have no sink or tap in the room. Prices vary according to the town and season but expect to pay DM16 to DM28 for a Category I room per person and DM12 to DM24 for a Category II room.

The price quoted is usually for a minimum three nights. If you're staying a shorter time (and you are usually welcome to), you'll have to pay 30% and sometimes as much as 50% more. The price of a private room never includes breakfast (DM6 to DM9 if available) or tourist tax. An extra bed is 20% on top of the other prices.

Some of the offices in the towns and cities mentioned earlier also have apartments available that can accommodate up to seven people. One for two people could go for as low as DM40 or as high as DM75 per night.

The CTEP office in Ljubljana (see the Useful Organisations section) publishes an annual brochure called *Rates for Accommodation and Private Rooms and Apartments*.

Colleges & Hostels
Only seven hostels in Slovenia are registered with the Holiday Association of Slovenia (Počitniška Zveza Slovenije; PZS), the national hostel organisation. They are in Bled, Bohinj, Koper, Ljubljana (two), Maribor and Rogla. Contact the PZS (☎ 061-312 156) at Parmova ulica 33 in Ljubljana. You are never required to have a Hostelling International (HI) card to stay at hostels here, but it sometimes earns you a small discount or cancellation of the tourist tax.

A large number of Slovenian pupils and students live away from home during the school year and sleep in a college dormitory *(dijaški dom)*. Some of the ones in Ljubljana, Maribor, Idrija, etc accept foreign travellers in summer for between DM15 and DM20 a night.

Guesthouses
Pensions are good value for solo travellers as rooms are often priced per person. They come by several names. A *penzion* is, of course, a pension but more commonly it's called a *gostišče*, or inn-restaurant with accommodation, called *prenočišče*, upstairs or behind the restaurant. They are more expensive than hostels but cheaper than hotels and often your only choice in small towns and villages. Generally speaking, a *gostilna* serves food and drink only but some have rooms available nowadays as well. The distinction between a gostilna and a gostišče isn't very clear – even to Slovenes.

Farmhouses
The agricultural cooperatives of Slovenia have organised a wonderful programme to accommodate visitors on 120 different working farms. The concept, which is less than 10 years old, was borrowed from Austria and is very popular with foreigners. You either stay in private rooms in the farmhouse itself or in Alpine-style guesthouses somewhere nearby. Many of the farms offer activities such as horse riding, kayaking or

cycling and allow you to help out with the farm work if you're interested.

The farms themselves can range from places where Old MacDonald himself would feel at home to little more than a pension with a vegetable patch. The latter is especially true at tourist destinations like Bled and by the coast. You'll find much more isolated farmsteads with livestock and vineyards in Štajerska and Dolenjska.

The Vas tourist office (☎ 061-132 8093), Miklošičeva cesta 4, in Ljubljana, oversees most farm-house accommodation in Slovenia. Their UK agent is Slovenia Pursuits (☎ 01763-852 646), 14 Hay St, Steeple Morden, Royston, Herts SG8 0PE, England.

Vas has very strict requirements and vets each farmhouse individually on an annual basis; it would be unusual to come across a dud if Vas listed it. They also control prices so you'll be sure to pay the same price for any farmhouse accommodation if you book through them: DM20 per person in a 2nd-category room with shared bath and breakfast in the low season (from September to mid-December and from mid-January to June) to DM39 per person for a 1st-category room with private bath and all meals in the high season (July and August). Apartments for groups of up to eight people are also available. There's no minimum stay but you must pay 30% more if it's less than three nights.

Farm stays are not for everyone – particularly when they are in areas far from a town or village – and many people don't know what to do with all that free time after a couple of days. But for a truly relaxing break, they are ideal.

Hotels

Hotels are more expensive than any of the other accommodation options and the rates vary according to season, with July and August being the peak season and September/October and May/June the shoulder seasons. In Ljubljana prices are constant all year. Many resort hotels, particularly on the coast, are closed in winter. As hotels seldom levy a surcharge for stays of one or two

nights, they're worth considering if you're only passing through.

As with many other countries in the region, hotel standards in Slovenia vary enormously, and the rating system is completely out of date. What that means is that if a small hotel is built or renovated and each room has a private shower (however tiny), it automatically gets more stars than a charming old-style hotel where a few of the rooms share the bath on the corridor. A lot of hotels are being renovated in Slovenia which will raise prices in the long term and disturb your sleep in the short term.

Among the finest and most expensive places to stay in Slovenia are the castle hotels at Otočec and Mokrice, and Podvin Castle in Mošnje near Radovljica. The Protocol Service of the Republic of Slovenia owns four other magnificent properties available for hire, including Brdo and Strmol castles near Kranj in Gorenjska, part of Snežnik Castle near Cerknica in Notranjska and Podrožnik Villa at Rožna Dolina in Ljubljana. For information, contact the Protocol Service (☎ 064-221 133; fax 221 551) at Brdo Castle in Predoslje.

FOOD

The most important thing to remember about Slovenian food is that it is heavily influenced by its neighbours' cuisines. From Austria, it's sausage *(klobasa)*, strudel *(zavitek)* and Wiener schnitzel *(Dunajski zrezek)*. The ravioli-like *žlikrofi*, *njoki* (potato dumplings) and *rižota* (risotto) are obviously Italian, and Hungary has contributed *golaž* (goulash), *paprikaš* (chicken or beef 'stew') and *palačinke*, thin pancakes filled with jam or nuts and topped with chocolate. Distinctively Slovenian dishes are prepared with *žganci*, groats that can be made from buckwheat, barley or corn. Slovenian bread *(kruh)* is generally excellent, especially the braided loaves made around the holidays. A real treat is 'mottled bread' *(pisan kruh)* in which three types of dough (buckwheat, wheat and corn) are combined into a roll and baked.

Most Slovenian meals start with soup,

usually chicken or beef broth with little egg noodles *(kokošja* or *goveja juha z rezanci)* and move on to a main course. This is for the most part meat *(meso)* with the favourites being pork *(svinjina)*, veal *(teletina)*, beef *(govedina)* and, in season, game such as deer *(srna)*. An excellent prepared meat is *pršut*, air-dried, thinly sliced ham that is nothing like the slimy Italian prosciutto from where it gets its name.

Despite the country's large number of chickens *(piščanec)*, it's rare to see them on a menu, though turkey *(puran)* and goose *(gos)* are popular. Slovenes are big eaters of fish *(riba)* and other seafood, though away from the coast it's usually trout *(postrv)*.

Slovenia is hardly paradise for vegetarians though you can usually find a few meatless dishes on any menu. Dumplings made with cheese *(štruklji)*, often with chives or tarragon added, are widely available as are dishes like *gobova rižota* (mushroom risotto) and deep-fried cheese *(ocvrti sir)*. Another boon for vegetarians is that Slovenes like fresh salad *(solata)* – a most un-Slavic partiality – and you can get one any place, even in a smoky gostilna in the countryside. Salad bars, however, are rare outside Ljubljana. A milk bar *(mlečna restavracija)* sells yogurt and other dairy products as well as *krofi*, jam-filled raised doughnuts that are very tasty.

Slovenian cuisine boasts two excellent and very different desserts. *Potica*, almost a national institution, is a kind of nut roll (though often made with savoury fillings, too) eaten after a meal or with coffee or tea during the day. *Gibanica* from Prekmurje is a rich concoction of pastry filled with poppy seeds, walnuts, apple and/or sultanas and cheese and topped with cream. It's definitely not for dieters.

You should have no problem getting a snack between meals in Slovenia; many people eat something hot at about 10 am. The most popular is a Balkan import called burek, flaky pastry stuffed with meat, cheese or apple not unlike Greek *tiropita* and sold at outside stalls throughout the land. It is very cheap and filling, but can be very greasy. Other snack foods include:

Čevapčiči
    Spicy meatballs of beef or pork
Pica
    Another way to spell 'pizza'
Pleskavica
    Spicy, Serbian-style meat patties
Pomfri
    Chips (French fries)
Ražnjiči
    Shish kebab
Vroča hrenovka
    Hot dog

Restaurants

'Restaurants' go by many names in Slovenia, but the distinction is not always precise. At the top of the heap, a *restavracija* is a restaurant where you sit down and are served. A gostilna or gostišče (there's supposed to be a difference) is more like an inn, with rustic decor and usually (but not always) national dishes. A *samopostrežna restavracija* is a self-service place where you order from a counter and sometimes eat standing up. An *okrepčevalnica* serves simple, fast food like grilled meats and sausages. A *bife* and a *krčma* may have snacks but the emphasis is on drinking. A *slaščičarna* sells sweets and ice cream while a *kavarna* has coffee and pastries.

Many restaurants and 'inns' have an inexpensive set menu at lunch *(dnevno kosilo)*

Potica

advertised on a blackboard outside. Three courses can cost less than 500 SIT.

It's important to remember that not many Slovenes eat in restaurants in cities or towns unless they have to because of work or they're entertaining. At the weekend, most will head five or 10 km out of town for a gostilna or gostišče they know will serve them good, home-cooked meals and local wine at affordable prices. For the traveller without a car, it can be difficult reaching these little 'finds', but we have included as many as practical.

Menu Reader

Almost every sit-down restaurant in Slovenia has a multilingual menu with dishes translated into English, Italian, German and sometimes even French. But the language used is sometimes inaccurate or less then appetising; 'Beef Mouth in Salad' and 'Farinaceous Dishes' would have most would-be diners scratching their heads or running for the door. And then there are all those lists with 'daily recommendations' *('danes priporočamo...')* that are frequently in Slovene only.

The following is a sample menu *(jedilni list)* with dishes listed in the way most Slovenian restaurants would group them. It's not complete by any means, but it will give you a good idea of what to expect. For more food and ordering words, see the Language heading in the Facts about the Country chapter.

It's customary to wish others at your table 'Dober tek!' (Bon appetit!) before starting your meal.

Cold Starters *(Hladne Začetne Jedi* or *Hladne Predjede)*
Domača salama
　Home-style salami
Francoska solata
　Diced potatoes and vegetables with mayonanaise
Gnjat/šunka s hrenom
　Smoked/boiled ham with horseradish
Kraški pršut z olivami
　Air-dried Karst ham with olives
Narezek
　Assorted smoked meats/cold cuts

Riba v marinadi
　Marinated fish

Soups *(Juhe)*
Dnevna juha
　Soup of the day
Gobova kremna juha
　Creamed mushroom soup
Goveja juha z rezanci
　Beef broth with egg noodles
Grahova juha
　Pea soup
Paradižnikova juha
　Tomato soup
Prežganka
　Toasted rye-flour soup thickened with cream
Zelenjavna juha
　Vegetable soup

Warm Starters *(Tople Začetne Jedi* or *Tople Predjedi)*
Drobnjakovi štruklji
　Dumplings of cottage cheese and chives
Omlet s sirom/šunko
　Omelette with cheese/ham
Ocvrti sir s tatarsko omako
　Deep-fried cheese with tartar sauce
Rižota z gobami
　Risotto with mushrooms
Špageti po bolonjska
　Spaghetti bolognese
Žlikrofi
　Ravioli of cheese, bacon and chives

Ready-Made Dishes *(Pripravljene Jedi* or *Gotova Jedilna)*
Bograč golaž
　Beef goulash served in a pot
Jota
　Beans, sauerkraut and potatoes or barley cooked with salt pork in a pot
Kuhana govedina s hrenom
　Boiled beef with horseradish
Kurja obara z ajdovimi žganci
　Chicken stew or 'gumbo' with buckwheat groats
Pečen piščanec
　Roast chicken
Prekajena svinjska rebrca s kislim zeljem
　Smoked pork ribs with sauerkraut
Svinjska pečenka
　Roast pork

Dishes Made to Order *(Jedi po Naročilu)*
Čebulna bržola
　Braised beef with onions
Ciganska jetra
　Liver Gypsy-style

Dunajski zrezek
    Wiener schnitzel (breaded cutlet of veal or pork)
Kmečka pojedina
    'Farmer's feast' of smoked meats and sauerkraut
Kranjska klobasa z gočico
    Carniolan sausage with mustard
Ljubljanski zrezek
    Breaded cutlet with cheese
Mešano meso na žaru
    Mixed grill
Ocvrti piščanec
    Fried chicken
Pariški zrezek
    Cutlet fried in egg batter
Puranov zrezek s šampinjoni
    Turkey steak with white mushrooms

Fish *(Ribe)*

Brancin z maslom
    Sea bass in butter
Kuhana/pečena postrv
    Boiled/grilled trout
Lignji/kalamari na žaru
    Grilled squid
Ocvrti oslič
    Fried cod
Orada na žaru
    Grilled sea bream
Morski list v belem vinu
    Sole in white wine
Pečene sardele
    Grilled sardines
Ribja plošča
    Seafood plate
Škampi
    Scampi (prawns)
Školjke
    Shellfish (clams, mussels, etc)

Side Dishes *(Priloge* or *Prikuhe)*

Ajdovi/koruzni žganci
    Buckwheat/corn groats
Bučke
    Squash
Cvetača
    Cauliflower
Grah
    Sweet peas
Korenje
    Carrots
Kruhovi cmoki
    Bread dumplings
Mlinci
    Small pancakes
Ocvrti krompir or *Pomfri*
    Chips (French fries)
Pražen krompir
    Fried potatoes

Pire krompir
    Mashed potatoes
Riž
    Rice
Špinača
    Spinach
Stročji fižol
    String beans
Testenine
    Pasta
Zelenjavne prikuhe
    Side vegetables

Salads *(Solate)*

Fižolova solata
    Bean salad
Kisle kumarice
    Pickled cucumbers
Kumarična solata
    Cucumber salad
Paradižnikova solata
    Tomato salad
Rdeča pesa
    Pickled beetroot (beets)
Sezonska/mešana solata
    Seasonal/mixed salad
Srbska solata
    'Serbian salad' of tomatoes and green peppers
Zelena solata
    Lettuce salad
Zelnja solata
    Cabbage salad

Fruit *(Sadje)*

Ananas
    Pineapple
Breskev
    Peach
Češnje
    Cherries
Češplja
    Plum
Grozdje
    Grapes
Hruška
    Pear
Jabolko
    Apple
Jagode
    Strawberries
Kompot
    Stewed fruit (many types)
Lešniki
    Hazelnuts
Maline
    Raspberries
Marelica
    Apricot

Orehi
Walnuts
Pomaranča
Orange
Višnje
Sour cherries (morellos)

Desserts/Cheese *(Sladice/Siri)*
Jabolčni zavitek
Apple strudel
Krofi
Raised doughnuts
Palačinke z marmelado/orehi/čokolado
Pancakes with marmelade/nuts/chocolate
Orehova potica
Slovenian nut roll
Prekmurska gibanica
Flaky pastry with fruit, nut and cheese filling and topped with cream
Sadna kupa
Fruit salad with whipped cream
Sirova polšča
Cheese plate
Sladoled
Ice cream
Torte
Gateaux (cakes)

DRINKS
Wine
Slovenia has been making wine since the time of the Romans, and many of their wines today are of a very high quality. Unfortunately, most foreigners know Slovenian wine – if at all – from the 'el cheapo' bottles of white Ljutomer Riesling or Laški riesling served at college parties. For the most part, these are dull, unmemorable wines (the Ljutomer can be slightly sweet), but a trip to Slovenia will convince you that most of the best wines stay home.

Slovenia counts 14 distinct wine-growing areas, but there are just three major regions. Podravje ('on the Drava') extends from north-east Štajerska into Prekmurje and produces whites almost exclusively. Eschew the insipid Ljutomer and Laški Rieslings in favour of Renski Rizling (a true German riesling), Beli Pinot (Pinot Blanc), Traminec (Gewürztraminer) or Šipon, all whites.

Posavje is the region running from eastern Štajerska across the Sava River into Dolenjska and Bela Krajina. This region produces both whites and reds but its most famous wine is Cviček, a dry, light-red, almost rosé wine that is distinctly Slovenian.

The Primorska wine region concentrates on reds, the most famous being Teran made from Slovenian Refošk grapes in the Karst region. It is a deep-red, peppery wine with almost a 'white wine' acidity that goes perfectly with pršut ham and olives. Other wines from this region are Malvazija, a yellowish white from the coast that is light and dry and good with fish, and red Merlot, especially the one from the Vipava Valley.

On a Slovenian wine label, the first word usually identifies where the wine comes from and the second word identifies the grape varietal: Vipavski Merlot, Mariborski Traminec, etc. But it's not always like that. Some bear names according to their place of origin such as Jeruzalemčan, Bizeljčan, Haložan.

There is no *appellation contrôlée* as such in Slovenia; *kontrolirano poreklo* is a trademark protection that usually (but not always) suggests a certain standard. When choosing wine, look for the words *vrhunsko vino* (premium wine) and a gold label, *kakovostno vino* (quality wine) and a silver label, and *namizno vino* (table wine) with a bronze label. They can be red, white or rosé and dry, semi-dry, semi-sweet or sweet. Vintage is not important with most Slovenian wines.

A	B	C
	D	
E	F	G

National icons – Hayracks and linden trees (SF)

A Double-linked hayrack *(toplar)*
B 350-year-old linden
C *Toplar* with corn and hay

D Detail of *toplar*
E *Toplar*

F Linden tree
G Hayrack *(kazolec)*

A	B
C	D
E	F

Ljubljana

A Brass band in Mestni trg (PCL)
B Schweiger House on Stari trg (SF)
C Castle Tower in winter (PCL)

D Outdoor café on Stari trg (PCL)
E Painted *Sax* pub in Trnovo (SF)
F View from Ljubljana Castle (SF)

The best sparkling wine is Zlata Radgonska Penina from Gornja Radgona. Valvasor is another label.

Slovenes usually drink wine with meals or socially at home; it's rare to see people sit down to a bottle at a café or pub. As elsewhere in Central Europe, a bottle or glass of mineral water is ordered along with the wine. It's a different story in summer when spritzers (wine coolers) of red or white wine mixed with mineral water are consumed in vast quantities.

All of the wine-producing areas have a 'wine road' *(vinska cesta)* that you can follow in a car or on a bicycle. These are outlined on the useful *Slovenian Wine Map* produced by a company called Imago and available in most bookshops in Ljubljana. Along the way, you can stop at the occasional cellar *(klet)* offering wine tastings or at one of the *vinoteke* in wine towns or cities (Maribor, Metlika, Ptuj, Rogaška Slatina, Dobrovo near Nova Gorica, Brežice).

Some important wine words are:

Arhivsko vino
Vintage wine
Belo vino
White wine
Brizganec
Spritzer/wine cooler
Buteljka
Bottle
Črno vino
Red (literally 'black') wine
Kakovostno vino
Quality wine
Kozarec
Glass
Kuhano vino
Mulled wine
Namizno vino
Table wine
Peneče vino
Sparkling wine
Polsladko
Semi-sweet
Polsuho
Semi-dry/medium
Rose
Rosé wine
Sladko or *Desertno*
Sweet wine

Špricar
Spritzer/wine cooler
Suho
Dry
Vino
Wine
Vinoteka
Wine bar
Vinska karta
Wine list
Vinska klet
Wine cellar
Vinski hram
Wine bar/room
Vrhunsko vino
Premium wine

Beer

Beer is very popular in Slovenia, especially outside the home and with young people. Štajerska hops grown in the Savinja Valley are used locally and are widely sought after by brewers from around the world. They have been described as having the flavour of lemon grass.

Slovenia has three breweries: Union in Ljubljana, Laško in the town of that name south of Celje and the smaller Gambrinus in Maribor. Union is lighter-tasting and sweeter than Zlatorog, the excellent and ubiquitous beer (it has about 50% of the market) brewed by Laško. Gambrinus is very popular around Maribor. Union also produces an alcohol-free beer called Uni and a decent stout. Laško's alcohol-free brew is called Lahko and it also makes a 'light' beer called Gren.

In a pub (pivnica) draft beer is drunk in 0.5-litre mugs or 0.3-litre ones. It is also available at pubs, shops and supermarkets in half-litre bottles or cans measuring one-third of a litre, both locally produced and imported. 'Na zdravje!' is how you say 'Cheers!'

Important beer words:

Malo pivo
One-third-litre glass
Pivnica
Pub/beer hall
Pivo
Beer

Svetlo pivo
    Lager
Temno pivo
    Dark beer/stout
Točeno pivo
    Draft beer
Veliko pivo
    Half-litre glass
Vrček
    Mug

Other Drinks

An alcoholic drink as Slovenian as wine is *žganje*, a strong brandy or eau de vie distilled from a variety of fruits but most commonly apples and plums. Another type is *medeno žganje* or *medica* flavoured with honey. But the finest is Pleterska Hruška made by the monks at the Pleterje Monastery near Kostanjevica na Krki in Dolenjska. They let a pear grow into an upside-down bottle, then pick bottle and pear together and pour brandy inside. Drink too much of this stuff and you'll see visions of the place the monks warn us about.

Many Slovenes enjoy a *špička* – slang for a little glass of schnapps – during the day as a pick-me-up. You'll probably get the invitation 'Pridite na kupico' ('Come and have a drop') more than once.

Most international brands of soft drinks are available in Slovenia, but mineral water from Radenci (Radenska) or Rogaška Slatina seems to be the most popular libation for teetotallers in pubs and bars. Juice *(sok)* is usually boxed fruit 'drink' with lots of sugar or a drink made with syrup.

Espresso is the type of coffee most commonly served but thick, sweet Turkish coffee is also popular (especially when the establishment does not have an espresso mach-ine!). If you don't want it too sweet, say 'Ne sladko, prosim'. Coffee is good everywhere except at hotel breakfasts when you'll almost invariably be served a cup of lukewarm, milky, ersatz coffee.

Local people drink lots of herbal teas and seem to prefer anything made with a berry, a blossom or a mint leaf over what they call 'Russian' (black) tea. Black tea is difficult to find in the shops so bring your own supply of tea bags.

Useful words include:

Brezalkoholne pijače
    Soft drinks
Brinjevec or *Brinovec*
    Juniper-flavoured brandy
Češnjevec
    Cherry brandy (kirsch)
Hruška
    Pear brandy
Jabolčni sok
    Apple juice
Jabolčnik
    Apple cider
Kava s smetana
    Coffee with whipped cream
Kapucinarja
    Cappuccino
Limonada
    Lemonade
Mineralna voda
    Mineral water
Planinski čaj
    Mountain-flower tea
Pomarančni sok
    Orange juice
Sadjevec
    Apple brandy (apple jack)
Slivovka
    Plum brandy
Sok
    Juice
Tonik z ledom
    Tonic water with ice
Viljemovka
    Pear brandy
Vinjak
    Wine brandy
Zeliščni čaj
    Herbal tea

There are more words and phrases in Slovene in the Language section of the Facts about the Country chapter and in the Glossary at the back.

ENTERTAINMENT
Classical Music, Opera, Ballet & Theatre

Slovenia has excellent high-brow entertainment on offer – particularly classical music and theatre. Ljubljana alone has seven theatres, an opera house where ballets are also staged and two symphony orchestras. Maribor has a resident opera company as well as a symphony orchestra, a ballet company and two theatres. There are also theatres in Celje, Kranj and Koper. Many other towns have chamber orchestras and string quartets that perform in churches, castles, museums and civic centres.

Cinemas

Foreign films are never dubbed in Slovenia but are shown in their original language with subtitles. The choice, even in Ljubljana, is not great – one film usually travels from one cinema to the next – but you're sure to find something of interest.

Discos & Casinos

Discos are the most popular form of entertainment for young people and are usually good fun. The biggest and most rollicking are in Ljubljana and on the coast, but you'll even find them in small provincial towns. Casinos are opening at a dizzying rate; the flashiest ones are in Nova Gorica, Potrorož and Bled.

Folk Music

Folk-music performances are usually local affairs and are very popular in Dolenjska and especially Bela Krajina. Črnomelj is the centre and as many as 50 bands playing stringed instruments such as the *tamburica*, the *berdo* (contrabass), the guitar-like *brač* and the *bisernica* (lute) are active in the area around Adlešiči. Flyers and posters in these areas are always announcing folk nights at halls and cultural centres. In Dolenjska, the most celebrated group is Fanti s Praprotna (Boys from Praprotno) headed up by Lojze Slak on the *frajtonarica*, a button accordion.

THINGS TO BUY

For folk craft and other souvenirs in Slovenia, it's best to go to the source where you will find the real thing and not just mass-produced kitsch: Idrija or Železniki for lace, Ribnica for basketry and household wooden utensils, Bohinj for carved wooden pipes with silver covers, Prekmurje for Hungarian-style black pottery, Kropa for objects made of wrought iron, Rogaška Slatina for crystal. Some people think they're tacky, but I like the traditional beehive panels (panjske končnice) painted with folk motifs, especially the ones showing a devil sharpening a gossip's tongue on a grindstone. I know a few people who should hang that one up at home as an icon.

The silver-filigree jewellery you'll see for sale in shops around the country, but especially on the coast, is not really Slovenian but a good buy nonetheless. Almost all of the shops are owned and run by ethnic Albanians who brought the craft here from Kosovo in the south of former Yugoslavia. Zlatarna of Celje makes some fine gold jewellery.

Ski equipment and skiwear are of very high quality. Elan skis are made in Begunje near Bled and Alpina boots at Žiri, north-east of Idrija. Look for Toper ski jackets from Celje.

Natural remedies, herbal teas and apian products such as beeswax, honey, pollen, propolis and royal jelly can be found in specialty shops around the country.

A bottle or two of Slovenian wine makes a great gift. Buy it from a vinoteka or a dealer with a large selection like Simon Bradeško in Ljubljana. A couple of monasteries, such as the Carthusian one at Pleterje in Dolenjska, sell their own brand of firewater made from fruits and berries. It's fragrant but very potent stuff.

Getting There & Away

AIR

The Slovenian national carrier, Adria Airways (☎ 061-133 4336 in Ljubljana; ☎ 064-221 441 at Brnik Airport), flies nonstop to Ljubljana from 15 European cities, including Copenhagen, Frankfurt, Istanbul, Leipzig, London, Manchester, Moscow, Munich, Paris, Rome, Skopje, Split, Tirana, Vienna and Zurich. Adria is not a particularly cheap way to go, however; at the end of 1994 the cheapest excursion fare (with endless restrictions and limited duration) from London to Ljubljana was £231 (against a regular full-fare economy ticket of £327) and from Frankfurt DM463 (full fare DM618).

Adria has about a dozen offices abroad, including the following seven:

Air Travel Glossary

Apex Apex, or 'advance purchase excursion' is a discounted ticket which must be paid for in advance. There are penalties if you wish to change it.

Baggage Allowance This will be written on your ticket: usually one 20 kg item to go in the hold, plus one item of hand luggage.

Bucket Shop An unbonded travel agency specialising in discounted airline tickets.

Bumped Just because you have a confirmed seat doesn't mean you're going to get on the plane – see Overbooking.

Cancellation Penalties If you have to cancel or change an Apex ticket there are often heavy penalties involved, insurance can sometimes be taken out against these penalties. Some airlines impose penalties on regular tickets as well, particularly against 'no show' passengers.

Check In Airlines ask you to check in a certain time ahead of the flight departure (usually 1½ hours on international flights). If you fail to check in on time and the flight is overbooked the airline can cancel your booking and give your seat to somebody else.

Confirmation Having a ticket written out with the flight and date you want doesn't mean you have a seat until the agent has checked with the airline that your status is 'OK' or confirmed. Meanwhile you could just be 'on request'.

Discounted Tickets There are two types of discounted fares – officially discounted (see Promotional Fares) and unofficially discounted. The lowest prices often impose drawbacks like flying with unpopular airlines, inconvenient schedules, or unpleasant routes and connections. A discounted ticket can save you other things than money – you may be able to pay Apex prices without the associated Apex advance booking and other requirements. Discounted tickets only exist where there is fierce competition.

Full Fares Airlines traditionally offer first class (coded F), business class (coded J) and economy class (coded Y) tickets. These days there are so many promotional and discounted fares available from the regular economy class that few passengers pay full economy fare.

Lost Tickets If you lose your airline ticket an airline will usually treat it like a travellers' cheque and, after inquiries, issue you with another one. Legally, however, an airline is entitled to treat it like cash and if you lose it then it's gone forever. Take good care of your tickets.

No Shows No shows are passengers who fail to show up for their flight, sometimes due to unexpected delays or disasters, sometimes due to simply forgetting, sometimes because they made more than one booking and didn't bother to cancel the one they didn't want. Full fare passengers who fail to turn up are sometimes entitled to travel on a later flight. The rest of us are penalised (see Cancellation Penalties).

On Request An unconfirmed booking for a flight, see Confirmation.

Open Jaws A return ticket where you fly out to one place but return from another. If available this can save you backtracking to your arrival point.

Austria

Mariahilferstrasse 32-34, A-1070 Vienna
(☎ 0222-522 3740)

Croatia

Praška 9, 41000 Zagreb (☎ 041-433 333)

France

38 Ave de l'Opéra, 75002 Paris (☎ 1-47 42 95 00)

Germany

Grosse Eschenheimer Strasse 43, 60313 Frankfurt 1 (☎ 069-29 02 74)

Maximiliansplatz 12a, 80333 Munich 2 (☎ 089-228 39 74)

Switzerland

Löwenstrasse 64, CH-8001 Zurich (☎ 01-212 63 93)

UK

49 Conduit St, London W1R 9FB (☎ 0171-734 4630)

Other airlines that serve Ljubljana include Aeroflot from Moscow, Austrian Airlines from Vienna, Palair Macedonian Airlines from Skopje and Swissair from Zurich.

There are international airports at Maribor and Portorož but only Brnik Airport (☎ 064-222 700), 28 km north-west of Ljubljana, receives regularly scheduled flights. The airport is open from 6 am to 10 pm and has

---

Overbooking Airlines hate to fly empty seats and since every flight has some passengers who fail to show up (see No Shows) airlines often book more passengers than they have seats. Usually the excess passengers balance those who fail to show up but occasionally somebody gets bumped. If this happens guess who it is most likely to be? The passengers who check in late.

Promotional Fares Officially discounted fares like Apex fares which are available from travel agents or direct from the airline.

Reconfirmation At least 72 hours prior to departure time of an onward or return flight you must contact the airline and 'reconfirm' that you intend to be on the flight. If you don't do this the airline can delete your name from the passenger list and you could lose your seat. You don't have to reconfirm the first flight on your itinerary or if your stopover is less than 72 hours. It doesn't hurt to reconfirm more than once.

Restrictions Discounted tickets often have various restrictions on them – advance purchase is the most usual one (see Apex). Others are restrictions on the minimum and maximum period you must be away, such as a minimum of 14 days or a maximum of one year. See Cancellation Penalties.

Standby A discounted ticket where you only fly if there is a seat free at the last moment. Standby fares are usually only available on domestic routes.

Tickets Out An entry requirement for many countries is that you have an onward or return ticket, in other words, a ticket out of the country. If you're not sure what you intend to do next, the easiest solution is to buy the cheapest onward ticket to a neighbouring country or a ticket from a reliable airline which can later be refunded if you do not use it.

Transferred Tickets Airline tickets cannot be transferred from one person to another. Travellers sometimes try to sell the return half of their ticket, but officials can ask you to prove that you are the person named on the ticket. This is unlikely to happen on domestic flights, on an international flight tickets may be compared with passports.

Travel Agencies Travel agencies vary widely and you should ensure you use one that suits your needs. Some simply handle tours while full-service agencies handle everything from tours and tickets to car rental and hotel bookings. A good one will do all these things and can save you a lot of money but if all you want is a ticket at the lowest possible price, then you really need an agency specialising in discounted tickets. A discounted ticket agency, however, may not be useful for other things, like hotel bookings.

Travel Periods Some officially discounted fares, Apex fares in particular, vary with the time of year. There is often a low (off-peak) season and a high (peak) season. Sometimes there's an intermediate or shoulder season as well. At peak times, when everyone wants to fly, not only will the officially discounted fares be higher but so will unofficially discounted fares or there may simply be no discounted tickets available. Usually the fare depends on your outward flight – if you depart in the high season and return in the low season, you pay the high-season fare. ■

a hotel booking desk in the arrivals hall and an information desk in the departure area. The Kompas travel agency has a representative office there, as do six car-rental firms, including Europcar, Hertz, Avis and Eurodollar. There's also a post office, duty-free shop and restaurant.

A departure tax of DM25 is collected from all passengers leaving Slovenia by air. This is usually included in the ticket price.

LAND
Bus

International buses not only arrive in and depart from Ljubljana, you can catch them from around the country. For an indication of international bus fares from the capital, see the Getting There & Away section in the Ljubljana chapter.

To/From Italy Nova Gorica is the easiest exit/entry point between Slovenia and Italy as you can catch up to seven buses a day to/from the Italian city of Gorizia or simply walk across the border at Rožna Dolina (Casa Rossa in Italian). Between eight and 11 buses a day make the run from the Italian border crossing at Lazaret, south-west of Trieste, to Ankaran, the first resort on the Slovenian coast.

Koper also has good connections with Italy. Up to 17 buses a day go to/from Trieste, 20 km to the north-east. Buses run from 6 am to 7.30 pm mostly on weekdays. The bus station in Trieste is immediately south-west of the train station in Piazza Libertà.

There's a daily bus from Ljubljana to Trieste at 6.25 am. Tarvisio in north-eastern Italy is linked with Kranjska Gora by a bus which runs every day but Sunday.

To/From Croatia The coastal towns of Koper, Piran and Portorož are the best places for making your way by bus to Croatian Istria. There are frequent services to Savudrija near the border at Sečovlje, Novigrad, Poreč, Pula and Rovinj. There's also at least one bus a day to Rijeka.

For cities in north-western Croatia like Varaždin and the capital, Zagreb, the Sloven-

ian gateways are in eastern Štajerska and Dolenjska. For Varaždin count on two buses a day from Celje, six from Ptuj and a dozen a day from Maribor. Zagreb-bound buses go from Ptuj (three a day), Maribor (eight), Novo Mesto (eight) and Brežice (one).

From Ljubljana there are daily buses to Novigrad, Rovinj, Split (at 7.40 pm) and Umag; two or three to Pula, Rijeka and Varaždin; and eight to Zagreb.

To/From Austria & Germany Many cities in Gorenjska, Koroška and Štajerska provinces have bus services to Austria and Germany. They can also be reached from Ljubljana. Be ready for a quick change of buses on the Austrian or German borders.

One weekday bus goes to Villach (Slovene: Beljak) in Austria from Kranjska Gora, and there are daily buses to Klagenfurt (Celovec in Slovene) from Dravograd and Maribor.

From Maribor and Rogaška Slatina, count on one bus a day to Graz and, from Ptuj, a twice-weekly service (on Monday and Friday). Daily buses also reach Frankfurt and Stuttgart from Maribor.

From Ljubljana, there are buses to Berlin with a stop in Frankfurt on Wednesday and Sunday at 7.30 pm, to Munich from Monday to Thursday at 7.30 pm (with several more on Friday), to Stuttgart on Wednesday and Thursday at 7.30 pm and to Klagenfurt on Wednesday at 6.15 am.

To/From Hungary From Ljubljana you can catch a bus to Budapest on Thursday and Friday at 10 pm. There's also a service twice a week (Tuesday and Thursday at 5.30 am) to Lenti. Otherwise take one of eight daily buses to Lendava; the Hungarian border is five km north. The first Hungarian train station, Rédics, is only two km beyond the border from where there are eight trains a day to Zalaegerszeg. From Zalaegerszeg there are three direct trains and three buses to Budapest.

Lenti is also served by two buses a week from Maribor and Celje (on Tuesday and Thursday).

Some bus and train timetables in Slovenia use the names in Slovene of cities and towns in neighbouring countries (Celovec for Klagenfurt, for example, or Trst for Trieste). See the Alternative Place Names appendix in the back of this book.

Train

Slovenia Railways (Slovenske Železnice; SŽ) links up with the European railway network to Austria (Villach, Salzburg, Graz, Vienna), Germany (Leipzig, Munich), Switzerland (Geneva), Italy (Trieste, Venice, Milan), Hungary (Budapest) and Croatia (Zagreb, Karlovac, Rijeka, Pula).

The international trains listed below are expresses and some require a seat reservation costing 296 SIT. The InterCity (IC) supplement is 200 SIT; the one EuroCity (EC) train serving Slovenia (the air-conditioned *Mimara* linking Leipzig and Zagreb via Munich and Ljubljana) charges a supplement of 218 SIT.

On two trains – the *Venezia Express* and the unnamed No 296/297 that goes from Zagreb to Munich via Ljubljana – sleepers are available in 1st class (8460 SIT) and 2nd class (5640 SIT). Couchettes in 2nd class cost 1920 SIT. Surprisingly, not all express trains have dining or even buffet cars. Bring along some snacks and drinks as vendors can be few and far between. SŽ trains are hardly luxurious but they are clean and punctual.

To reduce confusion, specify your train by the name listed under the following To/From sections or on the posted schedule when requesting information or buying a ticket. You can do both at the train stations, of course, but it is often easier to deal with the less-harried staff at the Slovenijaturist offices. They sell train tickets of all types and have branches at Celje, Ljubljana (including one at the train station), Koper, Maribor, Murska Sobota, Nova Gorica, Portorož and Rogaška Slatina.

Tickets are valid for four months on SŽ trains from the date of purchase but only for two months on other European systems, should you interrupt your journey.

Tickets & Discounts All fares to Croatia are reduced by 20%. BIJ (Billets Internationals de Jeunesse) tickets, available to people aged under 26 for 2nd-class travel on selected routes, offer discounts of up to 40%. Students up to 26 years old and holding an ISIC card get 30% off the fare on certain other trains. Both types of tickets must be purchased at Slovenijaturist offices – not the regular ticket windows in the train stations. Fare reductions are also available to children between six and 15 years of age (50%) and those over 60 years holding an international RES (Rail Europe S) card (30 to 50%).

Sample international one-way fares for 2nd-class travel from Ljubljana include: Berlin, 18,506 SIT; Budapest, 4243 SIT; Graz, 2311 SIT; Munich, 7016 SIT; Paris (via Geneva), 18,210 SIT; Rijeka, 847 SIT; Rome (via Venice), 5999 SIT; Trieste, 1229 SIT; Villach, 1333 SIT.

SŽ and Slovenijaturist sell Inter-Rail passes to those aged under 26. Theoretically, you must have resided in the country of purchase for six months. Inter-Rail divides Europe into seven zones (A to G). Passes for one, two, three or all seven zones are available. A 15-day pass valid in Zone G only (which includes Slovenia, Italy, Greece and the ferry companies serving the last two) costs 33,839 SIT. Other passes are valid for a month. A two-zone pass is 40,285 SIT, three zones cost 45,119 SIT and a pass for all seven zones (called Global) is 50,759 SIT. Inter-Rail cards should be treated as cash since you can make no claims in the event of loss or theft. Eurail passes and Flexipasses are not valid or sold in Slovenia.

Adult and youth Euro Domino passes with a validity of three, five or 10 days or a month are also available on SŽ. A five-day adult pass costs 5962 SIT, and 4199 SIT for those under 26. Passengers holding Euro Domino passes get a 25% discount on domestic fares in Slovenia.

SŽ also sells its own SlovenijaRail pass for domestic travel only. See Train in the Getting Around chapter for details.

To/From Italy Four trains a day link Trieste

with Ljubljana (165 km, three hours) via Pivka, including the IC *Venezia Express* from Venice to Zagreb and Budapest, the *Simplon Express* from Geneva to Zagreb, the IC *Drava* from Venice to Budapest and the IC *Kras* to Zagreb.

To/From Croatia To Zagreb (160 km, 2½ hours), there are eight trains a day from Ljubljana via Zidani Most. These include the EC *Mimara* from Leipzig, the IC *Venezia Express*, the IC *Arena* from Pula, the *Simplon Express*, the No 296/297 from Munich, the IC *Kras*, the *Bled* from Villach and the *Sava*.

To Rijeka (155 km, 2½ hours), there are two trains a day from Ljubljana via Pivka. Trains between Ljubljana and Pula (4½ hours) in Istria go via Divača. These include the IC *Arena* and a spur of the IC *Kras*.

To/From Austria & Germany The main train routes into Slovenia from Austria are Vienna to Maribor and Salzburg to Jesenice. There are two trains a day between Munich (453 km, seven hours) and Ljubljana via Salzburg. The EC *Mimara* travels by day while the IC 296/297 goes overnight in each direction. Four more trains make the run between Ljubljana and Salzburg, one with a change at Villach.

To get to Vienna (460 km, six hours) from Ljubljana, you have a choice between the morning IC *Croatia* from Zagreb (but you must connect at Maribor first) or the afternoon IC *Emona* from Rijeka.

When travelling by train to Austria, it's somewhat cheaper to take a local train to Maribor or Jesenice and buy your ticket on to Vienna or Salzburg from there. Domestic fares in Slovenia are much lower than the international fares.

To/From Hungary The IC *Venezia Express* and the IC *Drava* link Ljubljana directly to Budapest (500 km, 7½ hours) via north-western Croatia.

Car & Motorbike
Slovenia maintains 63 border crossings with

Italy, 49 with Austria, 34 with Croatia but only six with Hungary. Thanks to the policies of the former regimes, only rough secondary roads link Slovenia to Hungary and there are often long lines of trucks waiting to cross on each side of the two international border crossings, especially at Dolga Vas.

The following is a list of border crossings with each of Slovenia's four neighbours. They run clockwise from the south-western border with Italy. The name of the Slovenian border post appears first, followed by its location in brackets. Those crossings marked with an asterisk (*) have a Kompas MTS office which is authorised to make sales-tax refunds to foreigners (see Consumer Taxes in the Money section of the Facts for the Visitor chapter).

To/From Italy
Lazaret*
  (between Trieste and Ankaran)
Škofije*
  (between Trieste and Koper)
Kozina*
  (between Trieste and Rijeka)
Lipica*
  (near Trieste)
Fernetiči/Sežana*
  (between Trieste and Ljubljana)
Vrtojba*
  (near Nova Gorica)
Rožna Dolina*
  (between Gorizia and Nova Gorica)
Robič
  (32 km north-east of Udine)
Učeja
  (16 km south-west of Bovec)
Predel*
  (13 km south of Tarvisio)
Rateče*
  (12 km east of Tarvisio)

To/From Croatia
Petišovci
  (five km south of Lendava)
Središče ob Dravi*
  (20 km west of Čakovec)
Ormož
  (25 km east of Ptuj)
Dobovec
  (seven km south-east of Rogatec)
Rogatec
  (seven km east of Rogaška Slatina)

Bistrica ob Sotli
(nine km north-east of Podsreda)
Dobova
(eight km south-east of Brežice)
Obrežje*
(three km south-east of Mokrice)
Metlika
(between Novo Mesto and Karlovac)
Vinica
(18 km south of Črnomelj)
Petrina
(between Kočevje and Rijeka)
Babno Polje
(30 km south-west of Cerknica)
Jelšane*
(between Ilirska Bistrica and Rijeka)
Sočerga*
(between Trieste and Rijeka)
Dragojna*
(between Koper and Buje)
Sečovlje*
(seven km south-east of Portorož)

To/From Austria
Korensko Sedlo*
(20 km south-west of Villach)
Karavanke*
(at the seven-km tunnel between Jesenice and Villach)
Ljubelj*
(between Klagenfurt and Kranj)
Jezersko
(35 km north-east of Kranj)
Holmec*
(49 km east of Klagenfurt)
Vič*
(between Klagenfurt and Maribor)
Radlje
(43 km west of Maribor)
Jurij*
(13 km north-west of Maribor)
Šentilj*
(17 km north of Maribor)
Trate
(16 km east of Šentilj)
Gornja Radgona*
(41 km north-east of Maribor)
Gederovci*
(10 km west of Murska Sobota)
Kuzma*
(28 km north of Murska Sobota)

To/From Hungary
Hodoš
(60 km west of Zalaegerszeg)
Dolga Vas*
(between Lendava and Rédics)

SEA
Another way of getting to Slovenia from Italy is by boat. Between April and mid-October, the *Prince of Venice* catamaran sails between Venice and Portorož (2½ hours; DM50 one way and DM75 return) on the Slovenian coast at the weekend. Another catamaran called *Marconi* links Trieste with Piran (35 minutes; 2400 SIT return) twice a week between April and September. For more information, see the Getting There & Away sections for Portorož and Piran in the Primorska chapter.

TRAVELLING ON
All four countries bordering Slovenia can be reached by air, train, bus and private vehicle. For the appropriate border crossings, see the preceding Car & Motorbike sections.

Italy
Citizens of the USA, Canada, Australia and New Zealand can enter Italy without a visa for stays of up to three months. Those from the UK and other EU countries can enter on a passport or national identity card and remain as long as they like. If you are planning to work, apply for a *permesso di soggiorno* within 90 days.

Italy's currency is the lira (plural: lire) with about L1700 to US$1. Daily expenditure will vary dramatically according to one's budget, but a very prudent backpacker could get by on less than L40,000 a day. Mid-range travellers will find that they can live reasonably well for around L70,000 to L80,000 a day.

For more information, see Lonely Planet's *Italy: A Travel Survival Kit.*

Croatia
You must have a visa to enter Croatia if you are a citizen of the USA, Australia, Canada or New Zealand. Those from the UK and most other European countries can enter on a valid passport. Visas are issued by consulates and embassies and at border crossings free of charge. You should carry your passport or national identity card at all times in Croatia.

About 5 kuna (the new Croatian currency) is equal to US$1. Croatia is not cheap, and the government overvalues the kuna to obtain cheap foreign currency. A bare-bones visit here will cost at least US$30 a day, but you'll easily spend more if you indulge in life's little pleasures.

Both Lonely Planet's *Mediterranean Europe on a Shoestring* and *Eastern Europe on a Shoestring* guides cover Croatia.

Austria

Now a member of the EU, Austria has the same visa requirements as Italy. No other documents are needed while travelling around the country.

The schilling, Austria's monetary unit, is divided into 100 groschen; US$1 is equal to about AS9. Budget travellers can get by on AS250 to AS300 a day, but count on double that if you want to avoid self-catering or staying at hostels.

Both Lonely Planet's *Western Europe on a Shoestring* and *Central Europe on a Shoestring* contain chapters on Austria.

Hungary

Hungary requires visas for those carrying Australian and New Zealand passports; citizens of the USA, Canada and most European countries do not need them. Visas valid for 90 days cost between US$20 and US$25 at Hungarian embassies and consulates They are also issued at highway border crossings and at Budapest's Ferihegy Airport, but not on trains.

Hungary's currency is the forint divided into 100 fillér. The government continues to devalue the forint, but at the time of writing US$1 was worth about 120 Ft. Prices are on the increase but a budget traveller should be able to make do on about 3000 Ft a day. For anything more extravagant, think in the vicinity of 5000 Ft.

Lonely Planet's *Hungary: A Travel Survival Kit* is a complete guide to the country.

Getting Around

AIR

Little Slovenia has no scheduled domestic flights, but a division of Adria called Aviotaxi (☎ 221 441) will fly chartered Pipers (four seaters) and Cessnas (eight seats) to aerodromes and airstrips around the country. Sample return fares for three passengers are DM95 to Bled, DM185 to Slovenj Gradec and DM360 to Portorož.

BUS

Except for long journeys, taking the bus is preferable to the train in Slovenia and departures are frequent. In some cases you don't have a choice, as travel by bus is the only practical way to get to Bled, the Julian Alps, much of Dolenjska, Koroška and Notranjska and to Croatian Istria. But for a large part of the rest of the country you do have a choice.

You can buy your ticket at the bus station (avtobusna postaja) or simply pay the driver as you enter the bus anywhere in Slovenia. In Ljubljana you should book your seat a day in advance (70 SIT fee), particularly if you're travelling on Friday or to popular destinations in the mountains or along the coast before a holiday. Be aware that bus services are severely restricted on Sunday and holidays (and sometimes on Saturday, too). Plan your trip accordingly or you'll find yourself marooned until Monday morning.

Different national companies serve the country. It's Integral in Ljubljana, Kambus in Kamnik, Alpetour in Škofja Loka and Kranj and Slavnik in Koper. But this means little to travellers, and prices are uniform when services overlap or compete.

Some, but not all, bus stations have a left-luggage office (garderoba) and charge about 70 SIT per piece per day. Be careful: some of them keep almost banking hours. A better (and safer) bet is to leave your luggage at the train station, which is usually nearby and has longer hours. If your bag has to be checked in the luggage compartment below the bus it will be about 70 SIT extra, though most drivers don't mind you carrying it on the bus if it will fit between the seats.

The timetables at the stations are posted on a wall or column outside, and list all bus routes. If you cannot find your bus listed or don't understand the schedule, seek assistance from the information or ticket window (usually combined). *Odhod* means 'Departures' while *Prihod* is 'Arrivals'. *Blagajna Vozovnice* is the place for tickets.

Slovenian bus timetables use coloured numbers or abbreviation footnotes to denote which days of the week the buses run. The following lists cover most of the combinations you'll encounter.

Bus Timetable Colours

White	Daily
Green	Monday-Saturday
Blue	Monday-Friday
Orange	Monday-Friday and working Saturdays
Yellow	Days when school is in session
Red	Sunday and public holidays

Bus Timetable Abbreviations

Č	Thursday
D	Workdays
D+	Monday-Friday
N	Sunday
NP	Sunday and holidays
PE	Friday
PO	Monday
PP	Monday-Friday
SO	Saturday
SN	Saturday and Sunday
ŠP	Days when school is in session
SR	Wednesday
TO	Tuesday
V	Daily

TRAIN

SŽ runs trains on just over 1200 km of track, about 40% of which is electrified. Large stretches of the main line need to be upgraded and though SŽ rolling stock is not the most modern (4000 vehicles are still stranded in various locations of the former

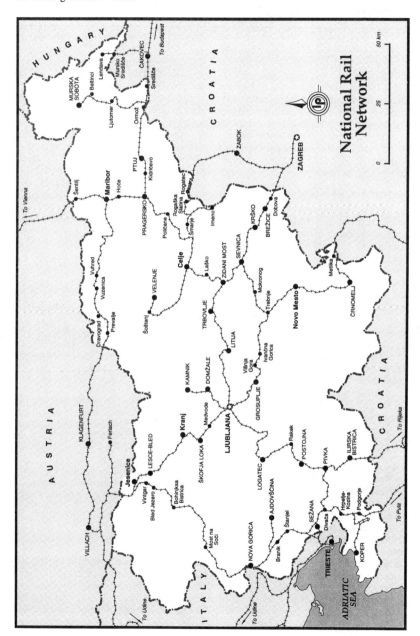

Yugoslavia), the service is reliable, fairly punctual and inexpensive, if a little slow. Very roughly, figure on covering about 60-65 km per hour.

Although many secondary lines link provincial cities and towns, all main lines converge on Ljubljana; to get from A to B it's almost always easier to return to the capital. Going from Maribor to Novo Mesto, for example, takes two or more changes if you refuse to backtrack. At the same time, large sections of the country (the Alps, Notranjska, western Dolenjska, central Primorska) are not served by rail, making the bus your only choice. Aside from Ljubljana, other important rail crossings are at Pivka, Divača, Zidani Most and Pragersko.

The domestic service runs rapid trains *(brzi vlaki)*, regional trains *(regionalni vlaki)* and city trains *(primestni vlaki)*, but the fastest are InterCity and InterCity Green Trains *(Zeleni Vlaki)*. IC trains levy a surcharge of 70 SIT. Fares on the IC Green Trains, which are calculated by the route not per km like IC trains, include the supplement, but you must book your seat on these for 70 SIT. If seat reservations are obligatory, the 'R' on the timetable will be boxed. An 'R' without a box means seat reservations are available.

Tickets are usually purchased in advance at the *železniška postaja* (train station) or a Slovenijaturist office. If you haven't been able to buy a ticket in advance, seek out the conductor, who will sell you one and charge you a supplement of 100 SIT. The extra charge is not made if the ticket window at the station was closed (yes, the conductor knows) or your connecting train was late. An invalid ticket, or trying to avoid paying, will earn you a fine of 800 SIT.

A return ticket *(povratna vozovnica)* is 20% less than double the price of a one-way ticket *(enosmerna vozovnica)*. A 1st-class ticket costs 33% more than a 2nd-class ticket.

SŽ is still under government subvention though it is free to set its own prices. SŽ has tried to keep prices down in competition with the more extensive bus network, so travelling by train is generally cheaper than going by bus. It's difficult to give an exact per-km charge as the price decreases as the journey lengthens. But very roughly, a 100-km journey costs 531 SIT in 2nd class and 796 SIT in 1st class.

Here are some one-way 2nd/1st-class domestic fares from Ljubljana: Bled, 348/522 SIT (51 km); Jesenice, 422/633 SIT (64 km); Koper, 724/1086 SIT (163 km); Maribor, 724/1086 SIT (156 km); Murska Sobota, 971/1456 SIT (216 km); Novo Mesto, 501/751 SIT (75 km).

SŽ sells SlovenijaRail passes that are valid for 10, 20 or 30 days of travel over a two-month period. They are available to individuals or 'groups' of two or more. Thus a 10-day pass is 5156 SIT for one person and 8540 SIT for a couple. Remember, though, that trains are generally convenient only for long-distance travel in Slovenia; once you reach a regional centre, you'll be making most day trips by bus. The only other discount schemes in effect for foreigners (students get 30% off only if they are enrolled in a Slovenian school) are a 30% discount for groups of six or more adults and 'mini-groups' of two adults and a child. Children up to the age of six travel for free if they don't occupy a seat. Otherwise they pay half the fare.

Depending on the station, departures and arrivals are announced by loudspeaker or on an electronic board and are always on a printed timetable. The yellow timetable with the heading *Odhod* or *Odhodi Vlakov* is 'Departures' and the white timetable with the words *Prihod* or *Prihodi Vlakov* is 'Arrivals'. Other important train words that appear often are: *čas* (time), *peron* (platform), *sedež* (seat), *smer* (direction) and *tir* (rail). Timetable symbols include:

�	Monday-Saturday (except public holidays)
⊗	Monday-Friday (except public holidays)
⊗	Monday-Saturday and public holidays

(V) Saturday and Sunday

(V) Saturday, Sunday and public holidays

(P) Sunday and public holidays

[7] No Sunday service

† Holiday service

If you expect to be taking a lot of trains in Slovenia, buy a copy of the official timetable book, *Vozni Red/Slovenske Železnice*, which is available at the Slovenijaturist branch at the Ljubljana train station for 500 SIT. It is published every year at the end of May and has explanatory notes in Slovene, German and French. Remember, too, when planning your trips that almost two-thirds of all rail passengers in Slovenia are commuters who only travel at peak times in the morning and late afternoon.

Left-luggage offices at some 30 stations around the country are supposed to be open 24 hours a day, but this is seldom the case (the posted hours in Rogaška Slatina, a '24-hour station', are 7 am till 3 pm). The charge is usually 70 SIT per piece. Ljubljana's garderoba is definitely open round the clock.

You can freight an automobile on the Maribor-Koper route for 3500 SIT one way (5600 SIT return). The charge for a bicycle, which can be transported on most trains with the exception of the IC Green Trains, is a flat 220 SIT.

Scenic Routes

Slovenia's most scenic rail route runs from Jesenice to Nova Gorica via Bled (Bled Jezero station), Bohinjska Bistrica and Most na Soči. This 89-km route through the Julian Alps and Soča River Valley opened for service in 1906. If you are travelling south, sit on the right-hand side of the train to see the emerald-green Soča at its sparkling best. A half-dozen local trains a day cover this route in each direction. The trip takes about two hours.

The 160-km train ride from Ljubljana to

Zagreb is also worth taking as the line follows the Sava River along most of its route through a picturesque gorge. Sit on the right side eastbound, the left side westbound.

Steam Trains

SŽ has a large stock of steam locomotives and antique wagons – a train-spotter's dream come true – and puts four of them to good use every year with its Oldtimer Train excursions in summer. The most popular trips cover the scenic route between Jesenice and Nova Gorica and Faak am See in Austria to Most na Soči (each section costs DM59/DM33 for adults/children under 14 years). There are also trips between Brežice and Sevnica (DM20/DM12), Ljubljana and Kamnik (DM10/DM7), Zidani Most (DM118/DM66) and Kočevje (DM59/DM33), Laško and Ormož via Celje and Ptuj (DM69/DM39) and Maribor and Ormož via Ptuj (DM99/DM56).

The trains only run a couple of times a month and the schedules and routings change each year. Contact any Slovenijaturist office (☎ 131 5206 or 131 5055 in Ljubljana) for the latest information.

CAR & MOTORBIKE

Perhaps more than anything else, Slovenes complain about their road system. OK, so the Los Angeles freeway system or France's sophisticated highway network it's not, but roads here are generally good – if a bit narrow. Driving in the Alps can be frightening, but never dangerous, with a gradient of up to 18% at the Korensko Sedlo pass into Austria. Many mountain roads are closed in winter and early spring.

There aren't all that many roads in the first place. Slovenia counts a total of 14,803 km of road, of which only 229 km are motorways. These go round Ljubljana as an outer ring road and extend south-west to Razdrto on the way to the coast, north-west to Naklo past Kranj, and to Grosuplje heading for Zagreb. There's also a stretch from Hoče, south of Maribor, to Arja Vas past Celje. They are numbered up to 10 and preceded by an 'A' (for *avtocesta*).

National highways contain a single digit and link cities. Secondary and tertiary roads have two sets of numbers separated by a hyphen; the first number indicates the highway that the road runs into. Thus road No 10-5 from Nova Gorica and Ajdovščina joins the A10 motorway at Razdrto. There are 627 km of international roads preceded with an 'E'. The most important of these are the E70 to Zagreb via Novo Mesto, the E63 to Klagenfurt via Jesenice and the E57 to Graz via Maribor.

A toll is payable on the motorways from Ljubljana to Kranj (25 km), Ljubljana to Razdrto via Postojna (56 km), and Maribor to Celje (54 km), but it's not expensive. From the capital to the turn-off on to highway No 10 for Koper and the coast, it costs 220 SIT for cars and motorbikes. Using the seven-km Karavanke Tunnel between Jesenice and Austria, however, is a different matter. That will set you back by more than 900 SIT.

Motorways and highways are well signposted, but secondary and tertiary roads are not; be sure to have your *Slovenia Atlas for Travellers* at the ready. Also, there seems to be a 'tradition' in certain parts of the country (notably around Ptuj) where vandals slice off the arrow of a sign indicating the direction. You could very well think you've arrived at your destination when you still have 10 km to go. Perhaps it's done by jealous tourism officials who want travellers to stay in their town and not move on elsewhere.

Private-car ownership in Slovenia (318 vehicles per 1000 inhabitants) is as high as it is in Germany so expect a lot of traffic, especially on Friday afternoons and in the summer when entire cities move to the countryside. The roads between Ljubljana and Celje, Celje and Maribor and Ljubljana and Koper can get very busy, and traffic jams are frequent. Lorries are banned from the highways between 5 and 8 pm so you might think of travelling those stretches then. Also, work is being carried out on major roads throughout the country so factor in the possibility of delays and diversions.

Petrol stations are usually open Monday to Saturday from 7 am to 8 pm, though larger towns have a 24-hour station as you enter the limits. Fuels of 91, 95 (unleaded) and 98 octane are available at most stations and are cheap by European standards: approximately 63, 66 and 73 SIT per litre respectively. Most stations also have diesel fuel costing 62 SIT per litre. Payment by foreign credit card is virtually impossible at petrol stations.

International vehicle insurance is compulsory in Slovenia. If your car is registered in the EU it is assumed you have it, but other motorists must buy a Green Card valid for Slovenia at the border (DM52 for 15 days, DM75 for a month).

The national automobile club is the Avto-Moto Zveza Slovenije (AMZS). For emergency roadside assistance, motorists should call them on ☎ 987. For information on road and traffic conditions, ring the AMZS in Ljubljana (☎ 061-341 341). All accidents should be reported to the police (☎ 92) immediately.

Road Rules

You must drive on the right. Speed limits for cars and motorbikes are the same throughout the country: 60 km/h towns and villages; 80 km/h on secondary and tertiary roads; 100 km/h on highways; 120 km/h on motorways. These are not always enforced as strictly as they should be, but just when you think you're in the clear you'll get caught in a speed trap.

The use of seat belts is compulsory and motorcyclists must wear helmets. But neither they nor motorists are required to show their headlights throughout the day outside built-up areas, as is the case in some other European countries. Many do, however. The permitted blood-alcohol level for drivers is 0.5 g/kg.

Parking is not a problem for the most part in the provinces, but many towns reserve large sections for pedestrians only. Ljubljana and the historic towns on the coast are a different matter. In these places you'll either have to use car parks (indicated on most maps by a 'P') where fees are charged, or buy special parking coupons from newsstands and kiosks and place them on the dashboard.

Car Rental

Car rentals from Kompas Hertz, Globtour Budget and Avis (all have offices in Ljubljana and some provincial cities) begin at around US$22 a day, plus US$0.22 a km, or US$365 a week with unlimited km for the cheapest car, usually a Renault Clio 4 assembled in Novo Mesto. Optional collision insurance is about US$8 a day extra, theft insurance another US$8 and passenger insurance US$5. There's also a 5% 'circulation tax' similar to VAT levied on all car rentals. Smaller agencies like Slavnik and Avtoimpex in Ljubljana have cheaper rates.

Hertz will rent to drivers aged from 18 to 23 only if they take full insurance coverage. Budget rents to those 19 years and over, Avis only to those 23 and over. Ask about one-way rentals with free drop-offs at other offices in Slovenia (eg Bled, Ljubljana, Maribor, Kranjska Gora, Portorož).

BICYCLE

Cycling is permitted on all roads except motorways. Many towns and cities, including Ljubljana, Maribor, Ptuj, Novo Mesto, Kranj and Škofja Loka, have bicycle lanes and some even have special traffic lights. The *Slovenia Tourist Map* available everywhere lists itineraries and some tourist offices have special cycling maps for their town or region. For more information see Cycling in the Facts for the Visitor chapter.

HITCHING

Hitchhiking is legal everywhere except on motorways and some major highways and is generally easy; even young women do it. Hitching can be difficult on Friday afternoon, before school holidays and almost impossible on Sunday. If you're heading north, don't count on many rides from Austrian motorists as they seem to have an aversion to this method of travel.

Hitching from bus stops is fairly common in Slovenia. Otherwise use motorway access roads or other areas where the traffic is not disturbed. See Hitching in the Getting There & Away section of the Ljubljana chapter for the best routes out of the capital.

Hitching is never a totally safe way of getting around and, although we may occasionally mention it as an option, we don't recommend it.

TOURS

All the big travel agencies – Kompas Holidays, Kompas Turizem, Emona Globtour, Slovenijaturist – as well as smaller agencies and some tourist offices organise excursions and tours for individuals and groups, usually out of Ljubljana. If you're pressed for time or want to squeeze in as much as possible over a short period of time, you can 'do' the entire country with them in a week for about US$450 including meals and accommodation, or a weekend for US$170. Both Kompas Holidays and Kompas Turizem have several good specialised tours, from horse riding and golfing programmes to folk and castle excursions.

ADDRESSES & PLACE NAMES

Streets are well signposted in Slovenian towns and cities, though the numbering system can be a bit confusing, with odd and even numbers sometimes running on the same sides of streets and squares.

Ljubljana and other cities have changed some of their street names since independence and almost anything recalling the *ancien régime* has been dropped. This can cause some confusion as many people still use the old names and, in some cases, streets have had to be renumbered. For example, Ljubljana's main drag, Slovenska cesta, and its northern extension, Dunajska cesta, were both Titova cesta until 1991. The houses and buildings on the latter have since had to be given new numbers.

In small towns and villages, houses are usually numbered along a single street which bears the same name as the community. Thus Ribčev Laz 13 is house No 13 in the village of Ribčev Laz on Lake Bohinj. As Slovenian villages are frequently made up of one road with houses clustered on or just off it, this is seldom confusing.

Place names with double-barrelled names like Novo Mesto (New Town) and Črna Gora (Black Hill) put the second word in lower case (Novo mesto, Črna gora) almost as if the names were Newtown and Blackhill. It's not a mistake, just the Slovenian way of doing it.

Slovene uses the possessive case frequently in street names. Thus a road named after the poet Ivan Cankar is Cankarjeva ulica while a square honouring France Prešeren is Prešernov trg.

Also, when nouns are made into adjectives they often become unrecognisable to a foreigner. The town is 'Bled', for example, but 'Lake Bled' is Blejsko Jezero. A street leading to a castle *(grad)* is usually called Grajska ulica. The words 'pri', 'pod' and 'na' in place names mean 'at the', 'below the' and 'on the'.

There are a lot of different words for 'street' in Slovene, and the following list will at least help you distinguish between a boulevard, a road and an alley. A more extensive list of words for use in reading maps appears in the Glossary in the back of this book.

avtocesta – motorway
breg – river bank
cesta (abbreviated *c*) – road
drevored – avenue
dvorišče – courtyard
gaj – grove
gora – hill, mountain
gozd – forest
hrib – hill
jezero – lake
most – bridge
nabrežje – embankment
naselje – colony, hamlet, estate
obvoznica – ring road
pot – trail
potok – stream
prehod – passage, crossing
prekop – canal
reka – river
sprehajališče – walkway, alley
steza – path
trg – square
ulica (abbreviated *ul*) – street
vrt – garden, park

Ljubljana

Though it only counts about 330,000 inhabitants, Ljubljana is by far Slovenia's largest and most populous city. It is also the nation's political, economic and cultural capital. As such, virtually everything of national importance begins, ends or is taking place in Ljubljana.

But it can be difficult to get a grip on the place. In many ways the city, whose name means 'Beloved' in Slovene, does not feel like an industrious municipality of national importance but a pleasant, self-contented little town with responsibilities only to itself and its citizens. You might think that way too, especially in spring and summer when café tables don't line but fill the narrow streets of the Old Town and street musicians (both free agents and hired help) entertain passers-by on Čopova ulica and Prešeren trg. Then Ljubljana becomes a Prague without the crowds, or a Latin Quarter minus the Parisian attitude.

With some 27,000 students attending Ljubljana University's 14 faculties and three art academies, the city feels young and offers all the facilities you'll need during your stay. Among the fine Baroque churches, palaces and quaint bridges, you'll see a lot of greenery. A large park called Tivoli and the hills beyond form the city's western border, and willow-lined walkways follow the Ljubljanica River and its canals. A much longer trail, a legacy of WW II, completely encircles the city as a kind of pedestrian 'ring road' and is a boon for those who want to escape the early-morning fog endemic to the city in autumn.

Slovenia is such a small country that a day trip can take you to its farthest reaches. Within an hour by train or bus from the capital, you can be hiking in the Alps of Gorenjska or enjoying the sun on Primorska's beaches.

HISTORY

Ljubljana first appeared in print in 1144 as the town of Laibach but a whole lot more had taken place here before that. The area to the south, an infertile bog called Ljubljansko Barje, was settled in the Copper Age by marsh dwellers who lived in round huts on stilts sunk into the soggy ground. Remnants of these dwellings can be seen in the National Museum. These early people were followed by the Illyrians and, in about 400 BC, the Celts, who settled along the Ljubljanica River.

But the first important settlement in the area came with the arrival of the Romans who built a military camp here in the century preceding the birth of Christ. Within 100 years, what had become known as Emona was a thriving town and a strategic crossroads on the routes linking Roman Pannonia in the south with colonies at Noricum and Aquileia. Legacies of the Roman presence – walls, dwellings, early churches – can still be seen throughout Ljubljana.

Emona was sacked and eventually destroyed by the Huns, Ostrogoths and Langobards from the 5th century, but the 'Ljubljana gate' remained an important crossing point between east and west. Tribes of Slavs settled here in the 6th century.

Ljubljana changed hands rapidly in the Middle Ages. In the 12th century the fortified town between Castle Hill and the Ljubljanica River was in the possession of the Dukes of Carinthia. Within 100 years it was transferred to the rulers of the new Duchy of Carniola, who made it their capital. The last and most momentous change came in 1335 when the Habsburgs became the town's new rulers. Except for a brief interlude in the early 19th century, they would remain the city's (and the nation's) masters until 1918.

The Habsburgs turned Ljubljana into an important trading centre and made it an episcopate; it would later become the centre of the Protestant Reformation in Slovenia. The town and its new hilltop castle (1415) were able to repel the Turks in the 15th century, but a devastating earthquake in 1511 reduced much of medieval Ljubljana to rubble. This led to a period of frantic construction in the 17th and 18th centuries which gave Ljubljana many of its pale-coloured Baroque churches and mansions – and the nickname 'White Ljubljana'. The town walls were pulled down to allow Ljubljana to expand and the southern marsh was partially drained. But the most important engineering feat was the construction of a canal to the south and east of Castle Hill that regulated the flow of the Ljubljanica River and prevented flooding.

When Napoleon established his Illyrian Provinces in 1809 in a bid to cut Habsburg Austria's access to the Adriatic Sea, he made Ljubljana the capital, as it remained until 1813. In 1821 members of the Holy Alliance of Austria, Prussia, Russia and Naples met at the Congress of Laibach to discuss measures to suppress the democratic revolutionary and national movements in Europe.

The railway linking Trieste and Vienna reached Ljubljana in 1849 and stimulated development of the town. By then it had become the centre of Slovenian nationalism under Austrian rule. Writers and nationalists France Prešeren and Ivan Cankar, among others, produced the bulk of their work here. Slovenes began to join the town government and emerged as a majority in 1882. But in 1895 another earthquake struck Ljubljana, forcing the city to rebuild once again. To Ljubljana's great benefit, the Secessionist and Art-Nouveau styles were all the rage in Central Europe at the time and many wonderful buildings were put up – structures the Communists would later condemn as 'bourgeois' and 'decadent' and raze to the ground.

Slovenia and its capital joined the Kingdom of the Serbs, Croats and Slovenes after WW I. During WW II the city was occupied by the Italians and then the Germans, who encircled the city with barbed-wire fencing creating, in effect, an urban concentration camp. Ljubljana became the capital of the Socialist Republic of Slovenia within Yugoslavia in 1945 and remained the capital after becoming independent in 1991.

ORIENTATION

Ljubljana lies in the Ljubljana Basin which runs to the north and north-west along the Sava River to Kranj. The basin forms two distinct parts: the non-arable Ljubljana Marsh (Ljubljansko Barje) to the south and the fertile Ljubljana Plain (Ljubljansko Polje) to the north and east. The city is wedged between the Polhov Gradec Hills to the west and Golovec Hills (including Castle Hill) to the east. The Ljubljanica River and the Gruber Canal have effectively turned a large part of central Ljubljana into an island.

All this geography is important in order to understand how the city has developed and continues to grow. If you look at a map or stand atop Ljubljana's landmark Skyscraper, you'll see that the city has had to expand fan-like to the north and east; hills and unstable ground have prevented growth in other directions.

Ljubljana is traditionally divided into five districts but only a few are of any importance to travellers. Center is the area on the left bank of the Ljubljanica to the west and north of Castle Hill and the Old Town. Tabor and Poljane are the easternmost parts of Center, and Bežigrad, where the bulk of the university buildings are, lies to the north. Two old suburbs to the south of Center – Krakovo and Trnovo – retain a lot of their old character.

Certain streets and squares (Čopova ulica, Trubarjeva cesta, Prešernov trg) and much of the Old Town are reserved for pedestrians and bicyclists. The Ljubljanica is crossed by a half-dozen road and foot bridges and some of them – Shoemaker Bridge (Čevljarski Most), Triple Bridge (Tromostovje) and Dragon Bridge (Zmajski Most) – are historically important. Work has begun on another foot bridge called Butcher Bridge (Mesarski Most), which will span the river between the last two. As in the past, it will contain shops and arcades.

The train and bus stations are opposite one another on Trg Osvobodilne Fronte – Trg OF – at the northern end of Center. Slovenska

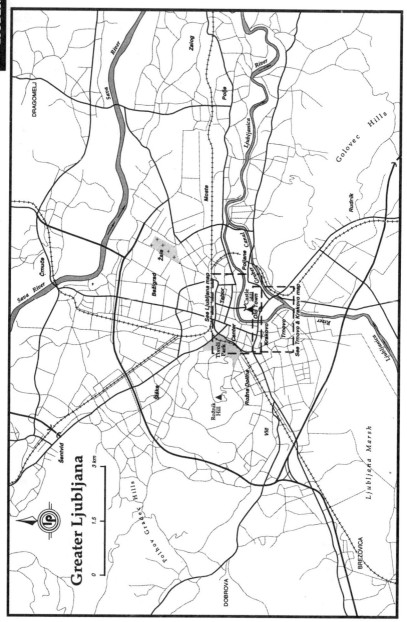

Greater Ljubljana

cesta is 350 metres west; catch bus No 9 to reach the TIC (800 metres). To get to Prešeren trg, head south on Miklošičeva cesta (600 metres).

INFORMATION
Tourist Offices
The best office in all of Slovenia for information is the TIC (☎ 061 215 412 or 224 222), at Slovenska cesta 35. The office employs students during the summer months who are very enthusiastic about their country and your interest in it. Though they can book accommodation only in Ljubljana, they can help with information on all of Slovenia. The TIC is open weekdays from 8 am to 7 pm and on Saturday and Sunday from 8 am to noon and from 4 to 7 pm. They can give you a map and brochures about Ljubljana as well as other parts of the country. Ask if the updated version of a multilingual map to all the buildings, bridges and parks designed by Jože Plečnik is available yet.

The Cultural Information Centre (☎ 061 214 025), next to Trg Francoske Revolucije 7, can answer questions about what's on in Ljubljana and has a free booklet listing all the city's museums and galleries. It's open from 10 am to 1 pm and 5 to 8 pm on weekdays and on Saturday morning.

The main office of the Alpine Association of Slovenia (☎ 061 312 553) is at Dvoržak-

GLAVNO MESTO SLOVENIJE • CAPITAL CITY OF SLOVENIA

ova ulica 9, a small house set back from the street. They have information about hiking throughout the country and some excellent maps and guides. The office is open from 8 am to 3 pm on weekdays only.

Motorists in need of assistance or advice can contact the Avto-Moto Zveza Slovenije (☎ 061 341 341) at Dunajska cesta 128, about three km north of Center.

Money
The currency-exchange office inside the train station is open 24 hours a day (no commission charged). They accept travellers' cheques and give a good rate. Upon departure they'll change excess tolars back into Deutschmarks or dollars.

There's an automatic currency-exchange machine outside the SKB Banka, Trg Ajdovščina 4, in the very centre of the modern shopping mall, which changes banknotes of 18 countries.

Some of the best rates of exchange in Ljubljana are available at Ljubljanska Banka at Trg Republike 2. It is open weekdays from 8 am to 5 pm and on Saturday from 9 am till noon. Three other central Ljubljanska Banka branches are at Slovenska cesta 35 next to the tourist office, in the beautiful Art-Nouveau City Savings Bank building (Mestna Hranilnica Ljubljanska) at Čopova ulica 3 and at Mestni trg 16 in the Old Town. These are open from 8.30 am till noon and 2 to 4.30 pm on weekdays and from 9 am till noon on Saturday.

Ljubljana is full of private exchange bureaux *(menjalnice)*. One called Hida is in the Central Market at Pogarčarjev trg 1 and has good exchange rates. It's open weekdays from 7 am to 7 pm and on Saturday to 2 pm.

Credit Cards The Atlas travel agency (☎ 061 222 711) at Mestni trg 8 is the Slovenian representative for American Express and can replace cards, make cash advances and hold clients' mail. They are open from 9 am to 5 pm on weekdays and till noon on Saturday.

A Banka, with a branch at Slovenska cesta 50, is the local rep for Visa and can issue a tolar cash advance on your card. They take a 1% commission for cashing travellers' cheques, though. A Banka is open from 8 am to 6 pm on weekdays and till noon on Saturday. If you have problems with your Visa card, you must go to the Visa Centre (☎ 061 302 055) in the office complex a few steps to the north at Slovenska cesta 56.

Eurocard and MasterCard holders should go to Ljubljanska Banka (☎ 061 125 0155) on Trg Republike.

Post & Telecommunications

The post office where poste restante is sent (counter Nos 17, 18 and 19) and held for 30 days is at Slovenska cesta 32 on the corner of Čopova ulica, so tell the folks at home to use the post code 61101. It is open weekdays from 7 am to 8 pm and on Saturday to 1 pm.

You can make long-distance telephone calls from here but the main telephone centre (open 24 hours a day) is to the north near the bus and train stations at Pražakova ulica 3. It is also a post office with service windows open from 7 am to 8 pm weekdays, 7 am to 6 pm on Saturday and 8 am to noon on Sunday.

There's a customs post office due west of the train and bus stations on Trg OF. This is where you must bring parcels that you wish to send abroad. Make sure you bring them open for inspection; the maximum weight is about 15 kg, depending on the destination. This post office is open weekdays from 8 am to 8 pm and on Saturday from 7 am to 1 pm.

Ljubljana's telephone code is 061. The postcode is 61000.

Foreign Embassies

For information about foreign embassies and consulates in Ljubljana, see Visas & Embassies in the Facts for the Visitor chapter.

Foreign Cultural Centres

The British Council (☎ 217 380) is located on the 3rd floor of Skyscraper at Štefanova ulica 1. It is open Monday, Wednesday and Friday from 11 am to 3 pm, Tuesday and Thursday from 3 to 7 pm and from 9 am to 1 pm on the first Saturday of every month.

The American Center (☎ 210 190), Cankarjeva ulica 11, is open Monday, Wednesday and Friday from 9 am to 4 pm and Tuesday and Thursday from 10 am to 5 pm.

The Centre Culturel Français (☎ 224 883) is at Slovenska cesta 19 and opens on weekdays from 8 am to 7 pm. Outside is a bust of the French Gothic novelist Charles Nodier (1780-1844), who lived and worked in Ljubljana in 1812-13.

Travel Agencies

All of the big agencies have offices in Center. Kompas Holidays (☎ 132 1053) is at Slovenska cesta 36, while Kompas Turizem (☎ 133 4180), which handles a lot of the incoming business, is at Pražakova ulica 4. Emona Globtour (☎ 213 843) is in the Maximarket passageway connecting Trg Republike with Plečnikov trg. Slovenijaturist (☎ 131 5288) at Slovenska cesta 58 and at the train station is your best source of information for rail travel. These offices are generally open from 9 am to 6 pm weekdays and till noon or 1 pm on Saturday.

Backpackers and students should head for the Erazem (☎ 133 1076) office at Trubarjeva cesta 7. They can provide information, make bookings and have a message board. They also sell ISIC cards (460 SIT) and, for those under 26 but not studying, FIYTO cards (500 SIT). Erazem is open weekdays from 10 am to 2 pm and from 4 to 7 pm. Mladi Turist (☎ 312 185), at Celovška cesta 49, is the office of the Slovenian Youth Hostel Association and sells hostel cards and makes bookings. They're open weekdays from 9 am to 3 pm.

The Vas agency (☎ 132 8093) at Miklošičeva cesta 4 (open from 9 am to 5 pm weekdays and till noon on Saturday) deals exclusively with rural tourism and farmhouse accommodation in Slovenia (see Places to Stay in Facts for the Visitor).

Bookshops

Mladinska Knjiga at Slovenska cesta 29 is the best bookshop in Ljubljana and has picture books, guides and maps to every corner of the country as well as books in English on other subjects. MK (as it's known here) has several smaller branches in the city, including one opposite the train station at Miklošičeva cesta 40 and another at Nazorjeva ulica 1. All shops are open from 9 am to 7 pm on weekdays and to 1 pm on Saturday.

A smaller chain with a knowledgeable and helpful staff is Cankarjeva Založba at Slovenska cesta 37, with another branch at Kopitarjeva ulica 2. They keep the same hours as MK.

The best selection of maps in Ljubljana can be found at a shop called Kam in Kod – meaning roughly 'Where and Which Way' – at Trg Francoske Revolucije 7 opposite the Križanke. Essentially an outlet for Slovenia's two largest cartographic companies, it stocks virtually every city, regional and hiking map produced in the country as well as imported maps and guides, including the Lonely Planet series. The small Geographical Museum is also based here.

There's a second-hand bookshop called Trubarjev Antikvariat at Mestni trg 25.

For foreign newspapers, go to the gift shop in the lobby of the Grand Hotel Union but don't expect them to be available on the day of publication. The *International Herald Tribune*, for example, always arrives a day late though it is only coming from Frankfurt. The shop is open weekdays from 9 am to 2 pm and from 6 to 10 pm. On Saturday it keeps roughly the same hours but closes for lunch at 1 pm and for the night at 9 pm. On Sunday it is open from 6 to 9 pm.

The small kiosk at the corner of Slovenska cesta and Trdinova ulica also has a decent selection, as does the Maximarket department store on the eastern side of Trg Republike.

Medical Services & Emergencies

You can see a doctor at the University Clinic Centre (Klinični Center; ☎ 131 4344) at Zaloška cesta 2. The emergency unit (marked 'urgenca') is open 24 hours a day. For emergency medical assistance, ring ☎ 323 060.

Either one of the two pharmacies (lekarne) will be open through the night: Centralna Lekarna (☎ 133 5044), Prešernov trg 5, or Lekarna Miklošič (☎ 314 558) at Miklošičeva cesta 24.

Laundry

This is a big problem in Ljubljana. A couple of the student dormitories (see Places to Stay – Colleges and Hostels) have washing machines and dryers that you can use; otherwise you'll have to cart your dirty clothes all the way to Cerjak Cvetka (☎ 316 834), a laundry at Kolodvorska ulica 10 south of the train station, or to Lavrih (☎ 212 390) at Vrtača ulica 1 south-west of Trg Republike.

THINGS TO SEE

The easiest way to see the best that Ljubljana has to offer and still enjoy a leisurely stroll is to follow the walking tour outlined on the map *Ljubljana: Capital of the Republic of Slovenia*. It is available free from the TIC as well as at many hotels and some restaurants around the city.

I've broken the tour up into eight sections which can be done individually or together with preceding or subsequent ones. If you run straight though them and make no stops, all eight shouldn't take much more than three hours. But count on a full day if you expect to see everything. Almost all the sights have plaques outside identifying and dating them in four languages, including English.

From June to September, a two-hour free guided tour in English departs at 5 pm from the town hall in Mestni trg.

Around Prešernov Trg

Begin the tour at Prešernov trg, a beautiful square which forms the link between Center and the Old Town. Taking pride of place in the square is the **Prešeren Monument** designed by Maks Fabiani and Ivan Zajc and erected in 1905 in honour of Slovenia's greatest hero. In summer, the steps at the base of the plinth (with motifs from Prešeren's poems) become a sitting area for Ljubljana's young bloods and foreigners alike.

To the east of the monument at No 5 is the

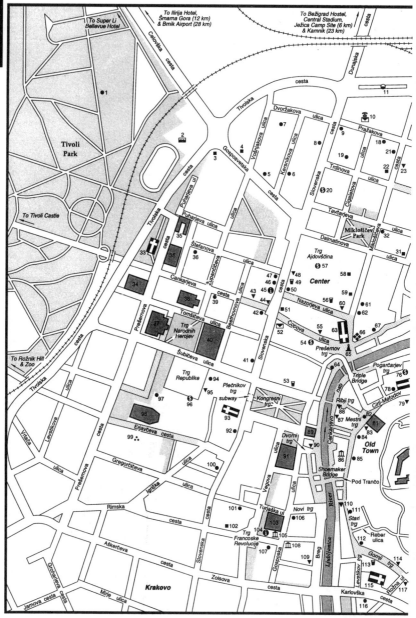

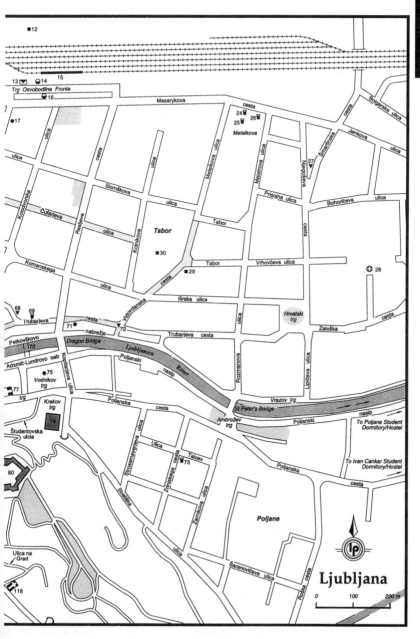

Ljubljana

0   100   200 m

LJUBLJANA

PLACES TO STAY

3	Tivoli Hotel
4	Lev Hotel
22	Austrotel
29	Park Hotel
30	Tabor Student Dormitory (HI)
31	Turist Hotel
51	Slon Hotel
58	Holiday Inn
59	Grand Hotel Union
102	Mrak Guesthouse

PLACES TO EAT

23	Marilyn/Kinoteka
27	Mao Tai
43	Daj-Dam
44	Dairy Queen
48	Šestica
55	McDonald's
60	Smrekarjev Hram
68	Napoli Pizzeria
72	Špageterija
79	Kolovrat
83	Rotovž
87	Maček
88	Zlata Ribica
90	Ljubljanski Dvor
95	Maximarket/Maxim Self-Service Restaurant
109	Napoleon-Pri Vitezu
110	Pizzeria Romeo
114	Sichuan
117	Marco Polo

OTHER

1	Tivoli Recreation Centre
2	Ilirija Swimming Pool
5	Adria Airways
6	Klub K4/University Student Centre
7	Alpine Association of Slovenia (PZS)
8	City Bus Ticket Kiosks
9	Slovenijaturist Travel Agency
10	Main Post Office/ Telephone Centre
11	Adria Airways Airport Buses
12	Ljubljana Fairgrounds/ Youth Theatre
13	Post Office (Customs)
14	City Airport Buses
15	Train Station
16	Bus Station
17	Kompas Cinema
18	US Embassy/Kompas Turizeu Travel Agency
19	Visa Centre
20	A Banka
21	Kompas Hertz Car Rental
24	Dvorana Club
25	Channel Zero Club
26	Club Magnus/Club Lilit
28	University Clinic Centre
32	Slavnik Car Rental
33	Serbian Orthodox Church
34	Museum of Modern Art
35	National Gallery
36	Globtour Budget Car Rental
37	National Museum
38	Opera House
39	American Centre
40	Parliament
41	Mladinska Knjiga Bookshop
42	Komuna Cinema
45	Tourist Information Centre (TIC)
46	Cankarjeva Založba Bookshop
47	Skyscraper/British Council
49	Holidays Pub
50	Kompas Holidays Travel Agency
52	Post Office (Poste Restante)
53	Babilon Disco
54	Art-Nouveau City Savings Bank Building (Ljubljana Banka)
56	El Dorado Disco
57	SKB Banka
61	Art-Nouveau Bank Buildings
62	Vas Travel Agency
63	Franciscan Church
64	Horse's Tail Café
65	Prešeren Monument
66	Urbanc Building/ Centromerkur Department Store
67	Erazem Travel Agency
69	True Bar
70	Butcher Bridge (under construction)
71	Hard Rock Music Shop
73	Club Cantina
74	Puppet Theatre
75	Vegetable Market
76	Seminary/Hida Exchange Bureau
77	Cathedral of Saint Nicholas
78	Bishop's Palace
80	Castle
81	Town Hall
82	Robba Fountain
84	City Gallery Café
85	Atlas Travel Agency (American Express)
86	Theatre & Film Museum
89	Filharmonija
91	University
92	French Cultural Centre
93	Ursuline Church
94	Emona Globtour Travel Agency
96	Ljubljanska Banka
97	UK Embassy
98	Cankarjev Dom/ Cultural Center
99	Ferant Garden/ Roman Ruins
100	National Drama Theatre
101	Glej Theatre/ Equrna Gallery
103	National & University Library
104	Cultural Information Centre
105	Kam in Kod Bookshop/Geographical Museum
106	Academy of Arts & Sciences
107	Križanke/Summer Festival Theatre
108	Municipal Museum
111	Schweiger House
112	Škuc Gallery/Bar
113	Atrium Bar
115	Church of St James
116	Gruber Palace
118	Church of St Florian

Italianate **Pharmacy**, which was a famous café for intellectuals in the 19th century, and to the north, on the corner of Trubarjeva cesta and Miklošičeva cesta, the delightful Secessionist **Urbanc** building (1903), now the Centromerkur department store. Diagonally across the square at No 1 is another Secessionist gem. The **Ura** building was once a shop for painters and thus very gaily decorated. Peer down Wolfova ulica and at No 4 you'll see a terracotta figure peering from a window. It's Julija Primic looking at the monument to her admirer France Prešeren.

The 17th century **Franciscan Church of the Annunciation** stands on the northern side of the square. The interior is not so interesting with its six side altars and enormous choir but to the left (west) of the main altar, designed by the Italian sculptor Francesco Robba, is a glass with the spooky remains of a saint. Like many churches in Ljubljana, the Franciscan church is open from morning to night but closes from about noon to 3 pm.

Attached to the church on the western side is the **Franciscan monastery**, with a very important library. Nearby in the south-west corner of the square is a bronze relief map of the city.

Walk north along Miklošičeva cesta from the Urbanc building and don't miss the several fine buildings along the way. The cream-coloured **People's Loan Bank** (1908) at No 4 is topped with the figures of two women holding a beehive and a purse – symbols of industry and wealth. The **Co-operative Bank** at No 8 was designed by Ivan Vurnik and the geometric patterns were painted by his wife Helena in 1922. You can take a small detour to **Miklošičev Park**, laid out by Maks Fabiani in 1902 and the only Art-Nouveau square in the city.

Market Area

From Prešernov trg, cross into the Old Town via the **Triple Bridge** (Tromostovje). Once the Špital Bridge dating from 1842, the prolific architect Plečnik added the two sides almost a century later to create something quite unique for Slovenia and the world. He also designed the covered walkway along the river called the **Plečnik Colonnade** that is part of the city's Central Market.

Walk through Pogarčarjev trg with its wonderful open-air market and old men and women selling everything from forest berries and wild mushrooms to homemade cheeses like soft white *sirček*.

The strange cone in Pogarčarjev trg was erected in honour of Plečnik in 1993. It represents the parliament building he designed but never realised for the top of Castle Hill. The building on the west side of Pogarčarjev trg is the Renaissance **Bishop's Palace** with a lovely arcaded courtyard. The **Seminary** (1749) to the east, with its pockmarked Atlases outside, contains some valuable Baroque furnishings and a library with priceless 16th century incunabula. It can be visited but only by appointment. There's a market in the basement of the Seminary.

Dominating the square is the **Cathedral of Saint Nicholas**, dedicated to the patron of fishermen and boatmen. A church has stood here since the 12th century but the existing twin-towered building is from the early 18th century. Inside it's a Baroque palace of pink marble, white stucco and gilt with frescoes by Matej Langus. Have a look at the magnificent carved choir stalls and the sweet faces of the angels of the main altar, another creation by Francesco Robba. The Pietà in the glass case on the outside southern wall is a copy.

If you want a closer look at what native Ljubljančans like to eat, continue on eastward to Vodnikov trg where there's yet another outdoor market. From here you could cross Ciril-Metodova trg and begin walking up Študentovska ulica to the castle, a relatively steep, 15-minute climb. (The city plans to erect a cable car that would whisk visitors up to the castle in seconds.) Instead, we'll continue walking west along Ciril-Metodov trg to one of the prettiest squares in the city.

Old Town

Mestni trg has two major landmarks. The **town hall** (Rotovž), seat of the city government, was erected in the late 15th century but rebuilt in 1718. The Gothic courtyard inside, arcaded on two levels, is where theatrical performances once took place and contains some lovely sgraffiti. If you look above the south portal leading to a second courtyard you'll see a relief map of Ljubljana in the second half of the 17th century. Every Saturday at 11 am in summer, trumpeters dressed in 18th century costumes play from the balcony above Mestni trg.

The town hall is topped with a golden dragon, the city symbol but quite a recent one. A wily mayor at the turn of the century apparently convinced the authorities in Vienna that Ljubljana needed a new crossing over the Ljubljanica River and the **Dragon Bridge** was built to the north-east. Ljubljančans say the dragons wag their tails whenever a virgin crosses the bridge.

Dragon Statue, Dragon Bridge

In the middle of Mestni trg stands the **Robba Fountain** (1751) modelled after the one in Rome. But the Titons with their gushing urns here represent something totally Slovenian: the three rivers of Carniola (Sava, Krka and Ljubljanica).

From Mestni trg you can make a small detour west into **Ribji trg** with perhaps the

oldest house in Ljubljana still standing at No 2 and a fountain with a girl in classical dress pouring water. The last time I visited Ribji trg, someone had sawed off the poor little thing's head.

Mestni trg leads into **Stari trg**, the true heart of the Old Town. More of a street than a square with 19th century wooden shop fronts, quiet courtyards and cobblestone passageways, Stari trg is a positive delight to explore. From behind the houses on the eastern side, paths once led to Castle Hill, a source of water. The buildings fronting the river had large passageways built to allow drainage in case of flooding.

Tranča at No 4 was the site of a prison until the 18th century, and those condemned to death were executed at a spot nearby in some fairly unpleasant ways (strangulation, drowning, being burned at the stake). Later it became the city's monopoly bakery – the only place where bread could be sold. Unscrupulous bakers who cheated customers got a dunking in the river.

A small street called Pod Trančo just beyond leads to **Shoemaker Bridge**. Like all the bridges here in the Middle Ages, this was a place of trade and an entrance into the town. Craftsmen worked and lived on the bridges (in this case 16 cobblers) to catch the traffic and avoid paying town taxes – a kind of medieval duty-free setup.

Between Stari trg 11 and 15 – the house that *should* bear the No 13 – there's a lovely Rococo building called **Schweiger House** with a large Atlas below the upper balcony. The figure has his finger raised to his lips as if asking passers-by to be quiet. But the owner, whose name meant the 'Silent One' in German, might have had something more than self-promotion in mind. In this part of the world, bordellos were traditionally located at No 13 and he probably got quite a few unsolicited calls.

In the middle of **Levstikov trg**, the southern extension of Stari trg, the large **Hercules Fountain** is a favourite meeting place in summer. Perhaps that's why a copy has replaced the original 17th century statue, which is now in the Town Hall.

The big church farther south on the square is the **Church of St James**. Far more interesting than the main altar (1732) by Francesco Robba is the one in the **Chapel of St Francis Xavier** with statues of a 'White Queen' and a 'Black King'. The **Column of Mary** south of the church was designed by Janez Vajkard Valvasor (well at least the statue was) and erected in 1682 in memory of the victory over the Turks at Monošter (now Szentgotthárd in Hungary) 18 years earlier.

Across Karlovška cesta is **Gruber Palace**, where the Jesuit priest Gabriel Gruber, who built the canal (Gruberjev Prekop) regulating the Ljubljanica, lived until 1784. It is in Zopf style, a transitional architectural style between late Baroque and neoclassicism, and now contains the national archives. If you look eastward on Karlovška cesta, you'll see a 'bridge of sighs' that was once Balkan Gate, the easternmost point of the Old Town. From here the town walls ran halfway up Castle Hill.

Gornji trg is the eastern extension of Stari trg. The four medieval houses at Gornji trg 9 to 15 have narrow side passages where rubbish was once deposited so it could be washed down into the river.

The most important building on this 'square' is the **Church of St Florian** built in 1672 and dedicated to the patron saint of fires after a serious blaze destroyed much of the Old Town. Beyond the church is an area of small houses once inhabited by Ljubljana's struggling artists. Venture into a courtyard or peer through an open door or window and you'll see that they left their mark.

A footpath called Ulica na Grad leads from the Church of St Florian up to Castle Hill.

Ljubljana Castle

There have been fortifications of some kind or another on Castle Hill at least since Celtic times, but the current structure mostly dates from after the 1511 earthquake. The castle has been under renovation for a couple of decades now and you still don't get to see much, but then it is a pretty big job.

The climb up the double wrought-iron staircase (150 steps) of the 19th century **Castle Tower** and a walk along the ramparts are worth it for the views down into the Old Town and across the river to Center. The ceiling in the newly renovated **Chapel of St George** (1489) features carved frescoes and the coats of arms of the Dukes of Carniola. In the **Pentagonal Tower** of the southern wing an archaeological collection is exhibited in an novel way: figures cut out of hard plastic show how earrings, amulets and necklaces were worn by their original owners. Weddings are held in the wing facing to the south-east on some days so the castle has complicated opening hours: from 11 am to 6 pm on Tuesday, Thursday and Sunday and from 1 to 6 pm on Wednesday and Friday. The tower, however, is open every day from 10 am to dusk.

A path from below the **Western Gate** will bring you to Reber ulica and Stari trg. Return to Pod Trančo and cross Shoemaker Bridge; the very narrow street a few steps to the north-west called **Židovska ulica** was the site of a synagogue and the centre of Jewish life in the Middle Ages.

Center

A lot of this district on the left bank of the Ljubljanica is worth exploring. If you go south from Shoemaker Bridge to **Breg**, the city's port when the Ljubljanica was still navigable this far (a steamboat once called from Vrhnika), and then west up Novi trg, you'll pass the **Academy of Arts & Sciences** on your left (No 3), which was once the seat of the Provincial Diet under the Habsburgs. The **National & University Library** (1941), Plečnik's masterpiece, is across Gosposka ulica. To appreciate more of this great man's philosophy, enter the main door on Turjaška ulica and you'll find yourself almost in darkness with all the black marble. But as you ascend the steps, you'll enter a colonnade full of light – the light of knowledge, according to Plečnik's plans. The reading room with huge glass walls has some interesting lamps also designed by Plečnik.

The **Municipal Museum** is a few steps farther south at Gosposka ulica 15. It has a well-preserved collection of Roman artefacts plus a scale model of Emona to help it all make sense. The rooms upstairs contain period furniture and household objects and one room is devoted to the work of the poet Oton Župančič (1878-1949). The museum is open Tuesday to Friday from 10 am to 1 pm and 4 to 6 pm and on Saturday and Sunday morning.

Diagonally opposite the museum in Trg Francoske Revolucije is the **Križanke**, a monastery complex that once belonged to the Teutonic Order of Knights and now serves as the headquarters of the Ljubljana Summer Festival. Its outside theatre alone seats 2000 people. The **Ilirija Column** in the square is dedicated to Napoleon and his Illyrian Provinces, during which time Slovene was taught in schools for the first time. Monsieur Bonaparte actually visited his 'capital'

Jože Plečnik, Architect Extraordinaire

Few architects anywhere in the world have had as great an impact on their birthplace as did Jože Plečnik, a name you'll hear again and again during your travels in Slovenia. And that's with good reason. His work is eclectic, inspired, unique – and found everywhere.

Born in Ljubljana in 1872, Plečnik was educated at the College of Arts in Graz and studied under the architect Otto Wagner in Vienna. From 1911 to 1921 he lived in Prague where he taught and helped renovate Prague Castle.

Plečnik's work in Ljubljana began in 1921 and continued until his death in 1957. Almost single-handedly he transformed Ljubljana adding elements of Classical Greek and Roman architecture, with Byzantine, Islamic, ancient Egyptian and folkloric motifs to the city's Baroque and Secessionist faces. The list of his creations and renovations is endless – from the National and University Library, colonnaded Central Market and cemetery at Žale in Ljubljana, to the delightful churches in Bogojina in Prekmurje and Ribnica in Dolenjska.

St Michael on the Marsh, near Ljubljana – another of Plečnik's creations

Plečnik was also a city planner and designer. Not only did he redesign the banks of the Ljubljanica River (including the Triple Bridge), entire streets (Zoisova ulica) and Tivoli Park, but he set his sights on monumental stairways (Kranj), public buildings (Kamnik) and outdoor shrines (Bled). An intensely religious man, Plečnik designed many furnishings and liturgical objects (especially chalices and candlesticks) for churches throughout the country.

Plečnik's eclecticism and individuality alienated him from the mainstream of modern architecture during his lifetime. But in the 1980s he was 'rediscovered' and hailed as a prophet of postmodernism. Oddly, he remained more or less in favour under the Communists because of his classicist phase.

One of Plečnik's designs that was never realised was an extravagant parliament house, complete with an enormous cone-shaped building. It was to be built on Castle Hill after WW II. However, such an extravagant building would have alarmed the federalist Josip Broz Tito so the Slovenes backed off. New life has been breathed into another of his projects. To celebrate the 850th anniversary of the founding of Ljubljana in 1994, plans for Plečnik's Butcher Bridge were unveiled. When completed it will span the Ljubljanica between Dragon and Triple bridges and will contain shops and arcades. ■

during this period and stayed at the Bishop's Palace.

Vegova ulica runs north from Trg Francoske Revolucije past a row of busts of Slovenian writers, scientists and musicians to the central building of **Ljubljana University**, established in 1919. The proclamation of independence was announced from the balcony facing **Kongresni trg** in 1991.

Named in honour of the Congress of the Holy Alliance hosted by Ljubljana in 1821, Kongresni trg is a somewhat scruffy place for all the important buildings it contains. The **Filharmonija** on the south-east corner is home to the Slovenian Philharmonic Orchestra, founded in 1701 and one of the oldest in the world. Haydn, Beethoven and Brahms were honorary members and Gustav Mahler was resident conductor during the 1881-82 season. The **Ursuline Church of the Holy Trinity** (1726) to the west is the most beautiful Baroque building in Ljubljana and contains a multicoloured altar made of African marble.

As you descend into the subway that will take you under Slovenska cesta, keep an eye open for a small gilded statue on top of a column. It's a copy (the original is in the National Museum) of the **Citizen of Emona**, dating from the 4th century. It was unearthed nearby in 1836 and probably formed part of a Roman necropolis.

Trg Republike is the main square in Center and contains the ugly **Parliament** (1959) to the north-east festooned with revolutionary reliefs in bronze and, to the south-west, **Cankarjev Dom** (Cankar Hall), the city's main cultural centre. To the south beyond Erjavčeva cesta in **Ferant Garden** are the remains of an early Christian church and baptistery with mosaics from the 4th century. It's open between April and October from 10 am to 6 pm on weekdays and to 1 pm on Saturday and Sunday.

Museum Area

The city's three most important museums are situated to the north-west of Trg Republike. They all keep the same hours – Tuesday to Saturday from 10 am to 6 pm and Sunday

from 10 am to 1 pm – and each costs 200 SIT (100 SIT for students) to visit.

The **National Museum** on Muzejska ulica at the western end of the park-like Trg Narodnih Herojev has sections devoted to history, natural history and ethnography as well as fine coin and mineral collections (the latter collected by Baron Žiga Zois in the early 19th century). The Roman glass and the jewellery found in 6th century Slavic graves is pretty standard fare; the highlight here is the **Vače situla**, a Celtic pail from the 6th century BC unearthed in a town east of Ljubljana. The relief around the situla shows men hunting stags, driving chariots, playing reed pipes (*trstenke*) and wrestling.

Other items on display – 16th century crossbows, a tiny 17th century strong box with a complicated locking system, an Art-Nouveau mirror from the turn of the century – are interesting but say little about Slovenian history and very few are labelled in English. Still, the museum building (1885) itself is impressive. Don't miss the ceiling fresco in the entrance hall featuring an allegorical Carniola surrounded by important Slovenes from the past and the statues of the Muses and Fates relaxing on the stairway banister.

The graceful **Opera House** on Župančičeva ulica to the north-east was opened in 1892 as the Provincial Theatre, and plays in both German and Slovene were performed here. After WW I it was renamed the Opera House and is now home to the Slovenian National Opera and Ballet companies. No doubt you'll hear someone practising scales as you walk by.

The **National Gallery** (1896) at Cankarjeva ulica 20 offers portraits and landscapes from the 17th to 19th centuries, copies of medieval frescoes and wonderful Gothic statuary. Although the subjects of the earlier paintings are the usual foppish nobles and lemon-lipped clergy, some of the later works are remarkable and provide a good introduction to Slovenian art. Take a close look at the works of the Impressionists Jurij Šubic and Rihard Jakopič *(Birches in Snow)*, the Pointillist Ivan Grohar *(Škofja Loka in* *the Snow)* and Slovenia's most celebrated woman painter Ivana Kobilca *(Summer)*. The bronzes by Fran Berneker are exceptional and, as long as you're here, have a look at the Art-Deco toilets, all black marble and green glass. The gallery's new wing to the north at Puharjeva ulica 9 is used for temporary exhibits. A glassed-in overhead walkway will link the two buildings and the Robba Fountain will be moved here from Mestni trg.

The **Museum of Modern Art** diagonally opposite at Cankarjeva cesta 15 is housed in an ugly modern building that is like stepping into a cold shower after walking around the other museums. The gallery shows part of its permanent collection of 20th century Slovenian art, which helps put some of the Socialist-inspired work of sculptors like Jakob Savinšek into artistic perspective. A large part of the building is given over to temporary exhibitions that a lot of people would consider 'fun' rather than 'serious' art. The Museum of Modern Art hosts the International Biennial of Graphic Art.

The interior of the Serbian Orthodox **Church of Sts Cyril & Methodius** north of the Museum of Modern Art is covered from floor to ceiling with modern frescoes that are still being created and it has a richly carved iconostasis separating the nave from the sanctuary. It is open Tuesday through Saturday from 3 to 6 pm.

Tivoli Park
You can reach the city's leafy playground (also called the Park of Friendship) via a subway from Cankarjeva cesta. Straight ahead, at the end of a monumental promenade designed by Plečnik, is the 17th century **Tivoli Castle** which contains the International Centre of Graphic Art and a small café.

Along with making use of the sport facilities at the Tivoli Recreation Centre (see Activities), you can climb to the top of **Rožnik Hill** (394 metres) for wonderful views of the city. The **Ljubljana Zoo** (Živalski Vrt), on the hill's southern slope, is open every day but Monday from 9 am to 4 or 6 pm.

Krakovo & Trnovo
These two attractive districts south of Center are Ljubljana's oldest suburbs and have a number of interesting buildings and historic sites. The Krakovo neighbourhood around Krakovska ulica with its two-storey cottages was called the 'Montmartre of Ljubljana' because of all the artists living here.

If you walk along Barjanska cesta, the southern extension of Slovenska cesta, you'll reach the **Emona Roman Wall** running along Mirje ulica. The pyramid is a Plečnik addition and the young people holding on to the bricks in the wall with their fingertips aren't being subjected to some cruel punishment: this is where novice mountaineers learn their stuff.

Within the **Jakopič Garden** at Mirje ulica 4, where the Impressionist painter once worked in his summer house, there are more Roman ruins including household artefacts and the remains of a sophisticated heating system.

Barjanska cesta ends at a picturesque canal called **Gradaščica**, which is a pleasant place for a stroll on a warm day. Spanning the canal to the east from Emonska ulica is the **Trnovo Bridge**, designed by Plečnik in 1932. Trees grow on the bridge and the railings are topped with curious pyramids. **The Church of St John the Baptist**, where France Prešeren met the love of his life, Julija Primic, is on the other side.

Farther south at Karunova ulica 4 is the house where Jože Plečnik lived and worked for almost 40 years. Today it houses the **Plečnik Collection**, an excellent introduction to this almost ascetically religious man, his inspiration and his work. It is open Tuesday and Thursday from 10 am to 2 pm.

Other Museums & Galleries
The following is a list of other museums in the Ljubljana area that may interest you. Some (but not all) can be visited while following the walking tours. They can have very convoluted and abbreviated opening times so check with the TIC before setting out.

Top: Shoemaker Bridge (Čevljarski Most) in Ljubljana (PCL)
Bottom Left: Robba Fountain and Ljubljana Cathedral from Mestni trg in the Old Town (SF)
Bottom Right: Winding staircase in the Castle Tower at Ljubljana Castle (SF)

Top: Bled Castle and Mt Stol (2236 metres) (Gorenjska) (SF)
Bottom Left: Lake Bled and the island church (Gorenjska) (SF)
Bottom Right: Medieval fresco of the beheading of St John the Baptist in Bohinj's Church of
St John the Baptist (Gorenjska) (SF)

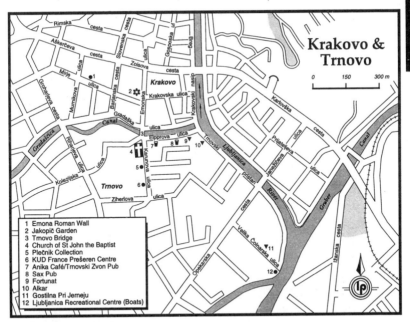

Krakovo & Trnovo

0   150   300 m

Krakovo

Trnovo

1 Emona Roman Wall
2 Jakopič Garden
3 Trnovo Bridge
4 Church of St John the Baptist
5 Plečnik Collection
6 KUD France Prešeren Centre
7 Anika Café/Trnovski Zvon Pub
8 Sax Pub
9 Fortunat
10 Alkar
11 Gostilna Pri Jerneju
12 Ljubljanica Recreational Centre (Boats)

Architecture Museum
    Fužine Castle, in the eastern suburb of Studenec (bus No 20)
Equrna Gallery
    Gregorčičeva ulica 3
Jakopič Gallery
    Slovenska cesta 7
Little Gallery (Mala Galerija)
    Slovenska cesta 35
Slovenian School Museum
    Plečnikov trg 1
Slovenian Theatre & Film Museum
    Mestni trg 17
Technical Museum of Slovenia
    Bistra Castle, 23 km south-west of Ljubljana (bus to Vrhnika)
Tobacco Museum
    Tobačna ulica 5 (bus No 1 or 6)

ACTIVITIES

The **Tivoli Recreation Centre** (☎ 131 5155), in the Tivoli Park at Celovška cesta 25, has bowling alleys, tennis courts, an indoor swimming pool, a fitness centre, a roller-skating rink and a popular sauna called the **Zlati Klub** with two saunas, a steam room, cold splash pools and a small outside pool surrounded by high walls so you can sunbathe in the nude. The Zlati Klub is open from 10 am to 10 pm (to 8 pm from July to September). Mixed days (men and women together in the buff) are Monday, Wednesday, Friday afternoon and all day Saturday and Sunday. Other times are for women only. Entrance costs 700 SIT (750 weekends) and it's 200 SIT if you don't have your own towel.

The **Ilirija** outdoor pool opposite the Tivoli hotel at Celovška cesta 3 is open in summer from 10 am to 7 pm on weekdays and from 9 am to 8 pm at the weekend.

You can rent rowing boats on the river from the **Ljubljanica Recreational Centre** (☎ 214 906) at Velika Čolnarska ulica 20 in Trnovo.

The **Zmajček Ballooning Club** (☎ 127 2534), south of the city at Ižanska cesta 305, has one-hour and 30-minute flights over the city for DM250 and DM125. For more information contact the TIC.

If you fancy a long but easy walk, you could follow the marked **Trail of Remembrance** (Pot Spominov) which runs for some 34 km along where German barbed wire once completely enclosed the city during WW II. Today it is especially favoured by joggers. The easiest place to reach it is from AMZS (Automobile Association of Slovenia) headquarters at Dunajska cesta 128 north of the Bežigrad hostel, but you can also join it from the south-western edge of Tivoli Park or the northern side of Žale Cemetery.

FESTIVALS

The number one event on Ljubljana's social calendar is the International Summer Festival of music, theatre and dance held in venues throughout the city but principally at the open-air theatre of the Križanke on Trg Francoske Revolucije. The festival, now in its fourth decade, begins in mid-July and runs through August.

A festival of Slovenian and other ethnic and folk music called Druga Godba takes place in the Križanke at the end of May, as does the Photo Antique Fair, where old photographs, cameras and other equipment are traded.

Ljubljana is at its most vibrant in July and August during the so-called Summer in the Old Town season when there are three or four cultural events a week in the city's historic squares and courtyards. All are free. There's a Jazz Festival in early July held at the Cankarjev Dom.

Vino is an international wine fair in early September for the trade and general public alike. It takes place at the Ljubljana Fairgrounds north of the train station at Dunajska cesta 18.

Numerous church concerts and street fairs are held throughout Ljubljana in December during the build-up to Christmas and the New Year.

The International Biennial of Graphic Art, at the Museum of Modern Art and several other venues, takes place in summer during odd-numbered years. The 22nd is in 1997.

PLACES TO STAY

If you're really down and out, you could crash at one of the squats in Metelkova, a former military camp between Metelkova ulica and Maistrova ulica about 500 metres east of the train and bus stations that has been taken over by a group of young Slovenes and others. Ask permission at the Channel Zero club there but don't expect many creature comforts; there's no water or power in most of the buildings. There's talk of converting one of the buildings into a hostel.

The tourist tax in Ljubljana is 135 SIT per person per night for most types of accommodation except for hostels and camping grounds, which charge 65 SIT and usually include it in the quoted price.

Camping

The only camp site really convenient to Ljubljana is the *Ježica* site (☎ 372 901) on the Sava River at Dunajska cesta 270a, about six km from the train and bus stations. You can reach it on bus No 6 or 8. Ježica, which is open all year, has an outdoor swimming pool, a fitness studio, bowling alley, tennis courts and a laundry room. It costs DM6 per person with a tent and DM10 with a caravan or car. Bicycles are available for 400 SIT per hour and daily permits for fishing in the Sava cost 1500 SIT. There are also 38 cramped little bungalows with two rooms costing from DM65 for two people.

The *Smlednik* camp site (☎ 061-627 002) in Dragočajna, 17 km north-west of Ljubljana, is located between two small lakes and the big draw here seems to be the nudist beach. Smlednik, open from May to mid-October, charges DM6 per person per night.

Private Rooms

There are relatively few private rooms available in Ljubljana. The TIC, for example, has only about 40 1st- and 2nd-class rooms on their list and just four are in Center. Most of the others would require a long bus trip up to

Bežigrad. Prices start at about DM16 per person.

Colleges & Hostels

Four student dormitories *(dijaški dom)* open their doors to foreign travellers in summer and are clean, cheap and friendly places to stay. A couple are near Center but many are quite a way out of town.

The closest one, which is affiliated with HI, is *Dijaški Dom Tabor* (☎ 321 067), Vidovdanska ulica 7, which can accommodate up to 60 people. They charge 1600 SIT for a single room and 1200 SIT per person for a bed in a double or triple. There is a discount of 10% if you pay three days in advance and breakfast costs 240 SIT. As usual, toilets and showers are on the corridor but all rooms have running water. Though there's a 'curfew' between 10 pm and 6 am, the security guard will let you in when you ring the bell. The Tabor is open in July and August only. It is a short walk from the bus and train stations.

The *Dijaški Dom Poljane* (☎ 327 494), about 1.5 km east of the Old Town at Potočnikova ulica 3, has 120 two-bedded rooms and is open in July only. The charge here is 1200 SIT per person (1360 SIT with breakfast), and you can eat in the student cafeteria. The big plus is that there's a laundry room and the Poljane doesn't have a curfew. To reach it, take Bus No 5 from Tavčarjeva ulica or No 13 from Kongresni trg and get off at the Poljane stop. The Poljane is where students of the Slovenian Language Summer School stay.

A bit closer to town but still in Poljane is the *Dijaški Dom Ivana Cankarja* (☎ 133 5274) at Poljanska cesta 26. It has 160 three-bedded rooms and charges 1500 SIT per person including breakfast (1200 SIT with a student card not including breakfast). Rooms don't have running water, but there are showers, toilets and TVs on each floor. The hostel is open in July and August only, but you may be able to find a bed here on weekends throughout the year. You can also reach here on bus Nos 5 and 13.

The *Dijaški Dom Bežigrad* (☎ 342 867) is at Kardeljeva ploščad 28 in the Bežigrad district two km north of the train and bus stations. It has singles/doubles/triples with shower and toilet for 1800/3000/3600 SIT and triples with shared facilities for 1000 SIT per person. None of the rates include breakfast. An HI card gets you 10% off, and the hostel is open all night long. The Bežigrad has 150 rooms available in summer but only about 15 the rest of the year. There's a laundry in the Kam student building at No 14 of the same street open 8 am till noon and 2 to 6 pm weekdays, and 8 am to 3 pm on Saturday. To get here from Slovenska cesta, take bus No 6, 8 or 21 and get off at the Triglavska stop.

Pension

The closest thing to a guesthouse in Ljubljana proper is the *Mrak* (☎ 223 412), west of Trg Francoske Revolucije at Rimska cesta 4, with 30 rooms. It's a charming place to find in the city and the Gostilna Pri Mraku downstairs has reasonably priced and generous Slovenian set menus from 530 SIT, but the rooms are small and quite expensive: DM54 for a single with shower and breakfast and DM75 for a double.

Hotels

Bottom End If you're absolutely desperate, the *Tivoli* (☎ 133 6131), a combination hotel and 'workers' hostel' at Tivolska cesta 30, has 30 tiny double rooms that cost a minimum of 2526 SIT for one person with shared shower and breakfast, and 4252 SIT for two. The Tivoli faces the park but is on the corner of two very busy and noisy streets.

One of the best deals in Ljubljana is the 15-room *Super Li Bellevue Hotel* (☎ 133 4049) on the northern edge of Tivoli Park at Pod Gozdom 12. There are no rooms with private baths but bright and airy singles with sinks are 2750 SIT, doubles are 5400 SIT and triples 7050 SIT. The disco/nightclub can get pretty noisy at the weekend.

The 110-room *Park Hotel* (☎ 133 1306; fax 321 352) at Tabor 9 is where everyone usually ends up as it's the city's only large budget hotel close to Center and the Old

Town. It's not a particularly nice place – the lifts work only sporadically, the rooms are spartan and the top couple of floors are used as a hostel for labourers from other parts of the former Yugoslavia and Albania, who seem to always stomp their cigarettes out on the threadbare carpets. But the prices are right: DM44 for a single with breakfast and shower and DM68 for a double. Rooms without showers are 20% cheaper and students with cards get a 20% discount. The staff are very helpful and friendly.

Middle The 120-room *Ilirija hotel* (☎ 159 3337; fax 159 3048) at Trg Prekomorskih Brigad 4 off Celovška cesta isn't anything special – in location or aesthetics. It's a fair walk from Center and the stations and although this two-storey hotel was renovated just a couple of years ago, there is already a sad feeling of neglect. It does back on to Debeli Hill and the Šiška district's leafy recreation area, however. Singles start at DM63, doubles at DM90.

The 196-room *Turist hotel* (☎ 132 2343; fax 319 291), at Dalmatinova ulica 15 and a mere 200 metres from Prešernov trg, is very central, but this six-storey place has a lot of drawbacks and is in bad need of renovation. Rooms are very small, the hotel very drab and noisy and the service is among the worst I encountered in Slovenia. Laundry came back not just damp but wet. If you do stay here, request a room looking southward to the Old Town and Castle Hill. Rates are DM72 for a single and DM104 for a double, including a generous breakfast buffet.

Top End Most of the expensive and luxury hotels in Ljubljana have all the things you'd expect from such high prices: satellite television, direct-dial telephones, minibars, etc.

In the thick of things is the 185-room *Slon hotel* (☎ 125 1232; fax 217 164) at Slovenska cesta 34, but try to get a room facing east to avoid the noise of Ljubljana's main drag. The 'Elephant' has a history going back more than four centuries – it is said that this was the spot where a pachyderm presented to the Habsburg emperor by an

African king tarried on its way to Vienna – though the present hotel dates from this century. There are five categories of single rooms starting at a minimum of about DM80, with doubles from DM138. The Slon has a floor reserved for non-smokers and a popular Italian restaurant which serves homemade pasta.

By now the *Lev hotel* (☎ 133 2155; fax 321 994) south of the landmark Union brewery at Vošnjakova ulica 1 should have completed its ambitious renovation programme, transforming the nondescript 209-room hotel into a glass-and-mirror tower. Rooms were DM90 to DM170 for a single and DM110 to DM195 for a double with all the mod cons. The Lev is within easy walking distance of the stations and most everything in Center.

The 56-room *Austrotel* (☎ 132 6133; fax 301 181) at Miklošičeva cesta 9 is Ljubljana's most modern hotel with distinctly 'modern' prices: DM158 to DM183 for a single, depending on the category of room, and DM238 to DM282 for a double. The Austrotel's pricey Steakhouse restaurant, with a salad bar and no-smoking section, is excellent and a welcome change from an overdose of burek. The only problem with this four-storey hotel is that the rooms facing Miklošičeva cesta are noisy. Parking is available.

The hotel with the most character in Ljubljana is the Art-Nouveau *Grand Hotel Union* (☎ 125 4133; fax 217 910), built in 1905 at Miklošičeva cesta 1. But beware: this 260-room hotel has rooms of different categories in an atmospheric old wing and in a boring new one from the late 1960s. Singles with breakfast and shower range from DM95 to DM136, with doubles between DM142 and DM190. The hotel has both a cellar and a lovely garden restaurant, and guests get to use the swimming pool and fitness centre (open from 3 to 10 pm) and car park of the *Holiday Inn* (☎ 125 5051; fax 125 0323) next door.

The 133-room Holiday Inn is the most expensive hotel in town – a minimum DM213 for a single and DM296 for a double

– and looks and feels like Holiday Inns from Cleveland, Ohio, to Kuala Lumpur. The Holiday Inn is one of the few hotels in the country with air-conditioning.

PLACES TO EAT

All the eateries listed here can be found in the areas described in the Things to See section in this chapter. Most inexpensive eating places are in Center; there are few bargains in the Old Town.

Around Prešernov Trg

Napoli Pizzeria off Trubarjeva cesta at Prečna ulica 7 is said to have the best pizza in town. It's open daily till midnight. *Špageterija*, 250 metres to the east at Trubarjeva cesta 52 and close to the Park hotel, is another place for decent pizza and pasta (though the decor suggests the owner originally had a Mexican restaurant in mind).

Marilyn opposite the Austrotel at Miklošičeva cesta 28 is an attractively decorated modern restaurant popular with office workers and staff from the nearby US Embassy. It has three-course daily set lunches for less than 700 SIT. Marilyn is open Monday to Saturday from 6.30 am to 11 pm and on Sunday from 4 pm.

Market Area

In the Plečnik Colonnade along the water in Pogarčarjev trg, there's a basement fishmonger's called the *Ribarnica Centre* with a stand-up bife on street level outside selling cooked fish and seafood. A large plate of deep-fried squid and whitebait should cost about 500 SIT.

The *Kolovrat* at Ciril-Metodov trg 14 opposite the cathedral is a renovated gostilna with reasonably priced Slovenian meals.

Old Town

A central place serving unexceptional pizzas (about 550 SIT) and with a rather sad salad bar (300 SIT) is *Pizzeria Romeo* at Stari trg 6. It is open every day from 11 to 1 am. As is fitting in a city called 'Beloved', opposite the Romeo is a bar/café called *Julija*. *Marco Polo* is a relatively expensive place at Gornji

trg 20 serving Italian food. It can be very difficult getting an outside table at this popular place in summer.

A favourite place for fish dishes is *Maček* at Cankarjevo nabrežje 15. But for my money (and to avoid the tourists), I'd head a few doors down to No 5 and the simpler, cheaper *Zlata Ribica*, a small pub-restaurant open from 8 am to 10 pm weekdays and from 9 am to 4 pm on Saturday.

If you hanker for a fix of Chinese food, the location of the *Sichuan* below St Florian's Church at Gornji trg 23 is wonderful, but the food is much more authentic at the *Mao Tai*, east of the train station at Šmartinska cesta 3. Main courses like *hui guo rou* (twice-cooked pork) and *mapo doufu* (spicy bean curd) are about 850 SIT at both places, but Mao Tai (whose owner is Japanese) can do half portions. It's open till midnight every day but Sunday.

A lovely place for a meal – if you can get in – is the *Vinska Klet* on the ground floor of the town hall on Mestni trg. The chef worked for many years for Josip Broz Tito, a man with a discriminating palate, so you can expect some good food.

The *Rotovž* next to the town hall at Mestni trg 2 is an expensive restaurant (900 to 1500 SIT for mains) that caters mostly to foreign tourists; you'll be lucky to get a seat, especially on the outside terrace. Some of the dishes (like the roast kid) are unusual and quite tasty; service is multilingual but cavalier despite the waiters' trendy braces and bow ties.

Center

There are burek stands everywhere in Ljubljana for a quick and filling lunch or snack and one of the best is opposite the train station on Masarykova cesta. If you want something more substantial, head for *Super 5*, which faces Slovenska cesta from the shopping mall on Trg Ajdovščina. They serve cheap and cheerful Balkan grills like čevapčiči and pleskavica, as well as klobasa, and are open very late.

One of the cheapest places to have a meal is at the *Maxim* self-service restaurant in the basement of the Maximarket shopping arcade on Trg Republike. Main dishes are between 250 and 300 SIT and there are set menus for 370, 400 and 450 SIT. It's open from 9 am to 6 pm and on Saturday till 3 pm. But don't expect cordon bleu food at those prices; it's real school cafeteria stuff. A similar place is *Daj-Dam* at Cankarjeva ulica 4, around the corner from the TIC. They have set menus (pay the cashier first), which you eat standing up, and a sit-down restaurant in the back with regular table service.

Ljubljanski Dvor at Dvorni trg 1 north of Breg has the second-best pizza in Ljubljana, according to aficionados. It opens daily except Sunday from noon till midnight.

If you must have Western-style fast food, Ljubljana can oblige. *Dairy Queen* has an outlet at Cankarjeva cesta 2 on the corner of Slovenska cesta (open Monday to Thursday from 9 am to 11 pm, to midnight on Friday and Saturday and from 4 to 10 pm on Sunday). *McDonald's* is upstairs on Čopova ulica 14. It is open Monday to Saturday from 9 am to 11 pm and on Sunday from 10 am. The best thing that can be said about this place is that it looks directly at the wonderful decorations of the Art-Nouveau City Savings Bank building (1904) opposite at No 3.

An up-market place is the *Napoleon-Pri Vitezu* restaurant at Breg 20. The atmosphere here is 'olde world' with a touch of Illyrian Provinces thrown in. Main courses such as beef Pohorje-style and chicken with apples run from about 900 to 1200 SIT. Salads are around 200 SIT.

Museum Area & Slovenska Cesta

An old stand-by – it's been around since 1776 – is the *Šestica* at Slovenska cesta 38. It's a very popular place with local people and serves up plates of *goveji golaž* (beef goulash) and fat Kranjska sausage with cabbage. Main courses are in the 500 to 800 SIT range. The back courtyard looks pleasant but gets a bit stuffy in summer.

Arguably the most stylish restaurant in Ljubljana is the *Smrekarjev Hram*, an Art-Nouveau jewel run by the Grand Hotel Union at Nazorjeva ulica 1. But without the rich aunt or uncle in tow, enter at your own peril: this place is very expensive. The new *Plečnikov Hram* restaurant in the Križanke is in the same league.

Tivoli Park Area

The *Pod Gozdom* below the Super Li Belle-vue Hotel and next to Celovška cesta 41 has some of the best salads in town.

Krakovo and Trnovo

The *Fortunat* at Eipprova ulica 1a has decent Italian food and the *Alkar* around the corner at Trnovski pristan 4 is where any budget-conscious local people go for fish. It's open daily except Tuesday until 10 pm.

A couple of inns that are a bit out of the way but get rave reviews from foreign residents of Ljubljana are *Gostilna Pri Jerneju* at Velika Čolnarska ulica 17, about 400 metres south-east of Eipprova ulica and the Gradaščica Canal, and *Gostilna Pri Žabarju* at Viška cesta 50, four km south-west of Center. You can reach the latter on bus No 6. Both places close on Sunday.

Cafés

The coffee house *(kavarna)* is nowhere near as much a part of the social fabric and daily routine as it is in, say, Budapest, but one or two may be worth a visit. The one at the Grand Hotel Union, open from 9 am to 9 pm and to 4 pm at the weekend, was once *the* venue to rub shoulders with the movers and shakers of Ljubljana. It still attracts an interesting assortment of characters.

Better yet, head for the *City Caffè* on the top (12th) floor of Skyscraper (Nebotičnik) at the corner of Slovenska cesta and Štefanova ulica. This was Ljubljana's tallest building for years after it was built in 1933 and it still looks like it could be part of a set for a King Kong film. The views – of the Old Town, castle, Tivoli Park, the Ljubljana Marsh to the south and the new glass-and-steel 72-metre-high World Trade Centre to the north – are the best in town and City Caffè is open daily from 8.30 am till midnight.

The *Anika* café at Eipprova ulica 19 in Trnovo has the best ice cream in town.

ENTERTAINMENT

Ljubljana enjoys a very rich cultural life so ask the TIC for its monthly programme of events entitled *Where to in Ljubljana?*, as well as any flyers they might have for the various theatres and concert halls. The theatre, concert and opera seasons last from June to September but there's always something going on in town.

Classical Music & Dance

Ljubljana is home to two orchestras: the Slovenian Philharmonic Orchestra and the RTV Slovenija Symphony Orchestra. Concerts are held in various locations all over town, but the main venue – with up to 700 cultural events a year – is *Cankarjev Dom* on Trg Republike. It has two large auditoriums (the Great Hall has perfect acoustics) and a number of smaller ones. The ticket office (☎ 222 815) is nearby at Prešernova cesta 10 and is open weekdays from 1 to 8 pm, Saturday from 9 am to 2 pm and an hour before performances. Also check for concerts at the beautiful *Filharmonija* at Kongresni trg 10. Tickets usually run between 500 and 1000 SIT.

The ticket office (☎ 331 950) of the *Opera House*, where ballets are also performed, at Župančičeva ulica 1 is open Monday to Saturday from 11 am to 1 pm and an hour before each performance.

For tickets to the Ljubljana Summer Festival and anything else staged at the *Križanke*, go to the booking office (☎ 126 4340) behind the Ilirija Column at Trg Francoske Revolucije 1-2. It is open weekdays from 11 am to 1 pm, 6 to 7 pm and one hour before performances.

Theatre

Ljubljana has seven theatres and nine companies so there should be something for everyone. Slovenian theatre is usually quite visual with a lot of mixed media so you don't always have to speak the lingo to enjoy the production.

The home of the national company is the *National Drama Theatre* (☎ 221 511) at Erjavčeva cesta 1. The *Youth Theatre* (Mladinsko Gledališče; ☎ 310 610) in the Festival Hall (Festivalna Dvorana) at Vilharjeva ulica 11 has staged some well-received productions of *Scheherazade* and *Alice in Wonderland* in recent years.

The *Glej Theatre* (☎ 216 679), Gregorčičeva ulica 3, is Ljubljana's foremost experimental theatre with three resident or affiliated companies, including Betontanc. They're often on tour at home or abroad and the theatre is closed in July and August. In other months your best chance to see a performance is on Thursday or Friday at 9 pm.

The *Puppet Theatre* (☎ 314 962) performs at Krekov trg 2 south of Vodnikov trg and has an office at Židovska ulica 1.

Cinema

For first-run films in Ljubljana, head for the *Kino Komuna* at Cankarjeva cesta 1. *Kino Kompas*, Miklošičeva cesta 38, screens art films as does the small cinema at the Slovenian Theatre & Film Museum at Mestni trg 17. The *Kinoteka* at Miklošičeva cesta 28 shows classic films at 6 and 8 pm. Tickets generally cost about 500 SIT and discounts are offered on Monday.

Jazz, Rock & Pop Music

Ljubljana has a number of excellent music clubs and all the ones listed below are highly recommended.

The *Klub K4* (☎ 131 3282) in the basement of the ŠOU (Student Organisation of the University of Ljubljana) building at Kersnikova ulica 4 is a very popular venue featuring both canned and live music nightly – from pop, rock and techno to jazz and Irish folk. Ask them for their monthly programme and make your choices. It's open from 10 pm to 2, 3 or 4 am and admission costs 400 to 900 SIT (200 to 500 SIT for students), depending on the night and the act.

The *KUD France Prešeren* (☎ 332 288), a 'non-institutional culture and arts society' at Karunova ulica 14 in Trnovo stages concerts of all kinds and is the headquarters of the *Ana Monro Theatre*, the only street theatre in Slovenia. KUD also has a great high-tech pub/café open daily from 3 to 10 pm where you can meet people.

The *ŠKUC* gallery and bar (☎ 329 185), run by the student cultural association at Stari trg 21, has music performances and exhibits art of the Neue Slowenische Kunst multi-media group and the IRWIN artists' cooperative.

For a truly alternative scene, head for Metelkova, Ljubljana's version of Christiania in Copenhagen minus the sleaze between Metelkova ulica and Maistrova ulica. There are two music clubs here – *Channel Zero* and *Dvorana* – with all sorts of music as well as performance-arts shows.

Discos

The most popular conventional discos are *El Dorado*, open daily to at least 2 am, at Nazorjeva ulica 6 and *Babilon* at Kongresni trg 2. Babilon is open Tuesday to Saturday from 10 pm to 4 am.

Klub K4 has a disco on some nights and when it runs, it rages. Doors open at 10 pm and the cover charge is around 500 SIT (300 SIT for students).

An excellent place to bop – with all kinds of hip music but a heavy Latino beat – is the *Club Cantina* near the Jesuit Church of St Joseph on Zrinjskega cesta in Poljane. Knock on the door to gain entry.

Pubs & Bars

Pedestrian Trubarjeva cesta from east of the Dragon Bridge to Prešernov trg is a lively street with plenty of pubs, bars, cafés and late-night pizzerias. One of my favourite places – especially for its name – is the *True Bar* at No 23 open nightly to 2 am. The *Reformator* at No 18 is also a pleasant place for a drink.

In the Old Town, the best place to meet people is in the *Atrium* at Gornji trg 4. *Holidays Pub* next to the Kompas travel agency at Slovenska cesta 36 is the closest thing to a real pub in Ljubljana, but it's more 'suity' rather than trendy and can get very crowded.

One of the best places for a drink in Ljub-

ljana if you just want to sit outside and watch the passing parade is the roped-off café/pub on the southern side of Prešernov trg that local people call the *Horse's Tail* (Konjski Rep). You'll probably bump into half the people you've met along the way in Slovenia here. It's open from June to October.

Down in the Trnovo district the *Sax* pub at Eipprova ulica 7, decorated with wonderful murals and graffiti, takes the spillover from the nearby KUD centre. The *Trnovski Zvon* in the same building as the Anika café at Eipprova ulica 19 isn't half as much fun but easier to get into.

Gay & Lesbian Clubs

Ljubljana is not the gayest city in Central Europe but there are a couple of decent options. The number one spot for both gays and lesbians alike in Ljubljana is the *Klub K4* on Sunday night when they put on the unfortunately named *Roza Noč* (Pink Night). The music takes no risks, but the crowd is lively and friendly. It's open from 10 pm to 4 am and costs 800 SIT (500 SIT for students).

In Metelkova there's a pub/café for gays called *Club Magnus* and one for lesbians called *Club Lilit*. It's in the small building to the left (east) as you enter the squat. Magnus is open most nights from 8 pm till midnight, but call the Roza Klub (☎ 132 4089) or Klub K4 for information and exact times.

The *City Gallery* Café at Mestni trg 5 (open 10 am till midnight) attracts something of a gay following, as does the *Zlati Klub* sauna at the recreation centre in Tivoli Park.

Spectator Sports

On Sunday at 3 pm there's often a soccer game at the Central Stadium (Centralni Stadion), designed by Jože Plečnik in 1925. It's an easy bus ride (bus No 6, 8 or 21 to the Stadion stop) or a 20-minute walk north up Dunajska cesta from Center.

Gambling

Ljubljana's Casino, next to the Austrotel at Miklošičeva cesta 9, has American roulette, blackjack, poker and slot machines. It's open daily from 7 pm to 2 or 3 am.

THINGS TO BUY

The TIC produces a commercial but useful guide called *Where to Shop* for Ljubljana and its surrounding areas. The best shopping areas are Nazorjeva ulica and the Old Town, but beware of the prices in the latter.

For general souvenirs and folk items, check out what's on offer at the Galerija Zibka in the Slon Hotel, the Dom shop at Mestni trg 24 or the Samec shop at Stari trg 15. They all have Prekmurje black pottery, copies of beehive panels with folk motifs, decorated gingerbread in the form of a heart, Easter eggs and so on.

There's an antiques and flea market on Pogarčarjev trg and Adamič-Lundrovo nabrežje on Sunday mornings till 1 pm. Another flea market takes place on Sunday in Rudnik south-east of Center. You can reach it on bus No 3.

Don't expect many bargains, but Carniola Antiqua at Trubarjeva cesta 9 and Antika at Mestni trg 19 in the Old Town have superb antiques.

Digitalia is a big music shop with CDs and cassettes of Slovenian folk music at Gregorčičeva ulica 9. It's open from 9 am to 7 pm and to 1 pm on Saturday. Another good place for more up-to-date music is the Hard Rock Music Shop at Trubarjeva cesta 40.

If you've forgotten your fishing rod, ski poles or hiking boots, head for Slovenijašport at Slovenska cesta 44. They're open on weekdays from 8 to 7.30 pm and on Saturday to 1.30 pm.

You may not like the idea but a shop called Kože Grčar at Cankarjevo nabrežje 13 sells furs, sheepskins and cow hides (to be used as floor coverings). They're open from 9.30 am till noon and 5 to 7 pm on weekdays only.

Sidro at Kongresni trg 3 sells natural remedies, herbal teas and other concoctions produced by the monks at the Stična Abbey in Dolenjska. The shop is open from 8 am to 4 pm and on Saturday to 1 pm. An interesting shop called Apiteka in a courtyard to the east of Trubarjeva cesta 23 sells all manner of bee-related items: wax candles, honey, pollen, propolis, etc. It's open from 9 am to 2 pm weekdays and till noon on Saturday.

Vinoteka Simon Bradeško at Dunajska cesta 18 has a a selection of some 400 Slovenian wines. It's open weekdays from 10 am to 7 pm and on Saturday from 9 am to 1 pm.

GETTING THERE & AWAY
Air

The main ticket office for Adria Airways (☎ 133 4336 or 131 8155) is at Kuzmičeva ulica in the Bežigrad district. A more convenient office is at Gosposvetska cesta 6 (☎ 313 312) near the Lev Hotel.

Other carriers with offices in Ljubljana are as follows.

Aeroflot
    Dunajska cesta 21 (☎ 313 312)
Austrian Airlines
    Dunajska cesta 107 (☎ 168 4099)
Lufthansa
    Slovenska cesta 54 (☎ 326 662)
Swissair
    Lev Hotel, Vošnjakova ulica 1 (☎ 317 647)

See also To/From the Airport in the following Getting Around section.

Bus

Buses to destinations both within Slovenia and abroad leave from the bus station – no more then a shed, really – opposite the train station on Trg OF. For information, ring ☎ 133 6136 or 133 4344. The number for seat reservations is ☎ 322 164. And good luck getting through... There's an information window inside the station across from the ticket windows. The staff are multilingual and reasonably helpful.

For the most part, you do not have to buy your ticket in advance; just pay as you enter the bus. But for long-distance trips on Fridays, just before the school break and public holidays, you are running the risk of not getting a seat. Book a seat the day before and reserve it for 70 SIT.

The bus station has a left-luggage office open from 5.30 am to 8.30 pm. If you think you'll arrive after closing time, leave your bags at the office in the train station; it's open 24 hours a day.

You can reach virtually anywhere in the country by bus – as close as Kamnik (every 15 minutes) or as far away as Vinica in Bela Krajina (three a day). If you're planning a trip to Bled or Bohinj, take the bus not the train. The train from Ljubljana to the former will leave you at the Lesce-Bled station, four km south-east of the lake. The closest train station to Lake Bohinj is at Bohinjska Bistrica, six km to the east, and it's on the line linking Nova Gorica with Jesenice. Buses leave Ljubljana about every hour for Lake Bohinj.

The timetable in the bus station lists all bus routes and times but here are some sample frequencies and one-way fares (return fares are double): Bled (every half-hour, 450 SIT); Bohinj (hourly, 620 SIT); Jesenice (hourly, 500 SIT); Koper (17 a day, 940 SIT); Maribor (every half-hour, 940 SIT); Murska Sobota (10 a day, 1300 SIT); and Novo Mesto (every half-hour, 500 SIT).

Buses from Ljubljana serve a number of international destinations as well, including: Berlin (Wednesday and Sunday, 12,300 SIT one-way); Budapest (Thursday and Friday, 3800 SIT); Frankfurt (Wednesday and Sunday); Klagenfurt (Wednesday); Lenti (Tuesday and Thursday); Munich (weekdays, 4000 SIT); Novigrad (daily); Prague (Tuesday, Thursday and Saturday at 9 pm); Pula (up to three a day); Rijeka (two a day); Rovinj (daily); Split (daily); Stockholm (Saturday at 3 pm); Stuttgart (Wednesday and Thursday); Trieste (daily, 830 SIT); Varaždin (three a day); Villach (Wednesday, 870 SIT); and Zagreb (eight a day).

The Eros travel agency on the main platform at the train station sells bus tickets to Belgrade (about 5000 SIT) and Skopje (about 7000 SIT), departing daily at 3.30 pm.

For more details on domestic and international bus services see the Getting There & Away and Getting Around chapters earlier in this book.

Train

All trains – both Slovenian and foreign – arrive at and depart from the train station (☎ 131 5167 or 316 768 for information) on Trg OF. It's a pretty dismal place but it's getting a face-lift and it does have *some* amenities. There's a 24-hour currency-exchange bureau and a grocery store that stays open late. The left-luggage office is on the platform inside the station (open 24 hours a day).

You can seek information and buy domestic train tickets in the station's main hall. The following are some one-way 2nd-class domestic fares from Ljubljana: Bled, 467 SIT; Jesenice, 422 SIT; Koper, 724 SIT; Maribor, 724 SIT; Murska Sobota, 971 SIT; and Novo Mesto, 552 SIT. Return fares are usually 20% cheaper than double the price and there's an 80 SIT surcharge on domestic IC train tickets.

The Slovenijaturist branch (☎ 316 768) behind the main hall and toward the platforms sells tickets for all international trains, including those to: Berlin, 18,253 SIT one-way; Budapest, 4185 SIT; Munich, 6980 SIT; Trieste, 1213 SIT; and Villach, 1314 SIT. Seat reservations (300 SIT) are mandatory on some trains and available on others. An extra 200 SIT is levied on foreign IC train tickets.

For more information on trains leaving Ljubljana, turn to the introductory Getting There & Away and Getting Around chapters.

Hitching

If you are leaving Ljubljana by way of thumb, take one of the following city buses to the terminus and begin hitching there. Do not actually go on to the motorway; use one of the access areas where the traffic is not disturbed.

To Postojna, Koper, Croatian Istria & Italy (Trieste)
  Bus No 6 south-west (stop: Dolgi Most)
To Bled, Jesenice & Austria (Salzburg)
  Bus No 1 north-west (stop: Vižmarje)
To Novo Mesto & Croatia (Zagreb)
  Bus No 3 south-east (stop: Rudnik)
To Maribor & Austria (Vienna)
  Bus No 6 north-east (stop: Črnuče)

GETTING AROUND
To/From the Airport

Adria Airways runs buses between Ljubljana

and Brnik Airport for all incoming and out-going flights – three to five departures a day with up to eight on Sunday. The bus follows the highway so it's a quick trip, and the fare is 400 SIT one-way.

City buses make the run 16 times a day and cost 210 SIT. They go via the back roads, a much more scenic but slower route. There are also seven buses a day from Brnik to Kamnik and up to 20 to Kranj.

From the bus station in Ljubljana, catch the city airport bus from platform 28 (east of the post office). The Adria airport bus leaves from the well-marked stop slightly to the west and in front of the post office on Trg OF.

A taxi from Brnik Airport to Ljubljana will cost between 3000 and 3500 SIT. To Bled, expect to pay about 4000 SIT and double that to Kranjska Gora.

Bus

From 1898 until 1958 public transport around Ljubljana was provided by trams; there's a wonderful picture book available in most of Ljubljana's bookshops recalling this nostalgic era. Until 1971 electric trolley buses did the job, when they were replaced by the internally clean but externally pollut-ing diesel buses that carry commuters around the city today.

The system, run by LPP (Ljubljanski Potniški Promet), is excellent and very user-friendly. Every bus stop has a name which appears on the plan in the bus shelter or is posted somewhere near the stop. There are a total of 22 lines with five of them (Nos 1, 2, 3, 6 and 11) considered main lines. These start at 3.15 am and run till midnight. The rest are in operation between 5 am and 10.30 pm. The main lines run about every five to 15 minutes for most of the day. Service is less frequent on other lines and on Saturday, Sunday and holidays.

The system is rip-off-proof. You can pay on board, which costs 70 SIT (the driver does not give change), or use a tiny yellow plastic token (50 SIT) available at Delo newsstands, tobacco shops and post offices.

Bus passes can be purchased from LPP's central office (☎ 159 4114) at Celovška ulica 160 or from the two kiosks marked 'LPP' on the pavement at Slovenska cesta 55 opposite what is, in fact, the system's main stop (Bavarski Dvor). They are available for a day *(enodnevna vozovnica*, 160 SIT), a week *(tedenska vozovnica*, 820 SIT) or even a month *(mesečna vozovnica*, 2000 SIT). The LPP office is open from 6.45 am to 7 pm Monday to Friday and to 1 pm on Saturday. You can reach the office on bus Nos 1, 8 and 15.

From the bus or train stations, bus No 2 will take you to the TIC (bus stop: Nama) or to Mestni trg (bus stop: Magistrat) in the Old Town.

Taxi

Taxis, which can be hailed on the street or hired from ranks such as those near the train station, in front of the Slon Hotel and at Mestni trg, cost 150 SIT at flag-fall and 120 SIT for each additional km. You'll never get away with paying less than 300 SIT though; the ride from the train station to Trg Republike costs somewhere around 500 SIT. You can call a taxi on seven numbers: ☎ 9700 to 9706.

Car & Motorbike

Parking is not easy in central Ljubljana and, if you're not prepared to pay in some form or another, you're bound to get a ticket for 500 SIT. In order to park on any street with blue lines painted by the kerb you are sup-posed to buy coupons from Delo or Tobak kiosks or petrol stations for 150 SIT (valid for one or two hours) and place them inside your car on the dashboard. Some Ljubljančans do but most don't and risk the fine. Inspections, they say, are not thorough in most parts of the city.

There are car parks throughout the city and their locations are indicated on most maps. To park in the underground garage beneath Miklošičev Park you'll pay 220 SIT for the first two hours (minimum) and 110 SIT for every additional hour.

Car Rental The international car-rental firms in Ljubljana are: Kompas Hertz (☎ 311

241), Miklošičeva cesta 11; Globtour Budget (☎ 126 3118), Štefanova ulica 13; and Avis (☎ 168 7204), Dunajska cesta 160. Ask the TIC about cheaper rates or try Avtoimpex (☎ 555 025), Celovška cesta 150, or Slavnik (☎ 321 351) near the Turist hotel at Tavčarjeva ulica 8a.

Bicycle

Ljubljana is a city of bicyclists and there are bike lanes and special traffic lights throughout the city. Unfortunately, only a very few places rent them. The biggest shop with bikes for rent is Bauer (☎ 453 710) at Šmartinska cesta 160. You can reach here on bus No 2 or 12 from the train station.

Dolinar (☎ 268 137), at Pod Jezom 59 in the south-western suburb of Vrhovci, has bicycles for between 800 and 1000 SIT a day. Get here on bus No 14 from Prešernov trg.

For information on tours, see Prava Pot (☎ 131 7114) at Slovenska cesta 55b.

AROUND LJUBLJANA

Let's face it: an awful lot in little Slovenia is 'around Ljubljana' and most of the towns and cities in Gorenjska, Primorska and Notranjska could actually be day trips from the capital. You can get to Bled in an hour, for example, and the coast in less than two hours. Škofja Loka, Kamnik and Velika Planina are less than 30 km away and Cerknica is only 50 km to the south-west.

Žale

Another Plečnik masterpiece, the monumental **cemetery** at Žale three km to the north-east of Center, has a series of chapels dedicated to the patron saints of Ljubljana's churches and the entrance is an enormous two-storey arcade. It is a very peaceful, green place and 'home' to a number of actors, writers, painters and Gospod Plečnik himself. You can reach Žale on bus No 2 or 7.

Šmarna Gora

This 669-metre hill above the Sava River some 12 km north-west of Ljubljana is a popular walking destination from Ljubljana and a mecca for hang-gliders and paragliders. Take bus No 15 from Slovenska cesta or Gosposvetska cesta to the Medno stop and begin the hike. Another way to go is via the Smlednik bus from the main station and then follow the marked path from 12th century **Smlednik Castle**. There's swimming and boating in **Zbilje Lake** nearby.

Gorenjska

Mountains and lakes are the big attraction in 'Upper Carniola', the province that feels more Slovenian than any other. The start of the Kamnik-Savinja Alps are a short drive from Ljubljana, and Gorenjska's Triglav National Park contains the bulk of Slovenia's share of the Julian Alps, with many peaks rising to well above 2000 metres. There's a lot of skiing here and Gorenjska offers some of the best hiking in Europe. A mountain trip is an excellent way to meet other Slovenes in a relaxed environment, so take advantage of this opportunity if you're in Slovenia during the hiking season.

The lakes at Bled and Bohinj are also popular centres for any number of outdoor activities, but Gorenjska also has many of Slovenia's most attractive historical towns. Škofja Loka, Kamnik, Kranj and Radovljica – to name just a few – are treasure troves of Gothic, Renaissance and Baroque art and architecture and wonderful bases from which to explore this varied and exciting province.

The people of Gorenjska have a reputation in Slovenia for being on the thrifty side. You won't see evidence of this yourself but you'll certainly hear a lot of jokes similar to the ones that are made about Scottish people.

KAMNIK (pop 9800)

A historical town 'in the bosom of the Alps' just 23 km north of Ljubljana, Kamnik ain't quite what she used to be. Established sometime in the 12th century under the Counts of Andechs and later boasting its own mint and school, Kamnik (Stein in German) competed with Ljubljana and Kranj for economic and cultural dominance in Kranjska (Carniola) throughout the Middle Ages. The town was known for its large numbers of artisans and craftsmen, and it was to this rising middle class that Emperor Charles IV donated the massive forests around Kamniška Bistrica in the 14th century.

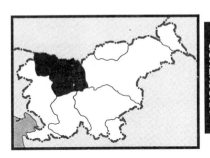

The tide turned, however, in the 17th century. Until that time Kamnik controlled the pass in the Tuhinj Valley to the east that was indispensable for moving goods from the coastal areas to Štajerska and Koroška. But when the route was redirected via Trojane to the south-east, Kamnik fell into a deep sleep and only awakened in the late 19th century when the town was linked by rail to Ljubljana.

Kamnik became a mecca for holidaying Ljubljančans at the turn of the century due to easy access to the Kamnik Alps and its popular thermal baths. The baths were destroyed during WW I and, while it remained a gateway in subsequent decades for hiking and skiing in the Velika Planina to the north, Kamnik began to industrialise and expand.

Today, Kamnik is frequently overlooked by travellers heading for the Alps. But the town's tidy and attractive medieval core, with its houses and portals of hewn stone, balconies and arcades, is well worth a visit. It was declared a cultural and historical monument in 1986.

Orientation

Kamnik lies on the left bank of the Kamniška Bistrica River south of the Kamnik Alps, which form part of the Kamnik-Savinja

GORENJSKA

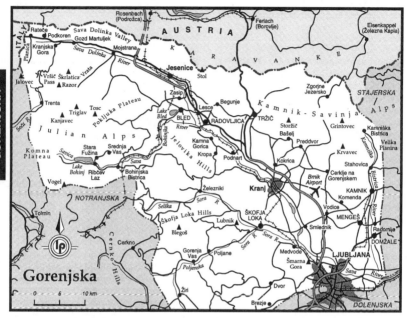

Gorenjska

chain. The Old Town consists of two parts: medieval Glavni trg and the newer 'suburb' of Šutna, really just a continuation of the square.

Kamnik's modern bus station is near the river east of Glavni trg at Maistrova ulica 18. The town has three train stations. The main one is on Kranjska cesta, south-west of Šutna. Kamnik Mesto, which is convenient for the Old Town and its sights, is on Kolodvorska ulica west of the Little Castle. Kamnik Graben, the terminus of the rail line, is north-west of Glavni trg on Tunjiška cesta.

Information

The staff at the tourist office (☎ 061 831 470) at Glavni trg 23 are among the most helpful and best informed in Slovenia. They will arrange bookings, find you keys to locked sights and organise guides for excursions into the mountains. The office produces a very useful brochure called *What & Where –*

The Municipality of Kamnik in English. It is open daily from 9 am to 8 pm. The Kamnik Alpine Society (☎ 061 831 345) at Šutna 38 will have advice about hiking in the Kamnik Alps and weather conditions there.

SKB Banka has a branch at Glavni trg 13 open from 8.30 am till noon and 2 to 5 pm on weekdays only. Next door, at No 14, you'll find a private exchange bureau called Avenida with slightly better hours. The post office, open from 7 am to 7 pm weekdays and till noon on Saturday, is at Glavni trg 27. It handles foreign exchange.

Kamnik's telephone code is 061. The postcode is 61240.

Things to See & Do

Nothing in Kamnik demands a visit, but it is a pleasant place for a stroll beginning from the tourist office.

The **Franciscan monastery** to the south-west at Frančiškanski trg 2 has a rich library of scientific manuscripts from the 15th to 18th centuries and some valuable paintings by early Slovenian artists. Ask one of the three priests still in residence if you can have a look. Next to the monastery is the **Church of St James** with a chapel designed by Jože Plečnik (1872-1955), who also worked on the attractive yellow-and-orange house on the eastern side of Glavni trg.

The **Little Castle** (Mali Grad), on a low hill above the southern end of Glavni trg, is Kamnik's most important historical sight. It has foundations going back to the 11th century, and this is where the town mint once stood. Beside the castle stand the ruins of a unique two-storey **Romanesque chapel** with 16th century frescoes in its lower nave and wall paintings by Janez Potočnik (1749-1834) in the presbytery. Ask the tourist office for the key if you care to have a look.

The Little Castle was home to Veronika, a legendary countess who was turned partly into a snake when she refused to help the Catholic faithful build a church. Not only was the old gal mean but she was spiteful too. In her rage at having been asked to contribute, she struck the entrance to her castle with her fist. If you look to the right of the portal as you go in, you'll see the imprint of her hand. Veronika continues to rule the treasure of the Little Castle and, in a way, the town of Kamnik too. She appears both on the town seal and on the license plate of every car registered here.

From the Little Castle, a walk along the quiet and attractive main street of Šutna is a trip back in time; check out the fine neoclassical house with columns at No 24, the stone relief of the Pascal lamb above the door at No 36 and the old butcher's shop sign at No 48.

In the centre of Šutna stands the **Parish Church of the Annunciation**, erected in the mid-18th century but with a detached belfry that shows an earlier church's Gothic origins. A short distance beyond at Šutna 33 is the **Sadnikar Collection**, a private museum – the first in Slovenia (1893) – of Gothic artwork, period furniture and paintings from the 18th century amassed by a local veteri-

narian and painter a century ago. It is opened by prior arrangement with the tourist office.

Zaprice Castle at Muzejski pot 3, with towers, walls and an interesting chapel, was built in the 16th century but later transformed into a manor house. Today it houses the **Kamnik Municipal Museum**, with some dull exhibits devoted to Kamnik's glory days and 18th century furniture. More interesting are the century-old **granaries** outside that have been moved from Tuhinj Valley east of Kamnik. The museum *should* be open on Tuesday, Thursday, Friday and Saturday from 9 am to noon and 2 to 6 pm but the opening hours aren't always certain. Ask the tourist office to call in advance.

The **Old Castle** (Stari Grad), a 13th century ruin above the right bank of the Kamniška Bistrica, can be reached from the end of Maistrova ulica on foot in about 20 minutes. There are excellent views of the Alps and the town from the top of the 585-metre hill.

On a hill east of Stahovica, a village about 4.5 km north of Kamnik, is the **Church of Sts Primus & Felician** with some of the best medieval frescoes in Slovenia. It's about a 40-minute walk up from the village of **Črna** but make this 'pilgrimage' only on Saturday and Sunday when the church door is open. The frescoes on the north wall depict the Flight into Egypt, the Adoration of the Magi and the Misericordia – the Virgin Mary sheltering supplicants under her cloak in a scene similar to the one at the church in Ptujska Gora (see Around Ptuj in the Štajerska chapter). The painting on the south wall shows scenes from the life of Mary and is dated 1504.

Some four km south of Kamnik is **Volčji Potok**, Slovenia's largest and most beautiful arboretum. With the heart-shaped park of a former castle as its core, the 79-hectare arboretum contains more than 4000 varieties of trees, shrubs and flowers from all over the world. The arboretum's greenery, ponds and nearby Kamniška Bistrica River make Volčji Potok a lovely place to visit on a warm summer's day. The entry fee is 500 SIT (200 SIT for children). Remember that while five

GORENJSKA

GORENJSKA

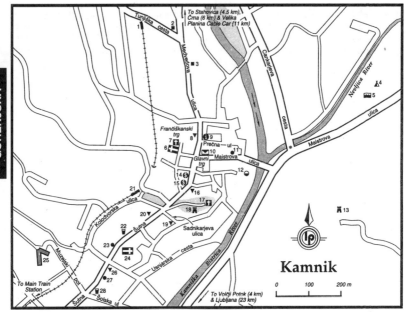

Kamnik

PLACES TO STAY

2   Pri Cesarju Guesthouse
3   Pri Bundru Guesthouse
4   Resnik Camp Site

PLACES TO EAT

8   Planinka Kenda Restaurant
16 Veronika Café
19 Napoli Pizzeria
20 Hram Lužar Restaurant
26 Sonček Delicatessen

OTHER

1   Kamnik Graben Train Station
5   Swimming Pool

6   Church of St James
7   Franciscan Monastery
9   Tourist Office
10 Post Office
11 Majolka Shop
12 Bus Station
13 Old Castle
14 SKB Banka
15 Avenida Exchange Bureau
17 Romanesque Chapel
18 Little Castle
21 Kamnik Mesto Train Station
22 Paradise Pub
23 Kamnik Alpine Society
24 Church of the Annunciation
25 Zaprice Castle/Kamnik Municipal Museum
27 Sadnikar Collection
28 Ideja Bar

buses a day arrive here directly from Kamnik on weekdays, there's only one on Saturday and Sunday. If you're stuck, take the Radomlje bus which stops not far away.

The outdoor Pod Skalco **swimming pool** near the camp site in Kamnik is open from mid-June to mid-September from 9 am to 10 pm.

The **Oldtimer Train** run by Slovenijaturist has occasional excursions between Ljubljana and Kamnik via Domžale. Contact them for further details.

Festivals

The big event in Kamnik is the National Costume Days festival held on the second weekend in September. A half-dozen stages are set up around town and feature music, dance, parades and general merrymaking. The event attracts people from all over Slovenia.

There are big flower and horticultural shows at Volčji Potok in late April and in early September.

Places to Stay

The tiny *Resnik* camp site (☎ 831 233) is north-east of the Old Town on the Nevljica River at Maistrova ulica 32. It is open from May to September and charges DM3 per person, DM2 per car and per tent and DM2 for a caravan. There's a tennis court and public swimming pool adjacent, as well as a popular bar open till midnight.

With Ljubljana so close, Kamnik doesn't seem to have much need for a hotel – or budget accommodation. The cheapest place to stay close to the Old Town is *Pri Bundru* (☎ 831 235), a rather dingy guesthouse at Medvedova ulica 24a, a couple of hundred metres north of the tourist office. Its five rooms have private showers but no toilet and cost 2400 SIT per person. If you can afford a bit extra, head a few metres north to Tunjiška cesta 1 and the much more salubrious *Pri Cesarju* guesthouse (☎ 832 917) with 12 rooms. They charge 4000 SIT per person.

Other accommodation can be found in the village of Stahovica on the road to Velika Planina and Kamniška Bistrica village. *Pri Planinskem Orlu* (☎ 825 410) at Stahovica 20 and *Pri Gamsu* (☎ 825 588) at Stahovica 31 are private houses with four or five rooms each. They both charge 2400 SIT per person.

Places to Eat

There's a good delicatessen called *Sonček* at Šutna 27 that sells sliced meat, cheese, salads and what they call *pommes frites* (chips/French fries).

The *Veronika Café* coffee shop at Glavni trg 6 is a good place to cool your heels over a cup of something warm and a slice of cake. It's the most popular café in town and doubles as an art galley. The *Napoli*, a pizzeria at Sadnikarjeva ulica 5 south of the Little Castle, is open from 9 am to 10 pm from Monday to Saturday and from noon on Sunday.

The most convenient restaurant in Kamnik is *Planinka Kenda* opposite the tourist office at Glavni trg 19. It is open from Monday to Saturday from 8 am to 10 pm and on Sunday from 10 am to 7 pm. The lunch menus at 450 SIT are good value. A better place for a meal, though, is *Hram Lužar* at Šutna 8 with a lovely courtyard at the rear. It's open from 9 am to 10 pm every day except Sunday, when its hours are 11 am to 8 pm.

Entertainment

Lira, Slovenia's first choir (founded in 1882) and still going strong, occasionally gives local concerts. Ask the staff at the tourist office.

There are a couple of good pubs in Šutna, including the *Paradise* at No 28. Farther south, at No 35 and opposite the start of Muzejski pot, is the very popular *Ideja Bar* open daily till 10 pm.

Things to Buy

Check out the interesting old clockmaker's shop at Maistrova 1 near the post office. At No 11 in the same street, a shop called Majolka sells souvenirs, paintings, porcelain and antiques. It is open from 9 am to 7 pm weekdays and till noon on Saturday.

Getting There & Away

Bus services are frequent to and from Domžale, Ljubljana, Mengeš, Radomlje and Stahovica. You can also reach Gornji Grad on between three and seven buses a day, Kamniška Bistrica (three), Ljubno (up to five), Logar Valley (one on Sunday), Mozirje

GORENJSKA

(one), Šentjakob (seven) and Volčji Potok (five on weekdays, one daily on weekends).

Kamnik is on a direct rail line from Ljubljana (24 km, one hour) via Domžale. Count on some 15 trains a day in each direction.

AROUND KAMNIK
Velika Planina
The highland area around Velika Planina, which reaches a height of 1666 metres, is a wonderful place to explore and is accessible to 1418 metres by cable car *(žičnica)* from the lower station 11 km north of Kamnik. The six-minute ride is not for the skittish! You can also walk to Velika Planina from Stahovica, taking in the Church of Sts Primus & Felician along the way, in about three hours.

Velika Planina is where traditional dairy farmers graze their cattle between June and September. If you follow the road from the upper station up the hill for about two km, you'll reach a highland plain filled with more than 50 shepherd's huts and a small church dedicated to Our Lady of the Snows. The low-lying rounded buildings with conical roofs are unique to Velika Planina, and the design may be a legacy of ancient shepherds as far back as the Bronze Age. Today's huts are replicas; the originals from around the turn of the century were burned to the ground by the Germans in WW II.

A circular walk of the plain and **Mala Planina** (1569 metres) to the south will take only a few hours. In summer, the friendly shepherds in their pointed, green felt hats will sell you sour milk, curd and white cheese.

Not too long ago Velika Planina was a popular ski area with six km of slopes. But the snow god hasn't blessed Velika Planina with the white stuff for several years now and the ageing T-bars have been shut down. The chair lift, which ferried skiers another 1500 metres up to Gradišče from the upper cable-car station, may be running again soon though.

Places to Stay There's a vast array of accommodation in Velika Planina. Just a few steps from the upper station, the *Šimnovec* hotel (☎ 831 425) has 24 rooms with shared showers for between DM25 and DM34 per person. Among the many mountain lodges offering accommodation daily between June and September and sometimes in winter are *Domžalski Dom* (☎ 376 005) and *Črnuški Dom* (☎ 724 316), each with nine multi-bedded rooms.

Places to Eat At the lower cable-car station you'll find something to eat at the simple *Bife Pri Žičnici* (along with picnic tables and barbecue pits) open from 7 am to 8 or 10 pm daily. In Velika Planina, the *Šimnovec* has a full restaurant, and there's a snack bar at Zeleni Rob about a km up the hill.

Getting There & Away In summer, the cable car runs every hour from Monday to Thursday from 8 am to 6 pm and Friday, Saturday and Sunday till 8 pm. During the rest of the year it goes every second hour till 4 or 5 pm on weekdays and till 6 pm at the weekend. A one-way ticket is 400 SIT (300 SIT for children); return is 600 SIT (500 SIT).

Kamniška Bistrica
Another three km north from the cable-car station is Kamniška Bistrica, a lovely little settlement in a valley near the source of the Kamniška Bistrica River. There's a *hostel* (☎ 825 544) here as well as a restaurant and a small chapel.

Kamniška Bistrica is the springboard for some of the Kamnik Alps' more ambitious and rewarding treks such as the ones to **Grintovec** (2558 metres, 11 hours return), **Brana** (2251 metres, eight hours) and **Planjava** (2394 metres, 10 hours).

The most popular hikes, though, are the easier, 3.5-hour ones north-west to the mountain pass or saddle at **Kokra Saddle** (Kokrško Sedlo; 1791 metres) and north to **Kamnik Saddle** (Kamniško Sedlo; 1903 metres). On the other side of the latter lies Rinka Waterfall and the Logar Valley (see the Upper Savinja Valley section of the Štajerska chapter). Each saddle has a mountain hut (☎ 831 345 for both) – *Coizova Koča* on

Kokrško Sedlo and *Kamniška Koča* on Kamniško Sedlo – open from 20 June to 10 October.

The main trails in the Kamnik Alps are well marked and pass numerous springs, waterfalls and caves. Guides are available from the tourist office in Kamnik, but the less energetic may be content to picnic around the lake near the hostel, cooling their drinks (or feet) in the blue Alpine water.

The cable-car station and Kamniška Bistrica can be reached from Kamnik on three buses a day.

ŠKOFJA LOKA (pop 12,400)

In 973 German Emperor Otto II presented the Bavarian Bishops of Freising with the valleys along the Poljanska Sora and Selška Sora rivers. The point where the two tributaries merge to form the Sora River began to develop as a town. Škofja Loka – 'bishop's field' – thus vies with Ptuj and Piran for being among the oldest settlements in Slovenia.

The Freising bishops held secular (and, naturally, spiritual) control over Škofja Loka (Bischoflack in German) for more than eight centuries – and two actually met their maker in the town. Bishop Leopold drowned in the 14th century when his horse slipped off the new bridge (no guard rails in those days) and Conrad was murdered by a covetous footman who wanted his 5000 gold ducats. In the Middle Ages Škofja Loka developed as a trade centre along the Klagenfurt-Trieste route, doing particularly well in iron, linen and furs. A circular wall with five gates protected by guard towers was built around the town in 1381 to ensure that this success continued.

But it was all for naught. An army of the Counts of Celje breached the wall and burned the town to the ground in 1457 and two decades later the Turks attacked. Then natural disasters struck: an earthquake in 1511 badly damaged the town and several great fires at the end of the 17th century reduced most of Škofja Loka's finest buildings to ashes.

In 1803 the Habsburgs took possession of the town and the advent of the railway later in the century put Škofja Loka on the road to industrialisation, especially in the field of textiles. Today the Old Town is protected as a historical and cultural monument and is among the most beautiful in Slovenia.

The castle and several other buildings are illuminated at night on the weekend, giving Šofja Loka the appearance of a fairytale village.

Orientation

The new part of Škofja Loka – without any redeeming qualities except that things of a practical nature are centred around Titov trg – lies on the northern bank of the Selška Sora River. The Old Town on the southern side of the river consists of two squares – long streets really – called Mestni trg and Spodnji trg, running southward from Cankarjev trg and the river. Mestni trg, which is the more beautiful and historically important, bans cars altogether while Spodnji trg (also known as Lontrg) remains a busy thoroughfare.

Škofja Loka's bus station is in Titov trg at the foot bridge leading to Cankarjev trg. The train station is three km to the east at the end of Kidričeva cesta in the industrial suburb of Trata.

Information

Tourist Office Škofja Loka's tourist office (☎ 064 620 268) is at Mestni trg 10 and opens on weekdays from 9 am to 7 pm and on Saturday till noon. Staffed by a group of enthusiastic young people who are keen to see you enjoy your stay in their town, the office sells maps and souvenirs and has a series of handouts on a wide range of subjects – from the history of the town and local lace-making to hiking, fishing and what farms offer accommodation.

Money Gorenjska Banka, near the Transturist hotel and Kompas at Titov trg 3a, is open Monday to Friday from 7 am to 6 pm and on Saturday till noon. There's an SKB Banka branch on Cesta Talcev behind the Church of

GORENJSKA

St Anne. It is open on weekdays only from 8.30 am till noon and from 2 to 5 pm.

Post & Telecommunications The post office, open on weekdays from 7 am to 7 pm and on Saturday till noon, is west of the bus station between the footbridge and Capuchin Bridge at Titov trg 9. It has an exchange service.

Škofja Loka's telephone code is 064. The postcode is 64220.

Travel Agency Kompas (☎ 620 960) has an office next to the Transturist hotel at Titov trg 4b. It is open weekdays from 9 am to 7 pm and on Saturday till noon.

Old Town

Parts of the **Parish Church of St James** in Cankarjev trg date back to the 13th century, but its most important elements – the nave, the presbytery with star vaulting and the tall bell tower – were added over the subsequent three centuries. On either side of the choir are altars made of black marble that were designed in about 1700. These are very unusual for a time and place when gilded wood and gypsum were all the rage. On the vaulted ceiling are bosses showing portraits of the Bishops of Freising, saints, workers with shears and a blacksmith, who was probably a generous contributor to the church. Two crescent moons in the presbytery area are legacies of the Turkish presence in Škofja Loka. The dozen or so modern lamps and the baptismal font were designed by Jože Plečnik.

Across from the church's main entrance on the south side is the **Priest's House**, part of a fortified aristocratic manor built in the late 16th century. Below the rounded projection on the corner are strange consoles of animals and human faces.

The colourful 16th century burgher houses on Mestni trg, rebuilt after the terrible earthquake of 1511, have earned the town the nickname 'Painted Loka'. Almost every one is of historical and architectural importance and plaques in English and Slovene explain their significance. Among the more impress-

ive is **Homan House** at No 2 with bits of frescoes of St Christopher and a warrior. The **town hall** at No 35 is remarkable for its three-storey Gothic courtyard and the 17th century frescoes on its facade. **Martin House** at No 26 leans against part of the old town wall. It has a wooden 1st floor, a late Gothic portal and a vaulted entrance hall. The **plague pillar** erected in the square in 1715 has recently been renovated.

Klobovsova ulica, a narrow street west of Homan House, leads to Loka Castle and the remains of **Krancelj Tower**.

Spodnji trg to the east of Mestni trg was where the poorer folk lived in the Middle Ages; after the devastating fire of 1698, most of them couldn't afford to rebuild the square so the houses remained two-storey and very modest. Of interest at the northern end is the 16th century **town granary** (Mestna Kašča), where the town stores collected as taxes were once kept, and the **Špital Church**, opposite No 29, with an opulent Baroque gold altar. The church was built in 1710 around the town's almshouse, and the poor lived in the cells of the courtyard building.

Loka Castle

The town castle, which looks down over Škofja Loka from a grassy hill west of Mestni trg on Grajska pot, was built in the 13th century but extensively renovated after the earthquake. Today it houses the **Loka Museum**, which has one of the best ethnographical collections in Slovenia.

The area around Škofja Loka was famous for its smiths and lace-makers, and there are lots of ornate guild chests. The copies of the 15th century frescoes from the churches at Crngrob and Suha (see Around Škofja Loka) in the corridors are much clearer than most of the originals *in situ*. Have a good look at these before you make the trip to visit the originals.

The Loka Museum is open daily except Monday mid-April to mid-November from 9 am to 5 pm. During the rest of the year it's open on Saturday and Sunday only. Entry is 100 SIT.

Other Attractions

The 18th century **Capuchin monastery** west of the bus station has a priceless library of medieval manuscripts, including the *Škofja Loka Passion*, a procession with dramatic elements performed here from around 1720. The library can be visited provided you phone ahead. Contact the tourist office or the monastery directly (☎ 620 970).

The stone **Capuchin Bridge** leading from the monastery's **Church of St Anne** (1710) dates from the 14th century and is an excellent vantage point for the Old Town and castle as well as the river with its deep gorge, dams, abandoned mills and 18th century barracks. The area north-west of the bridge is called Novi Svet (New World) because it was settled after the Old Town. The statue on the bridge is of St John Nepomunk, a Bohemian prelate who was martyred in the 14th century by being thrown from Charles Bridge in Prague, the city where executioners usually favoured windows.

A dry-goods market is held on Mestni trg and Cankarjev trg on the second Wednesday of every month from June to December.

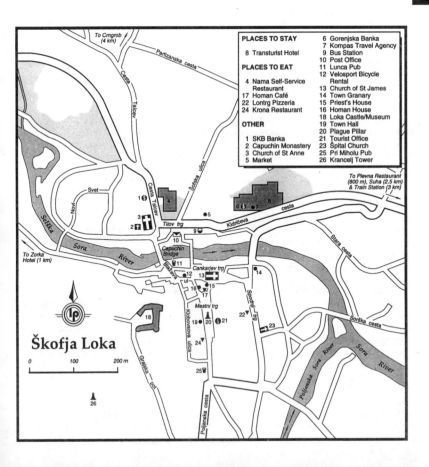

PLACES TO STAY
8 Transturist Hotel

PLACES TO EAT
4 Nama Self-Service Restaurant
17 Homan Café
22 Lontrg Pizzeria
24 Krona Restaurant

OTHER
1 SKB Banka
2 Capuchin Monastery
3 Church of St Anne
5 Market
6 Gorenjska Banka
7 Kompas Travel Agency
9 Bus Station
10 Post Office
11 Lunca Pub
12 Velosport Bicycle Rental
13 Church of St James
14 Town Granary
15 Priest's House
16 Homan House
18 Loka Castle/Museum
19 Town Hall
20 Plague Pillar
21 Tourist Office
23 Špital Church
25 Pri Miholu Pub
26 Krancelj Tower

Škofja Loka

GORENJSKA

Activities

The Škofja Loka Hills to the west, an area of steep slopes, deep valleys and ravines, is an excellent area for day walks or hikes of a longer duration and there are several huts with accommodation in the area. Before you set out, buy a copy of the 1:50,000 hiking map *Škofjeloško in Cerkljansko Hribovje* (Škofja Loka and Cerkno Hills).

One of the easiest trips is to **Lubnik**, a 1025-metre peak north-west of the Old Town, which can be reached on foot in two hours via Vincarje or the castle ruins near Gabrovo. Start the walk from Klobovsova ulica in Mestni trg. A mountain hut near the summit called *Dom na Lubniku* (☎ 620 501) has 21 beds and is open from March to December.

A hike to 1562-metre **Blegoš** farther west would be much more demanding, but it only takes about three hours from **Hotavlje**, a village a couple of km from Gorenja Vas and accessible by bus from Škofja Loka. There are two huts in the area. *Koča na Blegošu* (☎ 631 151) has 61 beds and is open every day from June to September and at weekends in May and October. *Zavetišče na Jelencih* (☎ 68 714), about two km to the south-west, has 20 beds and is open at weekends from October to May. If you don't want to hike all the way to Blegoš, there's the 12-bed *Slajka* mountain hut (☎ 68 550), which is less than three km from Hotavlje. It's open Thursday through Sunday but closes in winter.

The ski centre at **Stari Vrh**, 12 km west of Škofja Loka, is situated at an altitude of 1200 metres and covers 65 hectares of ski slopes and three km of trails. There are four T-bar tows and a chair lift. The only accommodation here, though, is at the *Koča na Starem Vrhu* (☎ 65 007), which is open daily in summer and winter and on Saturday and Sunday only in spring and autumn. The place has five rooms with 16 beds.

Festivals

The Glasbena Loka music festival takes place in late July and early August in Loka Castle.

Places to Stay

Smlednik camp site (☎ 061-627 002) in Dragočajna, 11 km to the east, is the closest camping ground to Škofja Loka. It is situated between two small lakes and has a nudist beach. Smlednik, open from May to mid-October, charges DM6 per person per night.

Škofja Loka is not overly endowed with places to lay your weary head. The tourist office can organise private rooms, including ones at Grajska pot 8 (☎ 620 509) and Suška cesta 1 (☎ 633 096), for about DM25 but they have a very short list. There are lots of *farmhouses* with accommodation but most are around Poljane, 13 km to the south-west. As in so many Slovenian towns, Škofja Loka offers that all-too-familiar choice: an over-priced guesthouse with cramped rooms or a monstrous concrete block that even George Orwell didn't see in his nightmares.

The first is the *Zorka* (☎ 620 986), a 'mini-hotel' in the suburb of Vincarje (house No 15) about a km west of the bus station. The rooms (all with shower) are clean but positively tiny and cost an outrageous 4000 SIT per person (3200 SIT if you are inclined to stay more than eight nights). The surrounding countryside is attractive and there is a swimming pool and three tennis courts, but I'd settle for a slightly bigger living space at a much lower price.

The 48-room *Transturist* (☎ 621 261; fax 621 994) at Titov trg 4b is grey, tall, depressing and expensive. Singles with breakfast and shower are 4800 SIT, while doubles are 7200 SIT.

Places to Eat

There's a cheap self-service restaurant at the *Nama* department store at Titov trg 1 opposite the post office. *Plevna*, a 'gallery restaurant' at Kidričeva cesta 16 about 800 metres to the east, is a very popular spot with Lokans. Dishes are simple but tasty and inexpensive. Plevna is open from Tuesday to Saturday from noon to 11 pm.

The *Homan* in historical Homan House at Mestni trg 2 is essentially a pub and a café but serves pizza and salads too. In warm weather, tables are set out on Mestni trg

The Hayrack: A National Icon

Nothing is quite so Slovenian as the *kazolec*, the hayrack seen almost everywhere in the country except in Prekmurje and parts of Primorska. Because the ground in Alpine and hilly areas can be damp, wheat and hay are hung from racks, allowing the wind to do the job of drying faster and more thoroughly.

Until the late 19th century, the kazolec was looked upon as just another tool to make a farmer's work easier and the land more productive. Then the artist Ivan Grohar placed it in the centre of many of his Impressionist paintings, and the kazolec became as much a part of the cultural landscape as the physical one. Today it is virtually a national icon, and a sure way to reduce *zamejci* (ethnic Slovenes living outside the national borders) to nostalgic tears is to send them a postcard or Christmas card of a kazolec on a distant slope covered in snow.

There are many different types of Slovenian hayracks: single ones standing alone or with sloped 'lean-to' roofs, parallel and stretched ones, and double hayracks *(toplarji)*, often with roofs and storage areas on top. Simple hayracks are not unknown in other parts of Alpine Central Europe, but toplarji, decorated or plain, are unique to Slovenia. The best places to see them are in Dolenjska (especially around Muljava) and in Gorenjska near Škofja Loka and Lake Bohinj.

Hayracks were traditionally made of hardwood (usually oak) and date back to the early 17th century. Some of the ornate double hayracks in the town of Studor near Bohinj date from the 18th century. Today the hayrack is made of concrete and the new stretched ones can go on for what seems forever. ■

under the giant linden trees. There's more pizza available at the *Lontrg* at Spodnji trg 33. It's open from 9 am to 9 pm daily except Monday.

Krona, in an old town house at Mestni trg 32, is the best restaurant in Škofja Loka, with tasteful artwork on the walls, flowers on the table, friendly service and reasonably priced meals. Try *Poljanski zvitki* (Poljane-style rolled beef) or the pizza. The Krona is open daily from 9 am to 10 pm.

There are fruit and food stands in the small market on Titov trg across from the bus station.

Entertainment

Škofja Loka has a number of pleasant pubs including *Lunca* at Blaževa ulica 10 and *Pri Miholu*, built into part of the defence walls at Poljane Gate at the southern end of Mestni trg (No 24). They are usually open till about 11 pm. There's a wine bar in the bottom of Loka Castle's western tower called *Freising* open on weekdays from 5 pm to midnight and on Saturday and Sunday from 3 pm.

Getting There & Away

Count on at least hourly buses to Gorenja Vas, Kranj and Ljubljana, but otherwise the service from Škofja Loka is only adequate. Other destinations include: Bled and Bohinj via Radovljica (one bus a day); Cerkno (three to five); Nova Gorica (one); Piran (one); Poljane (up to eight); Soriška Planina (two at weekends); Zali Log (five); Železniki (six to 10); and Žiri (six to 10).

Škofja Loka can be reached by up to 15 trains a day from Ljubljana (20 km; 20

minutes) via Medvode. An equal number continue on to Kranj, Radovljica, Lesce-Bled and Jesenice (44 km; 40 minutes). About half of these cross the border for Rosenbach (Podrožca) in Austria.

Getting Around

Local Alpetour buses (80 SIT) regularly make the run between the train station in Trata and the bus station on Titov trg in Škofja Loka.

Velosport at Blaževa ulica 3 rents mountain bikes and bicycles.

AROUND ŠKOFJA LOKA
Suha

The 15th century **Church of St John the Baptist** at Suha, about 2.5 km east of the bus station in Škofja Loka, is unexceptional except for the presbytery, whose interior is completely covered with amazing 15th century frescoes by Jernej of Loka. The paintings on the vaults show scenes from the life of Christ, the coronation of Mary and various Apostles. The panels below depict many male and female saints – some who were wise and some who were not. Inside the arch is a frightening scene from the Last Judgement.

If the church is locked, request the key from the house at No 45, the first building on the right as you enter Suha village and about 150 metres beyond the church.

Crngrob

The **Church of the Annunciation** at Crngrob, about four km north of Škofja Loka, has one of the most priceless frescoes in Slovenia. Look for it on the outside wall under a 19th century portico near the church entrance. Called *Holy Sunday* (*Sveta Nedelja*) and produced in the workshop of Johannes de Laibaco (John of Ljubljana) in 1460, it explains in pictures what good Christians do on Sunday (pray, go to Mass, help the sick) and what they do not do (gamble, drink, bowl or fight). The consequence of doing any of the latter, of course, is damnation – vividly illustrated with souls being swallowed whole by a demon. On the south wall there's a large fresco of St Christopher from the same period.

The interior of the church, which was built and modified between the 14th and 17th centuries, contains more medieval frescoes on the north wall as well as the largest gilded altar in Slovenia, built by Jurij Skarnos in 1652. The spectacular organ was made around the same time. The stellar vault of the presbytery, painted in light red, blue and yellow, has a number of bosses portraying the Virgin Mary, the Bishops of Freising and a man on a horse who was probably a benefactor.

The people at the house (No 10) nearest the church hold the keys. Don't be surprised if you hear a lot of shooting going on even though it's still several months to hunting season – an army camp is in the area. You can eat at *Gostilna Crngrob* at house No 13, which is open from 10 am to 11 pm every day but Wednesday, and there is accommodation and horses for rent at the *Porenta* farmhouse (☎ 631 626) nearby.

Crngrob is easily accessible on foot or by bicycle from Škofja Loka via Groharjevo naselje, which runs north from Cesta Talcev and the Capuchin monastery. An alternative is to take the bus bound for Kranj, get off at the village of Dorfarje and walk west for about 1.5 km.

KRANJ (pop 37,300)

Situated at the foot of the Kamnik-Savinja Alps with the snow-capped peak of Storžič (2132 metres) and others looming to the north, Kranj is Slovenia's fourth largest and most industrialised city, with its fair share of unemployment and graffiti (my favourite is the ubiquitous 'Kranjsterdam'). But the casual traveller wouldn't have to know anything about all that. The attractive Old Town sitting on an escarpment above the confluence of the Sava and Kokra rivers that barely measures one km by 250 metres contains everything of interest in Kranj (Krainburg in German).

A secondary Roman road linking Emona (Ljubljana) and Virunum (near today's

Klagenfurt in Austria) ran through Kranj until about the 5th century; 100 years later the Langobards established a base here. They were followed by the early Slavs, whose large burial grounds can be partly seen below the floor of the Gorenjska Museum and near St Cantianus Church in Glavni trg.

In the 11th century, Kranj was an important border stronghold of the German Frankish counts in their battles with the Hungarians and the town gave its name to the entire region: Kranjska (Carniola). It was also an important market and ecclesiastical centre and within 200 years Kranj was granted town status by the new rulers, the Bavarian Counts of Andechs. More wealth came with the development of iron mining and foundries and when the progressive Protestant movement reached Gorenjska, it was centred in Kranj.

Kranj grew faster after the arrival of the railway in 1870 and is now home to much of Slovenia's textile industry and Iskra, the electrical appliance company. As was the case in the Middle Ages, Kranj is known for its trade and industrial fairs.

Orientation

Kranj's Old Town is essentially three pedestrian streets running north to south. The main one begins as Prešernova ulica at Maistrov trg and changes to Cankarjeva ulica at Glavni trg, the main square and market place in medieval times. Cankarjeva ulica terminates, like everything else, at Pungert, the 'Land's End' at the tip of the promontory.

'New Kranj' spreads in every direction, but especially northward to Zlato Polje and to the south-east to Planina. Brnik Airport is 15 km east of Kranj.

The bus station is about 600 metres north of Maistrov trg on Stošičeva ulica. The train station lies below the Old Town to the west on the left bank of the Sava. To reach the Old Town from the station, follow Kolodvorkska cesta across the bridge and walk up Vodopivčeva ulica to the Plečnik-designed stairway. If you're headed for the Jelen or Creina hotels, continue north along Ljubljanska cesta after crossing the bridge.

Information

Tourist Office The tourist office (☎ 211 361) at Koroška cesta 29 is usually open from 8 am to 7 pm on weekdays and till 1 pm on Saturday; however, when I was last in Kranj staff reductions had severely limited opening hours. The office sells the English-language *Tourist Guide of Kranj and Its Environs* which could be very useful if you plan to spend a fair bit of time in this part of Gorenjska. It has eight day trips designed for motorists.

Money Gorenjska Banka's main branch is between the tourist office and the bus station at Bleiweisova cesta 1. It is open from 7 am to 6 pm on weekdays and till noon on Saturday. A smaller branch at Prešernova ulica 6 keeps shorter hours: 9 to 11.30 am and 2 to 5 pm on weekdays and till noon on Saturday. A Banka, at Bleiweisova cesta 14, is open weekdays from 7.30 am to 6 pm and on Saturday till noon.

Post & Telecommunications The main post office in Kranj is several hundred metres north-east of the bus station at Dražgoška ulica 8. A much more convenient branch, from where you can also make long-distance telephone calls, is at Poštna ulica 4 east of Glavni trg. It is open weekdays from 7 am to 7 pm and on Saturday till noon.

Kranj's telephone code is 064. The postcode is 64000.

Travel Agency Slovenijaturist (☎ 211 946) is in the same building as the tourist office at Koroška cesta 29; if you've got train enquiries ask here as the staff seems more keen to help than usual. It is open from 9 am till noon and from 2 to 5 pm on weekdays only. Kompas (☎ 218 473) at the Creina hotel opens weekdays from 8 am to 7 pm and to 1 pm on Saturday.

Bookshop Mladinska Knjiga at Maistrov trg 1 has maps as well as English-language guides and books. It is open from 8 am to 7 pm on weekdays and to 1 pm on Saturday.

GORENJSKA

Things to See

You can see virtually everything in Kranj by following Prešernova ulica and Cankarjeva ulica to Pungert and returning to Maistrov trg via Tomšičeva ulica. Most of the important sights have plaques in English and are marked with numbers. These correspond to the map included with the *Tourist Guide of Kranj and Its Environs*.

Maistrov trg was the site of the upper town gates in the 15th century and was the most vulnerable part of Kranj. The steep Kokra Canyon protected the town on the eastern side and thick walls did the trick on the west from Pungert as far as the square. The **Špital Tower**, one of seven along the wall, forms part of the shop at Maistrov trg 3. The unusual Art-Deco building with the three statues facing the square to the north is the former **Stara Pošta Hotel** built in the 1930s.

Kranj is a town of art galleries and many can be found on Prešernova ulica. **Prešeren House** (Prešernova Hiša) at No 7 was home to the poet France Prešeren for the last two years of his life (1847-49) and he died in the front bedroom. The Prešeren Memorial Museum in five rooms here is devoted to his life and work but, sadly for foreigners, the explanatory notes next to his letters, diaries and manuscripts are in Slovene only. The museum is open Tuesday to Friday from 10 am till noon and from 5 to 7 pm. On Saturday and Sunday it opens in the morning only. The 150 SIT admission charge allows entry to the Gorenjska Museum as well.

Glavni trg is a beautiful square of Gothic and Renaissance buildings; the ones on the western side with their painted facades, vaulted hallways and arched courtyards are masterpieces. The 16th century one (actually ones – they were two houses joined together) opposite at Glavni trg 4 was once the Town-Hall (Mestna Hiša). Today it contains the **Gorenjska Museum**.

Below the floor of the museum's vaulted vestibule some **Slavic tombs** from the 10th century can be seen through glass panels. The museum's upper floors contain a lovely Renaissance **great hall** with carved wooden

doors and ceiling (it is now used for civil wedding ceremonies), awful bronze sculptures by Lojze Dolinar (1893-1970) and history and folk-art collections. Among the eye-catching bits and pieces lying around is a large porcelain stove topped with a Turk's turbaned head, an embroidered sheepskin coat called a *kožuh* and a child's toy of a devil sharpening a gossip's tongue on a grindstone (a common motif in Slovenian folk art and one that always makes me wonder just how much Slovenes actually do like to gossip). The museum has the same hours and entrance fee as Prešeren House.

Glavni trg's pride and joy, though, is the **Church of St Cantianus** (Sveti Kancijan), which was built onto part of an older church starting in about 1400. It is the best example of a hall church – one with nave and aisles of the same height – in Slovenia and was the model for many others. There are some 15th century frescoes of angels with musical instruments on the stellar vaulting of the nave and beneath the choir. The relief illustrating the Mount of Olives in the arch above the main portal is worth a look, as is the modern altar designed by Ivan Vurnik (1884-1971).

On the northern side of the church exterior there are more old bones from early Slav graves and a medieval ossuary. On the south wall is a **lapidary** of medieval tombstones and nearby the **Fountain of St John Nepomunk**, with a stone statue of the 14th century Bohemian martyr complete with an sad-eyed octopus.

The **Prešeren Theatre** is across the plaza at Glavni trg 6. The portico near the **Prešeren Monument** (showing a rather rugged-looking and heroic Dr France) was designed by the architect Jože Plečnik in the early 1950s.

Walk down Cankarjeva ulica and you'll pass the **Church of the Holy Rosary**, built in the 16th century and a Protestant sanctuary during the Reformation. The church was 'attacked' by neo-Gothic restorers in 1892 and 'so renovated that it is of little importance artistically or historically', the plaque tells us. Beside the church are arcades, a

GORENJSKA

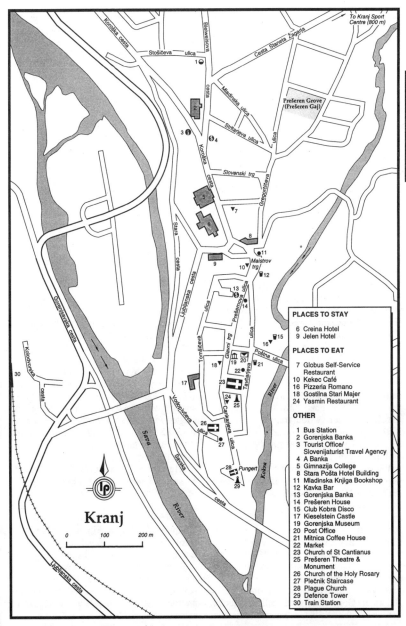

Kranj

0   100   200 m

PLACES TO STAY

6 Creina Hotel
9 Jelen Hotel

PLACES TO EAT

7 Globus Self-Service
   Restaurant
10 Kekec Café
16 Pizzeria Romano
18 Gostilna Stari Majer
24 Yasmin Restaurant

OTHER

1 Bus Station
2 Gorenjska Banka
3 Tourist Office/
   Slovenijaturist Travel Agency
4 A Banka
5 Gimnazija College
8 Stara Pošta Hotel Building
11 Mladinska Knjiga Bookshop
12 Kavka Bar
13 Gorenjska Banka
14 Prešeren House
15 Club Kobra Disco
17 Kieselstein Castle
19 Gorenjska Museum
20 Post Office
21 Mitnica Coffee House
22 Market
23 Church of St Cantianus
25 Prešeren Theatre &
   Monument
26 Church of the Holy Rosary
27 Plečnik Staircase
28 Plague Church
29 Defence Tower
30 Train Station

fountain and a staircase designed in the late 1950s by Plečnik to give Kranj a monumental entrance up Vodopivčeva ulica from the Sava River. This was where the lower town gates once stood.

Pungert is the end of the line for the Old Town. Here you'll find another old church, sometimes called the **Plague Church**, built during a time of pestilence in the 1470s. It contains some of the most important artwork in Kranj, including a painting dedicated to the three 'intercessors against the plague' (Sts Rok, Fabian and Sebastian) by the Austrian Baroque artist Martin Johann Kremser-Schmidt (1718-1801). It is now used by Orthodox Christians. A three-storey **defence tower**, the only one in Kranj entirely preserved, was built in the 16th century. There is a café and bar on the ground floor.

If you return to the Church of the Holy Rosary and head north on Tomšičeva ulica, you'll come to a restored section of the **town wall** and **Kieselstein Castle** (also spelled Khislstein) at No 44. Part of this stronghold was built during the Turkish invasions of the 15th century but mostly it's Renaissance. Today its glassed-in arcades and upper floors house the offices of several cultural institutes.

The future of the fearsome-looking **revolutionary statues** in Slovenski trg, opposite the attractive Gimnazija (1898) (college) and the Creina hotel, is doubtful and they may have been trucked to a zoo or a theme park by now. They were designed by Lojze Dolinar in 1961.

France Prešeren is buried in the parish cemetery, now called **Prešeren Grove** (Prešernov Gaj), about 400 metres north-east of Slovenski trg.

Activities

The Kranj Sport Centre at Partizanska cesta 37, about 1.5 km north-east of Maistrov trg, has tennis courts and both a covered and an outdoor swimming pool.

A very easy destination on foot is Šmarjetna Gora, a 643-metre hill three km to the west of the Old Town where a fort stood during the Hallstatt period. On top of the hill is the reconstructed Church of St Margaret and the *Bellevue Hotel*. The views from here of Kranj, the Alps and the Sava River are astonishing; on a clear day you might be able to see Bled and Ljubljana, some 30 km away in opposite directions.

Festivals

If you happen to be in Kranj in mid-July, follow the flocks to Jezersko for the annual Shepherds' Ball (Ovčarski Bal). The ball is a day and evening of folk music, dancing and drinking *žganje* (brandy) – an ovine alternative to the bovine event in Bohinj (see Festivals in that section). Jezersko, on the Austrian border 28 km north-east of Kranj and easily accessible by car or bus, was a popular health resort before WW II. Today it is an unspoiled area in the shadow of Grintovec with a delightful Alpine lake, hiking trails, old farmhouses and mountain huts.

Places to Stay

The tourist office can arrange *private rooms* for about DM20 per person, but only one family offers them in the Old Town itself; most are in the boring (and distant) housing estates to the north or north-east.

For what it offers, the *Jelen* hotel (☎ 211 466; fax 211 857), a run-down, three-storey pile at Ljubljanska cesta 1, is pretty pricey: singles with breakfast but no private shower are 3085 SIT, doubles 4170 SIT. If you want your own bathroom, add 500 SIT. They exchange cash only.

A few metres to the north at Koroška cesta 5, the brick-and-wood *Creina* hotel (☎ 213 650; fax 213 760) with 89 rooms is vastly superior in comfort, style and price; this is the place for Austrian business people, tour groups headed for the Alps and airline crews who don't want to travel all the way to Ljubljana. Singles with shower and breakfast are DM57, doubles DM79. Most rooms have TV and direct-dial telephones, but Koroška cesta is a busy street and it can get pretty noisy here. There's a vinoteka (wine cellar) in the basement.

The *Bellevue Hotel* (☎ 311 211), located at the top of Šmarjetna Gora, has 30 beds and a very pleasant restaurant.

Places to Eat

The cheapest place for a meal in Kranj is the *self-service restaurant* in the north-west corner of the Globus shopping centre opposite the Creina hotel. For 400 SIT you get half a chicken with potatoes or macaroni with some sort of meat and salad. It's open weekdays from 8 am to 7.30 pm and till 1 pm on Saturday.

Pizzeria Romano at Tavčarjeva ulica 31 north of the post office serves a novel triumvirate: pizza, pasta and 'dishes made from horsemeat'. It's open from 10 am to 10 pm Monday to Thursday, till midnight on Friday and Saturday and from 4 pm to 10 pm on Sunday.

Kekec at Maistrov trg 13 and open Monday to Saturday till 7 pm has decent sandwiches, while the stick-to-the-ribs Slovenian dishes at *Gostilna Stari Majer* at Glavni trg 16 will keep you going for longer than you'd think.

The best place for a meal in Kranj, though, is the *Yasmin* at Cankarjeva ulica 1, a combined café/restaurant, which serves well-prepared Continental food with a Slovenian touch and many unusual vegetarian dishes such as 'Wiener schnitzel' made with potato, mushrooms cooked with Gorgonzola and cheese *štruklji* (dumplings). The café is open daily from 9 am till midnight, the restaurant from noon.

The large *market* selling fruit and vegetables behind Petrček House at Prešernova ulica 5 is open from 6 am to 6 pm from mid-March to mid-October and from 7 am to 3 pm during the rest of the year.

Entertainment

Prešeren Theatre (☎ 222 681) at Glavni trg 6 is one of the most active theatres in Slovenia, staging about four plays with up to 200 performances a year. Concerts – both classical and popular – are held in the courtyard of Kieselstein Castle in summer.

Maistrov trg and Prešernova ulica are home to a number of pleasant pubs and cafés. One of the more unusual ones is *Kavka*, a lively bar/café/gallery up the stairs at Maistrov trg 8. It is open from 8 or 9 am till midnight Monday to Saturday and from 6 pm on Sunday. *Mitnica*, a lovely kavarna in the basement of a 16th century tollhouse at Tavčarjeva ulica 35, is just the place to relax in Kranj on a warm afternoon.

Club Kobra next to the Pizzeria Romano at Tavčarjeva ulica is the hottest disco and music club in Kranj at the moment and opens every day from 8 pm to 3 am. The *Gauloises Blondes* disco at the Creina hotel caters to a more mature and well-heeled set Thursday to Saturday from 9 pm to 4 am.

Getting There & Away

Bus Buses leave frequently for Bled, Bohinj, Brnik Airport, Cerklje, Ljubljana, Medvode, Piran, Preddvor, Predoslje, Radovljica, Rateče-Planica via Kranjska Gora, Škofja Loka, Tržič and Vodice.

You can also get to Bašelj via Preddvor six to 10 times a day, Bohinjska Bistrica (two), Bovec via Kranjska Gora and the Vršič Pass (one bus a day in summer), Brezje (one in summer), Jesenice (four), Jezersko (nine), Kamnik (eight), Kropa (three), Maribor (one), Novo Mesto (five), Rogaška Slatina (one), Vinica (one) and Zali Log (Sunday in summer). Three daily buses go to Zagreb in Croatia and there's another one to Varaždin.

Train Up to 15 trains a day pass through Kranj from Ljubljana (29 km; 30 minutes) via Medvode and Škofja Loka. They carry on to Radovljica, Lesce-Bled and Jesenice (35 km; 40 minutes), where about half cross the border for Rosenbach (Podrožca) in Austria.

Getting Around

Alpetour buses (80 SIT) make the run from the train station to the bus terminus on Stošičeva ulica if you don't feel like walking. You can ring a local taxi on ☎ 214 311.

Gostilna Dežman (☎ 218 956) at Golniška ulica 1a – the continuation of Bleiweisova cesta – north of Kranj in Kokrica, rents mountain bikes. It is open daily from 9 am to 11 pm.

With so many pedestrian areas, parking can be very difficult in Kranj.

AROUND KRANJ
Brdo Castle

Until quite recently, 16th century Brdo Castle, about five km north-east of Kranj at Predoslje, was for official state guests only. Though it is still managed by the Protocol Service of the Republic of Slovenia, now anyone can visit or even stay, provided they have the necessary cash.

The castle was long the property of the aristocratic and philanthropic Zois family, the Slovenian equivalent to the Széchenyi clan in Hungary. It has two towers on the northern side, corridors crammed with artwork and a library containing a priceless copy of the Bible translated by Protestant reformer Jurij Dalmatin (1547-89). Brdo is surrounded by lovely parkland and a protected forest of some 500 hectares. You can fish in one of 11 lakes stocked with trout, carp and pike (1300 SIT per day), play tennis or ride horses for 800 SIT per hour. Visitors not staying at Brdo may have to pay a fee of 300 SIT to enter the park. There are more horses 2.5 km to the west of Predoslje at the Bobovek Riding Centre (☎ 212 886).

Accommodation for most people here is at the 78-room *Kokra* hotel (☎ 221 133; fax 221 551), where very run-of-the-mill singles are DM65 and doubles DM100. Of course if you're not 'most people' and are very flush indeed, a 1st-class suite in *Brdo Castle* can be had for DM1000 (or a mere DM600 for a 3rd-class one). State guests, who also still stay here, probably get a discount.

Strmol Castle

The 15th century Strmol Castle, near Cerklje 10 km east of Predoslje, is another manor house in the Protocol Service's stable. Not a lot of recreational facilities here but if you want to live like a count or countess for a day, DM800 gets you a suite on the right, DM600 one on the left and DM300 a single room. Tourist tax is DM1.

Krvavec

The ski centre at Krvavec (☎ 421 180), 17 km to the north-east of Kranj, hasn't got much use in the past couple of years due to lack of snow but when it's up and running, it's one of the most popular (and crowded) in Slovenia. A cable car will bring you up to the centre at 1450 metres and a dozen chair lifts and T-bar tows serve the 25 km of slopes and six km of cross-country runs. Krvavec is also an excellent starting point for hikes in summer to **Kriška Planina** or **Jezerca**, about an hour's walk from the upper station of the cable car.

RADOVLJICA (pop 6200)

A charming town full of historical buildings, Radovljica enjoys an enviable position on top of an outcrop 75 metres above a wide plain called Dežela (Country). A short distance to the north-west, two branches of the Sava come together to form Slovenia's longest and mightiest river.

Radovljica (Ratmansdorf in German) was settled by the early Slavs and grew into an important market town by the 14th century. With increased trade on the river and the iron forgeries at Kropa and Kamna Gorica, Radovljica expanded and the town was built around a large rectangular square fortified with a wall and defence towers. Radovljica's affluence in the Middle Ages can be seen in the lovely buildings still lining this square – Linhartov trg – today.

Radovljica is an easy day trip from Bled, just six km to the north-west.

Orientation

The centre of old Radovljica is Linhartov trg, a protected historical and cultural monument; everything of importance in Radovljica is on it. The new town extends primarily northward along Gorenjska cesta toward Lesce.

Radovljica's bus station is 500 metres north-west of Linhartov trg on Kranjska cesta. The train station is below the town on Na Mlaki. To reach the square from the train station, walk up steep Kolodvorska ulica and turn right.

Information

The tourist office (☎ 715 300) is at Kranjska cesta 13.

The post office is beside the bus station at Kranjska cesta 1, while a Ljubljanska Banka branch can be found just opposite at Gorenjska cesta 16.

Radovljica's telephone code is 064. The postcode is 64240.

Linhartov Trg

Radovljica's main square, named in honour of Slovenia's first dramatist and historian Anton Tomaž Linhart (1756-95), who was born here, is lined with painted houses mostly from the 16th century and is a delight to explore. It has been called 'the most homogeneous Old Town core in Slovenia' and has interesting details at every step.

There are several lovely buildings opposite the Beekeeping Museum, including **Koman House** at No 23 with a Baroque painting on its front of St Florian, the patron saint of fires (he douses, not ignites) and **Mali House** at No 25 with a picture of an archer. But the most important one is 16th century **Šivec House** at No 22.

Šivec House is an interesting hybrid – Renaissance on the outside and Gothic on the inside. The fresco on the exterior shows the Good Samaritan performing his works of mercy; inside there is a vaulted hall on the ground floor and a wood-panelled drawing room with a beamed ceiling on the 1st floor. Šivec House is now used as a gallery and the paintings on exhibit when I last visited – Gothic-inspired dreams and fantasies of court jesters with wings and sea dragons by Marjeta Cvetko (1953-) – were a wonderful complement to this beautiful house. The gallery is open from 10 am to noon and from 4 to 6 pm every day but Monday.

To the east of the square, in an oddly shaped, shady courtyard, is the Gothic **Parish Church of St Peter**, a hall church modelled after the one in Kranj. The three portals are flamboyant Gothic and the sculp-

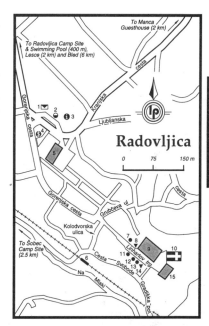

1   Post Office
2   Bus Station
3   Tourist Office
4   Ljubljanska Banka
5   Grajski Dvor Hotel
6   Train Station
7   Vidič House
8   Gostilna Lectar
9   Thurn Manor/Beekeeping Museum
10 Church of St Peter
11 Šivec House
12 Koman House
13 Mali House
14 Linhartov Hram Coffee Shop
15 Priest's House

tures inside were created by Angelo Pozzo in 1713. The building with the arcaded courtyard south of the church is the **Priest's House**. Parts of the old **town wall** can still be seen nearby.

To the north-west at Linhartov trg 3 is the 17th century **Vidič House** with a corner projection and colourfully painted in red, yellow and blue. Past the city park on Gorenjska cesta is the former **Savings Bank building** (1906) with a marvellous flowering tree in Secessionist style decorating the front.

Beekeeping Museum

Though it may not sound like a crowd-pleaser, this museum at Linhartov trg 1 is one of the most fascinating in Slovenia and there isn't a whole lot you won't know about things apiary after an hour inside.

The museum is housed in **Thurn Manor**, the largest and most important public building on Linhartov trg and also worth a look. Thurn Manor began life as Ortenburg Castle in the early Middle Ages but was rebuilt with a large hall on the ground floor after the earthquake of 1511. Subsequent alterations and expansions gave it the appearance of a large Baroque manor house. The cream-and-white structure has interesting reliefs and stucco work on its facade.

The museum's exhibits take a close look at the history of beekeeping in Slovenia (which was at its most intense in the 18th and 19th centuries), the country's unique contribution to the industry with the development of the species *Apis mellifica carniolica* – the Carniolan bee – and the research of men like Anton Janša (1734-73), who set up a research station in the Karavanke and is considered around the world to be the father of modern beekeeping. And it doesn't fail to pass on a few 'fun facts to know and tell'.

Did *you* realise that bees cannot see the colour red but go absolutely gaga over yellow, for example? The museum's great collection of illustrated beehive panels *(panjske končnice)* from the 18th and 19th centuries, a folk art unique to Slovenia, is the largest in the country. Thank-

fully, everything here is labelled in English and German along with Slovene.

The Beekeeping Museum has extremely complicated hours but this much is certain: it is always closed on Monday and in January and February. In spring and autumn, the hours are from 10 am till noon and 3 to 5 pm. The museum opens in summer from 10 am to 1 pm and from 4 to 6 pm. The entry fee is 200 SIT.

Activities

There's a public swimming pool open in summer at the northern end of Kopališka cesta and tennis courts nearby.

The Sport Riding Centre at Podvin Castle (☎ 738 881) in Mošnje, about four km southeast of Radovljica, has horses available for riding individually or with an instructor. The centre also has a new covered hippodrome.

Festivals

The Radovljica Festival in August is a series of concerts of ancient music and one of the country's most popular cultural events. The concerts take place in Thurn Manor.

Places to Stay

Radovljica's tiny *camp site* is next to the public swimming pool on Kopališka cesta. It is open from June to mid-September and costs between DM8 and DM10 per person, with an extra DM2 charged for a tent.

The largest (and some say the best-equipped) camp site in Slovenia, *Šobec* (☎ 718 104), is in Lesce about 2.5 km north-

Illustrated beehive panel *(panjske končnice)*

Top: View of Lake Bohinj and the Church of St John the Baptist (Gorenjska) (JŽ)
Bottom: Slovene folk band at the Cows' Ball festival at Lake Bohinj (Gorenjska) (SF)

Sheep grazing near the Vršič Pass in the Julian Alps (Gorenjska) (SF)

The Boards and the Bees

The keeping of honeybees (species *Apis*) has been an integral part of Slovenian agriculture since the 16th century when buckwheat was first planted on fallow ground to allow the more intensive use of farm land. Bees favour buckwheat and Slovenia, especially the Alpine regions of Carniola (Kranjska), was soon awash with honey for cooking and with wax for candles. The Renaissance scholar, Valvasor, discussed the subject at some length in his *The Glory of the Duchy of Carniola* published in 1689.

Originally bees were kept in hollow logs or woven baskets but the entire hive was damaged when the honeycomb was removed. The invention of the *kranjič* hive, with removable boxes that resembled a chest of drawers, solved the problem by creating individual hives. It also led to the development of Slovenia's most important form of folk art.

Kranjič hives have front boards *(panjske končnice)* above the entrance, and painting and decorating these panels with religious motifs soon became all the rage. Ethnographers still can't decide whether the illustrations were intended as religious appeals to protect the hives from fire or disease, as guides to lead the bees (which can distinguish colour) back home, or to help beekeepers identify the hives.

The first panels (from the mid-18th century) were painted in a 'folk Baroque' style and the subjects were taken from the Bible (Adam and Eve, the Virgin Mary, and patient Job, the patron of beekeepers) and from history (the Turkish invasions, the Counter-Reformation with Martin Luther being driven to hell by a devil, and Napoleon and the Illyrian Provinces). The most interesting panels show the foibles, rivalries and humour of the human condition. A devil sharpening a gossip's tongue on a grindstone, or two women fighting over a man's trousers (ie his hand in marriage). A very common illustration shows the devil exchanging old wives for nubile young women. Another – in a 'world turned upside down' – has the animals laying the hunter in his grave.

It is important to remember that these paintings were not 'art for art's sake'. The creators, not all of whom were 'artists', were primarily concerned with depicting the simple world around them and in doing so they produced some beautiful work.

The painting of beehive panels in Slovenia enjoyed its golden age between about 1820 and 1880. But the introduction of a new and much larger hive by Anton Žnidaršič at the end of the 19th century obviated the need for small illustrations and the art form degenerated into kitsch.

Today you will see the best examples of painted panjske končnice in museums (Radovljica, Maribor), but there are still a few traditional – and protected – ones around, such as those at Muljava in Dolenjska. An interesting twist is the beehive at Brdo Castle near Kranj painted in the 1970s by some of Slovenia's most outstanding artists. Most common are the large box hives painted bright yellow (a colour bees like) and the 'hives on wheels' which can be moved into the sun or to a promising meadow.

Bees are still kept in Slovenia for their honey and wax, but much more lucrative are by-products such as pollen, propolis and royal jelly used as elixirs and in homoeopathic medicine. Propolis is a brownish, waxy substance collected from certain trees by bees and used to caulk their hives. Royal jelly, so beloved by the European aristocracy of the 1920s and 1930s and by the Chinese, is the substance fed to the queen bee by the workers. ■

west of town. Situated on a small lake in a bend of the Sava Dolinka River, the camp site is huge – 19 square hectares – and can accommodate up to 2000 people, which this popular place often does in summer. Šobec is open from May to September and costs from DM11.50 to DM13 depending on the month.

You'll find lots more budget accommodation in nearby Bled but if you're determined to stay in Radovljica, the *Manca* guesthouse (☎ 712 020), which is a couple of km north of Linhartov trg at Gradnikova cesta 2, charges between DM40 and DM50 for singles with shower and breakfast and DM70 to DM80 for doubles.

Radovljica's only hotel, a four-storey concrete block called the *Grajski Dvor* (☎ 715 585; fax 715 878), is at Kranjska cesta 2 opposite the bus station and tourist office. Singles and doubles with shower and breakfast are DM55 and DM76. The hotel has 80 rooms.

If money is no object, you might treat yourself to a night at the *Grad Podvin* hotel (☎ 738 881; fax 738 885) in Podvin Castle, about four km south-east of Radovljica in the village of Mošnje. Depending on the season, singles with shower and breakfast are DM80 to DM105 while doubles are DM110 to DM140. Podvin Castle is surrounded by a lovely park and has tennis courts and a popular horse-riding centre. Its restaurant, *Pristava*, gets high marks.

Places to Eat
Gostilna Lectar, in yet another historical building at Linhartov trg 2, is open every day but Tuesday from 8 am till midnight. Across from Thurn Manor at No 26 is *Linhartov Hram*, a coffee shop and pub with snacks.

Getting There & Away
Buses leave Radovljica almost every half-hour for Bled and Ljubljana. They go hourly to Bohinj (via Bled), Kranj, Kranjska Gora, Kropa and Planica. Other destinations and their daily frequencies include: Bovec via Kranjska Gora and the Vršič Pass (one bus a day in summer); Brezje (one); Begunje (up

to nine); Jesenice (six); Novo Mesto (four); Podnart (five); Rogaška Slatina (one); Tržič (up to four); Vinica (one), and Zagreb in Croatia (three).

Radovljica is on the rail line linking Ljubljana (48 km; 50 minutes) with Jesenice (16 km; 20 minutes) via Škofja Loka, Kranj and Lesce-Bled. Up to 15 trains a day pass through the town in each direction. Several of the northbound ones carry on into Austria and Germany.

AROUND RADOVLJICA
Kropa (pop 1025)
While in Radovljica don't miss the chance to visit Kropa, a delightful little village tucked away in a narrow valley of the Jelovica Hills 10 km to the south-east. Kropa has been a workhorse for centuries, mining iron ore and hammering out the nails and decorative wrought iron that can be seen in many parts of Slovenia. Today Kropa (Cropp in German) has turned its attention to screws – the Plamen factory is based here – but artisans continue their work, clanging away in the workshop on the village's single street, and the work of their forebears is evident in ornamental street lamps shaped like birds and dragons, weather vanes and shutters. The fascinating collection in the **Blacksmith Museum** (Kovaški Muzej) at house No 10 traces the history of iron mining and forging in Kropa and nearby Kamna Gorica from the 14th to the early 20th centuries (with information in English, German and Slovene). Nail-making was the town's main industry for most of that period, and it is difficult to imagine that so many different types of nails existed, never mind that they were all made here. From giant ones that held the pylons in Venice together to little studs for snow boots, Kropa produced some 130 types in huge quantities. In Kropa you did not become a master blacksmith until you could fit a horseshoe around an egg – without cracking the shell.

The museum has working models of forges, a couple of rooms showing how workers and their families lived in very cramped quarters (up to 45 people in one house) and a special exhibit devoted to the work of master forger Joža Bertoncelj (1901-76), who turned out exquisite wrought-iron gratings, candlesticks, chandeliers and even masks. The museum shows a fascinating B&W documentary film about the town and its work produced in the very socialist 1950s. It's a real period piece.

The house itself was owned by a 17th century iron baron called Klinar and contains some valuable furniture and oil paintings. Among the most interesting pieces is a 19th century wind-up 'jukebox' from Bohemia. Ask the caretaker to insert one of the large perforated rolls and watch the piano, drums, triangle and cymbals make music.

The Blacksmith Museum keeps the same complicated hours as the Beekeeping Museum in Radovljica, including winter closure. The entrance charge is 200 SIT.

The **forgers' workshop** across from the museum at house No 7b is open for visits from 6 am to 2 pm on weekdays and from 9 am till noon on Saturday. The artisans sell their wares – none of it even approaching the work of Master Bertoncelj – at the shop next door (house No 7a).

An 18th century furnace called **Purgatory Forge** lies a short distance north of the museum near the Kroparica, the fast-flowing stream that once turned the wheels that powered the furnaces. Close by is the birthplace of the Slovenian painter Janez Potočnik, whose work can be seen in the Baroque **Church of St Leonard** on the hill to the east and in Kamnik. Kropa has many other lovely old houses, including several around Trg Kropa, the main square with an interesting old wayside shrine.

A medieval smelting furnace – the so-called **Slovenian Furnace** – dating from the 13th century is at Jamnik, about 3.5 km south of Kropa along a tortuously twisting road. There are trails from Kropa into the Jelovica Hills to the west, an area once rich in iron ore and timber for charcoal. In the early 19th century over 800 charcoal burners worked in this area alone.

There's no accommodation in Kropa but

you can eat at the *Kovaški Hram*, a pizzeria on the ground floor of the Blacksmith Museum, which is open from 9 am to 11 pm daily except Monday, or at *Pri Jarmu*, a gostilna at the southern end of Kropa in house No 2.

BLED (pop 5675)

With its emerald-green lake, picture-postcard church on an islet, medieval castle clinging to a rocky cliff and the highest peaks of the Julian Alps and the Karavanke as backdrops, Bled is Slovenia's most popular resort and its biggest money-spinner. Not surprisingly, it's overpriced, swarming with tourists and often less than welcoming. Many travellers make a beeline for the larger and far less developed Lake Bohinj, 30 km to the south-west.

But as is the case with popular destinations around the world, people come in droves – and will continue to do so – because the place *is* beautiful. On a clear day you can make out Mt Stol (2236 metres) and Mt Triglav (2864 metres, Slovenia's highest peak) in the distance and then the bells start ringing from the belfry of the little island church.

Bled was the site of a Hallstatt settlement in the early Iron Age but, as it was far from the main trade routes, the Romans gave it short shrift. More importantly, from the 7th century the early Slavs, no doubt attracted by the altitude (501 metres), the mild climate and the natural protection, came in waves, establishing themselves at Pristava below the castle, on the tiny island and at a dozen other sites around the lake. Bled has been linked with the myths and legends of these people for centuries, particularly the Slavic goddess Živa and her priestess Bogomila. France Prešeren gave this relationship new life in his epic poem *Krst pri Savici (Baptism at the Savica Waterfall)* in 1836.

Around the turn of the first millennium, German Emperor Henry II presented Bled Castle and its lands to the Bishops of Brixen in South Tyrol, who retained secular control of the area until the early 19th century when

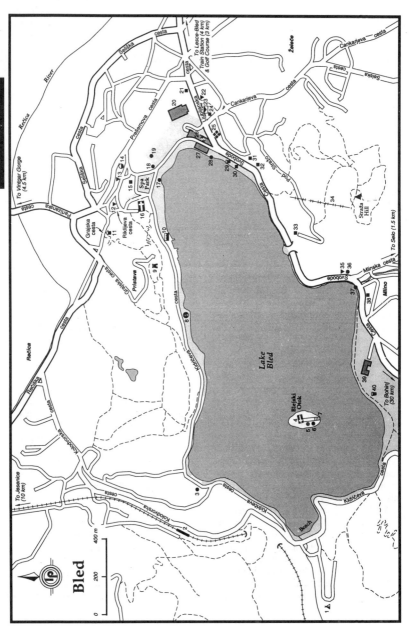

GORENJSKA

Bled

PLACES TO STAY

1	Zaka Camp Site
11	Bledec Hostel
15	Jelovica Hotel
21	Krim Hotel/Emona Globtour
24	Lovec Hotel
26	Park Hotel/Tourist Office/Gorenjska Banka
30	Grand Toplice Hotel
31	Trst Hotel
32	Jadran Hotel
33	Villa Viktorija Guesthouse
38	Gostilna Mlino
39	Villa Bled Hotel

PLACES TO EAT

12	Okarina Restaurant
13	Gostilna Pri Planincu
22	Lang Hai Restaurant
35	Gostilna Pletna
38	Gostilna Mlino

OTHER

2	Bled Jezero Train Station
3	Zaka Rowing Centre
4	Island Church
5	Provost's House
6	Chaplain's House
7	Island Stairway
8	Triglav National Park Office
9	Bled Castle/Museum
10	Castle Baths
14	Bus Station
16	Church of St Martin
17	Gondolas
18	Horse-Drawn Carriage Stand
19	Festival Hall
20	Ice-Skating Rink
23	Post Office
25	Shopping Centre/Kompas/SKB Banka
27	Casino/Park Café
28	Gondolas
29	Grand Toplice Café
34	Chair Lift
36	Svetina Gallery
37	Gondolas
40	Belvedere Café

the Habsburgs took it over. By that time a number of small villages, including Mlino, Želeče and Rečica, had grown up around the lake.

Bled's beauty and its warm waters were well known to medieval pilgrims who came to pray at the island church; the place made it into print in 1689 when Janez Vajkard Valvasor described the lake's thermal springs in *The Glory of the Duchy of Carniola*, his seminal work on Slovenian geography and history. But Bled's wealth was not fully appreciated at that time, and even in the late 18th century the keeper of the castle seriously considered draining Lake Bled and using the clay to make bricks.

Fortunately, along came a Swiss doctor named Arnold Rikli who saw the lake's full potential. In 1855 he opened baths where the casino now stands taking advantage of the springs, the clean air and the mountain light. With the opening of the railway from Ljubljana to Tarvisio (Trbiž) in 1870, more and more guests came to Bled and the resort was a favourite of wealthy Europeans from the turn of the century right up to WW II. In fact,

under the Kingdom of Serbs, Croats and Slovenes, Bled was the summer residence of the Karadžordževići, the Yugoslav royal family.

Orientation

'Bled' refers both to the lake and the settlements around it, particularly the built-up area to the north-east where almost all the hotels are located. This development is dominated by an unattractive new shopping centre called the Trgovski Shopping Centre, but known locally as the 'Khaddhafi Centre' because it was originally slated for Tripoli. Bled's main road, Ljubljanska cesta, runs eastward from here. Footpaths and a road called Cesta Svobode and then Kidričeva cesta circle the lake.

Bled's bus station is on the northern end of Cesta Svobode near the Jelovica hotel. There are two train stations. The station called Lesce-Bled is four km south-east on the road to Radovljica. It is on the line linking Ljubljana with Jesenice and Austria. Bled Jezero, on Kolodvorska cesta west of the lake and the Zaka rowing centre, is good for Jesenice to the north and Nova Gorica and Italy to the south-west.

Information

Tourist Office Bled's tourist office (☎ 741 122) is below the *Park* hotel at Cesta Svobode 15. Essentially it is a souvenir shop with information, maps and guides. They also handle currency exchange and sell fishing licenses for the lake. Ask for the helpful (and free) English-language publication *Bled Tourist News*. The office is open from 8 am to 6 pm from Monday to Saturday and from 10 am to 4 pm on Sunday.

Another important office to visit if you are headed for *the* mountain is the Triglav National Park information centre (☎ 741 188) at Kidričeva cesta 2 on the lake's northern shore. It is open from 8 am to 3 pm on weekdays only. The staff provide information about the park and climbing Mt Triglav, and can arrange guides.

Money Gorenjska Banka in the Park hotel shopping complex on Cesta Svobode is open from 8 am to 6 pm on weekdays and till noon on Saturday. SKB Banka has a branch in the shopping centre. It is open from 8.30 am till noon and from 2 to 5 pm weekdays only. There are other private exchange bureaus nearby.

Post & Telecommunications The main post office, open weekdays from 7 am to 7 pm and on Saturday till noon, is at Ljubljanska cesta 10. The long-distance call boxes have electronic metres telling you exactly how much you're spending as you talk.

Bled's telephone code is 064. The postcode is 64260.

Travel Agency Kompas (☎ 741 515) has an office in the shopping centre at Ljubljanska cesta 4. Emona Globtour (☎ 741 821) is in the western wing of the Krim hotel at Ljubljanska cesta 7. It is open Monday to Saturday from 8 am to 7 pm and on Sunday from 8 am till noon and 5 to 7 pm.

Bled Castle

Perched on a steep cliff more than 100 metres above the lake, Bled Castle (Blejski Grad) is how most people imagine all medieval forts to be, with towers, ramparts, moats and a terrace offering magnificent views on a clear day. The castle, which is built on two levels, dates back to the 11th century (though most of what stands here now is from the 16th century) and was the seat of the Bishops of Brixen, who seemed to have redecorated regularly, for 800 years.

The Baroque southern wing to the south houses a **museum** that traces the history of Lake Bled and its settlements from the Bronze Age to the middle of the 19th century. None of the furniture is original to the castle, but it helps give you an idea of how the leisured class actually lived in the Middle Ages.

There's a large collection of armour and weapons (swords, halberds and firearms from the 16th to 18th centuries), jewellery found at the early Slav burial pits south-west of the castle at Pristava and a few interesting carvings, including a 16th century one of the overworked St Florian, dowsing yet another conflagration. The small 16th century **chapel**, strewn with coins and paper money left by favour-seekers, contains a painting of Henry II and his wife Kunigunda above the altar.

Admission to the castle costs 300 SIT for adults and 100 SIT for children unless you're eating at the Blejski Grad restaurant, in which case you put down a 500 SIT deposit against your meal and get in for 'free'. The castle is open daily from 8 am to 7 pm, except in December and January when it opens at 9 am and closes at 4 pm.

You can reach the castle via two trails: from behind the hostel or from just north of the neo-Gothic **Parish Church of St Martin** on Riklijeva cesta. St Martin's Church (1904) was designed by Heinrich von Ferster who also designed the city hall and Votive Church in Vienna. The frescoes illustrating the Lord's Prayer were painted by Slavko Pengov in the late 1930s. Outside there's a small shrine designed by Jože Plečnik and the remains of defence walls built to subdue the Turks in the 15th century.

Bled Island

Tiny, tear-shaped Blejski Otok, the only true island in Slovenia, has been the site of a Christian church since the 9th century. But excavations have shown that the early Slavs worshipped at a pagan temple here at least a century before that.

Getting to the island is half the fun. The easiest way is to climb aboard one of the hand-propelled gondola *(pletna)* which are docked in front of the casino, to the east of the Castle Baths complex or in Mlino. The return fare is 800 SIT, and you get about half an hour to explore the island; all told the trip takes about 1½ hours. Alternatively, you can rent a boat from the Castle Baths pool complex (see the Activities section) or even swim to the island. But if you choose the latter you're going to have to drag some clothes along in a plastic bag. The powers-that-be will not let you into the island church in your swimming gear.

The boat lets you off on the island's south side at a dilapidated stairway built in 1655; as you walk up you pass the **Chaplain's House** and the **Provost's House** from the 17th and 18th centuries, with the Bishops of Brixen's coat of arms on the facades. Both houses are now restaurants.

The Baroque church contains some fresco fragments from the 14th century, a large gold altar and, under the floor of the nave, part of the apse of the **pre-Romanesque chapel**, the only one in Slovenia. Models in the porch illustrate the development of the site from an 8th century wattle-and-daub structure to the 17th century church standing here today. Outside is a 16th century **belfry** with a 'bell of wishes' that visitors can ring if they want to ask a favour. Naturally everyone and their grandmother does it – again and again and again. The church is open daily from 8 am to 8 pm.

Lake Walk

Lake Bled is not a large body of water – it measures only two km by 1100 metres – and the second-best way to see it is from the shore. A walk around the lake (six km) shouldn't take much longer than two hours at most and it is at its best in the early morning. Along the way, you'll pass willow trees hanging into the water, boat slips, wooden walkways, innumerable anglers, the beginnings of several hikes and a couple of interesting sights. Start at the Park hotel and walk clockwise.

In Mlino, the **Svetina Gallery** at Cesta Svobode 39 exhibits the sculptures of Tone Svetina. They're curious things really, made out of bits of old weapons, shrapnel and scrap metal and, like his popular *Boy's Own*-style historical novels, all express antiwar sentiments. You might catch the old man at work in his studio nearby at Mlinska cesta 10.

Around the bend and past the camp site is the **Zaka rowing centre**, from where an annual regatta is staged in June. The bronze statue of the *Boatman* by Boris Kalin is attractive but does little to obscure the dreadful staging built for an international rowing championship in 1989. The construction is *very* unpopular in these parts. The **Triglav National Park** (TNP) office at Kidričeva cesta 2 has a small nature exhibit concerned with mountain ecology and explains what you might encounter in the park. (It's unlikely you'll spot Zlatorog, the fearsome and immortal 'golden horned' chamois which guards the treasure of Mt Triglav.) The Castle Baths are a bit farther on.

An alternative to circling the lake on foot is to take a horse-drawn carriage *(fijaker)* from the stand (☎ 741 121) in front of the Festival Hall on Cesta Svobode. A twirl around the lake for four people costs 2500 SIT, and it's the same price for two people up to the castle. You can even get a carriage for four to and from Bohinj (15,000 SIT), Kropa (10,000 SIT), Radovljica (5500 SIT) and Vintgar (5000 SIT).

Activities

Swimming & Boating Bled's warm water (23° C) makes it suitable for swimming well into the autumn, and there are decent beaches around the lake including a gravel one near the camp site and a grass lido to the east of the TNP office. Just beyond the latter is the large Castle Baths (Grajsko Kopališče) complex with an indoor pool and protected enclosures in the lake itself where you can splash around among the lily pads. Entry is 250 SIT for adults and 100 SIT for children, with cabins costing 200 SIT. The baths are open from mid-April to October from 8 am to 8 pm.

This is also the place to rent boats for rowing on the lake or getting to the island (motorboats are banned here). Boats accommodating three people cost 500 SIT per hour, 1500 SIT for a half day and 2500 SIT for a full day. Paddle boats are 300 SIT for three hours' use.

Three hotels in Bled have indoor pools filled with thermal water and saunas too: the Grand Toplice, the Park and the Golf (opposite the shopping centre at Cankarjeva ulica 6). The pool in the basement of the Grand Toplice hotel costs 800 SIT to use. They also have boats for hire in the lake costing 600 SIT per hour.

Horse Riding The Villa Viktorija guesthouse has horses available for 1000 SIT per hour, a wonderful way to climb up Straža Hill or tour the lake. The stables are open from 10 am till noon and from 2 to 7 pm daily.

Tennis There are four tennis courts at the Zaka rowing centre at the western end of the lake.

Golf The Bled Golf & Country Club's 18-hole, 73-par course (☎ 718 230) is about three km to the east of the lake near Lesce. The club is open daily from April to October from 8 am to 7 pm. The green fees for a round are DM60, a half set of clubs costs DM15 and a hand cart is DM6 to rent. There's also a driving range (DM4 for 36 balls) and a pro who gives lessons for DM35 per hour.

Flying The Alpine Flying Centre (Alpski Letalski Center) (☎ 733 431) at Begunjska

cesta 10 in Lesce has panoramic flights over Bled, Bohinj and even Triglav, and in winter you can go 'para-skiing' in which you are dropped by parachute over a precipitous snow-bound slope – with skis!

Ice Skating The lake usually freezes in winter but if you're in Bled during a warm spell between October and March and feel like cutting up the ice, visit the ice skating rink *(drsališče)* at Ljubljanska cesta 5 in the park behind the Krim hotel.

Skiing The closest 'real' ski resort to Bled is Zatrnik (☎ 725 064), on the slopes of the Pokljuka Plateau eight km west of Bled, with skiing up to 1250 metres, a chair lift and four T-bars. But beginners will be content with the mini-ski centre at Straža (☎ 741 133) south of the Grand Toplice hotel. A chair lift takes you to the top of the 642-metre hill in three minutes; you'll be down the short slope in no time.

Steam Train Slovenijaturist's Oldtimer Train has several excursions throughout most of the year that either originate in Bled or pass through the resort. Others leave from Jesenice, 10 km to the north-west.

Festivals
A number of special events take place during the summer in Bled, including the International Rowing Regatta in early June, the Idriart Festival of Culture in late July, the Wake of Endurance swimming marathon and, in August, a touristy Farmers' Wedding Feast and the Okarina Festival of Slovenian Ethnic Music. The biggest event, though, is Bled Night on the third Sunday in July when there are fireworks and the entire lake is illuminated with candlelight.

Places to Stay
Befitting a resort of such popularity (and value to the national economy), Bled has a wide range of accommodation – from Slovenia's first hostel to a five-star hotel in a villa that was once the summer retreat of Josip Tito. The lake and surrounding areas

count some 4000 beds, more than 5% of the total available in Slovenia.

Camping *Zaka* (☎ 741 117) is a six-hectare camp site in a quiet valley at the western end of the lake, about 2.5 km from the bus station. The location is good and there's even a beach, tennis courts, a large restaurant and a supermarket, but Zaka fills up very quickly in summer. The camp site is open from April to mid-October and costs between DM8.50 and DM12.

Šobec (☎ 718 104), the largest camping ground in Slovenia, is in Lesce. See Places to Stay in the Radovljica section for details. It is strictly forbidden to camp elsewhere on the lake and the law is enforced.

Private Rooms Kompas and Emona Globtour have thousands of private rooms and apartments on their books. In the low season, the price per person for a room without breakfast ranges from DM13 to DM22, depending on the category. In summer, expect to pay between DM15 and DM24. Apartments for two start at about DM45. You'll have to pay 30% more if you stay in a private room or apartment for less than three days.

If you want to do your own investigating and strike a private deal, there are lots of houses with *sobe* (rooms available) signs around Bled, particularly to the north-west in Rečica. It's not exactly in the centre of things but it's a quiet area.

Hostel The *Bledec hostel* (☎ 78 230), below the castle at Grajska cesta 17, has a total of 28 beds in four rooms and costs DM15 per person (or DM20 with breakfast). Run by an amiable couple from Štajerska who are a fount of information about Bled and its surroundings, the hostel is open year-round except in October and November. Reception is open from 9 am to 9 pm and you'll be given a key to the front door if you expect to return late. Bledec is the place to have your laundry done if you're running low; a machine load washed and dried should only cost about 650 SIT.

Farmhouses Believe it or not, you can actually stay at a farm very close to Bled. It may not exactly be a Štajerska-style spread, but it will be a working farm nonetheless. Selo, a village 1.5 km south of Mlino, has several farmhouses with accommodation, and two of them have won national awards in recent years: *Povšin* (☎ 77 334) at Selo 22 with eight rooms and *Pavovc* (☎ 77 346) with six rooms at No 27. Prices range from about DM20 to DM27 per person, depending on the season and room category.

Pensions The attractive 11-room *Villa Viktorija* (☎ 77 344) below Straža Hill at Cesta Svobode 27a charges DM30 per person. The *Mlino* (☎ 741 404) in the next village at Cesta Svobode 45, better known for its restaurant than its accommodation, has 15 rooms. It is more expensive than the Viktorija, with singles (including shower and breakfast) costing DM41 to DM65 and doubles DM52 to DM100.

Hotels Not surprisingly, the cheapest hotels in Bled are a bit away from the water and on noisy streets. The *Lovec* (☎ 741 500), Ljubljanska cesta 6, has 138 beds in both an interesting old building and an ugly modern extension. Singles with shower and breakfast are DM49 to DM76 while doubles are DM58 to DM112. About 150 metres farther along the same street at No 7, the sprawling *Krim* (☎ 77 418), with 218 beds, has almost exactly the same rates for doubles as the Lovec though the singles are about 10% cheaper for some reason. Close to the bus station and fronting a pretty park that overlooks the lake, the 146-room *Jelovica* (☎ 77 316) has singles for DM41 to DM76 and doubles for DM58 to DM120. This is probably the best choice of the three.

Bled's largest hotel, the 217-room *Park* (☎ 77 945; fax 741 505), is opposite the casino and the lake and about as central as you are going to get. Singles are DM70 to DM110 while doubles are DM100 to DM180. Reception is on the 1st floor at Cesta Svobode 15.

If you really want to splurge or you have

a rich uncle or aunt in tow, there are two choices – both of them on the lake. The 100-room *Grand Toplice* (☎ 647 910; fax 741 841), Cesta Svobode 12, is Bled's 'olde worlde' hotel, with attractive public areas, rather dark rooms and superb views of the lake from its northern side. The cheapest singles are DM80 to DM105, depending on the season, while doubles are DM120 to DM170. The hotel's two extensions opposite – the *Trst* at Cesta Svobode 19 and the more attractive *Jadran* on the hill at No 23 – are much cheaper.

The five-star *Villa Bled* (☎ 77 436; fax 741 320), where Tito and his foreign guests once put their feet up, is even more expensive: DM161 to DM212 for a single and DM204 to DM255 for a double. Villa Bled is surrounded by a large park and has its own private beach and boat dock. It is at Cesta Svobode 18, west of Mlino village, and has 31 rooms and suites.

Places to Eat
Oddly, Bled is blessed with a lot of restaurants – good and otherwise. For pizza and vegetarian food, head for the large garden café and pub called the *Pod Kostanji* at the Jelovica hotel.

The *Lang Hai* is a – come on, guess – Chinese restaurant at Ulica Narodnih Herojev 3 opposite the Krim hotel. The *hui guo rou* (twice-cooked pork) and *mapo doufu* (spicy beancurd) aren't exactly what you'd get in Chengdu but, hey, this *is* Slovenia. Soups average about 200 SIT and main courses run from 600 to 800 SIT. The Lang Hai is open daily till 11 pm.

There are a couple of gostišča in Mlino, the main village on the lake's southern shore: *Pletna* at Cesta Svobode 37 and *Mlino* at No 45. The latter has decent Slovenian dishes with an emphasis on fish and is open till 11 pm.

My favourite restaurant in Bled is the homely *Pri Planincu* at Grajska cesta 8 just down the hill from the hostel. Excellent mushroom soup and grilled chicken with chips and salad shouldn't cost much more than 1000 SIT. Pri Planincu is open daily

from 9 am to 11 pm. It's been here since 1903.

Bled's most up-market restaurant (and some say it is the best one in Slovenia) is the *Okarina* at Riklijeva ulica 9. It has a lovely back garden lit with torches, great decor inside and even stages special cultural events from time to time. A multifaceted experience overall. The Okarina is open daily from 11 am to 1 am.

Entertainment
Summertime concerts (most often on Monday afternoon and Friday evening) take place at the castle, the island church and the parish church. While the island is a far more romantic venue for Bach or Handel, don't miss a concert at St Martin's; it has one of the finest organs in Slovenia.

Several pubs have lovely terraces with great views, which are open in the warmer months. Two of the better ones are the *Park Café* above the casino on Cesta Svobode and the *Grand Toplice Café* at Cesta Svobode 12a. But nothing beats the *Belvedere Café* on top of a tall tower near the Villa Bled. It closes in winter though.

Bled Casino (☎ 741 811) is open every day of the week – from 7 pm Monday to Thursday and from 5 pm at the weekend – till late.

Getting There & Away
Bus Buses are very frequent to Radovljica (via Lesce) and there is at least one an hour to Begunje, Bohinj, Kranj, Krnica, Ljubljana and Podhom-Zasip. Other destinations served from Bled include Bovec via Kranjska Gora and the Vršič Pass (one bus a day in summer), Celje (one), Jesenice (five), Kranjska Gora (one or two), Pokljuka (one or two), Piran (one a day in summer) and Rogaška Slatina (one). Two buses a day head for Zagreb in Croatia.

Train Lesce-Bled station gets up to 15 trains a day from Ljubljana (51 km; 55 minutes) via Škofja Loka, Kranj and Radovljica. They continue on to Jesenice (13 km; 15 minutes), where about half cross the border for Rosenbach (Podrožca) in Austria.

Up to six daily trains from Jesenice via Podhom pass through Bled Jezero station on their way to Bohinjska Bistrica (18 km; 20 minutes), Most na Soči and Nova Gorica (79 km; 1¾ hours). Two of these then head 40 km south-east to Sežana where you can change for Italy. This mountain railway is one of the most picturesque in Slovenia. If you are headed south-west to Nova Gorica, sit on the right-hand side of the train to see the valley of the emerald-green Soča River at its best.

Car Hertz Kompas rents cars from its office at Ljubljanska cesta 4. It is open weekdays from 7 am till noon and from 5 to 7 pm. It closes at 1 pm on Saturday.

Emona Globtour is affiliated with Budget and rents cars from its office at the Krim hotel.

Getting Around

You can order a local taxi on ☎ 741 118. Both Kompas and Globtour rent bicycles and mountain bikes. Prices are 300 SIT an hour, 600 SIT for half a day and 1000 SIT for a full day. Kompas has a bigger selection.

AROUND BLED

The area around Bled offers endless possibilities for excursions: the **Pokljuka Plateau** beneath Triglav to the west with a gorge some km long; the village of **Vrba**, where France Prešeren was born and site of the Romanesque-Gothic Church of St Mark with 14th century frescoes; **Begunje** with the ruins of Kamen Castle and the Church of St Peter, containing some of the most valuable medieval frescoes in Gorenjska done by Jernej of Loka. All of these destinations can be reached by well-marked trails that are outlined on the 1:25,000 scale map *Bled z Okolico (Bled with Surroundings)*.

Vintgar Gorge

One of the easiest and most satisfying day trips is to Vintgar Gorge, a mere 4.5 km north-east of Bled. A wooden footbridge built in 1893 hugs the rock wall for 1600 metres along the Radovna River, crisscrossing the raging torrent four times over rapids, waterfalls and pools before reaching **Šum Waterfall**. The entire walk is spectacular though it can get pretty wet and slippery. There are little snack bars at the beginning and end of the walkway and picnic tables at several locations along the way. Admission to the gorge costs 200 SIT for adults and 100 SIT for children, and it is open from mid-April to October from 8 am to 8 pm.

It's an easy walk to the gorge from Bled. Head north-west on Prešernova cesta then north on Partizanska cesta to Cesta v Vintgar. This will take you to Podhom, where signs show the way to the gorge entrance. To return, you can either retrace your steps or, from Šum Waterfall, walk over Hom Hill (834 metres) eastward to the ancient pilgrimage Church of St Catherine which retains some 15th century fortifications. From there it's due south through Zasip to Bled.

Those unable or unwilling to walk all the way can take the bus or the train (from Bled Jezero station) to Podhom. From there it's a 1.5-km walk westward to the main entrance. From late June to mid-September a special bus makes the run from Bled's bus station, stopping at the castle car park, to Vintgar two times in the morning and returns at about noon. One way is 120 SIT.

Climbing Mt Triglav from Pokljuka

The shortest – but hardly the most enjoyable – way to reach the summit of Mt Triglav is from Bled. But you must drive first to **Rudno Polje** (1345 metres) on the Pokljuka Plateau, 18 km south-west of the lake. From the Sport hotel a trail leads west below Mt Viševnik (2050 metres) to the Jezerce Valley, where it then turns south-west, zigzags over the Studor Saddle (1892 metres) and crosses the southern flank of Mt Tosc (2275 metres). Within three hours of setting out from Rudno Polje, you should be at the *Vodnikov Dom na Velem Polju* mountain hut (mobile ☎ 0609-615 621) at 1817 metres. It has 53 beds. The 62-bed *Dom Planika pod Triglavom* (mobile ☎ 0609-614 773), another hut at 2401 metres, is two hours' walk north-west from here. You can reach Triglav's summit in an hour from Dom Planika.

The very fit might attempt to do this trip in a day (Slovenian teenagers seem to manage), but most of us mortals stay at one of the huts overnight. For a more leisurely way of climbing 'Old Mr Three Heads', see the following section on Bohinj. You can also reach Triglav from the northern approaches described in the section on Triglav National Park at the end of this chapter.

BOHINJ

Bohinj, a larger and much less developed glacial lake 30 km to the south-west of Bled, is a wonderful antidote to Bled and one of my favourite spots in Slovenia. OK, so it doesn't have a romantic little island church or a castle looming high on a rocky cliff. But it does have Triglav itself visible from the lake when the weather clears and a wonderful naturalness that doesn't exist at Bled. Bohinj's handful of museums and historical churches will keep culture vultures busy during their visit, and for action types there are activities galore – from kayaking and mountain biking to scaling Triglav via one of the southern approaches.

Bohinj was densely settled during the Hallstatt period due to the large amounts of iron ore in the area, and a trade route linked the lake with the Soča Valley and the Adriatic Sea via a pass at Vrh Bače south-east of Bohinjska Bistrica. During the Middle Ages, when the area fell under the jurisdiction of the Bishops of Brixen at Bled, Bohinj was known for its markets and fairs held near the Church of St John the Baptist. Here people from the Friuli region around Trieste traded salt, wine and foodstuffs with Slovenian peasants for iron ore and livestock. As the population grew, herdsmen went higher into the Julian Alps in search of pasture while charcoal burners cleared the upper forests for timber to fuel the forges.

The iron industry continued to flourish here until the late 19th century when it was moved to Jesenice. But all was not lost for

Bohinj; a railway connecting the Sava Valley with Gorica and the coast opened in 1906, providing Bohinj with its first modern communications link.

There is no town called Bohinj; the name refers to the entire valley, its settlements and the lake. The largest town in the area is **Bohinjska Bistrica** (pop 3080), six km to the east of the lake. Other settlements on or near the southern and eastern shores include **Ribčev Laz**, **Ukanc** and the rustic villages of **Stara Fužina**, at the mouth of the Mostnica Gorge, and **Studor**, a veritable 'village of hayracks'. There are no towns on the northern side.

Triglav was 'conquered' from Bohinj for the first time in the late 18th century. Bohinj has also figured prominently in Slovenian literary history. The poet Valentin Vodnik (1758-1819) lived and worked in nearby Gorjuše and even left his name in pencil on the back of the high altar at St John the Baptist's Church. And most of the events in France Prešeren's epic poem *Baptism at the Savica Waterfall* take place around Bohinj. For those reasons Bohinj enjoys a much more special place than Bled in the hearts and minds of many Slovenes.

Orientation

Lake Bohinj, some 4.5 km long and up to 45 metres deep, lies in a valley basin 523 metres above sea level on the southern edge of Triglav National Park. The Savica River flows into the lake to the west while the Sava Bohinjka flows out from the south-eastern corner.

You'll find most everything of a practical nature in Ribčev Laz – more specifically in the shopping complex behind the Jezero hotel.

In Ribčev Laz, buses stop near the tourist office, and in Bohinjska Bistrica on Triglavska cesta near the post office and at the train station. Bohinjska Bistrica's train station is about 700 metres north-east of the town centre at Triglavska cesta 1.

Information

Tourist Office The helpful and very efficient

tourist office (☎ 723 370) at Ribčev Laz 48 is open daily from July to mid-September from 7 am to 9 pm. During the rest of the year it is open from Monday to Saturday from 8 am to 7 pm and Sunday from 8 am to 3 pm.

Money The tourist office can change money but the rate is not good and they take a high commission. The post offices in Ribčev Laz and Bohinjska Bistrica give a better rate. Gorenjska Banka has a branch in Bohinjska Bistrica at Trg Svobode 2b, about 100 metres east of Slovenijaturist. It is open weekdays from 8 am to 6 pm and on Saturday till noon.

Post & Telecommunications The post office at Ribčev Laz 47 is open Monday to Friday from 8 am to 6 pm with a couple of half-hour breaks and on Saturday till noon. Bohinjska Bistrica's post office, just east of Slovenijaturist at Triglavska cesta 35, is open weekdays from 8 am to 6 pm and on Saturday till noon.

The telephone code for the Bohinj area is 064. The postcode is 64265.

Travel Agency The main office of the Alpinum travel agency (☎ 723 441), which can organise any number of sport activities in Bohinj, is a couple of doors down from the tourist office at Ribčev Laz 50. They have an equipment-rental kiosk called Alpinsport (☎ 723 486) at house No 53 to the right just before you cross the stone bridge to St John the Baptist's Church from Ribčev Laz. Slovenijaturist (☎ 721 032) has a branch in Bohinjska Bistrica at Triglavska cesta 45. It is open from Monday to Saturday from 8 am to 8 pm and on Sunday morning in summer. In winter, its weekday hours are 8 am till noon and 2 to 7 pm. It also opens on Sunday morning till noon.

Churches & Museums
The **Church of St John the Baptist**, on the northern side of the Sava Bohinjka across the stone bridge from the Jezero hotel in Ribčev Laz, is what every medieval church should be: small, on a lake and full of exquisite frescoes. To my mind, it is the most beautiful and evocative church in all of Slovenia, with the possible exception of the Church of the Holy Trinity at Hrastovlje in Primorska. If the church is locked, ask the tourist office for the key. You are welcome to visit on your own but do *not* touch anything!

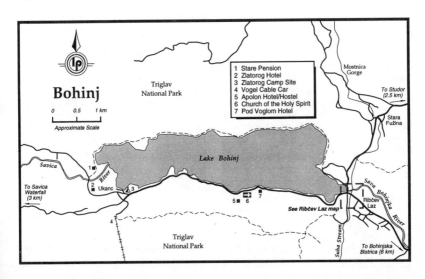

The nave is Romanesque while the Gothic presbytery dates from about 1440. A large portion of the latter's walls, ceilings and arches are covered with 15th and 16th century paintings too numerous to appreciate in one viewing. As you face the arch from the nave, look for the frescoes depicting the beheading of the patron saint on either side. On the other side of the arch to the right is a picture of Cain making his inferior offering to God (who is refusing it). Upon the shoulder of history's first murderer sits a white devil – a very rare symbol in Slovenia. Behind you on the lower walls of the presbytery are rows of angels with vampire-like teeth; look for the three men above them singing. Some of the men have goitres, once a common affliction in mountainous regions due to the lack of iodine in the diet. The carved wooden head of – guess who? – on one of the side altars dates from 1380.

Several paintings on the outside southern wall, one dating back to the year 1300, depict St Christopher. In the Middle Ages people believed they would not die on the day they had gazed upon an icon of the patron saint of travellers. No fools our ancestors, they painted them on churches near roads and villages, but apparently most folk forgot to look at least once as they're all now dead. The 18th century **Church of the Holy Spirit**, a couple of km to the west on the lake shore, has such a painting too.

The **Herders' Museum** at house No 181 in Stara Fužina, about 1.5 km north of Ribčev Laz, has a small but interesting collection related to Alpine dairy farming in the Bohinj Valley, once the most important such centre in Slovenia. Until the 1960s large quantities of cheese were still being made on 28 highland pastures, but now just one modern dairy in nearby Srednja Vas does all that.

The four rooms of the museum, a dairy itself once upon a time, contain a mock-up of a 19th century herder's cottage, fascinating old photographs, cheese presses, wooden butter moulds, copper rennet vats, enormous snowshoes and wonderful hand-carved crooks. It is open every day but Monday

from 10 am till noon and from 5 to 7 pm. Admission is 150 SIT.

While you're in Stara Fužina, take a walk over to the village of **Studor**, a couple of km to the east. Studor has an old peasant's house with a chimney-less 'black kitchen' turned into a museum at No 5, but its real claim to fame is its many *toplarji*, double-linked hayracks with barns or storage areas at the top. Look for the ones at the entrance to the village; some date from the 18th and 19th centuries.

The **Tomaž Godec Museum** over in Bohinjska Bistrica at Zoisova ulica 15 (about 100 metres south of Triglavska cesta) is a mixed bag of a place that does have its moments. Housed in a reconstructed tannery owned by Mr Godec, a Partisan who played a role in the formation of the Yugoslav Communist Party, the exhibits trace the history of iron-forging in the valley from earliest times, explain the long process of making leather (the small mill over the Bistrica River still turns) and examine the life of Comrade Godec.

Above the mill there is a small but fascinating collection called the **Small War Museum**, which deals graphically and often very poignantly with the horrors of the Isonzo Front in the Soča Valley during WW II. Josip Tito, who spent a few days here in 1939, returned 40 years later to open the museum. It's something the curator is very proud of. Along with weapons and bombs are many personal items from soldiers, including models of churches made from matchsticks by Russian prisoners of war and Italian helmets with holes punched into them for use as colanders when making pasta. It's really a peace museum and in many ways more moving and immediate than the much-publicised museum in Kobarid. It is open on Wednesday, Saturday and Sunday from 10 am till noon and from 4 to 6 pm. Admission is 200 SIT for adults and 100 SIT for children.

Savica Waterfall

Savica is one of the many reasons people come to Bohinj – to gaze at this magnificent

60-metre waterfall cutting deep into a gorge and perhaps carry on to the Triglav Lakes Valley or even Triglav itself.

Savica Waterfall, the source of Slovenia's longest and mightiest river, is four km from the Zlatorog hotel in Ukanc and can be reached by footpath from there along the northern side of the valley in about an hour. Cars go via a gravel road. From the Dom Savica restaurant, it's a 20-minute walk over rapids and streams to the falls. Entrance to the trail costs 200 SIT for adults and 100 SIT for children and it is open from 9 am to 5 pm.

The falls are among the most impressive sights in the Julian Alps, especially after a heavy rain, but bring something waterproof or expect to be soaked to the skin by the spray. Two huts to the west at about 1500 metres – *Dom na Komni* (☎ 721 475) and *Koča pod Bogatinom* (☎ 723 601), which served as a hospital during WW I – can be reached in about 2½ hours. Both have accommodation and food and are open most of the year.

Climbing Mt Triglav from Bohinj

That statue of four climbers – one of them pointing northward – may get you to thinking about higher ground: Mt Triglav, in fact. There are several ways to reach Triglav from Bohinj, though many prefer to use these paths to descend after scaling the mountain from the north or the east. They include routes from Savica Waterfall and Stara Fužina. One good route is to ascend by the former and return by the latter.

From the Savica Waterfall a path zigzags up the steep Komarča Crag. From the top of this cliff (1340 metres) there's an excellent view of Lake Bohinj. Farther north, three to four hours from the falls, is the *Koča pri Triglavskih Jezerih* (mobile ☎ 0609-615 235; 1685 metres), a 104-bed hut at the southern end of the fantastic Triglav Lakes Valley where you'll spend the night. If you want a good overview of the valley and its seven permanent lakes (the others fill up in spring only), you can climb to Mt Tičarica (2091 metres) to the north-east in about one hour. An alternative – though longer – route

from the waterfall to the Triglav Lakes Valley is via *Dom na Komni* and the Komna Plateau, a major WW I battlefield.

On the second day, you hike up the valley, which the immortal chamois Zlatorog is said to have created, past the largest glacial lakes then north-east to the desert-like Hribarice Plateau (2358 metres). You descend to the Dolič Saddle (2164 metres) where the *Tržaška Koča na Doliču* (mobile ☎ 0609-614 780; 2152 metres) has 60 beds. You would have walked about four hours by now from the Koča pri Triglavskih Jezerih and could well carry on to *Dom Planika pod Triglavom* (mobile ☎ 0609-614 773; 2401 metres), about 1½ hours to the north-east. But this 80-bed hut is often packed; it's better to stay where you're sure there's a bed.

From Dom Planika it's just over an hour to the summit of Triglav (2864 metres), a well-trodden path indeed. Don't be surprised if you find yourself being turned over to have your bottom beaten with a birch switch. It's a long-established tradition for Triglav 'virgins'.

You could return the way you came, but it's far more interesting to go back to Bohinj southward via Stara Fužina. This way passes the 50-bed *Vodnikov Dom na Velem Polju* (mobile ☎ 0609-615 621; 1817 metres) less than two hours from Dom Planika. There are two routes to choose from between Vodnikov Dom and Stara Fužina: down the Voje Valley or over Uskovnica, a highland pasture at about 1100 metres. The former takes about four hours; the route via Uskovnica is a little longer but affords better views. The trail to Rudno Polje and the road to Bled branch off from the Uskovnica route (see Climbing Mt Triglav in the Around Bled section).

If you decide to do the trip in reverse – starting from Stara Fužina and returning via Savica Waterfall – count on walking about seven hours to Dom Planika through the Voje Valley and eight hours via Uskovnica.

Other Activities

Hiking It's not all just Triglav at Bohinj. A circular walk around the lake (12 km) from

Ribčev Laz should take between three and four hours. Or you could just do parts of it by following the hunters' trail in the forest above the south shore of the lake to the Zlatorog hotel and taking the bus back, or go along the more tranquil northern shore under the cliffs of Pršivec (1761 metres). Much more difficult is the hike to Mt Vogel (1922 metres) from the cable car's upper station. Be very careful of the fog in these parts and don't set out if it looks like rain; Vogel is especially prone to lightning strikes. The whole trip should take about four hours.

The Bohinj area map available at the tourist office lists some 10 excellent walks and hikes. The Alpinum agency can arrange guides and excursions. It has a mountaineering school based at the Pod Voglom hotel where punters practise on artificial climbing walls. You can also take guided climbs ranging in grades from III to X. Serious stuff indeed.

Swimming & Boating Some of the beaches on Lake Bohinj's northern shore are reserved for nude bathing in summer. Several hotels have their own indoor swimming pools (should the fog drive you inside), including

Old Mr Three Heads
The 2864-metre-high limestone mountain Triglav has been a source of inspiration and devotion for Slovenes for more than a millennium. The early Slavs believed the mountain to be the home of a three-headed deity who ruled the sky, the earth and the underworld, but no one managed (or dared) to reach the summit until just two centuries ago. Today Triglav figures prominently on the national flag and seal.

As the statue of four men at Ribčev Laz constantly reminds visitors, Triglav's summit was first reached from Lake Bohinj by an Austrian climber and his three Slovenian associates in 1778 on the initiative of Žiga Zois (1747-1819), an iron magnate and patron of the arts. Under the Habsburgs in the 19th century, the 'pilgrimage' to Triglav became, in effect, a confirmation of Slovenian identity, and this tradition continues to this day. It's rare to meet a young Slovene who hasn't done the trek and even presidents and their ministers are known to do it together, as I discovered one warm Saturday in mid-September.

You too can do the hike to the summit, even if you have no experience in this sort of thing. But first a few words of advice and caution. Do some physical exercise for a few days before setting out – bicycling, walking, or swimming – and don't ignore some mental preparation; that's usually more than half the battle.

Triglav is inaccessible from late October to early June. June and July are the rainiest (and sometimes snowiest) summer months so August, and particularly September and early October, are the best times to go. Weather can be very unpredictable at altitudes above 1500 metres, with temperatures varying by as much as 20° C and violent storms appearing out of nowhere.

Under *no* circumstances should you make the trek by yourself. If you are travelling alone, hire a guide (roughly 1500 to 2000 SIT a day) through the Triglav National Park office in Bled or through a travel agency in Bohinj, or join a group that is setting out. Do the GRS (Gorska Reševalna Služba) volunteer rescue teams a favour; they have had to save dozens of people each year who the Bellevue and the Zlatorog. Outsiders can use the latter seven days a week between 3 pm and 8 pm and on Saturday and Sunday morning from 9 am till noon. Admission is 600 SIT; for 300 SIT more you get to use the sauna.

Alpinum rents kayaks and canoes for DM5 an hour or DM25 a day. As at Bled, no motorboats of any kind are allowed on the lake.

The Pod Voglom hotel organises a number of sporting activities, including rafting trips on the Sava Bohinjka River daily at 10 am and 2 pm and 'canyoning' through the rapids of the Mostnica Gorge safely stuffed into a neoprene suit, life jacket and helmet for DM70.

Fishing Lake Bohinj and the jade-coloured Sava Bohinjka are rich in various kinds of trout and grayling, and are among the most popular places for angling in Slovenia. But don't expect licenses to come cheaply: you'll pay DM50 a day for the lake and DM80 for the river as far as Soteska. The season on the lake extends from March to September depending on the type of fish, while on the river it's May to October. The tourist office

went on their own, ignored the trail markings and weather warnings, or tried to so something beyond their experience. Keep to the track marked with red-and-white circles and rest frequently. Remember that people die every year on Triglav simply because they did not follow these basic rules.

What to bring depends on personal preference but you want to travel absolutely as light as possible. Leave most of your kit down below, but wear sturdy hiking boots and warm, waterproof clothing. You might also consider carrying a compass and a torch (flashlight). Food, except for snacks like nutbars, is unnecessary as the mountain huts are well supplied. You should bring some water, but tea and other hot drinks are better for thirst.

There are some 52 mountain huts in the Julian Alps, most of them open between June and September. Others may extend their season a month in either direction and many huts at lower altitudes are open all year. Huts are never more than five hours apart. A mountain hut (*planinska koča* or *planinski dom*) almost always has accommodation (usually costing between 1000 and 1500 SIT) and food, with hearty dishes like *enoloncnica* (hotpot), *Segedin golaž* (goulash) and *ješprenj* (barley gruel). You'll never be turned away if the weather looks bad, but some huts on Triglav can be unbearably crowded at weekends, especially in August and September. Try to do the trek mid-week and phone the hut ahead if it has a mobile telephone, which is the case with about 20 of the huts. Some huts take bookings.

There are about 20 different ways to reach the top of Triglav, with the main approaches being from the south (Bohinj, Pokljuka) and the north (Vrata, Kot). All the routes offer varying degrees of difficulty and have their pluses and minuses. Experienced hikers tend to go for the more forbidding northern approaches, descending via one of the gentle southern routes. Novices usually ascend and descend near Bohinj. The route from Trenta in the Soča Valley is steep, but not impossible, and is less travelled due to its relatively remote start. Most treks require two overnight stops in the mountains.

Before you begin, arm yourself with a copy of *How to Climb Triglav*, a superb booklet with a dozen of the best routes and published by the Alpine Association of Slovenia (Planinska Zveza Slovenije). This 65-page publication, available everywhere for about 650 SIT, also has a useful illustrated section on Triglav's remarkable flora. It sure beats lugging around the 332-page pictorial *Flowers of Slovenia*! The much slimmer (and older) *An Alpine Guide* also includes Triglav trips among its other hikes.

Several maps to the area are available. Freytag and Berndt's 1:50,000-scale *Julische Alpen Wanderkarte* covers the whole of Triglav National Park. The Alpine Association publishes a two-sheet 1:50,000-scale map of the Julian Alps; for Triglav and the park you need the eastern part (*Julijske Alpe – Vzhodni Del*). They also publish some more detailed maps (1:20,000 scale), including *Julijske Alpe – Triglav* and *Julijske Alpe – Bohinj*. ∎

and Alpinum travel agency in Ribčev Laz sell the permits.

Tennis The tennis courts at the Kompas, Bellevue and Zlatorog hotels cost between DM6 and DM10 per hour to hire. Two rackets and balls are about DM5.

Skiing The main skiing station for Bohinj is Vogel (☎ 723 466), some 1540 metres above the lake's south-western corner and accessible by cable car. With skiing up to 1800 metres, the season can be long: sometimes from late November to early May. Vogel counts 36 km of ski slopes and cross-country runs served by three chair lifts and five T-bar tows. A daily ski pass costs about 2400 SIT, equipment costs about DM20 a day and there is accommodation near the cable car's upper station at the 63-bed *Ski Hotel* (☎ 721 471; fax 723 446), with singles in winter at DM49 and doubles DM78.

The cable car's lower station is about 250 metres up the hill opposite the Zlatorog hotel in Ukanc, about five km from Ribčev Laz. The cable car runs every half-hour year-round, except in November, from 7.30 am to 6 pm (till 8 pm in July and August). Adults pay 800 SIT for a return ticket while children pay 550 SIT.

The smaller and lower ski centre of Kobla (☎ 721 058) is about one km east of Bohinjska Bistrica. It has 23 km of slopes and 10 km of cross-country runs with three chair lifts and three T-bars. The Cross-Country Skiing World Cup is held between Bohinjska Bistrica and Lake Bohinj every year in mid-Decmber.

Steam Train The Oldtimer Train run by Slovenijaturist has several excursions between February and October that pass through Bohinjska Bistrica to or from Jesenice and Nova Gorica. For details about itineraries, schedules and prices, contact Slovenijaturist at Triglavska cesta 45 in Bohinjska Bistrica.

Festivals
The Kravji Bal (Cows' Ball) is a wacky event

staged every year on the second or third weekend in September in a field north of the Zlatorog hotel. Although it traditionally marked the return of the cows to the valley after a spring and summer on highland pastures of between up to 1700 metres, the ball has now degenerated into a day-long knees-up of folk dancing and music, eating and drinking and haggling over baskets, painted beehive panels and bowls carved from tree roots. Of course, if you want to say you've seen cows dance, then by all means, do go. Entry costs 300 SIT and the event attracts people from all over Slovenia and many parts of Slovene-speaking Italy and Austria.

On Midsummer's Night (23 June), everyone goes out on the lake in boats with candles and there are fireworks.

Places to Stay
Camping Bohinj has two camp sites. The large *Zlatorog* camp site (☎ 723 482) on the lake near the Zlatorog hotel is expensive, ranging from DM7 to DM14 depending on the season, but it's one of the best situated grounds in Europe. It's open from mid-May to September and you can use the Zlatorog Hotel's tennis courts.

The three-hectare *Danica* site (☎ 723 370) some 200 metres west of the bus stop in Bohinjska Bistrica is open from June to September and costs DM7.5 to DM10. It has its own tennis courts.

Private Rooms The tourist office can arrange private rooms in Ribčev Laz, Stara Fužina and neighbouring villages for as little as DM11 per person per night in the low season and up to DM18 in July and August (though there are 20% surcharges for stays of less than three days and for guests on their own). Breakfast usually costs about DM6 more, though you are sometimes allowed to use the kitchen yourself. One of the best places to stay is at the *Ardjelan* house (☎ 723 262), at Ribčev Laz 13.

Apartments for two people arranged through the tourist office run from DM40 to DM51, depending on the season. The Alpinum travel agency has some rooms and apartments but they are more expensive. Slovenijaturist in Bohinjska Bistrica also has apartments.

Hostel The *Apolon* hotel (☎ 723 469), about two km west of Ribčev Laz on the lake's southern shore at Ribčev Laz 63, doubles as a hostel all year except most of April and November. A bed in a room for two or three (many with their own showers) costs DM22 including breakfast.

Pensions & Farmhouses *Stare Penzion* (☎ 723 403) with nine rooms on the Savica River north of the Zlatorog hotel at Ukanc 128 has doubles with shower and breakfast for DM32 to DM36, depending on the season. If you really want to get away from it all without having to climb mountains, this is the place.

Several farmhouses in the area offer accommodation, including the four-room *Agotnik* (☎ 723 014) at house No 145 in Stara Fužina and *Pri Andreju* (☎ 723 509) with two rooms at house No 31 in picturesque Studor.

Hotels Bohinj has no shortage of hotels but the cheapest, the 49-room *Pod Voglom* (☎ 723 461) on the lake's southern shore at Ribčev Laz 60, is not very nice. It has singles with shared showers starting at DM27 and DM44 and doubles from DM48 to DM86, depending on the season.

In Ribčev Laz proper, you have a choice of three hotels. The 50-room *Jezero* (☎ 723 375; fax 723 376), used by the Gestapo during WW II, is the most central – a few steps from the tourist office and the lake at house No 51. Singles with shower and breakfast start at DM59 and DM69, depending on the season, while the cheapest doubles are DM78 or DM98. The 59-room *Bellevue* (☎ 723 331; fax 723 446), on a hill about 800 metres south of the Jezero at Ribčev Laz 65, has 115 beds and charges a minimum of DM30 to DM48 for singles and DM40 to DM76 for doubles. The 58-room *Kompas* (☎ 723 471; fax 723 161), off the road to Bohinjska Bistrica east of the post office, has

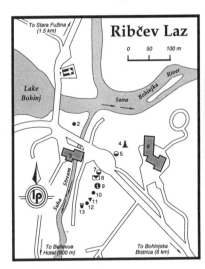

Ribčev Laz

1	Church of St John the Baptist
2	Alpinsport Kiosk
3	Jezero Hotel
4	Triglav Pioneers Statue
5	Bus Stop
6	Kompas Hotel
7	Bus Stop
8	Post Office
9	Tourist Office
10	Savica Supermarket
11	Pizzeria
12	Alpinum Travel Agency
13	Club Amor Disco

singles starting at DM44 and DM70, depending on the season, and doubles from DM58 and DM110.

Out of the way and pleasant because of it is the 43-room *Zlatorog* (☎ 723 381; fax 723 384), a hotel in Ukanc at house No 64 with lots of activities. Singles start at DM52 and DM58, while doubles are DM64 to DM76.

Places to Eat

The *pizzeria* next to the Alpinum travel agency at house No 50 in Ribčev Laz is one of the most popular places for the youth of Bohinj and a good place to eat and hang out.

If you've got wheels of any sort, head for *Gostilna Rupa* at house No 89 in Srednja Vas, about five km north-east of Ribčev Laz. It has some of the best home-cooked food in Slovenia including spectacular Bohinj trout and *ajdova krapi*, crescent-shaped dumplings made from buckwheat and cheese.

In Stara Fužina, the *Gostilna Mihovc* at house No 118 is a popular place which opens daily from 11 am till midnight. But if you want something light, head for *Planšar* opposite the Herders' Museum at house No 179. It specialises in home-made dairy products – hard Bohinj cheese, a strong-tasting soft cheese called *mohant*, curd pie, sour milk etc – and you can taste a number of them for about 400 SIT or make a meal of cheese and different types of grain dishes like žganci made from buckwheat, ješprenj from barley or močnik from white corn. Planšar is open Tuesday to Sunday from 10 am to 8 pm but only at weekends in winter. It's a taste sensation.

The *Zoisova Grad*, at Grajska ulica 14 in Bohinjska Bistrica about 200 metres east of the Tomaž Godec Museum, is a standard Slovenian restaurant in a rather dilapidated old manor house. It's open daily from 11 am till midnight. A place with pizza and cheap set menus nearby is the *Bistrica* at Trg Svobode 1.

There's a *supermarket* called Savica in Ribčev Laz open daily from 7.30 am to 7 pm.

Entertainment
The number one late-night venue around the lake these days is *Club Amor*, a disco next to the Alpinum travel agency.

Things to Buy
The traditional craft of Bohinj is a small, handcarved wooden pipe with a silver cover (gorjuška čedra) for tobacco or whatever. The real thing isn't so easy to find these days, but the tourist office will know which of the few remaining master carvers still sell their wares.

Getting There & Away
Bus Bus services to and from Ljubljana via

Bled, Radovljica, and Kranj are very frequent; count on up to a dozen departures a day. There are also three to five buses a day to Bohinjska Bistrica, one to Ljubljana via Trebovlje and one to Zagreb in Croatia. All of these buses stop near the post office on Triglavska cesta in Bohinjska Bistrica and in Ribčev Laz before carrying on to the Zlatorog hotel in Ukanc.

From the stops at the post office in Bohinjska Bistrica, buses also go to the lake via Bohinjska Češnjica, Srednja Vas, Studor and Stara Fužina up to seven times a day, to Jereka (up to five), and Gorjuše (up to three).

From mid-June to September a bus leaves Bled bus station every day at around 10 am for Savica Waterfall, returning at about 12.45 pm.

Train Lake Bohinj is not itself on a train line, though Bohinjska Bistrica is on the scenic line linking Jesenice (28 km; 35 minutes) and Bled Jezero to the north-west and Most na Soči and Nova Gorica (61 km; 75 minutes) to the south-east. Up to six trains a day pass through Bohinjska Bistrica in each direction. Two of the trains to Nova Gorica carry on another 40 km south-east to Sežana, from where you can board a train to Italy.

Car Alpinum in Ribčev Laz rents cars.

Getting Around
From the end of June to the middle of September, a bus runs between Bohinjska Bistrica and Savica Waterfall, stopping at Stara Fužina, the Bellevue hotel in Ribčev Laz, Pod Voglom and Zlatorog hotels and the Vogel cable-car station. From Monday to Saturday there are two trips in the morning and two in the afternoon. On Sunday, the schedule is reduced by one run in the afternoon.

Alpinum and the Kompas hotel rent bicycles and mountain bikes. The former charges DM5 an hour and DM25 a day.

KRANJSKA GORA (pop 2800)
The town of 'Carniolan Mountain', 40 km

north-west of Bled, is the largest and best-equipped ski resort in the country, but somehow it just doesn't seem Slovenian. The fact that the Italian *and* the Austrian borders are a half-dozen km to the west and north-west might help explain that impression. But there's a clinical feel here too – one that speaks with a Teutonic rather than Slavic accent.

Kranjska Gora (810 metres) is located in the Sava Dolinka Valley separating the Karavanke range from the Julian Alps. The valley has been an important commercial route between Gorenjska and Koroška for centuries; the 853-metre pass at Rateče is the lowest Alpine link between the Sava and Drava valleys. The first railway in Gorenjska – from Ljubljana to Tarvisio (Trbiž) in Italy – made use of this pass when it opened in 1870.

Kranjska Gora was just a small valley village (Barovška Vas) surrounded by mountains until the late 19th century, when skiing enthusiasts began to flock here. Planica, the cradle of ski-jumping south of Rateče, helped put the town on the world map earlier this century.

Kranjska Gora is at its best under a blanket of snow, but its surroundings are wonderful to explore in warmer months as well. The possibilities for hiking and mountaineering are endless in Triglav National Park on the town's southern outskirts, and there aren't many travellers who won't be impressed by a trip over the Vršič Pass (1611 metres), the gateway to the Soča Valley and the province of Primorska.

Orientation

Kranjska Gora sits at the foot of Mt Vitranc (1631 metres) and in the shadow of two higher peaks (Razor and Prisojnik/Prisank) that reach to 2600 metres. Rateče and Planica, famous for ski-jumping championships, are some six km to the west, while Jasna Lake, effectively Kranjska Gora's doorway to Triglav National Park, is two km south.

Kranjska Gora is a very small town with some unattractive modern buildings around its periphery and a more romantic older part along Borovška cesta. As you walk along this street, you might see tanners clipping and scraping sheepskins behind one of the ramshackle farmhouses. The chair lifts up to the ski slopes on Vitranc are at the western end of Borovška cesta.

The town's bus station (just a couple of bus stops really) is 150 metres south-west of the big TGC shopping centre at the main entrance to the town from the motorway.

Information

Tourist Office The tourist office (☎ 881 768) is at Tičarjeva cesta 2, a few steps east of the Prisank hotel. They have quite a few useful hand-outs on various activities and sell maps and guides to the surrounding areas (including Triglav National Park). The office is open Monday to Saturday from 8 am to 2 pm and from 3 to 7 pm.

Money Gorenjska Banka has a branch in the building behind the Gorenjka Ski School and south-west of the entrance to the Prisank hotel. It is open weekdays from 8 am to 6 pm and on Saturday till noon. You can also change money at the post office and at the Alpina Ski Centre at Borovška cesta 88a.

Post & Telecommunications Kranjska Gora's tiny post office is a few steps north of Emona Globtour at Koroška cesta 1; don't make long-distance calls from here if you need privacy though. It is open weekdays from 8 am to 7 pm and on Saturday till noon. During the high seasons (July and August and mid-December to mid-February), the hours on Saturday are extended to 7 pm.

Kranjska Gora's telephone code is 064. The postcode is 64280.

Travel Agency Most of the big agencies are represented in Krankska Gora, including Emona Globtour (☎ 881 055) on the corner of Koroška cesta and Borovška cesta and Kompas at Borovška cesta 98. Globtour is open Monday to Saturday from 8.30 am to 5 pm and on Sunday from 10 am to 3 pm. Kompas' hours are 7.30 am to 7 pm Monday

GORENJSKA

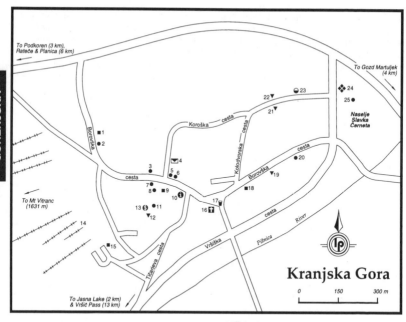

Kranjska Gora

0   150   300 m

PLACES TO STAY

1 Kompas Hotel
9 Prisank Hotel
15 Autocommerce Hotel
18 Kotnik Pension

PLACES TO EAT

12 Karavanke Bistro
19 Gostilna Borka
21 Maestro Pizzeria
22 Lipa Restaurant

OTHER

2 Kompas Travel Agency
3 Supermarket
4 Post Office
5 Emona Globtour Travel Agency
6 Alpina Ski Centre
7 Gorenjka Ski School
8 Horse-Drawn Carriage Stand
10 Tourist Office
11 Julijana Travel Agency
13 Gorenjska Banka
14 Ski Lifts
16 Church of the Assumption
17 Discoteca Club
20 Liznjek House
23 Bus Stops
24 TGC Shopping Centre
25 Delicatessen

to Saturday and from 8 am till noon on Sunday.

Things to See

Liznjek House One of the very few things to see in Kranjska Gora, this late 18th century house at Borovška cesta 63 contains quite a good collection of household objects and furnishings peculiar to this area of Gorenjska. But don't for a minute think that this 'folk Baroque' house was typical of the place and time; it belonged to an immensely rich landowner and was probably considered a palace in rural Slovenia 200 years ago. Among the various exhibits are some excellent examples of trousseau chests covered in folk paintings, several 19th century painted-glass icons and some linen tablecloths (the valley was famed for its flax and its weaving).

In the main room are two shuttered 'safes' for valuables; one was meant for the man of the house and one for the woman. The tiny fireplace was intended for light only. The chimney-less 'black kitchen' was used to smoke meats.

Antique carriages and a sledge are kept in the massive barn behind the house, which once held food stores as well as pigs and sheep. The 'stable' reserved for cows below the main building now contains a memorial room dedicated to the life and work of Josip Vandot (1884-1944), a writer born in Kranjska Gora who penned the saga of *Kekec*, the do-gooder shepherd boy who, together with his little playmate Mojca and trusty dog Volkec, battles the evil poacher and kidnapper Bedanec. It's still a favourite among Slovenian kids (and was a popular film), but he's a bit saccharine for my tastes. Kekec has become something of a symbol for Kranjska Gora, and there's a wooden statue of the little tyke outside the tourist office on Borovška cesta. Even the name of a monthly gay publication in Ljubljana bears the name *Kekec*.

Liznjek House is open Tuesday to Saturday from 10 am to 5 pm and on Sunday to 4 pm. Admission costs 150 SIT.

Church of the Assumption While the date on this Baroque-looking church in the nameless little square opposite Borovška cesta 78 says 1758, the net vaulting of the nave inside reveals its true age: the early 16th century. Most of the church is, in fact, late Gothic, and the belfry is even older.

Activities

Skiing The snow-covered slopes of the Sava Dolinka Valley, running for almost 11 km from Gozd Martuljek to Rateče and Planica,

are effectively one big ski piste. But the main ski centres are in Kranjska Gora and Podkoren, three km to the west, with ski-jumping concentrated at Planica. The season usually lasts from mid-December to early March, and there are snow cannons for making artificial snow on certain slopes.

Skiing in Kranjska Gora is on the eastern side of Vitranc, and some runs join up with those at Podkoren on Vitranc's northern face to an altitude of about 1600 metres. Kranjska Gora counts two chair lifts and nine tows; Podkoren, site of the Men's World Cup Slalom and Giant Slalom Competition (Vitranc Cup) in late December, has another two chair lifts and six tows. Generally, skiing is easier at Kranjska Gora than at Podkoren, where the two most difficult slopes – Ruteč and Zelenci – are located. In all, the two centres have 30 km of pistes and 40 km of cross-country courses.

The ski-jumping centre at Planica across the motorway from Rateče has six jumps with lengths of 25, 120 and 180 metres. The short lift near the Dom Planica hut reaches an altitude of 900 metres. There are also good possibilities at Planica for tobogganing and for cross-country skiing in the Tamar Valley. The Ski Jumping World Championships are held here every year in mid-March. The 100-metre mark was reached in 1936 and the 200-metre in 1994.

Ski passes for Kranjska Gora/Podkoren are DM30 a day for adults and DM21 for children, with a full seven days costing about DM180 and DM125 respectively. Needless to say, there are a lot of places offering ski tuition and rental equipment, but it's best to stick with the tried and true. Both Kompas and the Alpina Ski Centre (☎ 881 470), at Borovška cesta 88a next to the Razor hotel, have skis and other equipment for hire; a complete kit should cost about DM16 a day or DM96 a week. Alpina opens from 10 am to 1 pm and 2 to 6 pm on weekdays and on Saturday morning. For lessons, approach the Gorenjka Ski School (☎ 881 385) in the kiosk opposite the big supermarket on Borovška cesta. They do both Alpine and cross-country tuition in groups and on an individual basis. For one-on-one instruction, expect to pay about DM30 per hour.

Hiking The area around Kranjska Gora is excellent for hikes and walks ranging from easy to difficult. One of the best references available is *Walking in the Julian Alps* by Simon Brown and published by Cicerone Press in the UK. It also includes excursions from Bled and Bohinj in Gorenjska and Bovec in Primorska.

Between Podkoren and Planica is a beautiful area called **Zelenci** with a turquoise-coloured lake, the source of the Sava River. You can easily walk here on a path from Kranjska Gora via Podkoren and on to **Rateče** – both attractive Alpine villages with medieval churches, wooden houses and traditional hayracks – in about two hours. If you're still willing to carry on, there's a well-marked trail via *Planica to Dom v Tamarju* (☎ 876 055; 1108 metres) in the **Tamar Valley** six km to the south. The walk is spectacular, in the shadow of Mojstrovka (2366 metres) to the east and Jalovec (2645 metres) to the south. The Tamar hut is open every day and has a restaurant and accommodation for 70 people. From here, the Vršič Pass is less than three hours away on foot.

Another great walk from Kranjska Gora, and quite an easy one, takes you north and then east through meadows and pasture land to the traditional village of Srednji Vrh and **Gozd Martuljek** in a couple of hours. The views of the Velika Pisnica Valley and the Martuljek Mountains to the south are breathtaking. From Gozd Martuljek, it's only nine km east to Mojstrana, the starting point for the northern approaches to Triglav (see the Climbing Mt Triglav from Mojstrana section following).

Other Activities A couple of hotels in Kranjska Gora have indoor swimming pools and saunas, including the Larix, the Kompas and the Lek. You can hire one of several tennis courts at the Kompas hotel and Julijana (☎ 881 325), a small agency in a kiosk south-west of the Prisank hotel, rents racquets, balls and other sport equipment.

Horse-drawn carriages seating four people can be hired from the stand next to the Gorenjka Ski School office and the minigolf course on Borovška cesta. Prices are 800 SIT for a return trip to Jasna Lake return or 2500 SIT to Planica. Horses for riding are available at the Dom Porentov (☎ 881 436) just east of Kranjska Gora on the main road.

Fishing is possible in the Sava Dolinka and Jasna Lake but as always it's not for the budget-conscious. A total of three fish (the daily limit from the Sava) will cost you DM80. See Kompas if you want a fishing license for the river and the Gostišče Jasna for one for the lake.

Places to Stay

Camping The closest camping ground to Kranjska Gora is *Špik* (☎ 880 120) near the Špik hotel in Gozd Martuljek, some four km east of Kranjska Gora. The eight-hectare site is on the left bank of the Sava Dolinka below the peaks of the Martuljek range, and there's an outdoor swimming pool in the grounds. The overnight rate per person is DM9.

Private Rooms The tourist office has private rooms for between DM15 and DM30 depending on the category and the time of year. Its apartments for two people run between DM45 and DM60. If the office is closed or you want to check out the premises before you hand over your money, there are a lot of houses with rooms available (look for *sobe* or *Zimmer frei* signs) in the development called Naselje Slavka Černeta east of the TGC centre. The *Vidic* house (☎ 881 375) at No 19 and the small apartment at No 23 are especially good deals. There are also lots of private rooms and apartments available in Rateče.

Farmhouses If you feel like going rural, you will have to head out of Kranjska Gora in the direction of Rateče. On the Planica side of the road, the *Kvabišar* house (☎ 876 113) at Rateče 120 has three rooms. *Skubr*

(☎ 881 786), with four rooms, is at house No 78 in Podkoren. Both are open all year.

Hotels Kranjska Gora counts about a dozen hotels that are within easy walking distance of the ski lifts. Among the cheapest is the *Kotnik penzion* (☎ 881 564) with 20 double rooms costing from DM30 to DM35 per person, depending on the season. It's at Borovška cesta 75, in the centre of town.

The *Prisank* hotel (☎ 881 472; fax 881 359) has a total of 220 beds in two buildings at Borovška cesta 93 and 95. Singles range from DM40 to DM82, with doubles from DM62 to DM126. The nondescript *Autocommerce* hotel (☎ 881 584), with 27 rooms, is about as close to the lifts as you'll get. Singles are DM42 to DM45 and doubles are DM64 to DM70.

Singles at the 156-room *Kompas* (☎ 881 661; fax 881 176), Kranjska Gora's biggest and most expensive hotel, at Borovška cesta 100, start at DM58 and DM81, with doubles from DM76 to 134.

Places to Eat

One of the cheapest places for a quick meal in Kranjska Gora is the *Karavanke Bistro*, behind the Gorenjska Banka, with pizza, pasta and simple grills. More pizza is available at the *Lipa*, a lovely glassed-in café restaurant at Koroška cesta 14 open daily from 10 am to midnight, and at the *Maestro* opposite at No 16. The latter has 32 varieties of pizza and a good choice of fish dishes. The *Gostilna Borka* at Borovška cesta 71 has set menus (including roast suckling pig) for 800 SIT.

The restaurant at the *Kotnik*, one of Kranjska Gora's better eateries, with bits of painted dowry chests on the walls, serves a Shepherd's Snack (*Pastirjeva Malica*) of grilled meats for 950 SIT that should keep you going for awhile.

The huge *Emonamerkur* supermarket adjacent to the Prisank hotel on Borovška cesta is open Monday to Saturday from 7 am to 7 pm. There's a good *delicatessen* in the TGC shopping centre at Naselje Slavka Černeta 33.

Entertainment

The *Discoteca Club* just east of the Church of the Assumption on Borovška cesta is Kranjska Gora's most popular late-night venue. The *Hit Casino* (☎ 881 333), south of the town centre on the road to Jasna Lake, is open from 6 pm Monday to Friday and from 3 pm at the weekends.

Getting There & Away

Bus Buses depart frequently for Rateče-Planica via Podkoren and Jesenice and once an hour for Ljubljana via Mojstrana, Bled, Radovljica and Kranj. Other destinations include Villach (Beljak) in Austria (daily during the week), Tarvisio (Trbiž) in Italy (once a day except Sunday) and Zagreb in Croatia (two a day).

On Saturday and Sunday in June and in the second half of September and daily from July to mid-September, a bus from Ljubljana links Kranjska Gora with Bovec, 50 km to the south-west, via the Vršič Pass. Departure from Kranjska Gora is at 8.50 am, arriving in Bovec shortly after 11 am. It leaves Bovec at 3.45 pm and reaches Kranjska Gora two hours later before continuing on to Gozd Martuljek, Bled, Radovljica, Kranj and the capital

Car Globtour Budget rents cars from its branch at Koroška cesta 6.

Getting Around

Julijana, Alpina and Kompas rent bicycles. Kompas' rates are 250 SIT per hour, 600 SIT for half a day and 1000 SIT for a full day.

TRIGLAV NATIONAL PARK

Though there are some two dozen regional parks in Slovenia, this is the country's only gazetted national one, and it includes almost all of the Julian Alps lying in Slovenia. The centrepiece of the park is, of course, Mt Triglav but there are many other peaks here reaching beyond 2000 metres, as well as ravines, canyons, rivers, streams, forests and pastures. Triglav National Park (Triglavski Narodni Park) is especially rich in fauna and flora, including blossoms like pink Triglav

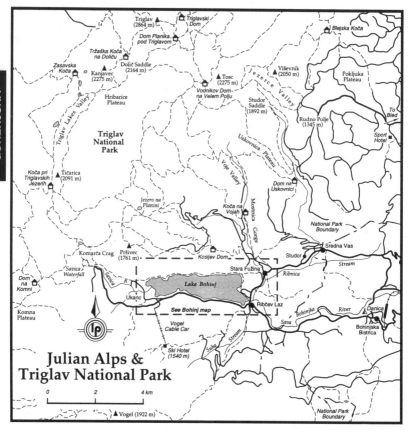

Julian Alps &
Triglav National Park

rose, blue gentian, yellow hawk's beard, Julian poppy and purple Zois bell flower.

The idea for a park was first mooted in 1908 and realised in 1924, when 14 hectares in the Triglav Lakes Valley were put under temporary protection. The area was renamed Triglav National Park in 1961 and expanded 20 years later to include most of the eastern Julian Alps. Today the park covers more than 84,800 hectares and stretches from Kranjska Gora in the north to Tolmin in the south, and from the Italian border on the west almost to Bled in the east. The bulk of the park lies in Gorenjska province, but once you've

crossed the awesome Vršič Pass and begun the descent into the Soča Valley, you've entered Primorska.

Excellent marked trails in the park lead to innumerable peaks and summits beside Triglav, and favourite climbs include those to **Mangart** (2678 metres) on the Italian border (the 12-km road that descends to the Predel Pass is the highest road in Slovenia) and the sharp ridges of **Razor** (2601 metres) and **Jalovec** (2645 metres) in the north. But the Triglav National Park isn't only about climbing mountains; there are easy hikes through beautiful valleys, forests and meadows too. Two excellent maps to consult are Freytag & Berndt's 1:50,000-scale *Julische Alpen Wanderkarte* and the Alpine Association of Slovenia's 1:50,000 *Triglavski Narodni Park*.

The park has a number of rules and regulations and most of the 'don'ts' are as obvious as Triglav on a clear day: no litter, no plucking flowers, no open fires etc. But also remember that this is a very fragile landscape and there is no camping, mountain bikes are banned from trails and the park tradition is to greet everyone you pass. That can get a bit tiresome after a while but a simple 'Dober dan' ('Hello') and/or a smile will suffice. You may notice that the roads running through the park aren't so great. The park commission refuses to upgrade them for fear that half of Europe will then descend on this little paradise.

For more information about Mt Triglav, also see Around Bled and the Bohinj section.

Climbing Mt Triglav from Mojstrana

Mojstrana, 13 km west of Kranjska Gora, is another gateway to Triglav, this time via one of the northern approaches. Without going into all the details, which can be gleaned from *How to Climb Triglav* or *An Alpine Guide*, the easiest route ascends through the **Kot Valley**, which is accessible by road three km south of Mojstrana. The road (and then trail) goes essentially due south past a meadow called Lengarjev Rovt, a spring and a big house called Pekel below Vrbanova Špica (2299 metres) before reaching the *Dom Valentina Staničev* (mobile ☎ 0609-614 772) at 2332 metres and it takes about five hours to reach. The hut has 78 beds. *Triglavski Dom na Kredarici* (mobile ☎ 0609-611 221), the main hut serving the northern routes, and at 2515 metres the highest accommodation in the land, is an hour away and the summit still another hour. While Triglavski Dom has 126 beds, it is often full; the best idea is to spend the night at Staničev Dom and make the ascent in the morning.

Side trips from Staničev Dom via marked and secure trails include Begunjski Vrh (2461 metres; 30 minutes' walk), Cmir (2393 metres; two hours), Vrbanova Špica (2299 metres; 1½ hours), and Rjavina (2557 metres; two hours).

A more difficult ascent is possible via the **Tominšek Trail** through the Vrata Valley, passing *Aljažev Dom v Vratih* (☎ 064-891 030), a 180-bed hut at 1015 metres. The hut can be reached by car from Mojstrana (11 km) but the gradient is very steep in parts. Walking should take about three hours, including a look at **Peričnik Waterfall**. You'll probably want to spend the night here as it is among the most beautiful sites in the park, with a perfect view of Triglav's north face. Nearby is a 10-metre boulder called Mali Triglav (Little Triglav) where you can practise your ascent of the Big One.

From Aljažev Dom, it's a 3½-hour walk via the north-west flank of Cmir and below Begunjski Vrh to a spring with excellent drinking water. From the spring you can choose whether to walk to Staničev Dom, 30 minutes to the south-west, or to Triglavski Dom, an hour to the south.

Kranjska Gora to Soča Valley

One of the most spectacular – and easy – trips in Triglav National Park is simply to follow the paved road open May to October from Kranjska Gora via the Vršič Pass to Bovec, about 50 km to the south-west and just outside the park. Between June and September, you can do the trip by bus. At other times, you'll have to have your own transport – be it a car or a mountain bike.

The first stop from Kranjska Gora is **Jasna Lake**, about two km south of town. It's a beautiful, almost too-blue glacial lake with white sand around its rim and the Pivnica River flowing alongside. A bronze statue of that irascible old goat Zlatorog stands guard.

As you zigzag to just over 1100 metres, you'll come to the **Russian Chapel** erected on the site where more than 400 Russian war prisoners were buried in an avalanche in March 1916. The POWs were in the process of building the road you are travelling on, so spare a moment for the repose of their souls.

GORENJSKA

GORENJSKA

Zlatorog and His Golden Horns

The oft-told tale of Zlatorog, the mythical chamois with the golden horns who lived on Mt Triglav and guarded its treasure, almost always involves some superhuman (or, in this case, super-antelopine) feat that drastically changed the face of the mountain. But don't let Slovenes fool you into believing that their ancient ancestors passed on this tale. The Zlatorog story first appeared in the *Laibacher Zeitung (Ljubljana Gazette)* in 1868 during a period of Romanticism and national awakening. It tells of how the chamois created the Triglav Lakes Valley, a wilderness of tumbled rock almost in the centre of Triglav National Park.

Zlatorog roamed the valley (at that time a beautiful garden) with the White Ladies, good fairies who kept the mountain pastures green and helped humans whenever they found them in need.

Meanwhile, down in the Soča Valley near Trenta, a greedy plot was being hatched. It seemed that an innkeeper's daughter had been given jewels by a wealthy Venetian merchant. The girl's mother demanded that her daughter's lover, a poor but skilled hunter, match the treasure with Zlatorog's gold hidden under Mt Bogatin. If not, he was at least to bring back a bunch of Triglav 'roses' (actually pink cinquefoils) in mid-winter to prove his fidelity – an impossible task.

The young hunter, seething with jealousy, climbed the mountain in search of the chamois, figuring that if he were to take even a piece of its golden horns, the treasure of Bogatin – and his beloved – would be his. At last the young man spotted Zlatorog, took aim and fired. It was a direct hit.

The blood gushing from Zlatorog's wound melted the snow and up sprang a magical Triglav rose. The chamois nibbled on a few petals and – presto! – was instantly back on his feet. As the chamois leapt away, roses sprang up from under his hooves, luring the hunter onto higher and higher ground. But as they climbed, the sun caught Zlatorog's shiny horns. The hunter was blinded, lost his footing and plunged into a gorge.

The once kind and trusting chamois was enraged that a mere mortal would treat him in such a manner. In his fury he gored his way through the Triglav Lakes Valley, leaving it much as it looks today. He left the area with the White Ladies, never to return.

And the fate of the others? The innkeeper's daughter waited in vain for her lover to return home. As spring approached, the snow began to melt, swelling the Soča River. One day it brought her a sad gift: the body of her young swain, his lifeless hand still clutching a Triglav rose. As for the innkeeper's rapacious wife, we know nothing. Perhaps she learned Italian and moved to Venice.

Observant travellers will see the face of Zlatorog no matter where they go in Slovenia. It's on the label of the country's most popular beer. ∎

The little wooden church is on a small hill and very simple inside. Services in memory of the victims were held jointly by the Russian patriarch and the archbishop of Ljubljana for the first time here in 1994.

The road meanders past a couple of huts as it climbs the next few km to **Vršič Pass** (1611 metres), about 13 km from Kranjska Gora. The area was the scene of fierce fighting during WW I, and a high percentage of the dead lay where they fell. The *Tičarjev Dom* mountain hut is 50 metres away. To the west is Mojstrovka, to the east Prisojnik/Prisank and to the south the valleys of the Soča and Mlinarica rivers point the way to Primorska.

A hair-raising descent of about 10 km ends at the **Julius Kugy Monument**. Kugy (1858-1944) was a pioneer climber and author whose books eulogise the beauties of the Julien Alps. He is shown meditating on 'his' Trenta Mountains to the north-west. From here you can take a side trip along the Soča Trail (Soška Pot) of about 2.5 km northwest to the Soča River source (Izvir Soče). Fed by an underground lake, the water bursts from a dark fissure before dropping 15 metres to the rocky bed from where the Soča begins its 136-km journey to the Adriatic.

Not long after joining the main road again you'll pass the entrance to the **Alpinum Juliana**, a botanical garden established in 1926 and showcasing the flora of all of Slovenia's Alps (Julian, Kamnik, Savinja and Karavanke), as well as the Karst. The elongated mountain village of **Trenta** (662 metres) is about four km to the south.

Trenta has a long tradition of mountain guides; shepherds and woodsmen made the first ascents of the Julian Alps possible in the 19th century and their bravery and skill is commemorated on a plaque just below the botanical garden. Na Logu in the upper part of Trenta is the gateway for the eastern approach of Triglav – a much less frequented and steeper climb than most of the others. It's about a four-hour walk from here to the Dolič Saddle (2164 metres) and the *Tržaška Koča* mountain hut, where you join the route from Savica Waterfall near Bohinj to the *Dom*

Planika and Triglav. Lower Trenta has a small **Mountain Museum** dedicated to the Trenta guides, the pioneers of Slovenian Alpinism and the park's flora and fauna. There's also an information office here.

The equally long village of **Soča** (480 m) is another 8.5 km down the river. The 18th century **Church of St Joseph** has paintings by Tone Kralj (1900-75). Completed in 1944 as war still raged in Central Europe, one of the frescoes depicts Michael the Archangel struggling with Satan and the foes of humanity: Hitler and Mussolini. The colours used are those of the Slovenian flag. Outside stands a lovely old linden tree and opposite, through the potato fields, the narrow Soča flows past.

Bovec, the recreational centre of the Upper Soča Valley (Gornje Posočje), is 12 km west of Soča. For details, see the following chapter on Primorska province.

Places to Stay & Eat The *Gostišče Jasna* overlooking Jasna Lake is a great place for a meal or a drink before pushing on to the Vršič Pass and points beyond. A lovely rear terrace opens in the warmer months.

Mihov Dom na Vršiču (☎ 881 190), a hut with food and accommodation at 1085 metres on the Vršič road, is open most of the year. *Tičarjev Dom* (☎ 883 066) right on the pass is open from May to October. A bed in a room for three is 1500 SIT, 1100 SIT in rooms with four to six beds and a bed in the attic is only 410 SIT.

Near the source of the Soča River at 886 metres, the *Koča pri Izviru Soče* (☎ 81 291) is open from May to October.

In Trenta the tiny *Orel* camp site (☎ 065-89 313) is right on the river at house No 33. *Koča Zlatorog v Trenti*, a mountain hut marking the start of the eastern approach of Mt Triglav, is open all year.

At house No 31 in Soča, the *Penzion Julius* (☎ 065-89 358) has accommodation and there's a decent restaurant attached. The small *Klin* camp site (☎ 065-89 356) about 4.5 km to the south-west at the start of the Lepena Valley is open all year.

GORENJSKA

Primorska

It may come as a surprise to learn that Primorska, the long, slender province that extends from Austria and Triglav National Park to Istria and the Adriatic Sea, means 'littoral' in Slovene. With Slovenia's coastline measuring only 47 km long (and never having been any longer), why such an extravagant name?

It all has to do with weather. Almost all of Primorska gets the warm winds from the coast that influence the valleys as far as Kobarid and Bovec and inland. As a result, the climate and the flora are distinctly Mediterranean right up to the foothills of the Alps. Yet the province has four distinct regions: the Soča Valley (covered partly under the Triglav National Park section in the Gorenjska chapter); central Primorska with the rolling hills of Idrija and Cerkno; the unique Karst; and the coast (occasionally called Slovenian Istria).

Primorska is a magical province offering unlimited activities and sights; it really is 'Europe in miniature'. In one day you can climb mountains or kayak in the Soča Valley, tour the wine-growing areas of the Vipava Valley or Brda Hills near Nova Gorica, explore the caves of Škocjan ride Lipizzaner stallions in the Karst or laze on the beaches of Piran or Portorož. Primorska is also an excellent gateway to Italy (eg from Nova Gorica or Ankaran) and Croatian Istrian from Sečovlje and Sočerga.

The Soča Valley

The Soča Valley (Posočje) stretches from Triglav National Park to Nova Gorica, including Bovec, Kobarid, Tolmin and Most na Soči. Its most dominant feature is the Soča River, which can widen to half a km and narrow to less than a metre but always stays a deep aquamarine colour. The valley has more than its share of historical sights and

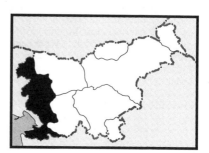

important artwork but most people come here for recreational pursuits such as rafting, hiking and skiing.

The Soča Valley has been an important trade route between Friulian Plain and the Alpine valleys since early times. It was the site of several Hallstatt settlements, evidenced by the rich archaeological finds unearthed at Most na Soči, Tolmin and Kobarid. During the Roman era the valley was on the important Predel road between Noricum and the province of Histria but lost its importance with their departure.

The proximity of Venice, and the Napoleonic wars of the late 18th and early 19th centuries, restored the valley's strategic role. The railway to Bohinj brought modern transport to the Sava Valley and Gorica in 1906 and during WW I millions of troops were brought to the battle front stretching from the Karst to Mt Rombon. Between the wars Primorska and the Soča Valley fell under Italian jurisdiction. Many Italians were expelled from the province after WW II.

BOVEC (pop 1775)

It is difficult to imagine an adventure-sports centre more diverse than Bovec, the 'capital' of the Upper Soča Valley (Gornje Posočje). With the Julian Alps above, the Soča River below and Triglav National Park behind, you could spend a week hiking, kayaking, mountain biking and, in winter, skiing at Slovenia's highest ski station without ever doing the same thing twice.

The area around Bovec (Plezzo in Italian) is first mentioned in documents dating back to the 11th century. At that time it was under the direct rule of the Patriarchs of Aquileia but was later transferred to the Counts of Gorica and, in about 1500, to the Habsburgs. The Turks passed through the basin on their way to the Predel Pass in the 15th century, and on two occasions (in 1797 and 1809) Napoleón's army attacked Austria from here.

Bovec suffered terribly in the fighting around the Soča Valley during WW I. Much of the town was destroyed but its reconstruction by the architect Max Fabiani in the 1920s gave Bovec an interesting combination of traditional and modern buildings. Further reconstruction took place after a severe earthquake in 1976.

Except for a period in the 17th and 18th centuries when the Bovec area was a centre of iron mining and forging, the people have traditionally worked as sheep and goat herders, climbing high into the mountains in search of pasture. The knowledge of these herders was highly prized by early alpinists, and many became guides – a tradition that continues to this day.

Orientation

Bovec, 483 metres above sea level, lies in a broad basin (Bovška Kotlina) at the meeting point of the Soča and Koritnica valleys. Towering above are several peaks well over 2000 metres, including Mt Rombon (2208 metres) and Mt Kanin (2587 metres). The Soča River flows past Bovec two km to the south at Čezsoča and widens from about a metre to almost half a km. The Italian border is 16 km to the south-west via the Učeja Pass and 17 km north at Predel.

The centre of Bovec is Trg Golobarskih Žrtev, about the only 'street' in Bovec which is named. Trg Golobarskih Žrtev is a long square that forms the main east-west drag and runs northward to the neo-Romanesque Church of St Urh and the holiday village of Kaninska Vas. Buses stop on Trg

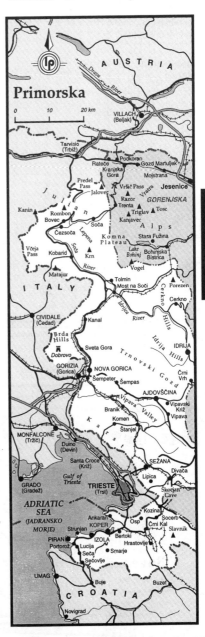

PRIMORSKA

Golobarskih Žrtev in front of the Letni Vrt (Summer Garden) restaurant at No 1.

Information

Money There's a Ljubljanska Banka branch next to the Alp hotel at Trg Golobarskih Žrtev 47 open from 8 am to 6 pm weekdays and till noon on Saturday.

Post & Telecommunications The post office and telephone centre is at Trg Golobarskih Žrtev 8 at the foot of the hill leading to the church and Kaninska Vas. It is open from 8 am to 3.30 pm and 4 to 6 pm on weekdays and till noon on Saturday.

The telephone code for Bovec is 065. The postcode is 65230.

Travel Agencies Bovec has no official tourist office but two agencies can handle your needs. The very knowledgeable and

helpful staff at the Hoteli Bovec agency (☎ 065 86 101) at Trg Golobarskih Žrtev 18 can arrange virtually any outdoor activity. The Avtopromet Gorica agency (☎ 065 86 123) between the Alp hotel and the bank can do the same, and they're particularly good with accommodation and transport. Avtopromet Gorica is open Monday to Saturday from 8 am to 6 pm and on Sunday from 9 am till noon. They also have exchange facilities.

Boating

Rafting, kayaking and canoeing on the beautiful Soča River (10% to 40% gradient; Degrees I to VI) are what attract most people to Bovec and so they should. They are exhilarating, frightening and educational sports.

The largest group dealing with these pursuits is Soča Rafting (☎ 32 221) next to the reception area at the Alp hotel. They are open weekdays from 9 am till noon and from 4 to

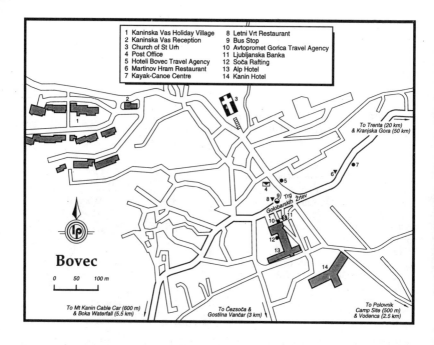

1 Kaninska Vas Holiday Village	8 Letni Vrt Restaurant
2 Kaninska Vas Reception	9 Bus Stop
3 Church of St Urh	10 Avtopromet Gorica Travel Agency
4 Post Office	11 Ljubljanska Banka
5 Hoteli Bovec Travel Agency	12 Soča Rafting
6 Martinov Hram Restaurant	13 Alp Hotel
7 Kayak-Canoe Centre	14 Kanin Hotel

To Trenta (20 km) & Kranjska Gora (50 km)

Bovec

0   50   100 m

To Mt Kanin Cable Car (600 m) & Boka Waterfall (5.5 km)

To Čezsoča & Gostilna Vančar (3 km)

To Polovnik Camp Site (500 m) & Vodenca (2.5 km)

Top Left: Main Square in Bovec (Primorska) (SF)
Top Right: Kayaking on the Soča River, Soča Valley (Primorska) (SF)
Bottom Left: Wild Lake near Idrija (Primorska) (SF)
Bottom Right: Fence separating Italy and Slovenia at Nova Gorica (Primorska) (SF)

Top: Limestone 'bowls' at the Škocjan Caves in the Karst region of Primorska (SF)
Bottom Left: Section of the Dance of Death fresco at the Church of the Holy Trinity at
Hrastovlje (Primorska) (SF)
Bottom Right: Teran grapes ripening near Hrastovlje (Primorska) (SF)

7 pm. On Saturday and Sunday the hours are 9 am to 6 pm.

The season lasts from mid-April to mid-September, but organised excursions are available daily only in July and August. At other times, they take place on Saturday and Sunday. Rafting is done in groups of six to eight (leaving at 10 am and 2 pm) while canoeing and kayaking can be practised individually or with a guide.

Raft trips on the Soča, taking 1½ hours with distances to 10 km, cost from DM45 to DM49 (including neoprene long john, wind cheater, life jacket, helmet and paddle). You should bring a swimsuit, T-shirt and a towel. A canoe for two is DM49 for the day and a kayak is DM30 (DM37 with life jacket, helmet etc). There are kayaking courses on offer in summer (eg a weekend for beginners costs DM100).

You can also book through the Kayak-Canoe Centre (☎ 195 524) on Trg Golobarskih Žrtev opposite the Martinov Hram restaurant. It is open May to September from 10 am to 1 pm and 5 to 7 pm.

Skiing

The **Kanin** ski centre (☎ 86 022) in the mountains north-west of Bovec has skiing up to 2200 metres – the only real high-altitude Alpine skiing available in Slovenia. As a result, the season can be long (God and Jack Frost providing) with good spring skiing in April and even May. The ski fields, 14 km of pistes and some 12 km of cross-country runs served by three chair lifts and two T-bars, are reached by a cable car in three stages. The lower station is 600 metres south-west of the centre of Bovec on the main road. Skiing at Kanin is generally more difficult than at centres like Kranjska Gora in Gorenjska and Rogla in Štajerska. You can rent your complete kit (skis, poles, boots) from the Hoteli Bovec agency.

The cable car runs constantly during the skiing season; in July and August it runs hourly from 8 am to 4 pm and in June and September every second hour from Thursday to Sunday. It's a lovely place to go when the weather is clear. From the cable car's

upper station (D Station) you could make the three-hour climb (difficult!) of **Kanin** (2587 metres) or reach the **Prestreljenik Window** (2499 metres) in about 1½ hours. For your troubles, you'll see all the way to Trieste and the Julian Alps.

Hiking

The 1:25,000-scale map called *Bovec z Okolico (Bovec and Surroundings)* lists a number of walks and hikes, ranging from a two-hour stroll south to **Čezsoča** and the protected gravel deposits in the Soča to an ascent of **Rombon**, which would take a good four hours one way. *Walking in the Julian Alps* by Simon Brown also lists a half-dozen walks in the area, including an easy trek to the source of the Soča River and a rather difficult ascent of **Kanin**. The Hoteli Bovec agency also has a lot of guided walks available such as one to the **Mangart Saddle** (2072 metres) along the highest road in Slovenia and **Krn Lake** above the Lepena Valley. They're expensive at about DM40 per person, but you certainly won't get lost. They also have a mountain walking tour of medium difficulty that follows the Soča Front lines (see the Kobarid section) to Rombon past trenches, old caverns, bunkers and observation posts. It takes between eight and 10 hours and costs DM80.

The most popular do-it-yourself walk in the area is to the **Boka Waterfall**, some 5.5 km to the south-west of Bovec. The waterfall drops more than 100 metres from the Kanin Mountains into the valley and is almost 30 metres wide – it's an impressive sight, especially in late spring when the snow melts. To get there you can either walk along the main road toward Tolmin, which more or less follows the Soča, or take the bus and get off after the Gostilna Žikar, a small restaurant and pub in Pod Čela. The trip to the falls (850 metres) and back takes about 1½ hours, but the path is steep in places and can be very slippery. If you are not up to climbing you can stand at the bridge on the main Bovec-Tolmin road and look up: the falls are on distant, but full, display.

PRIMORSKA

Other Activities

The Hoteli Bovec and Avtopromet Gorica agencies sell two types of fishing licences for hooking the famous Soča trout. One for the area east of Čezsoča as well as the Koritnica and Lepenjica rivers costs DM100 per day. To fish in the Soča below Bovec, where there is a lot more kayaking and boating, you must pay DM80 a day. The season lasts from April to October.

Tandem paragliding (ie with a pilot and a passenger), in which you descend from the upper cable-car station 2000 metres into the Bovec Valley, costs DM110, and there are hourly lessons in paragliding for DM25. This is available in March and April and from August to October.

You can also learn to pothole – descending with a guide through tunnels into the bowels of the earth – in the Kanin Mountains. This is real adventure stuff – there are no pretty stalactites, stalagmites or easy trails here. But prices are steep: DM100 for one person, DM160 for two and DM180 for three.

Places to Stay

Camping The closest camp site to Bovec is the *Polovnik* camp site (☎ 86 069), about 500 metres south-east of the Kanin hotel. It's small (just over a hectare) but in an attractive setting. Polovnik, which is open from May to mid-October, costs between DM7 and DM8.5 per person, depending on the month. The tiny *Liza* camp site (☎ 86 073) is farther afield in Vodenca, some 2.5 km south-east of the town centre at the point where the Koritnica River meets the Soča. It charges DM7 per person and is open from April to mid-October.

Private Rooms These are easy to find in Bovec with the agencies having a total of 320 beds on their lists. But they're not cheap. A single will cost between DM18 and DM20 while doubles are DM30 to DM36. There are lots of houses with *sobe* ('rooms available') signs, including one at Trg Golobarskih Žrtev 5, where you can make your own deal.

Hotels The Hoteli Bovec group runs two hotels and a 'village' of holiday houses at Kaninska Vas, 500 metres up the hill north-west of the town centre. The 93-room *Alp* hotel (☎ 86 040; fax 86 081), at Trg Golobarskih Žrtev 48, is not a particularly friendly place and charges DM60 to DM77, depending on the season, for singles with breakfast and shower and DM90 to DM123 for doubles. The *Kanin* hotel (☎ 86 021; fax 86 081), about 150 metres behind the Alp, is in slightly quieter surrounds and has an indoor swimming pool and a sauna. It has 122 rooms and the rates are the same as those at the Alp.

The *Kaninska Vas* complex (☎ 86 043; fax 86 081) has apartments for two people for between DM50 and DM80, depending on the season.

Places to Eat

The *Letni Vrt*, opposite the Alp hotel, has pizza, grilled dishes and trout at affordable prices. Its garden is lovely in summer. *Martinov Hram*, at Trg Golobarskih Žrtev 27, specialises in seafood and grills. It is open from 10 am to 11 pm every day except Monday.

If you want to eat where the locals do, head for *Vančar* (☎ 86 33) in Čezsoča (house No 48), about three km south of Bovec. It is open from 11 am to 10 pm but is closed Monday and Tuesday.

Getting There & Away

Buses are frequent to Kobarid and Tolmin, with between 10 and 12 departures a day (a lot less at the weekend as always). Other destinations and their daily frequencies are: Bled (one); Ljubljana via Tolmin and Most na Soči (five); Ljubljana via the Vršič Pass, Kranjska Gora, Bled and Kranj (one a day in summer) and Nova Gorica (five).

Getting Around

The Hoteli Bovec agency rents bicycles and mountain bikes. The latter cost 300 SIT per hour, 900 SIT per half-day and 1200 SIT for a full day. They also organise bike trips of varying lengths and degrees of difficulty.

PRIMORSKA

KOBARID (pop 1460)

Only a few things have changed since the American writer Ernest Hemingway described Kobarid (then Caporetto) in his novel about WW I, *A Farewell to Arms*. It was 'a little white town with a campanile in a valley,' he wrote, 'a clean little town and there was a fine fountain in the square'. The bell in the tower still rings on the hour, but the fountain has been replaced with a rather striking statue of the poet and priest Simon Gregorčič (1844-1906), who was born in nearby Vrsno.

Kobarid did have a history before WW I and things have happened since. It was a military settlement during Roman times, was hotly contested in the Middle Ages and hit by a devastating earthquake in 1976, which destroyed some historical buildings and farmhouses with folk frescoes (now preserved in the Kobarid Museum). But the world will remember Kobarid as Caporetto and the decisive battle of 1917 in which the combined forces of the Central Powers defeated the Italian army.

Still, you would be hard-pressed to think of a reason for coming to this place aside from visiting the award-winning (but disappointing) Kobarid Museum, which deals with the horrors of the 'war to end all wars', and perhaps paying your respects to the war dead on both sides.

Orientation & Information

Kobarid, some 21 km south of Bovec, lies in a broad valley on the west bank of the Soča River. Though it is surrounded by mountain peaks of more than 2200 metres, Kobarid feels more Mediterranean than Alpine. The Italian border at Robič is only nine km to the west and Cividale, where a good many people from Kobarid commute to work every day, is another 18 km to the south.

The centre of Kobarid is Trg Svobode, dominated by the Gothic Church of the Assumption and that famous bell tower. Buses stop in front of the Gostilna Kramar, on the eastern side of the square at No 9.

The tourist office (☎ 85 055) is on the ground floor of the Kobarid Museum and keeps the same hours. The post office, to the west of the church at Trg Svobode 2, is open weekdays from 8 am till 3 pm and from 4 to 6 pm. On Saturday it closes at noon. There's a Ljubljanska Banka branch in the market to the south at Trg Svobode 4 open weekdays from 8 am to 6 pm and on Saturday till noon. The small bookshop across from the church on Trg Svobode has a decent selection of maps and guides, including *How to Climb Triglav*.

The telephone code for Kobarid is 065. The postcode is 65222.

Kobarid Museum

This museum, which opened to great fanfare in 1990 and has won several European awards, is located in the 18th century Mašer House at Gregorčičeva ulica 10. It is devoted almost entirely to the Soča Front and is anti-war in tone, although not particularly strongly. Nor are the displays very well done.

Among the collection are 500 photographs documenting the horrors of the Soča (or Isonzo) Front, military charts, diaries and maps and two large relief displays showing the front lines and offensives through the Krn Mountains and the positions in the Upper Soča Valley the day before the decisive breakthrough. There's also a 22-minute 'multivision presentation' (slides with commentary) describing the preparations for the final battle, the fighting and its results. The observations made by soldiers on both sides are the most enlightening part.

The museum is on three floors and the displays are labelled in four languages, including English. The entrance hall on the ground floor has photographs of soldiers, tombstone crosses, mortar shells and the flags of all the countries involved in the conflict.

The rooms on the 1st and 2nd floors have themes: the **Black Room** shows horrible photographs of the dead and dying; the **White Room** describes the particularly harsh conditions of making war in the snow and fog in the mountains; and the **Rear Lines Room** which explains what life was like for

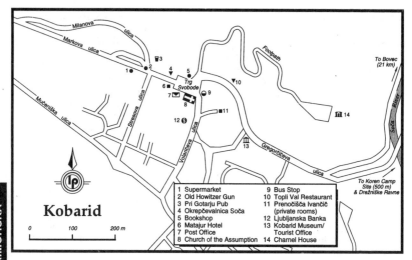

Kobarid

0   100   200 m

1 Supermarket
2 Old Howitzer Gun
3 Pri Gotarju Pub
4 Okrepčevalnica Soča
5 Bookshop
6 Matajur Hotel
7 Post Office
8 Church of the Assumption
9 Bus Stop
10 Topli Val Restaurant
11 Prenočišča Ivančič
   (private rooms)
12 Ljubljanska Banka
13 Kobarid Museum/
   Tourist Office
14 Charnel House

soldiers during pauses in the fighting and for the civilian population uprooted by war and famine. The **Breakthrough Room** deals with the events over three days (24-27 October 1917) when the combined Austrian and German forces met near Kobarid and defeated the Italian army. In one room an Italian soldier sits in his cavern shelter writing a letter to his father while the war rages outside. The intent is to put a human face to the war amid all the figures and weapons, but the martial music defeats the purpose and the sound effects are bad.

The Kobarid Museum is open daily from 9 am to 7 pm. Admission costs 300 SIT for adults and 150 for students and children.

Italian Charnel House

This huge ossuary *(kostnica* in Slovene) containing the bones of more than 7000 Italian soldiers killed on the Soča Front stands on the **Hill of St Anthony** (Sveti Anton) east of Trg Svobode.

After the war Austrian, German and Italian cemeteries littered the entire Soča Valley. During the Italian occupation of Primorska between the wars, the authorities

in Rome decided to collect what remains they could and deposit them at the charnel house. The opening in September 1938 was attended by Benito Mussolini.

The charnel house comprises three stacked octagons, each progressively smaller, and is topped with the 17th century **Church of St Anthony**, moved here from another location in 1935. Only one of several frescoes painted by Jernej Vrtav (1647-1725) survived the move.

You can reach it in 10 minutes by following the footpath leading north from Trg Svobode and lined with the Stations of the Cross.

Third Italian Defence Line

From the ossuary, a path several km long leads along the remnants of the 3rd Defence Line built by the Italians in 1915 to **Kozjak Waterfall**. The path crosses the Soča over a bridge that was built by the French in the early 19th century. Though the original was destroyed in May 1915, it is still called **Napoleon Bridge**.

After a short distance the path heads north and joins the cleared trenches which lead to gun emplacements, observation posts and a cavern used as shelter – not unlike that in the museum where the soldier writes his letter. About 500 metres after you cross a stone bridge over the **Kozjak Stream**, you reach the waterfall.

Places to Stay

The small *Koren* camp site (☎ 85 312) is about 500 metres north of Kobarid on the east bank of the Soča and just before the turn to Drežniške Ravne, a lovely village with traditional farmhouses at the foot of Mt Krn.

Koren is open from mid-March to October and costs DM8 per person.

The owners of the site also have accommodation in five rooms at the *Žvanč* farmhouse (☎ 85 312) in Drežniške Ravne (house No 33) throughout the year. The price per person is about DM20 to DM27, depending on the season and room category.

In Kobarid, the tourist office has a short list of families offering *private rooms* including *Prenočišča Ivančič* (☎ 85 307) between the museum and Trg Svobode at Gregorčičeva ulica 6c. They charge 1600

The Soča (Isonzo) Front

The breakthrough in the Soča Front (more commonly known to historians as the Isonzo Front) by the combined Austrian, Hungarian, German and Slovenian forces near Kobarid in October 1917 was one of the costliest battle in terms of human life the world has ever known. By the time the fighting had stopped 17 days after it had begun, hundreds of thousands of soldiers lay dead or wounded. They lay writhing and screaming in the blood-drenched earth, gassed and mutilated beyond recognition with limbs missing and faces torn away.

In May 1915, Italy declared war on the Central Powers and their allies and moved its army across the south-western border of Austria to the strategically important Soča Valley. From there they hoped to move eastward to the heart of Austria-Hungary. By then, however, the Austrians had fortified the lines with trenches and bunkers for some 80 km, from the Adriatic Sea and the Karst to the mountain peaks overlooking the Upper Soča Valley as far north as Mt Rombon. The 1st offensive launched by the Italians was successful, and they occupied Kobarid and Mt Krn to the north-east, where they would remain for some 29 months.

The Italians, commanded by General Luigi Cadorna, launched another 10 offensives over the ensuing months but the difficult mountain terrain turned it into a war of attrition between two entrenched armies. Territorial gains were minimal but the fighting was horrific, involving a total assault of light artillery, anti-aircraft guns, trench mortars and gas-mine throwers. With the stalemate, much of the fighting shifted to Gorica (Gorizia) on the edge of the Karst region.

On 24 October 1917 the stalemate broke. The Italians were dispirited by their lack of success and the weaker Austrian forces knew this. They formulated an unusual plan of attack based on surprise and moved hundreds of thousands of troops, arms and materiel (including six German divisions) into the area between Trnovo and Kobarid. The 12th offensive – the first by the Austrians – began with heavy bombardment.

The 'miracle of Kobarid' routed the Italian army and pushed the fighting back to the Friulian Plain as far as the Piave River, where the war continued for another year. The sketches of the breakthrough in the Kobarid Museum by one Lieutenant Erwin Rommel, who became known as the 'Desert Fox' while commanding Germany's North African offensive in WW II, are invaluable for understanding the battle. But nothing is more vivid than the description of the Italian retreat in Ernest Hemingway's *A Farewell to Arms*. Hemingway was wounded on the Gorica battlefield in the spring of 1917 while driving an Italian ambulance.

The 12th Offensive was the greatest breakthrough in World War I. It was also one of the most difficult mountain battles and the first successful 'lightning war' (blitzkrieg) in the history of European warfare. The Italians alone lost 500,000 soldiers and another 250,000 were taken prisoner. But if we count the casualties on the Soča Front for the entire 1915-17 period, that number grows to almost a million including soldiers on the battlefields and men, women and children behind the lines. ∎

SIT for a single. The *Topli Val* restaurant (☎ 85 071) has six rooms available for between DM20 and DM22 per person.

The only hotel in town is the 35-room *Matajur* (☎ 85 332; fax 81 007) at Trg Svobode 1. It is a decent enough place with three storeys and a pleasant glassed-in terrace, but it's expensive for what it is: DM48 to DM54 for a single, depending on the season, and DM76 to DM88 for a double. Wherever you stay, the church bell is sure to keep you awake all night as it did me. Not only does it ring on the hour every hour but two minutes later as well!

Places to Eat

The *Okrepčevalnica Soča*, opposite the Matajur hotel at Trg Svobode 12, has drinks and snacks, including pizza.

The best restaurant in Kobarid is the *Topli Val* at Gregorčičeva 1 open every day except Wednesday from noon to 10 pm. With a name meaning 'Warm Wave' and owners from Portorož, the speciality has to be fish. It's quite good but not cheap; a plate of mixed seafood and a salad will cost about 1200 SIT.

There's a large *supermarket* at Markova ulica 1 open daily from 7 am to 6 pm.

Entertainment

The *Pri Gotarju* pub, in a shady garden at the start of Milanova ulica, is a pleasant place for a drink in summer. In the grassy area near the petrol station opposite is a rusty 150-mm howitzer built in 1911 and fished out of the Soča River after WW I.

Getting There & Away

Buses are very frequent to Bovec and Tolmin, 15 km to the south-east. Other destinations include: Bled (one a day); Cerkno (up to five), Ljubljana via Idrija (six); Ljubljana via the Vršič Pass, Kranjska Gora, Bled and Kranj (one a day in summer) and Nova Gorica (five).

NOVA GORICA (pop 14,800)

When the town of Gorica, capital of the former Slovenian province of Goriška, was awarded to the Italians under the Treaty of Paris in 1947 and became Gorizia, the new socialist government in Yugoslavia set itself to building a model town on the eastern side of the border 'following the principles of Le Corbusier', the Swiss functionalist architect who has a lot to answer for. Appropriately enough they called it 'New Gorica' and erected a chain-link barrier between the two towns that stands to this day.

'Where the Latin and the Slavic worlds shake hands in the name of friendship' – and other tourist-brochure drivel notwithstanding – Nova Gorica itself offers travellers little more than a game of chance and an easy doorway into or out of Slovenia. With the Italian frontier running right through what was once united Gorica and a couple of flashy casino-hotels dominating the place, most people arrive here to try their luck or move on – sometimes both and in that order. The fence, the broken pavement and the unspeakably ugly barrack-like buildings bring to mind East Berlin circa 1975.

Still, Nova Gorica isn't all bad. It's a surprisingly green place with a couple of lovely parks and gardens, and its immediate surrounds – the Franciscan monastery at Kostanjevica nad Gorico to the south and the ancient settlement of Solkan in the north with several Baroque manor houses – offer some startling contrasts. Slovenian, Venetian, Friulian and Austrian influences can be felt everywhere.

Nova Gorica straddles two important wine-growing areas: the Brda Hills to the north-west and the wide Vipava Valley to the south-east. It's also an excellent springboard for some of Slovenia's most popular destinations: the Soča Valley, Bled and Bohinj in Gorenjska and the beautiful Karst region leading to the coast.

Orientation

Nova Gorica sits on a broad plain south of the Soča River. Across the Italian region of Goriziano to the north-west are the Brda Hills (Goriška Brda). The Vipava Valley (Vipavska Dolina) lies to the south-east. The

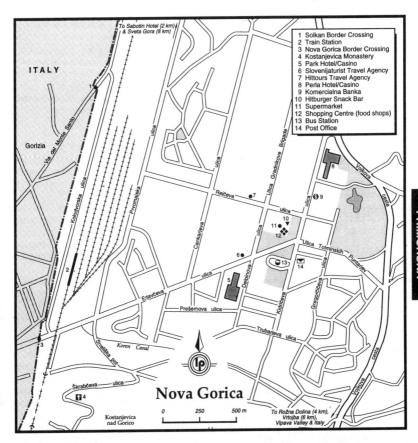

To Sabotin Hotel (2 km) & Sveta Gora (8 km)

ITALY

Gorizia

1 Solkan Border Crossing
2 Train Station
3 Nova Gorica Border Crossing
4 Kostanjevica Monastery
5 Park Hotel/Casino
6 Slovenijaturist Travel Agency
7 Hittours Travel Agency
8 Perla Hotel/Casino
9 Komercialna Banka
10 Hitburger Snack Bar
11 Supermarket
12 Shopping Centre (food shops)
13 Bus Station
14 Post Office

Nova Gorica

Kostanjevica nad Gorico

0   250   500 m

To Rožna Dolina (4 km),
Vrtojba (6 km),
Vipava Valley & Italy

PRIMORSKA

Karst region is south and south-east of the town.

Nova Gorica is an unusually long town, running about five km from the border crossing at Rožna Dolina (Casa Rossa) in the south to Solkan in the north. The bus station is in the centre of town at Kidričeva ulica 22, some 400 metres south-west of the Perla hotel. The train station is on Kolodvorska ulica, about 1.5 km to the west. To get to the train station from Kidričeva ulica, walk south-west on Erjavčeva ulica. When you reach the Italian border (and the fence) follow Kolodvorska ulica north to No 6.

Neither the border checkpoint you pass along the way nor the one farther north is open to foreigners (ie non-Slovenes and non-Italians). To cross into Italy you must travel four km south to Rožna Dolina or another two km to Vrtojba (Santa Andrea).

Information

About the only place to get information in Nova Gorica is Slovenijaturist (☎ 26 012), two hundred metres west of the bus station at Erjavčeva ulica 4, where the staff are helpful and friendly. It keeps 'Italian' hours:

from 9 am till noon and from 3 to 6 pm on weekdays and Saturday morning.

Hittours (☎ 28 202), a travel agency owned by the Hit hotel and casino company at Rejčeva ulica 4, will answer your questions provided you beg, roll over and/or play dead. That's just about how they treat you here. The office is open from 8 am to 7 pm and till 1 pm on Saturday.

Komercialna Banka Nova Gorica, south of the Perla hotel at Kidričeva ulica 11, opens from 7.30 am to 6 pm on weekdays and till noon on Saturdays. The post office lies opposite the bus station at Kidričeva ulica 19. It's open weekdays from 7 am to 8 pm and on Saturday to 1 pm.

Nova Gorica's telephone code is 065. The postcode is 65000.

Things to See & Do

Neither the neo-Baroque **basilica** built in 1927 nor yet another **WW I museum** perched atop Sveta Gora (Monte Santo) eight km north of Nova Gorica is worth the trip; you can see the church from the town anyway. But if you do walk up the 681-metre hill on a clear day, you'll be able to see up into the Soča Valley to the north with its impossibly blue river and across the Friulian Plain to the Gulf of Trieste in the south. The museum is open Wednesday to Friday from noon to 5 pm and on Saturday and Sunday from 11 am to 5 pm.

The **Kostanjevica Monastery**, on another hill 800 metres south of the train station, was founded by the Capuchin Franciscans in the early 17th century and has a wonderful library, which can be visited. The narrow, single-nave **church** nearby has interesting stuccos and in the spooky crypt lie the mortal remains of the last members of the French house of Bourbon.

If you have a few hours on hand and always did want to try **bungee jumping**, an outfit called Top (☎ 24 778) at Vojkova cesta 9 in Solkan will have you plummeting from Solkan Bride over the Soča River in a few hours (just be sure to bring clean pants). The mini-course and jumps are organised on Sat-

urday and Sunday between April and October.

The **Oldtimer**, a steam train run by Slovenijaturist, does several excursions to, from or through Nova Gorica during the season (roughly from February to October). For details about itineraries, schedules and prices, contact the Slovenijaturist office.

Places to Stay & Eat

Decent and affordable accommodation is at a premium in this transient town, and if you're looking for value for money, hop on the next train out.

In Rožna Dolina, the Pertout family at Ulica 25 Maja 23 has *private rooms* for about 1500 SIT per person. The house is scarcely 200 metres from the border crossing. In Solkan, about 2.5 km from the bus station, the 35-bed *Sabotin* hotel (☎ 28 221), in an old Baroque manor at Cesta IX Korpusa 35, has singles and doubles with shared shower for DM26 and DM46, including breakfast. If you want your own private bathroom, the rooms are DM37 and DM62.

The only other choices are a couple of expensive hotels. The 104-room *Park* (☎ 28 225; fax 22 381), at Delpinova ulica 5, is the cheaper of the two, charging DM80 for a single with shower and breakfast and DM114 for a double. The flashiest place in town – and arguably in all of Slovenia – is the 94-room *Perla* hotel (☎ 28 830; fax 28 886) attached to the casino at Kidričeva ulica 7. A favourite with Italians, this place could be anywhere – Hong Kong, Las Vegas, Euro Disney – and it's something local people are just a wee bit proud of. DM90 for a single and DM160 for a double gets you run of the place (pool, sauna, tennis courts, casino) and breakfast. The Perla's expensive *restaurant* (with an emphasis on Italian dishes – surprise, surprise) is one of the best in Slovenia.

The shopping centre north of the bus station is a warren of cafés, pubs and fastfood places, including the ever-popular *Hitburger*. There's also a large supermarket here called *Goriška* open Monday to Saturday till 7 pm.

Entertainment
Perla Hit Casino (☎ 28 890) is the company store – nothing makes more money in this town and it's all in lire from Italians denied access to casinos at home. So, if you want to gamble along with 50 million *italiani*, by all means beat a path to Kidričeva ulica 7 – it's open 24 hours a day. The town's other *casino*, at the Park hotel, is open daily from 3 pm to 3 am. Both casinos offer all the usual games – roulette, blackjack, poker, baccarat – with almost 800 slot machines.

Getting There & Away
Bus From Nova Gorica you can expect buses to Ajdovščina every half-hour and at least one an hour to Tolmin, Postojna and Ljubljana. Other destinations and their daily frequencies include: Bovec (two); Celje (two); Dobrovo (up to six); Idrija via Tolmin or Ajdovščina (two); Koper (up to five); Maribor (two); Piran (two); and Sežana (six). In July and August there's a daily bus to Kranjska Gora, Bled and Ljubljana via the spectacular Vršič Pass.

Up to seven buses a day cross the Italian border to Gorizia, and there's a daily bus to Trieste. For Croatia, count on a daily departure for Rijeka and Varaždin and one in summer for Novigrad.

Train About half a dozen trains head north-east each day for Jesenice (89 km; 1¾ hours) via Most na Soči, Bohinjska Bistrica (61 km; 70 minutes) and Bled-Jezero (79 km; 1½ hours) on what is arguably the country's most beautiful train trip. In the other direction, an equal number of trains go to Sežana (40 km; 55 minutes), where you can change for Ljubljana or Trieste in Italy (three trains a day).

If you're heading for Buzet, Pula or other towns in Croatian Istria by train, you must change at Divača, nine km south-east of Sežana. Pivka, another 24 km to the east, is where trains to or from Ljubljana go south for Rijeka.

Nova Gorica is linked to Ajdovščina, 26 km to the south-east, by two trains a day from Monday to Saturday year round except in July and August.

Getting Around
Local buses serve Solkan, Rožna Dolina, Šempeter and Vrtojba from the main station.

AROUND NOVA GORICA
It's sad but true. One of the nicest things you can say about Nova Gorica is that it is so easy to leave it – in every sense. If you want to have a look at **Goriška Brda**, the hilly wine region that stretches from Solkan west to the Italian border, catch a bus to **Dobrovo**, 13 km to the north-west. The town has a **Renaissance castle** dating from about 1600 that is filled with period furnishings and exhibits on the wine industry. Dobrovo Castle also has a very good restaurant and a vinoteka where you can sample the local vintages: white Rebula and the Pinot and Merlot reds. The very full red Teran (sometimes called after its grape varietal Refošk) is more closely associated with the Karst region than here. Goriška Brda is also known for its fabulous cherries in spring.

This area has been influenced by northern and central Italy since time immemorial and you'll think you've crossed the border as you go through little towns with narrow streets, houses built of karst limestone and the remains of feudal castles. One good example is **Šmartno** (San Martino), a pretty little fortified village with stone walls and a tower from the 16th century still standing.

South-east from Nova Gorica is the wide and fertile **Vipava Valley**, also famous for its wines; indeed, the first wine cooperative in Slovenia was established here in 1894. Some of the reds here are world-class, and a Vipava Merlot I drank was probably the best wine I've had in Central Europe. They also produce a decent rosé. The valley's mild climate encourages the cultivation of delicate stone fruits like peaches and apricots and in autumn, when the red sumac changes colour, the valley can look like it is in flames.

Vipava Valley is where the Romans first launched their drive into the Danube region. It was overrun by the Goths, Huns and

Langobards from the 4th to 6th centuries before the arrival of the Slavs. Along the valley, about 22 km south-east of Nova Gorica, is **Vipavski Križ** (Santa Croce), a walled medieval village with a ruined castle, a Gothic church and a 17th century monastery with some wonderfully illuminated medieval manuscripts.

Another four km to the west is **Ajdovščina** (Aidussina). This was the site of Castra ad Fluvium Frigidum, a Roman fort on the River Frigidus (Vipava) and the first important station on the road from Aquileia to Emona (Ljubljana). The border between Goriška and Kranjska provinces once ran nearby.

Vipava (Vipacco), the centre of the valley, is six km south-east, a not-unattractive town full of stone churches below **Nanos**, the karst plateau from where the Vipava River springs. Be sure to make a side trip two km to **Zemono**, a summer mansion built in the 17th century by one of the Counts of Gorica. Today the mansion, built in the shape of a cross inside a square with arcaded hallways and a raised central area, houses a posh restaurant and is used for wedding ceremonies. Have a peek at some of the **Baroque murals** near the entrance. They show symbols of fire (a phoenix) and water (subterranean cave). There are some excellent views down into the fertile valley.

Central Primorska

This is the area of Primorska 'between Alps and Karst' that is sadly so often overlooked by travellers heading for the 'sexier' Alps or beaches. It is a land of steep slopes, deep valleys and innumerable ravines with plenty of good hiking, the lovely Idrijca River and a couple of interesting towns.

Central Primorska is dominated by the Cerkno and Idrija hills, which eventually join the Škofja Loka Hills in Gorenjska to the east. They are the foothills of the Julian Alps. A major tectonic fault line runs below the region and Idrija was at the epicentre in

the catastrophic quake of 1511. It was at the time no more than an upstart mining town of wooden buildings and the damage was less severe than at Škofja Loka.

Nowhere in Slovenia can cultivated fields be found on such steep slopes and human dwellings in such remote locations as the regions around Idrija and Cerkno. The ravines and valleys were very useful to the Partisans during WW II and the region is dotted with monuments testifying to their heroic presence: the hospitals of Pavl and Franja (near Cerkno) and the Partisan printing house Slovenija at Vojsko, some 14 km north-west of Idrija.

IDRIJA (pop 6200)

When Slovenes think of Idrija, three things spring to mind: žlikrofi, lace and mercury. The women of Idrija have been taking care of the first two for centuries, stuffing the crescent-shaped 'Slovenian ravioli' with a savoury mixture of bacon, potatoes and chives as fast as they spin their web-like *čipka*. The men, on the other hand, went underground to extract the 'live silver' *(živo srebro)* that would make this town one of the richest in Europe in the Middle Ages.

Mercury was first discovered in 1490 at the site where the Church of the Holy Trinity now stands. The legend is that a man who made *suha roba*, or traditional wooden products, was busy at work on some tubs he was going to sell at the market in Škofja Loka. After he'd finished soaking them in a spring to ensure they wouldn't leak, he tried to lift one up but it was too heavy. At the bottom was a mass of silvery material that he'd never seen before. But some of the people at the market in Loka knew what it was and the 'mercury rush' to Idrija (Ydria in German) began.

So the story goes. The fact of the matter is that the first mine opened here in 1500, making it the second oldest mercury mine in the world after the one in Almadén in central Spain. By the 18th century, Idrija was producing 12% of the world's mercury and it was thought to be the purest and of the best

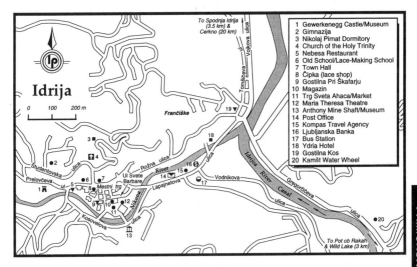

Idrija

1 Gewerkenegg Castle/Museum
2 Gimnazija
3 Nikolaj Pirnat Dormitory
4 Church of the Holy Trinity
5 Nebesa Restaurant
6 Old School/Lace-Making School
7 Town Hall
8 Čipka (lace shop)
9 Gostilna Pri Škafarju
10 Magazin
11 Trg Sveta Ahaca/Market
12 Maria Theresa Theatre
13 Anthony Mine Shaft/Museum
14 Post Office
15 Kompas Travel Agency
16 Ljubljanska Banka
17 Bus Station
18 Ydria Hotel
19 Gostilna Kos
20 Kamšt Water Wheel

quality. Its biggest markets were German towns, Venice, Trieste and Amsterdam.

All that meant money – for both the imperial court in Vienna and Idrija. Doctors (because of the toxic effects of mercury) and lawyers flocked here to work. The Idrija miner *(knap)* faced innumerable health hazards, but the relatively high wages attracted workers from all over the Habsburg Empire. In 1769, Idrija built Slovenia's first theatre and later could boast two of its finest schools. By the turn of the century, Idrija was second in size only to Ljubljana among the towns of Carniola (Kranjska).

The mercury market bottomed out in the 1970s and production of this once precious element has all but ceased in Idrija. The last pit is expected to close soon and most miners now work in factories north of town at Spodnja Idrija or Cerkno.

The mine has left the town a difficult and expensive legacy. Idrija sits on something like 700 km of shafts that go down 15 levels to 32 metres below sea level. The first four have now been filled with water and more have to be loaded with debris to stabilise the place. Otherwise the town will sink.

Some towns in Slovenia have just the right feel, and Idrija is one of them. Walking through the shaft where miners toiled for almost five centuries, across Mestni trg to the town's well-preserved castle or along the Idrijca River Canal to pristine Wild Lake on a warm summer's evening, you might just think so too.

Orientation

Idrija sits snugly in a deep basin at the confluence of the Idrijca and Nikova rivers. Surrounding the valley are the Idrija and Cerkno hills.

The centre of Idrija is Mestni trg, but everything of a practical nature is to the east on Lapajnetova ulica. The bus station is also near there, at Vodnikova ulica 2.

Information

Idrija does not have a tourist office though the staff at Kompas, (☎ 71 700) next to the post office on Lapajnetova ulica, will grudgingly answer your queries. They are open from 7 am to 3 pm on weekdays and on Saturday till 1 pm.

Ljubljanska Banka in the shopping centre opposite the bus station at Lapajnetova ulica 41 is open weekdays from 7 am to 6 pm and on Saturday till noon. The post office and telephone centre is to the west at No 35, near a small square with a fountain and a tiny statue of a mercury miner.

Idrija's telephone code is 065. The postcode is 65280.

Municipal Museum

The museum is housed in the enormous Gewerkenegg Castle on top of the hill to the west of Mestni trg at Prelovčeva ulica 9. Because the castle was purpose-built for the mine administration in 1529, local people call it Rudniški Grad from the Slovene word *rudnik* for mine. Visit here before you go into the Anthony Mine Shaft; you'll understand a whole lot more.

The collections, which deal with mercury and lace but not, sadly, žlikrofi, are exhibited in three wings centred around a courtyard. The 18th century **Rococo frescoes** of plants, scrolls and columns framing the windows and arcades have recently got a fresh coat of rather unattractive mustard-yellow paint.

Mercury (Hg on the periodic table) is the only metal that is in a liquid state at room temperature. It comes in a 'free' state (looking pretty much like the stuff in the thermometer) and can also be bound up with a bright-red mineral called cinnabar, which

must be burned at very high temperatures or treated with lime to free the silvery element inside. Mercury is a very heavy metal. In the castle's north wing, amidst a jungle of minerals and fossils, is a large cauldron of mercury with an iron ball floating in the middle since mercury is heavier than iron. If you touch the mercury (it is toxic if consumed or absorbed through the skin), remove any gold you have on or you'll risk losing it. Mercury amalgamates with gold.

Part of the **ethnographical collection** in this wing shows rooms in a typical miner's house at various times in history. A miner's job was one of status and they earned more than double the average salary in this part of Slovenia; the furnishings are more than adequate. The miners were well-organised and socialism was popular in the late 19th and early 20th centuries.

In the east wing, there's a mock-up of the 'call man', the unspeakable so-and-so who summoned miners to work every day at 3.30 am by hitting a hollow log with a mallet in the town centre. There's also an ingenious 'walking tour of Idrija' set up. Paintings and old photographs spaced between the windows allow you to compare old Idrija with the town that lies below you today.

One large room in the south wing is given over entirely to *klekljana čipka*, the **bobbin lace** woven in broad rings with distinctive patterns. Numbering up to 40, the motifs run the gamut from the usual hearts and flowers to horseshoes, crescents and lizards. Check out the table covering measuring 3 by 1.8 metres. It took 5000 hours to make and was intended for Madame Tito till she was banished into political limbo.

Another room is dedicated to the life and work of the novelist France Bevk (1890-1970), born in the village of Zakojca near Cerkno. One of Bevk's finest works is *Father Martin Čedermac* about the persecution of an Italian-Slovenian priest and his struggle against the Fascists before WW II.

The Municipal Museum is open every day from 9 am to 6 pm (3 pm in winter). Admission is 300 SIT (150 SIT for students and children).

Lace, as featured in the Municipal Museum

Anthony Mine Shaft

This 'living museum' on Kosovelova ulica south of Trg Sveta Ahaca allows you to get a brief feel for what work conditions were like for the mercury miners of Idrija. The entrance is the Anthony Shaft, built in 1500, which led to the first mine: 1.5 km long, 600 metres wide and 400 metres deep.

The tour, lasting about 1¼ hours, begins in the 'call room' of an 18th century building where miners were selected each morning and assigned their duties. Just imagine sitting on those hard, cold benches at 4 am with 10 hours underground to look forward to. There's an excellent 20-minute video in several languages (including English) which describes the history of Idrija and the mine.

Before entering the shaft, you must don coats with the miners' insignia, helmets with torches attached and wish each other 'Srečno!' ('Good luck!'), the traditional miners' farewell. You'll be thankful for those helmets every time you knock your head against one of the shaft's support beams.

As you walk into the shaft, you can see under a glass panel a model of the mine's levels. You won't be able to descend that far into the mine, but there are plans to make the shaft 200 metres longer and 20 metres deeper. There are some samples of live mercury on the walls which the miners painstakingly scraped to a depth of about five cm as well as some cinnabar ore. The 18th century **chapel** in the shaft is dedicated to Sts Barbara and Ahac, the patrons of miners here.

You can visit the mine with a guide on weekdays at 10 am and 4 pm only. On Saturday, tours depart at 10 am, 3 and 4 pm while they're at 11 am, 3 and 4 pm on

PRIMORSKA

On the Wings of Mercury

Why was mercury so important in the Middle Ages when they hadn't yet invented the thermometer? Well, mercury (or quicksilver as it was then called in English) had a lot of other important uses then, as it does today.

Alchemists, who named it after the fast-footed messenger of the Roman gods because of its fluidity, were convinced that all metals originated from mercury. They used mercury extensively in their search to obtain gold from other metals. But the biggest boon came in the 16th century, when amalgam processes for obtaining silver and gold were introduced by the conquistadors in Mexico and Peru. Since mercury bonds as an alloy to many metals, it can separate gold or silver from rock or ore.

Mercury was used as a medicine – it was an early antidote to syphilis – and in another form as an antiseptic. The Venetians needed it to make their mirrors and later milliners used it to lay felt for making hats. Mercury is a highly toxic substance and can affect behaviour; occupational mercurialism from vapours and absorption by the skin is a serious disorder. As a result many milliners went crazy and thus was the inspiration for the Mad Hatter in *Alice's Adventures in Wonderland* by Lewis Carroll. Idrija's miners didn't escape the ravages of mercurialism and one of the largest mental hospitals in the country is in the hills to the north of town.

In modern times, mercury has been used in industry to obtain caustic soda and chlorine, and to make drugs. It is an important element in certain light bulbs, batteries, laboratory monitoring equipment and power control switches. It has a place in the electrical industry as a conductor, in the paper industry, and has been used with silver to make amalgam for tooth fillings.

Its uses have not always been for peaceful purposes; it is a crucial ingredient in some detonators and bombs. Indeed, during the Vietnam War the US was one of the biggest importers of Idrija mercury from what was then socialist (and neutral) Yugoslavia.

Mercury mining in Idrija is coming to an end for several reasons. The use of heavy metals has been abandoned by many industries in favour of more environmentally-friendly substances and protective measures have been in place in some countries since the 1970s. More importantly, a 2.5-litre flask (about 34 kg) of mercury that sold for approximately US$800 in the 1960s was worth only $100 a decade later. Such prices no longer cover production costs. ∎

Sunday. Admission is 600 SIT for adults and 400 SIT for children.

Other Attractions

There are several fine neoclassical buildings on **Mestni trg**, including the **town hall** at No 1. To the west of the square opposite Prelovčeva ulica 1a is the **Lace-making School** in the Stara Šola (the 'Old School' built in 1876). Lace-making is still a required subject for girls in elementary school in Idrija. Visitors are welcomed daily from noon to 4 pm. The **Gimnazija Jurija Vege** (1901) to the north-west on Študentovska ulica educated many Slovenes who later rose to national prominence, including the painter Božidar Jakac (1899-1989).

The large 18th century building on the north side of **Trg Sveta Ahaca**, the centre of town in the Middle Ages, is the **Magazin**, a granary and warehouse where the miners, who were paid in food as well as cash, kept their stores. To the east at Trg Sveta Ahaca 5 is the **Maria Theresa Theatre**, the oldest in the country. Today it functions as a cinema.

Laid out across the slopes encircling the valley are Idrija's distinctive **miners' houses**. Large wooden A-frames with cladding and dozens of windows, they usually had four storeys with living quarters for three or four families. They must have appeared massive when they were first built in the 17th century.

North of Mestni trg is the **Church of the Holy Trinity** (1500), on the site where mercury was first discovered by our friend the tub-maker more than 500 years ago. To the north-east off Grilčeva ulica in the district of Frančiške is the last mine still functioning in Idrija. A warehouse nearby contains a mass of mining equipment from before WW I that still works on compressed air. If you're interested, ask the staff at the Municipal Museum about a tour.

One of the most interesting pieces of mining technology that still exists is the **Kamšt**, a 13.5-metre water wheel made of wood that was used to pump the water out of the flooded mines from 1790 until 1948. It is about 1.5 km south-east of Mestni trg just off

Gregorčičeva ulica, the main road. You could combine a visit here with a walk to Wild Lake, about three km south of the town centre.

Wild Lake

An excellent trail called Pot ob Rakah follows the Idrijca River Canal to Wild Lake (Divje Jezero) and the first of the barriers *(klauže)* that dammed the Idrijca and Belca rivers to float timber in the old days.

Wild Lake is a tiny, impossibly green lake fed by a karst spring 83 metres under the surface. After a heavy rain, water gushes up from the tunnel like a geyser and the lake appears to be boiling. Perhaps that's not the right word; the surface temperature never exceeds 10° C.

The lake has been declared a natural monument and little signboards around the shore (which should take you about 15 minutes to circle if you go at a snail's pace) identify the plants and trees and point out the lake's unique features. That body of water flowing from Wild Lake into the Idrijca just happens to be the shortest river in Slovenia. The Jezernica River is 55 metres long.

A couple of hundred metres south of the lake is the first of the water dams that were once called 'Slovenian pyramids' because of their appearance. This one was originally only stacked wood and rocks but was replaced with a permanent stone structure at the end of the last century. The two gates at the top stopped the flow of water to allow wood to float to the mine. Wood was an important commodity for two reasons. First, something had to support those 700 km of tunnels and, second, the heat needed to extract mercury from cinnabar required a lot of fuel. The dams continue for some 12 km down the Belca River.

The area of the Idrijca near the suspension bridge is good for swimming in summer, when the water averages about 20° C.

Festivals

The big event in Idrija is the annual Lace-making Festival during the last weekend in

August. The highlight is a contest in which up to 200 women compete.

Places to Stay & Eat

In summer the *Nikolaj Pirnat* student dormitory (☎ 71 052) at Ulica IX Korpusa 6 has 56 beds available in multi-bedded rooms.

The 26-room *Ydria* hotel (☎ 73 909) at Lapajnetova ulica 53 is the only hotel in town. While it is central and clean, the empty halls and restaurant give it a gloomy, neglected feel. Singles with shower and breakfast are a reasonable 2400 SIT, while doubles are 3600 SIT. Don't try to check in between noon and 6 pm when reception is closed.

Pri Škafarju ('At the Tub') is a very friendly restaurant at Ulica Svete Barbare 9, which also has rooms available. It is open weekdays to 10 pm and to 11 pm on Friday and Saturday nights. Pizza baked in a wood-burning tile stove is why most people come here, but they have plenty of other dishes on the menu as well. The upstairs dining area is reserved for non-smokers, very unusual in Slovenia.

Pri Škafarju does decent enough žlikrofi (350 SIT for a large plate of them), but the best place to have this most Idrijan of specialities is at *Kos*, a little pub and restaurant at Tomšičeva ulica 4 not far from the Ydria hotel. Don't be put off from entering what looks at first like a private club; the locals are friendly. The *Nebesa*, by the bridge over the Nikova River at Prelovčeva ulica 5, is a central place for lunch or a snack.

A *market* is held in Trg Sveta Ahaca on the 15th and 20th of every month.

Entertainment

Castle evenings of classical, folk and jazz concerts take place in the courtyard of Gewerkenegg Castle every second Friday or so in July, August and September. Contact the museum (☎ 71 135) for schedules and information.

Things to Buy

Idrija lace is among the finest in the world and a small piece, though not cheap, makes a great gift or souvenir. The best place to buy it is at a shop called Čipka (appropriately enough) at Mestni trg 12. The Vanda shop in Gewerkenegg has a smaller selection. They are open from 9 am till noon and 4 to 7 pm on weekdays and on Saturday morning.

Getting There & Away

Bus Idrija is not the easiest place in the world to reach. The town is not on a train line and bus service is fairly limited. There are hourly departures to Cerkno and Ljubljana, about five buses a day to Bovec, Črni Vrh and Tolmin, three to Ajdovščina and one to Nova Gorica (which then carries on into Italian Gorizia).

Car Rental Kompas Hertz rents cars from their office at Lapajnetova ulica.

CERKNO (pop 2170)

This town, 20 km to the north, has nothing like the history of Idrija. But it does have two particular features. This is the land of the *Laufarija*, the ancient Shrovetide celebration in which the key players wear artfully crafted wooden masks and 'execute' the Old Year. If you don't get a chance to come to Cerkno for Mardi Gras to see the famous show, you'll have to be content with looking at the masks in the town's museum. Cerkno is also known for its strange dialect (in a country where there are something like 50 dialects). People from outside the Cerkno region (Cerkljanska) always seem to smile when they hear what is the equivalent of an American Southern drawl.

Orientation & Information

Cerkno lies in the Cerknica River Valley about four km north-east of the main road linking Idrija and the Soča Valley. Glavni trg, the main square, is where the buses stop, and Ljubljanska Banka is here too, at No 18. The post office and telephone centre is in Sedejev trg next to the Cerkno hotel, whose helpful staff can provide information.

The telephone code for Cerkno is 065. The postcode is 65282.

PRIMORSKA

Cerkno Museum

The Cerkno Museum (Cerkljanski Muzej) is about 150 metres south-west of Glavni trg at Bevkova ulica 12. A large section of this small museum is given over to the work of the WW II Partisans in secret hospitals and printing presses around the region, but those displays are black, white and grey at best and labelled in Slovene only. Step into the room with the Laufarji masks. It's a lot brighter.

Ethnologists believe that the Laufarija tradition and the masks came from Austria's South Tyrol hundreds of years ago. *Lauferei* means 'running about' in German and that's just what they do as they nab their victim. The masks with the crazy, distorted faces on display are originals bought from one of the Laufarji clubs. Only one man in Cerkno still makes them – and he's on the shady side of 80.

Groups of boys and young men (and now a few girls and women) belonging to Laufarji societies (like the Mardi Gras clubs in New Orleans) organise the event every year and

about two dozen clubs perform. Those aged 15 and over are allowed to enter, but they must prove themselves as worthy apprentices by sewing costumes. Costumes – not masks – must be made fresh every year because many of them are made out of leaves, pine branches, straw or moss stitched onto a burlap (hessian) backing and can take quite a beating during Mardi Gras.

The action takes place on the Sunday before Ash Wednesday and again on Pustni Torek – Shrove Tuesday. The main character is the Pust, whose mask is horned and who wears a moss costume weighing up to 100 kilos. He's the symbol of winter and the old year and he must die.

The Pust is charged by people with a long list of 'crimes' – a bad harvest, inclement weather, lousy roads – and, of course, is found guilty. Some of the other two-dozen Laufarji characters represent crafts and trades – the Baker, the Thatcher, the Woodsman – while the rest have certain character traits or afflictions such as the Drunk and his Wife, the Bad Boy, Sneezy, the Sick Man who always plays the accordion. The Old Man wearing Slovenian-style lederhosen and a wide-brimmed hat executes the Pust with a wooden mallet and the body is rolled away on a caisson.

The Cerkno Museum shows a very dated video of the Laufarija in Slovene, but it is entertaining and illustrates how the masks and costumes are made and how the events unfold at Mardi Gras. It is open daily except Monday from 9 am to 2 pm and admission is 200 SIT (100 SIT for children).

Franja Partisan Hospital

This hospital hidden in a canyon near Dolenji Novaki, about five km north-east of Cerkno, treated wounded Partisan soldiers from Yugoslavia and those from another half-dozen countries from late 1943 until the end of WW II. Unlike other such memorials in Slovenia, Franja Hospital has nothing to do with political or economic systems. It is a memorial to humanism, courage and self-sacrifice. It is a moving and very worthwhile

Laufarji mask, Cerkno Museum

place to visit and the most popular WW II museum in Slovenia.

The complex, named after its chief physician, Dr Franja Bojc-Bidovec, was built in December 1943 for the needs of the IX Corps which included seven brigades and a large number of companies – a total of some 10,000 soldiers. By May 1945 it counted some 13 structures, including treatment sheds, operating theatres, X-ray rooms and bunkers for convalescence. More than 500 wounded were treated here and the mortality rate was only about 10%.

The complex, hidden in a ravine by the Pasica Stream with steep walls riddled with caves, had an abundance of fresh water which was also used to power a hydroelectric generator. Because of the hospital's isolated position noise was not a problem. Local farmers and Partisan groups provided food which was lowered down the steep cliffs by rope; medical supplies were diverted from hospitals in occupied areas or later airdropped by the Allies. The hospital came under attack by the Germans twice – once in April 1944 and again in March 1945 – but it was never taken.

The Franja Partisan Hospital is open April to September daily from 9 am to 6 pm and till 4 pm in March, October and November. From December to February it is open from 9 am to 4 pm on Saturday, Sunday and holidays only.

Raven Cave

The snow white aragonite crystals in the Raven Cave (Ravenska Jama) at Ravne, about seven km south-west of Cerkno are a very rare phenomenon. They are formed by karst springs containing magnesium as well as calcium and are very beautiful, resembling ice, needles and even hedgehogs. The cave is 682 metres long and you can see about half of it in three galleries. But to visit, you must seek permission from the Srečko Logar Caving Club (no telephone) at Ljubljanska cesta 5 in Idrija or from the Municipal Museum.

Hiking

The Cerkno Hills (Cerkljansko Hribovje) are excellent for hiking and the *Cerkno Map of Local Walks* available from the Cerkno hotel lists some eight walks, most of them fairly easy. They include walks to the **Franja Partisan Hospital** (No 7; 3½ hours return) and **Raven Cave** (No 2; four hours). The highest peak in the area is **Mt Porezen** (1632 metres) to the north-east, which has a mountain hut called *Dom na Poreznu* (☎ 75 711) with accommodation. It is open daily from June to September.

Skiing

The **Črni Vrh** ski centre, 10 km north-east of Cerkno, is situated at an altitude of 1290 metres and covers 50 hectares of ski slopes. In normal snow conditions (there are cannons for making artificial snow), four tows and two chair lifts operate. The closest accommodation is at Cerkno or Dolenji Novaki so you'll have to make it a day trip via one of the special ski buses which operate during normal snow conditions.

Festivals

The Laufarija festival in late February or early March takes place outdoors both in Glavni trg and Sedejev trg near the Cerkno hotel.

Places to Stay & Eat

The 75-room *Cerkno* hotel (☎ 75 111; fax 75 207) with some 140 beds is in a modern building in the heart of town at Sedejev trg 12. You wouldn't travel halfway across the world just to stay in a place like this, but it's comfortable enough with an indoor pool, sauna, gym and three clay tennis courts. Singles with breakfast and shower are DM55 to DM72, depending on the category and season, while doubles are DM90 to DM117. The hotel offers discounts for stays of more than two nights.

The *V Logu* inn (☎ 75 476) in Dolenji Novaki (house No 1) not far from the Franja Partisan Hospital is very popular with local people, particularly for lunch at the weekend. It is open daily from 11 am to 11 pm.

V Logu also has four rooms where you can stay for about DM50 for a double.

Getting There & Away

There are hourly departures by bus to Idrija and up to five a day to Ljubljana and Bovec via Most na Soči, Tolmin and Kobarid. Another five or so go just to Tolmin, where you can change for Nova Gorica and the coast.

Karst Region

The Karst region is a small limestone plateau stretching south of Nova Gorica to the Škocjan Caves in the south-east, west to the Gulf of Trieste and east to the Vipava Valley. Because it was the first such area to be researched and described in the 19th century, it is called the Classic, Real, True or Original Karst and always spelled with an upper-case 'K'. Other karst (from the Slovene word *kras*) areas around the world are similar but they get a down-graded 'k'.

Millions of years ago this part of Europe was covered by a deep sea which left thick layers of limestone deposits. When the sea dried up, craters and fissures began to appear, growing deeper and creating large stone fragments that were bleached white by the sun. Because most of the soil blew away, vegetation is scarce, giving the landscape a desolate, wild appearance.

Rivers, ponds and lakes can disappear and then resurface in the porous limestone through sinkholes and funnels. Some produce large underground caverns like the Škocjan Caves. The calcium bicarbonate from the dripping water below creates stalactites (the ones that hang down) and stalagmites (the ones that shoot up). When these underground caverns collapse – and they do periodically – they form a depression *(polje)* which collects soil (mostly red clay, the *terra rossa* of the Karst) and then vegetation. They are cultivated and because of all the sinkholes and underground water they tend to flood quickly in the heavy rain.

The Karst, with its olives, ruby-red Teran wine, air-dried pršut ham and old stone churches, is some people's favourite part of Slovenia. You can explore Rihemberk Castle at Branik or the walled village of Štanjel to the north, but the areas with the most to see and do are to the south.

Though the weather is very pleasant for most of the year with lots of sun and low humidity, don't be fooled into thinking it's all sweetness and light all the time. The bora *(burja* in Slovene), a fiercely cold northerly wind from the Adriatic Sea, can do a lot of damage in winter, ripping off roofs and uprooting trees. It does give the pršut its distinctive taste, though, they say.

ŠKOCJAN CAVES

The karst caves at Škocjan are far more captivating and 'real' than the larger one at Postojna, some 33 km to the north-east in Notranjska province. For many travellers a visit here will be a highlight of their trip to Slovenia – a page right out of Jules Verne's *A Voyage to the Centre of the Earth.* Heed the words of a French speleologist who wrote in 1955: 'In the Postojna Cave the speleologist sees everything he could desire, but the Škocjan Caves have no comparison in the world'.

The Škocjan Caves (Škocjanske Jame), five km long and 250 metres deep, were carved out by the Reka River, which originates in the foothills of Mt Snežnik to the south-east. The Reka enters the caves in a gorge below the village of Škocjan (San Canziano in Italian) and eventually flows into the Dead Lake (Mrtvo Jezero), where it disappears. It surfaces again – this time as the Timavo River – at Duino in Italy, some 40 km to the north-west, before emptying into the Gulf of Trieste.

The entrances to the caves were known by prehistoric people who used them for refuge or to make sacrifices to the gods of the underworld. They were also used for refuge throughout the turbulent Middle Ages. Janez Vajkard Valvasor described the caves and the phenomenon of the disappearing Reka in his encyclopaedic work *The Glory of the Duchy of Carniola* in 1689, but real exploration did not start until the mid-19th century. Organised visits followed soon afterward, but the caves never became the tourist Mecca that Postojna did; electric lighting was not even installed until 1959. Today visitors can explore about two km of these spectacular caves.

UNESCO included the caves and surrounding nature reserve in its World Natural Heritage List in 1986.

Orientation & Information

The caves are at Matavun, a small village about 1.5 km east of the main Ljubljana-Koper highway. The closest town of any size is Divača (pop 1750), about five km to the north-west. Divača's train station, where buses stop as well, is on Trg 15 Aprila about 600 metres west of this highway.

The information office (☎ 067 60 548) at the caves' reception area is open from 9 am until the last tour departs. The small shop there sells good guides and maps to the caves and surrounding areas, including a UNESCO 1:5000-scale map of the caves.

The telephone code for Divača and the Škocjan Caves is 067. The postcode is 66215.

Touring the Caves

If you have some time to spare before your tour departs, follow the path leading north from the reception area for 300 metres to the **lookout** (it is signposted 'Razgledišče/Belvedere' in Slovene and Italian). Extending before you is a superb vista of the Big Valley (Velika Dolina) and gorge where the Reka starts its subterranean journey (and close to where you will emerge from the caves). Across the 180-metre-deep gorge to the east is the village of **Škocjan** and the 17th century **Church of St Cantianus**. St Cantianus is the protector against evil spirits and

PRIMORSKA

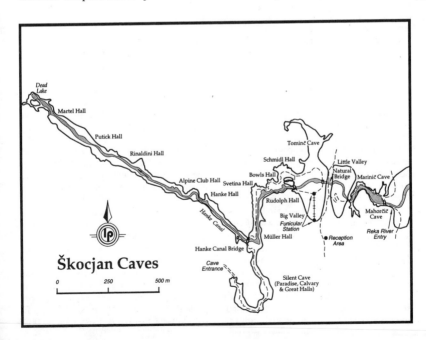

Škocjan Caves

0   250   500 m

floods and is also the caves' namesake. He's a good man to know in this volatile part of Slovenia.

Visitors to the caves assemble around the picnic tables across from the restaurant at the reception area and walk with their guides for about 500 metres down a gravel path to the main entrance in the Gločak Valley. Through an artificial tunnel built in 1933, you soon reach the head of the **Silent Cave** (Tiha Jama), a dry branch of the underground canyon that stretches for half a km. The first section, called **Paradise**, is filled with beautiful stalactites, stalagmites and flow stones; the second part (called **Calvary**) was once the river bed. The Silent Cave ends at the **Great Hall** (Velika Dvorana), 120 metres wide and 30 metres high. It is a jungle of exotic dripstones and deposits; keep an eye open for the stalagmite called the **Giant** and one named the **Organ**.

The sound of the Reka River rushing through cascades and whirlpools below signals your entry into the astonishing **Müller Hall**, with walls 100 metres high. To get over the Reka you must cross **Hanke Canal Bridge**, 45 metres high, narrow and surely the highlight of the trip. Count your blessings as you do (or don't) look down; the catwalk that allowed visitors to cross over into **Svetina Hall** before the bridge was built 60 years ago was 20 metres higher.

Only experienced speleologists are allowed to explore the caves and halls in the siphon that extends downward to the west ending at Dead Lake. Every century or so the siphon becomes blocked and the caves are flooded. This happened most recently in 1965.

From Svetina Hall you climb up a path hewn into the stone to **Bowls Hall**, remarkable for its rare bowl-like pans which were formed from calcium deposits when water flooding the cave churned and swirled up to the ceiling. They look like troughs or rice terraces. The final section, **Schmidl Hall**, opens on to the Velika Dolina. From here you walk past **Tominč Cave**, where finds from a prehistoric settlement have been unearthed, and over a walkway near a natural bridge to

the funicular, which carries you 90 metres up the rock face close to the reception area.

Having probably not seen much evidence of it, you will be surprised to learn that the Škocjan Caves are home to an incredible amount of flora and fauna: 250 varieties of plants and five different types of bats. The temperature in the caves is constant at about 13°C so you should bring along a light jacket or sweater. Good walking shoes (the way can get pretty wet and slippery in the high humidity) and a torch (flashlight) are also recommended.

The caves can be visited six times a day from June to September at 10 and 11.30 am and again at 1, 2, 3.30 and 5 pm. In April, May and October there are tours at 10 am and at 1 and 3.30 pm. From November to March, visits are allowed on Sunday and holidays only at 10 am and 3 pm. The entry fee is 1200 SIT for adults and 900 SIT for children. The tours, much less structured than at Postojna Cave, are given in five different languages (the guides will separate you) and they take about two hours.

Activities
The Farma Diomed (☎ 60 003) in Lokev, halfway between Divača and Lipica, has horses for hire. An excellent excursion would be to ride for a couple of km north-west to 803-metre-long **Vilenica Cave** (Jama Vilenica). This was the first Karst cave to open to the public in the early 19th century and guests are welcome every Sunday at 3 pm. **Divača Cave** (Divaška Jama), about three km north-east on the road to Divača, is open only by arrangement. It is only 672 metres long but has excellent dripstones and rock formations. Inquire at the Lipica Stud Farm or the Risnik pension.

Places to Stay & Eat
The closest *camp site* (☎ 82 689) to the caves is at Kozina, seven km south of Divača. It's a tiny place, barely covering a hectare, and is full of caravans and cars. It's open from May to September and costs DM9 per person.

In Divača, the *Risnik* pension (☎ 60 008)

at Kraška cesta 24, is the only place to stay near the caves unless you want to head for Sežana, a dull town nine km to the north-west where there are two small hotels: the *Tabor* (☎ 31 551) near the train station at Kolodvorska ulica 4 or the *Triglav* (☎ 31 361) at Partizanska ulica 1. They are both fairly nondescript but reasonable at about DM34 for a single with shower and breakfast and DM50 for a double.

The Risnik, about 400 metres north of the main highway to the caves and the coast, only has a dozen doubles (no singles) for 2400 SIT. It is very noisy here – with the highway, a busy petrol station opposite and buses and trains heading for the station.

The Risnik has a gloomy *restaurant* that serves fairly decent food. A much more pleasant place to eat in Divača is the *Klunov Hram*, a cellar restaurant 200 metres away at Kraška cesta 32. It has some good pasta dishes, like njoki, and pizza, as well as its own homemade Teran wine. The Klunov Hram is open daily, except Wednesday, from 11 am to 10 pm. Nearby is the 17th century Škratelj House, the oldest traditional Karst house in Slovenia.

There's a gostilna called *Pri Jami* at the caves' reception area open from 9 am to 8 pm.

Getting There & Away
The Škocjan Caves are about five km by road south-east of the Divača train station. Getting there by public transport can be tricky, but buses heading along the highway toward the coast might let you off at the access road (there are huge signs announcing the caves) from where you can walk the remaining 1.5 km. All in all, it's probably easier to go there on foot via a three-km path that leads south-east from Divača and through the village of Dolnje Ležeče to Matavun.

Destinations served by bus from Divača include Celje (five a day), Ilirska Bistrica (one), Koper (hourly), Kozina (two), Ljubljana via Postojna (eight), Maribor (three), Murska Sobota (one), Nova Gorica (five), Novo Mesto (two) and Piran (six).

Divača is on the rail line linking Ljubljana (104 km; 1½ hours) with Sežana (nine km; 10 minutes). Divača is also the railhead for the three daily trains to Buzet and Pula in Croatia.

LIPICA (pop 125)
The impact of Lipica, some 10 km south-west of Divača, on the world of sport has been far greater than its tiny size would suggest. In 1580, in what was then called Lipizza, the Austrian Archduke Charles, son of Ferdinand I, established a stud farm *(kobilarna)* to breed horses for the Spanish Riding School in Vienna.

The riding school had been founded eight years before to train horses for the imperial court and was looking for a lighter, more elegant breed for parades and military pur-poses. This would lead to the development of dressage. Andalusian horses from Spain were coupled with the local Karst breed that the Romans had once used to pull chariots and the Lipizzaner was born. They weren't quite the snow-white beauties we know today. Those didn't come about for another 200 years when white Arabian horses got into the act.

It's easy to see why both Charles and the nags liked the place. Though very much part of the region this 'oasis in the barren Karst', as Lipica is called, feels like Eden after all that limestone. Indeed, the word *lipica* in Slovene means 'little linden', after the trees that grow in such profusion here. The mod-erate, dry climate provides ideal conditions for breeding horses with speed, strength and stamina.

The stud farm remained the property of the court in Vienna until the end of WW I when the Italians took control of Primorska province. Herds were moved to Hungary and then Austria but the change in climate took its toll. In 1943, with WW II still raging, the Germans moved more than 200 horses to the Sudetenland in Bohemia (now the Czech Republic). When the area was liberated by American forces in 1945, most of the horses and the stud farm's archives were shipped to

PRIMORSKA

Italy. Sadly, only 11 returned when operations resumed at Lipica in 1947.

Today 180 Lipizzaners (and another 40 ponies) remain at the original stud farm while 'genuine' Lipizzaners are bred in various locations around the world: Croatia, Hungary, Italy, Slovakia and even in the American state of Illinois. The farm at Piber, north-east of Graz in Austria, now breeds the horses for the Spanish Riding School.

Orientation & Information

Lipica lies less than two km north of the Italian border and six km south of Sežana. The centre of everything, of course, is the stud farm in the south-west corner of the village and its two hotels nearby.

The information office (☎ 31 781) at the entrance to the stud farm can change money, but they take a 2% commission. The telephone code for Lipica is 067. The postcode is 66210.

Lipica Stud Farm

Tours of the 311-hectare stud farm begin

opposite the information and ticket office; simply wait by the sign naming the language you want (English, German, French, Italian or Slovene). The guide will find you.

A visit covers the stables, one of which dates from 1703, and the riding halls to give you an idea of what it's like to learn dressage and control a very large animal. But, frankly, it's a boring tour with endless facts, figures and horse pedigrees.

The highlight of a visit (if you can time it right) is seeing these elegant horses go through their complicated paces with riders *en costume*. It's not as complete a show as the one at the Spanish Riding School in Vienna or in as ornate surroundings, but watching great white horses pirouetting and dancing to Viennese waltzes sort of makes up for it. If you miss the performance, at least hang around for when the horses are moved from the stables to pasture at about 10.30 am and again in the late afternoon. It's stunning stuff as they gallop past.

You can visit the Lipica Stud Farm throughout the year, and it's open from 8 am

The Dancing Horses of Lipica

Lipizzaners are considered to be the finest riding horses in the world – the *haute cole* of dressage horse – and with all the trouble that's put into producing them, it's not surprising. They are very intelligent, sociable horses, quite robust and graceful.

Breeding is paramount and it is carried out with all the precision of a well-organised crime. Some six families with 16 ancestors can be traced back to the early 18th century and their pedigrees read like those of medieval royalty. When you walk around the stables at Lipica you'll see charts on each horse stall with complicated figures, dates and names like 'Maestoso Allegra' and 'Neapolitano'. It's all to do with the horse's lineage.

Lipizzaners foal between January and May and the colts and fillies suckle for six or seven months. They remain in the herd for about three years. They are then separated for training, which takes another four years.

Surprisingly, Lipizzaners are not white when they are born, but are grey, bay or even chestnut. The celebrated 'imperial white' does not develop until they are between five to 10 years old, when their hair loses its pigment. Think of it as just part of the old nag's ageing process. Their skin remains grey, however, so when they are ridden hard and sweat, they become mottled and are not so attractive.

A fully mature Lipizzaner measures about 15 hands, or about 153cm, and weighs between 500 and 600 kilos. They have long backs, short, thick necks, silky manes and expressive eyes. They live for 25 to 30 years and are particularly resistant to disease.

Lipizzaners are bred at Lipica, in Austria, and in the US as riding and show horses; they are known for their beauty, elegance and agility. However, Lipizzaners at Szilv sva'rad near Eger in Hungary, and at Jakovo near Osijek in Croatia, are raised primarily as carriage horses so as a result they are bigger and stronger than those found elsewhere. ■

to 6 pm. From May to September guided tours (mandatory) leave at 9.30, 10.30 and 11.30 am and on the hour till 5 pm. In April and October, the 5 pm tour is cancelled and from November to March there are only six tours a day: at 9.30, 10.30 and 11.30 am and again at 1, 2 and 3 pm. Tickets cost DM11 for adults and DM7.50 for children.

Exhibition performances take place from April to October at 2.30 pm on Tuesday and Friday and at 3.30 pm on Sunday. Admission to the performance, which includes the tour of the stud farm, is DM20 for adults and DM12 for children.

Activities

Some 60 horses are available for riding both in the ring and the countryside from 9 to 10.30 am and 3 to 5.30 pm Monday to Saturday and 9 am to 6 pm on Sunday. The cost is DM20 per hour. Also, there is a large choice of courses, including six two-hour lessons for beginners (DM300), for advanced riders (DM270) and in dressage (DM480; minimum L-level ability required). For children and/or the timid there are pony rides (DM12) and one-hour carriage jaunts (DM20).

The nearby Lipica Golf Course (☎ 72 930) has nine holes for a par 36. The green fees are about DM25 and you can rent clubs.

Places to Stay & Eat

There are two hotels in Lipica, both managed by one company and costing about the same: singles with breakfast and shower are DM67 to DM92, depending on the season, and doubles are DM96 to DM136. But these prices are discounted for stays of a week or more, and if you do a course.

The 65-room *Maestoso* (☎ 31 541: fax 72 818) has most of the amenities, including a swimming pool (closed Tuesday), sauna and tennis courts nearby. The 80-room *Klub Lipica* (☎ 31 849; fax 72 818) is generally reserved for those staying for longer periods. It has a pool (closed Monday) and is slightly closer to the stud farm.

The Maestoso has a *self-service restaurant* and a terrace café with food. The best (and most expensive) eatery in the complex is the *Lipica* wine cellar restaurant.

Entertainment

The *casino* at the Maestoso hotel is open from 4 or 5 pm to 3 am daily. The hotel also has a popular disco.

Getting There & Away

Most people visit Lipica as a day trip from Divača or Sežana, which are on the rail line to Ljubljana. You can reach both towns on one of two buses a day from Lipica.

HRASTOVLJE (pop 425)

Hrastovlje lies near the source of the Rižana River, its valley effectively forms the boundary between the Karst and the coast. From here northward to the village of Črni Kal and on to Osp, a row of fortresses were built below the limestone plains during the Bronze Age which the Illyrian tribe of Histrians later adapted to their needs. The valley and surrounding areas became safe havens for later inhabitants during the Great Migrations and the Turkish invasions.

The Romanesque church in this tiny village is the Istrian equivalent of St John the Baptist's Church in Bohinj. OK, so it's not on a lake. But it is small, surrounded by medieval walls with corner towers and it is covered inside with extraordinary 15th century frescoes.

Church of the Holy Trinity

This three-aisle church was built between the 12th and 14th centuries in the Istrian Romanesque style though the fortifications were added in 1581 in advance of the Ottomans. As you approach this structure of grey Karst stone at the southern end of the village of Hrastovlje, just imagine the fear in the hearts of the men, women and children who scrambled to protect what they most likely considered to the most important thing in their lives.

The sombre exterior does not prepare you for what's inside: the complete interior of the church is festooned with **narrative frescoes**

Church of the Holy Trinity

painted by Johannes de Castuo (John of Kastav near Rijeka) around 1490. The paintings are a *Biblia pauperum* – a 'Bible of the poor' to help the illiterate understand the Old Testament stories, the Passion of Christ and the lives of the saints. It is a unique way to understand how our ancestors viewed their lives, joys, hopes and sufferings. Spare the 20 minutes it takes to listen to the taped commentary that will guide you around the little church in English, German, Italian or Slovene. It's dull with a capital 'D', but there are a lot of things you'd miss otherwise.

Facing you as you enter is the main altar and central apse with scenes from the Crucifixion and portraits of the Trinity and the Apostles. On the arch Mary is being crowned Queen of Heaven. The central aisle has episodes from the **seven days of Creation**, including the story of Adam and Eve, as well as the murder of Abel by Cain – all easy stories for an unschooled 15th century peasant to comprehend. On the ceilings of the north (left) and south (right) aisles are scenes from daily life (sowing, hunting, fishing, making wine) as well as the **calendar year** and its seasonal duties. **Christ's Passion** is depicted at the top of the southernmost wall, including his descent into hell where devils are attacking him with blazing cannons.

Yes, I've saved the best bit for last. Below the Passion is what attracts most people to Hrastovlje and its little church: the famous **Dance of Death fresco** (also called the Danse Macabre) showing 11 skeletons leading an equal number of people to a freshly dug grave, a pick and shovel at the ready. A twelfth skeleton holds a list of the 'invited'. The line-up includes a child, a beggar, a burgher, a merchant, a noble, a monk, a bishop, a nun, a queen, a king and an emperor.

Ghoulish and strange though the Dance of Death may appear to be at first, it carries a simple message: we are all equal in the eyes of God no matter how important we (or others) think we are in this mortal life. It was a radical concept perhaps for the late 15th century in a remote part of Europe and it remains a sobering and thought-provoking one today.

Out in the churchyard have a look around at the two corner towers and ancient walls several metres thick. The strange cliffs of loose rock to the north make up the Kraški Rob – the very 'Edge of the Karst' – above the village of Črni Kal, marking the end of the stony limestone plateau and the start of a green valley leading to the sea. Could it be that this little church between two worlds was placed in this geographical limbo on purpose?

Entry to Holy Trinity Church costs 300 SIT for adults and 150 SIT for students and children. It is open every day from morning to evening but should you find it locked, seek the key from house No 30 in the village.

Getting There & Away

Hrastovlje is 31 km south-west of Divača off the main highway to the coast; Koper is 18 km to the north-west. Any bus heading along this road in either direction will drop you off just west of Črni Kal, but it's still another six km south to Hrastovlje. One of the three daily buses from Koper to Gračišče or to Buzet in Croatia could get you closer, but without a car or bicycle (or a horse or bullock cart) the only sure way of making it to Hrastovlje is by train.

Unfortunately it's not a very extensive or flexible schedule. A train leaves Divača every morning at 7.40, arriving at Hrastovlje at 8.15; the church is about one km to the north-west. The next train through this backwater is the 7.20 pm from Koper, which gets into Hrastovlje 20 minutes later. The train goes on to Divača, Postojna and Ljubljana.

The Coast

Slovenia's very short coast on the Adriatic Sea is both an area of history and recreation. Three important towns full of Venetian Gothic architecture and art (Koper, Piran and Izola) will keep even the most slavish sightseer busy and there are beaches, boats for rent and rollicking discos at Portorož and Ankaran.

But the coast is not everybody's cup of tea. It is very overbuilt, jammed from May to September and not especially clean. Most Slovenes give it a miss in favour of the unspoiled beaches of Istria or Dalmatia, leaving it to the Germans and Italians. If you want solitude, head for the hinterland to the south or east where 'Slovenian Istria' still goes about its daily life. Or spend an afternoon at the eerily tranquil salt pans of Sečovlje.

The Koper wine-producing area is known for its white Malvazija, Chardonnay and red Refošk. A number of cultural events take place during the Primorska Summer Festival in Koper, Izola, Piran and Portorož in July and August. If you're spending some time in this part of Slovenia, pick up a copy of the *Guidebook to the Coast*, a helpful 80-page booklet in English and German. Bear in mind that many of the hotels, camp sites, tourist offices and restaurants close down during the off-season from November to March or April.

KOPER (pop 25,300)
Koper is a workaday port city where tourism is barely given a second thought. It is much less crowded and smug than its ritzy cousin Piran, 17 km down the coast, but despite the

surrounding industry, container ports and high-rise buildings, Koper has managed to preserve its compact medieval centre. Its recreational area, the seaside resort of Ankaran, is to the north across Koper Bay.

Koper has been known by many names through its long and turbulent history. As an island separated from the mainland by a canal, it was called Aegida by ancient Greek sailors, Capris by the Romans (who found it being used to raise goats) and Justinopolis by the Byzantines. The Patriarchs of Aquileia, who took over the town in the 13th century and made it the base for their estates on the Istrian peninsula, renamed it Caput Histriae – 'Capital of Istria' – from which its Italian name Capodistria is derived. They fortified the town and erected some of Koper's most beautiful buildings, including its cathedral and palaces.

Koper's golden age was during the 15th and 16th centuries under the domination of the Venetian Republic. Trade increased and Koper became the administrative and judicial centre for Istria as far as Buzet to the south-east and Novigrad on the coast. It also had a monopoly on salt, which Austria desperately needed. But when Trieste, 20 km to the north-east, was proclaimed a free port in the early 18th century and the Habsburgs opened a railway line between Vienna and Trieste in 1857, Koper's fate was sealed. Many people moved inland to raise grapes, olives and stone fruits.

Between the two world wars, Koper was administered by the Italians, who launched an aggressive programme of Italianisation, closing bilingual schools and keeping close tabs on Slovenian intellectuals. After the defeat of Italy and Germany in WW II, the disputed areas of the Adriatic coast – the so-called Free Territory of Trieste – was divided into two zones. Under the London Agreement of 1954, Zone B and its capital Koper went to Yugoslavia while Zone A, including Trieste, fell under Italian jurisdiction.

Up to 25,000 Italian-speaking Istrians fled to Trieste, but 3000 stayed in Koper and other coastal settlements. Today Koper is the

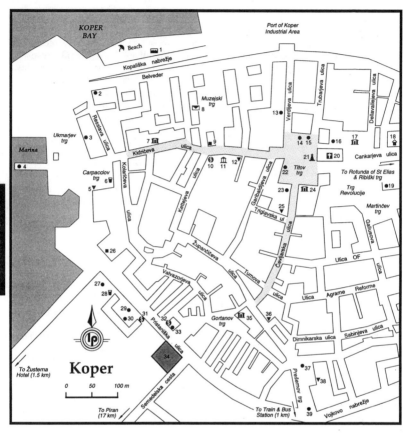

PRIMORSKA

Koper

To Žusterna
Hotel (1.5 km)

0   50   100 m

To Piran
(17 km)

To Train & Bus
Station (1 km)

centre of the Italian ethnic community of Slovenia and Italian is widely spoken. Indeed, Koper is one of the few places in Slovenia where English and German is often of little use when dealing with middle-aged and older people.

Koper has developed rapidly since the 1950s. Not only is it Slovenia's only shipping port (and Austria's main outlet to the sea) but also a business and industrial centre. It is by far the largest town on the coast.

island until the early 19th century when it was joined to the mainland by a causeway and later landfill. Today it's difficult to imagine it as a separate entity as you travel from the combined bus and train station, which is one km to the south-east at the end of Kolodvorska cesta.

The centre of the Old Town is Titov trg, a marvellous Gothic-Renaissance square with Venetian influences. The marina and tiny city beach are to the north-west of the square.

Orientation

Koper's semi-circular Old Town was an

Information

Money Splošna Banka Koper, which doesn't

PLACES TO STAY

9	Private Rooms
18	Dijaški Dom Koper
26	Triglav Hotel

PLACES TO EAT

5	Taverna Restaurant
12	Bife Vrt
25	Atrij Pizzeria
36	Istrska Klet Restaurant
38	Trgovina Restaurant

OTHER

1	Bath House
2	Italian Consulate
3	Slovenijaturist Travel Agency
4	Customs Wharf
6	Elite Disco
7	Totto Palace
8	Post Office
10	Splošna Banka Koper
11	Belgramoni-Tacco Palace/Regional Museum
13	Theatre
14	Loggia/Café
15	Koper Gallery
16	Baptistery (Carmine Rotunda)
17	Brutti Palace
19	Fontico
20	Cathedral of St Nazarius
21	City Tower
22	Town Hall
23	Jewellery Shop
24	Praetorian Palace
27	Park
28	Outdoor Café/Pub
29	Vegetable Market
30	Supermarket
31	Exchange Bureau
32	Exchange Bureau
33	Kompas Travel Agency
34	Department Store
35	Almerigogna Palace
37	Da Ponte Fountain
39	Muda Gate

charge a commission on travellers' cheques, has a branch at Kidričeva ulica 21 a few doors west of the regional museum. It is open from 8.30 am till noon and from 3 to 5 pm weekdays and Saturday morning. Compare their rates with those at the private exchange offices at Pristaniška ulica 13 next to Kompas and another in the east wing of the large shopping complex and market across the street. Both of these are open weekdays to 7.30 or 8 pm and on Saturday to 1 pm.

Post & Telecommunications The main post office and telephone centre is next to the train and bus station. It is open from 7 am to 8 pm on weekdays, to 7 pm on Saturday and from 8 am till noon on Sunday. Much more convenient is the branch at Muzejski trg 3. It is open weekdays from 7 am to 7 pm and on Saturday till 1 pm. As always, you can make telephone calls from this post office too.

Koper's telephone code is 066. The postcode is 66000.

Travel Agencies There is no tourist office as such in Koper; seek assistance from Slovenijaturist (☎ 21 358), opposite the marina at Ukmarjev trg 7 and open weekdays from 8 am to 7 pm and on Saturday to 2 pm, or from Kompas (☎ 22 555). The latter is opposite the outdoor market at Pristaniška ulica 17 and open on weekdays from 8 am to 7.30 pm and to 1 pm on Saturday. Slovenijaturist also has a counter (☎ 31 221) at the bus/train station open from 6 am to 7.30 pm daily. They change travellers' cheques for a 2% commission.

The Italian Consulate is at Belveder 2 opposite the bath house.

Things to See
The easiest way to see almost everything of interest in Koper's Old Town is simply to walk from the marina on Ukmarjev trg east along Kidričeva ulica to Titov trg and then south along Čevljarska ulica.

The first stop is **Carpacciov trg** behind the Taverna restaurant where the **Column of St Justina** commemorates the galley that Koper contributed to the Battle of Lepanto, in which Turkey was defeated by the European powers in 1571. Nearby is a large Roman basin.

On the north side of Kidričeva ulica you'll pass several disused churches and the 16th century **Totto Palace**. On the latter there's a relief of the winged lion of St Mark taken from Koper's medieval fortress. Opposite at No 33 are some wonderful old **medieval town houses** with protruding upper storeys painted red, yellow and green.

The **Koper Regional Museum** in 16th century Belgramoni-Tacco Palace at Kidričeva ulica 19, has old maps and photos of the port and coast, 16th to 18th century Italianate sculptures and paintings and copies of medieval frescoes. The museum is supposed to be open Tuesday to Sunday from 9 am to 1 pm and again from 6 to 8 pm, but you'll just have to try your luck. At least have a look at the wonderful bronze door knocker of Venus rising from the sea.

Titov trg, the centre of Koper, is a beautiful old square full of interesting buildings; mercifully, like much of the Old Town's core, it is closed to traffic. On the north side is the arcaded Venetian Gothic **Loggia** built in 1463. It contains a coffee house and the **Koper Gallery** open from 10 am to noon and from 6 to 8 pm Tuesday to Friday and Saturday mornings. To the south, directly opposite at No 3, is the **Praetorian Palace**, a mixture of Venetian Gothic and Renaissance styles dating from the 15th century and now the symbol of Koper. The facade of the palace, once the residence of Koper's mayor, is chock-a-block with medallions, reliefs and coats of arms of the rich and famous. The Praetorian Palace was once two separate buildings with the Loggia in the centre. When the latter was moved across the square, the wings were joined and the battlements added later.

On the square's western side at No 4, the **town hall** occupies what was an armoury four centuries ago. Opposite is the **Cathedral of St Nazarius** and its belfry, now called the **City Tower**. You can climb this 36-metre tower daily between 10 am and 1 pm and again between 4 and 6 pm.

The cathedral, partly Romanesque and Gothic but mostly dating from the 18th century, is the sixth church on this spot. It has a white classical interior with a feeling of space and light that belies the sombre exterior. The **carved stone sarcophagus**

behind the main altar is that of the cathedral's (and town's) patron, a 6th century bishop. Among the furnishings worth a look are choir stalls made from olive wood, an ornate 18th century **bishop's throne** on the north side and **paintings by Vittore Carpaccio** (1465-1526), a native of Koper. The cathedral doors are open daily from 7 am till noon and from 3 to 7 pm.

Behind the cathedral to the north is a Romanesque **Baptistry** (also called the Carmine Rotunda) dating from the 12th century.

Trg Revolucije, which joins Titov trg on its eastern side, is another square of fine old buildings, including the Baroque **Brutti Palace** to the north and on the eastern side the **Fontico**, a granary where the town's wheat was stored in the 14th century. **Ribiški trg**, a 10-minute walk to the north-east from here is an old fishing quarter with narrow streets and houses dating back to the 14th century. To get there from Trg Revolucije, walk east along Cankarjeva ulica and turn north on to Dijaška ulica. Along the way you'll pass the **Rotunda of St Elias**, a pre-Romanesque structure that may date to the 9th century. Bosadraga ulica, the next street on the right, leads into Ribiški trg.

From Titov trg continue the tour by walking south along **Čevljarska ulica** (Shoemaker's Street). As you walk under the arch of Praetorian Palace, have a look to the right. The little hole in the wall with the Italian inscriptions was the town's so-called lion's mouth, where anonymous denunciations of officials and others could be made.

Čevljarska ulica, a narrow pedestrian street, leads into Župančičeva ulica (Mayor's Street). Just below it, down the stairs in Gortanov trg (No 13) is the **Almerigogna Palace**, a painted Venetian Gothic palace and arguably the most beautiful in Koper. It's now a pub.

The Italian family which erected the **fountain** in **Prešernov trg** in the 17th century was named Da Ponte; thus it is shaped like a bridge. At the southern end is the **Muda Gate**, erected in 1516 and the last of a dozen such entrances to remain standing. On both sides of the archway you'll see the city seal: the face of a youth in a sunburst.

Activities

Koper's tiny – and dirty – beach is on the north-west edge of the Old Town on Kopališko nabrežje. It has a small bathhouse with showers, changing rooms, a grassy area for lying in the sun, a restaurant and a snackbar. It's open daily from 8 am to 8 pm in season.

Places to Stay

Camping The closest *camp sites* are at Ankaran, about 10 km to the north by road, and at Izola, eight km to the west. See those sections for details.

Private Rooms Slovenijaturist and Kompas have *private rooms* available for between DM16 and DM26, depending on the time of year. Both levy a 30% surcharge if you stay less than three nights. The vast majority of the rooms are in the new town beyond the train station, but not all: the family at Kidričeva ulica 16 has great rooms for rent in an old town house. *Apartments* for two start at about DM50.

Hostel Koper has one of Slovenia's six official youth hostels – but, as it is a student dormitory, most of it is open in summer only. *Dijaški Dom Koper* (☎ 24 172), a modern five-storey building at Cankarjeva ulica 6 in the Old Town, rents some 445 beds in three-bedded rooms at DM16 per person including breakfast in July and August. The rest of the year only 35 beds are available. You may have to show a hostel or student card to be admitted.

Hotels The only hotel in the Old Town, the 80-room *Triglav* (☎ 23 771; fax 23 598) at Pristaniška ulica 3, is relatively affordable: singles with shower and breakfast are DM35 to DM62, depending on the season, and doubles DM48 to DM90. The 100-room *Žusterna* (☎ 34 112), the Triglav's sister hotel about 1.5 km west on the main coastal road (Istrska cesta), is open from April to October only and has a swimming pool on the edge of the sea. Singles are DM41 to DM57, doubles DM54 to DM74.

Places to Eat

The *Bife Vrt*, at Kidričeva ulica 17 next to the regional museum, has very basic food and a lovely back courtyard. It's open weekdays till 7 pm and on Saturday till 1 pm. The inexpensive pizzeria called *Atrij* at Triglavska ulica 2 is open most days till 10 pm.

The *Trgovina* restaurant at Prešernov trg 4 lists three-course set meals on a blackboard at the entrance to the dining room. For 650 SIT, you'll get all you can eat plus a large beer. It's patronised mostly by local people and is good value.

One of the most colourful places in Koper for a meal is the *Istrska Klet* in an old palace at Župančičeva ulica 39. Filling set lunches go for 500 SIT, and there's draught wine straight from the barrel. This is the place to try Teran, the hearty red (almost purple) wine from the Karst and coastal wine-growing areas. Istrska Klet is open on weekdays till 9 pm.

The *Taverna*, in a 15th century salt warehouse at Pristaniška ulica 1 opposite the marina, is one of Koper's more up-market restaurants and has some decent fish dishes. The place is always filled with foreign sailors chatting in Spanish, Korean, Chinese or Tagalog.

The large shopping centre and outdoor *market* (open most days from 7 am to 2 pm) on Pristaniška ulica also contains a *supermarket*.

Entertainment

Koper's theatre at Verdijeva ulica 3, a street running north from Titov trg, puts on plays, dance performances and concerts.

Koper often feels more Italian than Slovenian and at dusk, as in most cities and towns across the Adriatic, the *passaggiata* – a lot of strolling and strutting – begins. You can watch some of it from the lovely *Loggia Café* at Titov trg 1, but the outdoor café-cum-pub at the west wing of the market on

PRIMORSKA

Pristaniška ulica facing the park and the marina is where the action is.

The *Elite* is a high-class nightclub and disco at Carpacciov trg 6, once the home of the painter Vittore Carpaccio. It is open every night except Sunday. There's also the *Camel Club* (as in the cigarettes) next to the Žusterna hotel on Istrska cesta, which opens its doors nightly at 10 pm.

Things to Buy
Koper has some very fine shops selling jewellery, textiles and folkcraft at the eastern end of Kidričeva ulica near Titov trg. The Široka jewellery shop at Čevljarska ulica 4 has lovely Art-Deco pieces in silver and onyx, coral etc. Most shops in Koper are closed during siesta, between about 1 and 4 pm.

Getting There & Away
Bus Although train departures are limited, the bus service to and from Koper is excellent. There are departures almost every 20 minutes on weekdays to Izola, Strunjan, Piran and Portorož and every 40 minutes at the weekend. The buses start at the train and bus station and stop at the big market on Koper's waterfront before continuing on to Izola.

Buses also leave hourly for Ankaran and Ljubljana via Divača and Postojna. Other destinations include: Branik (two buses a day); Celje (five); Črna na Koroškem (one); Gračišče (four); Ilirska Bistrica (five); Maribor (four); Murska Sobota (two); Nova Gorica (four); Novo Mesto (two); Sežana (three); Velenje (one) and Vrhnika (up to six).

Frequent service (up to 17 buses a day) to and from nearby Trieste makes Koper an easy entry/exit point to/from Italy. Buses run from 6 am to 7.30 pm mostly on weekdays. The bus station in Trieste is immediately south-west of the train station in Piazza Libertà.

Koper is also an excellent springboard for Istria. Destinations on the Croatian peninsula and their daily departures include: Buzet (three); Novigrad (four); Poreč (five); Pula

(two); Rijeka (one); Rovinj (one) and Savudrija (three). There are three buses a day to Zagreb.

Train Koper is on a minor railway linking it with Ljubljana (163 km; 2½ hours) via Divača. To get to Buzet and Pula in Croatia from here, you must change at Divača or Hrpelje-Kozina for one of the three trains a day.

Car Kompas has Hertz rental cars available from its office on Pristaniška ulica. Parking in much of the Old Town is restricted – or banned – between 6 am and 8 pm. Generally you can only park on the ring road or in the pay car park near Trg Revolucije.

Boat Interagent (☎ 456 100), in the Intereuropa building at the entrance to the commercial port east of the Old Town, handles the Transeuropa ferry to Durrës in Albania, which originates in Trieste. They also run boats from Trieste to Corfu, Igoumenitsa and Patras in Greece with varying frequencies throughout the year. Some of these might stop at Koper first.

Getting Around
Bus Local buses Nos 1, 2 and 3 go from the main bus and train station to the eastern edge of Cankarjeva ulica in the Old Town with a stop not far from Muda Gate.

Taxi Local taxis can be called on ☎ 21 451.

ANKARAN (pop 2820)
With Koper concerned primarily with container ships, the role of city playground has fallen to Ankaran (Ancarano in Italian), a seaside holiday village 10 km by road to the north. There's not much at Ankaran – the first of the Slovenian coastal resorts – apart from a large tourist complex with a camp site and a shopping centre. But it's a lush, very green place with a mild subtropical climate, and Italy is right around the corner. Just follow the main road north-west for 3.5 km to the checkpoint at Lazaret (Lazzaretto). Trieste is

directly across Muggia Bay (Miljski Zaliv) to the north.

Orientation
Ankaran lies on the southern side of the hilly Milje Peninsula, which is shared by Slovenia and Italy. The 'town' is essentially a stretch of the road (Jadranska cesta) that leads from the coastal highway to Italy and the scattered houses and vineyards above it. Buses stop in front of the shopping centre on Jadranska cesta. The Adria resort and camp site are opposite.

Information
Slovenijaturist maintains a tourist kiosk in the shopping centre car park from May to mid-September. At other times, seek assistance from the reception desk at the entrance to the Adria resort.

Splošna Banka Koper has a branch at Jadranska cesta 42. The post office, which also does exchange, is on the western side of the shopping centre at Regentova ulica 1. It is open on weekdays from 8 am to 7 pm and on Saturday to 1 pm.

Ankaran's telephone code is 066. The postcode is 66280.

Activities
The Adria holiday village, which can accommodate more than 2000 people at its hotel, cottages, bungalows and camp site, has a small pebble beach below a cement promenade, two large swimming pools (one faces south-east to the Istrabenz refinery) and sporting facilities, including four tennis courts, minigolf, table tennis, a basketball court and a fitness centre.

The Adria Kayak and Canoe Club (☎ 51 830), which gives lessons and rents equipment, is based at the camp site from May to September. See them any day between 9 am and noon and 4 and 7 pm.

Ankaran is the start (or finish) of the Slovenian Alpine Trail that goes all the way to Maribor via Škocjan Cave, the Cerkno and Idrija hills, the Julian Alps, the Kamnik-Savinja Alps and the Pohorje Massif. The whole trip would take a very fit person a

month of walking eight hours a day. Needless to say, most people find another way to get to Štajerska, where Maribor is located, from here. One of the first stops from Ankaran is **Mt Slavnik** (1028 metres), about eight km north-east of Hrastovlje. The *Tumova Koča na Slavniku* mountain hut (☎ 25 320) near the summit is open weekends and on holidays.

Places to Stay
Adria Camping (☎ 528 323) extends over an area of 12 hectares on the eastern side of the Adria resort and down to the sea. The price per person ranges from DM10 to DM14 depending on the season, and guests get to use all the facilities at the resort. Adria Camping is open from May to September.

The 125-bed *Študentski Tabor* (☎ 528 045), about 1.5 km north-west of the town centre at Jadranska cesta 88, has hostel-style accommodation in July and August.

The *Adria* resort complex (☎ 528 443; fax 528 320) contains a half-dozen different types of accommodation, ranging from cottages with balconies to self-contained seaside bungalows for five people. The cheapest place to stay at the resort just happens to be the most interesting. It's a two-storey hotel dead in the centre called the *Convent* that was once a Benedictine monastery and later became the summer residence of the aristocratic Madonuzza family from Koper. The price per person is DM33 to DM47 for a room with breakfast and shared shower; the differential depends on the season and which direction your room faces. The Convent is open year round; most of the other accommodation at the resort is available from May to September only.

The flashy new 25-room *Biser* hotel (☎ 526 050; fax 526 057), opposite the large (and quite famous) orthopaedic hospital at Jadranska cesta 86a, charges from DM50 to DM70 per person depending on the season. Suites start at DM60 and jump to DM90 in July and August. All the rooms come with air-conditioning, direct-dial telephones and satellite television. There's a fitness centre and a nightclub here as well.

PRIMORSKA

Places to Eat

The *Adria Bistro* at Regentova ulica 2 has light meals and snacks, but the emphasis is on liquid refreshment. The *supermarket* next door is open weekdays from 7.30 am to 7 pm and to 6 pm on Saturday.

Ever eat a pizza in church? The monastery chapel in the Adria resort is now the *Pizzeria Convent*.

The *Vera Gostilna*, about one km west of the Adria resort at Jadranska cesta 66, is one of the few independent eateries on the peninsula and popular with local people. It's open daily from 9 am to 11 pm.

Entertainment

There are a couple of popular discos at the Adria resort including one near the entrance with its own huge car park and the *Taverna* looking out over the Adriatic.

Getting There & Away

Buses make the run from the centre of Ankaran to the Italian border crossing at Lazaret between eight and 11 times a day. Up to a dozen buses go to Koper.

IZOLA (pop 10,300)

Izola, a scruffy fishing port seven km southwest of Koper, is the poor relation among the historical towns on the Slovenian coast. But it wasn't always that way. The Romans built a port called Haliaetum at Simon's Bay (Simonov Zaliv) west of the Old Town, and they say you can still see parts of the original landing when the tide is very low.

The vicissitudes of Izola in the Middle Ages are closely tied to those of Koper and, to a lesser degree, Piran. Struggle among various groups (and a brief period of independence in the 13th century) led to supremacy by Venice. At first Izola – at that time an island and thus its Italian name Isola – flourished, particularly in the trade of olives, fish and its celebrated wine, which travelled as far as Germany. But a devastating plague in the 16th century and the ascendancy of Trieste as the premier port in the northern Adriatic destroyed the town's

economic base. During the period of the Illyrian Provinces in the early 19th century, the French pulled down the town walls and used them to fill the channel separating the island from the mainland. Many of the medieval churches and buildings were also razed.

After several fish canneries were opened at Izola this century, the town began to industrialise. It remains the country's foremost fishing port, but Izola's glory days seem a million years ago as you walk through the narrow streets, where the houses look like they could topple over in the slightest wind. Still, for all that (and maybe because of it) Izola has its charms along with some of the best seafood in Slovenia. It's definitely worth a visit as long as you don't mind a slight fishy smell and very fat cats underfoot.

Orientation

Almost everything of a practical nature is centred around Trg Republike. Buses stop in front of the Slavnik Koper transport office at Cankarjev drevored 2 on the south-eastern edge of Trg Republike.

To reach the Old Town and Veliki trg, the main square facing a circular inner harbour, walk north along the waterfront promenade called Sončno nabrežje.

Information

The staff at the tourist office (☎ 62 901) at Sončno nabrežje 4 are among the friendliest and most knowledgeable in Slovenia. Save all your questions for here; they will bend over backward to make you feel welcome. The office is open Monday to Saturday from 8 am till noon and from 4 to 7 pm. On Sunday it is open from 9 am to 1 pm.

Splošna Banka Koper has a branch at Drevored 1 Maja 5 open from 8.30 am till noon and from 3 to 5 pm on weekdays and till noon on Saturday. A better rate for cash only is available from the Fiba exchange office at Pittonijeva ulica 1, the side street next to the bus office. Fiba is open from 8 am to noon and 4 to 6 pm weekdays and on Saturday morning.

The post office and telephone centre, open from 7.30 am to 7 pm weekdays and to 1 pm

Top: Piran from the old town walls (Primorska) (JŽ)
Bottom Left: Marina at Portorož (Primorska) (JŽ)
Bottom Right: Disused salt pans at Sečovlje near Portorož (Primorska) (SF)

Top Left: Snežnik Castle (Notranjska) (SF)
Top Right: Predjama Castle near Postojna (Notranjska) (SF)
Bottom: Views of 'disappearing' Lake Cerknica (Notranjska) (SF)

on Saturday, is opposite Slavnik Koper at Cankarjev drevored 1.

Izola's telephone code is 066. The postcode is 66310.

Things to See & Do

Izola isn't overly-endowed with important historical sights; Napoleon's finest took care of that. But there are one or two features worth a brief look, such as the 16th century **Church of Saint Maurus** and its landmark bell tower on the hill above the town, the **town hall** on Veliki trg and the Venetian Gothic **Manzoli Palace**, owned by a chronicler of Istria in the 16th century, on Manzoli trg near the waterfront.

Izola's most beautiful building is the Rococo **Besenghi degli Ughi Palace** on the corner of Gregorčičeva ulica and Bruna ulica below the church. Built between 1775 and 1781, the mansion has windows and balconies adorned with stuccos and wonderful wrought-iron grilles. Inside, a stairway decorated with illusionist paintings leads to a salon with a curious wooden balcony running below the ceiling. The palace is now a music school and headquarters of the local Italian Society.

There are **beaches** to the north and east of the Old Town, but the best is at Simon's Bay (Simonov Zaliv), about 1.5 km to the west. It has a grassy area for sunbathing and a water slide.

The tourist office sells fishing licences for 900 SIT a day and can organise a boat for about 500 SIT per person.

If you have your own transport consider an excursion to **Korte**, a village seven km south of Izola. This is a picturesque Slovenian Istrian village with stone houses and a lovely old church.

Places to Stay

Camping There are two camp sites within easy reach of Izola. *Avtokamp Jadranka* (☎ 61 202), a small site on the waterfront 1200 metres south-east of the Old Town, is open from May to mid-October. But it's right off the noisy coastal road and fills up quickly in summer. The charge is DM6.50 to DM8 per person, depending on the month.

Belvedere (☎ 67 115), on a bluff three km west of Izola with wonderful views of the port and the Adriatic, is larger than Jadranka, covering an area of three hectares and accommodating 700 campers among the

PRIMORSKA

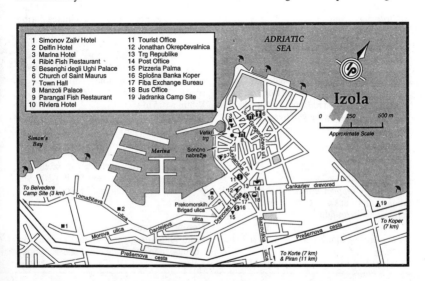

1	Simonov Zaliv Hotel	11	Tourist Office
2	Delfin Hotel	12	Jonathan Okrepčevalnica
3	Marina Hotel	13	Trg Republike
4	Ribič Fish Restaurant	14	Post Office
5	Besenghi degli Ughi Palace	15	Pizzeria Palma
6	Church of Saint Maurus	16	Splošna Banka Koper
7	Town Hall	17	Fiba Exchange Bureau
8	Manzoli Palace	18	Bus Office
9	Parangal Fish Restaurant	19	Jadranka Camp Site
10	Riviera Hotel		

ADRIATIC SEA

Izola

0   250   500 m

Approximate Scale

trees. It is open from May to October and costs from DM7 to DM12. A car is an extra DM3. The holiday village surrounding the camp has a large swimming pool.

Private Rooms The tourist office can arrange *private rooms* and *apartments* throughout the year, but the biggest choice is in summer. Single rooms are DM16 to DM28, depending on the category and the season, while doubles are DM25 to DM46. *Apartments* for two start at DM40 and DM50. Breakfast (when available) is usually DM6 extra, and you must pay a surcharge of 50% if your stay is less than three days.

Hotels Izola's cheapest hotel is the four-storey *Riviera* (☎ 62 925) overlooking the marina at Prekomorskih Brigad ulica 7. The catch is that its 175 beds are only available from mid-June to August; the rest of the year it serves as a dormitory for students attending Izola's catering and tourism school. Singles and doubles with breakfast and communal shower are DM29 and DM54. Rooms with their own bathroom are DM5 and DM14 extra.

The most central hotel in town is the 45-room *Marina* (☎ 65 325; fax 62 012) at Veliki trg 11. Singles start at DM41 in the low season, rising to DM66 in July and August. Doubles are DM60 and DM102.

If you don't mind being a bit out from the centre but still near the water, the *Delfin* (☎ 63 554; fax 63 411), Tomažičeva ulica 10, may be for you. It's a pleasant hotel on a hill about a km west of Trg Republike and has its own pool. It's big, with well over 100 rooms, and certainly isn't cheap: singles are DM40 to DM71 while doubles are DM58 to DM106.

Places to Eat
Jonathan Okrepčevalnica, at Drevored 1 Maja 6, has basic fast food in less-than-salubrious surroundings but it's pretty cheap. *Pizzeria Palma* next to the Splošna Banka Koper on Drevored 1 Maja, has far better pizza.

Why not skip a meal and splurge at one of the fish restaurants? Izola has a large selection but not all are reasonably priced or even very good. Stick with the local favourites: *Parangal* just up from the tourist office at Sončno nabrežje 18 or *Ribič* at Veliki trg 3, both of which are open till about 11 pm. But do be careful when you order (especially at Ribič) and ask the exact price of the fish. As seafood is sold by decagramme (abbreviated as *dag* on menus), you may end up eating (and paying) a lot more than you expected. For a list of fish dishes see the Menu Reader under Food in the Facts for the Visitor chapter. Be sure to have a glass or two of Malvazija, the yellowish local white wine that is light and reasonably dry.

In Korte, consider the *Livio* restaurant at house No 44. Italian-influenced specialities include *Istrska rižota* (risotto with shellfish and white wine) and *pašta fažol* (thick bean soup with noodles).

Entertainment
Izola's top disco is the *CC Club* behind the *Simonov Zaliv* hotel at Morovka ulica 6a in Simon's Bay.

Getting There & Away
Buses leave for Koper and for Strunjan, Piran and Portorož every 20 minutes during the week and every 40 minutes on Saturday and Sunday. Other destinations from Izola (via Koper) include: Celje (three buses a day); Črna na Koroškem (one); Ljubljana (up to 12); Maribor (four); Murska Sobota (two); Nova Gorica (one); Velenje (one); and Vrhnika (up to six).

International routes include eight buses a day (weekdays only) to Trieste in Italy and three to Zagreb in Croatia.

Like most of the towns on the coast, parking is severely restricted in Izola, and you'll have to pay between 50 and 100 SIT per hour for the privilege. The full day rate is 1000 SIT.

Getting Around
From June to August a minibus does a continuous loop from the Belvedere holiday village west of the Old Town to Simon's Bay,

the Izola Marina, Trg Republike and the Jadranka camp site and back. For a local taxi in Izola, call ☎ 62 333.

The Bele Skale travel agency (☎ 65 206) near the Marina hotel at Veliki trg 10 rents bicycles. They are open weekdays from 9 am to 2 pm and from 4 to 7 pm. On Saturday they close at noon.

AROUND IZOLA
Strunjan
For centuries, the people who lived at Strunjan, a peninsula halfway between Izola and Piran, were engaged in salt-making and you'll see the disused pans as you descend the main road from Belvedere. Today the area, protected as a regional park, attracts large numbers of waterfowl.

Though there has been much development around Strunjan Bay to the south-west, much of the peninsula is remarkably unspoiled. It is bounded by a high cliff – **Cape Ronek** – at its northernmost point and there are plans to turn the area into a nature reserve. The 16th century **Church of the Virgin Mary** nearby is a place of pilgrimage on 15 August.

The *Strunjan Health Resort* (☎ 78 882; fax 78 618) has all types of accommodation, but the cheapest is bungalows for two starting at DM50 during the low season and more than doubling in summer. Along with a beach, the resort has an indoor pool filled with heated sea water as well as tennis courts and other sport facilities. Much use is made of the salty mud found nearby for beauty and therapeutic purposes. *Avtokamp Strunjan* (☎ 73 638), which is open all year, has space for 350 campers. It charges DM8 per person, DM2 per car and DM2 for a caravan.

PIRAN (pop 4800)
Picturesque Piran (Pirano in Italian), sitting at the tip of a narrow peninsula, is everyone's favourite town on the Slovenian coast. It is a gem of Venetian Gothic architecture with narrow little streets, but it can be a mob scene at the height of summer. Some people might find the best thing about Piran at that time of year is getting out of it.

Piran has been settled since ancient times, and it is thought the town's name comes from the Greek word for fire *(pyr)*. In those days fires were lit at Punta, the very tip of the peninsula, to guide ships to the port at Aegida (now Koper). The Romans established a settlement here called Piranum after their victory over the Illyrians and Celts. They in turn were followed by the early Slavs, the Byzantines, the Franks and the Patriarchs of Aquileia.

Venetian rule began in the late 13th century and lasted in one form or another for over 500 years. Unlike Koper and Izola, whose citizens rose up against the Venetians time and time again, Koper threw its full support behind Venice in its struggles with Aquileia and Genoa. (The fact that Venice was Piran's biggest customer for the salt it produced was certainly an incentive.) The Venetian period was the town's most fruitful, and many of the most beautiful buildings and fortifications were erected then.

Economic stagnation under Austrian and particularly Italian rule from the early 19th century until after WW II meant Piran was able to preserve – at a price to its citizens – its medieval character. Today it is one of the best-preserved historical towns anywhere on the Adriatic and is entirely protected as a cultural monument.

Orientation
Piran's Old Town sits on the westernmost point of the Istrian Peninsula. Strunjan Bay is to the north; Piran Bay lies to the south: and Portorož, Slovenia's largest beach resort, to the south-east.

Tartinijev trg, north of Piran Harbour and the small marina, is the centre of the Old Town today, but in the Middle Ages the focal point was Trg 1 Maja (also written Prvomajski trg) in what is the oldest part of the Old Town. The bus station is along the waterfront, about 400 metres south of Trg 1 Maja at Dantejeva ulica 6. There is no left-luggage office here.

Information
Tourist Office Piran's tourist office (☎ 73

680) at Tartinijev trg 4 deals with private accommodation only and the staff seem to be of no assistance otherwise.

Money Splošna Banka Koper, at Tartinijev trg 12, changes travellers' cheques weekdays from 8.30 am till noon and 3 to 5 pm and on Saturday morning. Outside the bank is an automatic exchange machine that accepts banknotes from 13 countries. It's in operation 24 hours a day.

Post & Telecommunications The post office and telephone centre in the town hall, on Tartinijev trg 2, is open weekdays from 7.30 am to 8 pm and to 1 pm on Saturday. Piran's telephone code is 066. The postcode is 66330.

Travel Agency The Maona travel agency (☎ 746 228) at Cankarjevo nabrežje 7 has private rooms, organises a lot of activities and sells tickets for the *Marconi* catamaran to Italy and Croatia (see Boat in the Getting There & Away section). In summer, it is open Monday to Saturday from 9 am to 7 pm and on Sunday from 10 am to 1 pm and 5 to 7 pm. In winter, the opening hours are 9 am to 2 pm every day but Sunday.

Maritime Museum

This museum, housed in a lovely 17th century palace on the waterfront at Cankarjevo nabrežje 3, is named in honour of Sergej Mašera, a Slovenian naval commander whose ship was blown up off the Croatian coast in WW I.

The museum's excellent exhibits, labelled in Slovene and Italian only, focus on the three 'Ss' that have been so important to Piran's development over the centuries: sea, seafaring and salt-making. The salt pans at Sečovlje south-east of Portorož get most of the attention downstairs, and there are some excellent old photographs showing salt workers going about their duties in Asian-style straw hats, a wind-powered salt pump and little wooden weights in the form of circles and diamonds used to weigh salt under the Venetian Republic. The **antique**

model ships upstairs are very fine (especially the 17th century galleon and 18th century corvette); other rooms are filled with old figureheads and weapons, including some very lethal-looking blunderbusses. The folk paintings are **votives** that were placed on the altar of the pilgrimage church at Strunjan by sailors for protection against shipwreck.

The palace, with its lovely moulded ceilings, parquet floors and marble staircase, is worth a visit. The museum is open every day except Monday from 9 am till noon and from 3 to 6 pm. The admission charge is 250 SIT for adults and 150 SIT for children.

Tartinijev Trg

The **statue** of the nattily dressed gentleman in the centre of this oval-shaped square, once the inner harbour and filled in 1864, represents local composer and violinist Giuseppe Tartini (1692-1770). To the east, his birthplace at No 7, opposite the **Church of St Peter** (1818), contains the **Tartini Memorial Room** on the 1st floor open weekdays except Monday from 10 am till noon and 5 to 7 pm and at the weekend in the morning only.

The red **Venetian House** (Beneška Hiša), a lovely Venetian Gothic structure from the 15th century with tracery windows and a balcony at No 4, houses the 'tourist office' on its ground floor. There's a story attached to the stone relief of the lion with a ribbon in its mouth and the inscription *Lassa pur dir*. It seems a wealthy merchant from Venice fell in love with a beautiful local girl. But the latter was soon the butt of gossips. To shut them up and keep his lover happy, he built her this little red palace complete with a reminder for her loose-lipped neighbours: 'Let them talk.'

Opposite is the **Piran Art Gallery**.

The classical 19th century **town hall** and the **court house**, which has two 17th century doors, are on the north-west and western sides of Tartinijev trg. The **Aquarium**, less than 100 metres away along the harbour at Tomažičeva ulica 4, may be small, but there's a tremendous variety of sealife packed into its 25 tanks. It's open from 9 am

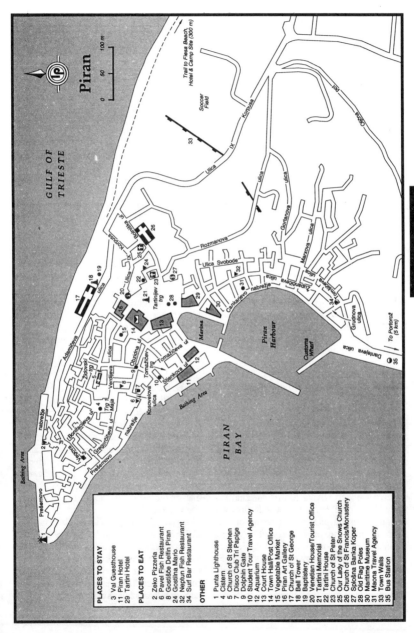

Piran

GULF OF TRIESTE

PIRAN BAY

Piran Harbour

Bathing Area

Prešernovo

Trail to Fiesa Beach,
Hotel & Camp Site (300 m)

Soccer Field

To Portorož
(5 km)

PLACES TO STAY

3 Val Guesthouse
11 Piran Hotel
29 Tartini Hotel

PLACES TO EAT

2 Zeko Pizzeria
6 Pavel Fish Restaurant
8 Gostišče Delfin Piran
24 Gostilna Mario
32 Neptun Fish Restaurant
34 Surf Bar Restaurant

OTHER

1 Punta Lighthouse
4 Cistern
5 Church of St Stephen
7 Disco Club Tri Papige
9 Dolphin Gate
10 Student Tour Travel Agency
12 Aquarium
13 Court House
14 Town Hall/Post Office
15 Vegetable Market
16 Piran Art Gallery
17 Church of St George
18 Bell Tower
19 Baptistery
20 Venetian House/Tourist Office
21 Tartini Memorial
22 Tartini House
23 Church of St Peter
25 Our Lady of the Snows Church
26 Church of St Francis/Monastery
27 Splošna Banka Koper
28 Old Flag Poles
30 Maritime Museum
31 Maona Travel Agency
33 Town Walls
35 Bus Station

to 8 pm and costs 200 SIT (half-price for children).

The two 15th century **flag poles** at the entrance to the square bear Latin inscriptions praising Piran, the town's coat of arms and a relief of St George, the patron. The strange engraving with numbers on one pole shows medieval linear measurements for fabric and firewood. No doubt it was used by both merchants and doubting customers alike.

Around the Church of St George

This Renaissance and Baroque church, Piran's most eye-catching structure, stands on a ridge above the sea north of Tartinijev trg. To the east runs a 200-metre stretch of the 15th century **town walls**, which can be climbed for superb views of Piran and the Adriatic. The walls once ran from the sea to the harbour and seven crenellated towers remain pretty much intact.

The church was founded in 1344 and was rebuilt in Baroque style in 1637. It's wonderfully decorated with paintings, marble altars and two statues of St George slaying the dragon. In the smaller of the two, a woman is curiously holding the monster on a leash.

The free-standing **bell tower** (1609) was modelled on the campanile of San Marco in Venice and can be climbed daily between 6 and 7 pm. The octagonal **Baptistry** from the 17th century next to it contains a **Gothic crucifix** (1300) called the Tree of Life because of its unusual shape and a Roman sarcophagus from the 2nd century later used as a baptismal font.

On your way to the church from Tartinijev trg, have a quick look inside **Our Lady of the Snows Church** (Sveta Marija Snežna) on Bolniška ulica. It contains a wonderful 15th century painting of the Crucifixion on the arch before the presbytery. The large complex across Bolniška ulica is the former **Franciscan monastery** with a lovely cloister and the **Church of St Francis** built originally in the 14th century but enlarged and renovated over the centuries. Inside the church is a giant clam shell used to collect donations.

Trg 1 Maja

This was the centre of Piran until the Middle Ages and the surrounding streets are a maze of pastel-coloured 'overhanging' houses, vaulted passages and arcaded courtyards. The square is surrounded by interesting Baroque buildings including the former town **Pharmacy** on the north side, now a bar. In the centre of the square is a large **cistern** that was built in the late 18th century to store fresh water; rain water from the surrounding roofs flowed into it through the fish borne by the stone cherubs in each corner.

If you're going to Tartinijev trg, walk along Obzidna ulica, one of Piran's oldest streets, which passes under the 15th century **Dolphin Gate** (Dolfinova Vrata). **Židovski trg**, the centre of Jewish life in Piran in the Middle Ages, is just to the east of Trg 1 Maja.

Activities

Piran has several 'beaches' – rocky areas along Prešernovo nabrežje where you might dare to get your feet wet. The beaches get a little better after Punta, the 'point' with a lighthouse and an old church, but I'd keep walking eastward for 900 metres to **Fiesa**, one of the best beaches on the Slovenian coast. Watch your step as you walk under the bluffs; the path can be slippery.

The beach at Fiesa is one of the cleanest and prettiest on the Slovenian coast, essentially because boating is very restricted here. It is terribly small though and is positively jammed with bathers in summer. From here you can see Strunjan and on a really clear day the Miramare Castle in Trieste and even Grado in Italy. Kayaks (300 SIT) and canoes (400 SIT) are available by the hour from the man on the beach who is also responsible for keeping the place tidy.

The DUFA Diving Club (mobile ☎ 0609-620 651) run by a jolly CMAS-qualified instructor is based near Fiesa beach between May and September. Equipment is available for rent and he gives lessons. For DM55 you get the entire kit (wetsuit, mask, flippers, tank, regulator) and a single dive for absolute beginners is DM70. There's also one for kids (DM12), lasting a half-hour and reaching a depth of only a metre. Remember that you're diving for the sport here; there ain't a whole lot in those waters.

Maona travel agency organises fishing trips (on Tuesday), night cruises (on Wednesday) and excursions to Trieste (daily; DM30) on a boat called *Lako*. Another boat called *Delfin* makes runs to the Saltworks Museum in Sečovlje (600 SIT return) and Strunjan (700 SIT) five days a week in season.

Festivals

Events of the Piran Musical Evenings/Primorska Summer Festival in July and August take place on Fridays in the vaulted cloister *(križni hodnik)* of the former Franciscan monastery. One very unusual event held in Piran is the 'mariners' baptism' of new recruits to the naval school held in early September. It involves a lot of pageantry.

Places to Stay

Camping One of the most secluded camp sites on the coast is *Camping Jezero Fiesa* (☎ 73 473) at Fiesa, four km by road from the Old Town. It's in a quiet valley by a small pond and close to the beach, but it's very crowded in summer. Camping costs between DM9 and DM12, and it's open from May to September.

Private Rooms The tourist office (☎ 73 680) on Tartinijev trg can arrange *private rooms* for between DM16 and DM28 for a single, depending on the category and season, and from DM25 to DM 46 for a double. *Apartments* for two start at DM40 and DM55. The office levies a 50% surcharge if you stay less then three nights. They are open in summer from 9 am to 1 pm and from 4 to 7 pm Monday to Saturday and on Sunday morning. In winter it is open from 9 am till noon on Monday, Wednesday and Friday and on Wednesday afternoon from 3 to 5 pm.

Maona travel agency and Student Tour (☎ 73 773) at Tomažičev trg 3 behind the Piran hotel have private rooms available between June and September.

Pension One of the cheapest places to stay in Piran and very central is the *Val* guesthouse (☎ 73 773) at Gregorčičeva ulica 38a on the corner of Vegova ulica. Open from late April to October, it has two dozen rooms with shared shower for between DM22 and DM25 per person.

Hotels From October to May, your best bet is the *Fiesa* (☎ 73 473), a 21-room hotel overlooking the sea near the Jezero Fiesa camp site. At that time this pleasant four-storey hotel charges DM34 per person for a room facing the hills and DM38 for one on the water. At other times, though, the price jumps to a minimum DM61.

Piran only has two really central hotels. The cheaper of the two, the *Piran* (☎ 746 185; fax 74 498) at Stjenkova ulica 1, has 70 rooms, many facing the sea. Singles and doubles with breakfast and shower start at about DM35 and DM55 in the lowest season but jump to a minimum DM64 and DM98 in July and August. The 45-room *Tartini* (☎ 746 221; fax 746 324) at Tartinijev trg 15 was once the Sidro hotel and a favourite with budget travellers. But now this five-storey place has been completely renovated and gone up-market: singles and doubles reach DM95 and DM146 in July and August, though there're only half that in the lowest season.

Places to Eat

Have a pizza at *Zeko*, about 150 metres east of the Punta lighthouse at Prešernovo nabrežje 26, and enjoy the uninterrupted views of the sea. Zeko is open from 9 am till midnight daily.

The *Surf Bar* at Grudnova ulica 1, a small street north-east of the bus station, is a good place for a meal or drink. It has a 'photo-album menu' with some 60 dishes – from ham and eggs and pizza to Slovenian specialities – and the staff speak a number of languages. It's open Monday to Saturday from 8.30 am to 10 pm and on Sunday from 11 am.

Gostilna Mario is a pleasant little restaurant with an outside terrace up the steps from

St Peter's Church at Kajuhova ulica 6. It specialises in fish dishes and is open daily except Wednesday until 10 pm.

Piran has a heap of seafood restaurants along Prešernovo nabrežje but most (including *Pavel* at the southern end of the promenade) are fairly pricey. Instead try the local favourites *Gostišče Delfin Piran* near Trg 1 Maja at Kosovelova ulica 4, or the *Neptun* at Župančičeva ulica 7 behind the Maona travel agency.

There's an outdoor *market* in the small square facing the Aquarium just off Kidričevo nabrežje.

Entertainment

Piran is not exactly raging but the pamphlet produced by the Erazem student travel agency in Ljubljana isn't entirely fair when it says that 'nothing really exciting here has happened since the Venetian Republic'. *Club Tri Papige*, at Prešernovo nabrežje 2, is Piran's top disco and lively enough. It's open Friday and Saturday from 10 pm to 4 am.

The *Porto Campo* bar at Ulica IX Korpusa 9 (open to 11 pm) has a gay clientele.

Getting There & Away

Bus Buses head for Portorož and for Strunjan, Izola and Koper about every 20 minutes in season and every 40 minutes at the weekend. Other destinations that can be reached from Piran include: Celje (five); Črna na Koroškem (one); Ljubljana via Postojna (12); Maribor (four); Murska Sobota (two); Nova Gorica (two); Novo Mesto (two); Sečovlje via Seča (10); and Sežana (two).

About six buses go to Trieste in Italy on weekdays, and there's a daily departure for the Croatian capital of Zagreb. One bus a day heads south for Croatian Istria, stopping at the coastal towns of Umag, Novigrad, Poreč and Rovinj.

Car & Motorbike Traffic is severely restricted in Piran and spaces are at an absolute premium. All cars must pay a parking fee if they intend to stay in the town for more than an hour and it's stiff – over six hours and

you'll have to pay 3000 SIT! Leave your car behind or in the lot south of the bus station, which charges only 100 SIT for up to six hours and 400 SIT for the day.

Boat Between April and September, the large catamaran *Marconi* glides between Trieste and Piran twice a week (35 minutes; 2400 SIT return). On Wednesday, Friday and Sunday, it goes down the Istrian coast in Croatia as far as the Brioni Islands (2¼ hours; 5500 SIT return), with stops at Umag and Rovinj. In Piran, contact the Maona travel agency for times. In Trieste, Agemar (☎ 040 463 222) at Piazza Duca degli Abruzzi Luigi Amedeo 1a, some 200 metres south-west of the train and bus stations, handles bookings and ticket sales.

The *Delfin* boat from Piran to Portorož (300 SIT one-way) via the Bernadin tourist complex (200 SIT) sails eight times a day in summer.

Getting Around

Bus Minibuses run by an outfit called Street Tour go from Piran to Portorož and as far as the camp sites at Lucija continuously from June to August. There is also a service to the beach and camp site at Fiesa.

Taxi For a local taxi in Piran, call ☎ 76 880 or ☎ 73 555.

Bicycle Student Tour near the Piran hotel rents bicycles. In summer, it is open weekdays from 8 am to 2 pm and 4 to 7 pm, on Saturday from 9 am to 1 pm and 4 to 7 pm and on Sunday from 9 am to 1 pm.

PORTOROŽ (pop 2980)

Every country with a sea coast has got to have a honky-tonk beach resort – a Blackpool, a Bondi or an Atlantic City – and Portorož is Slovenia's very own. The 'Port of Roses' is essentially a solid strip of high-rise hotels, restaurants, bars, travel agencies, shops, discos, beaches with turnstiles, parked cars and tourists, and it is not to everyone's liking. A senior Slovenian tourism official calls it 'Portobeton' (Port of Cement) while another said he hadn't been there for over 30 years, preferring (like the vast majority of Slovenes) to holiday in Croatian Istria or along the Dalmatian coast.

But Portorož ('Portorose' in Italian) isn't all bad. The sandy beaches are the largest on the coast and relatively clean, there is a pleasant spa where you can take the waters or cover yourself in curative mud and the list of other activities goes on and on. If you take it for what it is and let your hair down, Portorož can be a fun place to watch Slovenes, Italians, Austrians, Germans and others at play and in various states of undress. You may want to join in the fun.

Portorož may look like it was born yesterday but that's not the case. Though most of the development along the main drag Obala (Beach Road) dates from the late 1960s and 1970s, the settlement was first mentioned in the 12th century and its sheltered bay was fiercely contested over the next two centuries. In 1689, Portorož Bay was the centre of a pan-Istrian sailing competition in which over 100 galleons participated.

But Portorož didn't achieve real fame until the early 19th century when Austro-Hungarian officers came here to be treated with the mud collected from the salt pans at Sečovlje (see Around Portorož). Word spread quickly and the luxurious Grand Palace hotel was established in 1891. Sadly, the Grand Palace (not to be confused with the modern Palace hotel) is now closed.

Orientation

Portorož skirts a sandy bay about five km south-east of Piran. The main development looks onto the bay from Obala, but there are satellite resorts and hotel complexes to the west at Bernadin and south near the posh Portorož Marina at Lucija.

The bus station (which has facilities for left-luggage) is opposite the main beach on Postajališka pot. Portorož Airport is about seven km to the south-east near Sečovlje on the Croatian border. It is one of the three international airports in Slovenia, but only small chartered aircraft land here.

Information

Tourist Office The tourist office (☎ 76 372) is at Obala 16, a short distance west of the bus station. It's open from 8 am to 9 pm Monday to Saturday in summer but, like most of the travel agencies, in winter it's closed by 1 pm and at the weekend.

Money Splošna Banka Koper next to the Riviera hotel at Obala 33 is open from 8.30 am till noon and 5 to 7 pm on weekdays and on Saturday morning. It has an automatic exchange machine outside which accepts the banknotes of 18 countries. There are private exchange offices everywhere. Feniks, the exchange bureau next to the tourist office, gives a good rate and does not charge commission.

Post & Telecommunications The post office is located at K Stari cesta, next to the Palace hotel, and is open weekdays from 8 am to 7 pm and on Saturday till 1 pm. There's a row of public telephones outside, some of which accept Čip Impulz (not PTT Slovenija) telephone cards.

Portorož's telephone code is 066. The postcode is 66320.

Travel Agencies Almost all of the big Slovenian travel agencies are represented here, including Slovenijaturist (☎ 75 670) at Obala 18a, open in the warmer months Monday to Saturday from 9 am to 1 pm and 4 to 7 pm, and Kompas (☎ 73 160) at Obala 41, south of the post office. The latter opens Monday to Saturday from 8 am to 7 pm and Sunday from 9 am to noon in summer. Atlas (☎ 73 264) at Obala 55 just south of the bus station is the local representative for American Express.

Things to See

The **Maritime Museum Collection** in the Villa San Marco, Obala 58, is a branch of the Piran museum. This time, though, the emphasis of the museum is on the Slovenian shipping company Splošna Plovna Piran and its contribution to the development of the coast. It contains lots of ship models and

PRIMORSKA

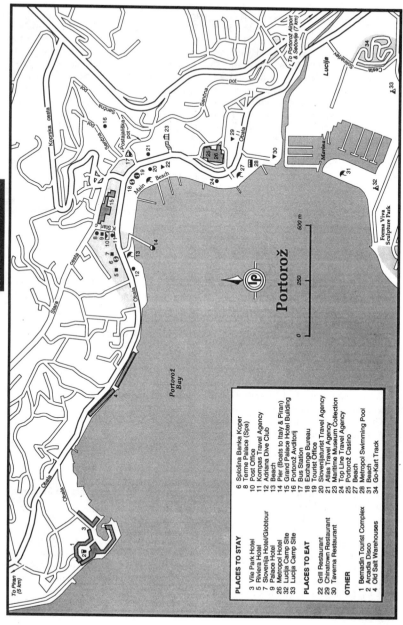

Portorož

Portorož Bay

To Piran
(5 km)

To Portorož Airport
& Sečovlje (7 km)

Lucija

Marina

Forma Viva
Sculpture Park

0   250   500 m

PLACES TO STAY

3   Vile Park Hotel
5   Riviera Hotel
7   Slovenija Hotel/Globtour
9   Palace Hotel
26 Metropol Hotel
32 Lucija Camp Site
33 Lucija Camp Site

PLACES TO EAT

22 Grill Restaurant
29 Chinatown Restaurant
30 Taverna Restaurant

OTHER

1   Bernadin Tourist Complex
2   Arcadia Disco
4   Old Salt Warehouses

6   Splošna Banka Koper
8   Terme Palace (Spa)
10 Post Office
11 Kompas Travel Agency
12 Adriana Dive Club
13 Beach
14 Pier (Boats to Italy & Piran)
15 Grand Palace Hotel Building
16 Portorož Avditorij
17 Bus Station
18 Exchange Bureau
19 Tourist Office
20 Slovenijaturist Travel Agency
21 Atlas Travel Agency
23 Maritime Museum Collection
24 Top Line Travel Agency
25 Portorož Casino

27 Beach
28 Metropol Swimming Pool
31 Beach
34 Go-Kart Track

naval paraphernalia. This collection is only for the truly devoted mariner. It's open Tuesday to Sunday from 9 am till noon and from 3 to 6 pm.

Forma Viva atop the Seča (Sezza in Italian) Peninsula near the first-category Lucija camp site, is an outdoor sculpture garden with over 100 works of art carved in stone. This is just one of several Forma Viva in Slovenia, which were international exhibitions where sculptors worked with local materials: stone at Portorož, wood at Kostanjevica in Dolenjska, iron at Ravne in Koroška and concrete in Maribor. This one, which is vaguely reminiscent of a cemetery, dates from 1961 and many of the sculptures are in sad shape. To be honest, the real reasons for coming are the fantastic views of Portorož and Piran bays and, if you walk a short distance to the south, the salt pans at Sečovlje. The peninsula is an excellent place for a picnic.

Activities
The **beaches** at Portorož, including the main one which accommodates some 6000 people, are 'managed' so you'll have to pay 200 SIT to use them. They have water slides and outside showers and are open from 7 am to 8 pm in season. On a hot summer's day they can be real zoos.

The Terme Palace **spa** (☎ 73 541), located on K Stari Cesta behind the modern Palace hotel, is famous for thalassotherapy (treatment using sea water and its by-products). The spa offers warm sea baths (800 SIT per half-hour), brine baths (2400 SIT), Sečovlje mud baths (2000 SIT) and a host of other therapies and beauty treatments Monday to Saturday from 7 am to 2 pm. The public swimming pool here is open daily, except Monday, from 7 am to 7 pm all year (400 SIT admission, sauna for two hours 800 SIT).

The large outdoor Metropol **swimming pool** opposite the Metropol hotel and north of the marina is open in summer (300 SIT admission). In the sports field attached there's minigolf, tennis courts and bowling alleys which are open 10 am to midnight daily.

The Atlas travel agency rents **boats** and you can also hire them on the grassy beach area directly west of the Metropol hotel. The Portorož Marina has 10-metre Elan 33' sailing boats seating six people for rent. They cost from DM250 to DM320 a day, depending on the month.

Adriana Dive Club, in the little round building near the beach opposite the Riviera hotel, rents scuba equipment and gives lessons daily at 9 am, 2 and 8 pm. As at Fiesa near Piran, don't expect to see much life under those waters.

There's a **go-kart track** (☎ 71 702) on Cesta Solinarjev north-east of the 2nd-category camp site at Lucija and east of the marina. Rides lasting 10 minutes (1000 SIT) are available every day in the afternoon and early evening.

Sightseeing by ultra-light plane is available at the Portorož Airport (☎ 79 001) near Sečovlje April to September from 8 am to 8 pm and from 3 and 5 pm the rest of the year. Flights over Portorož and Piran or the whole coast cost DM27 and DM45. There must be a minimum of two passengers.

Festivals
Portorož Night in July – an evening of celebration and fireworks – recalls the sailing competition held in the bay here in the 17th century.

Special events in summer are held in the large open-air theatre at the Portorož Avditorij (☎ 73 571), an auditorium at Senčna pot 12 located one block north-east of the bus station.

Places to Stay
Camping The *Lucija* camp site (☎ 71 027) has two locations. The 2nd-category site is south-east of the marina at the end of Cesta Solinarjev less than two km from the bus station. The 1st-category site, 600 km west of the 2nd-category site, is beside the water and just north of the Forma Viva sculpture park. Both camps are open from May to September and get very crowded in summer, with caravans jammed into every available nook and cranny. The charge per person

ranges between DM10 and DM14, depending on the site and the month.

Private Rooms The tourist office and Slovenijaturist, Atlas and Kompas all have *private rooms* and *apartments*. You can also book them through Globtour (☎ 73 356) in the Slovenija hotel at Obala 33 and at Top Line (☎ 74 480), Obala 20a. Generally prices start at about DM16 per person in the low season and double in July and August. Apartments for two are a minimum of DM40 and DM50. Some of the rooms are on the hillside, quite a walk from the beach. Getting a room for less than three nights or a single any time is difficult, and in winter many owners don't want to rent at all due to the low off-season rates in force.

Hotels Portorož has some 20 hotels not including the Grand Palace at Obala 45, the Art-Nouveau hotel that put Portorož on the map. Sadly, it has been 'under renovation' for five years now. Hotels in Portorož can be very expensive during the warmer months. Many close for the winter in October or November and do not reopen until April or even May.

The cheapest hotels in Portorož are the *Vile Park* (☎ 75 271; fax 75 491) in the Bernadin tourist complex and the more central *Riviera* (☎ 73 051; fax 76 603) at Obala 33. The Vile Park (that's the plural of 'villa' in Slovene not a comment on the establishment's quality) with some 362 beds has singles for DM43 to DM62, depending on the season and category, and doubles for DM66 and DM104. The Riviera and its annexe, with 200 rooms, charges DM44 to DM85 for singles and DM56 to DM126 for doubles. The Vile Park is closed from November to March, the Riviera from January to March.

Places to Eat
In summer, fastfood and pizza-pasta restaurants line Obala. But if you want a proper sit-down meal, the terrace at the *Taverna* in the sports field at Obala 22 looks out over the marina and the bay and the food is not bad.

It's open daily from noon to 11 pm. The *Grill* restaurant, often with something large being roasted on a spit near the entrance, faces the main beach at Obala 20.

If you find yourself craving Asian food, the *Chinatown* restaurant at the Barbara hotel, Obala 77, has large main courses for 450 to 550 SIT. The *Gostilna Ribič*, in Seča (house No 143) south of the Forma Viva sculpture park, has a wonderful setting and good fish dishes.

Entertainment
The most popular disco on the entire Slovenian coast is said to be *Arcadia*, near the old church tower in the centre of the Bernadin tourist complex. It opens nightly at 10 pm. For more 'mature' entertainment, there's also the *Club Venus* below the Riviera hotel, open till 4 am daily except Monday, and the *Tivoli Club* at the modern Palace hotel.

The *Portorož Casino* (☎ 73 049) at the Metropol hotel, popular with day-trippers from Italy, is open daily from 5 pm.

Getting There & Away
Bus Buses leave Portorož station for Piran, Strunjan and Izola about every 20 minutes on weekdays in season and every 40 minutes on Saturday and Sunday.

Other destinations from Portorož and their daily frequencies include: Celje (five); Črna na Koroškem (one); Ljubljana via Postojna (12); Maribor (four); Murska Sobota (two); Nova Gorica (two); Novo Mesto (two); and Sečovlje via Seča (10). International destinations include Poreč (three); Pula (two); Zagreb (two) in Croatia; and Trieste (eight a day on weekdays) in Italy.

Car & Motorbike Slovenijaturist and Atlas rent mopeds and both Atlas and Kompas have cars for hire. There are quite a few smaller agencies along Obala with both, so stroll along and compare prices. Portorož is one of the few places on the coast where parking is not severely restricted, but you'll be lucky to find a space in summer.

Boat On Friday, Saturday and Sunday

between April and mid-October, the *Prince of Venice*, a 40-metre Australian-made catamaran seating some 300 passengers, sails from Portorož to Venice (2½ hours; DM50 one-way and DM75 return). The boat leaves Portorož from the pier below the Ljubljana restaurant, Obala 14, at 8 am and departs Venice for the return journey at 5.30 pm. For information in Portorož contact Kompas. The Kompas Italia office in Venice (☎ 041 528 65 45) is at San Marco 1497. On other days of the week in the past the *Prince of Venice* has sailed to Poreč and Rovinj for about the same fare, but verify the prices and schedule at any Kompas office.

The *Delfin* boat sails from the same pier to Piran (300 SIT one-way) via Bernadin (200 SIT) eight times a day in summer.

Getting Around

Bus Street Tour minibuses make the loop from the Lucija camp sites to central Portorož and Piran throughout the day from June to August.

Taxi For a local taxi in Portorož, ring ☎ 73 555 or hail one by the post office.

Bicycle Atlas rents bicycles from its office at Obala 55 near the bus station.

AROUND PORTOROŽ
Sečovlje

The abandoned salt pans at Sečovlje, stretching 650 hectares from Seča to the Dragonja River on the Croatian border, have been turned into a regional park and nature reserve. In the centre is the wonderful **Salt-works Museum**, ranked in the top 12 by the European Museums Association.

The area, crisscrossed with dykes, channels, pools and canals, was once a hive of activity and one of the biggest money-spinners on the coast in the Middle Ages. Today it looks like a ghost town with its empty grey-stone houses and pans slowly being taken over by hardy vegetation. Part of a nature park, Sečovlje is eerily quiet except for the occasional cry of a gull, egret or heron.

Sečovlje is right on the border with Croatia. To reach it you must pass through Slovenian immigration and customs first (don't forget your passport). However, to reach the museum, you make a sharp turn to the right (east) before the Croatian checkpoint and continue along the unsealed, pot-holed road for just under three km. The two museum buildings stand out along one of the canals; they are the only renovated houses of the many still standing at Sečovlje.

At present, only one is open to the public. The exhibits relate to all aspects of salt-making and the lives of salt workers and their families: tools, weights, water jugs, straw hats, baking utensils and the seals used to mark loaves of bread baked communally. They are not in themselves very interesting (and labelled only in Slovene and Italian), but the surroundings are and you do get a feel for how the *solinarji* (salt workers) lived and worked. Out among the pans south of the museum is a **wind-powered pump** (just follow the earthern dykes to reach it) that still twirls in the breeze. The museum staff make use of it and other traditional tools to produce about 180 tonnes of salt every year.

The museum is open Tuesday to Friday from 9 am till noon and Thursday to Sunday from 3 to 6 pm. Admission is 250 SIT for adults and 150 SIT for children.

Getting There & Away

Buses stop at the town of Sečovlje (Sicciole in Italian), about 1.5 km north of the border so it is best to catch a bus heading into Istria if you can and get off before the Croatian frontier. An easier way to go in summer if you don't have a car or bicycle is to catch the *Delfin* boat which sails from Piran (600 SIT return) via Portorož (500 SIT) to the museum twice a day, five days a week. The Maona travel agency in Piran or the tourist office in Portorož have details.

Salt of the Sea

Although salt-making went on for centuries along the Slovenian coast at places like Sečovlje and Strunjan, the technique changed very little up to 35 years ago, when harvesting on a large scale came to an end.

Traditionally, sea water was channelled via three in-flow canals – the 'salt roads' – into shallow ponds separated by dykes, which were then dammed with small wooden paddles. Wind-powered pumps removed some of the water and the rest evaporated in the sun and the wind as the salt crystallized from the remaining brine. To stop the product from turning into a foul-tasting reddish-brown material, workers lined the pans with a hard, compressed material of microorganisms and gypsum called *petola* so that the salt would not mix with the mud and clay. The procedure dated to the 13th century.

The salt was collected, drained, washed and, if necessary, ground and iodised. It was then loaded onto a heavy wooden barge called a *maona* and pulled to salt warehouses at various locations on the coast. Examples of these old *skladišča soli* can still be seen on Obala between Portorož and the Bernardin tourist complex.

Salt is necessary in the human body to retain water and was once one of the few ways to preserve meat. Sea salt later became prized for its stronger and more pleasant taste (mined salt can taste somewhat metallic) and because it dissolves more quickly. Sea salt also became popular in the 19th century to treat rheumatism and other muscular disorders at the thermal spa at Portorož and elsewhere.

The lifestyle of the salt workers didn't change much over the years. Salt harvesting was seasonal work, lasting from April to September, when the autumn rains came. During that time most of the workers (both those who controlled the water and those who harvested the salt) lived with their families in the houses you can see lining the canals. They rented the houses and their 'salt funds' – the pans around each house – and divided the profits equally with the landowner.

The set-up of the houses was pretty much the same. The large room downstairs served as a storehouse and had two doors so that salt could be brought in from the fields and taken out onto boats in the canal. Upstairs there were two bedrooms and a combination living room and kitchen. All the windows and doors opened on both sides so that workers could observe changes in the weather – as crucial to them as to sailors. Rain and wind could wipe out the entire harvest if the salt was not collected in time.

In September, or during rainy periods, the workers returned to their villages to tend their crops and vines. For this reason – and the fact that they lived both on the land and 'at sea' – Slovenian salt workers were said to be 'sitting on two chairs'. ■

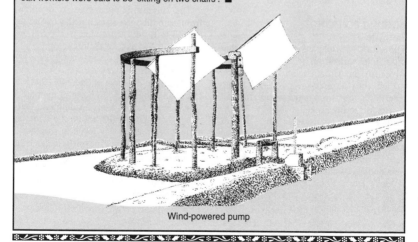

Wind-powered pump

Notranjska

'Inner Carniola', as Notranjska is called in Slovene, is the least developed of Slovenia's eight provinces. It is largely covered with forest – the setting of many of the country's myths and legends – but its most distinguishing characteristic is the many karst caves.

Notranjska is the most typical Dinaric region of Slovenia, but its karst is different from that of Primorska. Abundant rain and snow fall here but the ground is like a great slab of Gruyère cheese – the water vanishes into the ground and resurfaces on the fringes of karst fields called *polje*. The province is known for its underground rivers (Unica, Pivka, Ljubljanica, Rak) and 'intermittent' lakes at Cerknica and Planina.

Notranjska has traditionally had poor communications links with outside regions which has stunted development. Transport through the deep forests and valleys of this isolated province has been difficult for centuries and when the railway linking Trieste and Ljubljana opened in 1857, it sidestepped much of the province. Notranjska was hit by massive emigration (especially from around Cerknica) from the turn of the century until WW II. Today much of the province is given over to logging, especially on the Bloke Plateau and in the Lož Valley.

There is a move to make 60 sq km of the land around Lake Cerknica, west to Postojna and down to the border with Croatia into a regional park. Much of the country's wildlife, including the most aggressive animals, live in this region. There are already small regional parks at the Rakov Škocjan gorge and Snežnik Castle.

POSTOJNA (pop 8200)

The karst cave at Postojna is one of the largest in the world and is among Slovenia's most popular attractions. As a result, it is very commercialised, and many travellers prefer the less visited caves north of the town or the ones at Škocjan in Primorska. It's not

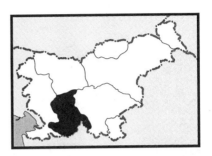

the end of the world if you miss Postojna; go to Škocjan and you'll see better caves.

The Postojna Cave (Postojnska Jama) system is a series of caverns, halls and passages 27-km long and two million years old that was hollowed out by the Pivka River, which enters a subterranean tunnel near the cave's entrance. The river continues its deep passage underground, carving out several series of caves, and emerges again as the Unica River. The Unica meanders through the Planina plain (Planinsko polje), a sunken field of porous limestone which becomes Lake Planina in the rainy season (see also the section on Lake Cerknica). But, as is the nature of what is called a ponor river, it is soon lost underground. It reappears near Vrhnika as the Ljubljanica River and continues its journey northward to the capital.

Postojna Cave has been known by residents of the area for centuries as you can see from the graffiti dating back seven centuries in the Gallery of Old Signatures by the entrance. But people in the Middle Ages knew only the entrances. The inner parts were not explored until April 1818, just days before the arrival of Habsburg Emperor Franz I (ruled 1792-1835). The following year the Cave Commission accepted its first organised tour group, which included Archduke Ferdinand, and Postojna's future as a tourist destination was assured.

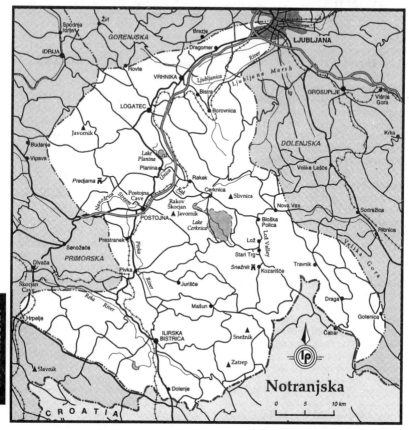

Notranjska

Even in those early days, the very poor region of Notranjska saw the potential economic benefits and in 1823 a guide to Postojna was published, which included the Škocjan and Vilenica caves as well as the mercury mine at Idrija. Since then 26 million people have visited the caves.

The town of Postojna (called Adelsberg in German) dates to the 12th century, but there is little of interest except for a small collection in the Karst Museum at Titov trg 2.

Orientation

The town of Postojna lies in the Pivka Valley at the foot of Sovič Hill (677 metres). The Pivka River, which was once lined with water mills, and the entrance to the cave are about 1.5 km north-west of Titov trg, the centre of town.

Postojna's bus station is at Titova cesta 36, about 250 metres south-west of Titov trg. The train station is on Kolodvorska cesta about one km south-east of Titova trg by road. If you're walking, the fastest way to get to the town centre from the train station is to go down the steps at the southern end of the station and follow Pod Kolodvorom to Ulica 1 Maja, which leads into Titov trg.

Information

Tourist Offices The tourist office (☎ 067 21 077) in town is at Tržaška cesta 4. It is open Monday to Saturday from 8 am to 7 pm. The tourist office by the entrance to Postojna Cave (☎ 067 25 041) at Jamska cesta 30 is open from April to September, 9 am to 6 pm daily.

Money Splošna Banka Koper has a branch at Tržaška cesta 2. It is open weekdays from 8.30 am till noon and 3 to 5 pm and on Saturday from 8.30 am to noon. You can also change money at the two tourist offices (cash only) and at Kompas travel agency, but they charge a hefty commission.

Post & Telecommunications The post office and telephone centre is at Ulica 1 Maja 2a about 150 metres south-east of Titov trg. Postojna's telephone code is 067. The postcode is 66230.

Travel Agency Kompas (☎ 25 439) at Titov trg 2a is open weekdays from 8 am to 8 pm and on Saturday from 9 am to 1 pm.

Things to See & Do

Postojna Cave Postojna Cave is located about two km north-west of the town. Visitors get to see about 5.5 km of the cave on 1½-hour tours, but the lazy or infirm should have no fear: about four km are covered by an electric train that will shuttle you along the so-called Old Passage. The remaining 1700 metres is on foot. Before you enter the cave, have a look at the Pivka River just opposite where it finds its way underground. That waterway has created everything you are about to see.

First you board the mini-train, just beyond the entrance, that runs for about three km to the **Big Mountain** (Velika Gora) cavern. Here you stand under one of the five signs identifying your language and a guide escorts you through numerous halls, galleries and caverns.

These are dry galleries, decorated with a vast array of white stalactites shaped like needles, enormous icicles and even fragile

spaghetti. The stalagmites take familiar shapes – pears, cauliflower and sand castles – but there are also bizarre columns, pillars and translucent curtains that look like rashers of bacon. All in all, it could be a nightmare for those who saw monsters in the dark as children.

Many of the dripstones are colourfully (and artificially) lit in reds, oranges, browns and whites. Only one of the halls is completely devoid of them. It was here that the Partisans blew up a Nazi fuel dump in 1944 and you can still see the blackened walls.

From the Velika Gora cavern you continue across the **Russian Bridge**, built by prisoners of war in 1916, through the 500-metre-long **Beautiful Caves** (Lepe Jame) filled with wonderful stalactites and stalagmites that form ribbons. In case you were wondering, it takes 10 years to produce one mm of a stalactite. The halls of the Beautiful Caves are the farthest point you'll reach in Postojna. From here a man-made tunnel stretches to the **Black Cave** (Črna Jama) and Pivka Cave, but you'll have to visit these caves from the entrance at the Pivka Jama camp site to the north.

The tour continues south through the **Winter Hall** (Zimska Dvorana) past the **Brilliant Stalagmite** and the **Pillar Column** which have become the symbols of the cave (and which look pretty silly when reproduced graphically on the guides' badges and bumper stickers). You then enter the **Concert Hall** (Koncertna Dvorana), which is the largest in the system and can accommodate 10,000 people for musical performances.

One of the last things you'll see before boarding the train for the trip back is a tank filled with pink salamanders. These bizarre (and rather rude-looking) little creatures are *Proteus anguinus*, a unique 'human fish' that was first described by the writer, scientist and historian Janez Vajkard Valvasor as the 'dragon's offspring'. *P. anguinus* is just one of 190 species of fauna (beetles, bats, cave hedgehogs etc) found in the cave and studied at the Biospeleological Station here.

The cave has a constant temperature of 8°

and humidity of 95% so a waterproof jacket is essential. Don't worry if you haven't got one; green-felt cloaks can be hired at the entrance for 100 SIT. Shoes are not as big an issue here as they are at the Škocjan Caves and a torch (flashlight) is not necessary as the cave has been lit by electricity since 1884.

From May to September tours leave daily on the hour between 9 am and 6 pm with one at 7 pm in July and August. Admission during this season is DM20 for adults and DM10 for children and students. From March to April and again in October there are tours at 10 am, noon, 2 and 4 pm with an extra one at 5 pm in April. Between November and February, tours go at 10 am and 2 pm on weekdays with extra ones added at noon and 4 pm on weekends and public holidays. Admission during the early and late seasons is DM16 for adults and DM8 for children/students.

Other Caves To the north of Postojna Cave lie several smaller but equally interesting caves created by the Pivka River and still part of the Postojna system. They too are open to the public.

Island Cave (Otoška Jama), a half-hour's

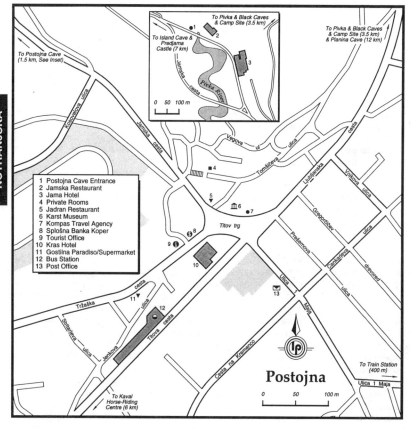

Postojna

1 Postojna Cave Entrance
2 Jamska Restaurant
3 Jama Hotel
4 Private Rooms
5 Jadran Restaurant
6 Karst Museum
7 Kompas Travel Agency
8 Splošna Banka Koper
9 Tourist Office
10 Kras Hotel
11 Gostilna Paradiso/Supermarket
12 Bus Station
13 Post Office

walk north-west from Postojna Cave, is very small (632 sq metres) and the tour takes only 45 minutes, but its stalagmites and stalactites are very impressive. There's no electric lighting so you'll need a torch (flashlight), and be ready for a temperature of 8° C, so bring a jacket.

The most popular caves after Postojna – **Pivka and Black caves** – are about five km to the north and the entrance is in the Pivka Jama camp site. You reach the four-km-long system by descending a couple of hundred stairs. A walkway has been cut into the wall of a canyon in Pivka Cave, with its two siphon lakes and a tunnel, and a bridge leads to Black Cave. This is a dry cavern and, as its name implies, its dripstones are not white. A tour of both caves takes 1½ hours.

Planina Cave, 12 km to the north-east near the unpredictable Lake Planina, is the largest water cave in Slovenia and its a treasure trove of fauna including *P. anguinus*. This is where the rivers Pivka and Rak join forces to form the Unica River. The cave's entrance is at the foot of a 100-metre rock wall. It's six km long and you can visit about 900 metres of it in an hour. There are no lights so take a torch (flashlight). Many parts of the cave are accessible only in low water or by rubber raft.

These caves are all open from June to September and can be visited between two and four times every day. For information about Island, Pivka and Black caves call the tourist office at Postojna Cave. For Planina Cave, ring ☎ 57 686. Admission is DM10 for adults and DM5 for children and students for each cave.

Horse Riding The Kaval Horse-Riding Centre (☎ 54 506) at Prestranek Castle, about 6.5 km south of Postojna, is one of the most professional stables in Slovenia and an excellent place for learning to ride or improving your skills. (The history of horse breeding at the castle goes back to the early 18th century.) The centre is open daily from 9 to 11 am and 4 to 8 pm in summer and 10.30 am to 12.30 pm and 2 to 5 pm in winter.

Places to Stay

Camping The *Pivka Jama* camp site (☎ 24 168) is located on a 2.5-hectare site in a pine forest near the entrance to Pivka and Black caves. It is open from May to September and costs DM13 per person. The two dozen box-like bungalows with four beds each are DM100; there's a swimming pool and if you're in a group this is a pleasant, friendly place to stay. You can walk to the camp site through the forest from Postojna via a marked trail in about 45 minutes.

Private Rooms Both the tourist office and Kompas organise *private rooms* in and around Postojna for about 1500 SIT per person. The rooms available at Tomšičeva ulica 3 above Titov trg are very central.

Hotels The only hotel in town is the ugly, 54-room *Kras* (☎ 24 071; fax 24 431) facing Titov trg at Tržaška cesta 1. Singles with breakfast and shower cost DM31 to DM47, depending on the season, with doubles DM53 to DM76.

Some 100 metres south-east of the entrance to Postojna Cave at Jamska cesta 28, the 143-room *Jama* (☎ 24 172; fax 24 431) costs DM44 to DM60 for a single and DM66 to DM96 for a double. There is little reason to stay out here though, unless you wanted to be the first person in the cave in the morning. The hotel has an indoor swimming pool and fitness centre.

Places to Eat

The *Jadran* restaurant on Titov trg has a good selection of fish dishes but they can be pricey. The fried sardines (550 SIT) and squid (800 SIT) are both good value.

The *pizzeria* at the Kras hotel is a local favourite while the *Gostilna Paradiso*, upstairs from the supermarket at Tržaška cesta 9, has a lot of simple grilled dishes. It's open from noon to 4 pm and 8 pm till midnight every day except Monday.

There are several places to eat in the complex near Postojna Cave, including another pizzeria and two self-service restaurants. The *Jamska* restaurant in a 1920s-style

Proteus Anguinus, the Human Fish

Proteus anguinus is one of the most mysterious creatures in the world. It's a kind of salamander but related to no other amphibians and is the largest permanent cave-dwelling vertebrate known to man. The blind little fellow lives hidden in the pitch black for up to a century and can go years without food. *P. anguinus* is now the symbol of Postojna and has been added to the town seal (just below the imperial eagle). It may even make it onto the 10 SIT coin when it goes into circulation one of these days.

The 17th century chronicler, Valvasor, wrote about the fear and astonishment of local people when an immature 'dragon' was found in a karst spring near Vhrnika, but he judged it to be 'an underground worm and vermin of the kind that is common in some parts'. Several other reports about this four-legged 'human fish' were made before a doctor in Vienna realised its uniqueness in 1768. In announcing its existence to the scientific world, he called it *'Proteus anguinus'*, after the protector of Poseidon's sea creatures in Greek mythology and the Latin word for 'snake'.

P. anguinus measures about 25 to 30 cm long and is a little bundle of contradictions. It has a long tail fin that it uses for swimming but can also propel itself with its four legs (the front legs have three 'fingers' and the back legs have two 'toes'). Though blind, with atrophied, almost invisible eyes, *P. anguinus* has an excellent sense of smell and is sensitive to weak electric fields in the water, which it uses to move around in the dark, locate prey and communicate. It breathes through frilly, bright-red gills at the base of its head when submerged but also has rudimentary lungs for breathing when it is outside the water. The human-like skin has no pigmentation whatsoever but it looks pink in the light due to blood circulation.

The question that scientists have asked themselves for three centuries is how does *P. anguinus* reproduce? This has never been witnessed in a natural state, and the wily creatures haven't been very cooperative in captivity. (One hasn't eaten in 12 years.) But it is almost certain that they hatch their young from eggs and that they don't reach sexual maturity until the age of 16 or 18.

Animal-rights activists will be happy to learn that the beasties in the tank in Postojna Cave call it home for only two or three months and are then returned to the 'wild'. Others aren't so lucky. The export of live *P. anguinus* is banned in Slovenia and the species is about to be included on the Washington Convention List, which prohibits the trade of endangered plants and animals. But that hasn't stopped unscrupulous dealers, and the little creatures keep appearing for sale in aquariums and pet shops in Italy and other European countries. The biggest customers, it is said, are scientists. ■

building at the entrance to the cave has set menus for 950 and 1400 SIT.

Entertainment

Musical performances are staged in Postojna Cave's Concert Hall in summer and on various holidays throughout the year, especially the week between Christmas and New Year. This is also the time when the 'Living Crèche' – the Christmas story performed by actors – takes place in the cave.

Getting There & Away

Bus All the buses travelling between Ljubljana and the coast stop at Postojna. Count on a bus about every half an hour to the capital and to Pivka, a town south of Postojna (and not the camp site). Buses bound for Nova Gorica leave every hour.

Other destinations and their daily frequencies include: Celje (five); Cerknica (four); Koper (eight); Koper via Ilirska Bistrica (three); Maribor (five); Murska Sobota (two); Izola (one); Piran (nine); Sežana (five); Stari Trg (five) and Žaga (four).

International destinations include Poreč (one bus a day), Pula (one), Rijeka (three) and Zagreb (three) in Croatia and Trieste (two) in Italy.

Train Postojna is on the main line linking Ljubljana (67 km; one hour) with Sežana and Trieste via Divača (37 km; 40 minutes). Up to 20 trains a day make the run from the capital to Postojna and back. You can also reach here from Koper (86 km; 1½ hours) via one of four trains a day.

Getting Around

For a taxi in Postojna, call ☎ 23 941. The Pivka Jama camping ground has bicycles for rent in summer.

AROUND POSTOJNA
Predjama Castle

Situated in the gaping mouth of a cavern half way up a hillside about nine km north-west of Postojna, this four-storey castle has a most dramatic setting. Although traces of other nearby structures can be dated back to the 12th century, the castle as you see it today is from the 16th century. It looks unconquerable perched in the centre of a 123-metre cliff.

The castle has a fascinating history. In the 15th century along came one Erazem Lueger, a robber baron who, like Robin Hood, waylaid wagons in the deep forest, stole the loot and handed it over to the poor. During the wars between the Hungarians, under King Matthias Corvinus, and the Austrians, behind Frederick III, Lueger supported the former. He holed himself up in the castle and continued his daring deeds with the help of a secret passage that led out from behind the rock wall. Frederick was furious.

In the autumn of 1483, the Austrian army attacked the castle, but it proved impregnable for months. All the while Erazem mocked the soldiers and showered them with fish, the occasional roast ox and even cherries to prove that he came and went as he pleased.

But Erazem proved to be too big for his breeches and met an ignoble fate. Having gone 'to where even the sultan must go alone' (as Valvasor described it), Erazem was hit by a cannon ball as he sat on the toilet. A turncoat servant, it seems, had betrayed his boss by marking the location of the water closet with a flag for the soldiers.

The castle is now in pretty bad shape and the eight **museum rooms** contain little of interest except for a portrait of Erazem and an oil painting of the 1483-84 siege. But Predjama's striking position and the views of the valley below are incomparable. And it does have all the features a castle should have: a drawbridge over a raging river, holes in the ceiling of the entrance tower for pouring boiling oil on intruders, a very dank dungeon, a 16th century chest full of treasure (unearthed in the cellar in 1991) and an eyrie-like hiding place at the top called **Erazem's Nook**. Just be careful when walking and climbing over the very uneven surfaces.

The **cave** below the castle, carved out by the Lokva and Nanoščica streams, is actually a seven-km network of galleries spread over five levels. Much of it is open only to speleologists, but casual visitors can see about 900 metres. There is no electric lighting and the trail is only partially constructed so you will need to don rubber boots and carry torches (flashlights), both of which are available at the entrance. For information, contact Postojna Cave or the castle (☎ 59 260).

Predjama is open year round from 10 am to 5 pm. In winter it closes on Monday, and from May to September the hours are extended so that it opens from 9 am to 7 pm. Admission is DM5 for adults and DM2.50 for children and students. Tours of Predjama Cave leave at 11 am and 1, 3 and 5 pm from June to September. Entry costs DM10/DM5.

If you want or need to stay out here (transport is tricky), the *Gostilna Požar* restaurant near the ticket kiosk has rooms. There's also accommodation at the *Erazem* guesthouse (☎ 21 168) about three km south-east near the village of Belsko. Singles with shower and breakfast cost DM29 to DM41, depending on the season. Doubles are DM45 to DM64.

Predjama is difficult to reach by public transport. As close as you'll get by local bus is Bukovje, a village about two km north-east of Predjama.

CERKNICA (pop 3500)

This is the largest town on the lake that isn't always a lake – one of Slovenia's most unusual natural phenomena. Cerknica itself is not important as a destination, but it is close to the 'intermittent' Lake Cerknica, the regional park around Rakov Škocjan gorge, Mt Snežnik and Snežnik Castle.

The area around the lake has been settled since prehistoric times, and a trade route once ran over the Bloke Plateau to the east, linking Slovenia and Croatia. During the Roman period, Cerknica was a stopover on the road leading from Emona (Ljubljana) to the coast. Cerknica was given town status in the 11th century.

But Notranjska is a good example of how important communication lines are for the development of town. The railway linking Trieste and Ljubljana opened in 1857 but it sidestepped Cerknica in favour of Rakek, five km to the north-west. The highway from Ljubljana toward the coast goes the same route and Cerknica remains a backwater. With some of Notranjska's most beautiful forests and their fragile ecosystems nearby, that may not be such a bad thing.

Orientation & Information

Cerknica lies north of Lake Cerknica and about 16 km north-east of Postojna. Cesta 4 Maja, the main street, is the centre of town. The bus station is on Čabranska ulica about 100 metres to the south-west.

Cerknica's tourist office (☎ 793 636) is at Cesta 4 Maja 51. It is open weekdays from 7 am to 3 pm and on Saturday and Sunday

from 8 am to noon. The post office, in the next building to the west at No 52, is open from 8 am to 6 pm weekdays and on Saturday from 8 am to noon. Ljubljanska Banka has a branch in the Mercator shopping centre opposite at Cesta 4 Maja 65. It is open weekdays from 8 to 11.30 am and 2 to 4.30 pm. On Saturday it is open from 8 to 11 am.

The telephone code for Cerknica and vicinity is 061. The postcode is 61380.

Parish Church of Our Lady

Sitting atop a gentle slope 200 metres north of Cesta 4 Maja, this church is the only real attraction in Cerknica. To reach it, walk up the street simply called Tabor, which is on the east of the shopping centre. This was called the 'Road of the Patriarchs' in medieval times when Cerknica was the centre of Aquileia's estates in the area.

The church sat in the middle of a fortified settlement, and the ramparts and two towers, built to withstand Turkish raids in the late 15th century, remain intact. On the Latin plaque in the wall, the number '4' of the year '1472' is written with a loop – the top half of an '8' – because '4' was considered unlucky in the Middle Ages.

Completed in the early 16th century, the Church of Our Lady is a hall church – with its nave and aisles of equal height – and not unlike the church at Kranj in Gorenjska. In the 18th century two side chapels were added and the bell tower was given its Baroque dome.

Lake Cerknica

This periodic lake has baffled people since ancient times, including the Greek geographer and historian Strabo (63 BC - 24 AD) who called the mysterious on-and-off body of water Lacus Lugeus (Mourning Lake). It wasn't until Valvasor explained how the water system worked at the end of the 17th century that it was fully understood. For his efforts, this great Renaissance man was made a member of the Royal Society in London, then the premier scientific institution in the world, in 1697.

Big Men for Big Times

Slovenian folklore and tales are rife with fairies, witches and things that go bump in the night, but among the most common stories are those describing the derring-do of 'supermen' whose strong wills and unusual strength enabled them to overcome evil and conquer their enemies.

The legends are not limited to one geographical area. Peter Klepec, who swept away his enemies with trees uprooted with his bare hands, lived on the Kolpa River and is associated with Bela Krajina province. Another hero called Kumprej ruled the Upper Savinja Valley in Štajerska with his mighty voice and fearsome blade. His shoes were five times larger than those of the average person and when he disappeared a poor couple made footwear for their entire family from them.

But perhaps the most popular stories revolve around the feats of Martin Krpan, the hero of the Bloke Plateau in Notranjska province. Krpan's traits and characteristics are familiar. He is an outlaw with a big heart hunted by the imperial guard for smuggling salt. When he is arrested, Martin Krpan proves his super-human strength to the emperor in Vienna by picking up and carrying his horse.

Realising his fortune at having such a powerful giant on his hands, the emperor sets Martin Krpan on Berdavs, the local scourge and personification of the marauding Turk. Martin Krpan defeats Berdavs and chops off his head with his magic axe – complete with a handle made of linden wood. For his pains the imperial court confers on him the privilege of the free transport and sale of salt.

The tales of Martin Krpan are traditional but reached a wider audience when the writer Fran Levstik collected and published them under the title *Martin Krpan* in 1858. This was during the period of national revival when authors around Europe were writing Romantic stories, raising the status of local legends and, in doing so, the local language. Thanks to Levstik, Slovenia had for the first time a hero that all Slovenes could admire. ■

Lake Cerknica is a polje, a field above a collapsed karst cavern full of sinkholes, potholes, siphons and underground tunnels that can stay dry for much of the year and then flood. From the south, Cerknica Polje is fed by another of those disappearing ponor rivers, the Stržen, and to the east and west it collects water underground from the Bloke Plateau and the Javornik Mountains. During rainy periods in the autumn and spring, all this water comes rushing into the polje. Springs flow and the water begins to percolate between the rocks, as though it were boiling. The sinkholes and siphons cannot handle the outflow underground and the polje becomes Lake Cerknica – sometimes in less than a day.

The surface area of Lake Cerknica can reach almost 40 sq km (Lake Bohinj in Gorenjska is a quarter that size), but it is never more than a few metres deep. During dry periods (July to September usually), farmers drive cattle down to the polje and haymakers come to work on the more than 4000 plots.

Lake Cerknica is a beautiful place – whether dry and under cultivation, full of water (and anglers and windsurfers and swimmers) or frozen solid. In fact, it is in winter that the lake becomes most glorious. The waves of the lake freeze into eerie ice formations, and mallard ducks and wild geese drift to and fro. Lots of people skate here.

The lake really begins at the village of Dolenje Jezero about 2.5 km south of Cerknica. If you continue south from the village along a trail which at first follows the Stržen River, you'll come to a little island called **Otok** which has farmland and a little village.

Rakov Škocjan This gorge six km west of Cerknica has been under protection as a regional park since 1949. The Rak River, en route to join the Pivka at Planina Cave, sculpted out 2.5 km of hollows, caves, springs and its two wonderful **natural bridges**. To the south lie the Javornik Mountains, including its tallest peak, **Veliki Javornik** (1269 metres). If you're coming from Rakek and want a place to stay, you can reach the Gostišče Rakov Škocjan on foot from the Rakek train station in about one hour.

Activities

When it's full, Lake Cerknica becomes a vast playground for boaters, anglers and swimmers. Ask the tourist office in Cerknica about fishing licences and boat rentals.

The tourist office can also help arrange tours around the lake by horse-driven carriage. The Kontrabanta farmhouse in Dolenja Vas, a village 1.5 km south-west of Cerknica and famous for its coloured pottery, has horses for rent for 800 SIT per hour. It's difficult to imagine a more enjoyable way of exploring Lake Cerknica and the surrounding hills.

The area around Cerknica is excellent for hikes, and the **Cerknica Mountain Trail** will lead you to the most interesting peaks in a very full two-day walk. The trail leads south-west from Cerknica to thickly forested Veliki Javornik. From here you can take a side trip of about two hours north to Rakov Škocjan and perhaps spend the night. From the side-trip turn off, the trail then skirts the southern shore of Lake Cerknica and carries on north to Križna Gora (856 metres) and its nearby cave and north-west to Slivnica (1114 metres). Slivnica, home of the witch Uršola and other sorcerers, has accommodation in a mountain hut. The next day you walk north to Stražišče (955 metres) and then south back to Cerknica.

You can do just parts of the walk, such as the stages to Rakov Škocjan, Veliki Javornik or Slivnica. The tourist office has a small guidebook with a basic map called *Planinski Vodnik Cerkniška Planinska Pot* but it is available only in Slovene. Ask the staff to point out the more salient features of the hike.

Festivals

Cerknica and its surrounds host two big events every year. The first is the Mardi Gras which takes place for four days before Ash Wednesday in late February or early March. This is the time when the enormous masks of Uršola and a half-dozen other legendary characters are dusted off and paraded up and down Cesta 4 Maja while being provoked by upstarts with pitchforks. It wasn't such a laughing matter during the Reformation, though. Valvasor reports that this part of Notranjska was the centre of witch-hunting and executions even in his day.

The second big occasion is Dormouse Night (Polharska Noč) in late September/early October held at Cerknica, Snežnik Castle or at Stari Trg in the Lož Valley, about 16 km south-east of Cerknica. This event takes place during the very brief open season for trapping the edible dormouse or loir *(polh)*. The dormouse is a tree-dwelling nocturnal rodent not unlike a squirrel that grows to about 30 cm and sleeps through several months of the year. It is a favourite food in Notranjska (in fact, it was once a staple), and the hunting and eating of it is tied up with a lot of tradition. According to one Slovenian belief, the polh is linked to the devil and thus deserves his fate in the stew or goulash pot.

Places to Stay & Eat

About the only place to spend the night in Cerknica town is the *Turšič* pension (☎ 791 354) between the tourist office and the Church of Our Lady at Partizanska ulica 14. A basic room with shared shower should cost about 1500 SIT per person.

The *Gostišče Rakov Škocjan* (☎ 791 066) is a restaurant with accommodation (20 beds) a short walk from the Little Natural Bridge (Mali Naravni Most) and the Zelške Caves at Rakov Škocjan. It is open May to September from 10 am to 9 pm and October to April from 11 am to 5 pm.

The *Dom na Slivnici* mountain hut (☎ 798 002) atop Slivnica has 25 beds and is open year round.

Cerknica has a couple of uninspiring restaurants in the centre of town, including

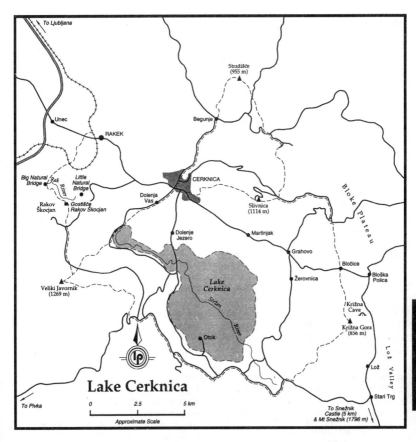

Lake Cerknica

0   2.5   5 km

Approximate Scale

Jezero opposite the tourist office on Cesta 4 Maja 4 and the *Cerknica* in the Mercator shopping centre. Cerknica is open from 9 am to 10 pm daily except Sunday. *Jezerski Hram* in Dolenje Jezero is a good place for a meal while having a look at the lake. There's a scale model of the lake inside.

Getting There & Away

Bus As is the case elsewhere in this part of Notranjska, bus services to and from Cerknica are not great. Buses run frequently to Ljubljana, Lož, Rakek and Stari Trg but other destinations are few and far between.

They include Bloška Polica (up to eight buses a day), Hrib-Loški Potok (one), Nova Vas (up to four), Postojna (four) and Snežnik Castle (one). Two buses a day go to Prezid in Croatia.

Train Luckily there's a train station at Rakek, about five km to the north-west, and it's on the line connecting Ljubljana with Sežana. About 15 trains a day stop at Rakek travelling to or from the capital. Heading south, all of these stop at Postojna and Pivka, but only about half carry on to Divača and Sežana.

NOTRANJSKA

Getting Around
The tourist office plans to start renting bicycles soon. It already has a map available detailing 10 excellent bike trips around the lake and farther afield.

AROUND CERKNICA
Snežnik Castle
This 16th century Renaissance castle near the village of Kozarišče, some 21 km southeast of Cerknica, is one of the loveliest and best-preserved castles in Slovenia. Because of its secluded position in the Lož Valley (Loška Dolina), it has been able to escape the fate of most other castles in the country and looks almost exactly as it did more than four centuries ago.

Its isolation makes it tough to reach by public transport. Without a car, bicycle or horse, you'll have to take a bus to Stari Trg and walk five km or try to get off at Pudob on the bus headed for Prezid in Croatia. The single bus to the castle leaves from Cerknica in the early evening.

Snežnik Castle (Schneeberg in German), which now houses a **museum**, stands in a large and tranquil park. The entrance is through a double barbican with a drawbridge and a moat. The exhibits in the main building are essentially the entire household inventory of the Schönburg-Waldenburg family, who used the castle as a summer residence and hunting lodge until WW II. The castle is crammed with tasteful period furniture. One room is done up with Egyptian handicrafts presented to Herman Schönburg-Waldenburg by a friend early this century. The castle also contains an **art gallery**.

Adjacent to the castle, a 19th century building that once served as a dairy contains a small **Dormouse Museum**. There's not much you won't know about this incredible, edible fellow's life and habits after a visit here.

Summer concerts are held as part of the Snežnik Evenings festival in July, August and September. Contact the museum (☎ 707 814) or the tourist office in Cerknica for details.

Snežnik Castle is open Wednesday to Friday from 10 am to 1 pm and 3 to 6 pm. On Saturday and Sunday it is open from 10 am to 6 pm. Admission is 350 SIT for adults and 250 SIT for children and students.

Snežnik Castle makes an excellent bicycle trip from Cerknica. If you make the necessary preparations in advance, you could stop at **Križna Cave**, about a km or so after you turn off the main Cerknica road. The cave, which was carved out by water from the Bloke Plateau, is eight km long and has 22 underground lakes filled with green and blue water, as well as a unique 'forest' of ice stalagmites near the entrance. It is one of the most magnificent water caves in the world and can be explored by rubber raft. But in order to do so you must contact the man in charge, Alojz Troha, in Bloška Polica (house No 7) or call ☎ 798 149. It's a long tour if you elect to do the entire cave. You should be dressed warmly and carry a torch (flashlight) as Križna Cave does not have lighting.

Lož, the next village, is a picturesque place with the ruins of a mighty **13th century castle** and a **fortified church**.

A stage of the E6 European Hiking Trail leads from near Snežnik Castle to **Mt Snežnik** (1796 metres), which has a snow-capped peak until well into spring. Snežnik, about 15 km south-west of Kozarišče, is the highest non-Alpine mountain in Slovenia and on a clear day you can see forever (well, as far as Trieste and Venice, the Julian Alps,

Snežnik Castle

the Karavanke on the Austrian border and the Pohorje Massif). There is accommodation at the *Planinska Koča na Velikem Snežniku* (mobile ☎ 0609-615 356). It is open on Saturday, Sunday and holidays from June to October and daily in August.

Dolenjska

'Lower Carniola' is a charming area of gently rolling hills, vineyards, forests and the Krka River flowing south-eastward into Croatia. Those white hilltop churches with their red tile roofs you'll see everywhere once protected the people from the Turks and other invaders; the ones on the flat lands are newer – Baroque and painted the mustard colour ('Maria Theresa yellow') so common in Central Europe. The castles along the Krka are some of the best preserved in Slovenia, as are the many monasteries and abbeys. You can't miss the distinctive 'double hayracks' *(toplarji)* of Dolenjska; they're here in spades.

Dolenjska was settled early and is famous for its Hallstatt ruins and tombs, especially near Stična, Šmarjeta and Novo Mesto. The Romans eventually made the area part of the province of Upper Pannonia (Pannonia Superior) and built roads connecting Emona (Ljubljana) with smaller settlements at Praetorium Latobicorum (Trebnje), Acervo (Stična) and Neviodonum (Drnovo).

In the Middle Ages, the people of Dolenjska clustered around the many castles along the river (Žužemberk, Otočec) and at parish centres like Šentvid pri Stični. Monasteries sprang up at Stična, Kostanjevica na Krki and near Šentjernej (Pleterje). Much of the region was part of the Slovenska Krajina, the 'Slovenian March' that became part of Carniola (Kranjska) in the 13th century.

Dolenjska declined after the Middle Ages and progress only came in the late 19th century when a railway line linked Novo Mesto with Ljubljana. This was extended (via Bela Krajina) to Karlovac in Croatia in 1914.

Many people say that the 'purest' Slovene is spoken around the village of Rašica, south of the town of Krka, but this may have more to do with the fact that Primož Trubar (1508-86), the 'father of the Slovenian literary language', was born and worked most of his life here.

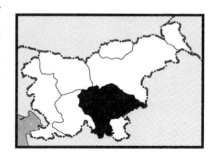

Dolenjska is the cycling capital of Slovenia. The E6 and E7 European hiking trails pass through Dolenjska and there are lots of chances to do some kayaking or canoeing on the Krka.

RIBNICA (pop 3300)
Though Ribnica is the oldest and most important settlement of western Dolenjska and just over the hills from the border with Notranjska, people in this region have traditionally affiliated with neither province. As far as they are concerned, this is Kočevsko, a forested, sparsely inhabited area with a unique history.

Ribnica was an important feudal centre during the Middle Ages and was ruled by a succession of lords including the Dukes of Celje before the Habsburgs arrived. It was also the centre of a large missionary area during the Christianisation of Slovenia. Like neighbouring Notranjska and Bela Krajina to the south-east, Kočevsko suffered greatly from the Turkish invasions of the 15th century. Bonfires would be lit atop peaks like Sveta Ana near Ribnica to warn the townspeople.

Among the inhabitants of the area at the time and up until the early days of WW II were many German-speaking Kočevarji who had been brought to Kočevsko by feudal lords a century before. Because the karst soil

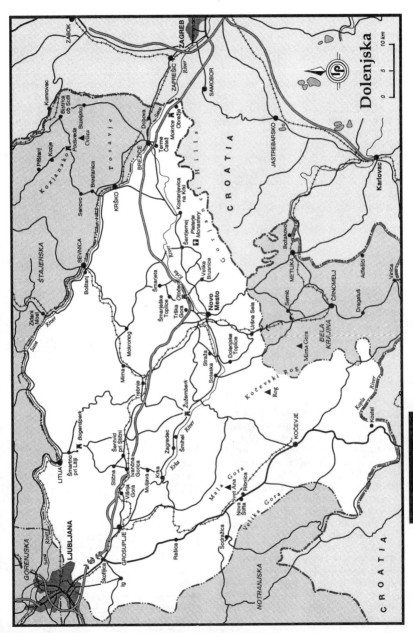

Dolenjska

DOLENJSKA

was too poor to make an adequate living from agriculture year-round, the Kočevarji supplemented their income with wooden products (suha roba, literally 'dry goods') they produced at home: pails, sifters, baskets and kitchen utensils. The men sold these products throughout the Habsburg Empire, and even the advent of the railway in 1893 did not put an immediate end to this itinerant way of life. Until well into the 20th century the sight of the suha roba peddler – his products piled high on his back and a staff in hand – was as Slovenian as a *kazolec* (hayrack). Wood carving remains an important cottage industry today.

Ribnica is 16 km north-west of Kočevje, another gateway to Kočevski Rog (see Around Dolenjske Toplice in this chapter), and on a main road to Croatia and the port of Rijeka.

Orientation

The town lies in the Ribnica Valley sandwiched between two ridges: Velika Gora and Mala Gora. The main street, Šeškova ulica, lies on the left bank of the tiny Bistrica River and runs parallel to it. Buses stop just in front St Stephen's Church.

Information

The cultural centre at Miklova Hiša (☎ 861 938), a lovely cream and white building dating from 1858, has a small gallery and will also provide information about Ribnica and surrounds. It is open from 10 am to noon and from 3 to 6 pm.

Ljubljanska Banka has a branch south of St Stephen's Church at Šeškova ulica 5b. It is open weekdays from 8.30 to 11.30 am and from 2 to 4.30 pm. SKB Banka keeps the same hours at the Ideal shopping centre on Kolodvorska ulica 9a.

The main post office is at Kolodvorska 2 opposite the shopping mall. It is open from 8 am to 6 pm weekdays and on Saturday till noon.

Ribnica's telephone code is 061. The postcode is 61310.

Things to See

Located on the right bank of the Bistrica at Gallusovo nabrežje 1, **Ribnica Castle** was originally built in the 10th century but was transformed and expanded over the centuries. Only a small section – a Renaissance wall and two towers – survived WW II bombing. Today the castle houses a small **ethnographic museum** (open Sunday only from 9 am to noon and from 3 to 6 pm) showcasing the traditional wood crafts and pottery made in the area. More interesting, perhaps, than the articles are the tools that are used to make them. The castle, set in an attractive semi-circular park with memorial statues and markers to Slovenian greats, is a popular venue for weddings on Saturday.

St Stephen's Parish Church on Šeškova ulica, built in the latter part of the 19th century on the site of an earlier church, would not be of much interest were it not for the two striking towers designed by Jože Plečnik (1872-1955) after WW II. As usual, Plečnik has mixed every conceivable style – and it works.

The plaque on the house opposite St Stephen's Church – **Štekličkova Hiša** – tells us that the 19th century poet and patriot France Prešeren had two years of education here (1810-12) in what was then the region's best known school, attracting students from throughout Slovenia as well as Croatia and Trieste.

Activities

Ribnica is the base for several excellent walks. A well-marked 'educational' trail leads north of the town for about 4.5 km up Mala Gora ridge to Sveta Ana, a rock wall or cliff (stena) 963 metres high with fantastic views of Ribnica and the Ribnica Valley. Along the way you'll pass the entrance to France Cave, the hilltop Church of St Ann and two huts selling food and drink.

From the *Jasnica Recreational Centre* (on the way to Kočevje and from where horses are for hire) a more difficult path leads north about six km to the junction with the Ribnica Alpine Trail. This eventually joins up with

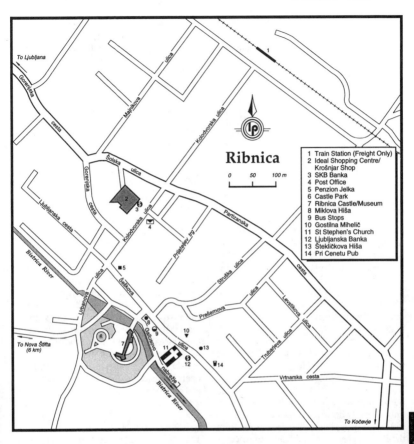

Ribnica

0   50   100 m

1 Train Station (Freight Only)
2 Ideal Shopping Centre/
   Krošnjar Shop
3 SKB Banka
4 Post Office
5 Penzion Jelka
6 Castle Park
7 Ribnica Castle/Museum
8 Miklova Hiša
9 Bus Stops
10 Gostilna Mihelič
11 St Stephen's Church
12 Ljubljanska Banka
13 Steklíčkova Hiša
14 Pri Cenetu Pub

the E7 European Hiking Trail about five km west of Velike Lašče.

A trail into the Velika Gora ridge west of Ribnica that leads to a comfortable mountain hut is more easily accessible from Nova Štifta (see the Around Ribnica section).

Festivals

Ribnica's main event is the Woodwork and Pottery Fair (Ribniški Semenj Suhe Robe in Lončarstva) held on the first Sunday in September though the entire weekend is given over to music, drinking and, of course, buying and selling things made of wood.

Places to Stay

The only place to stay in town is *Penzion Jelka* (☎ 861 637) centrally located on noisy Šeškova ulica at No 62. Doubles with breakfast and shower are DM54.

About four km south-east of Ribnica on the road to Kočevje, a guesthouse called *Izlaty* (☎ 864 515) in Prigorica (house No 115) has singles with shower and breakfast for DM35, doubles for DM40. Prigorica is less than a km from Dolenja Vas, a town noted for its clay pottery and clay whistles. But if you've come this far, continue on another four km to *Penzion Jasnica* (☎ 854

102) with 27 rooms in Gornje Ložine (house No 26) near the Jasnica recreational centre. The charge is from DM24 per person including breakfast.

Places to Eat

Ribnica's catering options are not much better than its accommodation ones. About the only central place for a meal is *Gostilna Mihelič* at Šeškova ulica 32 opposite St Stephen's Church. It is open from 9 am till 10 pm every day but Wednesday.

The far less salubrious *Pri Cenetu* on the same street at No 24 has 300 years of history under its belt but little in the way of food. Try it for a drink and a snack.

Things to Buy

You'll see lots of household articles made of wood for sale and the odd piece of pottery from nearby Dolenja Vas. Krošnjar at the Ideal shopping mall on Kolodvorska has a selection, as does Mercator at Šeškova ulica 15.

Getting There & Away

Buses run at least once an hour north to Ljubljana and south to Kočevje. The bus to Sodražica is good for Nova Štifta.

Ribnica is no longer served by passenger train. The line that includes Ribnica (Grosuplje-Kočevje) now handles freight only – mostly timber. But the Oldtimer Train run by Slovenijaturist has excursions from time to time between Ljubljana and Kočevje via Grosuplje. For details about itineraries, schedules and prices, contact any Slovenijaturist office.

Getting Around

You can order a taxi in Ribnica on ☎ 863 120.

AROUND RIBNICA
Nova Štifta

The **Church of the Assumption** at Nova Štifta, in the foothills of the Velika Gora six km west of Ribnica, is one of the most important pilgrimage sites in Slovenia. Completed in 1671 during the Counter-Ref-

ormation on a hilltop where mysterious lights had been seen, the Baroque church is unusual for its shape: both the nave and the presbytery are in the form of an octagon. The arcade on the west side fronting the entrance accommodated extra pilgrims on important holy days. But the church proved so popular that the painted stairway on the north side was added in 1780 to allow even more of the faithful to reach the clerestory, the upper story of the nave.

The interior of the church, with its three golden altars and pulpit carved by Jurij Skarnos, is blindingly ornate. Look for the painting of an aristocratic couple on stained glass on the north side of the presbytery. In the courtyard opposite the Franciscan monastery (where the church key is kept) stands a 350-year-old linden tree complete with a tree house.

Dom na Travni Gori (☎ 866 333 in Ravni Dol), a guesthouse 906 metres up with a restaurant and accommodation, can be reached by marked trail heading south-west from Nova Štifta in about 1½ hours. Prices are DM20 to DM27 per person including breakfast, depending on the type of room and the season. In winter one of Slovenia's smallest ski centres, Travna Gora (☎ 866 003), operates nearby with a 200-metre-long piste and one T-bar tow.

STIČNA (pop 1150)

The abbey at Stična (Sittich in German) is the oldest monastery in Slovenia and one of its most important religious and cultural monuments. At only 35 km south-east of Ljubljana and within easy walking distance of the train station at Ivančna Gorica (pop 2060), Stična can be visited as a day trip from the capital or en route to Novo Mesto, the lower Krka River Valley or Bela Krajina.

The monastery was established in 1136 by the Cistercians, a branch of the Benedictines that had been founded less than four decades before in France. The monks worked as farmers, obeying a vow of silence and communicating only through sign language. It became the most important religious, eco-

A	B
C	
D	E	F

Dolenjska (SF)

A Buildings at Baza 20 in Kočevski Rog
B Ruins of Žužemberk Castle
C Mobile beehive at Kočevski Rog

D Novo Mesto on the Krka River
E Vaulted cloister at Stična Abbey
F Church at Stična Abbey

Top: Festive Hall in Brežice Castle in the Posavje Region (JŽ)
Bottom: Indoor pool at Terme Čatež spa in the Posavje Region (J Ž)

Under the Lindens

If cities can have municipal animals – where would Rome be without the she-wolf that suckled Romulus and Remus? – and if US states can proclaim 'official drinks' (like tomato juice in New Jersey), why can't a country have a national tree? It's the linden (or common lime) in Slovenia, with its heart-shaped leaf, which has become the symbol of the national tourist board.

The stately linden *(lipa* in Slovene) can be found in abundance in Central Europe and was the most common tree in England thousands of years ago. Normally it grows slowly for about 60 years and then suddenly spurts upward and outwards, living to a ripe old age. It is said that a linden grows for 300 years, stands still for another 300, and takes 300 years to die.

Linden was used by the Romans to make shields and, as it is easy to work with, artisans in the Middle Ages carved religious figures from it, earning linden the title *sacrum lignum*, or 'sacred wood'. Tea made from the linden flower, which contains aromatic oils, has been used as an antidote for fever and the flu at least since the 16th century.

But the linden's ubiquity, longevity and many uses are not the only reasons it is so honoured by the Slovenes. For them it has an even more important past.

From earliest times, the linden tree was the focal point of any settlement in Slovenia – the centre of gossip, meetings, recreation and arbitration. A linden tree was always in the middle of the village and important decisions were made by town elders at a table beneath it. The linden, which could never be taller than the church spire, was also the place to gather after Sunday Mass.

So sacred has the linden tree become to Slovenes that its destruction is considered a serious offence. In discussing the barbarous acts committed by the Italians during the occupation of Primorska between the wars, one magazine article passionately points out that 'Kobarid had to swallow much bitterness... The Fascists cut down the linden tree etc.' Arbicide, it would appear, is a grave crime in these parts.

In today's Slovenia the linden represents not just hospitality but democracy – something that has not been lost on seekers of high office. No self-respecting politician fails to waltz around Slovenia's oldest linden, the Najevska Lipa under Mt Peca in Koroška, at least once a year. ∎

---

nomic, educational and cultural centre in Dolenjska.

The lives of the monks were disrupted continuously in the second half of the 15th century during the Turkish invasions. Ultimately the abbey was surrounded by walls (some eight metres high) and fortified with towers. But more damaging to the order was the edict issue by Emperor Joseph II in 1784 dissolving all religious orders in the Habsburg Empire. Stična was abandoned and the monks did not return until 1898.

The monastery has undergone steady reconstruction since WW II and today almost the entire complex is again in use though there are only a handful of monks in residence.

Orientation & Information

The village of Stična is about 2.5 km north of Ivančna Gorica, where the train station is.

The priests and staff at the monastery will be able to help you if you need information.

The telephone code for Stična and Ivančna Gora is 061. The postcode is 61295.

Stična Abbey

The entrance to the walled abbey, an incredible mix of Romanesque, Gothic, Renaissance and Baroque architecture, is on the east side across a small stream. This gives on to a large open courtyard bordered on the west by the abbey church and to the north by the Old Prelature, a Renaissance building dating to about 1600.

The **Old Prelature**, once the administrative centre of the abbey, contains exhibition rooms on two floors. The collection is a hotch-potch of antique clocks, paintings and furniture, farm implements mixed with chalices, monstrances and icons. (One particularly gruesome statue shows Saint Perpetua holding her two amputated breasts on

DOLENJSKA

a platter.) There are a few 16th century missals and medical texts in Latin and German, but all the medieval documents are facsimiles of the originals which were carted off to libraries in Vienna and Ljubljana when the order was banned in the 18th century. Two rooms are devoted to the accomplishments of two local sons who made good: the author Josip Jurčič (1844-81) from nearby Muljava whose *The 10th Brother* is considered the first full-length novel in Slovene; and the missionary Frederick Baraga (1797-1868), born in Trebnje. Baraga taught among the Chippewa Indians of Michigan and composed the first grammar of the Ojibwa language in 1843.

The video that the abbey shows visitors at the start of their tour is well produced but is only in Slovene with no subtitles.

If you want to drop out early, you can exit under the **Upper Tower** which is a few steps to the north-east of the Old Prelature. Just make sure you look up as you pass through. The ceiling is covered with stuccos from 1620 showing scenes of the Passion and Last Judgement.

Otherwise, across the courtyard to the west of the Abbey Church a door leads to Stična's celebrated **vaulted cloister**, mixing Romanesque and early Gothic styles. The cloister, which was once made of wood with stone corner pillars, served as an ambulatory for monks in prayer and connected the church with the monastery's other wings. The arches and vaults are decorated with frescoes of the prophets and Old Testament stories as well as allegorical subjects like the Virtues, the Four Winds etc. Look for the carved stone faces on the west side that were meant to represent human emotions and vices.

On the south side of the cloister is a typically Baroque monastic **refectory** with an 18th century pink ceiling and decorative swirls and loops made of white stucco. One floor above is the much impoverished **library**. **Neff's Abbey**, built in the mid-16th century by Abbot Volbenk Neff, runs westward. The arches in the vestibule on the ground floor are painted with a dense network of leaves, blossoms, berries and birds. You can gain access to the abbey church through a doorway in the north-east corner of the cloister.

The **Abbey Church**, consecrated in 1156, was built as a buttressed, three-nave Roman-

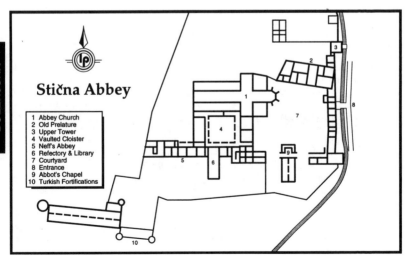

Stična Abbey

1 Abbey Church
2 Old Prelature
3 Upper Tower
4 Vaulted Cloister
5 Neff's Abbey
6 Refectory & Library
7 Courtyard
8 Entrance
9 Abbot's Chapel
10 Turkish Fortifications

esque cathedral. But except for the small windows at the top, you'd be hard-pressed to see much of that style today through all the Baroque reconstruction that took place in the early 17th century and again in the mid-18th century, just a few decades before the order was forced to vacate the premises. Apart from the ornate main altar and 11 side ones, the church contains several interesting elements. Look for the Renaissance red-marble tombstone of Abbot Jakob Reinprecht (who initiated the first Baroque reconstruction) in the north transept and the blue organ cupboard with eight angels (1747) in the choir loft. But the greatest treasures here are the **Stations of the Cross** painted by Fortunat Bergant in 1766. The artist signed the last one – 'Jesus is Laid into the Sepulchre' – spelling his surname with a 'W'.

One final building worth a look is the outer wing **Abbot's Chapel** closing off the southern portion of the courtyard. Built in the late 18th century as a kind of replacement to the grandiose halls seen in palaces and some larger monasteries, it contains a double staircase and a hall chapel of incredible lightness and vivacity.

The abbey can be visited from 8 am to noon and from 2 to 6 pm Tuesday to Saturday and on Sunday afternoon. Guided tours (available in Slovene, English and German) leave at 8.30 and 10 am, 2 and 4 pm Tuesday to Saturday and on Sundays and holy days at 2 and 4 pm. The entry charge is 200 SIT. The abbey can be very crowded with visiting school children in May and June.

Places to Stay & Eat
It is possible to spend the night at the monastery *guesthouse* (☎ 783 100) for about 1500 SIT per person, but you should make prior arrangements with the monks.

Perhaps less atmospheric but surely more comfortable is *Grofija* (☎ 778 141), a 19th century farmhouse with accommodation less than a km south-east of Stična in the village of Vir pri Stični (house No 30). Its four rooms cost DM28 per person for B&B, half board is DM32 and full board DM36; some rooms also have cooking facilities. Grofija (meaning 'county') is a working farm and horses are available for hire. If you're wondering what happens to the old ones, well, the speciality of the house is horsemeat *klobasa* (sausage). Of historical note: a major Hallstatt settlement dating from 800 BC once stood near the site of Grofija's tennis court. Grofija can also be reached directly from Ivančna Gorica (2.5 km) on the Šentvid bus.

In Ivančna Gorica, about 150 metres west of the train station at Ljubljanska cesta 38, *Gostilna Krjavelj* serves local Dolenjska favourites to an appreciative local crowd. Krjavelj (named after the hero in Jurčič's *The 10th Brother*) is open till midnight.

Things to Buy
The Cistercian monks sell many homemade products – bread, honey, wine, herbal teas and liqueurs – under their own label in a small shop in the Old Prelature.

Getting There & Away
Stična is served by up to 15 buses a day from Ljubljana but the number is halved on Saturday, and there are only three on Sunday.

Ivančna Gorica is on the rail line linking Ljubljana with Novo Mesto, Črnomelj and Metlika in Bela Krajina and Karlovac in Croatia. Up to 14 trains a day depart the capital and the 37-km trip to Ivančna Gorica takes just under an hour.

Getting Around
There are very infrequent buses (up to three a day) to and from Ivančna Gorica, but you can walk to Stična from the train station in about half an hour.

AROUND STIČNA
Bogenšperk Castle
About 20 km north of Stična is Bogenšperk Castle, in many respects the secular equivalent of the abbey. Here the Slovenian polymath Janez Vajkard Valvasor spent the most productive two decades of his life, writing and eventually publishing in 1689 *The Glory of the Duchy of Carniola*, his

Valvasor, Slovenia's Renaissance Man

Most of our knowledge of Slovenian history, geography, culture and folklore before the 17th century comes from the writings of one man, Janez Vajkard Valvasor, and more specifically his *The Glory of the Duchy of Carniola*. Not only did this truly great Renaissance man map large areas of Carniola and its towns for the first time, he explained the mystery of disappearing karst lakes and rivers, 'discovered' the unusual amphibian *Proteus anguinus*, introduced the world to Erazem Lueger, the 15th century Robin Hood of Slovenia, and catalogued early Slovenian folk tales.

Valvasor, whose name comes from *valvassores*, the burghers who lived in the towns of the Holy Roman Empire in the early Middle Ages, was born in Ljubljana in 1641 of a noble family from Bergamo. After a Jesuit education there and in Germany, he joined Miklós Zrínyi, the Hungarian count and poet, in the wars against the Turks. Valvasor travelled widely for a man of his time, visiting Germany, Italy, North Africa, France and Switzerland. He collected data on natural phenomena and local customs as well as books, drawings, mineral specimens and coins.

In 1672 Valvasor installed himself, his books and his precious collections (considered to be Slovenia's first museum) at Bogenšperk Castle, where he conducted scientific experiments (including alchemy) and wrote. In 1689 he completed his most important work. Published in German at Nuremburg under the title *Die Ehre des Herzogthums Crain* it ran to four volumes, containing 3500 pages with 535 maps and copper engravings. *The Glory of the Duchy of Carniola* remains one of the most comprehensive works published in Europe before the Enlightenment, a wealth of information on the Slovenian patrimony that is still explored and studied to this day.

As is so often the case with great men and women in history, Valvasor did not live to enjoy the success of his labour. Publishing such a large work at his own expense ruined Valvasor financially and he was forced to leave Bogenšperk in 1692. He died a year later at Krško, a town 65 km to the east on the Sava River. ∎

encyclopaedic work on Slovenian history, geography and culture.

The castle was built in the Renaissance style in the early 16th century by the aristocratic Wagen family, who named the place Wagensberg. Valvasor bought Bogenšperk in 1672 and installed his printing press, engraving workshop and an extensive library. But due to the enormous debts incurred in getting his *opus magnus* published, he was forced to sell the castle in 1692. He died a year later in Krško.

The castle passed from family to family and the last owners, the Windisch-Grätz family, left it in 1943. (They have recently expressed interest in reclaiming the prop-

erty.) During WW II, Bogenšperk was spared the total destruction that befell other castles in the area like Lichtenberg, Pogonik and Slatna.

The castle, with its rectangular courtyard and three towers (the fourth burned down in Valvasor's time) was renovated in 1972 and today houses a museum devoted to the great man, his work and Slovenian culture. Valvasor's **library** is now used as a wedding hall (complete with a cradle as is traditional in Slovenia), but his **study**, with its beautiful parquetry and painted ceiling, is pretty much the way he left it when he did his last alchemy experiments there. Other rooms contain examples of Valvasor's cartography and etching, four original volumes of his work donated by a Slovene from Trieste in 1993, a printing press similar to the one Valvasor used (which is in Munich) and the inevitable collection of hunting trophies, including a 132-kg brown bear shot in Kočevski Rog in 1978.

The most interesting exhibits, though, are the ones that deal with folk dress (life-size mannequins sport costumes modelled exactly on Valvasor's illustrations right down to the boots that have neither a right nor left), superstition and folk medicine through the ages in Slovenia. There are endless recipes to break spells, red crosses to ward off witches, votives and good-luck charms and vials of herbs and elixirs. The **Knights' Hall** on the ground floor is used for banquets and conferences, and the **castle chapel** near the entrance has artwork recently acquired from the abbey at Stična. The entrance to *Gostišče Valvasor*, a small restaurant with a vaulted ceiling, is by the fountain in the courtyard.

Bogenšperk does not have a posted schedule but is open most of the time. If not, the keeper of the castle key (about the size of a ukulele) lives in the house to the north of the main gate and says anyone is welcome any time. The entrance fee is 250 SIT for adults, 150 SIT for students.

Bogenšperk is only accessible from Stična by car or bicycle – and it's not a very good road. Even the public transport options from Ljubljana, 40 km west, are not good. Frequent trains and buses go to Litija but it's still another seven km south to Bogenšperk.

KRKA RIVER VALLEY

The Krka River springs from a karst cave south-west of Stična near the village of Trebnja Gorica and runs basically eastward for 111 km until it joins the mightier Sava River near Brežice. It is Dolenjska's longest and most important waterway.

If you are continuing on to other towns in Dolenjska and Bela Krajina and have your own transport, the ideal way to go is to follow the road along the Krka, which cuts a deep and picturesque valley along its upper course. The road is excellent for cycling and never gets too busy. From Ljubljana most buses and the train heading for Dolenjska follow the old medieval road, today's route No 1 (E70). Opt instead for the bus going to or via Žužemberk.

Muljava (pop 706)

This picturesque town of double hayracks (toplarji) and beehives (some with their original painted panels) is about five km south of Ivančna Gorica and just north of a tributary of the Krka. Muljava's claim to fame is twofold: it is the birthplace of the writer Josip Jurčič and is home to a small Gothic church with 15th century frescoes.

Things to See & Do The **Church of the Assumption** lies east of the main road and the key is available from the woman who lives next door (she's the bell ringer too). Not all of the paintings in the presbytery and on the vaulted arches are very clear – they show Cain and Abel making their sacrifices, symbols of the Apostles (including the winged lion of St Mark) and St Margaret – but the fresco depicting the death of the Virgin Mary on the south wall is still vibrant. The frescoes are signed by Johannes de Laibaco (John of Ljubljana) and dated 1456. The gilded main altar showing the Assumption dates from the late 17th century.

Josip Jurčič's birthplace, a small cottage typical of the region, is west of the main road and open every day, except Monday, from 10 am to noon and from 2 to 6 pm. Entry is 200 SIT. Behind the house is an open-air theatre in a dell where some of the writer's works are staged in summer.

One of the most popular places in Slovenia for fishing is the nine-km stretch of the Krka from its mouth to Zagradec, about halfway to Žužemberk. The season lasts from March to November, and brown and rainbow trout and grayling abound. But it's not a sport for the poor: foreigners pay DM80 for a daily fishing licence (DM200 for three days). Permits are available from the

Penzion Magovec (☎ 061-786 049) in Krka village (house No 13).

Places to Eat If you're hungry *Gostilna Obrščak* serves up hearty Slovenian fare like *klobasa in zelje* (sausage with sauerkraut). It is on the main road in the village centre and is popular with motorists.

Žužemberk (pop 3930)

The site of a mighty fortress from the early Middle Ages perched on a cliff over the Krka, Žužemberk is about 17 km from Muljava. The castle was completely rebuilt and the old walls fortified with round towers in the 16th century but was all but flattened during more than 20 air raids in WW II. Only one round tower has been reconstructed, but the sheer enormity and might of the place can still be seen from the opposite bank of the Krka.

Activities Kayaking and canoeing are excellent on the fast-flowing Krka, and Žužemberk is a good spot from which to set out. The Kayak-Canoe Club (☎ 068-87 230) in Prapreče (house No 1a), a km north-west of Žužemberk, can help with rentals and routes. Or contact the larger Rafting Club Gimpex (☎ 068-84 750) near Straža (Pod Srobotnikom 12).

Places to Eat *Gostilna Župančič* at Grajski trg 5 is a pizzeria with an outside terrace overlooking the Krka and is open till 11 pm every day except Monday. *Gostišče Pod Lipo* sits under a giant linden tree in front of the castle at Grajski trg 4.

Getting There & Away The bus stop is near the post office at Grajski trg 28. Up to a dozen buses a day go to Ljubljana, with eight to Dolenjske Toplice (13 km) and Novo Mesto (23 km), three to Črnomelj and two to Vinica.

DOLENJSKE TOPLICE (pop 800)

Within easy striking distance of Novo Mesto (13 km), this thermal resort is the oldest and one of the few real spa towns in Slovenia. Located in the karst Krka Valley below the wooded slopes of Kočevski Rog, Dolenjske Toplice is an excellent place in which to hike, cycle, fish or simply relax.

Although the curative powers of the thermal springs were known as early as the 14th century, the first spa was not built until 1658 when Ivan Vajkard, a member of the aristocratic Auersperg family, opened the Prince's Bath. Kopališki Dom (Bathers' House), complete with three pools, was built in the late 18th century and the first chemical analysis of the thermal waters was done. Within a century, Dolenjske Toplice had 30 rooms, basic medical facilities and its very own guidebook, but tourism did not really take off until 1899 with the opening of Zdraviliški Dom (Health Resort House). Strascha Töplitz, as it was then called (after the nearby town of Straža), was a great favourite of Austrians from the turn of the century up to WW I.

The complex was used as a military treatment centre in the 1920s and 1930s and part of it was a partisan hospital during WW II.

Orientation & Information

Dolenjske Toplice lies about 1.5 km south of the Krka River on an undulating stream called the Sušica. Virtually everything – including the two hotels of the thermal resort – is on or just off the main street, Zdraviliški trg.

Out-of-town buses stop on Zdraviliški trg just south of, or directly opposite, the post office. Dolenjske Toplice is not on a rail line.

The helpful staff at the Kopališki Dom (☎ 65 230) will answer all your questions about the spa and surrounding area. Ljubljanska Banka has a branch at Zdraviliški trg 8 and is open from 8 am to noon and from 2 to 4.30 pm weekdays. The post office is north across the car park at No 3. It is open from 8 am to 4 pm and on Saturday till noon and can change money.

Dolenjske Toplice's telephone code is 068. The postcode is 68350.

Thermal Baths

Taking the waters is the *sine qua non* of Dolenjske Toplice and you don't have to be a hotel guest to enjoy it. Outsiders pay 600 SIT on weekdays and 700 SIT at the weekend for the privilege. In reality, it's all taken very seriously; the warm mineral water (36-38°) gushing from 1000 metres below the two covered pools at Kopališki Dom is ideal for locomotive ailments such as rheumatism. But a recreational soak is still a lot of fun and will prevent backache. The health resort also offers other types of therapy, from underwater massage to paraffin baths.

The outside thermal pool *(športni bazen)* is 300 metres north of the two hotels and can be reached through a lovely little park. The unusual carved wooden statues of curling snakes and elongated human figures suggest the traditional occupation of this area: logging. The pool, which is open from 9 am till 7 pm in summer, has 27° water. The admission charge is 500 SIT on weekdays and 600 SIT at the weekend.

Hiking

A number of short (under five km), easy walks can be made from Dolenjske Toplice,

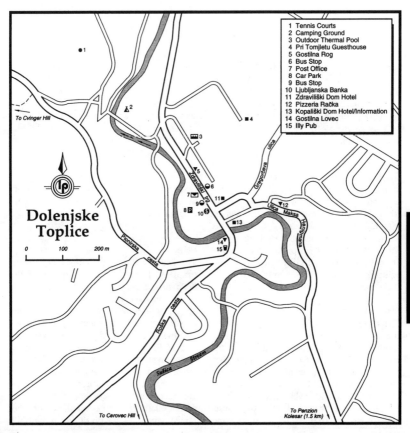

1 Tennis Courts
2 Camping Ground
3 Outdoor Thermal Pool
4 Pri Tomjletu Guesthouse
5 Gostilna Rog
6 Bus Stop
7 Post Office
8 Car Park
9 Bus Stop
10 Ljubljanska Banka
11 Zdravilišm Dom Hotel
12 Pizzeria Rača
13 Kopališki Dom Hotel/Information
14 Gostilna Lovec
15 Illy Pub

Dolenjske
Toplice

To Cvinger Hill

To Cerovec Hill

To Penzion
Kolesar (1.5 km)

DOLENJSKA

or you might consider hiking in the virgin forests of Kočevski Rog with Baza 20, the Partisan nerve centre during WW II, or even Mt Rog (1099 metres) as your destination (see the Around Dolenjske Toplice section).

Walks marked on the Dolenjske Toplice town map include a three-km walk south through the forest to Cerovec Hill (276 metres) and the Church of the Holy Trinity, affording pleasant views of the town, and a hike of four km west to Cvinger (263 metres), where Hallstatt tombs and iron foundries have been unearthed. Nature lovers may be interested in the 'educational forest walk' just west of Podturn (two km) which also takes in a small cave and the ruins of Rožek Castle.

Other Activities

The tennis courts on the hill west of the camping ground can be hired for 350 SIT per hour between 7 am and 8 pm. See the staff at the Kopališki Dom about renting racquets.

Daily permits valid for fishing in the Sušica and the middle course of the Krka, famous for its salmon trout, are available from the hotels.

The ski centre of Rog-Črmošnjice (☎ 65 230), 16 km south of Dolenjske Toplice, runs five T-bar tows on the slopes of Mt Gače at altitudes of between 730 and 930 metres. Depending on the snowfall, they operate from the end of December to the end of March. During the season a special ski bus carries skiers and instructors from Novo Mesto and Dolenjske Toplice. There are five km of cross-country trails at the centre, and equipment can be hired from the *brunarica* (ski shack) on site.

Places to Stay

The three-hectare *Dolenjske Toplice* camp site (☎ 65 230) is at the northern end of Zdraviliški trg opposite the outdoor swimming pool. It is open from May to September and can accommodate up to 120 guests. Daily charges are DM5 per person, DM3 per car and per tent and DM3.50 per caravan.

Pri Tomjletu (☎ 65 023) is a cosy guesthouse run by the friendly Tomlje family (the

son, Matjaž, is a famous racing-car driver) behind the open-air pool at Zdraviliški trg 24. None of the eight rooms has its own bathroom but all have sinks, and cooking facilities are available. The per-person charge including breakfast is DM20.

The eight-room *Penzion Kolesar* (☎ 65 003) is an even better deal – DM19 per person with bathroom and breakfast – and there's a very popular gostilna on the ground floor. But it's in Dolenje Sušice (house No 22), about two km south-east of Dolenjske Toplice, with no chance of catching a late-night bus.

The two spa hotels (☎ 65 230; fax 65 663) run by the Krka Health Resorts company – the four-star *Kopališki Dom* with 176 beds at Zdraviliški trg 11 and the three-star *Zdraviliški Dom* with 104 beds north across the plaza at Zdraviliški trg 19 – share the same facilities, including two indoor thermal pools, two saunas, fitness centre etc. Of the two, the Kopališki Dom has much better rooms and public areas. Depending on the season, singles with breakfast are DM51 to DM58 while doubles are DM76 to DM92. The Zdraviliški Dom has a large restaurant with a wonderful painted ceiling, but its rooms are badly in need of upgrading. Singles with breakfast here are DM44 to DM50 with doubles DM66 to DM80. Both hotels offer discounted weekend and week-long packages.

Places to Eat

The health resort's main restaurant is the ornately decorated dining room of the *Zdraviliški Dom* where most guests on half or full pension take their meals. It opens at 7 am and closes at 8.30 pm. Otherwise the choice in the immediate area is limited to two gostilne: the *Lovec* (Hunter) between the Gothic Church of St Anne and the small bridge over the Sušica or the *Rog* (Deer) in the park near the outdoor pool at Zdraviliški trg 22. Frankly, the 'Hunter' and the 'Deer' are much of a muchness though the Rog has decent salads. Both are open till 10 or 11 pm. *Račka* serves decent pizza and pasta daily until 11 pm in a newly renovated village house at Ulica Maksa Henigmana 13.

If you've got two or four wheels or don't mind walking three km, head south-west for *Gostilna Štravs* in Podturn (house No 28). It's one of the best small restaurants in the area and specialises in fresh-water fish and game.

Entertainment

The *Rog* has Slovenian folk music some nights, organised by the health resort. Otherwise it's early to bed and early to rise in this healthy place, although Dolenjske Toplice's young bloods have been congregating lately at the *Illy* pub south-west of the Kopališki Dom at Pionirska cesta 1.

Getting There & Away

There are buses to and from Novo Mesto about every 30 minutes and hourly service to Žužemberk. Up to half a dozen go to Črnomelj (two via Semič) every day with between seven and nine departures for Ljubljana.

Getting Around

The health resort has bicycles for rent for 300 SIT per hour and 500 SIT for two hours.

AROUND DOLENJSKE TOPLICE
Kočevski Rog

One of the most pristine areas in Slovenia, Kočevski Rog has been a protected nature area for more than 100 years. The region was – and is – so remote that during the early days of WW II the Partisans under the command of Marshal Tito headquartered here, building bunkers, workshops, hospitals, schools, even printing presses. The nerve centre was the so-called **Baza 20** (Base 20), about 10 km south-west of Dolenjske Toplice, which was reconstructed and turned into a national monument after the war.

During the old regime, Baza 20 was a favourite 'pilgrimage' spot for many Slovenes and other Yugoslavs, and busloads of 'the faithful' paid their respects every day. Nowadays Baza 20 is a shadow of its former self – its two dozen buildings ramshackle,

the access trail unkempt, the indicator maps all but illegible. Still, as an indication of how Slovenes view the recent past both now and then, it's worth a visit and the sheer beauty and tranquillity of the spot is a treat. There is no scheduled bus service to here, but Baza 20 is easily reached by sealed road on foot or bicycle from Podturn, seven km away. From the car park and *Gostilna MM* (open 10 am to 10 pm daily), it's a 15-minute walk up a mountain path to Baza 20.

The range's tallest peak, **Mt Rog** (1099 metres) is about five km to the south-west. The area is a popular hunting ground (brown bear, wild cat, boar) for rich Italian tourists and was a favourite of Tito and his cronies.

NOVO MESTO (pop 22,800)

Situated on a sharp bend of the Krka River, the inappropriately named 'New Town' is the political, economic and cultural capital of Dolenjska and one of its prettiest towns. For Slovenes, Novo Mesto is synonymous with the painter Božidar Jakac (1899-1989) who captured the spirit of the place on canvas, and the writer Miran Jarc (1900-42) who did the same in prose with his autobiographical novel *Novo Mesto*. For the traveller, Novo Mesto is an important gateway to the historical towns and castles along the lower Krka, the karst forests of the Gorjanci Hills to the south-east, Bela Krajina and Croatia. Indeed, Zagreb is a mere 74 km east of Novo Mesto via route No 1 (E70).

Novo Mesto was settled during the late Bronze Age in about 1000 BC, and helmets and decorated burial urns unearthed in surrounding areas suggest that Marof Hill above the Old Town was the seat of Hallstatt princes during the late Iron Age. The Illyrians and Celts came later, and the Romans maintained a settlement here until it was overrun by Germanic tribes during the late 5th century AD.

During the early Middle Ages, Novo Mesto flourished as a market because of its location and later became the centre of the estates owned by the abbey at Stična. In 1365, Habsburg Archduke Rudolf IV raised

DOLENJSKA

it to the status of a town, naming it Rudolphswert. By the 16th century, some 15,000 loads of freight passed through Novo Mesto each year. But plague, fires and raids by the Turks on their way to Vienna took a toll on the city and, within 100 years, Novo Mesto's main square had become grazing land for cattle. Yet, Janez Vajkard Valvasor wrote in *The Glory of the Duchy of Carniola* that despite the city's decline Novo Mesto was still 'the most remarkable town of the duchy after Ljubljana'.

Prosperity returned in the 18th and 19th centuries: a college was established in 1746, Slovenia's first National Hall (Narodni Dom) opened here in 1875 and a railway line linked the city with Ljubljana in the 1890s. After the capitulation of the Habsburgs in 1918, Novo Mesto began to industrialise. Bombardments during WW II, particularly in 1941 and 1943, severely damaged the city.

Today, Novo Mesto shows two faces to the world: the Old Town perched high up on a rocky promontory above the left bank of the Krka and a new town to the north and south which thrives on the business of Krka, a large pharmaceutical and chemical company, and Revoz, which produces Renault cars.

Orientation

Almost everything of interest in Novo Mesto is in the toe-shaped Old Town above the Krka River and dominated by the belfry of the Chapter Church. Glavni trg is a large, cobbled square – bigger than any in Ljubljana, as local people like to point out – lined with arcaded shops and public buildings. A bridge at its southern end leads to the suburbs of Kandija and Grm.

The bus station is south-west of the Old Town across the Krka on Roška cesta; to reach Glavni trg, follow Kandijska cesta for 800 metres and cross the bridge. Novo Mesto has two train stations: the main one about two km north-west of the Old Town and tiny Novo Mesto Center, at the start of Ljubljanska cesta at the western edge of the Old Town. From here it's a five-minute walk eastward to Novi trg, recently converted into a shopping mall and business centre.

Another 350 metres along Rozmanova ulica will take you to Glavni trg.

Information

Tourist Office Don't expect much help from the tourist office (☎ 068 322 512) on the ground floor of the town hall at Glavni trg 7; it seems to open according to the whim of whoever may be in the office. Instead, head for one of the two travel agencies.

Money The most centrally located banks are SKB Banka at Glavni trg 10 and another SKB branch at Novi trg 3. They are open weekdays from 8.30 am to noon and from 2 to 5 pm. A Banka's Novo Mesto branch is at Rozmanova ulica 38 just north of Novi trg.

Post & Telecommunications The main post office is at Novi trg 7, from where you can make international and domestic calls and change money. There's a call box outside the building that takes PTT Slovenija telephone cards. Novo Mesto's telephone code is 068. The postcode is 68000.

Travel Agencies There are two travel agencies in Novo Mesto: Kompas (☎ 321 338) at Novi trg 6 or Emona Globtour (☎ 323 376) at Rozmanova ulica 19, both of which are open from 7 or 8 am until 4 pm weekdays and till noon on Saturday.

Bookshop Mladinska Knjiga at Glavni trg 9, open from 7 am till 7 pm weekdays and till noon on Saturday, sells regional maps and guides.

Chapter Church of St Nicholas

Perched above the Old Town on Kapiteljska ulica, this Gothic church is Novo Mesto's most visible historical monument. And with a 15th century presbytery and crypt, painted ceiling, a belfry that was once a medieval defence tower and an altar painting of the eponymous saint supposedly done by the Venetian master Jacopo Tintoretto (1518-94), it is also its most important. But what strikes most visitors is the nave; it actually

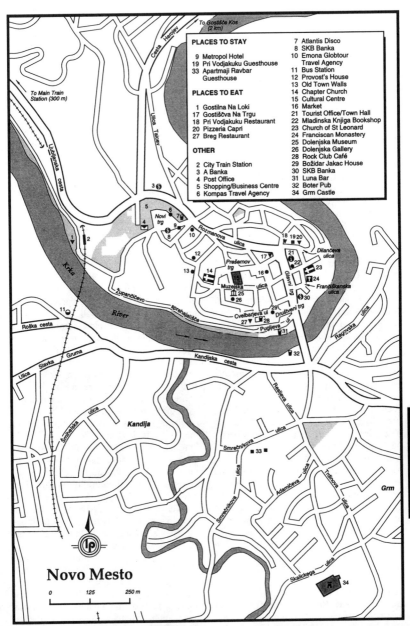

PLACES TO STAY

9 Metropol Hotel
19 Pri Vodjakuku Guesthouse
33 Apartmaji Ravbar
  Guesthouse

PLACES TO EAT

1 Gostilna Na Loki
17 Gostiščva Na Trgu
18 Pri Vodjakuku Restaurant
20 Pizzeria Capri
27 Breg Restaurant

OTHER

2 City Train Station
3 A Banka
4 Post Office
5 Shopping/Business Centre
6 Kompas Travel Agency

7 Atlantis Disco
8 SKB Banka
10 Emona Globtour
  Travel Agency
11 Bus Station
12 Provost's House
13 Old Town Walls
14 Chapter Church
15 Cultural Centre
16 Market
21 Tourist Office/Town Hall
22 Mladinska Knjiga Bookshop
23 Church of St Leonard
24 Franciscan Monastery
25 Dolenjska Museum
26 Dolenjska Gallery
28 Rock Club Café
29 Božidar Jakac House
30 SKB Banka
31 Luna Bar
32 Boter Pub
34 Grm Castle

Novo Mesto

0   125   250 m

DOLENJSKA

doglegs by some 17° before reaching the main altar.

The cream-coloured building to the north of the church is the **Provost's House**, built in 1623. If the church is locked, you'll find the key here. A section of the town's **medieval walls** can be seen just west of the church. They date from the 14th century.

Dolenjska Museum

Below the Chapter Church about 100 metres to the east at Muzejska ulica 7, the Dolenjska Museum complex is divided into five parts. The oldest building, which once belonged to the knights of the Teutonic Order, houses a valuable collection of archaeological finds unearthed in the southern suburb of Kandija in the late 1960s. The museum is divided into four periods: the Neolithic and Bronze ages; the Hallstatt period; the arrival of the Celts; and Dolenjska under the Romans. You can't miss the Hallstatt helmet dating from 800 BC with two enormous axe blows at the top, the fine bronze situlas from the 4th century BC with battle and hunting scenes and the Celtic ceramics and jewellery (particularly the bangles of turquoise and dark-blue glass) from nearby Beletov Vrt.

The **Dolenjska Gallery** hosts the Biennial of Slovenian Graphic Art during even-numbered years. It occasionally accepts non-Slovenian works; in 1994 at the 3rd Biennial sketches by the likes of Rembrandt (from a museum in Vienna) and Picasso (from Bremen) were admitted. The gallery's permanent collection includes regional works from the 16th to 20th centuries.

Other collections in the complex include one devoted to the liberation front and the Partisans during WW II and a small but excellent **ethnographic collection** with farm implements, commemorative jugs presented at weddings, gingerbread hearts and icons painted on glass. Take a look at the almost lifesize wooden statue of a French soldier from the Illyrian Provinces era. It was used as a beehive.

The museum also administers the **Božidar Jakac House** about 100 metres east at Društveni trg 2. The peripatetic and prolific Jakac visited dozens of countries in the 1920s and 1930s, painting and sketching such diverse subjects as Parisian dance halls, Scandinavian port towns, African villages and American city skylines. But his best works are of Novo Mesto: markets, people, churches and rumble-tumble wooden houses clinging precariously to the banks above the Krka. One unusual work is the almost surreal *Odkrivanje (Revelation)* of a man hiding his face before a parted curtain. In order to visit the collection you must be accompanied by a member of the Dolenjska Museum staff. As you approach the house via Mej vrti, don't miss the painted statue of Tito, abandoned in a garden to the left.

The Dolenjska Museum is open Tuesday through Saturday from 10 am till 6 pm and on Sunday till 8 pm. Entrance to all the exhibits is 500 SIT (300 SIT for students).

Other Sights

Novo Mesto's other interesting buildings are mostly on or just off Glavni trg. At No 7, the neo-Renaissance **town hall**, out of step with the square's other arcaded buildings, ostentatiously calls attention to itself at all hours with its bells and odd facade but especially at noon when an ear-piercing siren is sounded. The coat of arms on the front is that of Rudolf IV, the town's founder.

South of the town hall on Frančiškanske trg is the **Church of St Leonard**, which was originally built by Franciscan monks fleeing the Turks in Bosnia in 1472 but has an unusual 19th century neo-Gothic/Moorish gable, and the **Franciscan monastery**. The monastery library's collection of rare manuscripts, including many important 12th century incunabula, are now in Ljubljana. The **Gymnasium** founded by Maria Theresa in 1746 is north across Jenkova ulica. Today it houses a musical school, a public library and the provincial archives.

The only historical structure of note on the right bank of the Krka is **Grm Castle**, a manor house on Skalickega ulica with an ornately stuccoed central hall. Habsburg and socialist seals on the outside reveal its later incarnations: a public building from the late

Hallstatt Culture in Slovenia

Hallstatt is the name of a village in the Salzkammergut region of Austria where objects characteristic of the early Iron Age (from about 700 to 500 BC) were found in the 19th century. Today it refers to the late Bronze and early Iron Age cultures that developed in Central and Western Europe from about 1100 to 450 BC.

Many parts of Slovenia were settled during this period, particularly Dolenjska and Bela Krajina. Burial grounds and forts have yielded swords, helmets, jewellery and especially situlas, pails or buckets that are often richly decorated with battle and hunting scenes.

Hallstatt art is very geometric and typical motifs are birds and figures arranged in pairs. It was not until the advent of the late Iron Age – the La Tène culture (450 to 390 BC) of the European Celts – that S-shapes, spirals and round patterns developed. ■

Hallstatt Situla

19th century and then an agricultural school. It is now slated to become an office block.

Activities

Boating The Luna bar (☎ 321 612) rents canoes for 400 SIT per hour during the summer months. But don't expect to get very far; you can only paddle about two km upstream on the Krka and 200 metres downstream. More serious canoeing and kayaking is available nine km west on the Krka through the rafting club Gimpex in Straža (☎ 84 750) at Pod Srobotnikom 12.

Flying The Novo Mesto Aeroclub (☎ 21 107 or 20 472 in Novo Mesto) at Prečna, five km west of Novo Mesto, offers sightseeing flights over Novo Mesto and the Krka Valley in Cessna 172s and Piper 28-Warriors every day between 9 am and 7 pm. A 15-minute flight costs 4200 SIT for three passengers. Flying lessons are also available. The airfield is just over a km from the centre of Prečna, which is served by bus from Novo Mesto.

Horse Riding The Novo Mesto Sport Equestrian Centre (☎ 28 166) is in the village of Češča Vas, about three km south of Prečna. To find it from the main road, look for the sign marked 'Konjeniški Športni Center' and follow the dirt track for about 700 metres. The centre has 40 different Holsteiners and Arabians for riders of all levels. The charge is about 800 SIT per hour. You can ride any day, but you should book first.

Skiing Special buses link Novo Mesto with the ski centre of Rog-Črmošnjice (☎ 65 230) south of Dolenjske Toplice between late December and late March. See the staff at the Metropol hotel for more information.

Places to Stay

The accommodation options are not great in Novo Mesto. The closest *camp grounds* are at Otočec and Dolenjske Toplice, seven km and 12 km away respectively. Globtour has a few *private rooms* on its books, but they are quite a distance from town.

Apartmaji Ravbar (☎ 25 735), a family-run guesthouse at Smrečnikova ulica 15-17 across the Krka in Kandija, has five modern, spotlessly clean apartments (with kitchens)

DOLENJSKA

and two rooms for DM20 to DM30 per person. It's a very quiet area, full of trees and people walking their dogs. They also have a cottage available for rent in the vineyards of Birčna Vas, a village about nine km south of Novo Mesto.

The *Pri Vodjakuku* restaurant (☎ 321 584) on the corner of Dilančeva ulica and Glavni trg may have reopened its small guesthouse *(Prenočišča pri Vodjakuku)* by now. If not, the only other place to stay in Novo Mesto is the *Metropol* (☎ 322 226; fax 322 242) at Novi trg 1, a newly renovated 50-room business hotel run by the Krka group. Singles with shower and breakfast are 3500 SIT, doubles 5600 SIT. The Metropol has a decent restaurant and a pub that's open till 10 pm.

Places to Eat

The *Pizzeria Capri*, tucked away in a courtyard at Dilančeva ulica 7, has pizzas for between 320 and 500 SIT. The Capri is open from 9 am till 10 pm on weekdays and from 3 pm at weekends.

Gostišča na Trgu, the 'Inns on the Square' at Glavni trg 32, have no accommodation but count three eateries and a kavarna. On the ground floor is the café with sidewalk terrace, a pizzeria and a 'classic' restaurant with set-lunch menus from 500 SIT. All are open daily from 11 am to 10 pm. The self-service restaurant upstairs, with pleasant seating on a narrow balcony overlooking a courtyard, is much cheaper. It's open from 8 am till 8 pm.

For better (and more expensive) food, head deeper into the Old Town for the *Breg* restaurant at Cvelbarjeva ulica 7, birthplace of Božidar Jakac and once an important spot for artists and writers. Try *kurja obara z ajdovimi žganci* (chicken stew with buckwheat groats) along with a glass or two of Cviček, the uniquely Slovenian light, fresh red wine from Dolenjska. There's garden seating in warmer months. The restaurant is staffed by students from the local catering school who try very hard to please.

Na Loki, at Župančičevo sprehajališče 2, is not so much 'On the Meadow' as it is on the Krka River with restful views across to the Portoval peninsula. The speciality here is fish, particularly trout, and the restaurant is open daily from 9 am till midnight.

If you have your own transport *Gostišče Kos* at Ločna 7B on the left bank of the Krka about 2.5 km north-east of the Old Town gets excellent reviews for its home-style cooking. 'The Blackbird' is open for lunch and dinner weekdays and Saturday lunch.

There is an outdoor *market* selling fruit and vegetables on Forjanov trg in the centre of the Old Town.

Entertainment

The *cultural centre* (☎ 321 214) at Prešernov trg 5 has a cinema and sponsors occasional theatrical and musical performances. Ask the staff about summer concerts held in the atrium of the Provost's House.

Glavni trg has a number of small pubs and cafés with outside terraces which would be pleasant in the warm months if the traffic through the square wasn't so heavy. Leave them behind and head for *Luna* at Pugljeva ulica 2 or *Boter* behind Kandijska cesta 4, two outdoor café-pubs on opposite banks of the river. The Luna, with its lovely back garden, is more pleasant, but the Boter has better views of the Old Town from across the Krka, complete with jumping fish. It's all straight out of a Jakac painting.

The *Rock Club Café* next to the Breg restaurant on Cvelbarjeva ulica is where Novo Mesto's trendy set hangs out, but for a later night out head for the *Atlantis* disco at the eastern end of Novi trg opposite Rozmanova ulica 32. It's open nightly from 11 pm till 4 am.

Like the province of Bela Krajina to the south, Dolenjska has a tradition of folk music and flyers and posters around town are always announcing folk ensemble performances at music halls and cultural centres in neighbouring towns and villages.

Getting There & Away

Bus Bus service to and from Novo Mesto is good. There are very frequent departures to Dolenjske Toplice, Otočec, Šentjernej and Šmarješke Toplice and at least 10 a day to

Brežice, Črnomelj, Kostanjevica na Krki, Ljubljana, Metlika, Trebnje and Žužemberk. Other destinations served from Novo Mesto include: Bled (two buses a day); Celje (one); Koper (two); Kranjska Gora (two); Krško (six); Maribor (one); Prečna (five); and Vinica (eight). You can also reach Zagreb (eight buses a day) and Poreč (one) in Croatia.

Train Up to 14 trains a day serve Novo Mesto from Ljubljana (75 km; 1¾ hours) via Ivančna Gorica and Trebnje. Most of these continue on to Črnomelj (45 minutes) and Metlika (one hour), where you can make up to nine connections a day for Karlovac in Croatia. To reach anywhere else in Slovenia by train from Novo Mesto, you'll have to go to Ljubljana.

Car There's a Hertz office (☎ 323 925) above the bus station on Roška cesta open weekdays from 7 am till 3 pm and on Saturday till 1 pm.

Getting Around
Taxi Local taxis can be ordered on ☎ 21 777.

OTOČEC (pop 1885)
The castle at Otočec (Wördl in German), occupying a tiny island in the middle of the Krka River seven km east of Novo Mesto, is one of Slovenia's loveliest and most complete fortresses. Unfortunately, someone else thought so too and turned it into an up-market and very expensive hotel. But the area around Otočec, the gateway to the lower Krka and the Posavje region, has been turned into a recreational centre – somewhat commercial, some would say – and there is a wide choice of accommodation and activities.

The first castle at Otočec almost certainly stood on the right bank of the river. But during the Mongol onslaught in the mid-13th century (or even a century later during the wars with the Hungarians), a canal was dug on the south side, thereby creating an artificial island. The present structure probably lost its military significance almost as soon

as it was built in the early 16th century since the frontier had moved southward by then. In 1560 it was purchased by Ivan Lenkovič, the commander of the Vojna Krajina (Military March) who went on to defeat the Turks at Kostanjevica na Krki three years later.

Orientation
The castle (Grad Otočec hotel) is a km east of Otočec village on a secondary road running parallel to route No 1 (E70) and the river. The castle is reached via a rickety wooden bridge that probably should not handle cars. Cheaper accommodation is available up the hill a few steps north of the bridge and across the main road. The camping ground is south-west of the island on the right bank.

Information
Staff at the reception of the Grad Otočec hotel can provide information about the recreational facilities at Otočec and help with equipment rentals. You can change money here, at the reception of the Garni hotel, at the camp site or at the post office in Otočec village.

The telephone code for Otočec is 068. The postcode is 68222.

Otočec Castle
Though the castle is now a posh hotel, there's no harm in having a look around this historical site and perhaps having a cup of coffee at the terrace café in the courtyard if the weather is warm. The castle, which contains elements of late Gothic and Renaissance architecture, consists of two wings connected by a wall. There are four squat, rounded towers with very thick walls and narrow loopholes at each end. Together with the Dolenjska Museum in Novo Mesto, the castle hosts the Biennial of Slovenian Graphic Art during even-numbered years.

Activities
Otočec (and the Krka Valley in general) is a cycling centre; the Tour de Slovénie starts near here in early May, and Otočec is the host of the Krka Grand Prix bicycle race in June.

DOLENJSKA

The Garni hotel has bicycles and mountain bikes for rent for 400 SIT per hour.

The camp site rents canoes, rowing boats and rafts for use on the Krka. (The best areas for rowing are downstream from Struga.) The per-hour fee is 400 SIT.

While not as rich as the upper Krka, the river around Otočec is a popular fishing spot and will more than likely yield a couple of pike, perch or carp. Fishing permits from the hotel cost 1700 SIT per day.

The Struga Riding Centre (☎ 85 167) on the south river bank about 1.5 km north-east of the Otočec camp site has a number of horses available for dressage, cross-country riding and coach excursions. One hour of riding costs DM22; a day (five hours) including lunch is DM100. Lessons are DM26 per hour and a half-hour ride in an old coach is DM35. The centre, which is housed in another medieval castle complete with chapel, is open from 8 to 11 am and 5 to 9 pm every day except Tuesday. To get there from the castle, cross the second bridge, walk east for 600 metres on the paved road and then north for another 900 metres on the unsealed one.

Places to Stay

All the accommodation places listed here share the same contact numbers: ☎ 21 830 and fax 22 590.

The *Otočec* camp site is on a two-hectare strip of land running along the south bank of the Krka and can accommodate 200 people. To reach it from the castle, cross the second bridge, turn left (east) and walk for 300 metres. It has its own tennis court and pool and there's a 'beach' along the river. Daily charges are DM5 per person, DM3 per car and per tent and DM3.50 per caravan. It is open from May to September.

An unattractive area north of the castle includes the *Garni* hotel, a concrete-and-glass box at Grajska cesta 2 with a sauna, cocktail bar, disco and 78 rooms. Singles with shower and breakfast are DM69, doubles are 106. The nearby motel charges DM85 for its doubles including breakfast

and DM89 for bungalows accommodating two people.

The *Grad Otočec* hotel is one of the most attractive and luxurious hotels in Slovenia. Its two dozen rooms are enormous and have polished parquet floors, Oriental carpets, marble-topped tables and large baths. But don't expect all that to come cheap. Singles with bath and breakfast are DM151, doubles DM214.

If you want something a bit more rural and affordable, the *Šeruga* farmhouse (☎ 85 656) in the village of Sela pri Ratežu (house No 15) about two km south of Otočec village has doubles and triples (some with kitchen) for DM24 to DM27 per person including breakfast.

Places to Eat

The *Otočec* restaurant north of the castle has a large terrace that is very popular in summer. If you can't handle the crowds, try the small eatery at the camp site or the one at the Struga riding centre.

The *Castle* restaurant and the smaller *Knights' Hall* at the Grad Otočec will be out of most people's price range, but the ancient stone walls, chandeliers and game and fish specialities make them worth a splurge.

Entertainment

The *disco* at the Garni hotel is open till late on Thursday, Friday and Saturday. The *Hit Casino* (☎ 28 596), with blackjack, poker, American roulette and slot machines, is open from 5 pm to 2 am daily.

Getting There & Away

The bus linking Novo Mesto and Šmarješke Toplice stops at the bridge leading to the castle about once an hour on weekdays but less frequently at the weekend.

AROUND OTOČEC

There are a couple of excellent excursions accessible from Otočec on foot, mountain bike or even horseback. The first is to the vineyards of **Trška Gora** (428 metres), which can be reached by road and trail from Mačkovec, about five km south-west of

Otočec on the main road to Novo Mesto. The walk (or ride) is quite straightforward from there.

Follow the road north for a km to Sevno, where the farmhouse at No 1 has Dolenjska wines for tasting and sale, and then continue along the winding track for another two km to Trška Gora and St Mary's Church. From here there are wonderful views of the Gorjanci Hills, Kočevski Rog and the Krka Valley. Below the church is *Krkin Hram* (☎ 321 321), a 100-year-old wine cellar with a restaurant and accommodation. But make sure you call in advance; Krkin Hram isn't always open.

Farther afield is **Gospodična** (828 metres) in the Gorjanci Hills and its *Dom Vinka Paderšiča pri Gospodični* (☎ 24 920 in Novo Mesto), a mountain lodge with a restaurant and accommodation. Gospodična and the lodge are about 13 km south-east of Otočec in the shadow of **Trdinov Vrh** (1178 metres), the highest peak in the Gorjanci. This densely forested area is known for its mushrooms and a 'magic spring' in which first-time visitors should wash. The route from Otočec goes for five km south-east to **Velike Brusnice**, famous for its cherries and cherry festival in spring, then to Gabrje (4.5 km) and on to Gospodična (3.5 km).

ŠMARJEŠKE TOPLICE (pop 1860)

If all that Cviček wine is taking its toll, consider stopping at Šmarješke Toplice, a spa in a small, lush valley about five km north of Otočec. While it doesn't have anything close to the history or atmosphere of Dolenjske Toplice, 25 km to the south-west, it has lovely grounds and more than enough facilities to keep you busy and help recharge those batteries. The closest town to the spa is Šmarjeta.

The three natural pools that once stood on the site of the spa were used by local people as far back as the 18th century and were collectively known as the Lake Spa. Development did not come until 1950, when the first hotel was built, but even that remained a rather exclusive facility reserved for the

nomenklatura (Communist bosses) with failing hearts. Only in the last decade has Šmarješke Toplice really made it on the map as both a serious therapy centre for those with cardiovascular problems and a centre promoting relaxation and a healthier lifestyle.

Orientation & Information

The spa complex and its hotels are north of the tiny village of Šmarješke Toplice; the road to it passes a thermal-water stream and a pond with giant water lilies. Buses stop in front of the small restaurant (Gostilna Prinovec) and grocery store in the village. The post office, where you can change money and make phone calls, is next door and is open from 8 am to 4 pm weekdays and till noon on Saturday.

Šmarješke Toplice's telephone code is 068. The postcode is 68220.

Activities

The spa counts four pools fed by 32° spring water rich in carbon dioxide and minerals. Two are indoor at the hotel complex and are used for therapy. Nearby is a sauna, solarium and modern gym.

The large outdoor pool is below the sports centre. Visitors not staying at the spa pay 500 SIT (600 SIT at weekends). Because the basin of the older (and smaller) pool nearby is made of wood, the water temperature is 2° warmer.

The sports centre has four clay tennis courts available for hire (400 SIT per hour) and racquets can be rented. One of the courts is covered and illuminated at night. There are also facilities for table tennis (150 SIT), minigolf (110 SIT) and lawn bowls. Bicycles cost 200 SIT per hour.

The wine-growing areas surrounding Šmarješke Toplice make for excellent walking and there are trails and footpaths south-west to Trška Gora (see the Around Otočec section) and north-east to Vinji Vrh.

Places to Stay

All the accommodation places at Šmarješke Toplice, totalling just over 330 beds, have

DOLENJSKA

the same numbers: ☎ 73 230 and fax 73 107. Bear in mind that there's a DM15 supplement for guests staying in rooms on their own.

The cheapest place to stay in the spa itself is in one of the small *bungalows*, which cost DM50 per person, including full board. The J-shaped main complex is divided into three hotels. The *Toplice*, dating from 1950, is normally reserved for long-term guests with more serious medical problems. The *Krka*, the middle section built in 1983, costs DM52 to DM73 per person with full board. The newest (1991) and most attractive of the three hotels, the *Šmarjeta*, is DM60 to DM80 per person, including full board. Some of the rooms at the Krka and the Šmarjeta have small balconies with views of the nearby hills and forests.

A cheaper alternative to staying at the spa is the 18-room *Penzion Domen* (☎ 73 051) in Družinska Vas (house No 1), about 1.5 km south-east of Šmarješke Toplice. Rooms with shower are DM35 per person, but five rooms just under the roof share a shower and cost DM30 per person. The Domen has a tennis court, a football field and a decent restaurant.

Places to Eat

Most guests take all their meals at the huge hotel restaurant but if you are visiting or not staying on a full-board basis, try the *Topliška Klet* cellar restaurant.

In Šmarješke Toplice village, *Gostilna Prinovec* is a pleasant, inexpensive place for a meal, with an outside grill in summer. The restaurant at the *Penzion Domen* is open every day but Tuesday from 10 am till 10 pm.

Getting There & Away

Bus service is very frequent to Novo Mesto and Otočec, Šmarjeta and Brežice. There's also at least one bus a day to Ljubljana, Mokronog and Sevnica.

Getting Around

You can order a taxi in Šmarješke Toplice on ☎ 73 650.

KOSTANJEVICA NA KRKI (pop 765)

Situated on an islet just 500 metres long and 200 metres wide in a loop of the Krka River, Kostanjevica is Slovenia's smallest town. And, with a charter that dates back to 1252, it is also one of the oldest.

Kostanjevica was an important commercial centre in the Middle Ages and even had its own mint in the 13th century called Moneta Landestrostensis (Kostanjevica is still called Landstrass in German). Its coins were in circulation as far as what is now western Romania. In 1563, after repeatedly attacking the town, the Turks were defeated by Ivan Lenkovič, supreme commander of the Military March.

Kostanjevica's glory days have long since passed, however, and today the town is so sleepy it is almost comatose. Though it is dubbed 'the Venice of Dolenjska' by the tourist industry and under full protection as a cultural monument, most of its buildings are in very bad condition. The only one in the area that seems to be getting any attention is the former Cistercian monastery a km south of town.

Still, Kostanjevica is an important art centre and its location is magical. If you don't manage to flag down a helicopter to view the town from on high, at least take a look at the photographs of the town in *Slovenia from the Air* by Matjaž Kmecl (published in 1993).

Orientation & Information

Though most of Kostanjevica's historical sights are on the island, some others and things of a more practical nature are on the mainland to the north or south reached by two small bridges. Buses stop opposite the Pod Gorjanci guesthouse and restaurant.

The post office is at Kambičev trg 5 and is open weekdays from 8 am to 3 pm and till noon on Saturday. Ljubljanska Banka has a branch a few steps away at Oražnova ulica 3. It's open weekdays from 8 am to 2.30 pm and on Saturday from 7.30 to 11 am.

Kostanjevica's telephone code has four digits: 0608. The postcode is 68311.

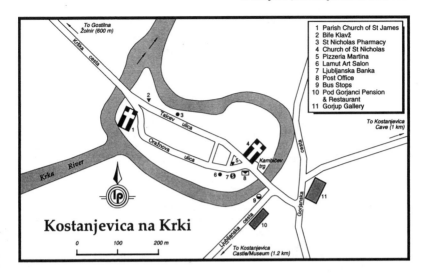

Kostanjevica na Krki

To Gostilna
Žolnir (600 m)

1 Parish Church of St James
2 Bife Klavž
3 St Nicholas Pharmacy
4 Church of St Nicholas
5 Pizzeria Martina
6 Lamut Art Salon
7 Ljubljanska Banka
8 Post Office
9 Bus Stops
10 Pod Gorjanci Pension
    & Restaurant
11 Gorjup Gallery

Krka cesta

Talcev ulica

Oražnova ulica

Krka River

Kambičev trg

To Kostanjevica
Cave (1 km)

Gorjanska cesta

Ljubljanska cesta

To Kostanjevica
Castle/Museum (1.2 km)

0   100   200 m

Walking Tour

No one is going to get lost or tired on a walking tour of Kostanjevica: some 500 metres up one street and 500 metres down another and you've seen the lot.

On Kambičev trg, across the small bridge from the bus stop, stands the **Church of St Nicholas**, a tiny late-Gothic structure dating from the late 16th century. The brightly coloured frescoes in the presbytery depicting scenes from the Old and New Testaments were painted by Jože Gorjup (1907-32). You can see more of this expressionist's work, including the wonderful *Bathers* series, at the **Gorjup Gallery** back over the bridge at Gorjanska cesta 2.

If you walk north-west along Oražnova ulica for about 100 metres, you'll reach a 15th century manor house at No 5 that now contains the **Lamut Art Salon**. The painter and graphic artist Vladimir Lamut (1915-62) completed a large portion of his work in Kostanjevica.

Continue along Oražnova ulica, passing an interesting *fin-de-siècle* house at No 24, to the **Parish Church of St James**, a 13th century Romanesque building at the island's northern tip with a mostly Baroque interior.

Above the carved stone portal on the western side, you can just make out geometric shapes and decorative plants and trees.

Talcev ulica, the island's other street, leads south-east back to St Nicholas Church and is lined with crumbling but quite attractive 'folk Baroque' houses. About halfway down on the left is the 200-year-old **St Nicholas Pharmacy**.

Kostanjevica Castle

The former Cistercian monastery – what most people here call Kostanjevica Castle – was begun in the mid-13th century and through donation deeds from the rulers of Hungary and Bosnia remained a very wealthy institution in the Middle Ages. It was abandoned by the order in the late 18th century and was severely damaged during WW II and again in an earthquake in 1984. Today, with renovations nearing completion, it houses a large and important art gallery. The castle is about 1.5 km south-west of the Pod Gorjanci restaurant on Grajska cesta 45.

The main entrance through two painted towers leads to an enormous courtyard enclosed by a **cloister** with some 260 arcades on three floors. To the west stands

DOLENJSKA

the disused **Church of the Virgin Mary**, containing elements from the 13th to 18th centuries – and a lot of free-flying sparrows. A set of steps near what was once the altar leads to the museum.

The **Božidar Jakac Gallery** contains 16th century frescoes taken from the church below, works by such Slovenian artists as Jakac, the brothers France (1895-1960) and Tone Kralj (1900-75) and Rihard Jakopič, the Impressionist painter whose likeness appears on the 100 SIT note. There is also a permanent collection of Old Masters from the Carthusian monastery at Pleterje.

Much of Jakac's work here consists of line drawings done while documenting the underground Partisan movement in 1943. Of all the artists, the expressionist France Kralj was the most versatile and prolific, turning out hundreds of works in oil, ink, bronze and wood; don't miss his sculptures *The Reapers* and *Mother and Child*. Some of Tone Kralj's early work (like *Veined Sunset)* is almost surreal but his later move to a kind of socialist realism obliterates all traces of it. The collection from Pleterje features works by French, German, Italian and Flemish artists of the 17th and 18th centuries. The oils are almost all portraits of saints and church noteworthies and pretty sombre stuff.

The castle grounds are used to exhibit over 100 large wooden sculptures from Forma Viva, an international exhibition once held in several places in Slovenia whereby sculptors worked with materials associated with the area. It was wood here, stone in Portorož, iron at Ravne in Koroška and (shudder) concrete in Maribor.

The castle is open every day except Monday from 9 am till 6 pm from April to September. During the rest of the year it closes at 4 pm. The entry fee is 150 SIT.

Kostanjevica Cave

This small cave, on an unsealed road about 1.5 km south-east of town, has 10 half-hour tours every day between 9 am and 6.30 pm for 150 SIT. The guide will lead you some 300 metres in (only 522 metres of the cave have been fully explored), past a small lake,

several galleries full of stalactites and stalagmites and, no doubt, a couple of specimens of *Paladilhiopsis kostanjevicae*, a snail unique to the cave which seems to enjoy the 12° temperature. There's a shaded picnic area in front of the cave on tiny Studena Stream.

Places to Stay

Not surprisingly, accommodation is very limited in a town as small as Kostanjevica. The *Pod Gorjanci* guesthouse (☎ 60 046) at Ljubljanska cesta 5 has seven rooms in total. Singles with shower and breakfast are DM40, doubles DM60.

A more pleasant though less central place is the *Žolnir* gostilna and guesthouse (☎ 60 133) about 700 metres north-east of the island at Krška cesta 4. Its six doubles are DM45, including shower and breakfast.

Places to Eat

There are a couple of bare-bones places for a quick meal or drink on the island, including *Pizzeria Martina* at Oražnova ulica 8 and *Bife Klavž* at the top of Talcev ulica.

The restaurant at *Pod Gorjanci* is very popular and the back garden is often crowded in summer. But for my money I'd head for the *Žolnir*, whose owners are very serious about the food they serve. It's open daily till 10 pm. A speciality of Kostanjevica is duck served with little *mlini* pancakes and, of course, accompanied by Cviček wine.

Getting There & Away

There are frequent departures from Kostanjevica to Novo Mesto and Brežice. Other destinations and their daily frequencies include Ljubljana (six), Krško (three), and in Croatia, Kumrovec, Bizeljsko and Zagreb (one each).

AROUND KOSTANJEVICA NA KRKI
Pleterje Monastery

You'll see more of the treasures of Pleterje, a huge monastery about three km south of Šentjernej, at Kostanjevica Castle than you will *in situ*. Pleterje (Pletariach in German) belongs to the Carthusians, the strictest of all monastic orders. The Gothic **Holy Trinity Church** (also called the 'old monastery church') is the only part of the complex open to the general public at present. But the monastery's location in a narrow valley between vine-covered slopes and the Gorjanci Hills is so attractive and peaceful, it's worth a visit.

The monastery was founded in 1407 by Herman II, one of the Celje counts, and its construction was supervised by an English abbot, Prior Hartman. The complex was fortified with ramparts, towers and a moat during the Turkish invasions and all but abandoned during the Protestant Reformation, which swept Dolenjska in the 16th century. The Carthusian order, like all monastic communities in the Habsburg Empire, was abolished in 1784. When the monks returned to Pleterje over a century later, they rebuilt the complex according to the plans of the order's charterhouse at Nancy in France.

You may catch a glimpse of the dozen or so white-hooded monks quietly going about their chores (they take a strict vow of silence and are vegetarians). But the ubiquitous signs reading *Klavzura – Vstop Prepovedan* ('Seclusion – No Entry') remind you that everything except the old monastery church – the ornate chapels, the inner courtyard, the cloisters, the library rich in medieval manuscripts – is off-limits.

Above the main portal of the church, built in 1420 and one of the most important Gothic monuments in Slovenia, is a fresco depicting Mary and the Trinity. Inside, the rib-vaulted ceiling and carved stone niches by the alter are worth a look, but what is most interesting is the medieval rood screen, the low wall across the aisle that separated members of the order from the rest of the faithful.

At the monastery office, you can ask to see a 30-minute video describing the Carthusian way of life and the history of Pleterje or buy some of the products the monks produce, including packs of beeswax candles (350 SIT), Cviček wine (175 SIT a bottle) and four types of brandy (750 to 1500 SIT): *sadjevec* (apple), *slivovka* (plum), *brinovec*

(juniper-flavoured) and *hruška* (pear). If you're wondering how they got that whole pear inside the bottle, it's simple: the bottle is placed over the immature fruit while still on the tree. When the pear ripens inside, the bottle is removed and filled with brandy. There is a traditional pottery workshop three km east of Šentjernej in Gruča (house No 2) with household items for sale.

Šentjernej is seven km west of Kostanjevica and can be reached on the Novo Mesto bus (return to Kostanjevica on the one headed for Brežice). There are also up to seven buses a day to Ljubljana and one each to Krško and Zagreb. Buses stop in front of the *Gostilna Majzelj* (☎ 42 014) at Trg Gorjanskega Bataljona 5, which is open daily except Tuesday till 10.30 pm. They can also arrange accommodation in town or in a vineyard cottage. You'll have to make your way on foot to Pleterje from the bus stop, though, as there is no local service.

POSAVJE REGION

Most of what is called Posavje, the area 'on the Sava River' as far as the border with Croatia, is in Štajerska, the province north of Dolenjska. But historically and geographically, Posavje is closely tied to Dolenjska and easily accessible from many of its towns.

Like Dolenjska, Posavje was settled early and is rich in archaeological finds from the Hallstatt, Celtic and Roman times. The Sava, of course, was paramount and while Jason and the Argonauts probably did not navigate the 'Savus' upstream as the legend tells us, the Romans certainly did, building a major port called Neviodunum near today's Drnovo. Slavic graves unearthed in the area date from the 7th century.

Posavje took centre stage during the Turkish invasions starting in the 15th century – that explains the large number of heavily fortified castles in the region – and again 100 years later during the Slovenian-Croatian peasant uprisings and the Protestant Reformation. River traffic increased in the 19th century after a 20-km stretch of the Sava was regulated, and the arrival of the railway in

DOLENJSKA

1862 linking Ljubljana and Zagreb helped the region develop industrially.

Posavje had more than its share of suffering during WW II. In a bid to colonise the area, the occupying German forces engaged in a brutal programme of 'ethnic cleansing' and expelled more than 15,000 Slovenes. Many of them were interned at a camp in Rajhenburg Castle at Brestanica before being deported to Serbia, Croatia or Germany.

Brežice (pop 6900)

Brežice is not the largest town in Posavje – that distinction goes to Krško, some 12 km upriver. But from a traveller's point of view, it is the most interesting.

Situated in a basin just north of where the Krka flows into the Sava, Brežice (Rhain in German) was an important trading centre in the Middle Ages and was granted a town charter in 1354. The town lies between the Orlica Hills to the north and the Gorjanci to the south and opens onto a vast plain to the east. The climate is milder and drier than elsewhere in Dolenjska.

Brežice's dominant feature has always been its castle, mentioned in documents as early as 1249, with a strategic position some 400 metres from the Sava. In the 16th century the original castle was replaced with a Renaissance fortress to strengthen the town's defences against the Turks and marauding peasants who, during one uprising, beheaded nobles at the castle and impaled their heads on poles. It was built with the help of Italian masters and is not dissimilar to the castles at Otočec, Sevnica and Mokrice in design. Over a century later, the castle's new owners, the Counts of Attems, renovated the building in the Baroque style and added several sumptuous rooms, including the largest function room in Slovenia. Today the castle houses the Posavje Museum.

Orientation & Information Brežice's main street is Cesta Prvih Borcev. Heading south it becomes Prešernova cesta and crosses the Sava. Going north it changes names to Cesta Bratov Milavcev. The main west-east artery is Bizeljska ulica.

The bus station is on Cesta Svobode, 200 metres north of Bizeljska ulica. The train station is farther afield on Trg OF, about 2.5 km north of the town centre.

There is no tourist office in Brežice, but the staff at the Posavje Museum will help you with any questions you have. The post office is at Levstikova ulica 1a and is open from 7 am to 6 pm weekdays and till noon on Saturday. There's a Ljubljanska Banka branch at Cesta Prvih Borcev 31 open on weekdays from 7 am to 6 pm and till noon on Saturday.

The telephone code for Brežice and surrounds has four digits: 0608. The postcode is 68250.

Posavje Museum Housed in the Renaissance castle at Cesta Prvih Borcev 1, this is one of provincial Slovenia's best museums, and its archaeological and ethnographic collections are particularly rich.

From the courtyard you ascend a staircase illustrated on the walls and ceiling with Greek gods, the four Evangelists and the Attems coat of arms. The first rooms contain bits and pieces from earliest times to the arrival of the Slavs; don't miss the skeletons from the 9th century BC unearthed near Dobova, the 5th century BC bronze bridle, the Celtic and Roman jewellery and a dented helmet that suggests the legionnaire wearing it got kicked in the head by a donkey. In the ethnographic rooms, along with the carved wooden bowls, decorated chests and plaited loaves of bread, is a strange beehive in the shape of a soldier from the early 1800s. On the top he's French and on the bottom Croatian.

Other rooms cover life in the Posavje region in the 16th century, focusing on the peasant uprisings in the area and the Protestant Reformation, and the time of the two world wars with emphasis on the deportation of Slovenes by the Germans during WW II. There's also a collection of Baroque oil

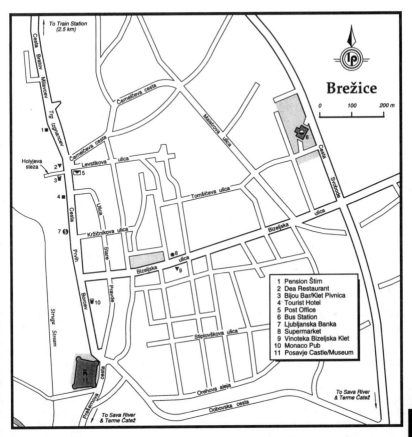

Brežice

0   100   200 m

1 Pension Štim
2 Dea Restaurant
3 Bijou Bar/Klet Pivnica
4 Tourist Hotel
5 Post Office
6 Bus Station
7 Ljubljanska Banka
8 Supermarket
9 Vinoteka Bizeljska Klet
10 Monaco Pub
11 Posavje Castle/Museum

paintings. Check out the ornate tile stoves in many of the rooms.

But the museum's real crowd-pleaser is the **Festival Hall** (Slavnostna Dvorana), an Italian Baroque masterpiece where everything but the floor is painted with landscapes, gods and heroes from Greek and Roman mythology, allegories, the Muses etc. You may vaguely recognise the place; some scenes from *The Winds of War* were filmed here and the staff is *still* talking about Robert Mitchum. The hall has near-perfect acoustics and concerts are held here from time to time.

The Posavje Museum is open Monday to Saturday from 8 am to 1 pm and on Sunday from 9 am till noon. The admission charge is 150 SIT.

Terme Čatež Rheumatics have been bathing in the thermal spring at Čatež (pop 1005) since the late 18th century. Today, while the huge spa complex some three km south-east of Brežice still attracts those suffering from such aches and pains, it is every bit as much a recreational area – and one of the friendliest in Slovenia. The spa counts seven thermal-water (28-34°) outdoor pools with huge slides, fountains and artificial waves over an area of 5700 sq metres. Indoors there are three pools, the newest one measuring 1200 sq metres. The outdoor complex is open from April to September and admission is 500 to 600 SIT depending on the day of the week. The indoor pools are open all year and cost 700 SIT. The spa also has a sauna, steam room, solarium, gym, a jogging track along the river and tennis courts. A guide is made available to guests every day between 9 and 11 am; tell him or her where you want to go and what you want to see.

Activities At Čatež, along with swimming in the Sava and taking the waters, you can rent a boat (800 SIT) or a bicycle (400 SIT per hour). In the nearby town of Čatež ob Savi, horses can be hired from the Zean Club at Rimska cesta 22 and ridden up Šentvid Hill (386 metres).

The Štirn guesthouse in Brežice can organise any number of activities in the area: canoeing on the Krka (DM10 half day, DM13 full day); fishing in the Sava or Krka (DM10 per day); horse riding (DM10 per hour) and tennis (DM7 to DM13 per hour).

The Oldtimer Train run by Slovenijaturist runs excursions from time to time from Brežice to Sevnica and back.

Places to Stay The *Terme Čatež* camp site (☎ 62 110), the largest in Slovenia, can accommodate up to 3000 guests. It's not cheap at DM17 per person, but campers get full run of the spa, including use of the swimming pools. It is open from April to October. There are also two-person bungalows nearby costing DM30 to DM33 per person per night depending on the season.

In Brežice, *Penzion Štirn* (☎ 65 613) at Trg Izgnancev 7 is an attractive little guesthouse with 22 beds that's been around for almost 70 years. Singles are DM25, doubles DM35. It's on a rather busy street so ask for one of the back rooms.

You might expect Brežice's only hotel, the *Tourist* (☎ 61 005) at Cesta Prvih Borcev 39, to have at least a little atmosphere; around the turn of the century it was the National Hall (Narodni Dom), the town's cultural,

political and business centre. Now it is one of the most depressing hotels in the land and expensive to boot: singles with shower and breakfast are DM45, doubles are DM60.

Terme Čatež has two expensive hotels (☎ 62 110; fax 62 721) at Topliška cesta 35. *Zdraviliški Dom*, with 118 beds, is generally reserved for those who are taking the spa seriously. Depending on the season, singles are DM67 to DM77, doubles are DM98 to DM116. The *Terme*, with over 250 beds, charges DM83 to DM94 for singles and DM120 to DM142 for doubles.

Places to Eat In Brežice, there's a fast-food place called *Dea* opposite the post office on Trg Izgnancev. *Vinoteka Bizeljska Klet* at Bizeljska ulica 10 opposite the supermarket serves food and wine from the Bizeljsko-Sremič wine region to the north and west of Brežice.

The gostilna at the *Pension Štirn* specialises in fish and seafood priced between 600 and 800 SIT for main courses. The Laški Rizling, a slightly fruity, medium dry wine from Bizeljsko, is not a bad accompaniment. But be warned that the area just behind the Štirn is marshy and if you sit in the courtyard in summer you'll be plagued by mosquitoes.

Entertainment Ask at the Posavje Museum office about concerts taking place in the castle's Festival Hall. *Monaco Pub* at Cesta Prvih Borcev 10 is a subdued place for a drink though it sometimes has a band playing folk music. It's open nightly except Sunday till 10 pm. For something a bit younger and louder, head for the *Bijou Bar/Klet Pivnica* at Holyjeva steza 1. They're open till late.

Getting There & Away Buses run hourly to Bizeljsko, Cerklje, Dobova, Krško, Novo Mesto and Terme Čatež and up to eight times a day to Ljubljana. There's also at least one departure a day for Celje, Orešje, Senovo, Zagreb (via Obrežje) in Croatia and Žužemberk. Some of these buses, like the ones to Čatež, can be boarded at the train station.

DOLENJSKA

As many as 15 trains a day serve Brežice from Ljubljana (107 km; 1¾ hours) via Zidani Most, Sevnica and Krško. Most of these trains then cross the Croatian border near Dobova and carry on to Zagreb (34 km; 40 minutes).

Getting Around Buses run between the bus station and the train station every half-hour throughout the day

Mokrice Castle

Mokrice Castle, about 10 km from Brežice, is the loveliest in the Posavje region and has been completely renovated and turned into a 30-room luxury hotel. With one of Slovenia's few 18-hole golf courses, a large stable with horses for rent and a 20-hectare 'English park' full of pear trees and rare plants, it makes a delightful excursion from Brežice.

The castle as it stands today dates from the 16th century, but there are bits and pieces going back to Roman times (inscription stones, part of a tower) built into the structure. Like many other castles in the region, it was built as a defence against the Turks and later turned into a baronial manor. The 19th

century German writer Count Friedrich von Gagern was born here and some of his novels are set in the castle and surrounds. As is the case with many of Slovenia's castles and manor houses, the ownership of Mokrice is being contested – this time by a Catholic diocese in Croatia.

There are a couple of interesting stories about the castle, one of which tells of a 17th century countess named Barbara who fell in love with a sailor called Marko. When he went to sea and failed to return, poor Barbara committed suicide. Her ghost still stalks the castle's secret passageways and staircases at night, and she is particularly active on St Barbara's feast day (4 December). The castle's coat of arms may strike you as odd; it portrays a raven with an arrow piercing his throat. Apparently a Turkish janissary shot the bird as it squawked to warn the inhabitants of an invasion in the 15th century.

The small Gothic **Chapel of St Ann** on the castle grounds not far from the drawbridge is in sad condition but has some interesting Baroque stucco work inside. The park is filled with Baroque statues.

If you want to stay at the *Grad Mokrice* hotel (☎ 57 000; fax 57 007), be prepared to shell out a minimum of DM136 for a double with breakfast or DM228 for one of the 240-sq-metre suites. The rooms have beamed ceilings and period furniture and some suites have fireplaces. The hotel restaurant is pretty formal with fancy game and fish dishes and classical music; the cellar has 60 different Slovenian wines available by the glass or bottle. Try some *viljemovka*, Mokrice's famous pear brandy.

The green fees for a round of golf at Mokrice is DM44 on weekdays and DM48 at weekends. A set of clubs costs DM15 to rent. There's also a pro giving lessons. Horse riding costs DM28 per hour and a carriage ride to Terme Čatež (seven km) and back costs DM30 per person.

You can reach Mokrice on the bus to Obrežje (get off just before Jesenice), but the ideal way to go would be by bicycle from Čatež, following the secondary road running parallel to route No 1 (E70).

Mokrice Castle

DOLENJSKA

Bizeljsko-Sremič Wine District

Bicycling all the way to Bizeljsko through the heart of the Bizeljsko-Sremič wine country might be pushing it for some (it's 18 km from Brežice), but there's a bus leaving every hour or so, allowing you to get off whenever you see a wine cellar *(vinska klet)* or gostilna that suits your fancy. In Bizeljsko, try some of the local medium-dry whites and reds at the *Vinska Klet Pintemič* at house No 115 or at *Gostilna Franc Šekoranja* at No 63.

From Bizeljsko (Wisell in German; pop 1940) you can either return to Brežice or continue your journey north for another seven km past Bizeljska Vas and the 15th century **Bizeljsko Castle** – now falling into ruin under a makeshift roof as an ownership dispute drags on – to Bistrica ob Sotli. From Bistrica ob Sotli, buses go north-west to Kozje via the village of **Podsreda**, site of the oldest castle in Slovenia (see the Štajerska chapter).

Bela Krajina

The 'White March' of south-eastern Slovenia takes its name from the endless stands of birch trees that cover this little province. It is a treasure trove of Slovenian folklore, and you'll see more traditional dance and hear more music here than anywhere else in the country, particularly around Črnomelj and Adlešiči. Many of the stringed instruments – the *tamburica*, the *berdo* (contrabass), the guitar-like *brač* and the *bisernica* (lute) are unique to the region or originated here.

Like Dolenjska, Bela Krajina is famous for its Hallstatt and Roman sites; a 3rd century shrine to the god Mithra near the village of Rožanec is one of the best preserved in Europe.

In the Middle Ages, Bela Krajina was the most remote part of Slovenia and some Slovenes say it still feels that way. Many of the peasant uprisings of the 15th and 16th centuries started here or across the border in Croatia.

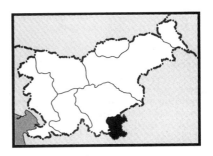

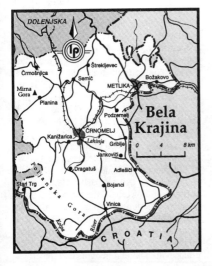

METLIKA (pop 3300)

One of Bela Krajina's two most important towns, Metlika (Möttling in German) lies in a valley at the foot of the Žumberak Hills surrounded by Croatia on three sides. The Kolpa River is two km to the south.

The area around Metlika was inhabited during prehistoric times, and there was a major Hallstatt settlement here during the early Iron Age. The Romans came too, establishing an outpost here, and Metlika was on a road leading to the important river port of Sisak in Croatia. In medieval times 'reggio que Metlica dicitur' ('the region called Metlika') included most of today's Bela Krajina, and the Metlika March was an important frontier region. Only a few km from the pilgrimage site of Tri Fare, Metlika grew into a market town and was given a charter in 1365.

Metlika was in the front lines during the wars with the Hungarians in the 14th century. The Turks attacked the town some 17 times beginning in 1408 and actually occupied the town in 1578 – something its rival Črnomelj points out never happened there. For many years, Metlika was the last outpost of Christianity in this part of Europe. Prosperity came briefly during the Reformation, but the Žumberak Hills sheltered outlaws and brigands from Croatia, who would continue to plague the town for centuries.

The Italians occupied Metlika during WW II and by the end of the war some 120 buildings had been burned to the ground. Though the kernel of the Old Town counts some buildings dating back several centuries, most of Metlika was rebuilt after 1945.

Orientation

Metlika's Old Town, consisting of three squares, stands on a ridge between a small stream called the Obrh and the main street, Cesta Bratstva in Enotnosti ('Avenue of Fraternity and Unity'). Reach it from the main street by walking up Ulica na Trg to Trg Svobode.

The modern bus station is 650 metres south of the Old Town on Cesta XV Brigade. To get to the train station, walk south along Cesta XV Brigade for 600 metres and then turn east on Kolodvorska ulica.

Information

The staff at the information window in the town hall (☎ 068 58 354) at Mestni trg 24 will help you out or you can try the reception at the Bela Krajina hotel.

Ljubljanska Banka has a branch at Trg Svobode 7 open from 8 am to 6 pm and till noon on Saturday and another one with reduced hours in the new shopping complex in Naselje Borisa Kidriča opposite the bus station. The post office, open from 7 am to 7 pm weekdays and till noon on Saturday, is in the same shopping centre.

Metlika's telephone code is 068. The postcode is 68330.

Things to See

Metlika Castle, with its L-shaped arcaded courtyard at Trg Svobode 4, houses the **Bela Krajina Museum**. The collection, exhibited in 18 rooms, includes archaeological finds taken from the area including Hallstatt buckles, bracelets and amulets from Pusti Gradac south of Črnomelj and a copy of the Mithraic relief from the Roman period found at Rožanec near Črnomelj. Artefacts collected from more recent periods are displayed in a mock-up of an old pharmacy and photo studio.

Much emphasis is placed on agriculture in Bela Krajina – everything you've ever wanted to know about beekeeping, fruit cultivation, fishing, animal husbandry is there – as well as folk art peculiar to the region, including decorated Easter eggs, glass paintings and religious icons in bottles. The artist and sculptor Alojzij Gangl, who was born in Metlika, is given pride of place, but I found his work mundane and some of it offensive, including *Žid*, a bronze caricature of a Jew with the requisite pot belly and huge nose.

A small building west of the castle entrance (Trg Svobode 5) contains the **Firefighting Museum**. Metlika was the first town in Slovenia to have a fire brigade and has thus earned the right to such a museum. It's a lot more interesting than it sounds, displaying old fire trucks with enormous wheels, ladders and buckets but no Dalmatians.

Firefighters, by the way, are the 'party animals' of Slovenia, hosting dances, parties and other booze-ups outside the *gasilski dom* throughout the summer. Some Slovenes say that's all they ever seem to do.

The **defence tower** opposite the Firefighting Museum dates from the 16th century. Both museums are open from 8 am to 2 pm on weekdays, till 1 pm on Saturday and from 9 am till noon on Sunday. The entrance fee is 200 SIT.

Mestni trg is a colourful, leafy square of 18th and 19th century buildings, including the neo-Gothic **town hall** (1869) at No 24. At the southern end of the square is the so-called **Komenda** (Commandery), which once belonged to the knights of the Teutonic Order, and its **Church of St Nicholas** from 1759. The interior, which is modelled after the Križanke's Church of the Virgin Mary in Ljubljana, has sobering frescoes of the Day of Judgement by Domenico Fabrio.

The Gothic **Church of St Martin** at the northern end of Cesta Bratstva in Enotnosti is one of the oldest structures in Metlika but is cracking from the bottom up and is no longer in use. It contains late Renaissance tombs with reliefs. Outside is a 'plague pillar' with a barely recognisable fresco.

PLACES TO STAY
3 Pri Veri Guesthouse
4 Bela Krajina Hotel
19 Goleš (private rooms)

PLACES TO EAT
1 Gostišče Kolednik
5 Na Dragah
10 Pri Batusu Restaurant

OTHER
2 Church of St Martin
6 Firefighting Museum
7 Metlika Castle/Museum
8 Ljubljanska Banka
9 Vinoteka Pinot
11 Town Hall
12 Church of St Nicholas
13 Komenda
14 Vinska Klet
15 Bus Station
16 Ghetto Disco/
     Hard Rock Caffè
17 Shopping Centre
18 Post Office

Veselica
Hill

Pot na Veseliko

To Vinomer
& Drašiči

Vinogradniška

Stara cesta

Cesta

Vinogradniška

cesta

Breg Revolucije

Cesta Bratstva in Enotnosti

Prečna pot

To Rosalnice &
Tri Fare Churches
(2.5 km)

Marentičeva ulica

Cesta Bratstva in Enotnosti

Partizanski trg

Trg
Svobode

Mestni
trg

Obrh

Obrh
Stream

Breg Revolucije

Na Obrh

Cankarjeva   cesta

Cesta XV Brigade

Metlika

0   100   200 m

To Primostek Camp
Site (2 km)

Cesta Bratstva in Enotnosti

Jardeva ulica

Ulica Maja

Župančičeva cesta

XV Brigade

Šestova ulica

To Train Station (600 m)
& Breza Beach (850 m)

BELA KRAJINA

Activities

The Kolpa is about the cleanest and certainly the warmest river (up to 28°) in Slovenia so you may want to go for a dip at Breza 'beach', a swimming complex at the end of Cesta Bratstva in Enotnosti about 1.5 km south of the Old Town. You can also swim in the Kolpa at the Primostek and Podzemelj camping grounds.

A daily fishing licence at the Podzemelj camp site costs 500 SIT a day. The Kolpa is known for its grayling, carp and brown trout but the area around Vinica is richer.

There are a lot of walks in the surrounding areas. A very easy one is up to Veselica, a small hill less than a km north of Metlika, with great views over the town. You can stop at *Gostišče Kolednik* at Pot na Veselico 5 for lunch. It's open from noon to midnight every day but Monday.

Festivals

Metlika's main event is the Vinska Vigred wine festival in early May.

Places to Stay

There are two camp sites in the Metlika area. One is the *Primostek* camp site (☎ 58 528) on the Lahinja River about 2.5 km to the south-west. The other is the larger *Podzemelj* (☎ 58 123) on the Kolpa near the village of Škrilje about seven km south-west of Metlika. Podzemelj measures 1.5 hectares in size and can accommodate some 200 people. The charge is DM6 per person and it is open from June to September. The buses to Črnomelj and to Griblje will let you off close to the camp sites.

Pri Veri (☎ 58 714) at Cesta Bratstva in Enotnosti 20 has two small double rooms, and the people at the *Goleš* house (☎ 58 612) at Ulica 1 Maja 6 a short walk east of the bus station have a room with six beds available for about DM20 per person.

The *Bela Krajina* hotel (☎ 58 123) at Cesta Bratstva in Enotnosti 28 has 24 fairly shabby rooms and charges DM25/DM50 for singles/doubles with shared shower and DM32 and DM58 for rooms with their own showers. Prices include breakfast.

Places to Eat

Pri Batusu at Mestni trg 6 is a pleasant place for a meal and is centrally located. The pizza at the *Bela Krajina* hotel restaurant is only a fair approximation of the real thing. The town's largest restaurant is the *Na Dragah* at Cesta Bratstva in Enotnosti 45, opposite the Bela Krajina hotel. It's open to 10 pm weekdays and to 2 pm at the weekend.

There's a wonderful place called *Gostilna Veselič* in Podzemelj (house No 17) not far from the camp site. It's a favourite of local people.

If you want to try some Bela Krajina wine but don't have time to get out in to the country, head for the *Vinoteka Pinot* at Trg Svobode 1, where you can sample Pinot Blanc, Chardonnay, Rieslings and sweet Gold Muscatel. The *Vinska Klet* at Cesta XV Brigade 2 is an old cellar with carved wooden barrels.

Entertainment

The town holds musical evenings in the castle from early July to early September. Ask for a programme at the museum or the Town Hall.

There's a disco called the *Ghetto* and a *Hard Rock Caffé* on the ground floor of the shopping centre in Naselje Borisa Kidriča.

Getting There & Away

Buses depart frequently from Metlika for Črnomelj, Drašiči, Jugorje, Karlovac in Croatia, Ljubljana, Novo Mesto and Vinica. Other destinations served include: Božakovo (two or three buses a day), Griblje (two) and Radoviča-Ostriž (three to seven).

Metlika is served by up to a dozen trains daily from Ljubljana (122 km; 2¾ hours) via Novo Mesto and Črnomelj. Some nine trains a day head for Karlovac in Croatia.

AROUND METLIKA
Tri Fare

The 'Three Parishes' in Rosalnice, 2.5 km east of Metlika, is a row of three graceful little churches which have been important pilgrimage sites for seven centuries. Though they were originally built in the late 12th century by the Templars, today's churches date from the 14th and 15th century. The one to the north – the largest of the three – is the **Church of the Sorrowful Virgin** and has a Gothic presbytery. The church in the middle – **Ecce Homo** – has a large tower over its porch. The one on the south with the buttresses and Gothic presbytery is the **Church of Our Lady of Lourdes**. Many of the gravestones in the churchyard are decorated with carved vines and grape leaves.

To the west of the churchyard entrance at house No 80 is *Gostilna Pri Treh Farah*, a pleasant place for lunch or a snack. There is actually a train station in Rosalnice south of the Three Parishes and the bus to Božakovo stops here, but it is just as easy to walk. From the Old Town, head north-east along Navratilova pot and follow Ulica Janka Brodariča eastward. Then turn south and east again.

Metlika Wine District

The hills to the north and north-east of Metlika are one of the most important wine-producing areas in Bela Krajina and produce such distinctive wines as Metliška Črnina, a very dark red, almost black, wine and a late-maturing sweet 'ice wine'. They are also superb areas for easy walking.

To get to Vinomer and Drašiči, two important wine towns about four and six km respectively from Metlika, you'll have to walk through *steljniki*, stands of birch trees growing among ferns in clay soil. For Slovenes, these 'forests' are the very symbol of Bela Krajina.

Drašiči is famous for its folk architecture – old peasant houses built over wine cellars. You can sample some local wines at several places, including the *Mavretič* farmhouse (☎ 58 644) at Drašiči 4a. Call in advance though; everyone might be out in the vineyards.

ČRNOMELJ (pop 5400)

The capital of Bela Krajina and its largest town, Črnomelj is situated on a promontory in a loop where the Lahinja and Dobličica

rivers meet. The town is not overly endowed with important sights, but it is Bela Krajina's folk 'heart' and its Jurjevanje festival attracts hundreds of dancers and singers from around the region.

Like Metlika, Črnomelj (Tschernembl in German) was settled very early on and the Roman presence is evident from the Mithraic shrine at Rožanec about four km north-west of the town. Črnomelj was an important market town and a bishopric as early as the 13th century and was given a charter in 1407.

During the Turkish invasions in the 15th and 16th centuries, the town was attacked incessantly, but due to its strong fortifications and excellent hilltop lookouts at Stražnji Vrh and Doblička Gora to the west, it was never taken. In fact, trade thrived under such protection and Črnomelj enjoyed something of a golden age in the 16th century. With the establishment of the Vojna Krajina (Military March) and the fort at Karlovac in Croatia in 1579, Črnomelj lost its military significance and prosperity. The town did not begin to develop again until 1914 with the opening of the railway between Novo Mesto and Karlovac.

Črnomelj played an important role during WW II. After Italy's surrender in 1943, the town functioned for a time as Slovenia's capital and was the centre of the Slovenian National Liberation Council and Partisan activity.

Legend has it that Črnomelj (a corruption of 'Black Mill') got its name when a beggar, dissatisfied with the quality of the flour he'd been given, put a curse on the local miller. Perhaps the man who the town's symbol represents – a smiling baker holding a pretzel – knew better than the miller the value of a 'beggar's curse'.

Orientation & Information

There are plans to open a new bus station a short distance west of the Jurjevanje fairground, but at present buses stop on Trg Svobode in the heart of the Old Town. Črnomelj's train station is about 200 metres from the Lahinja hotel located at

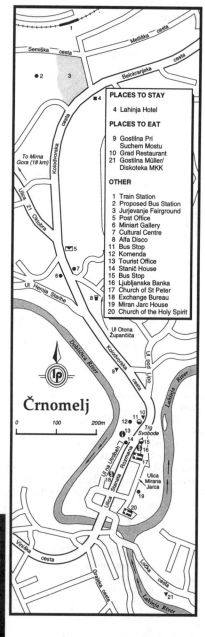

PLACES TO STAY

4 Lahinja Hotel

PLACES TO EAT

9 Gostilna Pri
   Suchem Mostu
10 Grad Restaurant
21 Gostilna Müller/
   Diskoteka MKK

OTHER

1 Train Station
2 Proposed Bus Station
3 Jurjevanje Fairground
5 Post Office
6 Miniart Gallery
7 Cultural Centre
8 Alfa Disco
11 Bus Stop
12 Komenda
13 Tourist Office
14 Stanič House
15 Bus Stop
16 Ljubljanska Banka
17 Church of St Peter
18 Exchange Bureau
19 Miran Jarc House
20 Church of the Holy Spirit

Črnomelj

Kolodvorska cesta 1, about 1200 metres
north of Trg Svobode.

There's a tourist office (☎ 51 011) at Ulica
na Utrdbah 2 south-west of Trg Svobode, but
as is often the case in Dolenjska and Bela
Krajina it does not keep regular hours. If you
find it bolted shut, seek help from the staff at
the Lahinja hotel.

Ljubljanska Banka has a branch at Trg
Svobode 2, which is open from 8 am to 6 pm
weekdays and till noon on Saturday. There's
also an exchange bureau at Ulica Staneta
Rozmana 22. Its hours are 7 am to 7 pm on
weekdays and from 8 am till noon on Saturday. Črnomelj's post office, open from 7 am
to 7 pm weekdays and till noon on Saturday,
is at Kolodvorska cesta 30 about halfway
between the train station and the Old Town.

Črnomelj's telephone code is 068. The
postcode is 68340.

Things to See & Do

Parts of **Stanič House** at Ulica Staneta
Rozmana 4 date back to the 13th century; this
is where the town's original castle stood. The
Komenda (Commandery) of the Teutonic
knights on Trg Svobode is a much larger and
more recent structure. Today it houses
offices of the county government.

The history of the **Parish Church of St
Peter** opposite Stanič House on Ulica
Staneta Rozmana also goes back more than
six centuries, but what you'll see today is a
standard-issue Baroque structure with a
single spire. You can still see Roman
tombstones built into the walls, and the large
fresco on the west side of St Christopher, the
patron saint of travellers, was meant to
remind passers-by that they, too, walked
with God. The Gothic **Church of the Holy
Spirit** at the southern end of Ulica Mirana
Jarca is undergoing extensive renovations.
The novelist and poet Miran Jarc was born
in the house at No 3 of the same street in
1900. It is now a music school.

Črnomelj counts a couple of small but
interesting art galleries including **Miniart** at
Kolodvorska cesta 37 with paintings, sculpture and antique musical instruments on
display.

Top: Churches of the Tri Fare (Three Parishes) at Rosalnice (Bela Krajina) (SF)
Middle: 19th century painted beehive panels, Maribor Regional Museum (Štajerska) (SF)
Bottom: Ptuj from the right bank of the Drava River (Štajerska) (SF)

Top: 440-year-old grape vine in the Lent district of Maribor (Štajerska) (SF)
Bottom Left: Lace-maker outside Ptuj Castle (Štajerska) (SF)
Bottom Right: Postmodern bus station in Maribor (Štajerska) (SF)

One of the most popular hikes in this part of Bela Krajina starts at the northern end of Ulica 21 Oktobra and carries on over hill and dale for 18 km north-west to **Mirna Gora** (1048 metres). Accommodation is available year round at the nine-room *Planinski Dom na Mirni Gori* (☎ 56 330).

Lahinja Regional Park about nine km south of Črnomelj is a protected karst area and the source of the Lahinja River with trails crisscrossing the area. Two small swamps in the park are home to a number of endangered plants and animals, especially birds, and the area around Pusti Gradac is a treasure trove of prehistoric finds.

Župančičev Hram (☎ 57 347), a restaurant with accommodation at house No 22 in the nearby town of Dragatuš, is an excellent starting point for walks in the park and one of the best eateries in Bela Krajina.

Festivals
Zeleni Jurij ('Green George') on 23-24 April is the day when young boys dressed in greenery go from house to house singing carols. Jurjevanje is a festival held on the first Sunday in June and one of the most important celebrations of folklore in Slovenia. The festivities begin in the centre of town at Trg Svobode and culminate at the fairground near the train station.

Places to Stay
The *Podzemelj* camp site (☎ 58 123) on the Kolpa River is about 10 km north-east of Črnomelj; see the Metlika section for details.

The only hotel in Črnomelj is the nondescript 30-room *Lahinja* (☎ 51 141) near the train station at Kolodvorska cesta 60. It charges DM24/DM45 for singles/doubles with shared shower and DM45/DM68 for rooms with private baths. Prices include breakfast. The hotel's terrace café is a pleasant meeting place in warm weather.

Places to Eat
The *Grad* restaurant in the courtyard of the Komenda at Trg Svobode 9 is an old-style eatery that hasn't changed a lot since the 1950s, but it serves decent pizza and local

Bela Krajina white wines like Chardonnay. Another option for snacks nearby is the *Gostilna Pri Suchem Mostu* at Kolodvorska cesta 17.

The best place for a meal in Črnomelj is the *Gostilna Müller* at Ločka cesta 6. It overlooks the Lahinja River and is very popular both as a restaurant and a night spot.

Entertainment
For information about what's on in Črnomelj, contact the *cultural centre* next to the post office at Ulica Otona Župančiča.

Črnomelj has two popular late-night venues. The *Alfa* disco at Ulica Otona Župančiča 6, a few steps from the cultural centre, is open weekdays till midnight and on Friday and Saturday till 4 am. *Diskoteka MKK* at the Gostilna Müller usually attracts an older crowd.

Getting There & Away
Departures to Adlešiči, Metlika, Novo Mesto, Semič, Vinica (via Dragatuš) and Žuniči are frequent; count on at least eight a day. Other destinations with less frequent departures include Dolenjske Toplice, Griblje, Jesenice, Ljubljana, Maribor and Žužemberk.

Črnomelj is served by up to a dozen trains a day from Ljubljana (107 km; 2½ hours) via Novo Mesto and Semič. Some nine trains daily depart Črnomelj for Karlovac in Croatia.

KOLPA RIVER VALLEY
The 124-km-long Kolpa, which forms Slovenia's south-eastern border with Croatia, is the warmest and about the cleanest river in the country. As a result, it has become a popular recreational area for swimming, fishing and boating, especially around the village of Vinica. Farther downstream is the village of Adlešiči, known for its vibrant folk culture and easy walks.

Things to See
In Vinica (pop 2288), the **Oton Župančič Memorial Collection** is in the house at No 35 where the celebrated Slovenian poet was

born in 1878, and the tower of the partially preserved **castle** has an interesting Gothic chapel. But most people visit Vinica (Weinitz in German) to go swimming, fishing or boating on the Kolpa.

The ruins of **Pobrežje Castle** about 1.5 km north-east of Adlešiči (pop 938) are worth exploring. While passing through the village of Purga, visit the **Čebelar Adlešič** farmhouse at house No 5. The family here are beekeepers and while there is no accommodation and meals are only prepared for groups, they will be happy to show you around, explain all things apiarian and give you a sample of their honey or *domača medica*, homemade mead that kicks like a donkey.

Activities

The Vinica camp site is the best source of information for all sporting activities in the area, and there is a decent grass beach adjacent to it. Žaga, a company with an office at the camp site, rents canoes and water scooters for 500 SIT an hour (800 SIT for two hours). The ambitious, though, will look into making the rapid-water kayak run from Stari Trg, some 20 km upriver, to Vinica. Fishing is good around Vinica, and the Kolpa is particularly rich in grayling, carp and brown trout. The camp site can sell you a daily fishing licence.

From Adlešiči, two easy hikes to nearby hills afford great views of the Kolpa, vineyards and surrounding towns. To get to **Mala Plešivica** (341 metres), walk south along a marked trail for about half an hour. A short distance to the west is a sinkhole with a water source called **Vodenica** which, according to local lore, was walled in by the ancient Illyrians. Steps lead down to the source, where you'll find a large stone vault.

Velika Plešivica (363 metres) is about an hour's walk north-west of Adlešiči. At the foot of the hill is a chapel dedicated to Mary; during attacks by the Turks in the Middle Ages, the faithful hid in the cave below it. On top of Velika Plešivica is another church dating back to the 12th century.

You can rent horses from the RIM farm-

house for DM20 per hour. There is a swimming area on the Kolpa just south of **Pobrežje Castle**.

Places to Stay

The *Kolpa* camping ground on the river at Vinica covers an area of about 1.5 hectares and can accommodate up to 300 people. The charge is DM8 per person, and the camp site is open from April to mid-October. There are also four double rooms above the main building which cost DM16.

One of the most interesting and attractive farmhouses with accommodation in Slovenia is *Erdeljc-Bio* (☎ 068-64 333) in the village of Zilje (house No 55), four km east of Vinica. Owned by a couple of marathon runners who drink salt water for stamina, Erdeljc-Bio serves macrobiotic dishes – seitan, chickpea spread, soba noodles, soya bread – made from vegetables and grains grown organically on the farm. Accommodation, which costs from DM24 per person including breakfast, is in an old peasant cottage with two bedrooms and a living room.

Among the accommodation near Adlešiči is the *RIM* farmhouse (☎ 068-57 718) in Jankoviči (house No 12). They charge from DM20 per person including breakfast. Meals are about DM8 per person.

Places to Eat

If you're staying at one of the farmhouses listed above, you'll probably want to eat there.

The *Kolpa* camp site has a full restaurant as well as a pub/snack bar open till 11 pm weekdays and till midnight at the weekend.

In the centre of Adlešiči, *Gostilna Milič* at house No 15 is one of the oldest eateries in Bela Krajina. Its drawing card is a large baker's oven that produces anything from pizzas to roast suckling pig.

Things to Buy

Erdelj-Bio sells many of its macrobiotic products already packaged; the soya biscuits are particularly good. The Čebelar Adlešič farm sells honey, mead, beeswax and pollen. An interesting souvenir is a vial of propolis, the sticky substance collected from certain trees by bees to cement their hives. It is supposed to be an elixir.

The RIM farmhouse contains a gallery of locally produced leather goods as well as some hand-woven linen, painted Easter eggs and other folk craft. They also have a range of local wines and brandies in beautifully crafted hand-blown bottles.

Getting There & Away

Bus connections to Črnomelj, Metlika and Novo Mesto from Vinica are very good. There is also one bus a day that passes through those three towns en route to Ljubljana and Kranj. It arrives in Vinica at about noon and departs at 3 pm.

There are frequent departures from Adlešiči to Črnomelj, 12 km away to the north-west. If you're heading for the RIM farmhouse, the Črnomelj-Žuniči bus should drop you off in Jankoviči.

BELA KRAJINA

Štajerska

It is difficult to characterise Štajerska (Styria in English, Steiermark in German). It is Slovenia's largest province but it does not have as much variety as Gorenjska and Primorska do. A lot of Štajerska is field but there are plenty of mountains too, like the Pohorje Massif to the north. Štajerska has more big farms than any other part of Slovenia (hops for making beer are an important crop as are wheat, potatoes and grapes for the province's excellent wines), but it also contains some of the country's largest and most historical cities and towns: Maribor, Celje and that little gem Ptuj.

Štajerska has been at the crossroads of Slovenia for centuries and everyone has 'slept here' – at least for a time: Celts, Romans, early Slavs and Habsburgs. In the 14th century the Counts of Celje were among the richest and most powerful feudal dynasties in central Europe and challenged the Austrian monarchy's rule for 100 years. Štajerska suffered terribly under the black leather boot of Nazism in WW II and many of its inhabitants were murdered, deported or forced to work in labour camps.

Some Slovenian guidebooks divide Štajerska up simply as the 'Maribor area' and the 'Celje area'. Here it is split into many more sections: the Kozjansko region in the south-east; the spa town of Rogaška Slatina above Kozjansko; historical Ptuj; Maribor, Slovenia's second-largest city; the Pohorje Massif; central Celje; and the Upper Savinja Valley bordering Gorenjska.

The geographical centre of Slovenia is at Spodnja Slivna, north of Litija in Štajerska. If you split the country in half, you'll see that virtually all of Slovenia to the east is Štajerska.

KOZJANSKO REGION

Kozjansko is a remote region along the eastern side of the Posavje Mountains and the 80-km-long Sotla River, which forms the

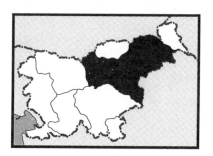

border with Croatia. It is an area of forests, rolling hills, vineyards and scattered farms.

Kozjansko's isolation made it suitable for settlement during the Great Migrations in the 5th century AD. In the Middle Ages it became the frontier region between Austrian Styria and Hungarian Croatia, which accounts for the large number of castles (Podsreda, Podčetrtek and Bistrica ob Sotli) and it became Slovenia's 'stormy corner' during the peasant uprisings of the 16th century.

Today, Kozjansko remains an underdeveloped region but with much to offer travellers: spas, castles, hiking and excellent wine.

Podčetrtek (pop 1155)

The town of Podčetrtek is about a km east of the Sotla River on a little bump of land extending into Croatia. Its castle, originally built in the 12th century, was an important fortification during the wars with the Hungarians 300 years later. Podčetrtek's name comes from the word for Thursday in Slovene – the day the market took place and the court sat.

The castle, the former Pauline monastery at Olimje and wonderful hikes into the surrounding hills are all major drawcards to Podčetrtek, but most people visit the town these days to relax at the Atomske Toplice thermal spa a short distance from the centre.

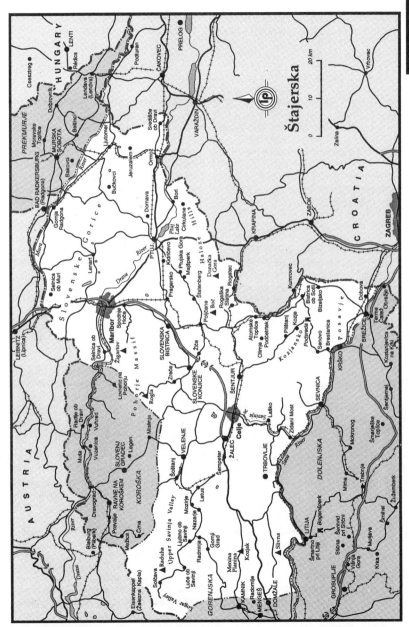

Štajerska

Orientation The centre of Podčetrtek is actually the junction of four roads: to the west is Olimje; to the north the castle; to the northeast the Atomske Toplice spa complex; and to the south Bistrica ob Sotli.

All buses stop here as well as at the spa and the camp site. There are three train 'stations'. For the town centre and the castle, get off at 'Podčetrtek'. 'Atomske Toplice' is good for the hotel, Atomska Vas and the Terme pool complex; while 'Podčetrtek Toplice' is the stop for the camp site.

Information The staff at the Atomske Toplice hotel (☎ 063 829 000; fax 829 024) assist travellers, answer questions and make bookings. They can change money and you can make telephone calls from here.

The post office, open from 7.30 am to 7 pm and till noon on Saturday, is 150 metres north of the main junction on the left. It too has exchange facilities. If the post office is closed, try the Srečno exchange office at house No 19a.

Podčetrtek's telephone code is 063. The postcode is 63254.

Podčetrtek Castle The giant castle on the hill to the north of town is not the original one. That was built by the Krško bishops in the 12th century but razed in the 15th century during the wars with the Hungarians. The present castle went up some time in the mid-16th century but it too was badly damaged – this time by an earthquake in 1974. The castle can be easily reached on foot by a trail marked 'Grad' from town. Along the way you'll pass the **Church of St Lawrence** with Baroque frescoes inside.

Atomske Toplice Though a serious thermal spa in its own right (the 30° to 36° C water is full of magnesium and calcium and recommended for those recovering from surgery or trying to cure rheumatism), this 'health and holiday resort', about 1200 metres north of Podčetrtek, puts most of the emphasis on recreation these days, with a total of eight pools, sauna, steamroom, solarium and sport facilities. The indoor and outdoor pools, con-

nected by an underwater passage at the new Terme complex, alone cover an area of 900 sq metres and there's a section reserved for nude bathing. The only drawback to the complex is that it overlooks a rather busy road.

Olimje The **Minorite monastery** three km west of Podčetrtek was built in about 1550. When Pauline monks took over what was then called Wolimia in German about a century later, they added the Baroque **Church of the Assumption**, which retains its original ceiling paintings in the presbytery and the **Chapel of St Francis Xavier**. On the ground floor of one of the four corner towers is the monastery's greatest treasure: a 17th century **pharmacy** – perhaps the oldest in Europe – painted with religious and medical scenes. One of the best scenes shows the cunning serpent tempting a rather plump Eve and Adam. The church and the pharmacy are open at 10 am and 3 and 4 pm daily except Wednesday. Admission is 100 SIT.

The **Ježovnik deer farm** in Sopote (house No 17) is 600 metres south of Olimje. From the monastery, walk 100 metres up the hill and turn left.

Horse Riding About 2.5 km along the road to Olimje and another 500 metres south is the **Amon Riding Centre** with horses for both beginners and the advanced. An hour in the paddock costs 1200 SIT, riding in the open countryside is 2100 SIT per hour and half-hour lessons are 2300 SIT.

Hiking & Cycling Some of the most rewarding hikes and bike trips in Slovenia can be made in this area, and the 1:18,000-scale *Podčetrtek-Atomske Toplice Tourist Map* lists dozens of excursions for walkers, cyclists and mountain bikers. The easiest walks on marked trails take an hour or two (though the circuitous north-east trail to the hilltop Church of St Emma lasts about four hours) and there are bicycle routes all the way to Kozje, Podsreda and Rogaška Slatina. The more demanding mountain bike routes head north to the Rudnica hills (600-

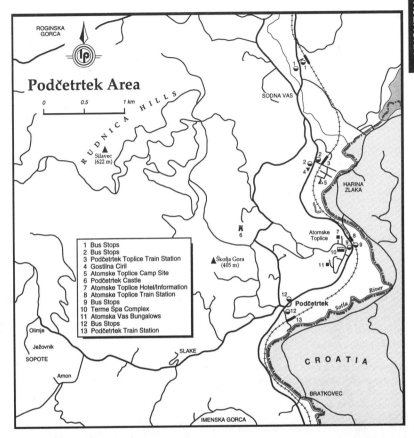

Podčetrtek Area

ROGINSKA
GORCA

SODNA VAS

R U D N I C A   H I L L S

Silavec
(622 m)

HARINA
ZLAKA

Škofja Gora
(405 m)

Atomske
Toplice

Podčetrtek

Sotla River

1 Bus Stops
2 Bus Stops
3 Podčetrtek Toplice Train Station
4 Gostilna Ciril
5 Atomske Toplice Camp Site
6 Podčetrtek Castle
7 Atomske Toplice Hotel/Information
8 Atomske Toplice Train Station
9 Bus Stops
10 Terme Spa Complex
11 Atomska Vas Bungalows
12 Bus Stops
13 Podčetrtek Train Station

Olimje

Ježovnik

SOPOTE

Amon

SLAKE

C R O A T I A

BRATKOVEC

IMENSKA GORCA

metre range), but there are some easier ones down through the Olimje forest and through the vineyards of Virštanj, Selo and Imeno.

Places to Stay The *Atomske Toplice* camp site (☎ 829 000; fax 829 024 for all accommodation here) is a km north of the main spa complex on the edge of the Sotla River; if you've checked in and you've got a guest card, you can take the shortcut through Croatia! The camp site covers an area of two hectares and can accommodate 450 guests. It's far enough off the main road, and the rail line running close by doesn't get much use.

The camp site has three outdoor and two indoor thermal pools; for the DM13 or DM15 (seasonal) charge, campers get to use these and the pools at the spa complex. The camp site is open from May to September.

The staff at the reception desk of the Atomske Toplice hotel have a list of about 10 families offering *private rooms* in Podčetrtek and Sodna Vas, two km north of the spa complex. Prices range from between DM13 and DM20 per person per night. The names also appear on the *Podčetrtek-Atomske Toplice Tourist Map* if you want to look on your own or check out the facilities in advance. The other private rooms on the list are in Harina Zlaka, literally a hop over the narrow Sotla and a few paces inside Croatia. You *should* have a visa, strictly speaking, but there is no border check here.

The *Atomska Vas* is a tourist 'village' south of the main hotel that does not look unlike a suburban development; if that's what you want, there are 25 houses with 136 apartments. One for two people (including kitchen, bathroom and bedroom) costs between DM64 and DM86, depending on the season.

The 104-room *Atomske Toplice* hotel is a strange, five-storey structure with roofs sloping off every which way and very tired-looking public areas. Singles in this over-priced place start at DM65; for a double you'll pay a minimum of DM100. The hotel has its own indoor thermal pool.

Places to Eat *Gostilna Ciril* in Sodna Vas (house No 49) on the main road across from the entrance to the camp site is a popular grill restaurant frequented by Slovenes and neighbouring Croats. The vine-covered terrace is lovely on a warm evening. *Gostilna Amon* at the riding centre in Olimje (house No 14) has better food, but it can get very crowded in the evening. Now that you've admired Bambi at the Ježovnik deer farm, why not eat one? The *Gostilna Ježovnik* serves them up and also has mushroom specialities in season.

Getting There & Away Up to nine buses a day cruise by Podčetrtek and Atomske Toplice on their way to Bistrica ob Sotli and Celje. You can also reach Bizeljsko (one bus a day), Kozje (two), Maribor (three), Rogaška Slatina (three) and Virštanj (one).

Podčetrtek and Atomske Toplice are on the rail line linking Celje (via Stranje) with Kumrovec in Croatia. Up to eight trains leave the main Podčetrtek station every day for Celje (38 km; 50 minutes) with about four departing for Croatia via Imeno.

Podsreda (pop 672)

If you're heading south to Bizeljsko, to Brežice in Posavje or to Dolenjska province, be sure to make a stop at Podsreda about 20 km to the south-west of Podčetrtek, site of the best preserved Romanesque castle in Slovenia. Transport to Podsreda from Podčetrtek is tricky if you don't have your own wheels; catch the bus to Kozje, change there for the one headed for Bistrica ob Sotli and descend at Podsreda village. The castle is perched on a hill, 475 metres high, south of the village. A five-km winding road leads to the castle but you can reach it via a relatively steep two-km trail from Stari Trg, less than a km south-east of Podsreda village.

Podsreda Castle (Herberg in German) looks pretty much as it did when it was built in 1200. A barbican on the southern side, with walls some three metres thick, leads to a central courtyard. The rooms in the castle wings, some with beamed ceilings and original chandeliers, now contain a boring glassworks exhibit (crystal from Rogaška Slatina, vials from the Olimje pharmacy, green Pohorje glass) and some hideous sculptures in bronze and plaster by the artist Jokov Brdar. But the tiny Romanesque chapel is worth the wait, and there's a wonderful collection of prints of Štajerska's castles and monasteries taken from *Topographii Ducatus Stiria* (1681) by Georg Mattäus Vischer (1628-96). The view from the castle windows of the surrounding countryside and the pilgrimage churches on Svete Gore above Bistrica ob Sotli is superb.

The castle is open every day but Monday from 9 am to 6 pm. The entry fee is 200 SIT. If you've built up an appetite climbing up and down those hills, there's a small **bife** called *Pod Gradom* in Podsreda village serving drinks and simple food.

Kozjansko Memorial Park, some 2.5 km east of Podsreda at Trebče, is dedicated to the Partisan effort during WW II and the pivotal role played by Tito. Tito was born in the Croatian village of Kumrovec just across the border from Bistrica ob Sotli in 1892 to Slovenian mother and a Croatian father.

ROGAŠKA SLATINA (pop 8586)

Rogaška Slatina is Slovenia's oldest and largest spa town. It's a veritable 'cure factory' with almost a dozen hotels, and therapies ranging from spruce-needle baths to painful-sounding 'lymph drainage'. It has 40,000 visitors a year. It's an attractive town set among scattered forests in the foothills of the Macelj range; its two highest peaks, Boč and Donačka Gora, are visible from the centre. The border crossing into Croatia at Rogatec is seven km to the east.

Legend says that the magnesium-rich spring was discovered by the winged horse Pegasus when Apollo advised him to eschew the 'make believe and glitter' of the magic Hippocrene fountain and drink instead at Roitschocrene. And the rest is history.

Well, not really. While it's true that the spring was known in Roman times, Rogaška Slatina didn't make it onto the map until 1574 when the then-governor of Styria, Wolf Ungnad, took the waters on the advice of his physician. A century later a publication entitled *Roitschocrene* examined the curative properties of the Slatina springs and claimed they helped the ailing viceroy of Croatia. The news spread to Vienna, visitors started to arrive in droves and inns were opened. By the early 19th century Rogaška Slatina (Rohitsch-Sauerbrunn in German) was an established spa town.

Today this 'Vichy of Slovenia' is as popular as a recreational and beauty resort as it is for health treatments, with a host of sporting facilities available. Hiking and cycling in the area is particularly good.

Orientation

The heart of Rogaška Slatina is the spa complex, an attractive (and architecturally important) group of neoclassical, Secessionist and Plečnik-style buildings surrounding a garden. This is called Zdravilíski trg (Health Resort Square). The ugly hotels and Terapija (Therapy Building) to the north and northeast are late 1960s and 1970s vintage and totally out of synch with the rest of the lovely square.

Rogaška Slatina's bus station is south of Zdravilíski trg on Celjska cesta next to the post office. The train station is about 300 metres farther south at Kidričeva ulica 29.

Information

The tourist office (☎ 814 414) at Zdravilíski trg 1 was in a state of reorganisation the last time I visited Rogaška Slatina, but it should be up and running by now. If not, talk to the people at reception at the Strossmayer hotel (☎ 811 6000) a few steps south at Zdravilíski trg 14. Slovenijaturist (☎ 814 488) has a branch at the train station open from 8 am till 3 pm and till noon on Saturday.

Banka Celje is at Kidričeva ulica 5 and is open from 8.30 to 11 am and 1.30 to 5 pm. On Saturday it closes at noon. Otherwise, try the Srečno exchange office in the little pavilion just opposite. The post office is next door to the bank at Kidričeva ulica 3 and has exchange facilities and a telephone box that accepts PTT Sloveniya phone cards. It is open from 7.30 am to 9 pm and till noon on Saturday.

Rogaška Slatina's telephone code is 063. The postcode is 63250.

Rogaška Spa

First and foremost, the mineral water (called Donat Mg here) is for drinking. The stuff is bottled and sold throughout Slovenia for both curative and refreshment purposes, but you might find the real thing a bit too salty and metallic. The water, which also contains calcium, sulphates, lithium and bromide, is said to eliminate stress, aid digestion and stimulate weight loss. The magnesium alone, I was told, regulates 200 bodily functions (most of which I didn't know were working for me).

You can engage in a 'drinking cure' of your own at the **Pivnica**, the round, glassed-in building just beyond the gazebo-like **Tempel**, which was built in the early 19th century above the central Slatina spring. A pass, valid for three days, costs DM9 but be sure you follow the advice in the pamphlet entitled *Catch Your Drop of Health*; you wouldn't want to overdo it. The Pivnica is open daily from 7 am to 1 pm and from 2 to 7 pm.

The centre of real action at the spa is the 12-storey **Terapija** building where those spruce-needle baths are being taken and those lymphs drained. Between the Donat hotel and Zdravilíski Dom containing the Grand hotel there's a Beauty Centre as well as an indoor thermal pool, sauna, steam room and gym. ·The outside swimming pool complex is next to the new shopping centre at Celjska cesta 5. It costs 360 SIT for adults and 240 SIT for children. Plans are afoot to build a series of thermal pools north of the Pivnica building.

The former Administration Building at Zdravilíski trg 4, the oldest structure at the spa, houses the little **Museum of Graphic Arts**, a collection of etchings and drawings dating from the 16th through to the 19th century that was donated by a satisfied Swiss patient. It's open on Tuesday, Thursday and Saturday only from 10 am till noon and from 2 to 6 pm.

Other Things to See & Do

The Sport Centre, a couple of hundred metres east of the Donat hotel and up the hill, has four indoor and six outdoor **tennis courts** available for hire starting at about 800 SIT and 1300 SIT per hour and a **squash court** for 650 SIT. Bicycles cost 430 SIT per hour or about 1050 SIT for the whole day. There's also minigolf, table tennis, archery and lawn bowling available.

South of the Sport Centre, on Janina Hill, is a tiny **ski slope** with three km of trails and two tows. A day pass costs DM11. Skis, poles and boots are another DM7 to rent.

Some 10 marked **trails** fan out from Rogaška Slatina into the surrounding hills and meadows, and the hikes can be as short as two km or as long as 20 km. No 8, for example, leads 14 km to **Sveti Florijan**, a hilltop church north-east of the spa, and Ložno, from where you can continue another five km to **Donačka Gora** (882 metres). If you want to do it an easier way, take a bus or train the six km to Rogatec, then walk to Donačka Gora in about two hours. Accom-

modation on the peak is at the *Rudljev Dom* (☎ 827 128). It's open on weekends and holidays from May to October.

In **Rogatec** (pop 1621), one of the oldest towns in Slovenia, there's a marginally inter-esting **open-air ethnographic museum** with traditional Pannonian farmhouses on display.

The walk to **Boč** (978 metres) north-west of Rogaška Slatina takes about four hours though you can drive as far as *Dom na Boču* (☎ 825 390), a mountain hut a couple of km south of the peak. Dom na Boču is open daily from January to September.

The Rogaška Riding Centre (☎ 824 110) near Podplat (Krtnice house No 11a), six km west of Rogaška Slatina, has eight horses and ponies available for hire for about DM20 an hour. Individual lessons are DM30 per hour, group ones DM20. The centre is open every day but Monday from 8 to 11 am and from 4 to 8 pm and bookings should be made in advance. Podplat can be reached on the Celje bus; the village of Krtnice is a short walk from the main road.

Festivals

Rogaška Musical Summer is a series of con-certs held in the Crystal Hall (where Franz Liszt tickled the ivories in 1846). Others are held *en plein air* at the Tempel pavilion. Concerts take place every two to three days at 8.30 pm from late June to late September. The information office (☎ 811 6487) on the 2nd floor of Zdravilíski Dom at Zdravilíski trg 11 will provide a list.

Rogaška Night is a knees-up of dancing, beer guzzling and general merrymaking in late August.

Places to Stay

The tourist office can arrange *private rooms* in the town and surrounding area for between DM14 and DM17 per person, depending on the season and the room category. If the office is closed, try the house at Strma cesta 7, a couple ·of hundred metres west of the train station.

With the exception of the high-priced *Sava* and *Donat*, two enormous (and very

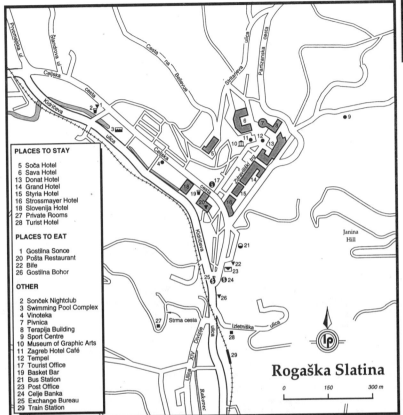

PLACES TO STAY

5 Soča Hotel
6 Sava Hotel
13 Donat Hotel
14 Grand Hotel
15 Styria Hotel
16 Strossmayer Hotel
18 Slovenija Hotel
27 Private Rooms
28 Turist Hotel

PLACES TO EAT

1 Gostilna Sonce
20 Pošta Restaurant
22 Bife
26 Gostilna Bohor

OTHER

2 Sonček Nightclub
3 Swimming Pool Complex
4 Vinoteka
7 Pivnica
8 Terapija Building
9 Sport Centre
10 Museum of Graphic Arts
11 Zagreb Hotel Café
12 Tempel
17 Tourist Office
19 Basket Bar
21 Bus Station
23 Post Office
24 Celje Banka
25 Exchange Bureau
29 Train Station

Janina
Hill

Rogaška Slatina

0   150   300 m

ugly) modern hotels with over 400 rooms at the end of Zdraviliški trg, prices at most of the spa hotels are standard: from DM40 to DM55 for a single with shower and breakfast and DM64 to DM96 for a double. Full board is recommended though not mandatory.

The hotels in Zdraviliški Dom (☎ 811 2000; fax 814636) – the *Grand*, *Styria* and *Strossmayer* – have seen better days though many of their rooms look out onto the lovely park. Choose instead the 55-room *Soča* (☎ 811 5000; fax 814 489) off on its own on the top of the hill to the west or, better still, the 50-room *Slovenija* (tel/fax same as the

Soča) at Celjska cesta 1, which is central to everything.

What was the cheapest place in town, the *Turist* hotel at Izletniška ulica 2 next to the train station, may have reopened by now. Ask at the tourist office.

Places to Eat

There's an inexpensive *bife* near the post office on Kidričeva ulica open from 7 am to 7 pm weekdays and till 2 pm on Saturday. Don't expect much.

Gostilna Bohor at Kidričeva ulica 23 has fish dishes and pizzas in the 350 to 600 SIT range. The *Kmečka Pizza* (Farmer's Pizza), with virtually everything from the barnyard thrown on top, is good. The Bohor is open daily from 9 am to 11 pm.

The *Pošta* restaurant at Zdraviliški trg 23 has a pleasant terrace for dining under the chestnut trees but the awful synthesizer music might drive you away. If so, head for the *Sonce*, a pleasant little gostilna with fish dishes at Celjska cesta 9 open till 11 pm.

One of the most pleasant places in the entire spa complex for a drink and a snack is the Zagreb hotel's *café* at Zdraviliški trg 5. It's open daily till midnight. The *Vinoteka*, in what was the very pink Trst hotel at Celjska cesta 3, has a selection of wines available from noon to 11 pm.

Entertainment

The *Casino* (☎ 814 711) at the Donat hotel is open nightly from 8 pm till 3 am. The Zagreb hotel has ballroom dancing in the café every night till midnight except on Wednesday and Saturday when the venue switches to the more elegant *Crystal Hall* in the Zdraviliški Dom.

Most visitors to Rogaška Slatina spend their evenings in the spa's bars and cafés; the *Basket Bar* attached to the Pošta restaurant but facing Celjska cesta is especially popular. But there's now a new *nightclub* below the Pošta restaurant (enter from Kidričeva ulica) and, on the raunchy side, a strip joint called the *Sonček* beneath the Sonce restaurant. The latter is open daily from 10 pm to 4 am.

Things to Buy

Rogaška Slatina is almost as celebrated for its crystal as it is for its mineral water. A showroom on the southern end of the Pošta restaurant has a large selection of drinking and wine glasses, vases and bowls.

Getting There & Away

Buses to Celje and Rogatec leave Rogaška Slatina at least once an hour. Otherwise, bus service is no more than adequate. The following other destinations can be reached from Rogaška Slatina: Bizeljsko (one); Bled (one); Dobovec and the Croatian border (eight); Ljubljana (four); Maribor (six); Murska Sobota (one); Ormož (one); Podčetrtek (three); and Ptuj (two). There is also one bus a day to Graz in Austria.

Rogaška Slatina is on the train line linking Celje via Dobovec with Zabok in Croatia, where you can change for Zagreb. Up to six trains a day go to Celje (36 km; 50 minutes) with another four heading eastward for Croatia.

PTUJ (pop 11,300)

Ptuj, the oldest town in Slovenia, equals Ljubljana in terms of historical importance. Ptuj's compact medieval core, with its castle, museums, monasteries and churches, can easily be seen in a day. But there are so many interesting side trips and activities in the area that you may want to base yourself here for awhile.

Ptuj, with a name in English that sounds like someone spitting from a great distance, began life as a Roman military outpost on the right bank of the Drava River and later grew into a civilian settlement called Poetovio on the other side. Unlike so many other Slovenian towns, Ptuj doesn't have to put a spade into the ground to prove its ancient origins: Tacitus mentioned it by name in his *Historiae* as existing as early as 69 AD.

Poetovio, then the largest Roman township in what is now Slovenia, lay on a major road linking Pannonia and Noricum provinces. It was famous for its large stone bridge spanning the Drava near today's Dominican monastery and an aqueduct brought water down from the distant Pohorje Massif. In the 2nd and 3rd centuries, Ptuj was the centre of the Mithraic cult, a new religion with origins in Persia that was popular among Roman soldiers and slaves. Several complete temples have been unearthed in the area.

But all this came to a brutal end when the Goths attacked the town in the 5th century. They were followed by the Huns, Langobards, Franks and then the early Slavs.

The hilltop castle at Ptuj (Pettau in German) was attacked by the Magyars in the

10th century but not taken. Ptuj received its town rights in 977 and over the next several centuries it grew rich through trade on the Drava. By the 13th century it was competing with the 'upstart' Marchburg (Maribor), some 26 km upriver, in both crafts and commerce. Two monastic orders – the Dominicans and the Franciscan Minorites – settled here and built important monasteries. The Hungarians attacked and occupied Ptuj for most of the 15th century though each of the half-dozen raids by the Turks were thwarted.

When the railroad reached eastern Slovenia from Vienna on its way to the coast in the mid-19th century, the age-old rivalry between Maribor and Ptuj became onesided: the former was on the line and the latter missed out altogether. Though Ptuj was rescued from oblivion in 1863 when the train to Budapest passed through it, the town remained essentially a provincial centre with a German majority and very little industry until WW I. Today Ptuj and its surrounds are agriculturally based, Ptuj being one of the few towns in Slovenia with farms on its very door step.

Orientation

Ptuj's lies on the left bank of the swift-flowing Drava, which widens into the artificial Ptuj Lake (Ptujsko Jezero) to the south-east. To the south are the Haloze Hills, one of the best wine-growing regions in Slovenia.

The castle, with its irregular shape and ancient walls, dominates the town from a 300-metre-high hill to the north-west. Though there is no real centre, much of historical interest lies on or near Slovenski trg, while Minoritski trg could be considered the gate to the town. Terme Ptuj, a spa and recreational area across the river, is a temptation on one of Ptuj's very hot summer days.

The bus station is about 450 metres northeast of Minoritski trg on Osojnikova cesta. The train station is another 200 metres farther along the same street.

Information

The tourist office (☎ 062 771 569) is at the bottom of the City Tower at Slovenski trg 14. It is open daily from 8 am to 7 pm (from 9 am on Sunday) and the staff are very knowledgeable and helpful. The Ptuj Alpine Society at Minoritski trg 5 has information about hiking in the area, but it is only open on Tuesday and Friday from 4 to 6 pm. Anyone planning to spend more than a day or two in Ptuj should pick up a copy of *Ptuj and Its Surroundings*, which provides a wealth of information on the town and neighbouring areas.

Ljubljanska Banka has a branch next to the Mitra hotel at Prešernova ulica 6. It is open on weekdays from 8.30 am till noon and from 2.30 to 5 pm (on Saturday till noon only). A Banka, in the lovely Gothic House opposite at Prešernova ulica 1, is open weekdays from 8 am to 5 pm and till 11 am on Saturday.

The main post office is at Minoritski trg 1a. It is open from 7 am to 7 pm and till 1 pm on Saturday. It has exchange facilities.

Ptuj's telephone code is 062. The postcode is 62250.

Ptuj Castle

Parts of the castle complex date back to the 11th century (notably the tower on the western edge of the hill) but what you see here is an agglomeration of styles dating from the 14th to the 18th century put into place by one aristocratic owner after another. The castle houses the collection of the **Ptuj Regional Museum** on its three arcaded floors, but a trip up here is worth it for the views alone.

As you enter the castle, you can't help but notice the red-marble **tombstone of Frederick V**, the last lord of Ptuj, who died in 1438. It was brought here from the Dominican monastery. The ground-floor castle contains a fascinating new exhibit of musical instruments dating from the 17th to 19th century – flutes, horns, drums, lutes, violas, harps, clavichords etc. As you approach each

STAJERSKA

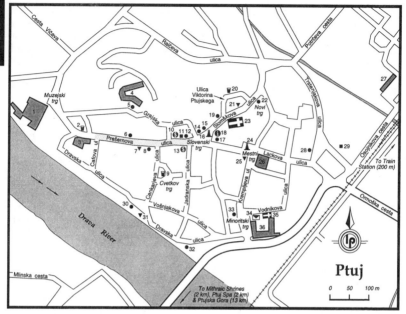

Ptuj

0   50   100 m

case, a tape plays the music they obviously still make.

The 1st floor is given over to period rooms, each with its own style and an impressive **Knights' Hall**. They are treasure troves of tapestries (many from Dornava Castle, eight km to the north-east), portraits, weapons and furniture left by the castle's last occupants, the Herbertsteins. You'll probably notice a coat of arms containing three buckles and the motto 'Grip Fast' in English. It belonged to the Leslies, a Scottish-Austrian family who owned the castle from 1656 to 1802. The buckles are said to have been added to the family escutcheon when Walter, Leslie saved a countess who had fallen into a well by pulling her up with belts buckled together.

Among some of the more interesting bits and pieces are the Chinoiserie decorations and wallpaper whose figures have curiously Caucasian features, the beautiful porcelain stoves which were fuelled through vents

from the outside corridors and the large collection of clocks, including an astronomical one from the 18th century, in the Music Room.

The 2nd floor is a gallery of Gothic statues and oil paintings dating from the 16th to the 19th century. Have a look at the scene of Ptuj in winter by Franc Jožef Fellner (1721-70) and one of the Church of St George marred by graffiti (in German) from the early 19th century. Two fine statues of St Catherine (with a wheel) and St Barbara (with a tower) carved from sandstone in about 1410 in the 'soft' Gothic style are among the museum's most priceless possessions. Check out the faces of the guards torturing Christ in the crucifixion scene nearby; they're really enjoying themselves.

The museum also has a large collection of Kurent masks from the Spuhlja-Markovci region used at Carnival celebrations and unusual 'Turkerie' portraits. These are paintings of Turkish aristocrats, generals and

PLACES TO STAY

| 11 | Mitra Hotel |
| 29 | Super Li Hotel |

PLACES TO EAT

7	Slonček Pizzeria
21	Pivnica Zlatorog
25	Evropa Café
31	Ribič Restaurant

OTHER

1	Dominican Monastery/Museum
2	Amadeus Pub
3	Little Castle
4	Ptuj Castle/Museum
5	Peruzzi Portal
6	Bistro M
8	Honey Shop
9	Metulj Disco
10	Ljubljanska Banka
12	Romanesque House
13	Late Gothic House/A Banka
14	Ljutomer House
15	Old Town Hall
16	Orpheus Monument
17	Ptuj Theatre
18	City Tower/Tourist Office
19	Provost's House
20	Pav Nightclub
22	Market
23	Church of St George
24	St Florian Column
26	Town Hall
27	Bus Station
28	Vinska Klet (wine cellar)
30	Anka Travel Agency
32	Drava Tower/Gallery
33	Bicycle Rental Stand
34	Post Office
35	Minorite Church
36	Minorite Monastery

courtiers commissioned by Count Johann Herbertstein in 1665 and painted in a Western style. Partly because of these paintings, Turkish dress became all the rage for a time in the 18th century.

The museum is open from 9 am to 4 pm in winter and to 6 pm in summer and visits are guided. Entry is 300 SIT and the ticket includes admission to the former Dominican monastery.

Things to See

Ptuj's Gothic centre, with its Renaissance and Baroque additions, is a joy to explore on foot. It's unlikely that you'll get lost in this small place but if you do, explanatory signs in four languages (including English) will tell you where you are. The arched spans that look like little bridges above some of the narrow streets are to support the older buildings.

Start a walking tour of Ptuj in Minoritski trg, site of the **Minorite monastery** that was built in the 13th century. Because the Minorites dedicated themselves to teaching, the order was not dissolved in the Habsburg edict of the late 18th century and it has continued to function in Ptuj for more than seven centuries.

The **monastery church**, on the northern side of the inner courtyard, was one of the most beautiful examples of early Gothic architecture in Slovenia until it was reduced to rubble by Allied bombing in January 1945. Only the presbytery, with a medieval altar, has been restored. The arcaded monastery, which dates from the second half of the 17th century, has two things worth seeing. The **summer refectory** on the 1st floor, which somehow managed to escape destruction during the war and served as the chapel until recently, contains beautiful 17th century stucco work and a dozen ceiling paintings of saints Peter (northern side) and Paul (southern side). One panel depicts the martyrdom of poor St Stephen, who was stoned to death by a group of pagans. Among them was Saul, who was later baptised as Paul. The monastery also contains a rich, 5000-volume **library** of important manuscripts, including part of a 10th century codex used to cover a prayer book around 1590 and an original copy of the New Testament (1561) translated by Primož Trubar, one of the most valuable documents of the Slovenian patrimony and kept in a shoebox in a lower cabinet. The monastery doesn't have regular opening hours, but you can ring the bell to the right of the church entrance and ask one of the four brothers in residence if you can visit.

If you walk northward on Krempljeva ulica, you'll soon reach Mestni trg, the rectangular square once called Florianplatz in honour of the **St Florian Column** (1745) in the centre. To the east, at No 1, is the neo-Gothic **town hall** (1907), designed by an architect from Graz and the most beautiful 'new' building in Ptuj.

Murkova ulica, with some interesting old houses at No 1 (have a peek at the courtyard) and No 7, leads westward to **Slovenski trg**, the heart of old Ptuj. This funnel-shaped square, which is higher than Mestni trg, contains the lion's share of Ptuj's most beautiful buildings.

The most obvious structure here is the **City Tower**, built in the 16th century as a belfry and later turned into a watch tower. Roman tombstones and sacrificial altars from Poetovio were incorporated into the tower's exterior in 1830; you can still make out reliefs of Medusa's head, dolphins and a man carrying huge bunches of grapes. In front of the tower stands the five-metre-high **Orpheus Monument**, a Roman tombstone from the 2nd century with scenes from the Orpheus myth. It was used as a pillory in the Middle Ages; the guilty were shackled to iron rings attached to the holes at the base. The attractive building on the right at No 13 is the **Ptuj Theatre**, built in the 18th century. Until 1918 it was exclusively German-speaking. The theatre was well-known for its avant-garde productions in the late 1930s.

Behind the City Tower is the **Provost's Church of St George**, which reveals a melange of styles from the Romanesque to neo-Gothic. The church contains some lovely 15th century choir chairs decorated with animals, a relief of the Epiphany dating from 1515 at the start of the south aisle, a 15th century stone Pietà and, in the baptismal chapel, the so-called Laib altar, a three-winged altar painting from 1460.

On the western side of Slovenski trg are several interesting buildings including the 16th century **Provost's House** with a Rococo facade at No 10, the **Old Town Hall** at No 6 and, next door, **Ljutomer House**, which was built by Italian workers in 1565 who were in Ptuj to fortify the town against the Turks.

The shortest way to the castle from here is to follow narrow Grajska ulica, which leads to a covered wooden stairway and the Renaissance **Peruzzi Portal**. But take time to explore pedestrian **Prešernova ulica**, the town's market in the Middle Ages.

The 15th century **Gothic House** at No 1 has an unusual projection held up by a black man's head while opposite, at No 4, is the **Romanesque House**, the oldest building in Ptuj. The house at No 6, for many years the **Hotel Osterberger**, has recently been turned into a hotel again. The rather unimpressive pile at Prešernova ulica 35 is the **Little Castle** (Mali Grad), home to the Bishops of Salzburg and a number of aristocratic families over the centuries and now being renovated. The building to the west once housed a **prison**, starting in the 19th century. During WW II many Partisans, including the local hero Jože Lacko, were tortured and died here. From the western end of Prešernova ulica you can follow the gravel path eastward to the castle.

Just past 'Sunny Park' at Muzejski trg 1 is the former **Dominican monastery**, which now contains the Ptuj Regional Museum's **archaeological collection**. The monastery was built in 1226 but abandoned in the late 18th century when Habsburg Emperor Joseph II dissolved all religious orders. The beautiful eastern wing has vaulted Romanesque and Gothic cloisters with 15th century frescoes of Dominican monks in their black and white garb, and there's a refectory with 18th century stucco work, a Gothic chapel and a large Roman coin collection. But the main reason for coming is to see the Roman tombstones, altars and wonderful mosaics unearthed in Ptuj and at **Mithraic shrines** at Zgornji Breg and Spodnja Hajdina, a couple of km west of town. A guide will explain the significance of all the stones and help bring them to life – from Mithra himself and the Sol deity that looks not unlike the US Statue of Liberty to the *nutrices*, the wet nurses who nourished the offspring of Roman aristocrats, and ancient tombstones of Jewish slaves in Hebrew. A guide will also accompany you to the Mithraic shrines themselves

Mithra & the Great Sacrifice

Mithraism, the worship of the god Mithra, originated in Persia. As Rome extended its rule into Asia, the religion became extremely popular with traders, imperial slaves and mercenaries of the Roman army and spread rapidly throughout the empire in the 1st and 2nd centuries AD. The Roman emperors eventually accepted the new faith, and Mithraism was the principal rival of Christianity until Constantine came to the throne in the 4th century.

Mithraism was a mystery religion with devotees sworn to secrecy. What little is known of Mithra, the god of justice and social contract, has been deduced from reliefs and icons found in temples like the ones at Ptuj and near Črnomelj in Bela Krajina. Most of these portray Mithra clad in a Persian-style cap and tunic sacrificing a white bull in front of Sol, the sun god. From the bull's blood and semen, grain, grapes and living creatures sprout forth. Sol's wife Soma, the moon, begins her cycle and time is born. The letters 'VSLM' that you see on many Mithraic stones are part of a secret code thanking Mithra for his good deeds and recognizable only to the faithful.

Mithraism and Christianity competed strongly because of the striking similarity in many of their rituals. Both involve shepherds, an ark built to escape a flood and a form of baptism. Devotees knelt when they worshipped and a common meal – a 'communion' – was a regular feature of the liturgy. ■

if you're interested. The Dominican monastery collection is open from mid-April to November from 10 am to 3 pm.

You can return to Minoritski trg by following Dravska ulica through Hrvatski trg and past the round **Drava Tower** (Dravski Stolp), a Renaissance water tower built by Italian workers for defence in 1551. It now houses a gallery featuring the works of the graphic artist France Mihelič. It is open on weekdays from 10 am to 1 pm and from 4 to 7 pm. At weekends it opens in the morning only.

Activities

Terme Ptuj, a thermal spa about two km north-west of town on the right bank of the Drava at Pot v Toplice 9, is primarily a recreational centre with two outdoor swimming pools, three indoor ones and eight tennis courts. Entrance to the pools is 400 SIT on weekdays, 500 SIT at weekends and 300 SIT at night. You can also rent bicycles there for 100 SIT per hour.

The Ribič restaurant rents a large boat – but usually only to groups – from its dock on the Drava River.

Licences for river fishing are available from the Anka travel agency (☎ 776 020) at Dravska ulica 10 near the Ribič.

The Oldtimer Train, run by Slovenijaturist, has several excursions between Maribor and Ormož via Ptuj and Laško and Ormož via Celje and Ptuj from time to time. Contact any Slovenijaturist branch for details.

Festivals

Kurentovanje – a rite of spring celebrated for i0 days up to Shrove Tuesday – is the most popular and best-known folklore event in Slovenia. Ask the tourist office for details about this year's festivities.

Some of the concerts staged as part of the Idriart Festival around Slovenia in July take place in Ptuj and surrounds (Minorite monastery, Church of St George, the Knights' Hall in Ptuj Castle, Borl Castle). There is also a series of concerts in Ptuj in September.

Two traditional 'peddlers' fairs' take place every year in Ptuj – one in late April and one in early August.

Places to Stay

The crowded camp site at the *Terme Ptuj* spa (☎ 771 721) charges between DM10 and DM12 per person and is open from May to September. Prices include use of the pools and other recreational facilities. Terme Ptuj also has *bungalows* available (DM48 for singles, DM75 for doubles) as well as

STAJERSKA

modern *apartments* in larger villas accommodating two people from DM60.

The tourist office can arrange *private rooms*, but they're not cheap (about 3500 SIT for a double) and most are on the right bank of the Drava near Terme Ptuj. *Pri Tonetu* (☎ 771 586), at Zadružni trg 13 on the way to the spa, charges DM30 per person.

The 22-room *Super Li* (☎ 779 821; fax 779 823) at Trstenjakova ulica 13 is the cheaper of Ptuj's two hotels: bright and airy renovated singles with shower and breakfast are 3400 to 4000 SIT and doubles are 5600 to 6000 SIT depending on the room. The Super Li is not a bad place but the disco and large outside *pivnica* below the rooms may make sleep just a tad difficult.

The new 24-room *Mitra* hotel (☎ 771 281; fax 771 111) at Prešernova ulica 6 is one of provincial Slovenia's more interesting hotels – complete with Mithraic artefacts – though the rooms are fairly ordinary. You can't beat the location but the prices are high: 5000 SIT for a single with shower and breakfast, 7000 SIT for a double and 9000 SIT for one of the four suites.

Places to Eat

The *Evropa* is a small restaurant-cum-café in an 18th century town house at Mestni trg 2. It's open daily from 7 am to 9 pm and on Sunday from 8 am to 8 pm.

Slonček at Prešernova ulica 19 serves pizza and some meatless dishes every day from 9 am to 10 pm. *Pivnica Zlatorog* at Slomškova ulica 20 also has pizza and is open weekdays from 9 am to 10 pm and on Sunday from 10 am.

Grajska Kavarna in the castle courtyard serves drinks and snacks weekdays from 9 am to 9 pm and at weekends till 11 pm.

The best restaurant in Ptuj, with excellent food, service and location, is the *Ribič* facing the river at Dravska ulica 9. The speciality here is fish – especially trout – and the mushroom soup is exceptional. If the oil on the

Kurent: Carnival Time in Ptuj

Ptuj, and many nearby towns, marks Shrovetide by Kurentovanje, a rite of spring and fertility that may date to the time of the early Slavs. Such celebrations are not unique to Slovenia; they still take place at Mohács in Hungary and in Serbia and Bulgaria. But the Kurentovanje is among the most extravagant.

The main character of the rite is Kurent, god of unrestrained pleasure and hedonism – a 'Slovenian Dionysus'. The Kurents (there are many groups of them) are dressed in sheepskins with cowbells dangling from their belts. On their heads they wear huge furry caps decorated with feathers, sticks or horns and coloured streamers. The leather face masks have eye-holes outlined in red, long, trunk-like noses and enormous red tongues that hang down to the chest.

The Kurents move from house to house in procession, scaring off evil spirits with their cow bells and wooden clubs topped with hedgehog spines. A devil *(hudič)* covered in a net to catch souls heads each group. Young girls present the Kurents with handkerchiefs (which they then fasten to their belts), and housewives smash clay pots at their feet for luck and good health. ■

Kurent Mask

salad tastes odd (nutty, a little smoky) that's because it's *bučno olje* (pumpkin-seed oil), a speciality of the Drava Plain region. Ribič, which has a group playing Slovenian folk music most nights, is open from 11 am to 11 pm (till 10 pm on Sunday).

Vinska Klet at Trstenjakova ulica 10 is the place to go if you want to taste or buy wine – it's one of the largest cellars in Slovenia. If you can't make it to the wine-growing regions to the south or east, try some Haložan, Šipon or Renski Rizling here. The cellar also has stocks of Zlata Trta, the 'Golden Vine' sweet wine dating from 1917. It is the oldest vintage in Slovenia.

There's a daily *market* selling fruit, vegetables and more on Novi trg.

Entertainment
Prešernova ulica has a couple of decent pubs and cafés, including *Bistro M* at No 20 and *Amadeus* at No 36, opposite the Little Castle. The large *pub* at the Super Li hotel has the cheapest beer in town: 200 SIT per litre.

There's a disco called *Metulj* at Cvetkov trg which can be reached by walking south along Cankarjeva ulica from Prešernova ulica. It's open on Friday and Saturday from 11 pm to 3 am. The *Pav* at Ulica Viktorina Ptujskega 4 is a nightclub for a more wizened crowd open from 9 pm till late.

Things to Buy
The shop at Prešernova ulica 15, open from 9 am till noon on Wednesday and Saturday only, sells all manner of bee products – honey, wax, pollen etc – from Apače, southwest of Ptuj. Anno 69 at Prešernova ulica 9 has up-market glassware and a good selection of Slovenian wine.

Getting There & Away
Bus Buses are frequent from Ptuj to Cirkulane, Kidričevo, Maribor, Majšperk, Ormož and Poljčane.

Other destinations and their daily frequencies include: Apače (four); Bučkovci (four); Celje (three via Maribor, two via Pragersko, two via Rogaška Slatina); Kranj (one); Lendava (one); Ljubljana (seven via

Maribor, Pragersko or Rogaška Slatina); Ljutomer (six); Murska Sobota (two); Nova Gorica (one); Pragersko (two); Rogaška Slatina (three); Slovenska Bistrica (five); and Vurberk (eight).

Two buses a week (on Monday and Friday) head for Graz in Austria. For destinations in Croatia, count on six buses a day to Varaždin and three to Zagreb (via Varaždin or Krapina).

Train You can reach Ptuj up to nine times a day by train from Ljubljana (155 km; 2½ hours) via Zidani Most and Pragersko. An equal number of trains go to Maribor (37 km; one hour). Two trains a day head for Murska Sobota and one goes to Budapest.

Getting Around
Bicycles are available for rent in warmer months from the stand in front of Minoritski trg 4 opposite the post office. It's open from 9 am till noon and from 4 to 7 pm. The charge is about 100 SIT per hour. The same company rents bikes at the Terme Ptuj spa.

AROUND PTUJ
Ptujska Gora (pop 1136)
The pilgrimage **Church of the Virgin Mary** at Ptujska Gora, 13 km south-west of Ptuj, contains one of the most treasured objects in Slovenia: a 15th century carved-wood **Misericordia** of the Virgin Mary and the Child Jesus sheltering both rich and poor under an enormous cloak held up by seven angels. The carving, which is above the main altar, is as important an historic document as it is a work of art. Among the life-like faces of the faithful are the Counts of Celje (Frederick II and the three Hermans). It rivals the altar carving (1489) by Wit Stwosz in Krakow's Church of Mary for its grace and beauty.

The church, built in the late 14th century, is the finest example of a three-nave Gothic church in Slovenia. Among some of the other treasures inside is a small wooden **statue of St James** on one of the pillars on the southern side, **15th century frescoes** of Christ's

Passion under the porch and medieval paintings of saints, including Sts Nicholas and Dorothy. The abstract stained-glass windows date from this century.

The church perches atop Black Hill (Črna Gora), an easy 10-minute walk from where the bus heading for Majšperk will let you off. There's a gallery with interesting artwork for sale to the left of the entrance at house No 38 and a small eatery called *Bife Dragica* at No 37.

Štatenberg (pop 173)

About nine km south-west of Ptujska Gora in the Dravinja Valley is Štatenberg, site of an 18th century Baroque manor house. The manor has impressive stucco work, frescoes and rooms full of antique (if a little motheaten) furniture and tapestries, but the main reason for coming is to spend the night in a castle – on a budget.

Štatenberg was built in the first half of the 18th century not far from the site of another castle that had been occupied by and razed by Slovenian and Croatian peasants under Matija Gubec in 1573. It was designed by an Italian architect for the Attems family.

The manor consists of a landscaped central courtyard enclosed by two side wings and the central building. On the ground floor of the latter is an arcaded hall with Baroque stucco work; seven residential rooms and the lovely **Great Hall** are on the 1st floor. The Great Hall has a frescoed ceiling with mythological scenes as well as statues of Greek and Roman gods in the corners. The other rooms contain carved armoires, rugs, 19th century portraits and a bed in which Empress Maria Theresa once slept. Štatenberg is open Wednesday to Sunday from 11 am till dark. The entrance fee is 100 SIT for adults and 50 SIT for children.

Places to Stay & Eat The *guestrooms* at the castle (☎ 818 916) are in the west wing and cost DM20 per person or DM100 for the nine-person apartment. There's also a small restaurant in the main building. The surrounding park has four small fishing ponds

and horses to ride (DM10 per hour). There are a couple of other restaurants in the area. The one on the main road across from the entrance to the castle is called *Gostilna Marof*. The other, *Gostilna Lesjak Karel*, is at house No 36 in Makole, a village on the Dravinja 1.5 km to the south-west.

Štatenberg can be reached on the Poljčane bus from Ptuj.

Wine Routes

Ptuj is within easy striking distance of two important wine-growing areas: the **Haloze** and the **Jeruzalem-Ljutomer** districts. They are accessible on foot, by car and, best of all, by bike.

The Haloze Hills extend for about 30 km from Makole south-west of Ptuj to Goričak on the border with Croatia. There's a footpath taking in this land of gentle hills, vines, corn and sunflowers called the Haloze Trail (Haloška Pot) accessible from near Štatenberg. But it's much easier to pick up the trail near **Borl Castle**, 11 km south-east of Ptuj. Borl was originally built in the 13th century and fell into Hungarian hands until the late 15th century. It changed ownership often and was used as a detention centre both by the Nazis and, after the war, the Communists. It was even a hotel and restaurant for a while. Today it's in pretty sad shape with very little of interest – a Baroque altar in a disused church, a few Kurent masks scattered about – though concerts are sometimes held in the courtyard in summer. There's a small restaurant near the entrance where you can try the local Haložan wine, and the surrounding parkland is lovely.

A road called the **Wind Rattle Route** (after the unusual wind-powered noise-maker called a *klopotec* used to scare the crows from the vines) follows a 50-km course from Ptujska Gora to Zavrč via Dolena, Gorca and Cirkulane. Ask the tourist office in Ptuj for a map.

The Jeruzalem-Ljutomer 'wine road' begins at Ormož and continues for 18 km north to **Ljutomer** (pop 3700), the main seat in the area, via the hilltop village of

Jeruzalem. There are quite a few cellars and small restaurants along the way where you can sample any of the region's local whites, especially around Ivanjkovci.

MARIBOR (pop 108,000)

Though it is the nation's second-largest city, Maribor counts only 40% of the population of Ljubljana and, frankly, feels more like a large provincial town than north-eastern Slovenia's economic, communications and cultural centre. It has the country's only university outside the capital and boasts an important museum, a number of galleries, a theatre (1786) and an attractive Old Town along the Drava River. Maribor is also the gateway to the Maribor Pohorje, a hilly recreational area to the south-west, and the Mariborske and Slovenske Gorice wine-growing regions to the north and the east.

Maribor has been inhabited continuously since the Neolithic period, but it did not rise to prominence until the Middle Ages, when a fortress called Marchburg was built on Piramida, a hill north of the present-day city, to protect the Drava Valley from the Magyar invasions. The settlement that later developed along the river was given town status in 1254. It grew wealthy through the timber and wine trade, financed to a large degree by the town's Jewish community, and the waterfront landing (Pristan) in the Lent district became one of the busiest ports in the country.

The town was fortified by walls in the 14th century to protect it against the Hungarians and then the Turks; four defence towers still stand along the Drava. Though its fortunes declined somewhat in later centuries – the Jews were expelled from the town in the late 1400s and it competed in commerce with Ptuj – most of the town's important buildings were erected then.

The tide turned in 1846 when the railroad from Vienna reached Maribor – the first town in Slovenia to have rail connections with the imperial capital – and by 1861 three main routes linking Vienna, Budapest and Trieste intersected at Pragersko to the south. The

town, by then known as Maribor, became the centre of Slovene-speaking Styria, a kind of counter-balance to German Graz in Austria, and began to industrialise. The bishopric was moved from Šent Andraž (now St Andrä near Wolfsberg in Austria) to Maribor in 1859 and two important Slovenian newspapers began publishing.

Maribor remained Slovenian within the Kingdom of Serbs, Croats and Slovenes after WW I due to the efforts of General Rudolf Maister and continued to develop in the 1920s and 1930s. But the air raids during WW II devastated the city and by 1945 two-thirds of it lay in ruin. New areas were opened up on the right bank of the Drava, and in the 1950s Maribor was Slovenia's most 'proletarian' city. Much of that is still evident from the factories and housing estates south of the Old Town.

Orientation

Maribor sits on both sides of the Drava but the Lent waterfront area and other parts of the Old Town are on the left bank. There are several main squares, with funnel-shaped Grajski trg the historical centre. The Maribor Pohorje lies to the south-west.

Maribor's enormous postmodern bus station – an urban 'prestige project' if there ever was one – is east of Grajski trg on Mlinska ulica. The train station is about 400 metres north on Partizanska cesta. Maribor Airport at Skoke, about eight km south-east of the Old Town, is one of only three international ones in the country but there are no scheduled flights, only charters.

Information

Tourist Office While the management of the Maribor Tourist Information Centre (MATIC) (☎ 211 262), Grajski trg 1, one of the few real tourist offices in Slovenia, couldn't be more excited about Maribor and its offerings, that eagerness has not filtered down to the staff, who seem to wonder what you are doing in Maribor and when you are going to leave. You may be able to extract a little information from them between 9 am and 6 pm (till noon on Saturday), but they won't even sell you a city map. The office does publish a monthly calendar of events but in Slovene and Germany only.

Money A Banka has a branch at Glavni trg 17 in the passageway connecting Gosposka ulica with Vetrinjska ulica. It is open from 8 am to 5 pm on weekdays and to 11 am on Saturday. To the right of MATIC, in a small passageway off Grajski trg, there's an exchange counter open from 8 am to 6 pm on weekends and till noon on Saturday. If you arrive in town tolar-less on a Sunday, go to the Slovenijaturist office at the train station.

Post & Telecommunications The main post office is near the train station at Partizanska cesta 54 and is open 24 hours a day. A more convenient telephone centre (but with shorter hours) is at Slomškov trg 10. It's open from 7 am to 8 pm on weekends and till 1 pm on Saturday and Sunday.

Maribor's telephone code is 062. The postcode is 62000.

Travel Agency Slovenijaturist (☎ 27 471) has an office next to the Orel hotel at Grajski trg 3a, open from 9 am to 1 pm and from 4 to 7 pm weekdays and on Saturday morning. Its train station branch (☎ 211 222), however, is open every day from 5 am till 8.30 pm. Kompas (☎ 26 751) at Trg Svobode 1 and Globtour (☎ 25 582) at the Slavija hotel (entrance on Sodna ulica) keep the same hours: 8 am to 6 pm on weekdays and till noon on Saturday.

Bookshop Mladinska Knjiga at Gosposka ulica 30 sells regional and city maps and a few guides in English. It also has the 1:50 000-scale *Pohorje-Vzhodni Del* map which includes the Maribor Pohorje.

Things to See

Start a walking tour of Maribor in **Grajski trg**, the centre of the Old Town and closed to traffic. In the middle of the square stands a 17th century **St Florian Column**. **Maribor Castle**, a successor to the Piramida castle, is on the north-eastern corner at Grajska ulica 2.

Along with the exhibits of the **Maribor Regional Museum**, the 15th century castle contains a **Festival Hall** with a remarkably disproportionate ceiling painting, a **Baroque chapel** and a magnificent **Rococo staircase** near the exit. The staircase, with its pink walls, stucco work and figures lounging on the bannisters, is worth a visit in itself.

The museum's collection, one of the richest in Slovenia, is arranged on two levels. On the ground floor there are archaeological, ethnographic and clothing exhibits with 19th century beehive panels painted with Biblical scenes from the Mislinja and Drava valleys, models of Štajerska-style hayracks, Kurent costumes and wax offerings from the area around Ptuj and heaps about the wine industry. Don't miss the mannequins displaying what the well-dressed Maribor woman wore in the 19th century or Marshal Tito's dress uniform as commander of the Yugoslav armed forces.

Upstairs you'll pass through a loggia with Greek and Roman statuary and 14th century Jewish tombstones. Farther on there are rooms devoted to Maribor's history and its guilds and crafts (glassware, wrought iron-work, clocks), a complete 18th century pharmacy and altar paintings and sculptures from the 15th to the 18th century. Taking pride of place among the sculptures are the exquisite **works of Jožef Straub** (1712-56) taken from the Church of St Joseph in the southern suburb of Studenci. The statues depicting the Angel of Grapes and Zacharias are especially fine.

The regional museum is open Tuesday to Saturday from 9 am to 5 pm and on Sunday from 10 am till noon. The entrance fee is 200 SIT (free on Sunday).

A few steps to the east is **Trg Svobode**. This and the two leafy squares to the north – Maistrov trg and Rakušev trg – would be unremarkable except for the honeycomb of **wine cellars** below that cover an area of 20,000 sq metres and can store seven million litres. The 160-year-old cellars are managed

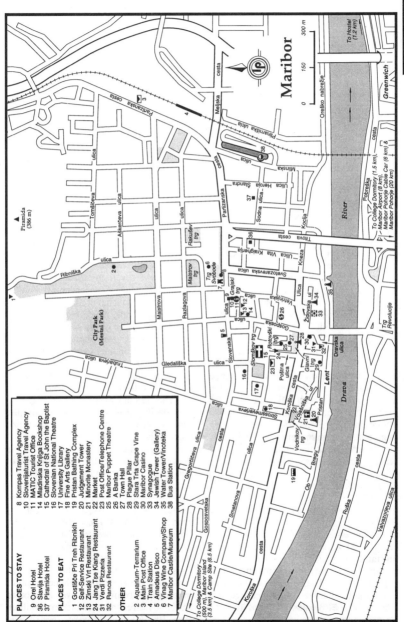

PLACES TO STAY

9 Orel Hotel
36 Slavija Hotel
37 Piramida Hotel

PLACES TO EAT

1 Gostišče Pri Treh Ribnikih
12 Self-Service Restaurant
13 Zimski Vrt Restaurant
24 Jang Tse Kiang Restaurant
31 Verdi Pizzeria
32 Ranca Restaurant

OTHER

2 Aquarium-Terrarium
3 Main Post Office
4 Train Station
5 Amadeus Disco
6 Vinag Wine Company/Shop
7 Maribor Castle/Museum

8 Kompas Travel Agency
10 Slovenijaturist Travel Agency
11 MATIC Tourist Office
14 Mladinska Knjiga Bookshop
15 Cathedral of St John the Baptist
16 Slovenian National Theatre
17 University Library
18 Fine Arts Gallery
19 Pristan Bathing Complex
20 Judgement Tower
21 Minorite Monastery
22 Market
23 Post Office/Telephone Centre
25 Maribor Puppet Theatre
26 A Banka
27 Town Hall
28 Plague Pillar
29 Stara Trta Grape Vine
30 Maribor Casino
33 Synagogue
34 Jewish Tower (Gallery)
35 Water Tower/Vinoteka
38 Bus Station

Maribor

by the Vinag wine export company at Trg Svobode 3 and are filled with old oak barrels, steel fermentation tanks and an 'archive' of vintage wine – all at a constant 15° C. There's a small cellar open to the public till 7 pm, but if you're serious about wine, ask for an extended tour at reception. The wine shop there has a large selection of local vintages, including Mariborčan, Laški Rizling, Chardonnay, Traminer and Gold Muscatel. It is open from 7.30 am to 2 pm.

Maribor's **City Park** (Mestri Park), a lovely arboretum with ponds, swans and a bandstand, has a rather pathetic **Aquarium-Terrarium** with about 40 small tanks filled with tropical fish and reptiles. It's open on weekdays from 8 am to 7 pm. On Saturday and Sunday the hours are from 9 am till noon and from 2 to 7 pm. The entrance fee is 250 SIT (200 SIT for children).

Several hundred metres north is **City Peak** (Mestni Vrh) and to the north-east **Piramida**, where the Titans of Marchburg once held sway. Today both hills are awash in vines that produce some of the best wine in north-eastern Slovenia. Three little ponds lie between them.

Return to the Old Town via Trubarjeva ulica and Gledališka ulica; the latter leads into **Slomškov trg**. The square is named after Anton Martin Slomšek (1800-62), the Slovenian bishop and politician who was instrumental in having the episcopate moved to Maribor and who is now a candidate for sainthood. That's him there seated in front of the cathedral near the **light pillar**, a 16th century lantern that once stood in the church cemetery.

The **Cathedral of St John the Baptist** dates from the 13th century and shows elements of virtually every architectural style from Romanesque to modern (including inept 19th century attempts to 're-Gothicise' certain bits). Of special interest is the flamboyant Gothic presbytery and the choir stalls with reliefs showing scenes from the life of the patron saint. The grand building across the park to the west is the **University Library**. The **Slovenian National Theatre** is on the northern side.

Maribor's **Fine Arts Gallery**, the most complete of the many in town, is south-west of Slomškov trg at Strossmeyerjeva ulica 6. It is open from Tuesday to Saturday from 9 am to 1 pm and from 3 to 6 pm. Sunday hours are from 9 am to 1 pm.

If you walk across Koroška cesta past the market and the dilapidated remains of the **Minorite monastery** to the waterfront, you'll come to the round **Judgement Tower** (Sodni Stolp), the first of four defence towers still standing. This is the start of Lent, Maribor's historical waterfront area.

A few steps along the Pristan embankment, at Vojašniška ulica 8, is Maribor's most celebrated possession, a 440-year-old grape vine called **Stara Trta** that is still producing some 35 litres of red wine each year. It is tended by a city-appointed viticulturist and small bottles of the almost black Žametna Črnina (Black Velvet) are distributed to visiting dignitaries as 'keys' to Maribor. They say it has a sour taste.

Glavni trg, which was Maribor's marketplace in the Middle Ages, is just north of the river. In the centre of the square is perhaps the most extravagant **plague pillar** found anywhere in Central Europe. Designed by Jožef Straub and erected in 1743, it includes the Virgin Mary surrounded by a half-dozen saints. At No 14 is the **town hall** built in 1565 by Venetian craftsmen living in Štajerska. The **Maribor Puppet Theatre** is in the lovely arcaded courtyard to the rear called Rotovški trg.

Running north from Glavni trg is **Gosposka ulica**, once the residential area of well-to-do burghers and now a fashionable shopping street for pedestrians. To the east is **Židovska ulica**, the centre of the Jewish district in the Middle Ages. The 15th century **synagogue** at No 4 is now being renovated, while the square **Jewish Tower** (Židovski Stolp) nearby has been converted into a small photographic gallery.

Opposite, at Usnjarska ulica 10, is the five-sided **Water Tower** (Vodni Stolp), a 16th century defence tower containing Slovenia's oldest vinoteka. You can taste some 300 different Slovenian wines from

9 am to 9 pm daily except for Sunday and Monday.

Activities

A great deal of the outdoor activities available in the Maribor area are centred in the Maribor Pohorje. See the Around Maribor below for details.

Maribor has several outdoor swimming pools, but the most pleasant ones are on Maribor Island (Mariborski Otok), a sandbank in the Drava about four km west of the Old Town. Swimming in the river is allowed here, and a sunbathing area has been reserved for nude bathing. It's open in summer only from 8 am to 7 pm and the entry fee is 400 SIT (300 SIT for children). Local bus No 15 from the train station will drop you off at the start of the footpath leading to the bridge and the island.

While Maribor builds a new thermal spa at Stražun, south-east of the Old Town, you'll have to be content with the Pristan bathing complex on the river west of Lent (entrance from Ob Bregu or Koroška cesta 33). It has an pool, sauna, gym and services such as massage. The pool is open from 7 am to 6 pm on weekdays and from 8 am to 7.30 pm at the weekend. The sauna is open from 8 am to 8 pm from Wednesday to Saturday.

The Maribor Flying Centre (☎ 691 506 for bookings) at the airport in Skoke has several sightseeing flights available including one that takes in Maribor, Ptuj and Slovenska Bistrica for DM35 per person or DM100 for a group of five people.

The Oldtimer Train, run by Slovenijaturist, has infrequent excursions between Maribor and Ormož via Ptuj.

Festivals

Maribor hosts a lot of events throughout the year, including the Youth Choir Competition in February, International Trade Fair in June and the Puppet Theatre Festival through most of the summer. But the biggest event on the city's calendar is Festival Lent, a two-week festival of folklore and culture in late June/early July with stages set up throughout the Old Town. Among the most colourful

ceremonies is the 'baptism' of the rafts on the Drava. Grapes are harvested from Stara Trta, the 'Old Vine' in Lent, in early October.

Places to Stay

Camping The *Jezero* camp site (☎ 621 640), in Bresternica about seven km west of Maribor, lies on a dammed-off portion of the Drava called Maribor Lake (Mariborsko Jezero). Though it's hardly central to town, it's a pleasant-enough place with a large amount of space (five hectares) for the 150 people it claims it can accommodate. The camp site is open from March to October and costs DM10 or DM11 a night per person. It also has expensive *bungalows* available all year: singles start at 5000 SIT, doubles at 6500 SIT. Local bus No 15 will drop you off outside reception.

Private Rooms Both MATIC and Slovenijaturist can organise *private rooms* – but never on a Sunday – for between DM15 and DM18 per person, depending on how many are sharing and the category.

Colleges & Hostel Several colleges have *dormitory rooms* available for travellers in July and August, including one at Titova cesta 24a (☎ 39 331) and one at Gosposvetska cesta 87 (☎ 212 848). The prices are right – a bed in a room for three is DM17 while singles are DM20 – but they are pretty far from the centre of things.

There's a *hostel* (☎ 511 800) at Železnikova ulica 12 on the right bank of the Drava in the south-eastern suburb of Pobrežje. From the train station take bus No 3 (which has an HI symbol on the front of it) and get off at the cemetery stop. Prices are the same as at the college dormitories. Reception is open from 7 to 10 am and again from 7 to 11 pm.

Hotels Maribor's three hotels cater almost exclusively to business travellers from Austria and Germany and charge accordingly; for cheaper hotel accommodation, you'll have to head for the hills of the

Maribor Pohorje (see the Around Maribor section).

The most central of the three city hotels, the rather gloomy *Orel* (☎ 26 171; fax 28 497) at Grajski trg 3, charges 7200 SIT for a single with shower and breakfast and 10,000 SIT for a double. The 120-room *Slavija* (☎ 23 661; fax 222 857), a modern 10-storey block facing a busy street at Ulica Vita Kraigherija 3, has singles for DM85 to DM95 and doubles for DM120 to DM130, depending on the season. The *Piramida* (☎ 25 971; fax 25 984), due east at Ulica Heroja Šlandra 10, is an old 80-room tourist hotel tarted up with a bit of paint and marble. Singles with shower and breakfast are 9600 SIT, doubles 12,800 SIT.

Places to Eat

One of the cheapest places in Maribor is the *self-service restaurant* on Volkmerjev prehod, the narrow passage on the southern side of the Orel hotel.

For pizza, head for *Verdi* just off Pristan at Dravska ulica 8; look for the sign with the three rats! Verdi is open from 10 am to 11 pm daily. Nearby at Vojašniškova ulica 4 and facing the Drava, *Ranca* serves simple Balkan grills like *pleskavica* and *čevapčiči* for between 350 and 500 SIT. The otherwise expensive *Ribja* restaurant at the Slavija hotel has good set lunches (including some vegetarian ones) for between 500 and 800 SIT.

If you really must have Chinese food, visit the *Jang Tse Kiang* Shanghainese restaurant at Poštna ulica 10 but don't expect authenticity. Mains run from 500 to 700 SIT and there are a couple of vegetarian stir-fries on the menu. It's open for lunch and dinner daily till midnight (10 pm on Sunday).

A great place for a meal if you want to get out of the city but don't feel like travelling is *Gostišče Pri Treh Ribnikih*, near the three fish ponds above City Park at Ribniška ulica 3. Oddly, its specialities are cheese *štruklji* (dumplings) and game dishes – not fish. The restaurant is open daily from 10 am to 10 pm.

The fanciest place in Maribor is the *Zimski Vrt*, a 'Winter Garden' restaurant with lots of marble, hanging vines and an atrium. It belongs to the Orel hotel but the entrance is around the corner at Gosposka ulica 30. It's open daily except Sunday till 11 pm.

There's a *market* selling produce at Vodnikov trg.

Entertainment

The *Slovenian National Theatre* has one of the best reputations in the county and its production of *Faust*, directed by Tomaž Pandur, has received critical acclaim throughout Europe. The city's ballet and opera companies also perform here. The ticket office, with extremely convoluted hours, is on the theatre's northern side at Slovenska ulica 27. Ring them at ☎ 221 206. Maribor's second famous theatre is the *Puppet Theatre*, at Rotovški trg 1, with productions year round.

Concerts are held in several locations, including the castle's *Festival Hall* and the cathedral. Ask at the tourist office for a list. The *Satchmo Jazz Club* meets in the Fine Arts Gallery building at Strossmeyerjeva ulica 6 nightly from 9 pm to 1 am.

The pubs and restaurants along the Drava in Lent are pretty lively on summer evenings. The beer in these parts is Gambrinus, brewed in Maribor for more than two centuries. If you're looking to bop, head for *Amadeus*, a disco down a little alleyway at Slovenska ulica 20 or *Paradiso* on Pobreška cesta in Greenwich. Greenwich is a suburb on the right bank of the Drava not far from the youth hostel. The *Café-Bar Stop* at the bus station is a busy gay venue after 8 pm.

Maribor Casino, at Glavni trg 1, is open daily from 6 pm to 2 am and offers slot machines, US and French roulette and blackjack.

Getting There & Away

Bus You can reach virtually any large centre in Slovenia (and ones in Austria, Hungary, Croatia and Italy) from Maribor. The bus station is huge, with some 30 bays, shops, bars, cafés and a large left-luggage office open from 7 am to 9 pm.

Bus service is very frequent to Celje,

Dravograd, Gornja Radgona, Lenart, Lendava, Ljubljana, Ljutomer, Lovrenc, Murska Sobota, Ptuj, Radenci, Selnica and Slovenska Bistrica.

Other destinations and their daily frequencies include: the Areh hotel (three); Bizeljsko (one); Črnomelj (one); Gornji Grad (one); Koper (five); Kranj (one); Majšperk (four); Moravske Toplice (three); Nova Gorica (two); Novo Mesto (one); Ormož (eight); Podčetrtek (three); Postojna (five); Ribnica (two); Rogaška Slatina (six); Rogatec (one); Slovenj Gradec (eight); Tržič (one); and Velenje (two).

Up to a dozen buses a day go to Varaždin in Croatia while eight head for Zagreb via either Varaždin or Krapina.

There are daily buses to Frankfurt and Stuttgart in Germany and Klagenfurt and Graz in Austria. For Lenti in Hungary, count on two buses a week.

Train Maribor is on the train line linking Zidani Most and Celje with the Austrian cities of Graz and Vienna. From Ljubljana (156 km; 2½ hours), you can reach Maribor on some 20 trains a day. About a half-dozen trains a day originating in Maribor go east from Pragersko to Ormož (59 km; 70 minutes), from where you can make your way into Croatia. Connections can be made at Pragersko for trains to Murska Sobota and Hungary.

About four trains head west each day for Dravograd (64 km; 1½ hours) and other stops in Koroška. Two of those trains cross the Austrian border at Holmec and carry on to Bleiburg (Pliberk).

Car Kompas Hertz (☎ 225 252) has an office at the Slavija hotel open from 9 am to 6 pm on weekdays and till noon on Saturday. Globtour also rents cars.

Getting Around

Bus Maribor and its surrounds are well served by local buses. They depart from stands about 200 metres north of the train station's main entrance.

Taxi For a local taxi, ring ☎ 27 755.

AROUND MARIBOR
Maribor Pohorje

Maribor's green lung and its central playground, the eastern edge of the Pohorje Massif (known as Mariborsko Pohorje in Slovene) can be easily reached by car, bus or cable car from town. The area has any number of activities on offer – from skiing and hiking to horse riding and mountain biking – and is a welcome respite from the city, especially in summer.

Skiing The ski grounds of the Maribor Pohorje stretch from the Habakuk hotel near the lower cable-car station to Žigartov Vrh (1347 metres) west of the Areh hotel. With some 40 km of slopes, 25 km of cross-country runs and 16 ski lifts, this is Slovenia's largest ski resort and long waits for tows – endemic elsewhere in Slovenia – are nonexistent here.

The season generally lasts from December to March, but there are snow cannons along the 870-metre run where the Women's World Cup Slalom & Giant Slalom Competition (Golden Fox trophy) takes place in late January or early February.

Ski equipment can be rented at the Bellevue hotel (1050 metres) or from the small cabin between the Areh hotel and the pretty little 17th century pilgrimage church nearby. A daily ski pass costs 2000 SIT (1700 SIT for children) and a weekly one is 10,000 SIT (8500 SIT). There's also a ski school here.

Hiking There are heaps of easy walks in every direction from the Areh hotel, but following a stretch of the marked Slovenian Alpine Trail (which originates in Maribor) west and then south-west for five km will take you to the two **Šumik waterfalls** and the virgin forest of **Pragozd** – one of the few in Europe left. A further six km to the south-west is **Black Lake** (Črno Jezero), the source of the swift-running Lobnica River, and Osankarica, where the Pohorje battalion of Partisans was wiped out by the Germans in January 1943. This is a remarkably beautiful hike and the joy of it is that with all the streams around you don't have to carry as much water as you normally would while hiking in summer.

Other Activities The Bellevue hotel rents horses for 350 SIT if you are content to sit in the paddock. Otherwise it costs 1000 SIT per hour. Both the Areh and the Bellevue hotels also have mountain bikes, an ideal way to explore the back roads of the Maribor Pohorje. The rental charge is 400 SIT per hour or 2000 SIT for the day. The Poštarski Dom mountain lodge has tennis courts.

Places to Stay & Eat There are plenty of places to stay in the Maribor Pohorje, including more than a dozen *mountain lodges* and *holiday homes* run by the Branik Ski Club (☎ 226 166). Its main office in Maribor at Mladinska ulica 29 will provide you with a list and basic map. Among those closest to main roads are *Ruška Koča*, *Poštarski Dom* and *Penzion Pohorc*. Generally they cost between 1200 and 1500 SIT per night with breakfast or 2400 to 2800 SIT with all meals. Most of the places have cooking facilities and are open all year.

The 25-room *Areh* hotel (☎ 603 260) is a very pleasant ski lodge with rustic, wood-panelled rooms, a pleasant restaurant and very helpful staff. Singles with shower and breakfast cost DM26 to DM29 while doubles are DM40 to DM54, depending on the season. The hotel has cupboards with locks in the basement for storing skis and bicycles.

The 40-room *Bellevue* (☎ 603 215) near the upper cable-car station is not as nice as the Areh but has pleasant outside terraces for eating and drinking in warm weather. Its singles with shower cost about the same as those at the Areh but ones without are DM22 to DM25 for a single and DM40 to DM54 for a double, depending on the season.

Getting There & Away You can drive or, if ambitious, cycle the 20 km from the Old Town in Maribor south past the Renaissance-style Betnava Castle, turning west at Spodnje Hoče before reaching a fork in the road at a

small waterfall. Go left and you'll reach the Areh hotel in about five km. A right turn and less than four km brings you to the Bellevue.

A much easier – and more exhilarating – way to get to the Bellevue and the heart of the Maribor Pohorje is to take the cable car *(vzpenjača)* from the station at Zgornje Radvanje six km south-west of the Old Town. The ride above the chestnut trees lasts only 15 minutes but offers excellent views of the city and surrounding countryside. There are even clamps on the outside of each car for skis and mountain bikes. Regular buses make the run between the Bellevue and Areh hotels.

From the train station in Maribor take local bus No 6, which leaves about every 20 minutes, and get off at the terminus at the Habakuk hotel (under renovation). The cable car runs continuously at the weekend from 7 am to 7 pm with one last trip again at 10 pm. On weekdays it runs every hour on the hour. A one-way trip is 400 SIT, return 600 SIT (300 and 400 SIT for children). Guests of the Bellevue and Areh hotels get a 10% discount.

CENTRAL POHORJE REGION

Travellers can easily sample Pohorje's recreational offerings along its eastern and western fringes from Maribor and Slovenj Gradec in Koroška. But the pear-shaped massif's most beautiful and highest area is in the centre.

While it's true that the Pohorje peaks can't hold a candle to those of the Julian Alps and the Kamnik-Savinja Alps – most here barely clear the 1500-metre mark – this is the only part of the country where you can appreciate the sheer vastness of the mountains without feeling hemmed in or dizzy. What's more, hiking and trekking in the winter is as good as it is in the summer. Though the Pohorje was once covered in forests, 19th century lumberjacks and charcoal-makers exploited the woods for the sawmills, forges and glassworks of Štajerska and Koroška. Many of the hillsides have been cleared and are now given over to brush, pasture and meadows. Others were replanted with oak trees.

Zreče (pop 3575), about 40 km south-west of Maribor, is the springboard for the central Pohorje region. Though certainly not Slovenia's most attractive town (the Unior tool-manufacturing company dominates the place), it has a modest spa called Terme Zreče and is within easy striking distance of the ski and sport centre around **Rogla** (1517 metres), 16 km to the north. The central Pohorje region is also very well-developed for rural tourism, with dozens of local farmhouses offering accommodation.

Orientation & Information

Staff at the Dobrava hotel at Terme Zreče, which is owned by the Unior Turizem travel group, can help with information. There's a Banka Celje branch next to Zreče's small bus station, some 150 metres from the spa's main entrance. It is open from 8.30 to 11.30 am and from 2 to 5 pm on weekdays only. The bus station also has an exchange office. The post office is near the bank and bus station.

The telephone code for Zreče and Rogla is 063. The postcode is 63214.

Terme Zreče

The thermal spa at Zreče is a serious treatment centre for post-operative therapy and locomotor disorders (especially sport injuries), but it is also a place to have fun. Along with an indoor thermal pool (water temperature: 34° C) and a couple of jacuzzis, there's a large covered recreational pool and two outdoor ones. A fee of 700 SIT (on weekdays) or 900 SIT (at the weekend) gets you use of the pool, saunas and steam room; it's 500/700 SIT for the pool alone. The spa complex also has one of the best-equipped gyms in Slovenia (700 SIT entry). A massage with aromatic oils or a medicinal mud treatment is something you won't soon forget.

Rogla

Rogla is a true sport centre and many teams come here to train. And why not? With all those spruce trees producing so much oxygen there's enough to go around for everyone – and then some. No matter where you look it seems that someone is bouncing,

lifting or pushing something and the hiking and skiing are excellent.

Hiking The *Rogla Footpaths* hiking map produced by Unior Turizem and available everywhere in Zreče and Rogla outlines seven trails (most of them open to mountain bikes) from Rogla. They all follow well-marked circular paths and are as short as two km (30 minutes) and as long as 32 km (eight hours). The latter is hike No 5 and covers much of the hike described in the earlier Around Maribor section – Šumik waterfalls, Black Lake, Osankarica – but from the other side of the Pohorje. Another good one is 12-km hike No 3 (three hours) that leads north-west to the **Lovrenc Lakes** (Lovrenska Jezera), a turf swamp with 19 lakes that are considered a natural phenomenon. This area is also known for its unique vegetation.

Skiing Rogla's 10 km of slopes and 30 km of cross-country trails are served by two chair lifts and 11 tows. The season is a relatively long one – from mid-December till April – and there are cannons for artificial snow. A daily ski pass in full season costs 2100 SIT (1700 SIT for children), a weekly is 11,000 SIT (8500 SIT). There's also a ski school, and you can rent equipment at the Planja hotel. Rogla has become the centre in Slovenia for snow-boarding, on which you 'ski' on something that looks like a skateboard (minus the wheels, of course).

Horse Riding The Rogla Horse Riding Centre (☎ 775 210 for bookings) is about three km north-east of Rogla at Koča na Pesku, a mountain hut with a small restaurant, and opens daily from 10 am to 5 pm. An hour's ride in the hills costs 1200 SIT. A 45-minute sleigh ride in winter is 800 SIT.

Other Activities The sport centre at Rogla has an indoor pool open from 9 am to 8 pm, a covered stadium for all kinds of team sports, jogging tracks, bowling alleys, squash courts and indoor and outdoor tennis courts. The tennis courts cost 400 to 800 SIT an hour to rent, depending on the type and the time of day. A racquet is 150 SIT. Mountain bikes are rented for 500 SIT an hour or 1500 SIT for four hours.

Places to Stay & Eat

The cheapest place to stay at the Rogla holiday centre (☎ 754 322; fax 754 096) is the *Jelka* youth hostel open from June to mid-October and December to March. For DM21, you get a bed in one of four dormitory rooms plus breakfast.

The *Brinje*, a poky 22-room annexe of the Planja hotel, charges DM25 to DM36 per person, depending on the season, while the hotel *bungalows* for two people are DM58 to DM93. The most expensive accommodation at Rogla is at the 116-room *Planja* hotel, which has a three-star and a four-star wing. Frankly, the cheaper wing's rooms are brighter and more attractive, but even they aren't a bargain: expect to pay a minimum of DM43 for one and DM62 for two in the low season. Prices shoot up to DM89 and DM138 in the high season.

A much better deal is available at the many *farmhouses* in the region, particularly along Cesta Kmečnega near Resnik, about seven km south-west of Rogla. The *Pačnik* farmhouse (☎ 762 202), at No 21, is open in summer and in winter and has five rooms, while *Kočnik-Kovše* (☎ 760 728) at No 33 has four rooms and is open all year. There are more farmhouses with accommodation in nearby Skormarje and Padeški Vrh and, closer to Zreče, Stranice and Križevec. The usual farmhouse prices apply: from DM20 to DM24 for bed and breakfast in the low season and DM22 to DM27 in the high season.

There's no particular reason for staying at Terme Zreče (☎ 762 451; fax 762 446); all the fun is up in Rogla anyway. But if you're a serious student of things thermal, the spa's 54-room *Dobrava* hotel, an unexceptional block near the entrance, has singles with shower and breakfast for DM58 and doubles for DM92. Make sure you get one of the rooms with a balcony, though. More pleasant (and expensive) are the 10 new *bungalows*

with four apartments each in a small wooded area behind the main spa building. Each apartment has a kitchen, eating area, sitting room and one or two bedrooms. Prices are DM70 to DM90 for an apartment for two and DM90 to DM110 for one for four people.

If you get tired of the restaurant at Terme Zreče and its *Zreška Klet* wine cellar, try the *Gostišče Brglez* for a light meal at Cesta na Roglo 3. *Paladin* is a pretty glam pizzeria at Obrtniška cesta 13. In Rogla, there's a cheap *self-service restaurant* in the Planja hotel and a *pizzeria* just north of the hotel near the ski lift. The *Stara Koča* is a rustic little bistro in one of Rogla's original wooden buildings.

Getting There & Away

There are regular connections from Zreče to Celje, Planina, Slovenske Konjice and Velenje. Two buses a day from Celje and at least three from Slovenske Konjice stop at Zreče and then carry on to Rogla. Local buses make the runs from Zreče bus station to Rogla and to Resnik. In winter there are special ski buses from both Zreče and Slovenske Konjice.

CELJE (pop 42,000)

Celje (Cilia in German) is not the largest city in Štajerska (Maribor, 60 km to the northeast, has almost three times as many people), nor is it the province's most attractive centre. But it has played a pivotal role in Slovenian history on at least two occasions.

Celje was settled by the Illyrians followed by Celtic tribes who were subdued by the Romans in about 15 BC. As Celeia, it was the administrative centre of the Roman province of Noricum between the 1st and 5th centuries, and roads linked it with other Roman settlements at Virunum (near Klagenfurt in Austria), Poetovio (Ptuj) and Emona (Ljubljana). Celeia was an affluent town as is evident from the large baths, mosaics and temples unearthed in the area. In fact, it flourished to such a degree that it gained the nickname *Troia secunda*, the 'second Troy'. Celeia's glory days came to an end when it was sacked by the Huns in

452 and overrun by subsequent tribes during the Great Migrations.

Celje's second Camelot came in the mid-14th century when members of the Žonek family took control of the area. The Counts (later the Dukes) of Celje, one of the richest and most powerful feudal dynasties in Central Europe, were the last on Slovenian soil to challenge the absolute rule of the Habsburgs and united much of Slovenia for a time. Under their rule, which lasted for just a century, Celje acquired the status of a town and they built the castles, town fortifications and most of the churches still standing today. The Counts of Celje left the town and the nation an invaluable legacy and a part of their emblem – the three gold stars forming an inverted triangle – has been incorporated into the Slovenian state flag and seal.

Celje was never able to repeat those glory days, and plagues, flooding, invasions and revolts struck the town over the ensuing centuries. Celje was in fact more German than Slovenian until the end of WW I, when the town government passed into local hands for the first time.

Orientation

Celje's compact Old Town – encompassing just about everything of interest to travellers – is bordered by Levstikova ulica and Gregorčičeva ulica to the north and north-west, the area around the Lower Castle to the west, the train lines to the east and the Savinja River to the south.

The town has two main squares: Glavni trg at the end of Stanetova ulica (a pedestrian street where most of the action is) and Krekov trg opposite the train station. The main bus station is 400 metres north of the train station opposite St Maximilian's Church on Aškičeva ulica. Local and suburban buses stop just south of the train station on Ulica XIV Divizije.

Information

Tourist Office The tourist office at Glavni trg 7 (☎ 29 445) is little more than a souvenir shop with ill-informed staff not particularly gifted in speaking foreign languages

(unusual in Slovenia). They will sell you a map and organise accommodation at one of a few households with private rooms for rent but little else. It would be better to try one of the travel agencies if you need more information. The tourist office is open from 8 am to 7 pm and till 1 pm on Saturday. In July and August, it closes between 1 and 4 pm on weekdays and at 12.30 pm on Saturday.

Money Banka Celje has a branch office at Vodnikova ulica 2 open from 8.30 to 11.30 am and from 2 to 5 pm on weekdays. It closes at noon on Saturday. A Banka is at Krekov trg 7 opposite the train station.

Post & Telecommunications While work is being done to the main post office at Krekov trg 9, business is conducted from the building just opposite at Aškičeva ulica 1 from 7 am to 8 pm weekdays, 7.30 am to noon on Saturday and 8 to 11 am on Sunday. Celje's telephone code is 063. The postcode is 63000.

Travel Agency Kompas (☎ 27 403), in a lovely Renaissance house at Glavni trg 1, can arrange accommodation and rent cars. Slovenijaturist (☎ 28 306), at the train station in Krekov trg, is open daily from 5 am till 10.30 pm. Globtour (☎ 29 302) has an office at Razlagova ulica 1 next to the Evropa hotel.

Bookshop Mladinska Knjiga, at Stanetova ulica 3, sells regional maps and guides including the useful *Celje Guide* published by EPSI.

Things to See

You can begin an easy walking tour of Celje, which takes in virtually everything of importance in the town, from the bus station.

Opposite, on the western side of Aškičeva ulica, is the **Church of St Maximilian**, named after the bishop who was beheaded in Celje in the 3rd century. The church was built in the Gothic style in the 15th century (as was the small chapel to the south) but has undergone many changes and additions since then.

STAJERSKA

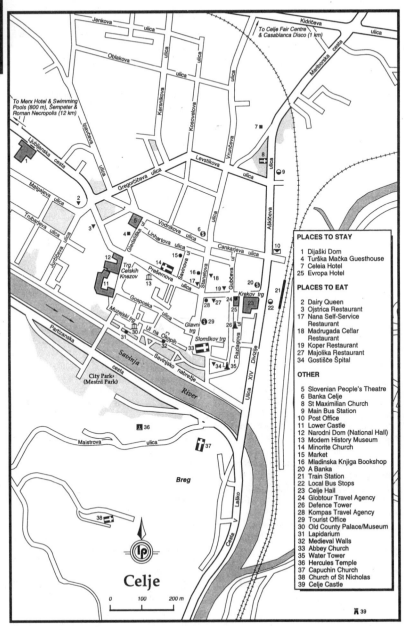

PLACES TO STAY

1 Dijaški Dom
4 Turška Mačka Guesthouse
7 Celeia Hotel
25 Evropa Hotel

PLACES TO EAT

2 Dairy Queen
3 Ojstrica Restaurant
17 Nana Self-Service
Restaurant
18 Madrugada Cellar
Restaurant
19 Koper Restaurant
27 Majolika Restaurant
34 Gostišče Špital

OTHER

5 Slovenian People's Theatre
6 Banka Celje
8 St Maximilian Church
9 Main Bus Station
10 Post Office
11 Lower Castle
12 Narodni Dom (National Hall)
13 Modern History Museum
14 Minorite Church
15 Market
16 Mladinska Knjiga Bookshop
20 A Banka
21 Train Station
22 Local Bus Stops
23 Celje Hall
24 Globtour Travel Agency
26 Defence Tower
28 Kompas Travel Agency
29 Tourist Office
30 Old County Palace/Museum
31 Lapidarium
32 Medieval Walls
33 Abbey Church
35 Water Tower
36 Hercules Temple
37 Capuchin Church
38 Church of St Nicholas
39 Celje Castle

Celje

Top Left: Celje Castle from across the Savinja River (Štajerska) (SF)
Top Right: Rinka Waterfall in the Logar Valley (Logarska Dolina) (Štajerska) (SF)
 Bottom: Wooden suspension bridge in the Upper Savinja Valley (Štajerska) (SF)

Top: Cycling in the Logar Valley (Logarska Dolina) (Štajerska) (JŽ)
Bottom Left: 13th century church in Spodnja Muta (Koroška) (SF)
Bottom Right: Stork nesting on a telephone pole at Bogojina (Prekmurje) (SF)

Continue southward along Stanetova ulica, past the **Banka Celje** building designed by Jože Plečnik in 1929 and the spot where the town gates stood in the Middle Ages. The shop on the corner of Prešernova ulica was once the **Merkur coffee house**, the most important gathering spot for Celje intellectuals in the 19th century. Prešernova ulica leads to Krekov trg with the **Evropa Hotel**, Celje's oldest, and **Celje Hall**, the social centre for the city's German citizens at the turn of the century.

South along Razlagova ulica, you'll pass a medieval **defence tower** on the right and, about 150 metres farther on, the **Water Tower**, part of the city wall and ramparts and built between 1451 and 1473. Many of the blocks used are of Roman origin.

From the Savinja embankment, at the point where the old **Capuchin Bridge** once stood, there's an excellent view of **Celje Castle** on an escarpment to the south-east. Directly opposite is **City Park**, the **Capuchin Church of St Cecilia** in Breg and, high up on the hill, the **Church of St Nicholas**.

A walk up to the castle, Slovenia's largest, via a footpath from Cesta na Grad, takes about half an hour from here. The castle was originally built in the early 13th century and went through several transformations, especially under the Counts of Celje in the 14th and 15th centuries. When the castle lost its strategic importance, it was left to deteriorate and subsequent owners used the stone blocks to build other structures, including parts of the Lower Castle and the Old County Palace. A surprisingly large portion remains intact, however, and has been restored, including the 35-metre-high **Frederick Tower**. The castle has a small display room and a restaurant.

On your way back to the Old Town, you can walk up to Nicholas Hill for a wonderful view of the castle, the Old Town and the Savinja River or explore the Breg area. Some 90 steps at Breg 2 lead to the Church of St Cecilia. The Germans used the nearby monastery (now apartments) as a prison during WW II. Between the church and the City Park off Maistrova ulica is the reconstructed

Roman **Temple of Hercules** dating from the 2nd century.

Back on the left bank of the Savinja, a birch-lined park on the embankment has a **lapidarium** of Roman remains unearthed in the Celje area. Just behind it at Muzejski trg 1a is the 16th century **Old County Palace**, a Renaissance building with a two-level arcade around a courtyard. The palace contains the **Celje Regional Museum**.

Needless to say, the museum places much emphasis on Celeia and the Counts of Celje, right down to exhibiting 18 of the nobles' skulls in glass cases. (They were taken from the Minorite church in 1956 and may be returned there soon. The one of Count Ulric is gruesome.) The museum has 13 rooms, many of them done up in styles from different periods (Baroque, neoclassical, Biedemeier, Secessionist), painted with various scenes and filled with fine furniture. Don't miss the 18th century cabinet with hunting scenes inlaid with ivory, the 20-drawer 'bank' desk and the neoclassical clock/music box that still works. But the museum's main draw is the **Celje Ceiling**, an enormous trompe l'oeil painting in the main hall of columns, towers, frolicking angels, noblemen and ladies looking down at you looking up. Completed in about 1600 by a Polish artist, the mural meant to lift the ceiling up to the sky and it does just that. Other panels represent the four seasons and show scenes from Roman and Greek mythology. The museum is open from 9 am to noon and from 2 to 4 pm from Tuesday to Friday and till noon at the weekend. The entry fee is 150 SIT.

Trg Celskih Knezov leads north from the western end of Muzejski trg. At the start of the square you'll find the **Lower Castle**, built in the 14th century as a residence for the Celje counts, and at No 9 the **Narodni Dom** (National Hall), the cultural and social centre for Celje's Slovenes at the turn of the century. Both buildings now contain art galleries open from 10 am till 1 pm and 4 to 6 pm Tuesday to Friday and on Saturday morning.

Walking eastward along Prešernova ulica,

you'll pass the **Museum of Modern History** in the former Town Hall building (1830) at No 17. The museum, which gives glory to our friends, the Counts of Celje, has a hodge-podge of items from WW II and – egad! – a dental surgeon's collection. It is open Tuesday to Friday from 10 am to 5 pm and on Saturady from 9 am till noon. It closes in August.

Opposite the museum is the **Minorite Church of Mary**, where the bones of the Celje counts were once stored and where they may yet rest again. Above the doorway leading from the nave into the sacristry is a relief depicting the Madonna and Child and counts Herman I and Herman II.

Prešernova ulica leads to Stanetova ulica, which takes you south to Glavni trg, the heart of the Old Town. It is filled with lovely 17th and 18th century town houses and, in summer, outdoor cafés. In the centre of the square, where a pillory once stood, is the requisite **plague pillar** dedicated to Mary (1776).

In Slomškov trg, a few steps to the south-east, you'll find the **Abbey Church of St Daniel** dating from the early 14th century. The church has some magnificent frescoes and tombstones, but its most important piece of art is the 15th century Pietà in the **Chapel of the Sorrowful Mother**. The walls are decorated with carved stone and the vaults with frescoes are from the early 15th century.

Parts of Celje's **medieval walls and ramparts** can be seen along Ulica na Okopih, west of St Daniel's Church.

Activities

There are a couple of open-air swimming pools behind the Merx hotel on Ljubljanska cesta and an indoor one at the Celje Fair Centre at Dečkova cesta 1 north-east of the Old Town. If you're not satisfied with these, you might consider a day trip 10 km south to the spa at **Laško**, a town equally celebrated for the beer brewed here since 1825 and a castle called **Tabor**. Some Slovenes say the gourmet restaurant at the castle is the country's finest.

The Šeško Riding Center (☎ 778 282) at

Socka (house No 33), 15 km north of Celje, has horses available for hire for experienced riders and offers lessons to beginners. The centre is in stunning countryside on the edge of the Pohorje Massif. It is open in summer from 8 to 11 am and 4 to 8 pm and in winter from 9 am to noon and from 2 to 6 pm.

The *Celje Guide* lists a number of walks and hikes into the surrounding countryside lasting between one and four hours. The longest one leads south-east to **Mount Tovst** (834 metres) and the picturesque village of **Svetina** via the Celjska Koča mountain hut. This can also be done by car or bike (28 km).

The Oldtimer Train, run by Slovenijaturist, has excursions from time to time between Ljubljana and Ormož via Celje and Ptuj. See Slovenijaturist at the train station for details.

Places to Stay

The tourist office has a few *private rooms* on its accommodation list ranging in price from DM24 to DM30 per person including breakfast. It may also have information about *dormitory rooms* at the Dijaški Dom (☎ 28 013), at Ljubljanska cesta 21, some 300 metres west of Dairy Queen.

The cheapest hotel in Celje is the 76-room *Celeia* (☎ 29 141), an ugly, nine-storey brick block opposite the bus station at Mariborska cesta 3. Singles and doubles with shared shower and breakfast are DM30 and DM50. If you want your own shower, add DM5 and DM10 respectively.

The evocatively named *Turška Mačka* (Turkish Cat) (☎ 21 041; fax 28 521), a 25-room guesthouse hard by the Slovenian People's Theatre at Gledališka ulica 5, is the nicest place to stay in Celje, with small but comfortable rooms, a good restaurant and friendly staff. Singles with shower, TV and breakfast are DM45, doubles DM80.

The *Evropa* (☎ 21 233; fax 24 126), an historical hotel with 80 rooms, has seen better days and, despite its good location near the train station at Krekov trg 4, is a gloomy and depressing place. Singles with breakfast, shower and TV are DM50, doubles DM90.

The far-flung *Merx* hotel (☎ 21 917; fax

21 401), at Ljubljanska cesta 39, with only 36 beds may not be very convenient to the Old Town, but it is as close as you'll get to the Savinja River and there are public swimming pools behind it. Singles with shower and breakfast are DM55, doubles are DM80.

Places to Eat

There's a very basic (and very cheap) self-service restaurant called *Nana* at Stanetova ulica 17, open from 8 am till 8 pm. Two pizza places almost opposite one another at the eastern end of Prešernova ulica can be recommended. *Majolika* at No 3 is open daily from 9 am to 9 pm. *Koper* at No 2 has both pizza and pasta dishes. It is open weekdays from 9 am to 7 pm and on Saturday from 11 am to 2 pm.

The *Ojstrica* at Ljubljanska cesta 5 is one of the oldest eateries in Celje but its claims to fame (it was the meeting place of an important Slovenian cultural society in the late 19th century) do nothing for the food. If you want something a bit more recent, cross Jurčičeva ulica to the new *Dairy Queen* where a meal (of sorts) will set you back about 600 SIT. It's open till 11 pm (9 pm on Sunday).

One of the most interesting places in Celje is the *Gostišče Špital*, a small, tastefully decorated restaurant attached to a medieval hospice church at Slomškov trg 5. It's open from 5 pm to midnight every day but Sunday. Another up-market place is the *Madrugada* cellar restaurant at Stanetova uliva 4. This would be a good place to try some of the better whites from the Ljutomer wine-growing region to the east of Celje.

There's an outdoor *market* selling fresh fruit, vegetables and other foodstuffs on the corner of Savinova ulica and Linhartova ulica behind the Minorite church.

Entertainment

The *Slovenian People's Theatre* at Gledališki trg 5 stages six plays a season, not always in Slovene. The box office (☎ 25 332) is open weekdays from 9 to 11 pm and from 5 to 7 pm.

A couple of popular discos are *Jungle* in the north-western suburb of Lava (house No 7) and *Casablanca* at the Celje Fair Centre at Dečkova cesta 1. The *pub* next door to the Dairy Queen is a popular hangout for Celje young bloods.

Getting There & Away

Bus For places like Šempeter, Škofja Vas and Šentjur, go to the bus stops south of the train station on Ulica XIV Divizije.

Intercity buses, which leave from the main station, run at least once an hour to Dobrna, Hrastnik, Laško, Ljubljana, Maribor, Rimske Toplice, Rogaška Slatina, Slovenske Konjice and Velenje. Other destinations accessible by bus from Celje and their daily frequencies include: Bled (one); Bistrica ob Sotli (nine); Brežice (one); Črnomelj (one); Črna (two); Dravograd (three); Gornji Grad (three); Koper (five); Kranj (two); Krško (five); Lendava on the Hungarian border (four); Logar Valley (Logarska Dolina; four); Murska Sobota (eight); Mozirje (eight); Nova Gorica (two); Novo Mesto (one); Ormož (three); Piran (five); Podčetrtek (nine); Ptuj (five); Sevnica (two); and Zreče (three). International destinations include Varaždin in Croatia (two a day) and Lenti in Hungary (on Tuesday and Thursday).

Train Celje is one of the few rail hubs in Slovenia and for once you have a real choice between taking the train and bus. Celje is on the line linking Zidani Most (connections to and from Ljubljana and Zagreb) with Maribor and the Austrian cities of Graz and Vienna. From Ljubljana (89 km; 1½ hours) you can reach Celje up to two dozen times a day, and there are just as many services from Celje for to Maribor (67 km; 70 minutes).

Another line links Celje with Velenje (38 km; 70 minutes) via Šempeter up to 10 times a day in each direction. A third one connects Celje with Zabok in Croatia via Rogaška Slatina (36 km; 50 minutes), Rogatec and Dobovec. Up to six trains arrive and depart each day.

Car Kompas and Globtour rent cars.

Getting Around

Parking can be difficult in Celje's Old Town and you will have to pay for the privilege: 600 SIT per day. To summon a local taxi ring ☎ 442 200.

AROUND CELJE

Šempeter (pop 3935)

Some 12 km west of Celje and accessible by bus and train, Šempeter is the site of a **Roman necropolis** reconstructed between 1952 and 1966. The burial ground contains four complete tombs and scores of columns, steles and fragments carved with portraits, mythological creatures and scenes from daily life.

The marble stones, quarried in the Pohorje near Slovenska Bistrica between the 1st and 3rd centuries, were washed away and buried during flooding in the Savinja River in 268 AD. They have been divided into about two dozen groups linked by footpaths.

The **oldest tomb** (No I) was commissioned by Gallus Vindonius, a Celtic nobleman who lived on a nearby estate in the 1st century, while the largest is the **Priscianus tomb** (No II) raised in honour of a Roman official and his son. (Notice the kidnapping scene on the side relief.) But the most beautiful is the **Ennius tomb** (No III), with reliefs of animals and, on the front panel, the princess Europa riding a bull. If you compare these three with the more recent tomb erected in honour of Secundanius in about 250 AD, it is obvious that Roman power and wealth in these parts was already very much on the decline in the mid-3rd century.

The necropolis is open daily from 8 am to 6 pm and costs 200 SIT to visit. There's a small bistro called *Rosa* near the entrance, but if you want something more substantial, try the *Gostišče Štorman*, one of the first private restaurants to open in Slovenia during the Tito years. It's Šempeter at house No 5a, about two km east of the site on the road to Celje, and is open from 7 am till midnight except on the first Sunday of every month.

UPPER SAVINJA VALLEY

The Upper Savinja Valley (Zgornja Savinjska Dolina) refers to the drainage areas and tributaries of the Savinja River from its source in the eastern Savinja Alps to a gorge at Letuš, some 12 km north-west of Šempeter. Bounded by forests, ancient churches, traditional farmhouses and Alpine peaks of more than 2000 metres, the valley is a land of incomparable beauty. And there's activities here to suit every taste – from hiking, mountain biking and rock climbing to fishing, kayaking and swimming in the Savinja.

The Savinja begins its rapid flow above Rinka, at 90 metres Slovenia's highest waterfall, enters the Logar Valley (Logarska Dolina) and continues past isolated hamlets and farmland. The region beyond the gorge at Ljubno is quite different, with a number of towns – really overgrown villages – of historical importance, including Radmirje, Gornji Grad, Nazarje and Mozirje.

Tools found in a cave at Mt Olševa, north-west of Solčava village, suggest that the Upper Savinja Valley was inhabited during the Stone Age, and remains of three Roman settlements have been unearthed around Mozirje. The valley has been exploited for its timber since the Middle Ages, and until WW II the Savinja was used to power some 200 sawmills. Raftsmen transported the timber from Ljubno to Mozirje and Celje and some of the logs reached as far as Romania. The trade brought wealth and special rights to the valley, evident from the many fine buildings still standing.

The following itinerary follows the 45-km valley road from Mozirje to Rinka Waterfall, with a side trip to Radmirje and Gornji Grad. It can be done by bus or car but it is tailor-made for a bicycle trip.

Orientation & Information

The small English-language brochure entitled *Zgornja Savinjska Dolina – The Short Guidebook* is helpful if you intend spending a fair bit of time in the area. It lists numerous trails, the best places for rock climbing, isolated farmhouses with accommodation etc.

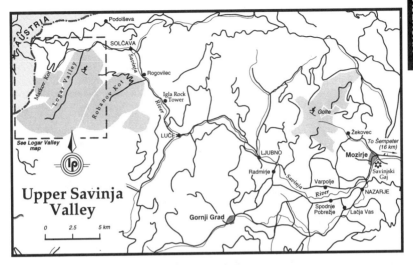

Upper Savinja Valley

0   2.5   5 km

Serious hikers should pick up a copy of the 1:50 000 map *Savinjska Dolina in Širša Okolica* (Savinja Valley and Surrounding Districts).

In Mozirje, the Turist guesthouse (☎ 831 022), at Na Trgu 32, is also a travel agency and can provide information. Ljubljanska Banka has a branch in the centre of town at Na Trgu 9. The post office is 200 metres to the south around the bend in the road, and the bus station just beyond that.

In Nazarje there's a Ljubljanska Banka in the complex next to Vrbovec Castle open from 8 to 11 am and 1 to 3 pm on weekdays and on Saturday morning.

In Gornji Grad, the little kiosk near the courtyard behind the massive Baroque church houses a tourist information centre. Buses stop in Attemsov trg, the main square in front of the church. The post office is nearby at house No 79. It is open weekdays from 8 am to 2 pm and on Saturday till noon.

There's an information office at the entrance to Logar Valley Regional Park. All buses stop here before continuing on to the falls.

The telephone code for all the towns and areas listed here is 063.

Things to See & Do

Mozirje The administrative centre of the Upper Savinja Valley on the river's left bank, Mozirje (pop 1900) is a town with a long history yet it has little to show for its past except for the much rebuilt Gothic **Church of St George** at the western end of Na Trgu. You might walk over to **Savinjski Gaj**, a botanical park with a new **open-air ethnographic museum** south of town across the river (open April to October) or in winter continue four km north-west to Žekovec, where a cable car runs to the ski centre at **Golte** (☎ 831 111), with slopes at up to 1500 metres. Otherwise, there's little to hold you in this one-horse town.

Nazarje The town of 'Nazareth' (pop 1835) is two km due south of Mozirje on the Savinja. **Vrbovec Castle**, a 15th century pile at the confluence of the Savinja and Dreta rivers, has a couple of enormous towers; today the castle houses a music school and offices of a logging company, the industry that built Nazarje.

Towering above the town, on Gradišče Hill, is the **Franciscan monastery** and its **Church of the Virgin Mary**, which were all but flattened by Allied bombs during WW II but have since been rebuilt. The twin-spired church has a choir loft with fine grill work; the original chapel, built by Bishop Tomaž Hren of Ljubljana in the early 17th century, now serves as the presbytery. The monastery, now inhabited by an order of nuns, has a lovely garden surrounded by an arcaded courtyard. You can drive up to the monastery or climb the 193 steps that lead here.

The Burger Horse Riding Centre (☎ 831 265) at Lačja Vas, in a beautiful valley three km south-west of Nazarje, has horses for rent. Carriage rides are also available if there are enough of you.

Radmirje The road to Radmirje (pop 440), a village some nine km to the west, is very picturesque with hayracks, little white churches and stone farmhouses larger than most in Slovenia. About 500 metres before the turn to Radmirje, the Prodnik Sport Centre (☎ 841 504) organises canoe and kayak trips on the Savinja and rents equipment.

Radmirje is famous for two churches. The **Church of St Michael** in the centre of town dates from the late 14th century. The **Church of St Francis Xavier**, on Straža Hill southwest of the centre, has been rebuilt several times over the centuries; the present structure is only about 200 years old. St Francis was established as a pilgrimage church by the bishop of Gornji Grad during a period of great fires and the plague. European monarchs paid homage to the site and the church's rich **treasury** contains Mass vestments presented by the kings of Poland and France and a gold chalice from Empress Maria Theresa. There's an old road marker *(znamenje)* with folk paintings in the little valley below the church.

Gornji Grad This windy town (pop 1845), in the Zadrečka Valley some six km southwest of Radmirje, was the site of a large castle until the last days of WW II when it was flattened. Today all that is left is the entrance to the fortification.

Gornji Grad (Oberburg in German) was associated for centuries with the Ljubljana diocese. The former **Benedictine monastery**, for example, was converted into a manor house for Ljubljana's bishops in the 15th century. Today one of its towers contains a small **folk collection** with everyday objects relating to life on the Menina Planina, an area of mountain pastures and slopes south of Gornji Grad.

In the same complex, the **Church of Sts Hermagoras & Fortunatus**, one of the largest Baroque churches in Slovenia, was built in the mid-18th century and modelled after Ljubljana's cathedral. Its enormous 55-metre dome notwithstanding, the interior of the church is surprisingly light and airy. The altar pictures by the 18th century Austrian Baroque artist Martin Johann Kremser-Schmidt (1718-1801) are especially fine. Outside, near the entrance, are bits and pieces from an earlier church, including a 16th century altar. The fountain in the courtyard still appears to be a meeting place for local people.

Ljubno After this town the Upper Savinja Valley begins to feel truly alpine with the mountains so close you can almost touch them and the houses built entirely of wood. The road continues along the winding Savinja, past wooden foot bridges, more hayracks and, in a gorge four km beyond **Luče**, a curious rock tower called **Igla** (Needle). Just before **Rogovilec**, the usual starting point for canoe and kayak trips on the Savinja, there's a turn south to **Robanov Kot**, a pristine valley and protected area with trails and farmhouse accommodation.

To the north-east of Robanov Kot below Mt Raduha (2062 metres) there's an ice cave called **Snežna Jama** (actually 'Snow Cave') open to the public at the weekend in summer. It is accessible by car via a forest road.

Solčava The highest town in the valley (642 metres), Solčava has some road markers with folk icons and painted barns. To the north is the Alpine village of **Podolševa**, where you can spend the night. The road from Solčava to Podolševa that continues west to the Church of the Holy Spirit and down into the Logar Valley is one of the most panoramic in the country.

Logar Valley Most of the Logar Valley – eight km long and only 500 metres wide – has been a regional park since 1987. This 'pearl of the Alpine region' is a wonderful place to explore for a few days with more than 30 natural attractions such as caves, springs, peaks and waterfalls.

The park is open every day year round, but cars entering between May and September must pay 300 SIT; cyclists, hikers and bus passengers get in free. A single road goes past a small chapel and through the woods to **Rinka Waterfall**, the main event here, but there are plenty of trails to explore and something like 20 more falls in the area. The bottom of Rinka Waterfall is only about 10 minutes from the car park, and you can climb to the top in about 20 minutes. It's not very difficult but it can get slippery; you'll probably encounter several people using ski poles for balance. From the top of the falls to the west you can see three peaks reaching higher than 2200 metres: Kranjska Rinka, Koroška

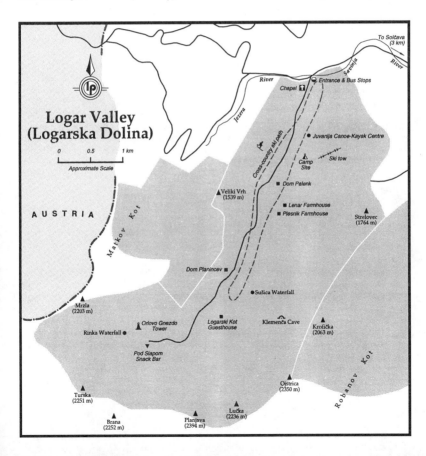

Logar Valley (Logarska Dolina)

0   0.5   1 km
Approximate Scale

To Solčava (3 km)

River

Savinja River

Entrance & Bus Stops

Chapel

Jezera

Cross-country ski path

Juvanija Canoe-Kayak Centre

Camp Site

Ski tow

Veliki Vrh (1539 m)

Dom Palenk

Lenar Farmhouse

Plesnik Farmhouse

Strelovec (1764 m)

AUSTRIA

Makov Kot

Dom Planincev

Sušica Waterfall

Mrzla (2203 m)

Orlovo Gnezdo Tower

Logarski Kot Guesthouse

Klemenča Cave

Krofička (2063 m)

Rinka Waterfall

Pod Slapom Snack Bar

Robanov Kot

Turska (2251 m)

Ojstrica (2350 m)

Brana (2252 m)

Planjava (2394 m)

Lučka (2236 m)

Rinka and Štajerska Rinka. Until 1918 they formed the triple border of Carniola (Kranjska), Carinthia (Koroška) and Styria (Štajerska).

About 1200 metres from the entrance of the park is the Juvanija Canoe-Kayak Centre (☎ 840 071), which organises trips, gives lessons and rents equipment. The Lenar farmhouse, to the south at Logarska Dolina (house No 11), has horses for rent (600 SIT per hour for lone riders or 900 SIT with a guide), which is an excellent way to explore the valley. Opposite Dom Planincev is a trail leading to **Sušica Waterfall** and **Klemenča Cave**.

Another magnificent and much less explored valley, the six-km-long **Matkov Kot**, runs parallel to Logar Valley and Austria. You can reach here by road by turning west as you leave the Logar Valley. Some think this valley was once a lake. There are several farmhouses with accommodation.

Places to Stay & Eat

In Mozirje, the *Turist* guesthouse (☎ 831 022) at Na Trgu 32 has 12 double rooms priced at between DM12 and DM15, depending on whether you want your own shower or not. The *Turist* restaurant is a simple but inexpensive affair; for something better try the *Gaj* restaurant at the botanical garden. The *Levec* farmhouse (☎ 831 861), not far from Savinjski Gaj in Loke (house No 19), has seven rooms and is open all year.

Some three km west of Nazarje, you'll find a couple of *camp sites* on opposite sides of the river that charge between DM7 and DM10 per person. *Menina* (☎ 831 787) is in Varpolje on the left bank while *Savinja* (☎ 831 463) is in Spodnje Pobrežje on the right. The owners of the Savinja have rooms available at the *Petrin* farmhouse in Spodnje Pobrežje at house No 11. In Nazarje, the *Grad Vrbovec* restaurant is in the new complex next to the castle on Savinjska cesta.

In Gornji Grad, the 30-bed *Trobej* guesthouse (☎ 842 006) at Attemsov trg 12 has double rooms with showers for DM50. There's a decent *pizzeria* at Attemsov trg 25, but if you need something more substantial, try *Gostilna Pri Jošku* at Gornji Grad 77, one of the oldest traditional eateries in Slovenia. Its specialities are boiled beef with horseradish and *žlikrofi* (Slovenian 'ravioli' made with cheese, bacon and chives). Pri Jošku is open daily except Wednesday till 10 pm.

In the Logar Valley, the *Trik* camp site lies about 1.5 km from the park entrance. About the same distance farther south two farmhouses – *Lenar* (☎ 846 500) at Logarska Dolina (house No 11) and *Plesnik* (☎ 846 501) at (house No 13) – have simple rooms available all year. *Logarski Kot* guesthouse, about two km from Rinka Waterfall, is an attractive little place under a cliff face with rooms for 900 SIT per person (or 2200 SIT including all meals). There is no shortage of restaurants either. *Dom Palenk* (☎ 846 088), near the two farmhouses, is a bit up-market, while *Dom Planincev* (☎ 846 096), three km from Rinka, has a much more relaxed, rustic feel. Both also have accommodation. There's a simple snack bar called *Pod Slapom* near the Rinka car park and another in a tall wooden tower called *Orlovo Gnezdo* overlooking the falls.

Getting There & Away

From Mozirje, there is bus service to Celje, Gornji Grad, Nova Štifta and Velenje. Up to four buses a day originating in Celje continue along the valley road to the Logar Valley and the trail to Rinka Waterfall.

From Gornji Grad, buses go to Celje (three a day), Kamnik (up to five), Ljubljana (five), Ljubno (four), Maribor (one), Mozirje (10), and Velenje (two). There's an early morning bus on Sunday from Gornji Grad to Logar Valley (Logarska Dolina) from May to September only.

Koroška

Koroška (Carinthia in English, Kärnten in German) is Slovenia's smallest province – and a mere shadow of what it once was. Until the end of WW I, Carinthia included a very large area as well as the cities of Klagenfurt (Celovec) and Villach (Beljak) now in Austria.

In the plebiscite ordered by the victorious Allies after WW I, Slovenes living on the other side of the Karavanke, the 120-km-long rock wall that separates much of north-west and north-central Slovenia from Austria, voted to put their economic future in the hands of Vienna while the mining region around the Mežica River and two other valleys went to Slovenia. Understandably, the results of that vote have never sat very well with the Slovenes on the southern side of the mountains. In fact, under the communist regime, school children were taught a very different version of what actually took place in 1920.

The fact remains that the Slovenian nation lost 90,000 of its nationals to Austria (along with 400,000 to Italy and 5000 to Hungary – one-third of its total population) and it still rankles. In one popular guide to Slovenian art and architecture published in Ljubljana, Slovenian Koroška is referred to as the 'Carinthian corner'.

Koroška has a special place in the hearts and minds of most Slovenes. Karantanija, the first Slovenian (and Slavic) state dating back to the 7th century, was centred here and the word 'Carinthia' is derived from that name. The region was heavily fortified with castles during the Middle Ages and, from the 12th century onward, was an important cultural and artistic centre. Development came to western Koroška in the early 19th century with the opening of the iron mines at Prevalje and Ravne na Koroškem, and in 1863 a railway linked Maribor with Klagenfurt via the mountain pass at Holmec. Ironically, Holmec was the site of the last battle fought during WW II.

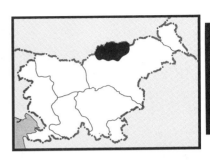

Koroška, a region of dark forests, mountains and highland meadows, is essentially just three valleys bounded by the Pohorje Massif on the east, the last of the Karavanke peaks (Mt Peca, where good King Matjaž is said to rest) on the west, and the hills of Kobansko to the north. The Drava Valley runs east to west and includes the towns of Dravograd, Muta and Vuzenica. The Mežica and Mislinja valleys fan out from the Drava; the former is an industrial area with towns like Ravne and Prevalje while the latter's main centre is Slovenj Gradec.

Koroška is an excellent area for outdoor activities, including skiing, flying, horse riding and especially hiking. The E6 European Hiking Trail running from the Baltic to the Adriatic enters Slovenia at Radlje, and the Slovenian Alpine Trail from Maribor to Ankaran passes through the heart of Koroška. Parts of these trails can be easily covered from many towns in the area.

SLOVENJ GRADEC (pop 6800)

Slovenj Gradec is not the capital of Koroška – that distinction goes to the industrial centre of Ravne to the north-west – but it is certainly the cultural and recreational centre of the province. A number of museums, galleries and historical churches line its main square, and the sporting facilities in the Pohorje Massif to the east are seemingly endless. It

is a wonderful place for a brief stopover en route to Štajerska or Austria.

The history of Slovenj Gradec is closely tied to Stari Trg, a suburb south-west of the Old Town where there was a Roman settlement called Colatio from the 1st to the 3rd centuries. At that time an important Roman road from Celeia (Celje) to Virunum (near Klagenfurt in Austria) passed through Colatio. A castle (called Grez) to the west of the Old Town is first mentioned in the late 11th century though a fort had probably stood on the site as early as the late Iron Age.

Slovenj Gradec came into its own when the settlement shifted to an area between the Mislinja and Suhodolnica rivers in the 12th century. It was an important trade centre in the Middle Ages and minted its own coins. Later it became an important cultural and artistic centre with many artisans and craft guilds. But the town did have its share of troubles: the Turks raided from the 15th century; the Mislinja Valley was ravaged by locusts in 1477; and Slovenj Gradec was captured by the Hungarians under King Matthias Corvinus, 11 years later.

Among the prominent Habsburg nobles based in Slovenj Gradec over the centuries were members of the Windisch-Grätz family, a variant of the German name for the town (Windisch Graz). Windisch was the German for 'Slovenian' until the 19th century. 'Gradec' is Slovene for 'Graz'.

Orientation

Slovenj Gradec's main street is Glavni trg, a colourful 'square' of old town houses and shops. Castle Hill and Stari Trg are to the west and south-west; the northern side of the Old Town is scarred by saw mills and paper factories.

The modern bus station is at Pohorska cesta 15 about 400 metres north-east of the tourist office. Slovenj Gradec is not on a train line.

Information

The tourist office (☎ 0602 41 940) at Glavni trg 24 can provide information, arrange accommodation and sells guides to the region, including the useful (but expensive at 1500 SIT) *Guide to Mislinjska Valley* in English. It is open weekdays from 8 am to 6 pm and from 9 am till noon on Saturday and Sunday. Kompas (☎ 0602 41 145), at Glavni trg 38, will answer general questions and book accommodation. They are open from 8 am to 1 pm and 4 to 6 pm weekdays and till noon on Saturday and Sunday.

Ljubljanska Banka at Glavni trg 30 is open from 7 am to 6 pm and till noon on Saturday and there's an A Banka branch in the former Rotenturn mansion at Šolska ulica 5. The post office is at the northern end of Glavni trg at Francetova cesta 1. It is open Monday to Friday from 8 am to 6 pm and till noon on Saturday.

Mladinska Knjiga bookshop, at Glavni trg 6, has regional maps if you've arrived in Koroška unprepared and want to do some hiking. It is open from 7.30 am to 6.30 pm weekdays and from 8.30 till noon on Saturday.

Slovenj Gradec's telephone code has four digits: 0602. The postcode is 62380.

Things to See

The **Gallery of Fine Arts** and the **Koroška Regional Museum** are housed in the former town hall building at Glavni trg 24 above the tourist office. Admission to both of these is 100 SIT.

The regional museum, open from 9 am to 6 pm Tuesday through Friday and till noon on Saturday, has exhibits on the 2nd floor devoted to the history of Slovenj Gradec and the Koroška region – from local sport heroes' awards and farm implements to models of wartime hospital rooms and schools – and a very good archaeological collection on the ground floor. Most of the town hall deals with the Roman settlement of Colatio and includes jewellery and other effects taken from a Slavic burial ground at Puščava near Castle Hill. This part of the town hall served as a German prison during WW II.

The gallery, which is open on the same days as the regional museum but closes between noon and 3 pm on weekdays, is on the 1st floor. It has rotating exhibits but counts among its permanent collection African folk art, bronze sculptures by Franc Berneker (1874-1932) and naive paintings by Jože Tisnikar (1928-). Tisnikar is among

the most interesting and original artists in Slovenia, and his obsession with corpses, distorted figures and oversized crickets (perhaps inspired by that locust attack in the late 15th century) is at once disturbing and funny. Don't miss *Rojstva in Smrt (Birth and Death)* and *Stopala (Feet)*. The paintings are all very black and blue.

The interesting **sculpture** in the courtyard is of the French poet Guillaume Apollinaire done by Ossip Zadkine in 1946. Outside the Town Hall is the odd, life-size **Venetian Horse** by contemporary sculptor Oskar Kogoj. It is becoming something of a symbol for the town.

The items on display at the **Sokli\u010d Museum**, in the rectory at Trg Svobode 5, were amassed by Jakob Soklič (1893-1972), a pack-rat priest who began squirrelling away bits and bobs in his 40s. Among the mediocre watercolours and oils of peasant idylls and the umpteen portraits of Hugo Wolf (a Slovenian composer who was born at Glavni trg 40 in 1860) are green goblets and beakers from nearby Glažuta, an important glass-manufacturing town in the 19th century, local embroidery and linen, religious artefacts and some 18th century furniture. The statue of a saint holding a chalice with a snake coming out of it represents St John the Evangelist. (In quite a reversed role for a biblical reptile, a serpent once warned the apostle that he was about to quaff poisoned wine.) The museum is opened on request; ask at the regional museum or the tourist office.

The sombre **Church of St Elizabeth** (1251), the town's oldest structure, is at the end of Trg Svobode. But aside from the Romanesque nave and a couple of windows, most everything here is Baroque, including the massive gold altar and the altar paintings done by local artist Franc Mihael Strauss (1647-1740) and his son Janez Andrej Strauss (1721-82). Far more interesting is the 15th century **Church of the Holy Spirit** next door with an interior covered with Gothic frescoes. The 27 panels on the north wall represent the Passion of Christ; the scenes on the archway are of the Final Judgement. As

Slovenj Gradec

0   100   200 m

PLACES TO STAY

4 Pohorje Hotel
15 Kompas Hotel

PLACES TO EAT

1 Pizzerija Turist
10 Pri Grofu Restaurant

OTHER

2 Bus Station
3 Post Office
5 Crafts Market
6 Pod Velbom Bar/Café
7 Mladinska Knjiga Bookshop
8 A Banka
9 Rotenturn Mansion
11 Tourist Office/Museums
12 Ljubljanska Banka
13 Perger Shop
14 Kompas Travel Agency
16 Soklič Museum
17 Church of St Elizabeth
18 Church of the Holy Spirit

always, the most disturbing frescoes are those of the devil leading the damned down, down, down...

Stari Trg, where the Romans once frolicked, is nothing but an empty field now, but on Castle Hill (530 metres) there is the 13th century **Parish Church of St Pancras**, the oldest church hall in the country, with a bell tower that is part of the 17th century fortifications. Castle Hill is about a 25-minute walk north-west from Stari Trg; just follow the **Calvary** and its Baroque **Stations of the Cross** up the hill. If you continue along the path past the church you'll reach Puščava.

Activities

There are plenty of opportunities for recreation near the airfield in Mislinjska Dobrava some six km south-east of Slovenj Gradec; take the Velenje road for five km and then turn east for another 800 metres. The bus to Mislinja or Velenje will drop you off along the main road.

First you'll come to the Slovenj Gradec Riding Club (☎ 53 547), which has horses for riding both within the hippodrome and cross-country, and some tennis courts. Next is the Koroška Aeroclub (☎ 53 630), which offers 10-minute sightseeing flights of the

Mislinja Valley for 2500 SIT for one person (4800 SIT for up to three), 15-minute flights of Ravne, Velenje and Dravograd for 3700 SIT (6900 SIT for three) and 20-minute flights over Mozirje and Radlje for 4800 SIT for one person (9000 SIT for three).

Three ski slopes are within striking distance of Slovenj Gradec but the closest is Kope, 1380 metres above the Mislinja Valley on the western edge of the Pohorje Massif. The ski grounds have nine km of runs and seven lifts on Mala Kopa and Velika Kopa peaks. To reach Kope, follow the Velenje road for three km and turn west. The ski area is another 13 km at the end of the road. The town runs special ski buses in winter, depending on the snowfall.

The *Guide to the Mislinjska Valley* outlines a number of hikes and bicycle trips in the area, including sections of the E6 and Slovenian Alpine trails. Pohorje is unique in Slovenia in that there is no real 'off-season' for hiking; the meadows and paths are generally as good in the winter as they are in summer.

The Slovenian Alpine Trail passes through Stari Trg and the centre of Slovenj Gradec before continuing up to Mala Kopa (1524 metres) where it meets the E6. There is a mountain hut here – *Partizanski Dom* (☎ 53 415) – and it is open all year. The E6 heads north through Vuhred and Radlje to Austria while the Slovenian Alpine Trail carries on eastward to Rogla and Maribor. There is more accommodation at Velika Kopa (1543 metres) in the *Grmovškov Dom* (☎ 53 410), which is open all year as well. If you are going to do a fair amount of hiking in the western Pohorje, pick up a copy of the 1:50 000-scale map *Pohorje-Zahodni Del* before setting out.

Festivals

The Gallery of Fine Arts hosts an exhibition of folk crafts and art in early June, and there is a bonfire and celebration on Midsummer Night (Kresna Noč) on 23 June.

Places to Stay

The *Medeni Raj* camp site (☎ 53 483) is just

beyond the airfield in Mislinjska Dobrava. 'Sweet Paradise' is a small, friendly place set among pine trees and costs DM10 per person. The camp site also has bungalows (DM40 single including breakfast, DM60 double) and the small restaurant is open till 10 pm.

The tourist office can arrange accommodation in *private rooms* both in and out of town for about DM20 per person, but their list is very short.

By now the 24-room *Pohorje* hotel (☎ 42 291), above the dumpy Pohorje restaurant on Glavni trg, may have reopened. If not, the only hotel option in town is the 60-room *Kompas* (☎ 42 295; fax 43 179) at Glavni trg 43. Singles with shower and breakfast are 3200 SIT, doubles 5600 SIT and small suites are 7800 SIT. The rooms are no great shakes and the dark corridors seem to go on forever, but some of the public areas, including a pleasant courtyard out back, have been redone.

Places to Eat

The *Pizzerija Turist* at Francetova cesta 14 serves something round and doughy with tomato sauce on top, but you wouldn't want to call it pizza. Still, it's cheap enough and the people are friendly. It's open till 9.30 pm. *Gostilna Murko*, about 400 metres north at Francetova cesta 24, is a rather chi-chi establishment popular with Austrian tourists on the move. It's open daily till 10 pm.

The fanciest place in Slovenj Gradec for a meal is *Pri Grofu*, in the former Rotenturn Mansion at Šolska ulica 5. It has seating both inside (naff 'knight's hall' decor) and outside in a lovely arcaded courtyard with a fountain. But don't expect Slovenian specialities here: this is definitely the cordon-bleu-pork-with-gorgonzola school of cooking. Pri Grofu is open daily except Mondays (and Sundays in July and August) from noon till midnight.

If you've got wheels, a farmhouse restaurant called *Tina*, about four km north-west of Slovenj Gradec in Gmajna (house No 30), is an excellent choice. Among the specialities of the house is obara z ajdovimi žganci, a rich stew with buckwheat groats. In Stari Trg at

house No 251, *Na Klancu* has fish specialities and wine from its own vineyard.

Entertainment

If you're interested in chatting up Austrian
business people, head for the *nightclub* at the
Kompas hotel between 10 pm and 3 am.
Otherwise, one of the best places for meeting
people is the *Pod Velbom* bar and café at the
start of Poštna ulica. It attracts a young
crowd.

Things to Buy

Basketry, a speciality of this region, and
other local crafts are on sale at a small market
on the corner of Poštna ulica and Glavni trg.
A shop called Perger at Glavni trg 32 has a
good range of honey, heart-shaped honey
cakes, candles and other products produced
in part by our little stinging friends.

Getting There & Away

Buses are very frequent to Črna, Dravograd,
Mislinja, Radlje, Ravne na Koroškem and
Velenje. Other destinations served by bus
from Slovenj Gradec include: Celje (three a
day); Gornji Grad (one); Ljubljana (six);
Legen (eight); Maribor (eight); Piran (one);
Sele (three); and Vuhred (four).

DRAVOGRAD (pop 3500)

Situated on the left bank of the Drava,
Slovenia's second-longest river (144 km),
'Drava Castle' is much smaller than its sister
city 12 km to the south but just as old, with
a recorded history that dates back to the 12th
century. It was then that the castle, the ruins
of which can be seen on the hill to the north
of town, was built. Situated on a bend in the
Drava at the point where the smaller Meža
and Mislinja rivers flow into it, the castle and
the town were of great strategic importance
for centuries.

Today, Dravograd is a sleepy place with
few sights of its own. But it is a good springboard for exploring the Kobansko Hills to
the north and the Drava Valley to the east.
The Austrian border (crossing at Vič-

Rabenstein) is just 3.5 km north-west of
Dravograd.

Orientation & Information

While Dravograd's historical centre and its
main street, Trg 4 Julija, is on the left bank
of the Drava, the train and bus stations and
the town's only hotel are about one km to the
south-east on the right bank.

Dravograd has no tourist office, but the
friendly staff at the Košenjak hotel can help.
Ljubljanska Banka has a branch at Trg 4
Julija 42, open from 7 am to 6 pm and till
noon on Saturday. The post office is at the
eastern end of Trg Julija just before you cross
the Drava. It is open from 8 am to 6 pm and
till noon on Saturday.

Dravograd's telephone code is the same as
Slovenj Gradec's: 0602. The postcode is
62370.

Things to See & Do

The **Church of St Vitus**, at the western end
of Trg 4 Julija, is one of the most important
Romanesque buildings extant in Slovenia.
Built in the second half of the 12th century
and only recently renovated, it is a solid
structure of light brown stone with a high
tower between the nave and the small circular presbytery. While the occupants in the
house next door are more than happy to hand
over the key, there's not much to see inside
except for a beamed ceiling and a fresco of
Sts Cyril and Methodius. The church is used
almost exclusively for wedding ceremonies;
Mass is said only on the patron's feast day in
June. The Gothic-style **Church of St John**,
on a bend in the Drava a short distance to the
west of St Vitus, has a fine Baroque interior.

The basement of the **town hall**, at Trg 4
Julija 7, was used as a Gestapo prison and
torture chamber during WW II and its five
cells have now been converted into a
Museum of Nazi Terror open weekday
mornings. The hydroelectric dam on the
Drava nearest Dravograd was built by
German soldiers during the war, and many
of them were lodged in town. The remains of
a bombed out bridge run parallel to a new
one over the Drava.

It's an easy hike north from Dravograd to the **castle ruins** (really just a wall) but the energetic may want to carry on farther into the Kobansko Hills, where you might encounter some traditional charcoal makers. A circular section of the Kozjak Mountain Trail leads north past Goriški Vrh to Mt Košenjak (1522 metres) and returns to Dravograd via Ojstrica. A lodge is under construction near Košenjak; ask at the hotel or the tourist office in Slovenj Gradec whether it is now accepting guests.

Festivals
A mock 'country wedding' (Koroška Ohcet) used to be staged in July in Dravograd. Though aimed at tourists, it attracted enough local people to at least give it something of a party feel. Ask at the Košenjak hotel if there are any plans to revive it.

Places to Stay
The only hotel – the only form of accommodation for that matter – in Dravograd is the 16-room *Košenjak* (☎ 83 073) at Meža cesta 3 by the train and bus stations. The price is right (DM20 for a single and DM32 for a double with shared shower, DM37 for a double with private shower) but the rooms are shabby, trains stop practically in front of the reception desk and they're building (very noisily) a shopping complex nearby.

Places to Eat
Trg 4 Julija has a handful of bistros, cafés and small restaurants, including the *Bife Okrba* next to Ljubljanska Banka. Far more pleasant, though, is *Na Klancu* restaurant with a back terrace overlooking the Drava.

Local people say that the best restaurant in Dravograd is *Korošica* at the Košenjak hotel. It specialises in fish and seafood dishes.

Getting There & Away
If you're headed for Črna, Maribor via Radlje, Prevalje, Slovenj Gradec or Velenje, count on a bus about every half hour. Three buses a day go to Celje, one to Gornji Grad,

five to Ljubljana and two to Piran. There's one bus a day to Klagenfurt in Austria.

Dravograd is on the rail line linking Maribor and Bleiburg (Pliberk) in Austria. Up to five trains a day depart for Maribor (64 km; 1½ hours) via Vuzenica and Vuhred. Only a couple leave for Austria via Ravne na Koroškem and Prevalje (12 km; 20 minutes).

AROUND DRAVOGRAD
An excellent bike trip follows the spectacular Drava Valley through the Pohorje and Kobansko Hills some 60 km east to Maribor. The river, whose highest flow is reached at the start of the summer, is at its most scenic at Brezno and just above Fala where it narrows into a gorge. Just before Maribor the Drava widens into a lake with the help of a major dam.

You don't have to go that far to see some great scenery, though; **Vuzenica** and **Muta**, two very attractive villages, are just 14 km from Dravograd. The road is popular with cyclists though there are no bike lanes. The two towns can also be reached on the bus bound for Maribor.

If you have your own transport and would like to get away from it all, consider spending a night or two in one of the dozen or so farmhouses in the picturesque village of Šentanel in the Mežica Valley some six km north of Prevalje. Prevalje is 12 km southwest of Dravograd and easily accessible by bus and train. The *Ploder* farmhouse (☎ 31 104), open in July and August, has 15 rooms while the more remote *Marin* farmhouse (☎ 31 409), open all year, has 11. Both charge between DM20 and DM27 per person per night including breakfast. (Prices depend on the room and the season.)

Vuzenica (pop 2916)
The **Church of St Nicholas** at Vuzenica on the Drava's right bank was built in the 12th century and expanded later. Among its outstanding features is a star-shaped vaulted ceiling typical of Koroška, 15th century frescoes in the porch and an original fortified wall surround the churchyard. The ruins of a

16th century **castle** can be seen on Pisterjev Vrh north-east of town.

Muta (pop 3727)

This two-tier village across the Drava from Vuzenica, has churches on both levels but it's the one in the Lower Town (Spodnja Muta) by the road that you want. The **Church of St John the Baptist**, one of the oldest churches in Slovenia, is an austere round structure built in the early 1200s. Its shape, wooden roof and steeple are typical of Koroška, and the tiny church looks quite content with itself sitting in a field with the hills far behind it. There are 14th century frescoes in the choir inside which you can see if you can manage to wrest the key from the farmhouse to the west. The larger **Church of St Margaret**, up in Zgornja Muta, is 'new' – from the 17th century.

Prekmurje

Prekmurje is Slovenia's forgotten corner – mostly a broad plain that extends for kilometres 'beyond the Mura River'. Its isolation is rooted in history; until 1924 not a single bridge spanned the sluggish Mura and crossings were by ferry only. As a result, Prekmurje has preserved some traditional music, folklore and architecture in its distinctive Pannonian farmhouses.

Until the end of WW I, almost all of Prekmurje belonged to the Hungarian crown and a sizeable Magyar minority still lives here, especially around the spa town of Lendava, Slovenia's easternmost town and oil capital, and Murska Sobota (which Hungarians call Muraszombat). In many ways Prekmurje looks and feels more like Hungary than Slovenia, emphasised by the abundance of white storks, large thatched farmhouses with attached barn and other farm buildings under a single roof, a substantial Gypsy population and the occasional Hungarian-style *čarda* (inn) for good measure.

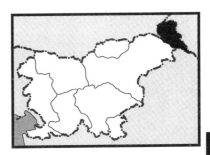

For most Slovenes, Prekmurje means a local version of goulash cooked with paprika, *gibanica* cake and a people who are more volatile and quick-tempered than most others in the nation. For travellers the province is a crossroads into Austria or Hungary and a place to relax and enjoy one of the many thermal spas in the region. Winters can be very cold on the plain, though, and summers very hot.

MURSKA SOBOTA (pop 13,800)

Now the capital and administrative centre of Prekmurje, Murska Sobota was little more than a market town (its name means Mura Saturday indicating the day of the market) until two events took place this century.

The first was the opening of the railway in 1907 which linked Murska Sobota with Hungary proper via Šalovci to the south. The second event was ultimately even more significant for the city. With the formation of the Kingdom of Serbs, Croats and Slovenes in 1918 and the transfer of territory, Murska Sobota found itself more or less in the centre of the new province and development really began. The area was occupied by the Hungarians during WW II.

Today Murska Sobota is an economically depressed industrial town with little to show for its past except for an odd architectural mix of neoclassical, secessionist and social-

White storks are abundant in Prekmurje

305

PREKMURJE

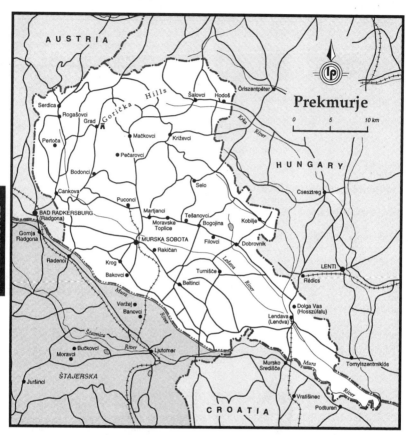

ist Baroque buildings. But the gentle countryside, little potters' villages and thermal spas make it well worth a stopover.

Orientation

The centre of Murska Sobota, Trg Zmage, lies south-east of large, shady City Park (Mestni Park). The train station is about one km south-east of the square. Just follow Slovenska ulica, the main street lined with fruit and other stands, southward and turn east on Ulica Arhitekta Novaka. The bus station is some 400 metres south-west of Trg Zmage.

Information

Murska Sobota does not have a tourist office, but the folks at Slovenijaturist (☎ 069 21 296), at Slovenska ulica 1, or at Kompas (☎ 069 22 332), on the south side of the Diana hotel, should be able to help you with questions and arrangements. Slovenijaturist is open from 8 am to noon and from 2.30 to 6 pm weekdays and on Saturday morning. Kompas opens from 8 am to 4 pm weekdays and to noon on Saturday.

Pomurska Banka has a branch at Trg Zmage 7. It is open from 7 am to 6 pm and on Saturday to 11.30 am. A Banka is at Ulica

Staneta Rozmana 5, east of Trg Zmage. The post office, which is next door to Pomurska Banka on Trg Zmage facing City Park, is open weekdays from 7 am to 7 pm, on Saturday till noon and on Sunday from 9 to 11 am.

Dobra Knjiga, a bookshop at Slovenska ulica 11, has a decent selection of regional maps if you plan to do any hiking in the area. It is open from 7 am to 5 pm on weekdays and till noon on Saturday.

Murska Sobota's telephone code is 069. The postcode is 69000.

Things to See

Soba Castle, a 16th century fortress with Renaissance and Baroque elements, is in the centre of City Park and houses the **Murska Sobota Regional Museum**. The largest collection of the museum, which may have reopened after extensive renovations, is an ethnographic exhibit devoted to the culture and traditional lifestyles of the Prekmurje region. Anyone who has visited such collections in Transdanubia just across the border, will find the farm implements, painted jugs, costumes and woodcarvings in the vaulted rooms almost identical to their Hungarian counterparts. The museum is usually open daily from 10 am to noon only.

The castle structure itself is interesting. Have a walk around the outside to spot the two Atlases supporting the balcony on the east side, the older chapel on the west and the lovely Baroque gable on the north side.

You may be surprised to see heavy artillery guns and statues of Yugoslav and Soviet soldiers at the park's main (eastern) entrance. This is the **Liberation Monument** which has somehow managed to stay in place despite the 'house cleaning' being done so anxiously around the rest of the region.

Opposite the park entrance is the neo-Gothic **Evangelical Church**, the main Lutheran seat in Slovenia. Prekmurje has long been a Protestant stronghold and the vast majority of Slovenian Protestants live in this province. The church dates only from 1910, but its ceilings painted with geometric shapes and muted shades of blue are a welcome relief from overwrought Baroque gold and marble.

The **Parish Church of St Nicholas** near the train station is a turn-of-the-century structure built around a Gothic presbytery with 14th century frescoes.

Activities

The Grad Rakičan Riding Centre is located on the grounds of a historical castle three km south-east of Murska Sobota at Lendavska ulica 28. It's all pretty serious stuff, with experienced riders trotting along the Mura or into the Gorička Hills to the north for 1450 SIT per hour, but absolute beginners can give it a go in the paddock for 1200 SIT. The centre is open daily, except Monday, from 9 am till noon and 2 to 8 pm. There's a very nice restaurant in a wing of the castle open till 10 pm.

Places to Stay

The closest camp site to Murska Sobota is at Moravske Toplice, about seven km to the north-east (see that section). The *Banovci* camp site at a small spa near Veržej about 13 km south of Murska Sobota is one of the few naturist camp sites in Slovenia. Nearby on the Mura River is the last of the famous floating mills.

The 33-room *Zvezda* hotel (☎ 32 040), in a four-story neoclassical building at Trg Zmage 8, has singles and doubles with shower and breakfast (but communal WC) for 2600/4700 SIT. The *Čarda* motel (☎ 48 118), about 2.5 km north of town in the village of Nemčavci, charges the exact same rates.

The most expensive place to stay in Murska Sobota is the 97-room *Diana* hotel (☎ 32 530; fax 38 688), a garishly painted concrete block at Slovenska ulica 52. Its singles with shower and breakfast are DM55, doubles are DM98. At those rates, you should indeed get 'unlimited use' of the indoor swimming pool as advertised.

Places to Eat

There's an inexpensive *bife* south of the Zvezda hotel, open weekdays till 8 pm and

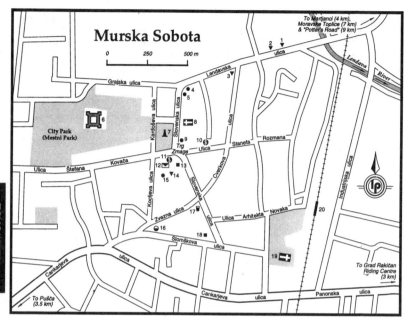

Murska Sobota

City Park
(Mestni Park)

To Martjanci (4 km),
Moravske Toplice (7 km)
& "Potter's Road" (9 km)

To Grad Rakičan
Riding Centre
(3 km)

To Pušča
(3.5 km)

PLACES TO STAY

13   Zvezda Hotel
18   Diana Hotel

PLACES TO EAT

1   Adria Restaurant
2   Prekmurski Hram Restaurant
3   Rajh No 1 Pizzeria
14   Bife

OTHER

4   Slovenijaturist Travel Agency
5   Dobra Knjiga Bookshop
6   Sobota Castle/Museum
7   Liberation Monument
8   Evangelical Church
9   Grocery Store
10   A Banka
11   Pomurska Banka
12   Post Office
15   Market
16   Bus Station
17   Rdeči Baron Pub
19   Parish Church of St Nicholas
20   Train Station

on Saturday to 2 pm. The restaurant in the *Zvezda* hotel is no great shakes but in warmer months, the outside terrace under the chestnut trees becomes the focal point of Murska Sobota. It is open to 10 pm (till midnight on Friday and Saturday).

You'll find better restaurants along Lendavska ulica a few minutes' walk from Trg Zmage. *Prekmurski Hram* at No 39 has regional specialities; this is a good place to try some of the local Laški Rizling wine from one of Prekmurje's wine-growing areas. *Adria*, at No 39e, specialises in fish dishes while *Rajh No 1* on the corner of Lendavska ulica and Cvetkova ulica is an upmarket špagetarija and picerija. All are open till 10 pm.

The *market* behind the Zvezda hotel sells fresh fruit and vegetables. A small *grocery store* at Slovenska ulica 25 keeps odd hours (for Slovenia anyway): from 6.30 am to 9 pm on weekdays, till 3 pm on Saturday and till noon on Sunday.

Entertainment
The castle courtyard is the site of occasional concerts and at least one folklore festival in summer; ask at one of the travel agencies as to what's going on.

A couple of pleasant pubs can be found along Slovenska ulica, including *Rdeči Baron* (no prizes for guessing that *rdeči* means 'red' in Slovene) at No 42. The *disco* at the Diana hotel rages till 4 am on Friday and Saturday.

Getting There & Away
Bus Buses depart Murska Sobota at least 10 times a day for Dobrovnik, Gornja Radgona (via Radenci) on the Austrian border, Lendava near the Hungarian border, Ljutomer, Mačkovci, Maribor, Moravci, Petrovci, Rakičan and Turnišče via Dobrovnik or Beltinci. Other destinations include: Beltinci (five departures daily); Celje via Ljutomer (seven); Grad (six); Hodoš on the Hungarian border (eight); Ljubljana via Maribor or Ljutomer (eight); Ormož (five); Piran (two); and Ptuj (three).

International destinations served by bus from here are Lenti in Hungary (one bus a day), Vienna (one on Friday and on Sunday) and Varaždin in Croatia (one a day).

Train Murska Sobota is on a spur that connects it with a main line (to Ljubljana, Maribor, Vienna and Budapest) at Ormož (39 km; 45 minutes). There are up to eight departures a day, and the train stops at Beltinci, Ljutomer and sometimes Veržej.

AROUND MURSKA SOBOTA
The **Parish Church of St Martin** at Martjanci, four km north of Murska Sobota on the road to Moravske Toplice, contains wonderful frescoes painted in the late 14th century by Johannes Aquila of Radgona. The best are on the presbytery's vaulted ceiling and walls; they depict angels bearing inscriptions, apostles, scenes from the life of St Martin and even a self-portrait of Master Aquila himself. Not to be outdone, the church's donor had his likeness appear in several scenes on the north and west walls of the arch leading to the presbytery.

Though it's not a tourist attraction, the village of **Pušča**, about 3.5 km west of Murska Sobota, contains one of the largest Gypsy settlements in Slovenia.

MORAVSKE TOPLICE
The thermal spa of Moravske Toplice at Moravci (pop 700), seven km north-east of Murska Sobota, can boast the hottest water in Slovenia: 72° C at source and cooled to 38° for use in its many pools and basins. Though it's one of the newest spas in the country (the spring was discovered in 1960 during oil drilling), many young Slovenes consider the clientele too geriatric for their liking, preferring the small *au naturel* spa at Banovci. But Moravske Toplice is every bit a health resort geared for recreation, with enough sport facilities to cater to every taste.

Thermal Spa
The resort counts seven indoor and outdoor pools filled with thermal water and two large outdoor ones with ordinary heated water. The thermal water is recommended for relief of rheumatism and certain minor skin problems, and there are enough therapies and beauty treatments available to keep you occupied for a week. Many visitors, though, simply come to sit in the warm water, cycle in the countryside or walk in the nearby vineyards. If you're staying at the resort you get use of the pools for free. Otherwise you'll pay 850 SIT (1000 SIT at the weekend) for the indoor pools and 450 SIT (550 SIT at the weekend) for the outdoor ones.

Moravske Toplice also has tennis courts, a fitness room/gym and saunas.

Places to Stay & Eat
All the accommodation at the Moravske Toplice resort share the same contact numbers: ☎ 069-48 210; fax 48 607.

The *camp site*, measuring five hectares, can accommodate 400 guests and is open all year. Use of the swimming pools is included in the daily charge (DM17 per person), and bicycles are available for hire.

PREKMURJE

The resort's two hotels – big modern structures of little interest – are expensive. Singles with shower and breakfast at the 274-bed *Ajda* are DM97 to DM105 and doubles are DM154 to DM170, depending on the season. The 252-bed *Termal*, while cheaper, is still going to cost you a minimum of DM74 for a single and DM118 for a double.

The only other option at the resort is to stay in one of the attractive *bungalows* done up to look like traditional Prekmurje peasant cottages with thatched roofs and cool white-washed walls. They cost DM61 to DM73 for one person and DM73 to DM116 for two depending on the time of year.

The *Flisarovi* farmhouse (☎ 069-48 411), about three km north of the resort at Dolga ulica 213, has five double rooms costing about DM20 to DM22 per person. Closer to the resort, at house No 5b in Moravske Toplice village, is the *Gostilna Kuhar* (☎ 069-48 215), a restaurant with accommodation.

One of the best places to sample Prekmurje's food specialities like *bograč golaž* (goulash in a pot) served with rye bread, *ciganska pečenka* ('Gypsy roast') and *gibanica* (a rich dessert of pastry, fruit and sweet cheese) is *Gostišče Kamin*, about 700 metres north of the spa at Dolga ulica 61. It's a friendly place with excellent food and outside seating with views of surrounding farmland and vineyards. Kamin (which means 'fireplace') is open every day, except Tuesday, from 10 am to 10 pm.

Getting There & Away

Buses leave hourly for Murska Sobota, and there are about a dozen a day to Dobrovnik. Other destinations include: Kobilje (five buses a day); Lendava via Turnišče (six); Ljubljana (two) and Maribor (three). There are two buses a week to Vienna (on Friday and Sunday).

AROUND MORAVSKE TOPLICE

An excellent **bike trip** (also accessible on the Dobrovnik and Kobilje buses from the spa) is along what could be called **potter's road**

which runs south-east from the spa. The road passes through the villages of Tešanovci, Bogojina and Filovci; to the north are the low Gorička Hills covered in vineyards. This is not Prekmurje's most important wine-growing region – that distinction goes to the areas around Lendava to the south-east and Gornja Radgona to the west – but it is just as lovely.

Tešanovci (pop 1080), less than two km from Moravske Toplice, is noted for its pottery and you can visit workshops at house Nos 51 and 53 on the main road. Otherwise, Tešanovci is not an especially interesting place; it is more rewarding to travel another 2.5 km to **Bogojina** (pop 1530), which should be awarded the most attractive and tidiest village in Prekmurje.

The main draw here is the **Parish Church of the Ascension**, redesigned by Jože Plečnik in the 1920s and one of his most characteristic works. The church is at the northern end of the village on a low hill; from the main road, proceed past peasant houses bedecked with flowers, as well as storks nesting on chimneys and telephone poles, to No 147.

To the original Romanesque and Baroque structure, Plečnik added two asymmetrical aisles and a round tower reminiscent of a crow's-nest. The interior is an odd mixture of black marble, brass and wood; the oak-beamed ceiling is fitted with ceramic plates collected from the area. On your way back to the main road, don't miss the leaning cottage of Bogojina, which looks like it may tumble down at any moment – if it hasn't already.

Filovci (pop 522), another two km beyond Bogojina, is famed throughout Slovenia for its *črna keramika* (black pottery), which can also be found in parts of southern and eastern Hungary. One of the best workshops to visit is at house No 29, where Alojz Bojnec and his wife work the wheel and fire their pots and jugs in an old brick oven. The workshop is about 200 metres south-west of the main road past the small church and over the bridge.

If you are hungry, there are a couple of

Prekmurje's Farmhouses

Along with *gibanica* cake and storks, Prekmurje is known for its traditional L-shaped farmhouses, among the most uniform regional dwellings in Slovenia. Anyone who has crossed the border into Hungary will recognize them; they are almost exactly like the *kerített házak* ('fenced-in houses') found in southern Transdanubia.

The thatched roof of a Prekmurje farmhouse extends into the central courtyard, and this sheltered 'portico' *(podsten)* allows access from the outside to all the rooms when it rains. It is also used as a work area and a place to gossip with the family or neighbours on a warm summer afternoon.

Traditionally, the main living area consisted of a central entrance hall, which also served as the kitchen. The large open hearth was used to cook and also to heat the tile stoves in the rooms on either side: the 'first room' *(prva iža)*, with table and chairs, decorated trousseau chests and religious icons, and the 'back room' *(zadnja iža)*, used for sleeping. Connected to the house (though accessible only from the *podsten)* were the work and storage shed, the barn and the stable.

Another distinctive feature of Prekmurje houses (though not uncommon in south-western Hungary) are the floral designs *(pojas)* stencilled on the outside walls about a metre from the ground. They give a little colour to the stark, whitewashed walls and vary from one house to another. ■

decent gostilne in Dobrovnik, 3.5 km beyond Filovci. *Pri Lujzi* is at house No 273a. *Lipot*, a few doors down at No 277a, has outside seating. Both are open till 10 or 11 pm.

RADENCI (pop 5750)

Strictly speaking, Radenci isn't part of Prekmurje province because it is not 'beyond the Mura'. In fact, it lies about a km from the river's right bank and is thus 'on the Mura' (Pomurje). But let's not get technical. Radenci has always been closely tied historically and geographically with Prekmurje, and it is easily accessible from Murska Sobota, 13 km to the east.

Radenci is best known for its health resort, parts of which still feel like a full-of-itself 19th century spa town. Indeed, as one Slovenian wag put it: 'Radenci remains the preserve of highbrow intellectuals and rumble-tumble chamber music.' But when most Slovenes hear the name they think of Radenska Tri Srca – the Radenci Three Hearts mineral water bottled here that is consumed in every restaurant and café in the country.

Orientation & Information

Radenci lies west and north of the Radgona-Kapel wine-growing area. To the north is a triangle of Austrian territory inhabited mostly by Austrian Slovenes. The border crossing is at Rakersburg (Radgona in Slovene), six km north-west of Radenci.

For general information, go to reception in the Radin hotel or to the Marika travel agency at the bus station, which is south-east of the spa complex. Marika, which also does exchange, is open from 8 am to 3 pm and till noon on Saturday.

Thermal Spa

The health resort has three claims to fame: mineral water rich in carbon dioxide for drinking, thermal water high in minerals for bathing that comes out at 41° at source and sulphuric mud for smearing all over yourself. All three play a role in the therapeutic and beauty treatments so popular here.

Springs of mineral water were discovered in the early 19th century and the bottling of Radenska began in 1869. By the turn of the century, the water had become so popular that is was being dispatched to the imperial court in Vienna and to the pope in Rome. The spa itself opened in 1882.

Today, three modern (and ugly) blocks overlook the older Victorian-style buildings and a large wooded park with paths, a chapel, pavilions and tame red squirrels. The complex counts three pools: indoor recreational, outdoor thermal with a temperature of about 35° and Olympic-size outdoor. Guests can use the pools at will; outsiders pay 300 to 500 SIT depending on the pool.

There's a small museum in the park devoted to the history and development of the spa and its famous mineral water.

Activities

The tennis courts just south of the hotel complex can be rented for 700 SIT per hour. Racquets (200 SIT) and balls (350 SIT) are available from the small booth there from 8 am to noon and 2 to 8 pm. Lessons for one or two people are 1500 SIT per hour. For badminton, table tennis and minigolf, go to the large outdoor pool. Mountain bikes from the resort cost 1000 SIT per day while regular 10-speeds are 600 SIT.

Excellent cycling excursions can be made into the surrounding wine country; head south-west along the 'wine road' *(vinska cesta)* for about four km to Janžev Vrh and an old vineyard cottage called Janžev Hram, or even farther south to Kapelski Vrh and Ivanjski Vrh. Almost all the wines produced here are whites; try the popular local one called Janževec or the sparkling Zlata Penina 'champagne'.

Places to Stay

There are lots of *private rooms* available on Panonska cesta to the west and south of the spa's main entrance, including some at house No 23. But to save time and energy, ask the staff at the Radin hotel for their list of private accommodation. The price should be about DM20 per person.

The three spa hotels (☎ 069-65 006; fax 65 054), with a total of some 600 beds, are much of a muchness and certainly no bargain. Singles at the cheapest of the three – the *Terapija* – range from DM48 to DM59, with doubles DM80 to DM102 depending on the season. Prices at the three-star *Miral* and four-star *Radin* are generally about 25% and 40% higher than those at the Terapija.

Places to Eat

Radenci is supposed to have some of the best food in Slovenia, but great cuisine proved elusive for me; perhaps you'll be luckier. The *Park* restaurant in the middle of the resort's large wooded park is a pleasant place for a meal in summer but the mosquitoes may consume you first.

For something a little more colourful, head north-west for two or three km on the road to Austria to *Gostilna Klobasa* in Šratovci at house No 8 or to *Gostilna Adamič* in Mele at house No 27a. They're both open till 10 pm, but the former closes all day on Wednesday.

Entertainment

The spa puts on its famous chamber-music concerts in summer. Two venues catering to the less highbrow are *Diskoteka Srček* in the park and the *Vikend* disco near the bus station at Panonska cesta 2.

Getting There & Away

Departures are very frequent to Maribor, Murska Sobota and Rakersburg (Radgona), in Austria. Other destinations include: Koper (two a day); Ljubljana (eight); Ljutomer (six); Nova Gorica (two); Ormož (two); Piran (two); and Varaždin in Croatia (one).

Passenger trains do not run on the line that passes through Radenci, which is for freight only.

Glossary

If you can't find the word you're looking for here, try the Language section in the Facts about the Country chapter, the Food and Drinks sections in the Facts for the Visitor chapter or the Addresses & Place Names section in the Getting Around chapter.

AMZS – Automobile Association of Slovenia
avtocesta – motorway, highway

bife – snack and/or drinks bar
bivak – bivouac (basic shelter in the mountains)
breg – river bank
burja – bora (cold north-east wind from the Adriatic Sea)

čakalnica – waiting room
cenik – price
cerkev – church
cesta – road

delovni čas – opening/business hours
dijaški dom – student dormitory, hostel
dolina – valley
dom – house; mountain cottage or lodge
Domobranci – collaborationist Slovenian 'Home Guards' during WW II
drevored – avenue

fijaker – horse-drawn carriage

gaj – grove, park
garderoba – left-luggage office
gora – mountain
gostilna – inn-style restaurant sometimes offering accommodation (plural: gostilne)
gostišče – inn-style restaurant usually with accommodation (plural: gostišča)
gozd – forest
greben – ridge, crest
GRS – mountain-rescue service

Hallstatt – late Iron Age culture (700-400 BC)

hrib – hill

izhod – exit
izvir – source (of a river, stream, etc)

jezero – lake
jug – south

Karst – limestone region of underground rivers, gorges and caves in Primorska. It is from this region that other areas in the world with similar geographic characteristics take the name 'karst'
kavarna – coffee house, café
kazolec – hayrack distinct to Slovenia
koča – mountain cottage or hut
kot – glacial valley
kotlina – basin
kras – karst
krčma – drinks bar (sometimes with food)

ljudska glasba – traditional folk music
ljudski ples – traditional folk dance
lekarna – pharmacy
LPP – Ljubljana city bus network

moški – men (toilet)
most – bridge

na – on
nabrežje – embankment
naselje – colony, development
nasip – dyke, embankment

občina – administrative division; county or commune
obvoz – detour
odhod – departure
odprto – open
okrepčevalnica – snack bar
Osvobodilne Fronte – Anti-Fascist Liberation Front in WW II
otok – island

panjska končnica – beehive panel painted with Slovenian folk motifs

PD – 'circulation tax' similar to Value-Added Tax (VAT)
pivnica – pub, beer hall
planina – Alpine pasture
planota – plateau
pod – under, below
polje – collapsed limestone area often under cultivation
pot – trail
potok – stream
prehod – passage
prekop – canal
prenočišče – overnight accommodation (plural: prenočišča)
pri – at, near, by
prihod – arrival
PZS – Alpine Association of Slovenia

regija – province or region
reka – river
restavracija – restaurant
rini – push
rob – escarpment, edge

samopostrežna restavracija – self-service restaurant
sedežnica – chair lift
sedlo – pass, saddle
sever – north
SIT – tolar (international currency code)
situla – embossed pail
slaščičarna – shop selling sweets, ice cream
sobe – rooms available
soteska – ravine, gorge
sprehajališče – walkway, promenade
stena – wall, cliff
steza – path

SŽ – Slovenian Railways

terme – Italian for 'spa' (in common use)
TIC – Tourist Information Centre
TNG – Triglav National Park
toplar – double-linked hayrack unique to Slovenia (plural: toplarji)
toplice – spa
trg – square

ulica – street

vas – village
vhod – entrance
vinoteka – wine bar
vinska cesta – wine road
vinska klet – wine cellar
vleci – pull
vozni red – timetable
vozovnica – ticket
vrh – summit, peak
vrt – garden, park
vrtača – sinkhole
vzhod – east
vzpenjača – cable car, gondola

zahod – west
zaprto – closed
zavetišče – mountain 'refuge' with refreshments and sometimes accommodation
zdravilišče – health resort, spa
žegnanje – a patron's festival at a church or chapel
ženske – women (toilet)
žičnica – cable car
znamenje – religious road sign, way marker

Index

PLANET TALK
Lonely Planet's FREE quarterly newsletter

We love hearing from you and think you'd like to hear from us.

When...is the right time to see reindeer in Finland?
Where...can you hear the best palm-wine music in Ghana?
How...do you get from Asunción to Areguá by steam train?
What...is the best way to see India?

For the answer to these and many other questions read PLANET TALK.

Every issue is packed with up-to-date travel news and advice including:

- *a letter from Lonely Planet founders Tony and Maureen Wheeler*
- *travel diary from a Lonely Planet author - find out what it's really like out on the road*
- *feature article on an important and topical travel issue*
- *a selection of recent letters from our readers*
- *the latest travel news from all over the world*
- *details on Lonely Planet's new and forthcoming releases*

To join our mailing list contact any Lonely Planet office (address below).

LONELY PLANET PUBLICATIONS

Australia: PO Box 617, Hawthorn 3122, Victoria (tel: 03-9819 1877)
USA: Embarcadero West, 155 Filbert St, Suite 251, Oakland, CA 94607 (tel: 510-893 8555)
TOLL FREE: (800) 275-8555
UK: 10 Barley Mow Passage, Chiswick, London W4 4PH (tel: 0181-742 3161)
France: 71 bis rue du Cardinal Lemoine – 75005 Paris (tel: 1-46 34 00 58)

Also available: Lonely Planet T-shirts. 100% heavyweight cotton (S, M, L, XL)

Lonely Planet guides to Europe

Central Europe on a shoestring
From the snow-capped peaks of the Austrian Alps, the medieval castles of Hungary and the vast forests of Poland to the festivals of Germany, the arty scene in Prague and picturesque lakes of Switzerland, this guide is packed with practical travel advice to help you make the most of your visit. This new shoestring guide covers travel in Austria, Czech Republic, Germany, Hungary, Liechtenstein, Poland, Slovakia and Switzerland.

Eastern Europe on a shoestring
This guide has opened up a whole new world for travellers – Albania, Bulgaria, Czechoslovakia, eastern Germany, Hungary, Poland, Romania and the former republics of Yugoslavia.
'...a thorough, well-researched book. Only a fool would go East without it.' – *Great Expeditions*

Mediterranean Europe on a shoestring
Details on hundreds of galleries, museums and architectural masterpieces and information on outdoor activities including hiking, sailing and skiing. Information on travelling in Albania, Andorra, Cyprus, France, Greece, Italy, Malta, Morocco, Portugal, Spain, Tunisia, Turkey and the former republics of Yugoslavia.

Scandinavian & Baltic Europe on a shoestring
A comprehensive guide to travelling in this region including details on galleries, festivals and museums, as well as outdoor activities, national parks and wildlife. Countries featured are Denmark, Estonia, the Faroe Islands, Finland, Iceland, Latvia, Lithuania, Norway and Sweden.

Western Europe on a shoestring
This long-awaited guide covers all of Western Europe's well-loved sights and provides routes for cycling and driving tours, plus details on hiking, climbing and skiing. All the travel facts on Andorra, Austria, Belgium, Britain, France, Germany, Greece, Ireland, Italy, Liechtenstein, Luxembourg, Netherlands, Portugal, Spain and Switzerland.

Baltic States & Kaliningrad – travel survival kit
The Baltic States burst on to the world scene almost from nowhere in the late 1980s. Now that travellers are free to move around the region they will discover nations with a rich and colourful history and culture, and a welcoming attitude to all travellers.

Britain – travel survival kit
Britain remains one of the most beautiful islands in the world. All the words, paintings and pictures that you have read and seen are not just romantic exaggerations. This comprehensive guide will help you to discover and enjoy this ever-popular destination.

Czech & Slovak Republics – travel survival kit
The Czech and Slovak Republics are two of the most exciting travel destinations in Europe. This guide is the essential resource for independent travellers. It's full of down-to-earth information and reliable advice for every budget – from five stars to five dollars a day.

Dublin – city guide
Where to enjoy a pint of Guinness and a plate of Irish stew, where to see spectacular Georgian architecture or experience Irish hospitality – Dublin city guide will ensure you won't miss out on anything.

Finland – travel survival kit
Finland is an intriguing blend of Swedish and Russian influences. With its medieval stone castles, picturesque wooden houses, vast forest and lake district, and interesting wildlife, it is a wonderland to delight any traveller.

France – *travel survival kit*
Stylish, diverse, celebrated by romantics and revolutionaries alike, France is a destination that's always in fashion. A comprehensive guide packed with invaluable advice.

Greece – *travel survival kit*
Famous ruins, secluded beaches, sumptuous food, sun-drenched islands, ancient pathways and much more are covered in this comprehensive guide to this ever-popular destination.

Hungary – *travel survival kit*
Formerly seen as the gateway to eastern Europe, Hungary is a romantic country of music, wine and folklore. This guide contains detailed background information on Hungary's cultural and historical past as well as practical advice on the many activities available to travellers.

Iceland, Greenland & the Faroe Islands – *travel survival kit*
Iceland, Greenland & the Faroe Islands contain some of the most beautiful wilderness areas in the world. This practical guidebook will help travellers discover the dramatic beauty of this region, no matter what their budget.

Ireland – *travel survival kit*
Ireland is one of Europe's least 'spoilt' countries. Green, relaxed and welcoming, it does not take travellers long before they feel at ease. An entertaining and comprehensive guide to this troubled country.

Italy – *travel survival kit*
Italy is art – not just in the galleries and museums. You'll discover its charm on the streets and in the markets, in rustic hill-top villages and in the glamorous city boutiques. A thorough guide to the thousands of attractions of this ever-popular destination.

Poland – *travel survival kit*
With the collapse of communism, Poland has opened up to travellers, revealing a rich cultural heritage. This guide will help you make the most of this safe and friendly country.

Prague – *city guide*
Since the 'Velvet Revolution' in 1989, Prague and its residents have grasped their freedom with a youthful exuberance, even frenzy. This thoroughly comprehensive guide will show you the sights and hidden delights of this vivacious city.

Switzerland – *travel survival kit*
Ski enthusiasts and chocolate addicts know two excellent reasons for heading to Switzerland. This travel survival kit gives travellers many more: jazz, cafés, boating trips...and the Alps of course!

Turkey – *a travel survival kit*
This acclaimed guide takes you from Istanbul bazaars to Mediterranean beaches, from historic battle-grounds to the stamping grounds of St Paul, Alexander the Great, Emperor Constantine and King Croesus.

USSR – *travel survival kit*
Invaluable advice on getting around and beating red tape for individual and group travellers alike. This comprehensive guide includes an unsanitised historical background and complete information on art and culture. Over 130 reliable maps, and all place names are given in Cyrillic script. Includes the independent states.

Vienna – city guide
There's so much to see and do in Vienna and this guide is the best way to ensure you enjoy it all.

Trekking in Greece
Mountainous landscape, the solitude of ancient pathways and secluded beaches await those who dare to extend their horizons beyond Athens and the antiquities. Covers the main trekking regions and includes contoured maps of trekking routes.

Trekking in Spain
Aimed at both overnight trekkers and day hikers, this guidebook includes useful maps and full details on hikes in some of Spain's most beautiful wilderness areas.

Trekking in Turkey
Few people are aware that Turkey boasts mountains with walks to rival those found in Nepal. This book gives details on treks that are destined to become as popular as those further east.

Also available:
Central Europe phrasebook
Languages in this book cover travel in Austria, the Czech Republic, France, Germany, Hungary, Italy, Liechtenstein, Slovakia and Switzerland.

Eastern Europe phrasebook
Discover the most enjoyable way to get around and make friends in Bulgarian, Czech, Hungarian, Polish, Romanian and Slovak.

Mediterranean Europe phrasebook
Ask for directions to the galleries and museums in Albanian, Greek, Italian, Macedonian, Maltese, Serbian & Croatian and Slovene.

Scandinavian Europe phrasebook
Find your way around the ski trails and enjoy the local festivals in Danish, Finnish, Icelandic, Norwegian and Swedish.

Western Europe phrasebook
Show your appreciation for the great masters in Basque, Catalan, Dutch, French, German, Irish, Portuguese and Spanish (Castilian).

Greek phrasebook
Catch a *ferrybot* to the islands, laze the day away on a golden *baralia*, and say *stin iyia sas!* as you raise your glass to the setting sun... you can explore *tin acropoli* another day.

Turkish phrasebook
Practical words and phrases that will help you to communicate effectively with local people in almost every situation. Includes pronunciation guide.

Russian phrasebook
This indispensable phrasebook will help you get information, read signs and menus, and make friends along the way. Includes phonetic transcriptions and Cyrillic script.

Moroccan Arabic phrasebook
Essential words and phraes for everything from finding a hotel room in Casablanca to asking for a meal of *tajine* in Marrakesh. Includes Arabic script and pronunciation guide.

Lonely Planet Guidebooks

Lonely Planet guidebooks cover every accessible part of Asia as well as Australia, the Pacific, South America, Africa, the Middle East, Europe and parts of North America. There are five series: *travel survival kits*, covering a country for a range of budgets; *shoestring guides* with compact information for low-budget travel in a major region; *walking guides*; *city guides* and *phrasebooks*.

Australia & the Pacific
Australia
Australian phrasebook
Bushwalking in Australia
Islands of Australia's Great Barrier Reef
Outback Australia
Fiji
Fijian phrasebook
Melbourne city guide
Micronesia
New Caledonia
New South Wales
New Zealand
Tramping in New Zealand
Papua New Guinea
Bushwalking in Papua New Guinea
Papua New Guinea phrasebook
Rarotonga & the Cook Islands
Samoa
Solomon Islands
Sydney city guide
Tahiti & French Polynesia
Tonga
Vanuatu
Victoria
Western Australia

North-East Asia
Beijing city guide
China
Cantonese phrasebook
Mandarin Chinese phrasebook
Hong Kong, Macau & Canton
Japan
Japanese phrasebook
Korea
Korean phrasebook
Mongolia
North-East Asia on a shoestring
Seoul city guide
Taiwan
Tibet
Tibet phrasebook
Tokyo city guide

South-East Asia
Bali & Lombok
Bangkok city guide
Cambodia
Indonesia
Indonesian phrasebook
Jakarta city guide
Laos
Lao phrasebook
Malaysia, Singapore & Brunei
Myanmar (Burma)
Burmese phrasebook
Philippines
Pilipino phrasebook
Singapore city guide
South-East Asia on a shoestring
Thailand
Thailand travel atlas
Thai phrasebook
Thai Hill Tribes phrasebook
Vietnam
Vietnamese phrasebook

Middle East
Arab Gulf States
Egypt & the Sudan
Arabic (Egyptian) phrasebook
Iran
Israel
Jordan & Syria
Middle East
Turkey
Turkish phrasebook
Trekking in Turkey
Yemen

Indian Ocean
Madagascar & Comoros
Maldives & Islands of the East Indian Ocean
Mauritius, Réunion & Seychelles

Mail Order

Lonely Planet guidebooks are distributed worldwide. They are also available by mail order from Lonely Planet, so if you have difficulty finding a title please write to us. US and Canadian residents should write to Embarcadero West, 155 Filbert St, Suite 251, Oakland CA 94607, USA; European residents should write to 10 Barley Mow Passage, Chiswick, London W4 4PH; and residents of other countries to PO Box 617, Hawthorn, Victoria 3122, Australia.

Indian Subcontinent
Bangladesh
India
India travel atlas
Hindi/Urdu phrasebook
Trekking in the Indian Himalaya
Karakoram Highway
Kashmir, Ladakh & Zanskar
Nepal
Trekking in the Nepal Himalaya
Nepali phrasebook
Pakistan
Sri Lanka
Sri Lanka phrasebook

Africa
Africa on a shoestring
Central Africa
East Africa
Trekking in East Africa
Kenya
Swahili phrasebook
Morocco
Arabic (Moroccan) phrasebook
North Africa
South Africa, Lesotho & Swaziland
Zimbabwe, Botswana & Namibia
West Africa

Central America & the Caribbean
Baja California
Central America on a shoestring
Costa Rica
Eastern Caribbean
Guatemala, Belize & Yucatán: La Ruta Maya
Mexico

North America
Alaska
Backpacking in Alaska
Canada
Hawaii
Honolulu city guide
USA phrasebook

Europe
Baltic States & Kaliningrad
Baltics States phrasebook
Britain
Central Europe on a shoestring
Central Europe phrasebook
Czech & Slovak Republics
Dublin city guide
Eastern Europe on a shoestring
Eastern Europe phrasebook
Finland
France
Greece
Greek phrasebook
Hungary
Iceland, Greenland & the Faroe Islands
Ireland
Italy
Mediterranean Europe on a shoestring
Mediterranean Europe phrasebook
Poland
Prague city guide
Scandinavian & Baltic Europe on a shoestring
Scandinavian Europe phrasebook
Slovenia
Switzerland
Trekking in Spain
Trekking in Greece
USSR
Russian phrasebook
Vienna city guide
Western Europe on a shoestring
Western Europe phrasebook

South America
Argentina, Uruguay & Paraguay
Bolivia
Brazil
Brazilian phrasebook
Chile & Easter Island
Colombia
Ecuador & the Galápagos Islands
Latin American Spanish phrasebook
Peru
Quechua phrasebook
South America on a shoestring
Trekking in the Patagonian Andes
Venezuela

The Lonely Planet Story

Lonely Planet published its first book in 1973 in response to the numerous 'How did you do it?' questions Maureen and Tony Wheeler were asked after driving, bussing, hitching, sailing and railing their way from England to Australia.

Written at a kitchen table and hand collated, trimmed and stapled, *Across Asia on the Cheap* became an instant local bestseller, inspiring thoughts of another book.

Eighteen months in South-East Asia resulted in their second guide, *South-East Asia on a shoestring*, which they put together in a backstreet Chinese hotel in Singapore in 1975. The 'yellow bible' as it quickly became known to backpackers around the world, soon became *the* guide to the region. It has sold well over half a million copies and is now in its 8th edition, still retaining its familiar yellow cover.

Today there are over 140 Lonely Planet titles in print – books that have that same adventurous approach to travel as those early guides; books that 'assume you know how to get your luggage off the carousel' as one reviewer put it.

Although Lonely Planet initially specialised in guides to Asia, they now cover most regions of the world, including the Pacific, South America, Africa, the Middle East and Europe. The list of *walking guides* and *phrasebooks* (for 'unusual' languages such as Quechua, Swahili, Nepali and Egyptian Arabic) is also growing rapidly.

The emphasis continues to be on travel for independent travellers. Tony and Maureen still travel for several months of each year and play an active part in the writing, updating and quality control of Lonely Planet's guides.

They have been joined by over 50 authors, 110 staff – mainly editors, cartographers & designers – at our office in Melbourne, Australia, at our US office in Oakland, California and at our European office in Paris; another five at our office in London handle sales for Britain, Europe and Africa. Travellers themselves also make a valuable contribution to the guides through the feedback we receive in thousands of letters each year.

The people at Lonely Planet strongly believe that travellers can make a positive contribution to the countries they visit, both through their appreciation of the countries' culture, wildlife and natural features, and through the money they spend. In addition, the company makes a direct contribution to the countries and regions it covers. Since 1986 a percentage of the income from each book has been donated to ventures such as famine relief in Africa; aid projects in India; agricultural projects in Central America; Greenpeace's efforts to halt French nuclear testing in the Pacific; and Amnesty International.

Lonely Planet's basic travel philosophy is summed up in Tony Wheeler's comment, 'Don't worry about whether your trip will work out. Just go!'